June 17–20, 2014
Rome, Italy

I0047540

**Association for
Computing Machinery**

Advancing Computing as a Science & Profession

EICS'14

Proceedings of the 2014 ACM SIGCHI Symposium on
Engineering Interactive Computing Systems

Sponsored by:
ACM SIGCHI

Supported by:
HIIS Laboratory, CNR-ISTI, Pisa, Italy

**Association for
Computing Machinery**

Advancing Computing as a Science & Profession

The Association for Computing Machinery
2 Penn Plaza, Suite 701
New York, New York 10121-0701

Notice to Past Authors of ACM-Published Articles
ACM intends to create a complete electronic archive of all articles and/or other material previously published by ACM. If you have written a work that has been previously published by ACM in any journal or conference proceedings prior to 1978, or any SIG Newsletter at any time, and you do NOT want this work to appear in the ACM Digital Library, please inform permissions@acm.org, stating the title of the work, the author(s), and where and when published.

ISBN: 978-1-4503-2725-1 (Digital)

ISBN: 978-1-4503-3092-3 (Print)

Additional copies may be ordered prepaid from:

ACM Order Department
PO Box 30777
New York, NY 10087-0777, USA

Phone: 1-800-342-6626 (USA and Canada)
+1-212-626-0500 (Global)
Fax: +1-212-944-1318
E-mail: acmhelp@acm.org
Hours of Operation: 8:30 am – 4:30 pm ET

Printed in the USA

Foreword

It is our great pleasure to welcome you to the *6th ACM SIGCHI Symposium on Engineering Interactive Computing Systems – EICS'14* held in Rome (17-20 June 2014). EICS is an international conference devoted to all aspects of engineering usable and effective interactive computing systems. EICS focuses on tools, techniques and methods for analysis, design and development of interactive systems.

The conference brings together people who study or practice the engineering of interactive systems, drawing from the fields of Human-Computer Interaction (HCI), Software Engineering, Requirements Engineering, Computer-Supported Collaborative Work (CSCW), Ubiquitous & Pervasive Systems, and Cognitive Engineering.

We hope that you will find this year program interesting and thought provoking. The symposium will provide you with a valuable opportunity to share ideas with other researchers and practitioners from institutions around the world. We believe that with this sixth EICS edition, by increasing the diversity of paper presentations, posters, workshops, tutorials, demonstrations and doctoral presentations, we obtained an exciting and interactive program, which stimulates fruitful discussion in the relevant research fields.

The work presented here describes recent innovations in the area of engineering of interactive computer systems. There are papers on model-based approaches and tools for analysis and engineering of interactive systems, adaptive systems, tangible user interfaces, development frameworks for multi-device and multi-user environments including public display systems, as well as languages and tools for designing and developing multimodal systems, approaches for engineering collaborative environments, and analytical methods for safety-critical systems.

Since its beginning EICS has witnessed a growing number of submissions. This year the program contains 16 full papers carefully chosen from a total of 88 submissions (18% acceptance rate). There are also 18 late breaking papers (6 of them are presented as posters) as well as a number of doctoral reports and demonstration descriptions. The competition was strong and the selection difficult. The published material originates from 17 countries from various parts of the world including North and South America, Canada and New Zealand.

Our keynote speakers, Yvonne Rogers and Krzysztof Gajos, provide interesting novel perspectives on key topics for the engineering community in the coming years – user experience and adaptation in ubiquitous systems – which should provide further useful content for interesting discussions on the future of user interface software and technologies.

We thank all who contributed to EICS 2014 for their hard work, particularly the Program Committee and the many external reviewers listed in the proceedings, the chairs for doctoral consortium, workshops, demonstrations and tutorials. We also thank Giulio Galesi for his invaluable support in managing various aspects of the conference logistics and organisation. Our special thanks go to our sponsor, ACM SIGCHI, for their continued support of the EICS successful symposia.

Lastly, we also wish the best to the next edition, EICS 2015, which will be held in Duisburg, Germany in June 2015.

Fabio Paternò
CNR-ISTI
Conference Chair

Carmen Santoro
CNR-ISTI
Paper Co-Chair

Jürgen Ziegler
University of Duisburg-Essen
Paper Co-Chair

Paolo Bottoni
Sapienza University of Rome
LBR Co-Chair

Michael Nebeling
ETH-Zurich
LBR Co-Chair

Table of Content

Multimodal and Web Applications Session

Model-based UIs Session

Touch and Gesture-based UIs Session

Demo Session

Late Breaking Results Session

Keynote II

Analytic Techniques Session

Prototyping and Development Frameworks Session

Workshop Summaries

EICS 2014 Symposium Organization

General Chair: Fabio Paternò *(CNR-ISTI, Italy)*

Paper Chairs: Carmen Santoro *(CNR-ISTI, Italy)*
Jürgen Ziegler *(University of Duisburg-Essen, Germany)*

Late Breaking Results Chairs: Paolo Bottoni *(Sapienza University of Rome, Italy)*
Michael Nebeling *(ETH Zürich, Switzerland)*

Demonstrations Chairs: Giulio Mori *(CNR-ISTI, Italy)*
Giuseppe Ghiani *(CNR-ISTI, Italy)*

Doctoral Consortium Chairs: Kris Luyten *(Hasselt University, Belgium)*
Laurence Nigay *(Université Joseph Fourier, France)*

Workshop Chairs: Gaëlle Calvary *(University of Grenoble, France)*
Gerrit Meixner *(Heilbronn University, Germany)*

Tutorial Chairs: Simone Barbosa *(University PUC-Rio, Brazil)*
Marco Winckler *(IRIT-ICS, University Paul Sabatier, France)*

Local Organisation Chair: Giulio Galesi *(CNR-ISTI, Italy)*

Program Committee: Simone Barbosa *(University PUC-Rio, Brazil)*
Marco Blumendorf *(DAI Labor Technische Universität Berlin, Germany)*
Matthew Bolton *(NASA Human Systems Integration, USA)*
Paolo Bottoni *(Sapienza University of Rome, Italy)*
Judy Bowen *(University of Waikato, New Zealand)*
Gaëlle Calvary *(University of Grenoble, France)*
José C. Campos *(University of Minho, Portugal)*
Stéphane Chatty *(ENAC, France)*
Keith Cheverst *(Lancaster University, UK)*
Anke Dittmar *(University of Rostock, Germany)*
Peter Forbrig *(University of Rostock, Germany)*
Giuseppe Ghiani *(CNR-ISTI, Italy)*
Michael Harrison *(Newcastle University, UK)*
Hermann Kaindl *(Vienna University of Technology, Austria)*
Christian Kray *(University of Münster, Germany)*
Kris Luyten *(Hasselt University, Belgium)*
José A. Macías *(Universidad Autónoma de Madrid, Spain)*
Michael Nebeling *(ETH Zürich, Switzerland)*
Jeffrey Nichols *(IBM Research Almaden, USA)*
Laurence Nigay *(Université Joseph Fourier, France)*
Nuno Nunes *(University of Madeira, Portugal)*
Philippe Palanque *(University of Toulouse 3, France)*
Fabio Paternò *(CNR-ISTI, Italy)*
Andreas Pleuss *(Lero, Ireland)*

x

Additional reviewers (continued):

Michael Katchabaw
Rick Kazman
Thomas Kirste
Bernhard Klein
Clemens Klokmose
Andrea Kohlhase
Floor Koornneef
Dean Kramer
Matthias Kranz
Yann Laurillau
Effie Law
Luis A. Leiva
Catherine Letondal
Bo Li
Steffen Lohmann
María Lozano
Leilah Lyons
Christian Maertin
Jalal Mahmud
Apostolos Malatras
Marco Manca
Célia Martinie
Paolo Masci
Maristella Matera
David McGookin
Gerrit Meixner
Pierrick Milhorat
Andreas Möller
Giulio Mori
Cosmin Munteanu
Lennart Nacke
David Navarre
Luciana Nedel
Gerrit Niezen
Ian Oakley
Zeljko Obrenovic
Philipp Oehme
Patrick Oladimeji
Aditya Pal
Celeste Paul
Evan Peck
Lucas Pereira
Greg Phillips
Marcelo Pimenta
Vesna Popovic
Roman Popp
Benjamin Poppinga

Manoj Prasad
Victor M. R. Penichet
Nitendra Rajput
David Raneburger
Lionel Reveret
António Nestor Ribeiro
Guillaume Rivière
Paola Johanna Rodriguez Carrillo
Gustavo Rossi
Daisuke Sakamoto
Vagner Santana
João Saraiva
Stefan Sauer
Antonio Schiavone
Johannes Schöning
Hartmut Seichter
Audrey Serna
Marcos Serrano
Haifeng Shen
Beat Signer
José Luís Silva
J. David Smith
Shamus Smith
Anthony Sorel
Jean-Sébastien Sottet
Kenia Sousa
Gunnar Stevens
Mark Sujan
Kåre Synnes
Aurélien Tabard
Rami Tabbah
Federico Tajariol
Daniela Trevisan
Heli Väätäjä
Alain Vagner
Vero Vanden Abeele
Marijke Vandermaesen
Radu-Daniel Vatavu
Arnold Vermeeren
Jo Vermeulen
Chi Vi
Markel Vigo
Chris Vincent
Jean-Luc Vinot
James Wallace
Gerhard Weber
Mark Whiting

EICS 2014 Sponsor & Supporters

Sponsor:

SIGCHI

Supporters:

HIIS Laboratory
The Human-Computer Interaction Group

ISTITUTO DI SCIENZA E TECNOLOGIE
DELL'INFORMAZIONE "A. FAEDO"

ifip wg 2.7/13.4 on
user interface engineering

Making the Web More Inclusive with Adaptive User Interfaces

Krzysztof Z. Gajos

Harvard School of Engineering and Applied Sciences
33 Oxford St., Cambridge, MA 02138, USA
kgajos@eecs.harvard.edu

Abstract

I build user interface that adapt their structure, appearance and behavior to the goals, abilities, preferences and cultural norms of their users. Prior work in adaptive user interface community has demonstrated that adaptive and adaptable interfaces can improve users' performance and satisfaction. These findings alone should make adaptation a core component of the user interface design practice. But I argue that adaptive interactive systems are even more fundamentally important: they help overcome implicit biases built into most interfaces and they are a scalable approach for democratizing access to digital resources. To convince you of it, I will first present several examples of situations in which the typical one-size-fits-all user interfaces can be a source of unintended, but systematic discrimination causing some groups to be less likely than others to take advantage of a digital resource in the first place, or causing them to have a less efficient or substantially different experience compared to their peers. I will then present examples of several adaptive user interfaces that successfully provided more equitable experiences to broader populations compared to traditional non-adaptive designs. I will conclude by reflecting on the major challenges that stand in the way of broad adoption of adaptive techniques in practice. In particular, I will highlight the mismatch between the abstractions needed to develop effective adaptive user interfaces and the current software engineering practice.

Categories and Subject Descriptors

H.5.m. Information Interfaces and Presentation (e.g. HCI): Miscellaneous

Keywords

Adaptive user interfaces

Short Bio

Krzysztof Gajos is an associate professor of Computer Science at the Harvard School of Engineering and Applied Sciences. Krzysztof is broadly interested in interactive intelligent systems, a research area that bridges artificial intelligence, machine learning and human-computer interaction. Recent projects pursued by his group touched upon areas such as personalized adaptive user interfaces, computer accessibility, peer learning, creativity support tools, crowdsourcing, and tools and methods for engaging broader publics in research.

Prior to arriving at Harvard, Krzysztof was a postdoctoral researcher at Microsoft Research. He received his PhD from University of Washington and his M.Eng. and B.Sc. degrees from MIT. In the Fall of 2005, he was visiting faculty at the Ashesi University in Accra, Ghana, where he taught Introduction to Artificial Intelligence. Krzysztof is a coeditor-in-chief of the ACM Transactions on Interactive Intelligent Systems. He is a recipient of a Sloan Research Fellowship.

EICS'14, June 17–20, 2014, Rome, Italy.
ACM 978-1-4503-2725-1/14/06.
http://dx.doi.org/10.1145/2607023.2611454

.

Dynamically Adapting an AI Game Engine Based on Players' Eye Movements and Strategies

Stefanie Wetzel   Katharina Spiel   Sven Bertel[*]

{stefanie.wetzel, katharina.spiel, sven.bertel}@uni-weimar.de
Usability Research Group, Bauhaus-Universität Weimar
Bauhausstr. 11, 99423 Weimar, Germany

ABSTRACT

Artificial intelligence (AI) game engines have frequently been used to drive computational antagonists when playing games against humans. Limited work exists, however, on using human players' psychophysical measures to directly parametrise AI game engines. Instead, parameters to optimise AI performance are usually derived from general play-related data or user models. This paper presents novel research on using eye movement data in addition to data on users' strategies to adapt the live play of a computational antagonist in the visuo-spatial strategy game, *Hex*. It offers a set of suitable parameters for both types of data. A systematic evaluation of the approach showed, among other things, that using eye movement data led to significantly better gameplay experience for human players, as they experienced less frustration with sufficient challenge. Findings are discussed not only with regard to designing gameplay experience, but also their more general ramifications on using live psychophysical data for intelligent interactive systems.

Author Keywords

Interaction Technologies; Adaptive Gameplay; User Experience Design; User Studies; Eye Movement Tracking; Intelligent Systems.

ACM Classification Keywords

H.5.m. Information Interfaces and Presentation (e.g. HCI): Miscellaneous

INTRODUCTION

The design of antagonists in adaptive games is often based on machine learning techniques (e.g. [43]) or employ artificial intelligence (AI) game engines (e.g. [40]) in order to delineate the gameplay of a computational agent. Their goal is to maximise the strength of the antagonist's gameplay.

---

[*]Contact author.

EICS'14, June 17 - 20 2014, Rome, Italy
Copyright is held by the owner/author(s). Publication rights licensed to ACM.
ACM 978-1-4503-2725-1/14/0615.00.
http://dx.doi.org/10.1145/2607023.2607029

Parameters used for adapting the performance of AI components in games, such as of an AI game engine, are usually derived from game- and situation-related data. In turn-based games, this involves a game's current state, and possibly intelligence on the last moves made by the human player or the computational agent (e.g. [5]). More sophisticated approaches involve deriving parameters from models of a player's behaviour with respect to that player's preferred strategies or tactics (see [11] for full discussion). Such parameters can be used to continually configure AI components during a game (i.e., to provide *adaptivity*), or to establish general and longer-lasting settings for a player or group of players, thus adding aspects of *adaptability* to a game.

This paper presents a novel practical approach to the use of psychophysical data in adaptive games based on live interpretation of a player's eye movements while playing the strategy game, *Hex*, against computational antagonists. For some of these, data derived from eye movements was used to directly parameterise an AI game engine during gameplay. We chose to broaden the set of criteria associated with suitable antagonist behaviour by not including only those centred on optimal gameplay, gameplay strength and maximising the antagonist's prospect of winning. Instead, we also considered a range of softer criteria relating to user experience, such as fun and frustration. As we will show, this approach involved constructing antagonists that, based on an underlying AI game engine, *satisfice* rather than *optimise* in their game play, thereby incidentally conforming to some classical descriptions of human intelligence offered by AI research [38].

Next, we will discuss relevant related research on antagonistic adaptive gaming and the use of psychophysical data for it. We will then introduce foundations of our approach, as well as, briefly, *Hex*, *Six* (an AI game engine for *Hex*), and relevant fundamentals of eye movement tracking and measures. The fourth section will present our series of *Hex*-playing antagonists and some of their respective properties. We will discuss a user study and its results in the fifth section. In the concluding section, we will inspect what the results of our user study can tell beyond the game of *Hex*—specifically, for the design of more intelligent adaptive games and computational game agents, as well as, generally, for the design of user interfaces that make use of live psychophysical user data.

PSYCHOPHYSICAL DATA IN ADAPTIVE GAMES

Research into adaptive games has recently seen progress across a range of conceptually diverse approaches. These include general work on modelling play and players, such as those based on schema theory [30], as well as on constructing (or discussing how to best construct) adaptive games involving AI system components (e.g., [14]). However, current research employing AI components does not also employ psychophysical user data.

Those approaches to adaptive gaming that do use parameters and mechanisms derived from psychophysical measures do not also include AI components. Among these are applications of brain-computer interfaces (BCIs) which adapt to a user's mental state. This is often achieved by adapting classification functions to the individual user. For example, [22] present the design of an adaptive self-paced brain-computer interface for *Hangman*, which significantly outperforms a non-adaptive control system by adapting classificators to variations in player fatigue.

Parametrisation of adaptive environments via psychophysical measures has been conducted and discussed (e.g. [4]), however, in a range of non-game related contexts, such as intelligent learning environments (e.g. [33]), visualisation tasks (e.g. [41]) or human-robot interaction (e.g. [3] or [16]). When eye tracking is used to parametrise adaptiveness in games, this has not yet been done with a focus on game experience, but rather, for example, with a focus on "effectiveness and efficiency of [serious] games" [29].

In recent years, there has been an increase in the number of adaptive BCI systems for interactive applications, including games. In a current survey, [20] point out the potential of increasing general interaction quality through adapting interactive systems based on user BCI data. Video games in particular are expected to benefit from such adaptation [31]. Similar approaches and analyses exist for data derived via eye movement tracking instead of BCI interfaces, including for video game control [39] or for context-aware games [9].

FOUNDATIONS

User Experience in Games
Adapting an agent to a user's gameplay can involve setting the strength of its play to that of the user. Motivation for playing computer games, however, does not simply depend on winning or losing games, but additionally on dimensions such as fun or frustration, which can positively influence the user's game experience.

As [12] argues, game designs should specifically allow for adaptive choices modifying the balance between challenge and abilities without interrupting the player's core activities' (i.e., gameplay). While their position suggests player involvement in determining values for those choices, we propose an adaptive automated process.

Hex
Hex is a visuo-spatial game with strategic components. We chose *Hex* because it is based on relatively simple rules but still offers challenges for experienced players. The game was selected from a larger class of comparable visuo-spatial board games such as *Go* or *Nine Man Morris*. We expect approach and findings to be similar for other games of that class.

The parameters used were designed to be applicable or easily adaptable to other games.

Hex was developed separately by Piet Hein and John Nash [17] as a two-player game. It is played on a field of $n \cdot m$ hexagonal cells, with usually $n = m$ (cf. Fig. 3). Two players alternately place tokens on unoccupied cells. Each player tries to lay an uninterrupted line of tokens across the board, attempting to connect opposite edges.

Common Strategies
Hex is a deterministic game with a winning strategy [10]. A detailed description of *Hex* strategies can be found in [8]. The selection of strategies we used to calculate strategy values are described and mapped onto goals in Table 1. Those also coincide with strategies that are often employed by fairly inexperienced players; it is those fairly inexperienced players that were in the focus of our study.

Eye Movement Data
We decided to capture eye movements during gameplay and use related measures to track a player's behaviour against different antagonistic setups and to provide input to adaptive system components. We used data derived from eye movements for our approach, since collecting it is non-invasive, largely unobtrusive, and quick to set up. Furthermore, it has been shown that players' game expertise and eye movements are related (c.f. [37] in reference to [15]). Importantly, as the focus of visual attention often corresponds to the point of gaze, eye movement data has been successfully employed to track and model human mental processes in tasks that involve visuo-spatial representations, such as reading maps or reasoning with diagrams (e.g., [6]).

Eye Tracking
Videoocculography is today the most commonly used non-invasive technique for eye tracking. The setup consists of one or two cameras directed at the eye, which are mounted on a headband or placed in front of a user. Mechanisms for counteracting small head movements are often incorporated. Gaze points recorded by the cameras are normally mapped onto screen or scene coordinates, using reference points obtained via calibration procedures (see [18] for methods; [27] for use in human-computer interaction).

Eye Movements and Measures
Two types of eye movements relevant to our approach are fixations and saccades. While the eye moves constantly, a fixation is a period during which it stays relatively stable (i.e., registered gaze positions show low spatial dispersion). For various visuo-spatial tasks, fixations have minimum durations between 100–150ms, and typically last for 250–300ms [42]. Visual input processing happens during fixations, resulting in an inspection of scenes in a sequential, piecemeal fashion. Saccades are spatially larger, temporally shorter, high-velocity eye movements, which happen between fixations. For a discussion of eye movement types and measures, see [7, chap. 4–5].

The choice of suitable methods and measures for interpreting eye movement data gathered during interaction with a user

Table 1: Mapping of strategies on goals

Strategy	Description	Goal	Calculation
First Move	The first move indicates the strength of the following game, which specifies who has the winning strategy.	Start at a strong position. The closer it is to centre lines, or to the central field of the board, the stronger the move.	Based on move's distance to board's centre. On a field of size $11x11$, strength values are chosen from $[0,1]$ in steps of 0.2.
Bridges		Secure more space than covered by the actual tokens by securing the connection between two tokens.	Binary decision: bridge or no bridge; value in $\{0,1\}$.
Distance Blocking	Preparation of moves that will eventually cut through the opponent's planned path.	Obstruct future moves of an opponent.	Ratio of tokens belonging to the player or the opponent in the neighbourhood of the placed token. Range: $[0..1]$.
Forced Moves		Force the opponent to a specific next move.	Binary decision, forced move or not; value in $\{0,1\}$.
Ladders		Force the opponent to take a certain route that eventually leads to an own win.	Length of line of tokens, without twists, over line length; range of $[0..1]$.

interface depends highly on the current task and stimuli, as well as on the properties of the tracking devices (e.g., temporal and spatial resolutions, temporal lag in data availability), among other issues. It is a continuing topic of scientific debate. We followed recommendations on measures by [36], whenever this is not otherwise noted.

Fixations are commonly interpreted as loci of visual focus. In visual search tasks, the more fixations are made, the less efficient the visual search is. A high spatial density of fixations in a particular area can be interpreted as it attracting increased user attention. Fixation length hints towards effort, such as perceptual or cognitive processing loads [28].

A shift in the current focus of attention precedes an actual saccade [25], and while focus and gaze location can be discrete, moving both simultaneously to different locations is hard [35]. Larger saccadic amplitudes (i.e., saccade lengths) indicate that the player's attention is drawn to more remote areas of the board and, possibly, that information relevant to current mental processes, such as the planning of a move in *Hex*, is spread out across larger distances.

A transition is a pair of subsequent fixations that fall into different designated areas. We refer to these as areas of interest (AOIs). [36] suggest following [24] and [21] to inspect the matrix of all transitions over a time period to determine the user's uncertainty during a task. High transition frequencies between two AOIs can point to a mental integration of the contents in these areas via integrative saccades (cf. [26]).

A scanpath [34] refers to a series of subsequent fixations. The concept is useful to check for recurring patterns of fixations,

which may indicate repeating patterns in mental processing. When seen two-dimensionally, scanpaths can help distinguish the areas that were covered (i.e., inspected) by the user from those that were not.

Components
The weights of the parameters were determined by a top-down theory-driven approach. Other weight combinations were tried in a pilot study but dismissed, as they produced too small component or overall CAP value (please see the next section below for a discussion of these values).

Play Related Components
Play related components are calculations which are solely based on both sides' current play. Adaptivity is created by reacting not only to the the player's recent moves but also to the current game state and the antagonistic strategy. Some of the calculations might seem specific to *Hex*. However, they can be generalised for other visuo-spatial games as well.

Calculating Game Progress is only needed for the antagonist's moves, the simple formula $\frac{2}{n}$ where n is set to the count of moves already played can represent part of the desired strength of the antagonist as the game goes on. Incorporating this parameter in the adaptive antagonist's calculations ensures that its first move is not too weak. Especially in games like *Hex*, a weak starting move leads to a weak game more than a weak move towards the end of the game.

Since the difference between Win and Loss situations for every side in *Hex* can be theoretically calculated at any point and, if that is impractical, be estimated fairly well, we included this important value as a forecast parameter in our

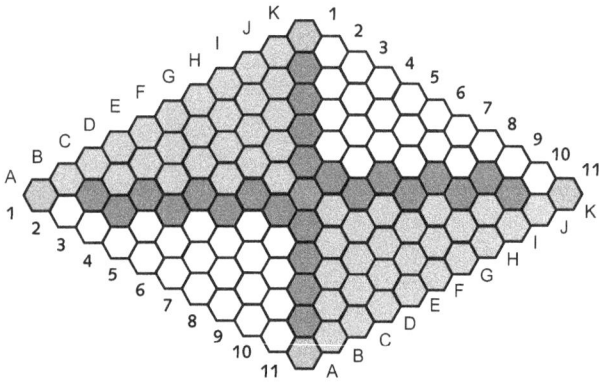

Figure 1: Board zones — red: middle of board, green: neutral cells, blue: bordering zones, grey: area of player, white: area of antagonist (adapted from [8])

adaptivity calculations for CAP. The value of interest is the numeric assessment of the best possible move as evaluated by the *Six* game engine. This forecast helps in adjusting the strength of the antagonist's moves.

There are two types of strategy analysis incorporated in our play related components, the Antagonistic Strategy and the Player Strategy. They are both calculated in the same way. These parameters reflect some part of the history of the game. While this goes only one or two moves back, these moves are also based on previous decisions. The calculation is a two-step process: First, for each possible strategy (e.g., bridge moves or ladders), a strength value is determined (see also Table 1). In the second step, these values are compared and the highest reflects the strength of the previous move. In this context, the player strategy has a stronger influence in the adaptivity formula than the antagonistic strategy.

In *Hex*, the Player Attitude can be determined from the location of the most recently placed token. Figure 1 shows how the cells on a *Hex* board can be interpreted. The value for this parameter is determined by a calculation determining the distance to the player zone. It increases the more aggressive the player acts and ranges between [0..1]. Values above 0.5 describe moves in the antagonist's zone, whereas values below this threshold describe moves in the player's zone, which are seen as more defensive play.

Eye Movement Data Components
As psychophysical component, Adapt-EM uses, firstly, the Scanpath in order to set allowed cells for the antagonist. Those limit the cells into which the antagonist can place its next move. All cells which have been actively examined by the player tell the antagonist that these attracted the player's attention. In *Hex*-related calculations, all cells within a certain radius around the last player and antagonist moves are also considered to be allowed. The radius is based on the general adaptivity value calculated, but with a minimum value to allow for strategies such as bridges.

[36] suggested a transition matrix to determine uncertainty. We only recorded transition changes and calculated the relationship as $\frac{time}{\# \, of \, transitions}$. The lower this value gets the more

uncertainty can be seen. Hence, the Transition Value gives information about the depth of the player's uncertainty. For *Hex* we defined one cell as an area of interest (AOI), so the transition value reflects how often the player refocused on different cells of the board. The lower this value, the more uncertain the player was about which cells to consider, which can be interpreted as general uncertainty.

Confidence is a parameter based on human interaction in games. It can be seen to reflect the antagonist's equivalent of hubris or self-consciousness. The confidence parameter includes play-related and eye movement data components and is the parameter with the most historic knowledge. The confidence value C is modelled by using the following formula, which approximates the findings of [19] best:

$$C = sig\left(\frac{(\text{PS} + 2 \cdot \text{WL} + \text{TV})}{4}\right)$$

(with $sig = \frac{1}{10 \cdot e^{-10x+2.8}+1}$, PS: Player Strategy, WL: Win and Loss Ratio, TV: Transition Value)

The initial value is set at the middle of the $[0;1]$ range of the sigmoid function, where the antagonist's modelled hubris and self-consciousness are in a balanced state. In subsequent moves, confidence is calculated in three steps: (1) Take the mean of the value for player strategy, transition value and twice the win/loss value. (2) Use the mean as input for the sigmoid function as the new confidence value. And, (3) compare the calculated confidence with the confidence of the previous move with a maximum change in confidence of 10% (to prevent unreasonable drastic changes).

Table 2: Types of antagonists

Antagonist	Behaviour	Principle
Baseline	optimising	*Six*
Adapt	satisficing	*Six* + individual play-related data
Adapt-EM	satisficing	*Six* + individual play-related data (incl. user's eye movements)

APPROACH

Types of Antagonists
In order to verify the usefulness of different parameters that may be used by adaptive antagonists, we defined three different types; one of them employs eye movement data in a novel way to create step-wise adaptivity (see also Table 2).

Baseline
While *Hex* is a deterministic game, so far, only opening positions up to a $9x9$ field size have been weakly solved [2]. Every game engine for *Hex* hence incorporates algorithms to address the lack of computability for larger board sizes. We chose the *Six* engine by Gábor Melis[1] as the Baseline antagonist. *Six* is one of the leading competitors among optimising *Hex* engines [23]. It optimises its play by incorporating

---

[1]available via **http://six.cetes.hu**

a two-ply truncated-width alpha-beta search [1]. The only global adaptability offered by this engine is setting game levels. Doing so determines the search width of the game search tree. We chose the lowest level available for the Baseline.

Six was also chosen as a foundation for the two adaptive antagonists described next, as it is available as open source, permits granular alterations of the search width, and permits to restrict the set of legal cells for an individual move.

In the Baseline setup, no modifications were made to *Six* and neither one of the two options of alteration – cap value for the depth of the alpha-beta search or limiting available cells to a set of allowed fields – were used.

Adaptive Antagonist (Adapt)

The basis for the adaptive antagonist (Adapt) is *Six*. It additionally makes use of game- and play-related measurements to determine its next move. Each individual move is calculated according to the player's current move, but also considers its own last move. It adapts solely by calculations that can be extracted from the game state itself and from those player strategies that can be determined from moves.

The parameters of the play-related components below are combined in a formula which calculates the cap value CAP; *Six* can return moves of strength up to CAP (PS: Player Strategy, WL: Win and Loss Ratio, GP: Game Progress, AS: Antagonistic Strategy, PA: Player Attitude; all values in $[0, 1]$):

$$\frac{1.5 \cdot \text{PS} + 2 \cdot \text{WL} + 0.5 \cdot \text{GP} + (1 - \text{AS}) + (1 - \text{PA})}{2} + 0.5$$

The individual values of the parameters differ in their effective value ranges, so that weights partially serve as range normalizing factors. The resulting CAP value ranges between $[0.5..3.5]$ and is passed on to *Six* for the computation of Adapt's next move. The higher CAP is, the stronger a move is, and the stronger the antagonist will react to it. This means, effectively, that the pruning of results in the search tree expanded by *Six* for possible moves is performed according to the strength of the whole game until this point and even more so according to that of the previous move. Adapt, hence, incorporates a user model that relies simply on the player strategy and their game attitude.

Adaptive Antagonist Using Eye Movement Data (Adapt-EM)

In addition to all parameters used by Adapt, Adapt-EM also considers eye movement data in order to extrapolate more of the human player's skill and strategies (see also Figure 2). This is supposed to create an antagonist that is more fun to play against, since especially eye movements can reveal key elements of a player's strategising [32]. Furthermore, Adapt-EM employs a concept of play confidence.

Adapt-EM incorporates eye movement data: Firstly, within the formula for the cap value CAP, secondly, in the calculations of the confidence value C and the transition value TV (for explanations, see below). For Adapt-EM,

$$CAP = \frac{\text{Adapt-Params} + 2 \cdot (1 - \text{C}) + \text{TV}}{3} + 0.5$$

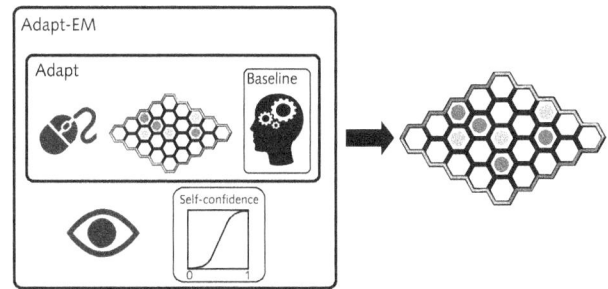

Figure 2: Schematic of AI components

The term Adapt-Params simply includes all parameters used in the numerator of the CAP formula in the Adapt condition described above.

Possible moves of Adapt-EM are restricted to fields adjacent to the last move of the antagonist and to fields around the last move of the player. Any field with user's eye fixations in it is also considered. The resulting set of allowed fields and computed CAP value are passed on to *Six* for the computation of Adapt-EM's next move.

Adapt-EM's user model is broader and considers more aspects of a player's state than the user model employed in the Adapt condition. Due to the differences in the three setups, the respective intrinsic game difficulty is also different. Our hypothesis is that adaption in a system changes intrinsic difficulty for each user according to the user's skills.

USER STUDY

In order to have solid grounds for the development of the approach described above, we conducted a series of studies in which we tested where players of *Hex* and especially novices look during a game and how this information is useful for an adaptive antagonist. Finally, we also conducted a user study to compare the Baseline, Adapt and Adapt-EM types.

In our laboratory setup, we used an *EyeLink II* eye tracker by *SR Research* in monocular mode and with fixation detection at 250 Hz in combination with an in-house eye tracking framework to drive experiments and register data. For the

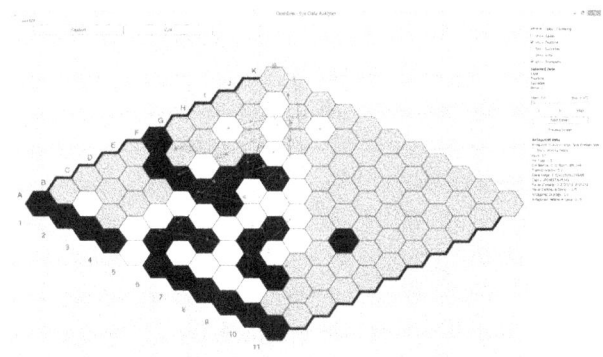

Figure 3: *OpenEyes* — Analysing eye movement data with our custom visualisation tool

analysis of the eye movement data, we employed the *SR Research DataViewer* as well as our own *OpenEyes* tool.

Method

To acquire a sufficient amount of data, we had 31 test subjects in a mixed in-between/within subject study. While all test subjects played against every antagonist, only 16 of them were told that eye movement data may be used to adapt the antagonist's behaviour. Participants played three training games followed by two games against each antagonist in randomised order for a total of six games recorded for every participant. They were allowed to take a break after three games played. A brief questionnaire after each game and a final questionnaire concluded each session.

The test subjects' age ranged from 21 to 60 years with a median of 25 years. 21 of them had a background in Computer Science, most of those were students. None of them had any particular knowledge about *Hex*, but most of them were familiar with digital or board games. All test subjects participated in the study out of their own free will with no extra incentive.

Due to technical problems some of the games were not properly recorded. In total, we were able to analyse 176 games; 60 for the Baseline setup, 59 for Adapt and 57 for Adapt-EM. The evaluation concerning eye movement data is based on the human player's moves.

Selected Hypotheses

First of all, we expected that, compared to playing against other antagonists, players would experience the most fun when playing against Adapt-EM (hypothesis H1a). We also expected that subjects would report a lower degree of frustration and challenge, respectively (H1b).

We assumed that the win rates in Baseline and Adapt/Adapt-EM conditions would differ and that they would also differ between Adapt and Adapt-EM. We expected furthermore that Adapt-EM would have a winrate of about 50% (H2).

Knowledge about the use of eye movement data against a player was also been deemed to be a framing parameter that would influence player behaviour. We expected to be able to detect differences in saccadic amplitudes between players of different conditions (H3).

Results

We statistically analysed our data with SPSS. Significance was tested with U-tests, Kruskal-Wallis tests and Jonckheere-Terpstra tests, since our data was not normally distributed. The strength of an effect was interpreted according to [13] for behavioural data, where $r = 0.1$ indicates a small effect, $r = 0.3$ describes a medium effect, and $r = 0.5$ can be interpreted as strong effect.

Self-Reported Results

Self-reported results were taken from a short questionnaire after every game, which asked the test participants to rate the game that they had just played on attributes of challenge, frustration, fun, and nervousness; each on a Likert-scale with six options ranging from affirmation (6) to disagreement (1) to the statements presented (such as "The game was fun."). In

the study, we mixed the polarity of statements to deal with possible positivity bias. For analysis, the values were reoriented to the same polarity, so that high values indicate high estimates for given parameters, and vice-versa for low values.

The results of a Kruskal-Wallis test showed no effect for fun ($H(2) = 3.42$, $p = 0.189$), which means that hypothesis H1a had to be rejected.

However, the values reported for challenge and frustration differ significantly. All effects are reported at $p < 0.05$. This means that challenge ($H(2) = 11.38$) as well as frustration ($H(2) = 13.27$) were significantly affected by the chosen setup. Jonckheere's test revealed a trend in the data: there is a development of lowering the means for both to acceptable values (challenge: 4.19, frustration: 2.42). Note, that the value for challenge on the Likert scale should not go under the possible mean of 3.5 whereas the mean for frustration should not go over this possible mean for the values to be acceptable. They are acceptable for both adaptive setups, but not in the Baseline setup (3.55), and significantly better in Adapt-EM compared to Adapt (challenge: $J = 4106$, $z = -1.18$, $r = -0.08$; frustration: $J = 4320$, $z = -2.34$, $r = -0.17$). Hence, H1b can be accepted. It can be inferred that eye movement data does not change the subjective evaluation of the games, however, step-wise live adaptivity does.

Performance of Adapt/Adapt-EM

The rates at which the different antagonist types won games differed highly significantly ($H(2) = 71.37$, $p < 0.001$, $r = 0.64$). While no test participant was able to beat the Baseline, 75% won against Adapt and 53% against Adapt-EM. This allows us to accept hypothesis H2.

We also found a significant difference ($U = 727557$, $z = -2, 44$, $p < 0.05$), albeit with a very small effect ($r = 0.05$), in the recorded transition values for Adapt (mean: 0.42) and Adapt-EM (mean: 0.39, with values ranging from 0 to 1). This means that against Adapt, test participants were less insecure and, hence, a little more confident in their play than against Adapt-EM. However, participants were also more likely to win against Adapt, which might make them more confident in general. These differences can be seen as a proof of concept more than as a result giving implications for future development and analysis, especially due to the small effect size.

Framing through Knowledge

Knowing about the use of eye movement data in an antagonistic setup frames the gameplay tremendously. Figure 4 shows how all of the self-reported parameters significantly differ in comparison of those test participants who were told that eye movement data might be used against them and those who were not told beforehand. An inspection of the values shows higher levels of fun and lower levels of frustration, challenge, and nervousness for those test participants who were made aware of the use of their psychophysical data.

In the final questionnaire we also asked the participants to subjectively judge whether they had behaved differently when they knew about the use of eye movement data, or whether they thought that they would have had behaved differently,

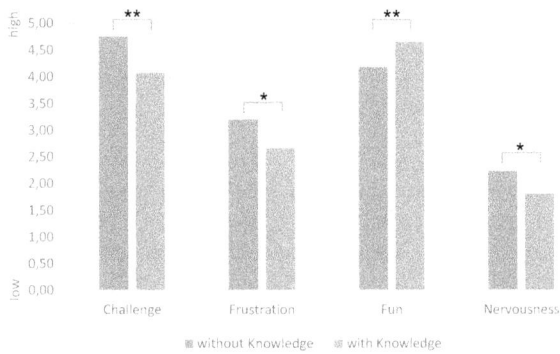

Figure 4: Results of questionnaire according to knowledge

Table 4: Results of U-tests on three measures of eye movement data by two categories of players' pre-game knowledge about the use of eye movements against them (K/C). $\alpha = 0.05$. Significant differences are marked by grey shading.

	Mean K	Mean C	K vs. C	Effect size r
Fixations per Move	15.47	12.88	$p < 0.001$	0.05
Saccades per Move	15.45	12.94	$p = 0.001$	0.05
Fixation Durations in ms	301.84	333.10	$p < 0.001$	0.08

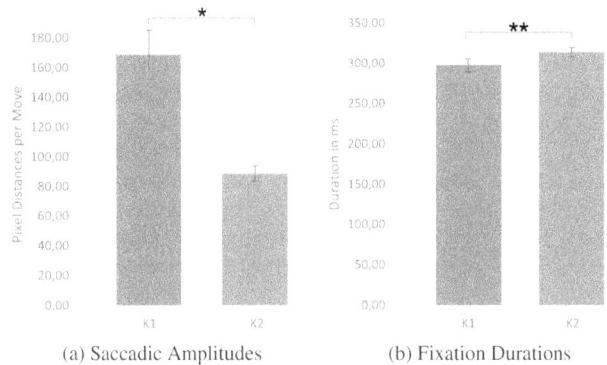

(a) Saccadic Amplitudes   (b) Fixation Durations

Figure 5: Saccadic amplitudes and fixation durations according to self-reported behaviour

had known about it beforehand (see Table 3). We compared the self-reported results with the values for saccadic amplitudes and the fixation durations. While the saccadic amplitudes did not differ, contrary to our hypothesis, we find that there were more and shorter fixations when players had knowledge about the use of eye movement data (see Table 4).

We investigated further into possible differences in behaviour when it was self-reported as such (K1 vs. K2 in Table 3). For this, we excluded the Baseline antagonist against which all participants quickly lost and hence did not have the option for much strategic coordination. There are significant differences in saccadic amplitudes and the fixation durations as can be seen in Fig. 5, in such that there are larger amplitudes, but longer fixation durations for K1, but smaller amplitudes combined with short fixations for K2.

Table 3: Frequency counts based on post-hoc questionnaire on subjective interpretation of behaviour. Knowledge (K): subjects were told before games that data on their own eye movements would be used against them; they were asked if they had changed their behaviour (group K2), or had not (group K1). No knowledge (C): subjects were not told before games that eye movement data would be used against them; they were asked if they would have changed their behaviour (group C2) had they been been told, or would not have changed their behaviour (group C1).

	Same Behaviour	Different Behaviour
K ($n = 15$)	7 (K1)	8 (K2)
C ($n = 15$)	3 (C1)	12 (C2)

CONCLUSION

The presented research investigates the use of eye movement data as a form of psychophysical data to provide adaptivity in games through parameterising an AI game engine. To do so, we compared three different antagonists: Baseline, Adapt and Adapt-EM.

We evaluated player frustration as high for the Baseline and as significantly lower for the Adapt and again significantly lower for the Adapt-EM condition. Similar findings can be reported for the subjective evaluation of the challenge of a

game. These two parameters are important to watch out for when assessing user experience in games. Frustration can also be understood as a factor which influences a player's productive motivation — as long as occurring frustrations can be resolved within the game. An antagonist should thus best aim to create, and to maintain, a medium level of user frustration throughout a game.

It is also important to give novices a chance to win in a game. Based on this, Adapt-EM offers the relatively best grounds for creating a satisfactory level of user experience for novice players: The players have leverage to improve their game and their use of strategies. It can be assumed then, that players stick longer to a game when it offers them sufficient, though not too many, challenges, which let them continually learn according to their current skills, but which also offer them positive reinforcement through winning games. Since these properties are desirable for creating a good user experience, we propose to measure the performance of an antagonist not simply based on the highest winning rate. An ideal antagonist should offer its players individual adaption to their skills so they can improve and are neither overtaxed nor underengaged.

Knowing about the use of eye movement data enables the players to judge the situation correctly. Players reported on significantly lower frustration and challenge values when they knew about the use of eye movement data. Reports on fun value were not significantly different. It can be concluded, that players who know that their eye movements were (supposedly always) used against them were subjectively under a lower level of stress during their play than the control group. These findings give room to interpretation. It could be that players actually prefer playing against antagonists that act (or, better, react) more similar to how a human player would. Alternatively, it could be that players reported lower frustration and challenges, as playing against a system that uses their eye movements was a novel experience, with novelty in itself affecting self-reported measures. Further studies are needed to investigate which of these is the case. Further studies seem also indicated into why frustration and challenge value showed significant differences, but fun and nervousness did not.

The difference in the number of fixations and saccades as well as in fixation durations show that there is significantly more cognitive effort involved when players are not fully informed about the setup. In that case, they focus more on smaller and distinct areas of the game. Since players were told only vaguely that their eye movement data was used, but not exactly how, it can be assumed, that they tried to consciously move their gaze away from their actual location of interest instead of visually exploring the board more thoroughly.

However, the possibility exists that players who knew eye movements were used tried to game the system. While there were only novices present in the user study on which we have reported here, we would expect experienced players to try to exert some strategic control of their eye movements while playing against an antagonist known to track and analyze them. Assumedly, this can also happen between two human players playing *Hex*. Incorporating this in one's strategy can also be an aspect of fun in a game. Hence, self-reported data as well as eye movement data might change, if experienced players are part of a future user study.

Players can also accurately judge whether their behaviour is different from usual behaviours. Analysis of the eye movement data revealed significant differences in the visual analysis of the board. This indicates that there are probably differences in strategic behaviour as well, mostly through concentrating on smaller areas of the board when test participants reported that they actively changed their behaviour.

These results show the viability of our approach and how step-wise adaptivity as used in Adapt and Adapt-EM creates a better user gameplay experience than general adaptability. The use of eye movement data has been shown to work well to influence win rates and, hence, improves the conditions for better game experience and mastering the game during play. Use of eye movement data should be strongly considered as an option for the design of intelligent adaptive games.

OUTLOOK
The research described above offers practically applicable insights into the parameterisation of an adaptive intelligent antagonist that uses live eye movement data to enhance its adaptivity. While eye movement data was employed for the present study, this work can be adapted to other types of psychophysiological data. Several future research options as well as other use cases for eye movements in adaptive interactive software are here discussed.

Phase Recognition
Eye movement data gathered during a game may be clustered according to phases a player goes through (cf. [28], [6]). This could be applied to establish specific phase-dependent rules for adapting interaction. Similarly, players will fall into different types based on patterns in the eye movements which they produce, even when given the same task and stimulus. Adapting interaction rules to such player types thus seems a viable course of future work as well. As a first step, phases in playing and types of players would have to be determined. Core elements of global phases would likely include win or loss situations, advantages players have, as well as whether a play is more aggressive or defensive. It can be assumed that, similar to findings of [28], among others, there exist phases which are repeated in a similar fashion for every individual turn in a turn-based game (such as situation assessment, planning, and execution). With knowledge about typical phase repetitions and the clustering of certain phases, be it during a move or during the game, eye movement data can be given stronger weights for strategically important phases.

Adaption Based on Individual Eye Movement Data
Adapt-EM uses eye movement data and interprets it in the same way for every human player who plays the game. However, gathered data was different for individual players. On a player-by-player basis, it could be useful to compare eye movement behaviour at a certain point during the game with previous eye movement data, and to generate hypotheses about the player's strategy and cognitive state. Certain types of players might also show type-specific behaviour in their eye movement data, possibly permitting player classification based on their eye movement data. Furthermore, such approach might allow the use of eye movement data which is highly variable between individuals such as pupil dilation.

Further Research into Parameters
While we focused on the use of eye movement data along with data derived about players' strategies, the other parameters still require some extra effort to make sure that they are suitable and reliable to influence adaptivity. As the weight choice regulates the system's effectiveness, a more quantitative and data-driven approach is desirable for future system versions, e.g., modeling parameter interdependence.

Additional parameters could be explored, such as regarding the times used for a move. It might also be fruitful to explore the usefulness of the parameters presented here for other games and other game types. Another option would be to incorporate other types of psychophysical data into the setup, such as EEG or skin conductance data.

Also, generalising the presented parameters for the adaption of other strategic games (e.g. Chess) and game types (e.g. First-Person-Shooters) will require some work. As a more direct aspect, further research should be conducted in user studies comparing a version of Adapt that also models confidence and nervousness without eye movement data to Adapt-EM to further evaluate when and how using eye movement data is beneficial.

Effects of Framing

The effects of framing (i.e., whether player were, or were not, told that data about their eye movements would be used by the antagonist) on self-reported player emotions as well as on player strategies on which we reported here, and the mechanisms that produce those effects, certainly merit further research. We are currently designing a new line of user studies which will particularly address effects of framing for a setup of antagonists that is very similar to the one used in the study described here. Players on different levels of game expertise will be included for this study. We expect that eye movement patterns (e.g. regarding transitions) and strategies that reflected in these patterns will depend on player expertise as well as on measures of a player's current emotional state and general personality type.

Other Applications

For fields other than games, the presented research could well be used to enhance interaction with intelligent software that benefits from modelling user states. Areas that come to mind are e-learning, tutor and expert systems (c.f. [33]), information visualisation (c.f. [41]), etc. Analysing eye movement data in live contexts permits us to infer those screen areas that are currently especially important to the user. Such focus can be guided or strengthened appropriately according to a user's eye movements and the task at hand. Key moments important for good interaction can then better be supported as needed, and, as shown by our approach, with less frustration and more enjoyment for the user.

ACKNOWLEDGEMENTS

We would like to thank Jannis Harder and Florian Madeya as members of the initial student project that led to this work; Jakob Gomoll for setting up the in-house eye tracking experimentation software framework; Maximilian Schirmer for theoretical and critical support; Kearsley Schieder-Wethy for proof reading; and five anonymous reviewers for their helpful and constructive comments. Katharina Spiel would like to acknowledge financial support by the Heinrich-Böll-Stiftung.

REFERENCES

1. Arneson, B., Hayward, R., and Henderson, P. MoHex Wins Hex Tournament. *ICGA Journal 32*, 2 (2009), 114–116.

2. Arneson, B., Hayward, R. B., and Henderson, P. Solving Hex: Beyond Humans. In *Computers and Games*. Springer, 2011, 1–10.

3. Atienza, R., and Zelinsky, A. Active Gaze Tracking for Human-Robot Interaction. In *Proceedings of the 4th IEEE International Conference on Multimodal Interfaces*, IEEE Computer Society (2002).

4. Bednarik, R. Potentials of Eye-Movement Tracking in Adaptive Systems. In *Proc. 4th Workshop on Empirical Evaluation of Adaptive Systems, 10th Intl. Conf. on User Modeling UM2005, Edinburgh* (2005), 1–8.

5. Bergsma, M. H. J., and Spronck, P. Adaptive Spatial Reasoning for Turn-based Strategy Games. In *AIIDE*, C. Darken and M. Mateas, Eds., AAAI Press (2008).

6. Bertel, S. Towards Attention-Guided Human-Computer Collaborative Reasoning for Spatial Configuration and Design. In *Foundations of Augmented Cognition (Proc. HCI International 2007, Beijing)*, LNCS 4565, Springer; Berlin (2007), 337–345.

7. Bertel, S. *Spatial Structures and Visual Attention in Diagrammatic Reasoning*. Pabst Science Publishers; Lengerich, 2010.

8. Browne, C. *Hex Strategy - Making the Right Connections*. AK Peters, 2000.

9. Bulling, A., Roggen, D., and Tröster, G. EyeMote – Towards Context-Aware Gaming Using Eye Movements Recorded from Wearable Electrooculography. In *Proceedings of the 2nd International Conference on Fun and Games*, Springer-Verlag (2008), 33–45.

10. Campbell, G. On Optimal Play in the Game of Hex. *INTEGERS: Electronic Journal of Combinatorial Number Theory 4*, 2 (2004), 1–23.

11. Charles, D., Kerr, A., McNeill, M., McAlister, M., Black, M., Kücklich, J., Moore, A., and Stringer, K. Player-Centred Game Design: Player Modelling and Adaptive Digital Games. In *Proceedings of the Digital Games Research Conference* (2005).

12. Chen, J. Flow in Games (and Everything Else). *Communications of the ACM 50*, 4 (2007), 31–34.

13. Cohen, J. *Statistical Power Analysis for the Behavioral Sciences (2nd Edition)*, 2 ed. Routledge, July 1988.

14. Conroy, D., Wyeth, P., and Johnson, D. Modeling Player-Like Behavior for Game AI Design. In *Proceedings of the 8th Intl. Conference on Advances in Computer Entertainment Technology*, ACM (2011), 9.

15. De Groot, A. D., and de Groot, A. D. *Thought and Choice in Chess*, vol. 4. Walter de Gruyter, 1978.

16. Decker, D., and Piepmeier, J. A. Gaze Tracking Interface for Robotic Control. In *System Theory, 2008. SSST 2008. 40th Southeastern Symposium on*, IEEE (2008), 274–278.

17. Demaine, E. D. Playing Games with Algorithms: Algorithmic Combinatorial Game Theory. In *Mathematical Foundations of Computer Science 2001*. Springer, 2001, 18–33.

18. Duchowski, A. T. *Eye Tracking Methodology: Theory and Practice*, second ed. Springer, London, 2002.

19. Einhorn, H. J., and Hogarth, R. M. Confidence in Judgment: Persistence of the Illusion of Validity. *Psychological Review 85*, 5 (1978), 395–416.

20. Ferreira, A. L. S., de Miranda, L. C., de Miranda, E. E. C., and Sakamoto, S. G. A Survey of Interactive Systems Based on Brain-Computer Interfaces. *SBC Journal on 3D Interactive Systems 4*, 1 (2013), 3–13.

21. Goldberg, J. H., and Kotval, X. P. Computer Interface Evaluation Using Eye Movements: Methods and Constructs. *International Journal of Industrial Ergonomics 24*, 6 (1999), 631–645.

22. Hasan, B. A. S., and Gan, J. Q. Hangman BCI: An Unsupervised Adaptive Self-Paced Brain–Computer Interface for Playing Games. *Computers in Biology and Medicine 42*, 5 (2012), 598–606.

23. Hayward, R. B. Six Wins Hex Tournament. *ICGA Journal 29*, 3 (2006), 163–165.

24. Hendrickson, J. J. Performance, Preference, and Visual Scan Patterns on a Menu-Based System: Implications for Interface Design. In *ACM SIGCHI Bulletin*, vol. 20, ACM (1989), 217–222.

25. Hoffman, J. Visual Attention and Eye Movements. In *Attention*, H. Pashler, Ed. Psychology Press, Hove, 1998, 119–153.

26. Holsanova, J., Holmberg, N., and Holmqvist, K. Reading Information Graphics: The Role of Spatial Contiguity and Dual Attentional Guidance. *Applied Cognitive Psychology 23*, 9 (2009), 1215–1226.

27. Jacob, R. J. What you Look at is what you Get: Eye Movement-based Interaction Techniques. In *Proceedings of the SIGCHI Conference on Human factors in Computing Systems*, ACM (1990), 11–18.

28. Just, M., and Carpenter, P. Reading and spatial cognition: Reflections from eye fixations. *Eye movement research: Physiological and psychological aspects 2* (1988), 193–213.

29. Kickmeier-Rust, M. D., Hillemann, E., and Albert, D. Tracking the UFO's Paths: Using Eye-Tracking for the Evaluation of Serious Games. In *Virtual and Mixed Reality-New Trends*. Springer, 2011, 315–324.

30. Lindley, C. A., and Sennersten, C. C. Game Play Schemas: From Player Analysis to Adaptive Game Mechanics. In *Proc. 2006 International Conference on Game Research and Development* (2006), 47–53.

31. Lotte, F. Brain-Computer Interfaces for 3D Games: Hype or Hope? In *Proceedings of the 6th International Conference on Foundations of Digital Games*, ACM (2011), 325–327.

32. Meijering, B., van Rijn, H., Taatgen, N. A., and Verbrugge, R. What Eye Movements can Tell about Theory of Mind in a Strategic Game. *PloS One 7*, 9.

33. Merten, C., and Conati, C. Eye-tracking to Model and Adapt to User Meta-Cognition in Intelligent Learning Environments. In *Proc. of the 11th Intl. Conference on Intelligent user interfaces*, ACM (2006), 39–46.

34. Noton, D., and Stark, L. Eye Movement and Visual Perception. *Scientific American 224*, 6 (1971), 34–43.

35. Peterson, M. S., Kramer, A. F., and Irwin, D. E. Covert Shifts of Attention Precede Involuntary Eye Movements. *Perception & Psychophysics 66* (2006), 398–405.

36. Poole, A., and Ball, L. J. Eye Tracking in Human-Computer Interaction and Usability Research: Current Status and Future Prospects. In *Encyclopedia of Human Computer Interaction*, C. Ghaoui, Ed. IGI Global, December 2005.

37. Reingold, E. M., Charness, N., Pomplun, M., and Stampe, D. M. Visual Span in Expert Chess Players: Evidence from Eye Movements. *Psychological Science 12* (2001), 48–55.

38. Simon, H. Rational Choice and the Structure of the Environment. *Psychological Review; Psychological Review 63*, 2 (1956), 129.

39. Smith, J. D., and Graham, T. Use of Eye Movements for Video Game Control. In *Proc. 2006 ACM SIGCHI Intl. Conf. on Advances in Computer Entertainment Technology (ACE)*, ACM (2006), 20.

40. Spronck, P., Ponsen, M., Sprinkhuizen-Kuyper, I., and Postma, E. Adaptive Game AI with Dynamic Scripting. *Machine Learning 63*, 3 (2006), 217–248.

41. Steichen, B., Carenini, G., and Conati, C. User-Adaptive Information Visualization: Using Eye Gaze Data to Infer Visualization Tasks and User Cognitive Abilities. In *Proc. 2013 International Conference on Intelligent User Interfaces (IUI)*, ACM (2013), 317–328.

42. Viviani, P. Eye movements in Visual Search: Cognitive, Perceptual and Motor Control Aspects. In *Reviews of oculomotor research (4): Eye movements and their role in visual and cognitive processes*, E. Kowler, Ed. Elsevier, Amsterdam, 1990, 353–393.

43. Zook, A., Lee-Urban, S., Drinkwater, M., and Riedl, M. Skill-Based Mission Generation: A Data-Driven Temporal Player Modeling Approach. In *Proceedings of the 7th International Conference on Foundations of Digital Games* (2012).

What Should Adaptivity Mean
to Interactive Software Programmers?

Mathieu Magnaudet
Université de Toulouse - ENAC
7 avenue Edouard Belin
31055 Toulouse, France
mathieu.magnaudet@enac.fr

Stéphane Chatty
Université de Toulouse - ENAC
7 avenue Edouard Belin
31055 Toulouse, France
chatty@enac.fr

ABSTRACT

Works about adaptability and adaptivity in interactive systems cover very different issues (user adaptation, context-aware systems, ambient intelligence, ubiquitous computing), not always with the explicit goal of supporting programmers. Based on examples that highlight how weakly discriminative the present terminology is, we propose to separate two concerns: adaptivity as a purely analytical concept, relative to a given viewpoint on the software rather than to its very structure, and its programming as a non specific case of reactive behavior. We describe how simple adaptive behaviors can be programmed with simple interactive behavior patterns, and how more complex patterns can be introduced for intelligent adaptation. Finally we describe an application where, relying on the principles exposed in this paper, interaction and adaptation are combined in a simple and innovative manner.

Author Keywords

Adaptive software, plasticity, responsive design, context-sensitive applications, software architecture, programming, theory of interactive systems.

ACM Classification Keywords

H.5.2. Information Interfaces and Presentation: User Interfaces: D.2.11.Software engineering: Software Architectures

INTRODUCTION

Software adaptivity is a long time concern in the research domain of interactive computing systems that can be traced back at least to 1975 and John H. Holland's seminal work [22]. In the early 80s, the adaptivity of user interfaces, broadly understood as the self-modification of a system under context variations, arose as a significant issue in the improvement of usability [23]. However subsequent works in this domain forked in various directions depending on the context considered: while early works focused on user adaptation and user modeling [29], the spreading of new execution platforms, such as PDAs, tablet PCs and smartphones, shifted the focus to interaction devices [36, 16]. In the meantime, the generalization of small sensors in computing systems (light, temperature, humidity, etc.) raised the more general issue of adapting software applications to their physical environment [21]. At the same time, progress in distributed architectures brought forward the issue of adaptation to new services or new software components in the execution context of an application [6].

During this process a number of sub-communities addressing specific issues have emerged: user modeling, sensor modeling, middleware, adaptation policy, model-based adaptation, to cite but a few. Each sub-community has developed their own concepts and vocabulary (e.g. adaptation, plasticity, context-aware application). From a theoretical point of view this situation is quite unsatisfactory: if we agree that the science of human-computer interaction is also a theoretical endeavor and cannot be reduced to a collection of methods or good practices, we have to work toward the clarification of its basic concepts and progress toward their unification.

But this is not simply a matter of theoretical aim. Heterogenous concepts yield heterogenous software tools, introducing unnecessary complexity for programmers. Developing an adaptive software that includes several of the dimensions cited above (natural environment, input devices, user's cognitive abilities for example) can be a daunting task. This might explain why the computing industry has introduced "responsive design", a less ambitious but more practical concept for adapting interactive applications to their execution environment. If we want support for adaptivity to find its way into operating systems, like it happened for touch interaction and gesture recognition, eliciting concepts that are simple enough to be embedded in programming tools is a key step.

This article is a contribution toward this goal. We show that the entanglement of programming issues and adaptivity concepts from the state of the art can be untangled into separate concerns: an analysis framework of software adaptivity on the one hand, a set of simple programming concepts on the other hand.

Firstly, we propose a new analysis framework for software adaptation. We show that there is no clear cut division that emerges from previous works between programming adaptation and programming interactive behavior. We propose a definition in which adaptivity appears as quality of interactive behavior, that often has no particular relevance to programming. We then turn to the practical consequences of our definition. We obtain confirmation on standard adaptation situations that no dedicated primitives are required to program adaptive processes: the simple "event - control - action" schema can be tailored for this purpose. Finally, we further validate these principles by demonstrating them on a full-size concrete application, using an existing reactive programming framework.

PREVIOUS WORK

Adaptation to the user
Adaptive interfaces emerged as a research topic in the 1980s (cf. [29] for a review). Simply stated, the idea was that the software must adapt to users rather than the opposite. Users were mostly considered for their cognitive skills, and the topic was strongly associated to cognitive ergonomics. According to Greenberg and Witten [18] for instance, the condition of interface adaptation is that the software manages a model of its users. They proposed to define adaptation as the automatic transformation of this model during the use of the software. They also introduced a now common distinction between automatic transformations and transformations operated by the user via configuration parameters, or by a designer in a process of reengineering.

In this context, adaptive user interface were considered a consequence of the automatic transformation of a user model. The main difficulty was to find the rules allowing to infer the (cognitive) state of users from their actions. This goal created a clear connection between adaptation and the field of artificial intelligence [27]. In more recent works, the focus has moved toward neuroscience with the introduction of physiological sensors and neuroimaging [31, 34]. With these techniques, the user model has been enriched with new dimensions such as affective state [37] or stress level [20], but the principles of adaptation remain the same.

Adaptation to the context
With the 1990s and the increasing variety of computer form factors (larger display sizes, then PDAs, mobile phones, tablet PCs), and more recently new sensors (acceleration, light, pressure, humidity, etc.), new adaptation concerns appeared. We can distinguish at least three of them: adaptation to the execution platform [36, 28], adaptation to the environment [33], adaptation to the applicative context [30]. These various dimensions of adaptation are often gathered under the general expression "context-aware systems". Many of these works propose model-based solutions to the problem of context variation. Models range from complex ontologies [12, 19] to more partial models of the context or of some parts of the software system [17, 13]. They are usually associated with algorithms, inference rules or policies specifying how to modify an application according to the modeled context dimensions (cf. [3] for a review).

There is no consensus, however, about what exactly must be included in the context of an application: authors each choose their own focus of interest and propose their own characterization of what they take to be the relevant context of an application. This ranges from technicalities to topics that are closer to user-centered adaptation: physical properties, surrounding objects, user emotional state, etc.). By contrast Dey and Abowd [14] propose a general definition:

> *Context:* any information that can be used to characterize the situation of entities (*i.e.*, whether a person, place, or object) that are considered relevant to the interaction between a user and an application, including the user and the application themselves. Context is typically the location, identity, and state of people, groups, and computational and physical objects.

This definition clarifies the common focus of all these works: the interaction between the user and the software. It is pragmatic and flexible, with the drawback that it does not provide an absolute definition, independent of any application.

Adaptation in software architecture
Another area of research is more focused on the pragmatics of implementing software. Historically this was first documented when the domain of interactive software architecture emerged in the 1980s from the need to adapt existing applications to graphical user interfaces. The Dialogue layer in the Seeheim model [32] partly serves this purpose. The Functional Core Adapter in the Arch model has the explicit role of permitting the adaptation of a functional core to various interaction layers, and reciprocally [4].

Note that this is quite remote from the definition proposed by Greenberg and Witten for adaptation: here, adaptation is not even a matter of configuration parameters but of sheer reengineering. The adaptation is not relative to the user or the environment, but to the programming interface of software components. It is only recently that connections have appeared with context adaptation, with the proposal to handle software components and input devices through a unified component model [10].

Meanwhile, this type of adaptation has become a general issue in software engineering. Software reengineering, Web services and ubiquitous computing each have brought their own needs, leading to various solutions. This even includes network security, where adaptive architectures have been proposed to manage the variations in the security level of physical networks [5]. Solutions such as aspect-oriented programming [24] or component-based architectures (Enterprise Java Beans, Corba Component Model) are related to this issue of supporting programmers who manage the adaptation of software components [26].

Lessons learned
From this overview of previous works we propose two lessons. The first is that adaptivity encompasses a huge variety of works, especially when context and context-aware systems are understood in such a wide sense as in Dey's and Abowd's definition. Building a set of core concepts that can be derived for each kind of adaptation could help to offer more integrated support for adaptivity.

The second lesson is that, in contrast with what happened in the software engineering field, research on adaptation in interactive software has been carried out in relative independence from research on programming concepts. Studying how the core concepts of adaptivity relate to those of interactive software programming could also be beneficial.

In the next two sections we study these two lessons in more detail so as to propose an analysis of adaptivity and its relations to interactive software programming.

ADAPTIVITY, A MATTER OF POINT OF VIEW

From the above overview, can we derive a definition of software adaptivity that may be used for providing support to programmers? For this, we need to overcome a few difficulties and come back to the roots of the concept of adaptivity.

Software adaptivity: from a fuzzy concept...

A closer look at the concept of software adaptation as it is presented in the literature reveals some ambiguities. The first resides in the distinction between the transformations that are applied automatically and those that are applied by the user via a configuration menu for example. Only the former are usually considered as adaptations *proprio sensu*, but sometimes the difference can be tenuous. In [34], for example, the authors investigate the possibility to detect the mental load of the user so as to adapt the user interface accordingly. But, interestingly, other works propose to use the exact same technique as a means to add an explicit control device to a system, *i.e.* as a new input modality [38]. Technically and from the information processing point of view, there is no significative difference between these two situations: in both cases the goal is to enable the software to react to a specific brain process detected by a neuroimaging device. The difference lies in the voluntary versus involuntary nature of a specific brain process of the user; the former will be classified as interaction the latter as adaptation. Equally ambiguous situations can be found with eye tracking, RFID or movement detection. In these cases, the difference is more in the eye of the observer of the human-machine interaction than in the software itself. This raises an even wider question, that of the actual difference between adaptivity and plain interactivity: if the same piece of interactive software can be used for both, what use is the distinction to programmers?

Even if we take the more relaxed definition of context adaptation, we are faced with similar difficulties. While this is not often stated in the literature, it is useful to remind that context is a relative concept: it can only be defined with regard to something, a task or an event for example. For adaptive user interfaces, the context is usually that of the current activity of the user and, taken in a wide sense, it encompasses everything that can affect this activity. But, here too, the difference between an activity and the context of this activity seems to lie very much in the eye of the observer (the user, the designer, the scientist). Consider for instance the accelerometers that are now embedded in most smartphones. They typically allow to adapt the graphical interface to the orientation of the phone, but they are also used as an input modality in many applications, especially games. Thus what was considered as a "context sensor" for some activities is also an input modality for other activities. Once again, not only is it difficult to come up with a clear cut application of the proposed definition, but we also have two processes that are similar from from the programmer's point of view and different from other points of view.

... to a relative concept

The above examples emphasize how much the categorization of a process as an adaptive one depends on the chosen point of view on the human-machine system. The distinction works well enough if we consider users and their activities, or what a given designer takes to be the users' task, or the human-computer interaction itself. From these points of view, adaptivity encompasses all transformations that are not directly caused by deliberate actions of the user. The other transformations, voluntarily triggered by the user, are considered as classic cases of interaction.

On the contrary, from the pure software point of view there is no difference. Programmers are concerned by the interactions of their software with its whole environment, not only with the user. May the action be voluntary or not, the intention explicit or not, the process can always be described as an association between an event and a transformation: detection of a change in the environment (user's actions included), then modification of the state of the software.

Thus, if one is interested by the usability of a system, the concept of adaptation can be useful as an analysis tool for the processes that surround the user's activity. But for those involved in the programming of these processes, this concept does not seem to offer very much.

Alternatively, the distinction is sometimes founded on what is considered to be the function of a software system. In these cases, adaptation characterizes software transformations that maintain its main functionality. This is perfectly illustrated by the works on plastic interfaces [9], where transformations of the user interface are oriented toward the maintenance of the functionality of the software. Here too, adaptation offers an analysis tool to identify what must be transformed and when. However this tells little about how to program such processes.

Also note that other points of view on systems are possible. Consider for instance an air traffic control room with a number of "open positions", each consisting of a workstation and two operators. The control room, considered as a system, adapts to the level of traffic: when the level increases, controllers trigger de-grouping transformations in which the software helps them to move part of the traffic to newly opened positions. This makes the whole human-computer system adaptable to its context. What is particularly interesting here is that a system engineer would perceive this as an adaptation process, while neither the programmers nor the users or the interaction designers would. Still, the software needs to support it.

The notion of point of view seems crucial to understand adaptive processes in interactive software. This will appear more clearly by analyzing the very concept of adaptivity.

Back to the roots

Adaptivity is a concept inherited from biology. It refers to the ability of a system to self-modify according to the evolutions of its environment in order to maintain or enhance its viability. Adaptivity is not an all or nothing phenomenon but rather a continuum. Systems are more or less adaptive, depending on both the variation range of the environmental properties and the number of these properties. Moreover, not all evolutions are viable; adaptation is a process of transformation under constraints that must maintain the system in its so-called viability kernel [2].

The fact that adaptive processes are oriented toward an end (*i.e.* the maximisation of the viability of a system) is a crucial feature of this phenomenon. Indeed, this is what distinguishes adaptation from a simple mechanical transformation. Thus, the expansion of an iron bar caused by heat is not considered as an adaptive processes. But the thermoregulation mechanisms of the living organisms are considered as such because they are aimed at maintaining properties that are essential to survival. Adaptivity of artificial systems obeys to the same schema with the noticeable difference that viability criteria are not intrinsic but defined from the outside, *i.e.* by the designer, the human factors expert, the user, or any stakeholder involved in the lifecycle of the system.

A new definition

Therefore, we propose to define adaptation as *a function that maps changes in an environmental state affecting the viability of a system to evolutions in the state space of the system (i.e. transformations) in order to maintain its viability.*

Here, environment and transformation are taken as observer-relative concepts. Each observer chooses to delineate a system and its boundaries, the environment is everything that is outside these boundaries, and transformations are all the changes within the boundaries. For programmers, the system consists of the software components they are in charge of, the environment is everything else, and the transformations are the modifications of the software components and their data. These transformations may come out as graphical changes, behavior changes, etc.

With this definition, software adaptivity clearly appears as an external property that is relative to the criteria chosen by each stakeholder to characterize the viability of a system. For instance, from the point of view of the usability expert the viability will be assessed against the usability criteria. Alternatively, the software architect may characterize the viability of a software as its ability to support updating processes, or the addition of new components.

We are now able to explain why the same transformation process may be characterized in the same time as an adaptive one and as a simple interaction: it simply depends on the analysis criteria. The automatic change of the luminosity of a screen according to the variation of the ambient light is a simple interaction in the eye of the programmer. But it is also an adaptive process for the ergonomist who studies how the ambient light affects the visibility of a graphical component (and then, the viability of the software) and how the change of the screen luminosity can correct this issue.

Moreover this definition allows to qualify the roles of various stakeholders in the engineering of adaptive software. Usability experts or systems engineers are interested by the viability of a transformation, that is by the relevance of a software transformation for the maintenance of its function. Designers are interested in the exploration of the transformations space.

Programmers are more interested in the means to observe the environmental state and to relate it to a set of transformations. Adaptivity becomes an explicit concern for them only in specific cases. This may be when the adaptation criterion is embedded in the software itself, and they need to implement it. This is typically the case of learning algorithms that have to check whether a transformation is successful. Such software could arguably be qualified as "self-adaptive" software.

Finally, this definition is broad enough to include the cases of software adaptation triggered by software or platform evolutions. For example the adaptation of an x86 application to an ARM architecture and the refactoring of a component to adapt it to a new version of a protocol, match the definition as much as the resizing of a window to adapt to a new display.

PROGRAMMING ADAPTIVE SOFTWARE

The above definition is general enough to encompass the whole range of adaptive phenomena. It also clarifies the distinction between a process of transformation and the finality of this process. From this, we can infer that the programmer is more concerned by the building of the transformation process than by the specification of its finality. But we still need to understand how programmers build the transformation process into their programs: what are their responsibilities, what support do they need? For this, we propose to use an analysis framework specifying the dimensions that structure this space.

Extending an analysis framework

In [36], Thevenin and Coutaz propose a framework that characterizes adaptation along four axes: actor, time, means, target. However, if adaptation is a relational property that depends on a specific point of view on the mapping from environmental changes to system transformations, then the framework must be adapted to reflect this.

We propose to consider that software transformations are themselves particular cases of software actions, along with interactive behaviors such as beeps or color changes. Calling "interaction" or "transformation" the effect of an action results from the same choice of point of view as above. In other words, *all the software transformations considered for adaptation are reactive behaviors and can be analyzed in the unifying framework of reactive processes.* Consequently, we propose to consider that the framework describes reactive processes in general, and to supplement it with an axis representing the possible observers of the system and their adaptation criteria. It is along this axis that adaptive processes can be distinguished from simple interaction.

The other dimensions of Thevenin and Coutaz remain fully relevant in that they point to important distinctions regarding the structuring of an interactive application. For instance, there will be significant differences in the building of a software if one wants it to react, at runtime, to a change of the screen size rather than to recode it for each specific hardware target. However, in order to more accurately capture the range of possible reactive processes, we propose two additional extensions (Figure 1):

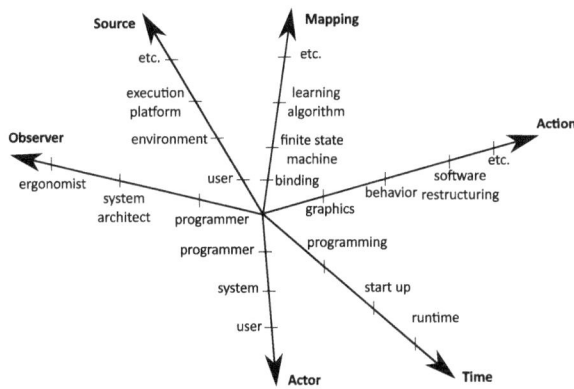

Figure 1. Analysis framework for reactive software processes, derived from Thevenin and Coutaz [36]

- refine the Target and Means axes into Source, Mapping and Action so as to denote what causes the process, what it triggers, and how the decision is made;

- enrich the Actor and Time axes to capture such cases as the redesign of a graphical component and the recompilation of an application after the notification of an API change.

The result is a design space with five axes describing what happens, how, when, whence and by whom, and one that characterizes whether this qualifies as an adaptation process.

Where the application programmer's work lie

Using our variant of Thevenin and Coutaz's analysis framework makes it easy to sort out what should be in the hands of application programmers. It suffices for that to identify which dimension in the design space should be assigned to whom. Not only does this help defining responsibilities for programmers and programming environment architects and ensuring the independence of their design choices. It also helps understanding what support programming primitives must offer in priority to the programmers of adaptive applications.

- The Observer dimension is not relevant to programming and can safely be ignored.

- What Sources and what Actions are used in a given application are the programmers' choice. However, defining the range of available sources and actions is the responsibility of the programming framework: does it provide support for multitouch devices, or only for classical pointing devices? Does it allow the design of rich graphical components, or only classical WIMP widgets? Consequently, these dimensions should be assigned to the framework programmer rather than the application programmer.

- Similarly, the Time and the Actor of the transformation strongly depend on the programming environment. Consider for instance the adaptation of an application to a new processor architecture. Currently, programmers must decide and implement this adaptation themselves because the application is unable to do it. In the future, this might become a feature of a programming environment that includes support for adaptation. As above, these dimensions

concern more the framework programmer than the application programmer.

- The Mappings between sources and actions are where the intrinsic programming complexity resides. For any interactive behavior, the task of application programmers it to select the right mapping between sources and actions, or to build the appropriate mapping if necessary. This applies to adaptive software as well. All user interface frameworks support variants of "when this then that", and some offer state machines. For more complex cases, such as intelligent adaptation, programmers must build their own solutions from the basic mappings available. This is similar to using the control structures of standard programming languages to build dedicated algorithms, potentially very complex.

The proposed definition and analysis framework hence translate to the following hypothesis regarding application programmers: their task consists in using and creating mappings between events and transformations, therefore any programming environment that provides the appropriate primitives for creating mappings can be used without introducing dedicated primitives.

ADAPTATION IN A REACTIVE ARCHITECTURE

If the above hypothesis is valid, the primitive constructs of a classical reactive programming framework should be sufficient to address the whole range of adaptive processes delineated by our design space. We now test this hypothesis with the "event-control-action" schema from the reactive programming paradigm, refined into a an "event-control-transformation" schema. We show how this simple schema can be used to account for a series of classical adaptation scenarios.

Coupling sources and transformations

Simple (source, transformation) couples can be used to express a wide variety of behaviors:

- event sources, taken in a very broad sense as described in [11] ou [10], may be an input device consciously manipulated by a user, a physiological sensor, a physical sensor, a software component reporting the hardware configuration of the execution platform (displays, network, processor, etc.), and so on. The only requirement is that the programming environment provides these sources to the programmer so as to cover the desired part of the design space.

- Transformations can range from a simple variation of a graphical property to a complex restructuring of a component tree or to the loading of new software modules. Just as for the event sources, the limits to the expression of interactive processes are those of the actions made available by the programming environment.

With this schema in hand, we can easily describe some classic cases of adaptive processes. For instance, a Web service provider announces a change in their protocol through a dedicated service, application vendors develop an event source that catch such announcements and couple a rebuild action to it. Or a physiological sensor detects inappropriate attention patterns in a user, this is coupled to an animation that make the display vibrate so as break the attention pattern.

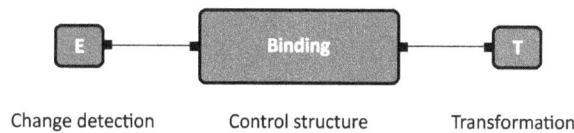

Figure 2. Simple binding between an event and a transformation

Continuous change

Another classic adaptive process is the adaptation to a continuous change in the application context. For example the continuous variation of ambient light, or more usual, the progressive resizing of the application window. In such cases we need a mapping that propagates the current value each time it changes, this is a typical dataflow mapping. However, the connected transformation does not need to be equally continuous, it may respond to various thresholds. In this case the mapping must be composed of a data flow block supplemented with a switch that will point to one branch or the other (figure 3).

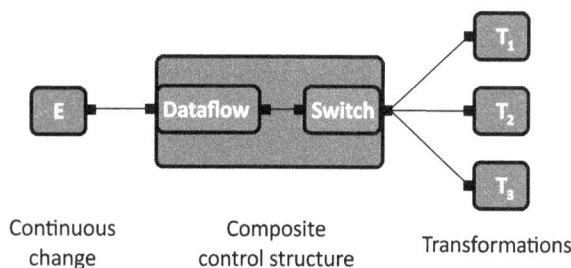

Figure 3. Composition of a dataflow and a switch

Dynamicity

The appearance and disappearance of an object in the surroundings of an application are classic sources of adaptive processes. Object is here taken in a very wide sense that includes input devices, users, software components, and so on. Such processes can be modeled by a component that encapsulates a monitoring process and that sends events when detecting that objects have appeared or disappeared. The appropriate control mapping is a simple binding that will trigger a specific transformation when receiving this event (figure 2). Of course the transformation itself may be complex, for example a transformation of the behavior of some interactors when a specific input device is plugged, however the mapping linking event and transformation is quite simple.

Complex algorithms

At first sight, artificial intelligence seems to offer a more challenging example of adaptation for our analysis schema. However it is no more the case if we regard it as a mapping of a higher degree of complexity. A neural network, for example, is an input/output structure that may be connected to one or several event sources on one side and to a set of transformations on the other side. The specificity of this mapping is that

the link between events and transformations may change with time according to the change in the connection weights made by a learning algorithm.

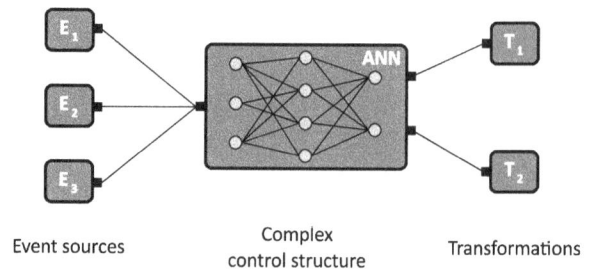

Figure 4. Learning algorithms as a complex mapping

Discussion

As we have seen, the proposed schema (event - control - transformation) provides an analysis tool that accounts for various classical adaptation scenarios. This provides initial validation not only of the schema, but also of part of the definition it is derived from: it makes sense to reduce adaptive behavior to interactive behavior as far as the programmer is concerned.

The above analysis also shows how the chosen schema helps to clarify in what cases programmers need to perform adaptation-specific programming tasks. Arguably, only the creation of dedicated control structures can be considered as such. This would be consistent with the classical distinction between adaptation in general and self-adaptive systems: the level of self-adaptation is probably correlated to the complexity of the algorithms involved in the control structures.

In order to further validate the proposed definition through the chosen programming schema, we have applied it to the implementation of an actual interactive software.

EXAMPLE APPLICATION

The djnn programming framework [1] implements the general event - control - action schema. We used it to implement a software prototype featuring various cases of interaction and adaptation, relying solely on the event - control - transformation principle.

A ground control station for UAVs

In the context of a research project dedicated to cooperation between humans and machines, we have developed a prototype ground control station for squad of civil unmanned aerial vehicles (UAV). This prototype is aimed at replacing the user interface of the open source Paparazzi system [7] in the future. Some of the requirements for this software are related to our concerns:

• the ground station must run on a classical desktop computer as well as on a tablet PC equipped with a touchscreen and stylus;

• it must be ready for multimodal interaction;

• the user interface must automatically adapt to changes in the operational configuration (network connectivity between the UAVs, current phase in the mission).

This makes it a concrete example of the issue we are discussing in this paper. We could have dealt with the requirements by choosing some conceptual frameworks from the literature, one for shared control and one for multimodality. But for our programmers, most concepts derived from these frameworks would have been irrelevant for the task. For example the question of who must take the control on the system and when is not their concern but those of the designer or the architect of the system. They are just interested in how to map a specific control source onto a specific set of transformations.

In the following, we illustrate how the principles described in the previous section can be used to build such mappings, which provide additional examples of the wide variety of mappings that the reactive architecture allows.

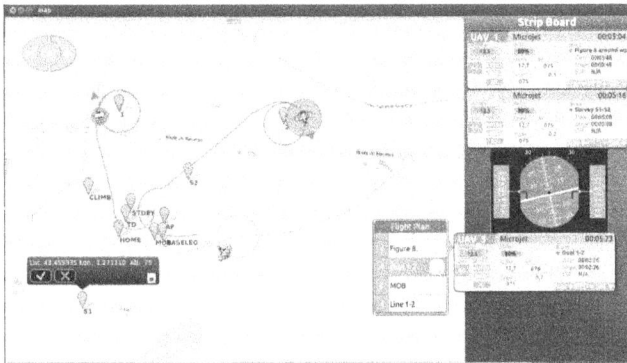

Figure 5. The main window of the UAV application

Application structure

This application is visually architectured in two main parts: a map picturing the flight area and a side panel containing various state indicators about each vehicle (figure 5). These indicators are packed in what is classically called a strip (figure 6). The flight plan of the UAVs are organized in series of waypoints that can be displayed and handled on the map. When the user selects a vehicle, various components appear and allow the user to interact with the UAV, by selecting a waypoint in its flight plan for example.

The application is implemented with the Java API of Djnn, a programming environment that implements the principles of reactive programming described earlier. In particular, Djnn comes with a series of control structures that all rely on the source-action principle and that correspond to the various mappings described in the previous section.

In addition, Djnn implements a model-based architecture in which the structure of an application is represented by components that can be created, assembled and destroyed in exactly the same way as the data manipulated by the application. This allows to trigger transformations of the application (e.g. the replacement of a visualization panel) with the same mechanisms as simple color or position changes. Consequently, all transformations of the software can be programmed according to the same source-action mappings, provided that the necessary event sources are available.

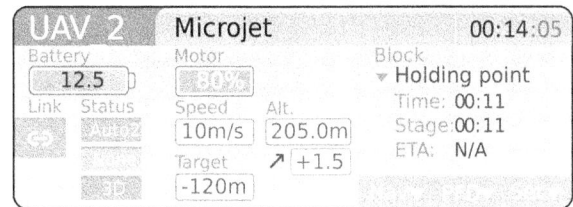

Figure 6. "Strip" gathering the various state information of a vehicle

Event sources

The application is sensitive to events from the UAV squad as well as user events.

UAVs are equipped with autonomous squad flight capabilities and the communication between the UAVs and the ground station relies on a dynamic routing protocol. Changes in the squad configuration or in the routing configuration, as well as alarms from UAVs (e.g. "short fuel") are transmitted to the application and must trigger reconfigurations of the user interface. For instance, in case of an emergency the application should restructure the interface so as to force the operator to focus on a UAV, with all the relevant information easily available. A first implementation step has consisted to make all these messages from the UAVs and routers available to the rest of the application in the same form as input events.

The user events are the usual ones: mouse clicks, touch panel touches, etc. A future version of the application includes unconscious input, provided by physiological sensors (EEG, near infra red). For this reason, and because the application must run on various platforms, the application must be able to transform its internal wiring according to the available devices. As above, this is possible because events such as the connection and disconnection of input devices are available to the rest of the application.

In the following we give an overview of three kinds of coupling between events and transformations of the application. All are implemented according to very similar patterns, with the same mappings. From the user's point of view, some of these couplings will appear as simple interaction, others as adaptive processes, others with no clear status. The homogeneous implementation model allows to explore design spaces where the difference between adaptation and interaction is not important.

Basic interaction

Like most of the graphical user interfaces, our application proposes many examples of simple interactions such as state change on mouse press or graphical object dragging. This is the case for the waypoints, which can be in four different states (figure 7). The transitions between the states are triggered by the user's actions on a mouse or a touch screen.

The coupling between events and changes is described with a finite state machine that governs the branches of a switch as explained in [11]. Each transition corresponds to a coupling, where the event is for instance a mouse press or a screen touch and the transformation is the activation or the deactivation of a graphical object.

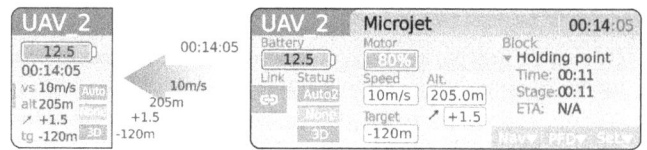

Figure 8. Animated strip adaptation, or manual strip resizing

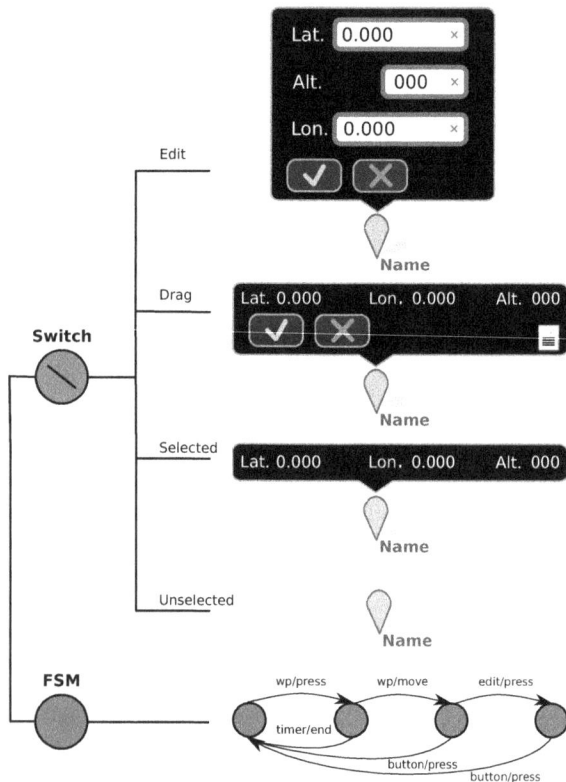

Figure 7. Waypoint state change triggered by a user action

graphical reorganization. The first is a simple size reduction of the panel itself when the main display becomes too small. The second level is a complete reorganization of the strips themselves when the panel becomes too small. This can happen when the application is run on a smaller display, when the main window is resized or when the user decides to reduce the size of the panel. In addition, when the user acts on the panel she directly takes the control over the animation of a smooth graphical transformation inspired from [15] (figure 8).

This transformation cannot be described by a simple finite state machine because of its progressiveness. The mapping involved here is a combination of dataflow components and finite state machines. The interesting point is that the same transformation can be triggered and controlled in two different ways, either automatically on window resizing or manually on direct user action. In other words the same component, driven by the same mapping, can be triggered in both a way that is pure interaction and a way that is a fairly complex case of adaptation.

Adapting interaction styles

The third kind of coupling proposed by our application concerns the modification of the behavior of some graphical components according to the hardware architecture and the available input devices. The transition from a classic computer equipped with a mouse and a keyboard to a tablet PC with a touchscreen raises several known problems. One of them is the fact that a finger on a touchscreen can hide a too small target, leaving the user without feedback. The usual solution [25] that we have adopted consists in the addition of a deported feedback over small components (figure 9). The other issue comes from the fact that most touchscreens have no hovering events [8]. It is thus necessary to transform the state machine that governs the buttons according to the current input device.

Recomposing the visual architecture

The reorganization of the visual architecture is a classic case of adaptation [35]. In its current version, our application offers two kinds of such a reorganization. The first one is triggered by an alarm coming from the anti-collision system of the UAVs. The event is a message received on a software bus, that contains the ID of the concerned vehicles as well as the avoidance strategy they have adopted. In our application, this message is encapsulated in a *TCAS-alert* component that represents the various properties of the alert. When a message arrives, this component is activated. This activation is bound to the activation of visual components that display the alert parameters. Consequently, the user's current activity is interrupted by the disappearance of all the usual displays (flight plan, altitude controller, etc.), that are replaced by the altitude of the vehicles involved, their slope and the avoidance strategy.

This transformation implements a new distribution of authority. It is aimed at improving the awareness of operators and preventing them from further actions on the flight parameters that could jeopardize the automatic avoidance strategy. While this can be described as a typical scenario of adaptation, the event mappings involved in this process are the same as in the previous case: a subscription to an event *TCAS-alert* that activates a few components.

Another classic case of graphical reorganization is the one motivated by a change in the dimensions of a container (window, panel, widget, etc.). The strip panel offers two levels of

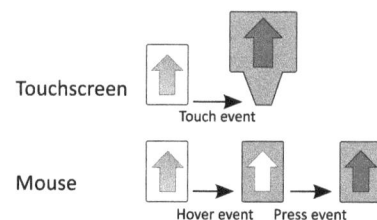

Figure 9. Dual behavior of the buttons

Here, we have two kinds of transformation, a graphical one and a behavioral one, both triggered by appearing/disappearing of an input device. The corresponding adaptation is obtained by coupling these transformations to events such as "new touchscreen available" and "new mouse available". For simple hardware configurations (one mouse or one touch-screen), it is enough to group these couplings in a finite state machine, which is not much different from that of section "Basic interaction" above. The only significant difference is the nature of the events that trigger the transitions.

This series examples demonstrate that if some situations can be distinguished from the user's point of view, or from the observer of human-computer interaction, from the programmer's point of view they can be analyzed according to the same canonical schema. Furthermore, some combinations can be imagined that defeat all attempts at strict categorization of software behavior.

CONCLUSION

In this article, we have addressed support for adaptation under a new angle: the point of view of programmers of interactive software. We have untangled the concerns from software architecture and those from adaptive systems so as to propose two independent albeit compatible models.

On one hand we came up with a definition and a design space for software adaptivity that is grounded in the more general definition of system adaptivity. On the other hand creating adaptive software comes through as a straightforward application of the reactive programming model. In simple cases, adaptation can managed with usual software patterns for interactivity. In more complex cases, control patterns are required but the reactive model still holds.

Not only does this offer some clarifications on software adaptivity, it also opens new opportunities for designing control structures for elaborate adaptive behaviors. This paves the way to innovative combinations of interaction and adaptation, and to a better integration of interactive software and intelligent systems.

ACKNOWLEDGEMENTS

This work was funded by the ARTEMIS JU and the French government through project D3CoS. The authors are grateful to Stéphane Conversy and to the reviewers of a previous version of this article for their constructive comments.

REFERENCES

1. http://djnn.net.

2. Aubin, J.-P., Bayen, A., Bonneuil, N., and Saint-Pierre, P. *Viability, Control and Games: Regulation of complex evolutionary systems under uncertainty and viability constraints*. Springer, 2005.

3. Baldauf, M., Dustdar, S., and Rosenberg, F. A survey on context-aware systems. *International Journal of Ad Hoc and Ubiquitous Computing 2*, 4 (2007), 263–277.

4. Bass, L., Pellegrino, R., Reed, S., Seacord, R., Sheppard, R., and Szezur, M. R. The Arch model: Seeheim revisited. Presented at the CHI'91 User Interface Developers Workshop, Apr. 1991.

5. Ben Mahmoud, M., Larrieu, N., Pirovano, A., and Varet, A. An adaptive security architecture for future aircraft communications. In *Proceedings of IEEE/AIAA DASC 2010* (2010), 3.E.2–1–3.E.2–16.

6. Bencomo, N., and Blair, G. Using architecture models to support the generation and operation of component-based adaptive systems. In *Software Engineering for Self-Adaptive Systems, LNCS 5525*. Springer, 2009.

7. Brisset, P., and Hattenberger, G. Multi-UAV control with the paparazzi system. In *Conference on Human Operating Unmanned Systems* (2008).

8. Buxton, W. A. S. A three-state model of graphical input. In *Proceedings of INTERACT'90*, Elsevier (1990).

9. Calvary, G., Serna, A., Kolski, C., and Coutaz, J. *Transport: a fertile ground for the plasticity of user interfaces*. ISTE Ltd and John Wiley & Sons, Inc., 2011, 343–368.

10. Chatty, S., Lemort, A., and Valès, S. Multiple input support in the IntuiKit framework. In *Proceedings of Tabletop 2007*, IEEE computer society (2007).

11. Chatty, S., Sire, S., Vinot, J., Lecoanet, P., Mertz, C., and Lemort, A. Revisiting visual interface programming: Creating GUI tools for designers and programmers. In *Proceedings of UIST'04*, Addison-Wesley (Oct. 2004), 267–276.

12. Chen, H., Finin, T., and Joshi, A. An ontology for context-aware pervasive computing environments. *The Knowledge Engineering Review 18*, 3 (2003), 197–207.

13. Collignon, B., Vanderdonckt, J., and Calvary, G. Model-driven engineering of multi-target plastic user interfaces. In *Proceedings of ICAS 2008*, IEEE Computer Society Press (2008), 7–14.

14. Dey, A. K., Abowd, G. D., and Salber, D. A conceptual framework and a toolkit for supporting the rapid prototyping of context-aware applications. *Human-Computer Interaction Journal 16*, 2 (2001), 97–166.

15. Dragicevic, P., Chatty, S., Thevenin, D., and Vinot, J.-L. Artistic resizing: A technique for rich scale-sensitive vector graphics. In *Proceedings of UIST'05*, ACM (2005), 201–210.

16. Dragicevic, P., and Fekete, J.-D. The input configurator toolkit: Towards high input adaptability in interactive applications. In *Proceedings of AVI'04*, ACM (2004), 244–247.

17. Gajos, K., and Weld, D. S. Supple: Automatically generating user interfaces. In *Proceedings of IUI'04*, ACM (2004), 93–100.

18. Greenberg, S., and Witten, I. H. Adaptive personalized interfaces - a question of viability. *Behaviour and Information Technology 4*, 1 (1985), 31–45.

19. Gu, T., Pung, H. K., and Zhang, D. Q. A service-oriented middleware for building context-aware services. *Journal of Network and Computer Applications 28*, 1 (2005), 1–18.

20. Healey, J., and Picard, R. Detecting stress during real-world driving tasks using physiological sensors. *IEEE Transactions on Intelligent Transportation Systems 6*, 2 (2005), 155–166.

21. Henricksen, K., and Indulska, J. Developing context-aware pervasive computing applications: Models and approach. *Pervasive and Mobile Computing 2*, 1 (2006), 37 – 64.

22. Holland, J. H. *Adaptation in natural and artificial systems*. MIT Press, 1975.

23. Innocent, P. Towards self-adaptive interface systems. *International Journal of Man-Machine Studies 16*, 3 (1982), 287 – 299.

24. Kiczales, G. Aspect-oriented programming. *ACM Computing Surveys 28*, 4es (1996).

25. Martin, B., Isokoski, P., Jayet, F., and Schang, T. Performance of finger-operated soft keyboard with and without offset zoom on the pressed key. In *Proceedings of Mobility'09*, ACM (2009), 59:1–8.

26. McKinley, P., Sadjadi, S., Kasten, E., and Cheng, B. H. C. Composing adaptive software. *Computer 37*, 7 (2004), 56–64.

27. McTear, M. User modelling for adaptive computer systems: a survey of recent developments. *Artificial Intelligence Review 7*, 3-4 (1993), 157–184.

28. Nilsson, E. G., Floch, J., Hallsteinsen, S., and Stav, E. Model-based user interface adaptation. *Computers and Graphics 30*, 5 (2006), 692–701.

29. Norcio, A. F., and Stanley, J. Adaptive human-computer interfaces: A literature survey and perspective. *IEEE Transactions on Systems, Man, and Cybernetics 19*, 2 (1989), 399–408.

30. Papazoglou, M., Traverso, P., Dustdar, S., and Leymann, F. Service-oriented computing: State of the art and research challenges. *Computer 40*, 11 (2007), 38–45.

31. Parasuraman, R. Neuroergonomics: Research and practice. *Theoretical Issues in Ergonomics Science 4*, 1-2 (2003), 5–20.

32. Pfaff, G. E., Ed. *User Interface Management Systems*. Eurographics Seminars. Springer, 1985.

33. Schmidt, A., Beigl, M., and Gellersen, H.-W. There is more to context than location. *Computers and Graphics 23*, 6 (1999), 893 – 901.

34. Solovey, E. T., Girouard, A., Chauncey, K., Hirshfield, L. M., Sassaroli, A., Zheng, F., Fantini, S., and Jacob, R. J. Using fNIRS brain sensing in realistic HCI settings: experiments and guidelines. In *Proceedings of UIST'09*, ACM (2009), 157–166.

35. Stuerzlinger, W., Chapuis, O., Phillips, D., and Roussel, N. User interface façades: Towards fully adaptable user interfaces. In *Proceedings of UIST'06*, ACM (2006), 309–318.

36. Thevenin, D., and Coutaz, J. Plasticity of user interfaces: Framework and research agenda. In *Proceedings of INTERACT'99*, IOS Press (1999).

37. Wang, H., Prendinger, H., and Igarashi, T. Communicating emotions in online chat using physiological sensors and animated text. In *CHI '04 Extended Abstracts*, ACM (2004), 1171–1174.

38. Wolpaw, J. R., Birbaumer, N., McFarland, D. J., Pfurtschellere, G., and Vaughan, T. M. Brain-computer interfaces for communication and control. *Clinical Neurophysiology*, 113 (2002), 767–791.

Updating Database Schemas Without Breaking the UI: Modeling Using Cognitive Semantic Categories

Evangelos Kapros, Simon McGinnes
School of Computer Science and Statistics
The University of Dublin, Trinity College
Dublin 2, Ireland
{evangelos.kapros, simon.mcginnes}@scss.tcd.ie

ABSTRACT

Data management user interfaces are ubiquitous in information systems and web-based applications. From the oldest spreadsheet to the most modern database, end users and administrators alike have interacted with tabular data. Usually, each concept is represented by a *table* and *columns*. Change to the structure of each concept requires structural change to the tables and columns, which is costly. Tailor-made database and web applications may overcome this obstacle by designing UIs on top of the data layer, providing some degree of data independence. However, changes in their schemas do not automatically propagate into the user interface, and so their maintenance is expensive.

In this paper we present a user interface that lets the end user alter the schema without the need for programming skills, eliminating the need for expensive software maintenance. To this end we propose an automatically generated user interface to include schema and data management functions. We built and evaluated an Adaptive Information System user interface (AIS UI), incorporating schema evolution functionality. In usability testing, first-time users were able to perform various data management tasks equally fast or faster than users using Microsoft Access, and on average ~43% faster than users using Microsoft Excel. Task completion rates using the AIS significantly exceeded those using Microsoft Access and were comparable (>95%) with those using Microsoft Excel.

Author Keywords

Adaptive information systems; databases; spreadsheets.

ACM Classification Keywords

H.5.2. Information interfaces and presentation (e.g., HCI): User Interfaces–*Graphical user interfaces (GUI)*. H.2.m. Database Management: Miscellaneous.

INTRODUCTION

Data management applications are a main production force in office environments. Many SMEs, NGOs, and other small organisations depend on so-called "productivity applications" such as Microsoft Access databases or Google Docs spreadsheets.

These organisations often lack the luxury of the "buy or build" choice, since their resources may be too limited to build bespoke data management solutions or to purchase expensive enterprise software applications. Instead they use spreadsheet (SPR) and database (DB) software to create their own ad hoc data management systems.

However, relying on systems of this type can be problematic. One reason for this is that the systems need to be maintained and enhanced over time. For example, change can occur due to disagreement over semantics (the so called "Tower of Babel" problem), miscommunication, and change in business needs.

In many cases the maintenance and enhancement of a system requires amendment to its underlying data schema (which may be either explicit, as in a relational database, or implicit, as in a spreadsheet). Changing the schema of a database or spreadsheet makes it necessary to re-write queries or formulas and to re-design the user interface, to reflect the changes in the schema. This can be costly, since expert IT skills are required (typically from the IT departments of these small organisations or external contractors). However, IT departments and external vendors are not always best-placed to understand user needs, and are not necessarily trained in user-centered design methods, so the results are not necessarily ideal.

In this paper, we propose that the end users themselves should be able to adjust the schemas of their own data management applications. To this end, we have defined an adaptive data model for data management, by including concepts (tables) and attributes (columns) in extended "soft" schemas, so that end users can manage entities and relationships without breaking the UI. Operations on the schema are performed using the familiar desktop metaphor.

We implemented this idea in an "Adaptive Information System" UI (AIS UI), a web application that allows the manipulation of arbitrary databases and database structures using a desktop-like GUI. Our AIS UI is a tool for editing and managing a database that allows the user to work primarily with a graphical representation of the schema; in this sense, it is important to note that the adaptivity in our approach lies predominantly on the Information Systems end of the system rather than just the UI. We evaluated our approach by conducting a laboratory-based user study with 30 participants. Each participant used either our system, database software (Microsoft Access), or spreadsheet software (Microsoft Excel). We recorded the performance time and the completion rate of the participants performing a scenario of eight tasks, and we used a System Usability Scale (SUS) questionnaire to evaluate the relative usability of the three types of software.

RELATED WORK

Spreadsheets
Research has shown that most organisations rely on spreadsheets for their data management [3, 12]. There are several reasons for this, including a lack of usable end-user systems. End users have been reported to "shun enterprise solutions" [12] and 70% use spreadsheets frequently or occasionally, most commonly for "sorting and database facilities" [3].

However, spreadsheets are notoriously error-prone; because they lack critical database management functionality, serious issues of data integrity can arise. There are real risks in the widespread dependence on spreadsheets [16]. In response, research has looked at ways of achieving database-like functionality in spreadsheets, such as the management of relationships [1]. However, the underlying issue of schema evolution in the spreadsheet context has received little attention. Work on "semantic spreadsheets" has improved modelling capabilities in spreadsheets, but maintains the problematic distinction between the roles of authoring and use [15, 10].

Relational Databases
Codd proposed the relational model as a way to translate concepts into data structures. Although his original work provided the theoretical tools for a versioning system of tables and relationships [17], this system has not reached production. One can imagine that Codd's original grasp of relational databases successfully addressed schema evolution issues, however there is no implementation of his original model; even Codd himself later abandoned the idea.

Relational databases have offered little flexibility for end users, who had to depend on professional database administrators to deploy any change. Research in Schema

Evolution focuses on this very problem of adapting a database schema to changes. This research field has shown that changes in schemas represent a significant cost to organizations. In [4] changes in the database schema are reported to affect up to 70% of queries, which have to be manually reconfigured. Some theoretical models to address this problem have been constructed, but real systems incorporating schema evolution functionality are hard to find [5].

NoSQL Databases
NoSQL is an umbrella term for databases that reject some or all of the constraints of the relational model. Such databases include document databases and graph databases. These technologies allow fast querying of large volumes of data, and they can accommodate schema evolution more smoothly than relational databases. However, the data in a NoSQL database must be communicated to the end user via a user interface. At present it is not clear how the schema change would be accommodated by user interfaces in a non-discontinuous manner and without the need for expert IT skills.

User Interfaces for Data Management
User interfaces for relational databases typically use tabular views for data, which may or may not be programmable. The following convention is followed: data are viewed in tabular form; relationships are displayed in a different screen and might use lines to illustrate how tables are linked; database administrators and end users have separate views; end users can have custom-designed interfaces which have to be amended once the tables or the relationships change. A notable novel approach of querying databases can be found at [24] and even though querying is beyond the scope of this paper it is an approach worth mentioning as it brings visual interface affordances to data management.

Applications such as HyperCard and FileMaker have facilitated metaphors similar to the desktop for data management. However, they also suffer from the "Tower of Babel" problem, as each application developer has to build their own user interface, as views are not embedded in the authoring environment.

Automatically-Generated Interfaces
Our goal is to allow end users to change the schema of an application without having to reprogram its user interface. This means that the interface must be re-generated in some way. Work has been done on automatically-generated interfaces exists and addresses various issues. For example, some early theoretical work on interfaces which can be adapted to various devices is ability-based [7]. Other work has facilitated adaptation to end users' capabilities (personalisation) [23] or users' tasks [24]. The majority of this work has provided various formalisations of user-interface languages to facilitate adaptation (e.g. [4, 23, 24]). Research on [23] is of particular interest with regard to

letting end-users themselves retrieve information at a semantic web setting.

Moreover, work on ontology evolution has given useful results on change in semantics while using an automatically generated interface [13, 14]. These results use annotated ontologies and, in many case, the interfaces are generated semi-automatically [5]. Similarly, work on dynamic data management has given useful results [15,16,17] but has not, in general, addressed user-interface or usability issues.

Other relevant research has used cognitive semantics to create non-domain-specific top-level ontologies that can be used as a basis for arbitrary schemas [9]. This idea is explored in the next section.

THE ADAPTIVE INFORMATION SYSTEM

We approach the problem of schema evolution by turning conceptual models (schemas) into data rather than, for example, hard-coded table structures, and by allowing "lazy" transformation of existing data following schema change. To test these ideas, we built and evaluated a prototype Adaptive Information System (AIS) (see Figure 1 and Figure 4). Current application design practice requires conceptual models to be hardcoded into software structures (classes, windows, tables, etc.) Our AIS avoids this practice. Instead, the AIS is constructed from generic, domain-independent structures and reusable functionality. The model-as-data is termed a soft schema; in our prototype it is stored as XML, although any logically-equivalent way of storing data would suffice. The soft schema is read and interpreted by the AIS at run-time (see Figure 2 and Figure 3). The soft schema is a properly normalised relational data model, with some additions, but it is stored as data rather than being hardcoded in application structure.

To provide domain-specific functionality, yet also exhibit conceptual data independence, the AIS meets several conditions. First, it reacts at run-time to a soft schema, providing a user interface which looks and behaves similarly to those of conventional domain-specific applications. To date we do not provide specialised behaviour for different types of data by responding to semantic categories embedded in the soft schema, but this is planned. Currently we present all data in tabular form (Figure 1).

The AIS can store and retrieve data corresponding to multiple soft schemas with guaranteed data integrity. The AIS has no advance knowledge of the schemas it will be used with, and how they may change. The data corresponding to each soft schema must be able to co-exist and be used with data stored for other soft schemas, regardless of their structures. Therefore we store data in a domain-independent way, but retain intact the conceptual structure for each instance of data. Our prototype meets that requirement by storing the data using XML and using XML tags to denote structure. But, again, any logically-equivalent storage mechanism would suffice. For example, another

prototype uses a graph database to represent the same information in a natural way but with the potential for improved runtime performance.

Archetypal categories

The AIS provides domain-specific behaviour by responding to the currently active soft schema. Each concept (entity type) in the soft schema represents something that data can be stored about. Therefore, the AIS provides CRUD (create, read, update, delete) functionality in respect of every concept in the schema. Design heuristics are applied automatically to produce a "reasonably usable" interface directly from the conceptual model. The principle has been applied and tested in a number of web and client-server application environments [18]. Dialog design takes into account general rules of interaction and layout, as well as responding specifically to the data types used for attributes in the soft schema, the relationships between concepts, and so on.

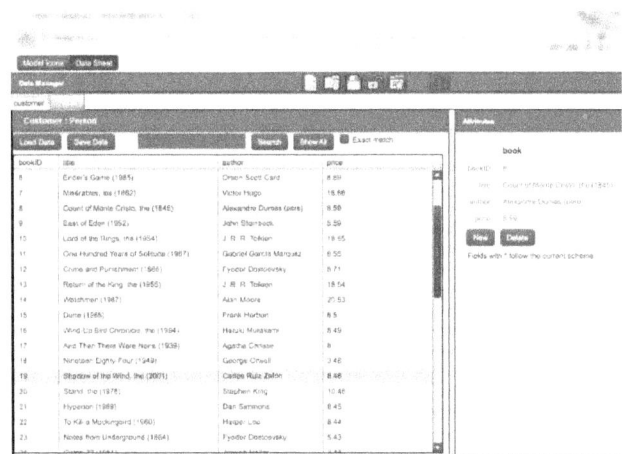

Figure 1. The Data Manager tab of the AIS UI.

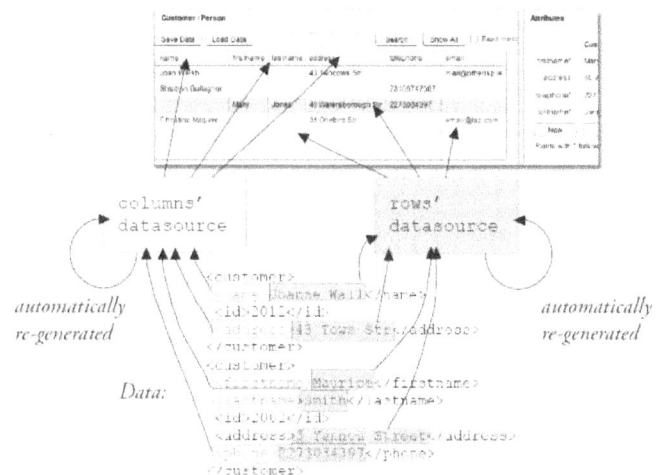

Figure 2. The concepts of the soft schema form the columns of the data grid, while the attributes its cell contents.

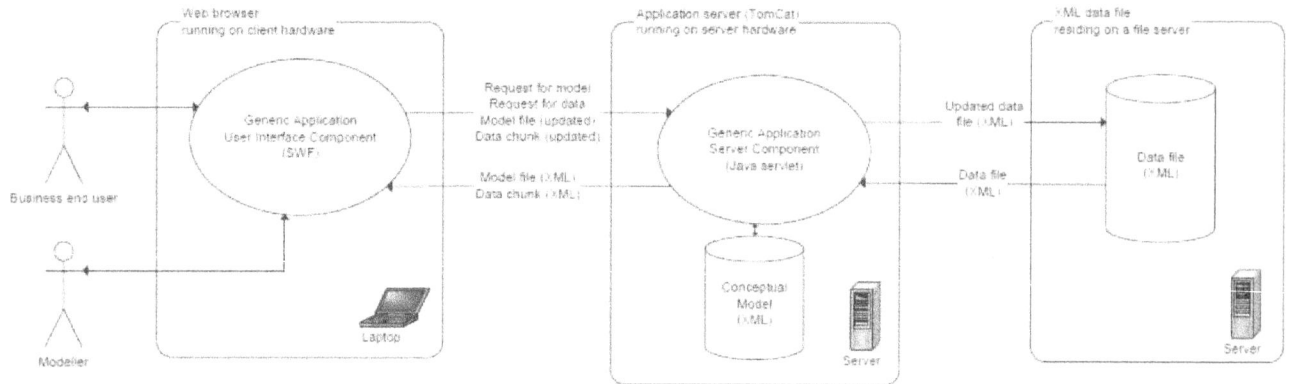

Figure 3. Architecture of the AIS UI.

We therefore sought to embed data and attributes into soft schemas, so that it could be used automatically by an AIS to render more domain-specific behaviour. It is achieved by linking each concept in the soft schema with a particular archetypal category (major cognitive semantic category [19,20,21]). The prototype AIS uses nine archetypal categories: *people, organisations, places, documents, activities, physical objects, conceptual objects, systems and categories* [18]. Using archetypal categories presents advantages during modelling; for example, it allows aspects of models to be predicted, helping to speed up modelling and reduce error. This makes end-user modelling easier, opening up the prospect that end users could use a suitable AIS to provide application functionality they want without recourse to IT specialists [22]. That is, these categories serve as a "top-level ontology" thus facilitating the flexibility, interoperability, and integrity of software applications.

End users can manipulate the model using the icons at the desktop-like representation of the soft schema (see Figure 4) and manipulate data and attributes using the tabular view of Figure 1. Using the archetypal categories to generate the UI means that the latter does not break when the end users make changes to the schema.

Relationships between concepts are accommodated implicitly. The end user can simply add a concept as an attribute of another concept, thus creating an implicit relationship. For example, a user might use the concepts tab of Figure 4 to locate the concept *purchase*. Then, they might go to the Attributes panel on the right hand side and click "New…" to add a new attribute, so as to define what is a purchase. There, they could add an attribute *purchaseDate* of the predefined *date*, or they could add a *location* which, as can be seen at the Concepts tab, is of category *places*. Thus, the end user has implicitly made the relationship "a purchase has-a location".

An Example: The "Bookplace" Database

As an illustration of the AIS in use, let us consider a simple example. A bookstore called "Bookplace" has stores in five locations, and each customer purchases one or more books.

The Bookplace manager can use the AIS UI to create icons in the model manager for this schema: they can make a new icon for the store location, which they can label as a place, an icon for the purchases, which they can label as activities, another for customers (people), etc.

Once the end user has made a *customer* concept, which falls under the category *people*, they can click on the icon to bring up the customer tab in the attributes panel on the right-hand side of the screen. There, they can make new attributes by clicking "New", choosing from a menu what type of attribute they want (e.g., text), and naming their attribute (e.g., first name).

Thus, the attributes panel represents a "has-a" relationship (i.e., the customer *has a* first name). The same mechanism is used to create joins; we can add an icon of another concept to the window to represent the fact that the two concepts are related (e.g., a purchase has a location). This is similar to the desktop metaphor in the sense that the desktop is (often) agnostic about the meaning of each icon: a folder might include an icon of a document or an icon of a folder or of a software application.

Double clicking the customer icon will bring up the data manager tab. There, the user will be able to click on "new" to add new customers, or open a file with existing customers. Moreover, the user can delete, edit, or search for a customer on this tab.

Adding and opening the contents of a concept follows usual desktop conventions: clicking on an icon operates on the icon itself; double clicking opens the content related to this icon.

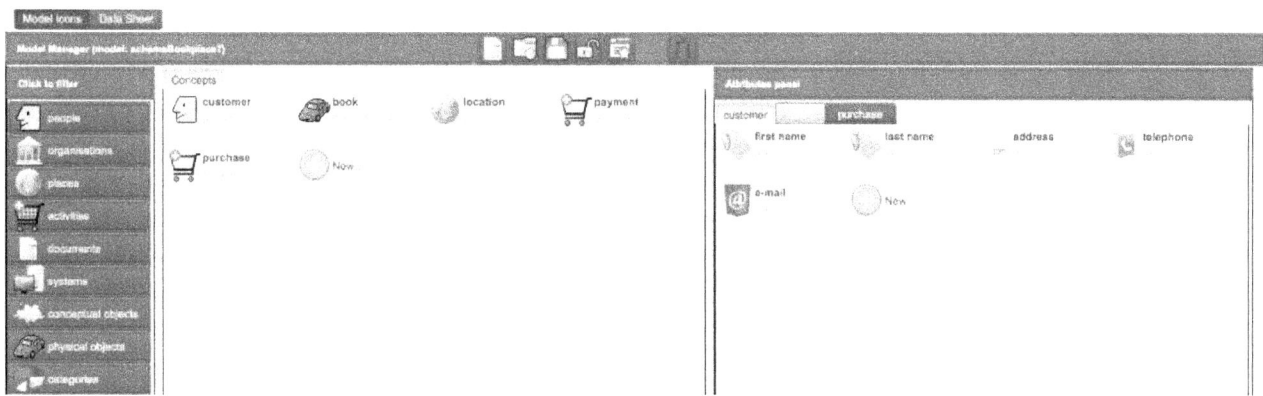

Figure 4. The Model Manager tab of the AIS UI.

Managing schema changes is as easy as managing desktop icons. Assuming that the manager of the "Bookplace" want to add a new payment method, they would only have to select the icon for *purchase* and add a new attribute icon, then go to the data tab and change the data accordingly. Note that this change will require no middleware/UI reprogramming. Data migration is optional; it can be done immediately or at a later time, or not at all.

Now, let us assume that the solution of modelling the relationship "purchase has-a purchase method" by representing purchase method as an attribute proves to be insufficient, so the Bookplace manager makes a decision to represent purchase methods as a new concept. Then, the end user can make a new concept *purchase method*, and the existing functionality will not break. Then, they can relate the new concept to the concept *purchase*, and (if they want to) migrate their data to this new structure.

In addition, users can right click an item to edit its properties; that is, they can set the cardinality of a relationship to allow-one or allow-many, or make an attribute mandatory. So far, relationships are modelled implicitly: allowing-many *book* items in a *purchase* will model a 1:N relationship. If a user would want to model an N:M relationship they would have to allow-many *purchase* at the *book* window. In the future we plan to provide a different menu in a drop-down fashion to accommodate this functionality.

USER EVALUATION
The evaluation of the AIS UI included a usability study in a laboratory environment where users conducted a set of tasks. The users consisted of thirty individuals in the 25-35 age range. All were students in the information systems/computer science area. Most had at least two years' work experience.

The experimental procedure was as follows. Each user was given a simple model of a bookstore, implemented in either AIS UI, Microsoft Access (DB), or Microsoft Excel (SPR). The allocation of software to user was made at random. Each user carried out a scenario of eight tasks, as follows.

1. Add new data of various types.

2. Add new attributes, e.g., a new payment method.

3. Make changes to the model, e.g., each purchase will change so as to have many product types.

4. Search for a particular piece of data.

5. Add and rename a concept.

6. Edit and delete a piece of data.

7. Handle missing relationships, e.g., enter a purchase where a location is missing.

8. Handle missing attributes, e.g., enter a payment where the payment method is missing.

The starting schema was constructed by the authors in Excel, then exported to XML, and finally imported to Access and the AIS UI in order to create the three instances of the database to be evaluated.

The users loaded the schema and then followed instructions on a website given to them which had a detailed description of the tasks. Beside each task were two fields for the users to fill in: the time it took them to perform a task, and a checkbox to report if they actually finished the task successfully. No explicit talk-aloud protocol was enforced, although some participants voluntarily made comments.

After completing the tasks, the users were asked to fill in a System Usability Scale (SUS) questionnaire [26].

Addressing Bias
The experiment was designed to address potential sources of bias in the following ways.

Completion rate

System Usability Score

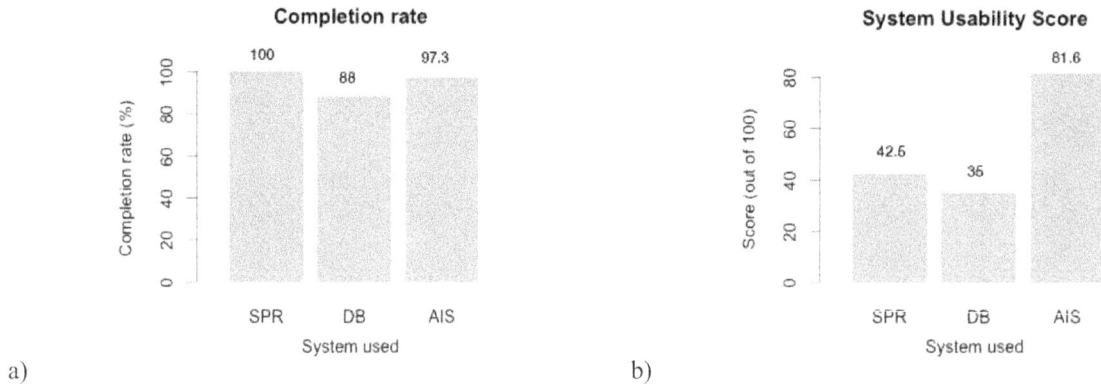

a)   b)

Figure 5. a) Completion rate for the eight tasks per system, b) reported usability score using SUS.

Ideally, the experiment would have taken place in a real working environment. However, a laboratory setting was used due to limitations in resources, and thus attention was paid to recruiting subjects who would represent the target users as much as possible. The users were professionals who were attending an evening information systems course, and came from a non-expert, non-computer-science background. While they might have occasionally had some computer related topics while studying, e.g., economics or mathematics, they were not programmers but typical users of productivity software at their workplace. Thus, we approached our target user, who is the non-expert office professional.

The experimenters supervised the procedure to make sure that the users were filling in the actual time employed. Moreover, the experimenters collected the final .xls, .mdb, and .xml files (from MS Excel, MS Access, and the AIS UI respectively) after the users had finished the experiment to make sure that the tasks, which have been reported as completed successfully, were indeed correct. However, the users were briefed that all tasks were voluntary and could leave the experiment at any time, so 11 of them either chose not to finish the scenario, or finished the scenario but didn't complete the SUS questionnaire.

Concerning the selection of the tasks, these were based on previous work [3] so as to form a realistic scenario according to what has been reported to be a common set of tasks among spreadsheet users. The intention for this choice was to fit the experiment to the common tasks and not vice versa.

Undoubtedly, one source of bias which was unavoidable was that all users were completely new to the AIS UI but had used Excel and Access before. The users were given a short brief concerning the experiment, but the results might still be potentially biased in favour of Access and Excel.

RESULTS

Analysis

Out of the 30 recruited users, 19 finished the scenario *and* filled in SUS questionnaires. We analysed the 19 entries that had both a finished scenario and a SUS questionnaire submitted.

The completion rate was 97.3% for the AIS UI, 100% for Excel, and 88% for Access.

	Estimate (minutes)	Std. Error	t-value	P-value
AIS	18.500	3.652	5.066	0.000115***
DB	24.714	4.977	1.249	0.229741
SPR	31.333	5.165	2.485	0.024403*

Table 1: Linear regression results for the user completion time per system.

	Estimate (minutes)	Std. Error	t-value	P-value
AIS	17.833	4.257	4.189	0.000413***
DB	23.333	6.020	0.914	0.371323
SPR	31.333	6.020	2.242	0.035862*

Table 2: Linear regression results for the total task time per user.

To accommodate statistical significance analysis, given the fact that there were missing data due to varying completion rates, we considered two cases: one where we interpolated performance time values for uncompleted tasks, and a more conservative case, where we set the time of each completed task to zero. In both cases normality (Q-Q) and homoscedasticity (Bartlett) tests showed the following.

Uncompleted task time interpolated.
The results passed the homoscedasticity and independence of error tests, so a linear regression analysis of the results was performed (Table 1). For the homoscedasticity hypothesis we have Bartlett's K-squared=1.0988, df=2, and p-value=0.5773, so the hypothesis holds (p-value>0.05).

Uncompleted task time set to zero.
These results also passed the homoscedasticity and independence of error tests, so a linear regression analysis of the results was performed (see Table 2). For the homoscedasticity hypothesis we have Bartlett's K-squared=3.3443, df=3, and p-value=0.3415, so the hypothesis holds (p-value>0.05). Also, we have lag=1, autocorrelation=-0.0605187, D-W statistic=2.04625, and p=value=0.612. The alternative hypothesis is: rho!=0. Since p-value>0 we do not reject the null hypothesis of rho=0. There is no autocorrelation and independence of the error hypothesis holds.

The SUS score for AIS UI was 81.6, for SPR it was 42.5, and for DB it was 36.

Discussion
The results show a statistically significant performance improvement when using the AIS UI instead of spreadsheets, up to 43% (Δ=13.500 minutes, p<0.05). In addition, the AIS UI users performed equally or better than database users (Δ=6.214 minutes, p=0.23) (see Figure 4).

In addition, completion rates for the AIS UI were similar to the ones of popular spreadsheet and database production software (88<97.3<100) (see Figure 5.a). More specifically, the completion rate of 97.3 for the given scenario means that only one user did not accomplish one task using the AIS UI.

These performance metrics are important and demonstrate some advantages of our system. However, it is the usability metrics that fully demonstrate the potential impact of this approach. Our system scored 81.6 points at the Systems Usability Scale, that is more than double than the database which scored 35 points, and almost double points than the 42.5 points of the spreadsheet (see Figure 5.b).

Where does this difference in usability lie? A qualitative observation might give us a hint. As noted before, a talk-aloud protocol was not enforced; however, two users who were using the AIS UI made useful comments, having been rather surprised by the interface they were using:

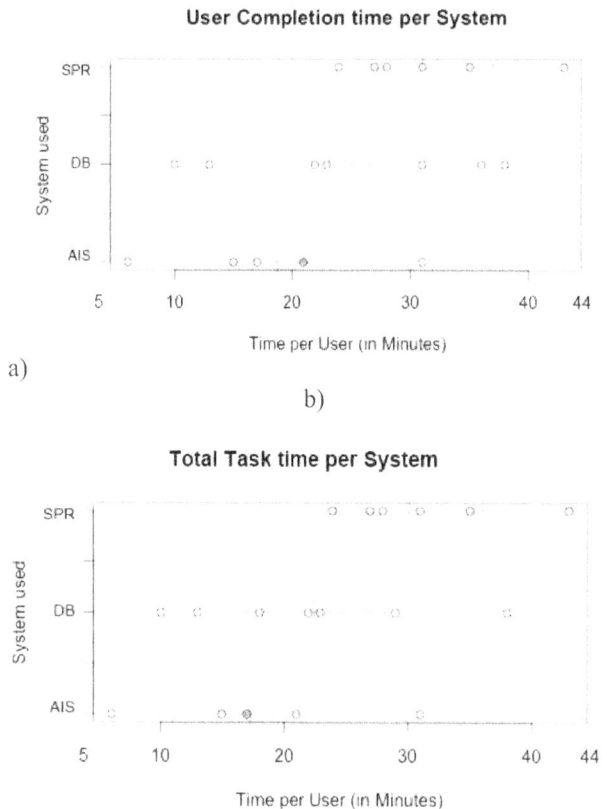

a)

b)

Figure 4: User performance per system. Each white circle represents one user; each gray circle represents two users. The mean is drawn as a vertical line, the standard error from the mean drawn as a horizontal bar. a) Scenario completion time per system, regardless of the completion rate for each system. b) Total task time per system (Uncompleted task duration = 0 min).

*"It makes perfect sense to use icons instead of columns, it's so more **usable** this way." (User 28)*

"I cannot believe that we've not been using this all this time—what were we thinking?" (User 30)

This supports the view that there is merit in extending the desktop metaphor to data management. Looking closely to the performance time of each task, we see that spreadsheet users performed well at direct data manipulation, i.e., tasks 1 and 5 (add, search average time=2.7 minutes) but not at managing relationships, i.e., tasks 3, 7, and 8 (average time=13.7 minutes). In contrast, database users performed better than spreadsheet users at managing relationships, especially at task 3 (avg.=5.2 min), but not better than AIS UI users (avg.=4.3 min). The average time to change the cardinality of a relationship was just 1.3 minutes for database users, 3 minutes for AIS UI users and 3.3 minutes for spreadsheet users (to find a working solution).

These results suggest that, in edge cases such as pure data manipulation and intensive schema change, the spreadsheet and the database respectively are fit for purpose (ignoring other potential concerns such as security, data integrity, system integration, etc.).

However, we propose that the AIS UI, with its familiar metaphor, offers a middle way and good performance for end users who need a fair bit of both schema and data management, where their resources do not allow them to invest in a bespoke solution or enterprise software.

The results show that it is beneficial indeed to manipulate schemas and data graphically, according to the motivation we presented at the introductory section. That is, large organisations that can afford experts on relational or document databases might not avail much of a desktop-like representation of schemas. Similarly, individuals who need to organise a single collection of data, e.g., personal finances, might be better off using a spreadsheet. Since the vast majority of organisations, SMEs, and NGOs do not lie in these categories, but need a middle level of data management complexity, it is probable that they will find a system like our AIS UI not only usable, but also useful.

FUTURE WORK
Future work includes building an AIS UI which is more scalable and which includes specific views for each archetypal category.

In addition, the scenario of this usability study demonstrated the usability of changing an existing schema but not of merging two or more similar schemas. Thus, further usability testing needs to be conducted. We plan to achieve this by putting the AIS UI into trial in small organisations to apply it to real-world situations instead of a laboratory experiment. We anticipate that evaluating with users in organisations onsite might provide a larger pool of users, too.

Moreover, we plan to implement a version based on graph databases. We anticipate that we will be able to improve relationship modelling, e.g., by explicitly joining attributes of concepts through a visual dropdown-like menu.

CONCLUSION
In this paper we presented the Adaptive Information System UI, which adapts and augments the desktop metaphor to facilitate data management. Our implementation allows direct manipulation of icons to perform operations on concepts, attributes and relationships. We evaluated our system by conducting a user study that compared the AIS UI with Microsoft Excel and Microsoft Access when used in a simple business data management scenario. The AIS UI performed equally well to or better than Access and significantly better than Excel (~43% on average), and its SUS usability score was almost double that of the scores of Access and Excel.

REFERENCES
1. Bakke, E., Karger, D.R., and Miller, R.C. A Spreadsheet-Based User Interface for Managing Plural Relationships in Structured Data. In *Proc. CHI 2011*, ACM Press (2011), 2541-2550.

2. Canfield Smith, D., Irby, C., Kimball, R., and Harslem, E. The Star User Interface, In *Proc. AFIPS NCC 1982*, AFIPS Press (1982), 515-528.

3. Chan, Y.E., and Storey, V.C. The use of spreadsheets in organizations: determinants and consequences. *Information & Management 31*, 3 (1996), 119-134.

4. England, D., Randles, M., and TalebBendiab, A. Runtime user interface design and adaptation. *Proc. BCS-HCI '09*, BCS (2009), 463-470.

5. Ertl, D., Kaindl, H., Arnautovic, E., Falb, J., and Popp, R. Generating high-level interaction models out of ontologies. *Proc. IUI SEMAIS'11*, CEUR (2011), 467-468.

6. Evamy, M. *World Without Words*. Laurence King Publishing, London, UK, 2003.

7. Gajos, K., and Weld, D.S. 2004. SUPPLE: automatically generating user interfaces. *Proc. IUI '04*, ACM Press (2004), 93-100.

8. Horton, W. *The Icon Book*. John Wiley & Sons, 1994, 13-16.

9. Kapros E., McGinnes S. Cognitive Semantic Categories as a Basis for Adaptive Information Systems. In *Semantic Models for Adaptive Interactive Systems*, Springer, London, UK, 2013, 43-57

10. Kohlhase, A., and Kohlhase, M. Spreadsheets with a semantic layer. *Electronic Communications of the EASST Volume X*, (2010).

11. McGinnes, S., and Amos, J. Accelerated Business Concept Modeling: Combining User Interface Design with Object Modeling. In *Object Modeling and User Interface Design: Designing Interactive Systems*, Addison-Wesley, Boston, MA, USA, 2001, 3-36.

12. Raden, N. *Shedding light on shadow IT: Is Excel running your business?* Hired Brains, Inc., Santa Fe, NM, USA, 2005.

13. Wach, E.P. Automated ontology evolution as a basis for adaptive interactive systems. *Proc. IUI SEMAIS'11*, CEUR (2011), 467-468.

14. Whitehouse, R. The uniqueness of individual perception. In *Information Design*. MIT Press, Cambridge, MA, USA, 2000, 103-129.

15. Zhao, C., Zhao, L., and Wang, H. A spreadsheet system based on data semantic object. *Proc. ICIME 2010*, IEEE (2010), 407-41.

16. Dahalin, Z., 2005. Risks of user-development application in small business. *International Journal of Management Studies (IJMS)*, 12(2), pp.41–52.

17. Codd, E. F. A relational model of data for large shared data banks. *Communications of the ACM, 13*(6) (1970), 377-387.

18. McGinnes, S.: Systems and Methods for Software Based on Business Concepts. 20050289524, *USPTO* (2005)

19. Moore, C.J., Price, C.J.: A Functional Neuroimaging Study of the Variables that Generate Category-Specific Object Processing Differences. *Brain 122*, 943-962 (1999)

20. Markman, A.B.: Similar and Different: The Differentiation of Basic-Level Categories. *Learning, Memory 23*, 54-70 (1997)

21. Caramazza, A., Mahon, B.Z.: The Organization of Conceptual Knowledge: the Evidence from Category-Specific Semantic Deficits. *Trends in Cognitive Sciences 7*, 354–361 (2003)

22. McGinnes, S.: Conceptual Modelling: A Psychological Perspective. Ph.D Thesis, Department of Information Systems, London School of Economics, University of London (2000)

23. Karger, D., Bakshi, K., Huynh, D., Quan, D., and Sinha, V. Haystack: A General Purpose Information Management Tool for End Users of Semistructured Data. *CIDR*, (2005), 13-26.

24. Borges, C., and Macías, J. 2010. Feasible database querying using a visual end-user approach. *Proc. EICS '10.* ACM, 187-192.

25. Puerta, A.R. A Model-Based Interface Development Environment. *IEEE Software 14*, 4, 1997, 41-47.

26. Brooke, J. SUS: a "quick and dirty" usability scale. In *Usability Evaluation in Industry.* London: Taylor and Francis. (1996).

Towards a Multi-Stakeholder User Interface Engineering Approach with Adaptive Modelling Environments

Alfonso García Frey, Jean-Sébastien Sottet and Alain Vagner
Public Research Center Henri Tudor
29 Avenue John F. Kennedy L-1855 Luxembourg
{alfonso.garcia, jean-sebastien.sottet, alain.vagner}@tudor.lu

ABSTRACT

Human-Computer Interaction (HCI) addresses the study, planning and design of the interaction between people and computers through User Interfaces (UIs). The co-design and co-development of these UIs involve different stakeholders as *Developers*, *Functional Analysts*, *Usability Experts* and *Interaction designers* among others, all of them responsible for different UI elements (respectively *implementation*, *functional requirements*, *usability* and *interaction workflow*). Collaboration between stakeholders has been identified as a key factor for UI development.

This article investigates how concepts and methods from model-driven engineering (MDE) can contribute to UI development through a collaborative approach. We discuss how UI views (extra-UI, mega-UI) can be useful for multi-stakeholder engineering, and how MDE acts as the backbone that supports them. The global approach is implemented through a first prototype of an Adaptive Modelling Environment (AME) illustrated through a case study. A screencast of the tool is also provided.

Author Keywords

Human-Computer Interaction; Model-Driven Development; Multi-Stakeholder Engineering; User Interfaces; Tools; IDE; Collaborative Modelling;

ACM Classification Keywords

D.2.2 Software Engineering: Design Tools and Techniques; H.5.2 Information Interfaces & presentation: User Interfaces

INTRODUCTION AND PROBLEM STATEMENT

The development of User Interfaces "is a time-consuming and error-prone task" [36]. Approximately 50% of development resources are devoted to UI implementation tasks [30]. According to [35] one of the causes is "the lack of an integrated view" that "often forces developers to implement suboptimal solutions". This lack of integrated views affects not only how

individuals work during the UI development process, but also how individuals collaborate in such process. A potential solution to overcome the lack of integrated views and thus, enhance individual and collaborative work "is to develop more flexible tools" [31]. According to Schmidt [35] and Kimelman [25] these views should help individuals to understand how the artifacts that are manipulated during the UI development process are related to each other and, in consequence, provide a better comprehension of the UI development.

These integrated views refer to two different aspects. Firstly, the artifacts that are manipulated by the stakeholders as, for instance, *usability criteria* (e.g., *cognitive workload*, *guidance*) managed by usability experts, *widgets*, *mockups* and *wireframes* conceived by designers, and *functions* programmed by the developers to implement behavior. Secondly, integrated views refer to how these artifacts are interconnected with each other, for instance, what *cognitive workload* or *guidance* means in terms of *widgets*.

Most of the existing tools for UI development do not take into account the lack of integrated views neither for individual work nor for collaborative UI development. Some solutions are envisioned by related work in order to cope with a multiple stakeholder's involvement in the context of model-based UI development ([2, 8, 33]). However, many research questions remain open: how to make each stakeholders' artifact explicit in the context of model-based UI development? How to provide means for adapting these artifacts to multiple stakeholders? How to make links among stakeholders' artifacts explicit? How to make them manipulable?

Finally and because of these questions, there is a lack of UI development tools supporting a multi-stakeholder engineering approach. In particular, there is a lack of visualization tools allowing to explore, understand and modify stakeholders' artifacts and their interconnections.

To this end, this paper provides a first overview of AMEs, Adaptive Modelling Environments that aim at supporting both individual and collaborative work in order to improve model-based UI development. AMEs support collaborative modelling by providing initial answers to the previous questions by means of integrated views.

The remaining of the article is structured as follows. The first section defines the context of collaboration and its scope, eliciting requirements for a multi-stakeholder engineering approach. An AME is then introduced through a case study first, and depicted through HCI and MDE concepts next. Afterwards, the article ends with a discussion of the conclusion and future work.

COLLABORATION

This section defines and delimits the concept of collaboration in the frame of model-based UI development, eliciting requirements for collaborative modeling of UI.

Definition and Scope

One accepted model for describing collaboration is the 3C model introduced by [11] and refined by [13]. According to the 3C model (figure 1), *collaboration* is composed of the next three complementary elements:

- *Cooperation*: "the joint operation of members of the group in a shared space, seeking to execute tasks, and generate and manipulate cooperation objects."[13].
- *Coordination*: "inter-dependencies between tasks that are carried out to achieve a goal"[13].
- *Communication*: "Conversation to negotiate and make decisions through an augmentation process"[13].

In the context of model-based UI development, *coordination* can also be understood as the process (in a computational sense) organising cooperation actions. *Communication* also involves the exchange of information and knowledge among the team. Awareness is fostered by the three components. Results showed [20] that "the highest degree of users' awareness about their activities and other system users contribute to a decrease in their errors and in the inappropriate use of the system".

Eliciting Collaboration Requirements

A tool supporting collaborative modeling is in fact a groupware dedicated to modeling activities. The Johansen's matrix [24] for groupware (i.e., collaborative software) classification enables us to decompose *cooperation, coordination* and *communication* into the *time* and *space* dimensions. The *time* dimension measures if collaboration is synchronous or asynchronous. The *space* dimension captures whether the actors involved in the collaborative task share the same location or not. Thus, collaboration should ideally be supported through *cooperation, coordination* and *communication* both synchronously and asynchronously, and either in co-located and remote environments.

Moreover and according to [28], UI design teams can be considered as adhocratic organizations since all members have highly specialized profiles, are highly autonomous and the coordination between them is made through mutual adjustments. In consequence, collaboration support should provide means for flexible coordination in order to manage the unpredictable workflows of the adhocracy. In this way, [40] asserts that groupware UIs should be flexible to adapt itself to users needs, and thus, supporting collaboration.

Finally, [40] shows that groupware flexibility can be considered at two different levels: the *microscopic level*, i.e., the (UI) mechanisms that will improve collaboration at the individual level, and the *macroscopic level*, i.e., flexibility for

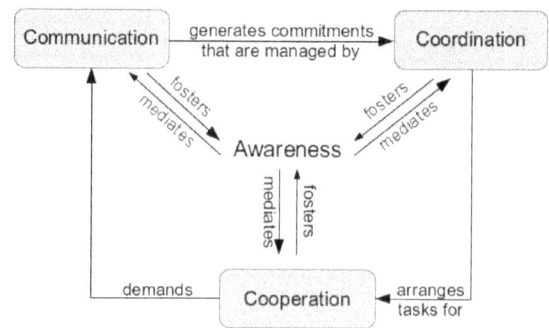

Figure 1. The 3C model as defined by Fuks et al. [13].

adapting to the organizational aspects including the stakeholders inter-relationships and the organizational processes. These macroscopic and microscopic levels follow the MDE idea of "modeling in the large and modeling in the small" proposed by [3].

In summary, good collaborative environments in the context of model-based UI development should support flexibility both by providing integrated views for making stakeholders' artifacts directly manipulable and by providing means for adapting the representation of such artifacts. Collaboration should be supported via communication, coordination and cooperation. Microscopic and macroscopic collaboration should be supported as well. The concept of integrated view is orthogonal to both collaboration types. Finally, synchronous and asynchronous collaboration should be possible in both co-located or remote environments. In order to fulfill these requirements, the next section introduces an AME.

ADAPTIVE MODELLING ENVIRONMENTS

AMEs aim at supporting collaborative modelling in two ways. Firstly, providing stakeholders with specific views on their artifacts, represented with customizable representations. Secondly, providing views that make explicit the relationships between different stakeholders' artifacts. The combination of both are illustrated in the case study described next.

Case Study

The AME (figure 2) shows multiple integrated views of an online shopping website being developed. The shopping website provides several catalogues to the users, each of them containing a family of products. Once one or more products have been added to the cart (products can be either added or removed from the cart), users can checkout. To checkout or modify the account details, users are requested to login.

The figure shows four different views (three inside the AME plus the AME itself) addressing different stakeholders. These stakeholders are all involved in the co-design and co-development of the shopping website. These views and their stakeholders are depicted next.

1.- Interaction Workflow View
The Interaction Workflow View enables *interaction designers* to define the interaction workflow. The interaction workflow (already used by languages like IFML [7]) captures all the different workspaces (orange ovals) in which the UI is decomposed. The main workspace is the *Home website* from

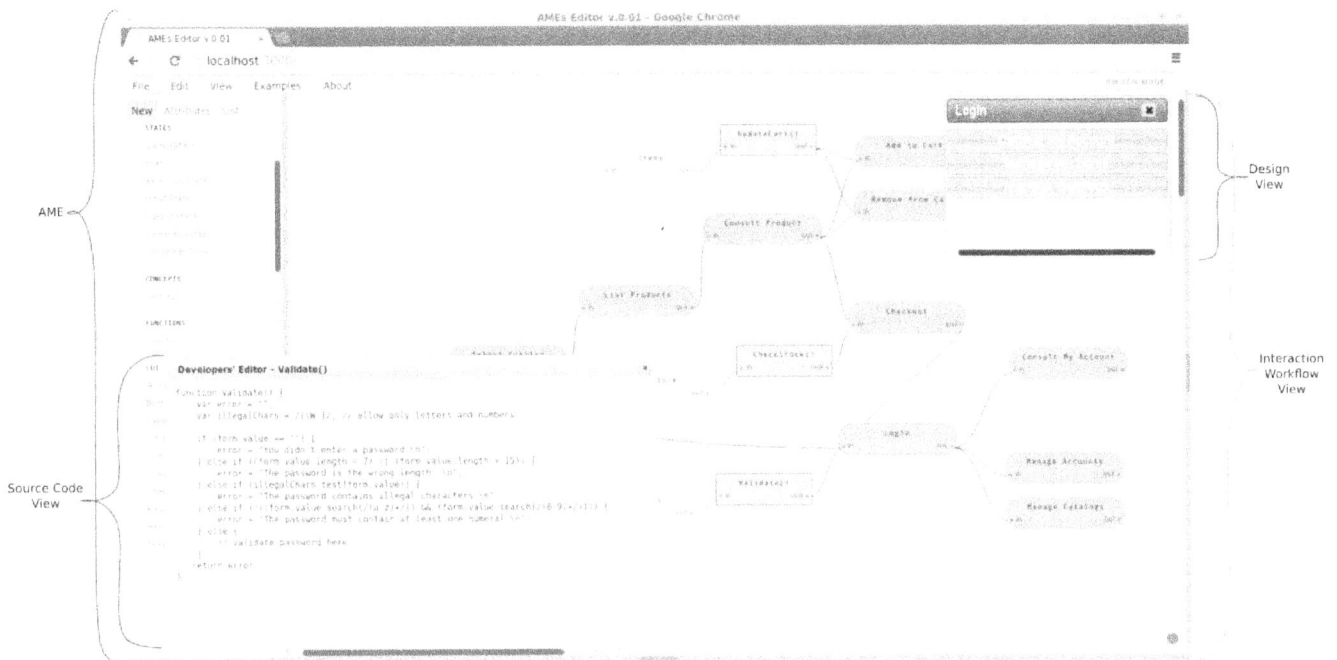

Figure 2. AME interactive online editor. The *Interactive Workflow View* enables stakeholders to (meta)model their artifacts. The figure shows a model done by the *interaction designers* and the *functional analysts*. Inter-artifacts relationships are explicitly represented. The preview window corresponds to the highlighted *container state* named "Login". A video of the whole modeling process is available at `https://www.youtube.com/watch?v=Mz_kSuraFe0&hd=1`.

which users can navigate to *Select Catalogue*. From here, the products of the catalogue are available through the *List Products* workspace.

The interaction designer of the case study has a graphical design background and concentrates on page flow. The manipulated artifacts are thus the *workspaces* composing the interaction workflow of the website plus the *relationships* between them that enable navigation. Note that navigation from a workspace to another could eventually require external information. For instance, *Checkout* requires confirmation by the *CheckStock()* function. Other examples are saving the state of the application and updating some information in the UI. These relationships are all examples of cases involving different stakeholders' artifacts (*workspaces* and *functions*). *Functional analysts* define these function signatures (blue boxes) that trigger functional core methods from the functional core.

2.- Source Code View

The source code view (figure 2, bottom-left window) enables *developers* to implement functional aspects previously identified by *functional analysts*. *Developers* are also involved in the interaction workflow to implement functionality classically associated to the dialog controller of the UI, as for instance, navigation between workspaces. Regarding the chosen development methodology, *developers* can also discuss with *functional analysts* the relevance of defined functions and potential discrepancies between models and developments. The artifact manipulated in this view is the *source code* implementing the function signatures that interface the functional core. The source code view, opened by double clicking the *Validate* function, illustrates the implementation of the *Validate()* function used in the login workspace.

3.- Design View

The design view enables designers to have a first preview of the UI being designed. The preview is computed at runtime and updated according to stakeholders' actions. The preview provides designers with the benefits of rapid prototyping. This view is interactive but not directly modifiable.

4.- AME View

The AME is itself a view on the models of the application that enables for observation and modification by stakeholders. The left sidebar provides access to the (meta)models proposed by the AME. Custom (meta)models can be imported through the *File* menu. Importing (meta)models will populate the sidebar accordingly. Classical (meta)modelling exchange formats such as *Ecore* and *XMI* are used for the (meta)models whereas plain *CSS* is used for customising their representations. When stakeholders do not provide custom representations for the imported (meta)models, a default one is provided by the AME. Next section explains the concepts sustaining these views and how they are supported by MDE.

HCI Views and their MDE support

The example views previously introduced are particular cases of the following HCI concepts ([39]):

- *Extra-UIs*, that give access to the models (e.g., model editors). Extra-UIs are the main HCI design tools; these tools often remain dedicated to specialists, being rarely designed for collaboration. Some UI design tools pay attention to collaborative edition of models, but only providing role-based collaboration such as Quill[1].

---

[1] http://www.w3.org/wiki/images/b/bb/Quill-2012-01-18.pdf

- *Meta-UI* that provides access to the modelling language specification (i.e., metamodel) These UIs are not usually provided by design tools and are more dedicated to tool providers themselves. Modelling language design environments such as MetaEdit+[2] also provide collaborative features, mainly based on asynchronous role-based access to (meta)model elements.
- *Trans-UIs* give access to transformations. Transformations play a central role in MDE processes as they capitalize designers know-how. The trans-UI concept is very rarely explored in the literature. One notable work is UMLx [Willink03], a UML profile for their representation.
- *Mega-UIs* give access to the holistic view, encompassing all modelling artifacts and their relationships. The mega-UI provides a way to visualize and modify different levels of abstraction of the core model elements and their relations. As a result, they permit to align, discuss and evolve the various models (i.e. views) on the interactive system.

These UIs are the necessary backbone for a collaborative modelling environment such AMEs, because each of them can effectively contribute to stakeholders' views through an orthogonal consideration of different stakeholders as illustrated in figure 2.

Our approach aligns with MDE as follows: stakeholders' artifacts are captured into (and represented with) models conforming to some metamodels. These artifacts are manipulated and transformed using model transformations. Flexibility is thus supported at different levels. First, interconnections between different artifacts and their relationships are captured, represented, and made manipulable through the concept of megamodel. Second, adaptation is investigated through mechanisms that able stakeholders to customise the representation of the models, metamodels and transformations. By these contributions, AMEs aim at providing support for multi-stakeholder engineering.

COVERAGE OF COLLABORATION REQUIREMENTS AND CURRENT LIMITATIONS

Figure 3 shows how AME instantiates the 3C model. Firstly, *communication* is supported through the models that underly each view through view updates. Rather than fixing the *communication* to a single channel, i.e, the views, the AME provide views with a double objective. First, views aim at enriching the communication by providing representations that are understandable by the involved stakeholders, so they can serve as a common ground for discussion. The current version of the AME provides default representations for new artifacts in case no representation is provided by the stakeholder. Second, the views enable direct manipulation of the (meta)models and transformations. The discussion of design alternatives benefits from the rapid prototyping preview provided by the design view. The current version of the AME provides limited support for transformations (merge and filtering) through transformation views (trans-UIs).

Support for *cooperation* is provided by construction by most of the views. Consider for instance the central workspace of

[2]http://en.wikipedia.org/wiki/MetaEdit+

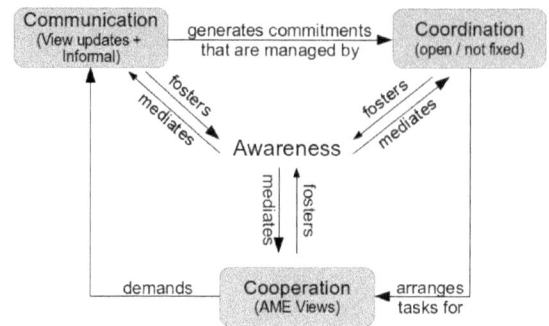

Figure 3. Instantiation of the 3C model by the AME.

the AME, implemented through a megamodel and accessible through a mega-UI. This central workspace illustrates the *interaction workflow* view in which cooperation among different stakeholders takes place.

Finally, the presented AME does not fix any *coordination* mechanism. This design choice has been made to allow the AME to be adapted to different organizational processes that orchestrate how model-based UIs are generated. Explicit coordination support could be added if further evaluations reveal significant benefits.

The microscopic flexibility is managed in the AME by single metamodel instances (each model), whereas the megamodel supports the macroscopic flexibility. In particular, the AME supports micro- and macroscopic collaboration as follows:

- *microscopic collaboration* when only one model is impacted (e.g., co-design of the UI).
- *macroscopic collaboration* where many interrelated models are affected (i.e., megamodel).

Both micro and macro levels have been illustrated in the case study through different interfaces (extra-UI, mega-UI). Regarding the dimensions proposed by the Johansen's matrix, the AME has been designed as an online tool to maximize the collaboration possibilities specially in non co-located environments. Co-located stakeholders are already supported by the AME. Support for synchronization among stakeholders is not currently provided.

RELATED WORK

Model-Based approaches are suited for UI development for several reasons. First, a number of frameworks and languages [26, 32, 6] structure the way UIs are generated from models. Models are defined in [4] as "an artifact that conforms to a metamodel and that represents a given aspect of a system". Thus, thanks to this conformance relationship, models are successively transformed and combined using transformations to finally generate the code of the UI. Moreover, using model-based approaches for UI development provides a number of significant advantages like easier evolution and reuse [22], dynamic adaptation to the context of use [9, 5], end-user programming [10], greater quality [12, 18, 29, 38] and automatic generation of support [17, 16] among others.

AMEs are thus model-based UIs themselves that aim to support collaborative modelling in the context of UI development. Indeed, some works prove that collaborative modelling for one single type of models provides significant advantages (e.g. [14]). As a consequence, providing support for multiple models should reiterate (and possibly increase) such benefits.

However, collaborative modelling has been only lately considered, (e.g. in [23]). Existent collaborative environments such as Synergo [2], Space-Design [8], CoolModes [33] or Gambit [34] lack of integrated modelling views for multiple stakeholders or focus on a predefined set of models. On the contrary, our proposition does not fix neither the models nor their representations.

Most model-driven engineering tools[3] do not support collaborative modelling and when they do, collaboration is diluted into classical modelling editors without focusing on the relationships between different stakeholders' artifacts. Moreover, the models managed and generated by these tools are predefined at design-time whereas AME provides means for both (meta)modelling and importing existent (meta)models.

Most model-based UIs development tools (e.g., Cedar Studio [1], MASP [5], Leonardi[4], GrafiXML [27], UsiComp [19], WebRatio [7], MuiCSer [21], Xplain [15]) also lack of support for remote collaboration and/or integrated views, or have fixed (meta)models.

CONCLUSIONS AND PERSPECTIVES

This paper introduces AME, an Adaptive Modelling Environment that firstly, enable stakeholders to visualize and manipulate the metamodels, models and transformations, or any of their internal elements, that are relevant to their specific tasks in the context of model-based UI development; secondly, the AME should help stakeholders to understand the full stack of models by means of integrated views in which custom representations of the manipulated artifacts and their interconnections are displayed. An AME in the form of an online Integrated Development Environment -IDE- has been introduced. The AME has been depicted through a case study including four different stakeholders each of them working with their own (meta)models.

Future work will use adequate evaluation techniques of the so called *groupware usability* to test the suitability of AMEs with real stakeholders and compare its performance against existing collaborative modelling tools. Some modifications to the 3C model have been purposed in the literature. These improvements should be considered and compared to other collaboration models. Explicit support for coordination (through process modelling) and more support for communication (e.g., via chat) will be evaluated. Finally, research on improving trans-UIs to provide a more fine control of transformations [37], support for remote collaboration and inclusion of visualization techniques for better interaction will be addressed in future evolutions of the software.

ACKNOWLEDGMENTS
This work has been supported by the Luxemburgish FNR MoDEL project (C12/IS/3977071).

---

[3]http://wiki.eclipse.org/images/d/dc/Report.external.bvs.pdf
[4]http://www.leonardi-free.org

REFERENCES

1. Akiki, P. A., Bandara, A. K., and Yu, Y. Cedar studio: An ide supporting adaptive model-driven user interfaces for enterprise applications. In *Proc.of the 5th ACM SIGCHI Symposium on Engineering Interactive Computing Systems*, EICS'13, ACM (New York, 2013).

2. Avouris, N., Margaritis, M., and Komis, V. Modelling interaction during small-group synchronous problem-solving activities: the synergo approach. In *Proc. of the Workshop on Designing Computational Models of Collaborative Learning Interaction, 7th Conf. on Intelligent Tutoring Systems, ITS*, Springer (2004).

3. Bézivin, J., Jouault, F., Rosenthal, P., and Valduriez, P. Modeling in the large and modeling in the small. In *Proceedings of the 2003 European Conference on Model Driven Architecture: Foundations and Applications*, MDAFA'03, Springer-Verlag (Berlin, Heidelberg, 2005).

4. Bézivin, J., Jouault, F., and Valduriez, P. On the need for megamodels. *Proc. of OOPSLA/GPCE: Best Practices for Model-Driven Software Development workshop, 19th Annual ACM Conf. on Object-Oriented Programming, Systems, Languages, and Applications* (2004).

5. Blumendorf, M., Feuerstack, S., and Albayrak, S. Multimodal user interaction in smart environments: Delivering distributed user interfaces. In *Constructing Ambient Intelligence*, vol. 11 of *Communications in Computer and Information Science*. Springer, 2008.

6. Botterweck, G. Multi front-end engineering. In *Model-Driven Development of Advanced User Interfaces*, vol. 340. Springer, 2011, 27–42.

7. Brambilla, M., and Fraternali, P. Large-scale model-driven engineering of web user interaction: The webml and webratio experience. *Science of Computer Programming* (2013).

8. Bravo, C., Duque, R., and Gallardo, J. A groupware system to support collaborative programming: Design and experiences. *J. Syst. Softw. 86*, 7 (July 2013).

9. Calvary, G., Coutaz, J., Thevenin, D., Limbourg, Q., Bouillon, L., and Vanderdonckt, J. A unifying reference framework for multi-target user interfaces. *Interacting with Computers 15*, 3 (2003).

10. Dittmar, A., García Frey, A., and Dupuy-Chessa, S. What can model-based ui design offer to end-user software engineering? In *Proceedings of the 4th ACM SIGCHI Symposium on Engineering Interactive Computing Systems*, EICS'12, ACM (New York, 2012).

11. Ellis, C. A., Gibbs, S. J., and Rein, G. Groupware: some issues and experiences. *Commun. ACM 34* (1991).

12. Fernandez, A., Insfran, E., and Abraho, S. Integrating a usability model into model-driven web development processes. In *Web Information Systems Engineering - WISE 2009*, vol. 5802. Springer, 2009, 497–510.

13. Fuks, H., Raposo, A., Gerosa, M. A., Pimental, and Mariano. *Encyclopedia of E-Collaboration*. 2008, ch. The 3C Collaboration Model.

14. Gallardo, J., Molina, A. I., Bravo, C., Redondo, M. A., and Collazos, C. A. Groupware: Design, implementation, and use. Springer-Verlag, Berlin, Heidelberg, 2008, ch. Comparative Study of Tools for Collaborative Task Modelling: An Empirical and Heuristic-Based Evaluation, 340–355.

15. García Frey, A., Calvary, G., and Dupuy-Chessa, S. Xplain: an editor for building self-explanatory user interfaces by model-driven engineering. In *EICS* (2010).

16. García Frey, A., Calvary, G., and Dupuy-Chessa, S. Users need your models!: exploiting design models for explanations. In *BCS HCI*, British Computer Society (2012), 79–88.

17. García Frey, A., Calvary, G., Dupuy-Chessa, S., and Mandran, N. Model-based self-explanatory uis for free, but are they valuable? In *INTERACT (3)*, vol. 8119 of *Lecture Notes in Computer Science*, Springer (2013).

18. García Frey, A., Céret, E., Dupuy-Chessa, S., and Calvary, G. Quimera: A quality metamodel to improve design rationale. In *Proc. of the 3rd ACM SIGCHI Symposium on Engineering Interactive Computing Systems*, EICS'11, ACM (New York, 2011), 265–270.

19. García Frey, A., Ceret, E., Dupuy-Chessa, S., Calvary, G., and Gabillon, Y. Usicomp: an extensible model-driven composer. In *EICS* (2012), 263–268.

20. Gava, V. L., Spinola, M. d. M., Tonini, A. C., and Medina, J. A. C. The 3c cooperation model applied to the classical requirement analysis. *JISTEM Journal 9* (2012).

21. Haesen, M., Coninx, K., Bergh, J., and Luyten, K. Muicser: A process framework for multi-disciplinary user-centred software engineering processes. In *Proc. of the 2nd Conf. on Human-Centered Software Engineering and 7th Inter. Workshop on Task Models and Diagrams*, HCSE-TAMODIA '08, Springer (2008), 150–165.

22. Hamid, B., Radermacher, A., Lanusse, A., Jouvray, C., Grard, S., and Terrier, F. Designing fault-tolerant component based applications with a model driven approach. In *Software Technologies for Embedded and Ubiquitous Systems*, vol. 5287. Springer, 2008.

23. Izquierdo, J. L. C., Cabot, J., Lopez-Fernandez, J. J., Cuadrado, J. S., Guerra, E., and Lara, J. Engaging end-users in the collaborative development of domain-specific modelling languages. In *Cooperative Design, Visualization, and Engineering*. Springer, 2013.

24. Johansen, R. *Groupware: Computer support for business teams*. The Free Press, 1988.

25. Kimelman, D., and Hirschman, K. A Spectrum of Flexibility-Lowering Barriers to Modeling Tool Adoption. In *ICSE 2011 Workshop on Flexible Modeling Tools* (2011).

26. Limbourg, Q., Vanderdonckt, J., Michotte, B., Bouillon, L., and López-Jaquero, V. Usixml: A language supporting multi-path development of user interfaces. In *EHCI/DS-VIS* (2004), 200–220.

27. Michotte, B., and Vanderdonckt, J. GrafiXML, a multi-target user interface builder based on UsiXML. In *ICAS* (2008), 15–22.

28. Mintzberg, H., and Romelaer, P. *Structure et dynamique des organisations*. Editions d'organisation, 1986.

29. Montecalvo, E., Vagner, A., and Gronier, G. Proposal of a usability-driven design process for model-based user interfaces. In *Proc. of the 2nd Inter. Workshop on USIXML* (2011).

30. Myers, B. A., and Rosson, M. B. Survey on user interface programming. In *Proceedings of the SIGCHI Conference on Human Factors in Computing Systems*, CHI '92, ACM (New York, 1992), 195–202.

31. Ossher, H., van der Hoek, A., Storey, M.-A., Grundy, J., Bellamy, R., and Petre, M. Workshop on flexible modeling tools (flexitools 2011). In *Proceedings of the 33rd International Conference on Software Engineering*, ICSE '11, ACM (New York, NY, USA, 2011).

32. Paternò, F., Santoro, C., and Spano, L. D. Maria: A universal, declarative, multiple abstraction-level language for service-oriented applications in ubiquitous environments. *ACM Trans. Comput.-Hum. Interact. 16*, 4 (Nov. 2009), 19:1–19:30.

33. Pinkwart, N., Bollen, L., and Fuhlrott, E. Group-oriented modeling tools with heterogeneous semantics. In *In Proceedings of ITS 2002 (eds. Cerri, Gouardères & Paraguacu*, Springer (2002), 21–30.

34. Sangiorgi, U., and Vanderdonckt, J. Gambit: Addressing multi-platform collaborative sketching with html5. In *Proc. of the 4th ACM SIGCHI Symposium on Engineering Interactive Computing Systems*, EICS'12, ACM (New York, 2012), 257–262.

35. Schmidt, D. C. Guest editor's introduction: Model-driven engineering. *Computer 39*, 2 (2006).

36. Schramm, A., Preußner, A., Heinrich, M., and Vogel, L. Rapid ui development for enterprise applications: Combining manual and model-driven techniques. In *Proc. of the 13th International Conference on Model Driven Engineering Languages and Systems*, MODELS'10, Springer (Berlin, 2010), 271–285.

37. Sottet, J., and Vagner, A. Defining domain specific transformations in human-computer interfaces development. In *2nd Conf. on Model-Driven Engineering for Software Developement, Modelsward* (2014).

38. Sottet, J.-S., Calvary, G., Coutaz, J., and Favre, J.-M. Engineering interactive systems. Springer-Verlag, 2008, ch. A Model-Driven Engineering Approach for the Usability of Plastic User Interfaces, 140–157.

39. Sottet, J.-S., Calvary, G., Favre, J.-M., and Coutaz, J. Megamodeling and metamodel-driven engineering for plastic user interfaces: Mega-ui. In *Human-Centered Software Engineering*, Human-Computer Interaction Series. Springer London, 2009, 173–200.

40. Tarpin-Bernard, F. La flexibilité dans les collecticiels. *Le temps, l'espace et l'évolutif* (2000), 449–458.

Design Space for Focus+Context Navigation in Web Forms

Johannes Harms, Christoph Wimmer, Karin Kappel, Thomas Grechenig
INSO Research Group, Vienna Univ. of Technology, Austria
Firstname.Lastname [at] inso.tuwien.ac.at

ABSTRACT

Navigation in long forms commonly employs user interface design patterns such as scrolling, tabs, and wizard steps. Since these patterns hide contextual form fields outside the viewport or behind other tabs or pages, we propose to apply the focus+context principle from information visualization to form design. This work presents a design space analysis to support usability engineering of focus+context form navigation. We evaluated the design space's usefulness and applicability in a case study and found the design space has fostered creativity and helped to clearly document design decisions, indicating it can be a valuable support for engineering intelligent, form-based user interfaces.

Author Keywords

Navigation; Focus + Context; Web Form Design; HCI

ACM Classification Keywords

H.5.4. Hypertext/Hypermedia: Navigation

INTRODUCTION

Forms are widely employed as user interface metaphor for data entry and subsequent editing [21, 23]. Their proper design is considered crucial for smooth information exchange [3, 23, 36]. This work primarily understands 'long' forms in a spatial sense (e.g., number of fields), as opposed to form filling time or cognitive complexity. Long forms are considered a bad design practice – e.g., an empirical study [36, p.294] and guidelines [3] recommend against long forms and unnecessary questions – but they cannot always be avoided. Long forms can result from application requirements for editing large sets of data in domains such as business administration, social networking, e-health and e-government, see Table 1. Furthermore, vertically spatious forms result from design recommendations [3] [23, p.164] to avoid multiple columns and to only ask one question per row.

Hence, given the length of many forms, users need effective means for navigation. Existing navigation solutions are problematic because either the whole form is shown on one page and requires a lot of scrolling, or else the form is split into tabs

Domain and Form	Number of Fields
Business Adm.: Editing a person in JFire	35
Social Networking: Profile page in Xing	66
E-Health: OpenClinica Docetaxel sample study	143
E-Government: US 1040 tax return form	246
Software Eng.: Eclipse preferences dialog	> 300

Table 1. Examples of long forms in different domains. Number of fields counted as input fields and options, without headings, labels and buttons.

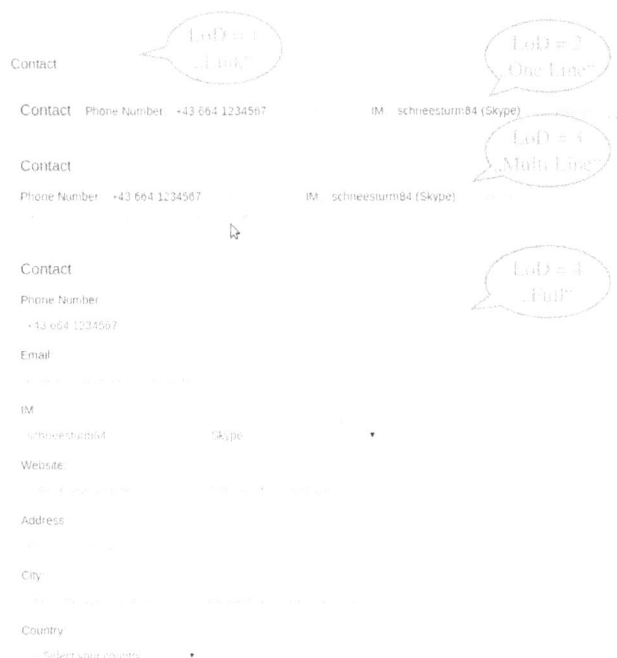

Figure 1. Focus+context navigation in long forms, as designed in the case study. The level of detail (LOD) depends on the user's degree of interest.

or pages. Both options hide the majority of contextual form fields (either outside the viewport or in other tabs), leading to a loss of context for the user. The underlying 'loss of context' problem has been addressed in other domains using the focus+context technique in information visualization [7, 18].

Methodologically, this paper analyzes the design space for how the focus+context principle from information visualization (infovis) can be applied to web form design in order to improve navigation in long forms. The primary contribution of the paper consists of the design space and its evaluation regarding usefulness and practical applicability in a case study where form navigation was redesigned in a social network profile page scenario (see Figure 1).

Form Design

Best practices for form design are captured in guidelines [3] and books [23, 36]. Related research has been classified [3] into five areas: form content, layout, input types, error handling, and submission. Directions for future research are provided in [21], seeking to make the form user interface metaphor more interactive and application-like. Navigation in long forms is treated in [13] with a focus on button placement in web survey design. Linear form filling scenarios with a predictable number of steps can be supported with progress indicators [23, 36] that should communicate scope (overview of the overall steps), position (the current page), and status (of the form submission) [36]. Designers may force linear navigation by using the 'wizard steps' design pattern, allowing them to adapt the form based on previous input. In contrast, non-linear form filling is typical in the domains shown in Table 1: to fill, revise, and complete these forms, users navigate freely around the various form sections.

Navigation

Navigation is a widely used concept in HCI research that metaphorically likens information seeking in electronic environments to navigation in the physical world [14, 16]. An overview of research in mobile, wearable, embedded, 3D, and desktop systems is provided in [34]. The cognitive processes involved in human navigation are detailed in [32]. One branch of navigation research has examined navigation *between* documents, e.g., in hypertext environments [10, 14, 29] and websites [30], or when trying to find the right form to fill in an enterprise resource planning system [33]. In contrast, research on *within*-document navigation investigates topics such as reading long documents [1, 9, 20], navigation in lists [18] and tree-like structures [8], and navigation in long web forms [13], as examined in this paper.

A formal, graph-based model where nodes represent views and edges represent possible transitions allows to formulate two requirements for efficient navigation [19]. Firstly, the out-degree of each node must be relatively small because given limited display size, each view can only show a small number of outgoing navigation links. Consequently, navigation is likely to include multiple steps, which leads to the second requirement: the maximum length of all navigation paths should be short to make navigation efficient. Focus+context techniques fulfill the first requirement by only showing contextually relevant information that users can navigate to, and the second requirement if the contextual information provides shortcuts that abbreviate navigation paths.

Adaptive UIs

As a defining characteristic, adaptive systems modify their behavior based on models of user attributes and actions in order to improve the interaction with the user [22, 26]. To implement such adaptation, software architectures of adaptive systems employ runtime models of the UI to reflect and manipulate the current state of the interactive system [5]. In focus+context approaches, the runtime model computes the users' degree of interest (DOI) and calculates the level of detail (LOD) for UI elements [8], compare Figure 2. A taxonomy of adaptive UIs is provided in [26], allowing to classify

Classification criteria	Classification of this work
Initiating agents	User, system.
Type of adaption	Manner of presentation.
UI-Level of adaptation	Visible
Scope of adaptation	User behavior, etc. [1]
Goals of adaptation	Make complex systems usable
Methods of adaptation	Switching.
Strategy of adaptation[2]	During use.

[1] More options are considered in the design space section of this paper.

[2] Strategy refers to the timing of adaptation: pre / post / during use.

Table 2. Classification of the focus+context form navigation proposed in this work as an adaptive user interface, using the taxonomy from [26].

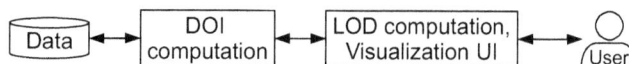

Figure 2. Architecture of focus+context systems, as in [8], Figure 1.

the present work as shown in Table 2: the overall goal of focus+context form navigation is to make complex systems usable; to achieve this goal, the manner of presentation of specific form sections is switched upon user initiative, and upon system initiative when the UI is initially displayed.

Related work has used adaptive systems to improve performance in navigation [22] and menu selection [17] tasks and to reduce visual clutter in form design [25]. Forecasts of future user behavior have been used to improve navigation [2]. Evaluations of adaptive systems have mostly focused on performance, but the users' emotional response and how much they learn from using the system is also important [22]. Adaptive systems have been criticized for introducing additional complexity [35]. It is therefore important to design simple interactions to avoid drawbacks in efficiency and satisfaction.

The Focus + Context Principle

The focus+context principle, as formulated in the infovis discipline by Card et al. [7], states that users simultaneously need detailed information (at the user's focus of interest) and overview (context). It suggests these two kinds of information to be combined into a single, dynamic display that balances global overview and local detail [18]: specific areas of interest are shown in great detail to make interaction feasible while other areas give a compact overview of the global context the user is operating in. A taxonomy of infovis techniques used for navigation design [11] includes zooming (temporally separated views), overview+detail (spatially separated views), focus+context (interwoven focal and contextual views), and cue-based techniques (highlighting of focal elements). The focus+context principle is relevant to existing form navigation patterns where most of the context is hidden either outside the scrolling viewport or behind other tabs or pages. A link between focus+context techniques and navigation is also established in [18]: "Context is not only needed to interpret a static view of an item, providing meaning. It is also critical for moving around effectively". Related work has likewise proposed applying the focus+context principle to navigation in long forms [21] but did not provide a specific solution.

Design Space: Design questions and corresponding options

DOI: Degree of Interest Computation
A-priori importance of form elements:
– Manually assigned by form author
– Automatically derived from form schema
Modelling the user's interest:
– Single focal point
  (with spatial / structural / semantic distance calculation)
– Multiple foci of interest
– Discrete or continuous distributions of interest
Granularity of DOI computation:
– Per control, field, fieldset, section or page
Timing of DOI computation:
– During use, pre-use, post-use
Influencing factors:
– User characteristics, user behavior, context of use, domain

LOD: Level of Detail Computation and Visualization
Influencing factors:
– DOI values and (optionally) total available display space
The number of LODs:
– Multiple, discrete LODs vs. an infinite number of continuous LODs
Techniques for 'making space':
– Semantic approaches: Filtering, aggregation
– Visual approaches: Scaling, distortion, highlighting
– Layout: Block movement, deformation, overlay, outside allocation
Designing LODs by applying the above techniques to:
– Labels, values, form controls
– Hints, validation errors
– Selection fields and corresponding options
– Composite fields, fieldsets, form layout

Table 3. The proposed design space for focus+context form navigation.

A DESIGN SPACE FOR F+C FORM NAVIGATION

Based on the above findings, we suggest applying the focus+context principle to navigation in long forms. The user's focus of interest determines which part of the form is fully shown; the rest of the form is shown in a more compact, aggregated, read-only way. Since this can be designed in various ways, the concept of design spaces is apt to systematically describe design options and their implications. Design spaces have been proposed as a semi-formal notation of design questions (i.e., key issues to be addressed in a design project), design options (possible answers to design questions), and evaluation criteria (implications of design options, used for choosing between design options) [24]. In order to make our proposed design space reusable across multiple projects and domains, we present questions and options in a generic way, see Table 3. Project-specific evaluation criteria and decisions made in one specific scenario are presented in the case study.

The overall structure of the proposed design space can be seen in Table 3, consisting of design options for the two essential components of focus+context visualization as described in [8, 18] and depicted in Figure 2. The degree of interest (DOI) computation component determines the most relevant subset of information. The visualization component computes the levels of detail (LOD) for elements of the UI based on DOI computation and considering the limited display space.

DOI: Degree of Interest Computation

Degree of interest is used to model the instantaneous interest a user is likely to have in various parts of the UI. Furnas [18] describes a generalized fisheye formalism to estimate a user's

DOI in various features of large information structures based on current user activity, defined as

DOI of feature = A-priori importance - Distance from focal point,

where a-priori importance describes the static, intrinsic importance of the features of an information structure, and the focal point describes one specific point of heightened activity.

In form design, *a-priori importance* can be manually assigned by the form author based on the domain-specific importance of form fields. Additionally, a-priori importance can be derived automatically from a given form schema, e.g., an algorithm may assign higher initial DOI values for fields that were marked as 'required' by the form author. Furthermore, the importance of specific fields may be adapted based on the characteristics of individual users or user groups, such as physical and cognitive abilities, preferences, expectations, and experience, compare [26]. E.g., user characteristics based on market segmentation in e-commerce could be used by an algorithm to adapt shopping forms.

Modeling a user's interest in various UI elements as a single *focal point* has been proposed [8, 18] as a highly simplified but practical abstraction. In form design, distance from the focal point may be calculated spatially using a metric on the visualization space (e.g., pixel distance in the UI), structurally using a metric on the form schema (e.g., distance measured in number of fields or fieldsets), or semantically based on the domain-specific similarity or co-relevance of specific form sections. Related work has also considered multiple, discrete focal points [4]. In an even more general form, DOI can be modeled as distribution of interest values over elements of a UI (or elements of the underlying data structure). In form design, DOI can be distributed with different granularity across form elements: per control, field (whereas one field may contain multiple controls), fieldset, section, tab or page.

Different *timings* have been proposed for adapting system behavior [26]. During-use adaptation is the most dynamic option, able to adapt the system while in use. This is required for DOI computation in focus+context visualizations to adapt the system to the user's fluctuating focus of interest. Pre-use adaptation corresponds to the a-priori importance of features in the above formula for DOI computation. Post-use adaptation relates to adapting the system between usage sessions.

Many *factors* can be exploited to influence DOI computation. Related work in infovis has mostly included user behavior such as mouse position and movement, mouse click and hover events, and keyboard input. Other input modalities include taps and gestures on touch devices and other means of interaction such as gestures or eye gaze. Form-specific factors that can be exploited for DOI computation include previously entered data, focus and blur events of input fields and fieldsets, validation errors, and unfilled but required fields. Advanced approaches have considered the social behavior of multiple users [15] or tried to predict future behavior [2]. Context of use has also been proposed as an influencing factor [26]. E.g., in form design, DOI values may depend on mobile vs. stationary usage in private versus public environments.

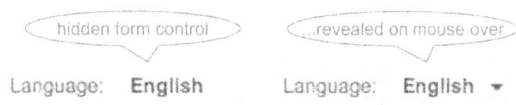

Figure 3. Form controls may be hidden to reduce visual clutter. Screenshot from youtube.com, where the control is revealed on mouse over.

Figure 4. Deselected values may be hidden in lower LODs.

LOD: Level of Detail Computation and Visualization

The visualization component of focus+context user interfaces must be able to display UI elements with different levels of detail (LOD) [11]. The computation of LOD values is a function of DOI values and available display space. Since DOI values change over time, the visualization component must continually recalculate the below formula, compare [8, 9] and Figure 2 for corresponding software architectures.

LOD of feature = f (DOI of feature, total display space).

The above formula for LOD calculation shows that in addition to DOI values, the available display space can be used to influence the LOD computation. E.g., the visualization component may be designed to "squeeze" the entire UI into one screen as in [9]. Another possible aim is to fit a printable form on one sheet of paper as in [23, p.102].

Designing lower LODs immediately raises the question what to omit in order to make space [18]. Previous research in infovis has explored a large variety of techniques for selective reduction of information based on the DOI formalism. Semantic approaches address *what* parts of a structure to display, visual approaches address *how* to display them [18]. "What" corresponds to techniques for filtering and aggregating information, "how" corresponds to techniques for scaling, distorting and highlighting of visual representations [7, 18]. More specific techniques for 'making space' within textual documents are described in [9]. Block movement moves neighboring elements apart to make space. Deformation scales or deforms elements. Overlay allows elements to be rendered on top of others. Outside allocation creates an empty space outside the current view, such as a page margin, and uses it to display additional information.

A varying *number of LODs* may be used in focus+context designs. Multiple, discrete LODs can be designed using filtering, aggregation and highlighting techniques. An infinite number of continuous levels of detail can be designed using distortion and scaling techniques. Note that in traditional form design, the whole form is rendered with just one LOD, but interactive form features such as tooltips and selection-

dependent expanding of form sections [36, ch.12] can be likened to additional levels of detail.

The design of form elements should result in a semantically meaningful *progression of levels of detail*. Many design options exist because all of the before-mentioned visualization techniques (filtering, scaling, highlighting...) can be applied to the various form elements. E.g., *Labels* may be omitted for non-empty fields, if the field's content is self-explanatory. *Values* may be truncated to save space, especially for text-areas with potentially long contents (compare LoD 2 and 3, Figure 1). The *type of form control* may be hidden to reduce visual clutter, as shown in Figure 3. *Hints and help* may be hidden in lower LODs. *Validation errors* may be compacted in lower LODs, e.g., by only showing a warning icon. *Deselected options* in selection fields (such as unchosen radio buttons and check boxes) can be hidden, see Figure 4. *Composite fields and fieldsets* may be compacted by filtering the most important information (compare LoD 3 and 4, Figure 1). The *form layout* may be adjusted to use less space, e.g., by decreasing whitespace, by removing line breaks, and by changing the labels' placement (compare LoD 2, 3 and 4, Figure 1).

The *transition between different LODs* should be smooth to avoid confusion. Scaling, distortion, and block movement techniques can be improved using spatial animations to avoid abrupt changes. Filtering and aggregation techniques can be improved by highlighting the focused element so the user does not lose sight of it during a transition. Highlighting may use graphic styles such as color and font weight to differentiate important from less important elements. Alternatively and additionally, highlighting may use the temporal dimension by showing important elements at once, but fading in less important elements with a delay; a method termed "ephemeral adaptation" which has performed better than graphic highlighting in menu selection tasks [17].

Intended Use of the Design Space

The above design space can be employed as design tool for supporting usability engineering and UI design of navigation in form-based UIs. Methodologically, the design space is best used in early to medium phases of usability engineering. Within Mayhew's Usability Engineering Lifecycle [27], the design space can be used in levels 1 and 2 for prototyping and UI design activities. Within Jarret and Gaffney's form design process [23], it can be used in the conversation layer of form design, seeking to "make the form flow easily" [23].

To use the design space, designers should first define users, tasks, and the intended form schema, as described in the relationship layer in [23]. Based on this knowledge, they can draft a concept for DOI computation using options from the DOI section of our design space as inspiration. Design decisions will depend on the specific project, e.g., different information may be available to influence DOI computation. Designers can then proceed to the more visual design of the different levels of detail, inspired by options in the LOD section of our design space. These activities can and should be iterated using prototyping and formative usability evaluations.

CASE STUDY

To evaluate the design space's practical usefulness and applicability, it was employed in a case study, choosing social network profile pages as scenario. The scenario comprises both initial filling and subsequent revising in a stationary usage context – similar to forms in productivity applications and different from, e.g., registration forms and questionnaires.

Application of the Design Space within the Case Study

One senior designer (> 5 years in UI design) and one junior designer (student in HCI) were tasked with employing the design space (presented to them in textual and tabular representations, as in this paper) for redesigning navigation in a social network profile page prototype. The prototype was neutrally styled and consisted of 75 form controls arranged in 27 fields and 6 fieldsets. Prior to using the design space, the designers analyzed the scenario, describing form filling to be non-linear, sparse (irrelevant fields are left empty), to some degree explorative, and not strictly goal-directed, compare [20] for more on goal directedness. The designers performed three iterations joined by two formative usability tests. Their design decisions are documented in the following paragraphs. The resulting visual design is shown in Figure 1.

When designing *DOI (degree of interest) computation*, a constant a-priori importance was applied to all form elements. User interest was modeled using per-fieldset granularity and a single focal point, with linearly decreasing DOI values for neighboring fieldsets. DOI values are computed during use, based on focussing of form fields by clicking or tabbing.

LOD (level of detail) computation is performed whenever a DOI value changes. The corresponding algorithm is similar to [9] in that it takes the available screen space into account: the algorithm first assigns the maximum LOD to the focussed fieldset. It then tries to fit the remaining fieldsets into the available screen space and otherwise resorts to scrolling. Four levels of detail were designed as shown in Figure 1, using the visualization techniques of filtering, aggregation, highlighting, block movement, and overlay. Specifically, lower LODs use a more compact form layout, omit empty fields, truncate long textual values, omit non-chosen radio buttons and check boxes, and reduce visual clutter by hiding the type of form control (but reveal it on mouse over). The lowest LODs go even further, truncating an entire fieldset's representation to one line or even a single word. Switching between LODs is eased using animations and graphical highlighting.

Lessons Learned, Evaluation Results

Applicability and Usefulness: Designers reported a mostly positive experience with the design space, stating they had successfully applied the design space and benefited from using it. They criticized they had not been able to choose some design options because of the generic nature of the prototype given to them (e.g., specific user profiles would have opened additional options) – we conclude that the prototype's purposely generic nature was a trade-off in study design between realism and generalizability. The designers had very positive opinions on the general applicability of the focus+context

principle to form design, based on their experiences in the case study.

Creativity: The designers reported their biggest benefit while using the design space was that it fostered creativity by providing a list of design options, thus enabling them to discuss options they would otherwise not have considered. The amount of options was initially overwhelming, but later appreciated for inspiration. Additional options suggested by the designers were later added to the design space.

Decision making: The designers found the design space supported their making of design decisions. Its textual description particularly provided helpful details and explanations.

Documenting design decisions: The designers found the design space's structure (particularly its tabular representation) has helped documenting design decisions in a structured way.

Usability Evaluation: To evaluate the resulting focus+context design, we performed a preliminary usability test with 30 novice users, using tabbed and scrolled designs as control conditions. There was no significant effect of navigation design on either navigation performance (measured as task completion time) or subjective satisfaction. All users could easily work with the prototype without needing help or assistance.

CONCLUSION AND FUTURE WORK

This paper introduces a generic design space for focus+context navigation in long forms, based on two critical issues elicited from literature: computation of the user's degree of interest and subsequent visualization of form elements in varying levels of detail. An initial evaluation of the design space within a case study supports its applicability and usefulness for usability engineering and user interface design. Firstly, the design space's applicability and the general feasibility of focus+context form designs can clearly be seen from the prototype resulting from the case study (see Figure 1). Even novice users could easily work with the prototype with similar performance as in tabbed and scrolled designs, as evaluated in a preliminary usability test. Secondly, the designers' experience within the case study strongly supports both the applicability and usefulness of the design space: they found it fostered creativity and helped making and documenting design decisions. Future work should quantify the effect of focus+context form design on performance and user satisfaction in different scenarios and should further evaluate the design space by using it in other projects.

REFERENCES

1. Alexander, J., and Cockburn, A. An empirical characterisation of electronic document navigation. In *Proc. Graphics Interface '08*, Canadian Information Processing Society (2008), 123–130.

2. Anderson, C. R., Domingos, P., and Weld, D. S. Relational markov models and their application to adaptive web navigation. In *Proc. Knowledge Discovery and Data Mining '02*, ACM (2002), 143–152.

3. Bargas-Avila, J., Brenzikofer, O., Roth, S., Tuch, A., Orsini, S., and Opwis, K. Simple but crucial user interfaces in the world wide web: Introducing 20

guidelines for usable web form design. In *User Interfaces*, InTech, 2010, ch. 1.

4. Björk, S., and Redström, J. Redefining the focus and context of focus+context visualizations. In *Proc. Information Vizualization '00*, IEEE (2000), 85–89.

5. Blumendorf, M., Lehmann, G., and Albayrak, S. Bridging models and systems at runtime to build adaptive user interfaces. In *Proc. EICS '10*, ACM (2010), 9–18.

6. Brooke, J. SUS – a quick and dirty usability scale. *Usability evaluation in industry 189* (1996), 194.

7. Card, S., Mackinlay, J., and Shneiderman, B. *Using Vision to Think*. Morgan Kaufmann, 1999.

8. Card, S. K., and Nation, D. Degree-of-interest trees: a component of an attention-reactive user interface. In *Proc. Advanced Visual Interfaces '02*, ACM (2002), 231–245.

9. Chang, B.-W., Mackinlay, J. D., Zellweger, P. T., and Igarashi, T. A negotiation architecture for fluid documents. In *Proc. UIST '98*, ACM (1998), 123–132.

10. Chen, C., and Rada, R. Interacting with hypertext: a meta-analysis of experimental studies. *Hum.-Comput. Interact. 11*, 2 (June 1996), 125–156.

11. Cockburn, A., Karlson, A., and Bederson, B. B. A review of overview+detail, zooming, and focus+context interfaces. *ACM Comput. Surv. 41*, 1 (Jan. 2009), 2:1–2:31.

12. Cockburn, A., Quinn, P., Gutwin, C., and Fitchett, S. Improving scrolling devices with document length dependent gain. In *Proc. CHI '12*, ACM (2012), 267–276.

13. Couper, M. P., Baker, R., and Mechling, J. Placement and design of navigation buttons in web surveys. *Survey Practice 4*, 1 (2013).

14. Dillon, A., McKnight, C., and Richardson, J. Navigation in hypertext: A critical review of the concept. In *Proc. INTERACT '90*, North-Holland (1990), 587–592.

15. Dörk, M., Lam, H., and Benjelloun, O. Accentuating visualization parameters to guide exploration. In *CHI '13 Extended Abstracts*, ACM (2013), 1755–1760.

16. Dørum, K., and Garland, K. Efficient electronic navigation: A metaphorical question? *Interacting with Computers 23*, 2 (2011), 129 – 136.

17. Findlater, L., Moffatt, K., McGrenere, J., and Dawson, J. Ephemeral adaptation: The use of gradual onset to improve menu selection performance. In *Proc. CHI '09*, ACM (2009), 1655–1664.

18. Furnas, G. A fisheye follow-up: further reflections on focus + context. In *Proc. CHI '06*, ACM (2006), 999–1008.

19. Furnas, G. W. Effective view navigation. In *Proc. CHI '97*, ACM (1997), 367–374.

20. Guiard, Y., Du, Y., and Chapuis, O. Quantifying degree of goal directedness in document navigation: application to the evaluation of the perspective-drag technique. In *Proc. CHI '07*, ACM (2007), 327–336.

21. Harms, J. Research goals for evolving the 'form' user interface metaphor towards more interactivity. In *Human Factors in Computing and Informatics*, vol. 7946 of *LNCS*. Springer, 2013, 819–822.

22. Höök, K., and Svensson, M. Evaluating adaptive navigation support. In *Social Navigation of Information Space*, Computer Supported Cooperative Work. Springer, 1999, 237–249.

23. Jarrett, C., and Gaffney, G. *Forms that work: designing web forms for usability*. Morgan Kaufmann, 2008.

24. MacLean, A., Young, R. M., and Moran, T. P. Design rationale: the argument behind the artifact. *SIGCHI Bull. 20*, SI (Mar. 1989), 247–252.

25. Malinowski, U. Adjusting the presentation of forms to users' behavior. In *Proc. IUI '93*, ACM (1993), 247–249.

26. Malinowski, U., Kühme, T., Dieterich, H., and Schneider-Hufschmidt, M. A taxonomy of adaptive user interfaces. In *Proc. HCI '92*, Cambridge University Press (1993), 391–414.

27. Mayhew, D. J. *The Usability engineering lifecycle: A practitioner's handbook for user interface design*. Morgan Kaufmann, 1999.

28. Mizoguchi, K., Sakamoto, D., and Igarashi, T. Overview scrollbar: A scrollbar showing an entire document as an overview. In *Human-Computer Interaction – INTERACT 2013*, vol. 8120 of *LNCS*. Springer, 2013, 603–610.

29. Nielsen, J. The matters that really matter for hypertext usability. In *Proc. HYPERTEXT '89*, ACM (1989), 239–248.

30. Pilgrim, C. J. Website navigation tools – a decade of design trends 2002 to 2011. In *Australasian User Interface Conference (AUIC 2012)*, vol. 126 of *CRPIT*, ACS (2012), 3–10.

31. Rummel, B. System usability scale (translated into german). www.sapdesignguild.org/resources/sus.asp, last retrieved March 12th, 2014.

32. Spence, R. A framework for navigation. *Int. J. Human-Computer Studies 51*, 5 (1999), 919 – 945.

33. Tomasic, A., Cohen, W., Fussell, S., Zimmerman, J., Kobayashi, M., Minkov, E., Halstead, N., Mosur, R., and Hum, J. Learning to Navigate Web Forms. In *Workshop on Information Integration on the Web* (2004).

34. Vainio, T. A review of the navigation HCI research during the 2000's. *Int. J. Interactive Mobile Technologies 4*, 3 (2010), 36–42.

35. Woods, D. D. The price of flexibility. In *Proc. IUI '93*, ACM (1993), 19–25.

36. Wroblewski, L. *Web Form Design. Filling the Blanks*. Louis Rosenfeld, 2008.

A Framework for the Development of Multi-Display Environment Applications Supporting Interactive Real-Time Portals

Chi Tai Dang, Elisabeth André

Augsburg University, Human Centered Multimedia, Department of Computer Science

Universitaetsstr. 6a, 86159 Augsburg, Germany

{dang, andre}@informatik.uni-augsburg.de

ABSTRACT

Advances in multi-touch enabled interactive tabletops led to many commercially available products and were increasingly deployed at places beyond research labs, for example at exhibitions, retail stores, or showrooms. At the same time, small multi-touch devices, such as tablets or smartphones, became prevalent in our daily life. When considering both trends, occasions and scenarios where tabletop systems and mobile devices form a coupled interaction space are expected to become increasingly widespread.

However, application development or research prototypes for those environments will foreseeable require considerable resources when considering nowadays heterogeneity of device platforms and the functionality to establish a connected interaction space. To address these concerns, this paper discusses challenges and answers questions that arose during design and implementation of the Environs framework, a multi-display environment software framework that eases development of interactive distributed applications. In particular, Environs enables applications utilizing video portals that put high requirements on responsiveness and latency.

Author Keywords

Multi-display environments; portal; latency; design; tabletop; mobile devices; tablets.

ACM Classification Keywords

D.2.6 Programming Environments: Interactive environments; H.5.2 Information Interfaces and Presentation: Miscellaneous

INTRODUCTION

The last decade has shaped the landscape of mobile touchscreen devices tremendously by generating a variety of device classes such as small smartwatches, smartphones, paper sheet sized tablets, or touch enabled notebooks. Even intermediate form factors, such as notepad sized "phablets" or hybrid devices with detachable keyboards (e.g. Microsoft Surface, Asus Transformer Pad) emerged and the variety of device classes is expected to develop further since the technology has matured out of its infancy and variations can be manufactured easily. Along with larger screen sizes, the equipment of those devices, such as CPU, GPU, connectivity features, or sensors, has been improved constantly making them nowadays well suited for demanding applications. Due to this trend and along with drop in cost and high availability, those devices meanwhile became prevalent in daily life. Hence, people got used to absolute input devices [11] in addition to the relative input of traditional mice, which also alleviates comprehension for interactive tabletop interaction.

At the same time, proliferation of large immobile touchscreen devices, such as interactive tabletops, has risen at smaller paces but yet constantly. More and more interactive tabletops became commercially available (e.g. Microsoft Surface tabletops[1], SmartTech SMART Table[2], ideum Touch Tables[3]) and increasingly deposited at public places beyond research labs, for example museums, showrooms, customer service places, or airports. Considering both trends, environments composed of multiple mobile displays working together with interactive tabletops are expected to become increasingly commonplace, also at home. Such environments, called MDEs (Multi-Display Environments), promise for novel applications, usage scenarios and interaction techniques spanned across multiple displays [22, 23]. A quite challenging example for an MDE application is to establish wireless video portals between devices which is the primary application domain of this work, see Figure 1. Portals replicate part of a large workspace to the smaller workspace on a mobile device at hand, for instance to enable a world-in-miniature view [7], to create a virtual loupe [26], to enable collaborative visual exploration [17], or, more general, as an extension in collaborative interactive spaces [1, 8, 13]. These recent research efforts indicate a growing interest of the HCI community in real-time video portals for interactive spaces or appropriate interaction techniques, which essentially require applicable and scalable MDE and portal realizations for todays mobile devices.

---

[1] http://www.pixelsense.com (Apr. '14)

[2] http://smarttech.com/ (Apr. '14)

[3] http://ideum.com/products/multitouch/ (Apr. '14)

Figure 1. Interactive Real-Time Portals.

On the other hand, with a foreseeable heterogeneous device environment comprised of different kinds of mobile device and tabletop platforms, it is also a hassle to establish the functionality and infrastructure required to couple devices, identify devices and users, perform and synchronize distributed application logic, and establish interactive portals. This is not only an issue for research prototypes, but also for engineering of commercial interactive applications for MDEs. Instead of developing all the aforementioned functionality from scratch for each application, those best fit into a framework that can be used for application development. Such a framework help reduce development effort and time and optimize the process of engineering interactive application prototypes for research studies or products for consumer market.

To address these issues, we have implemented a software framework called *Environs* aimed at alleviating the development of MDE applications. The framework supports nowadays heterogeneous device environments and particularly addresses *low latency* and *high resolution video portals* for interactive applications. It consists of self-contained platform specific libraries that manage available application counterparts within the MDE, dynamically couple each other, establish video portals, and enable user interaction and applications spanned across multiple displays.

This paper gives an overview over the Environs framework and answers questions that we encountered in designing and implementing the framework, for example how to design the architecture/infrastructure, what components are required, how to couple application counterparts and establish communication, or how to distribute responsibilities over components. We also present two example applications that employ our framework to enable research for interactive video portal applications within MDEs. Even though parts of Environs provide service concepts typical of middlewares, we use the term framework for Environs because of the more general meaning of frameworks.

RELATED WORK
The research literature related to MDEs provides studies for interaction techniques [5, 13, 19, 22, 28], interaction

metaphors and gestures [23, 24, 27], or example applications [7, 17, 26]. However, no work has yet considered the requirements and challenges on appropriate application frameworks. In particular, interactive video portal applications for MDEs have a strong demand on low latency for the presentation. Therefore, we discuss related work in terms of interactive portals in conjunction with latency issues in the light of touch interaction.

Interactive Portals
A large body of research for interactive portals draws on user interface and interaction metaphors, for example a toolglass [6], a peephole [9, 10, 29], or a magic lens [6, 10, 21]. They applied mobile augmented reality techniques to enable a portal, where the device's back facing camera was used to capture the portal source in order to augment the captured portal and ultimately to display the result on the device's display [9, 10, 21]. While this approach works well for the underlying metaphor, it also pose limitations of the application area. For example, navigation or zoom interaction is intrinsically tied to the mobile device's physical position and orientation.

Alternative portal approaches include having the whole portal content preloaded on the mobile device as proposed by Yee et al. [29] or restricting the portal content to geometrical drawings as demonstrated by Holmquist et al. [12]. Only few realized a portal for mobile devices that overcome the former described limitations [7, 13, 25, 26], however, they still suffer from restricted applicability for mobile devices. For example, Tsao [25] or Baudisch [3] facilitated portals based on VNC[4], which was originally designed to transmit screen captures on an event triggered request mechanism. Thus, VNC is not particularly designated for real-time streaming a portal in video quality.

Latency
Besides visual quality and applicability of portal implementations, latency is an equally important quality. In this work, we define latency as the duration for changes on the portal source to be visible on the portal destination. While prior works neglected latency issues, the impact of latency on user interaction and user experience increasingly became the focus of attention of recent research efforts [2, 4, 14, 15, 20], emphasizing the negative effects of high latency on task performance and error rates.

Since early work in 1968 by Miller [18], the "100ms rule of thumb" has been widely asserted for an upper recommendation for GUI feedback to *seem instantaneous*, whereas the evolution of technology educed increasing performance gains of mobile processors and new forms of devices, applications, and corresponding interaction techniques. Consequently, researchers focused again on system latency, for example, Jota et al. [14] studied the effect of latency in direct-touch pointing tasks and showed how task performance significantly decrease and error rates increase as latency increase. Thus, reinforcing an earlier Fitt's law study of MacKenzie [16] who identified *latency as a major bottleneck for usability*. Ng and colleagues [20] proposed to explicitly consider latency in user

---
[4]http://www.realvnc.com (Apr. '14)

interface design to cope with system latency. In addition, latency also has an effect on user experience where users perceive lower latency as more responsive [2]. Overall, portal implementations suffering from high latency in visualization and interaction not only has a negative effect on task performance, but also becomes annoying for users which in turn declines user experience [2].

CONTRIBUTION

The contribution of this paper for the research community is twofold. Firstly, we address questions regarding design, architecture, and implementation, that arise when engineering frameworks for MDEs supporting high resolution and low latency video portals. Secondly, we describe the software architecture and implementation details of our approach to enable interactive applications for MDEs. This work seeks to help advance research for interactive portal applications in MDEs that also account for user experience in which user expectations on applications rise with increase of mobile device performance.

EXAMPLE APPLICATIONS

Before describing concepts and technical details of Environs, this section aims at giving the reader an impression of the framework's functionality by depicting example applications and scenarios. Thus far, we have realized two example applications employing the Environs framework to prove the usefulness of the framework's capabilities and its advantages in terms of easy integration as well as reduced development cost. Those applications also served to conduct research for appropriate interaction techniques in MDEs through interactive portals.

MediaBrowser

The MediaBrowser is a distributed application consisting of an application for tabletop surfaces and mobile devices. The applications are designed for collaborative reviewing or examining of media data on large tabletop displays. They aimed at studying interaction techniques that best support collaborative tasks within such an interactive MDE scenario.

Users who run the MediaBrowser on their mobile device are first presented a list of available MediaBrowser devices and tabletops that were detected by the framework. The framework updates this list automatically allowing users to participate in an ad-hoc fashion. Upon being presented with the list of application counterparts, users may transmit different kinds of media data, such as images or text-documents, with each other through the MediaBrowser. Media data transmitted to the tabletop are immediately shown on the tabletop display where all media objects can be manipulated through multi-touch input.

In Figure 2, the MediaBrowser shows multiple images which can be moved or scaled with multi-touch gestures. Bystanders who want to take part in the collaborative task just place their device on the tabletop surface whereupon a video portal between the devices is automatically created. As depicted in Figure 1 and 2, the mobile devices appear as transparent windows that show the tabletop surface area occluded by the device. In order to detect mobile devices on the tabletop surface,

Figure 2. Example application: Media Browser.

every mobile device has a Microsoft Surface supported visual byte tag[5] attached at the backside, see Figure 3. The portal

Figure 3. Microsoft Surface byte tag attached at the back side of a mobile device.

stays connected and updated if a device is lift off from the tabletop surface allowing users to virtually pick up a piece of the tabletop surface by means of their personal device. Users can further input multi-touch gestures on their mobile device which are directly applied to the media on the tabletop surface. By this way, multiple users collaboratively interact with the tabletop surface in parallel while the presentation of the large tabletop surface does not suffer from space conflicts or occlusion issues due to too many arms and hands of collaborators. However, users are still able to interact on the tabletop surface if the collaborative task requires for. Development of the application hugely benefited from the Environs framework's functionality allowing developers to focus mainly on user interface and presentation related logic.

Public Display Toucher

The second example application *Public Display Toucher*, as shown in Figure 4, consists of an application for public displays and mobile tablets. This application demonstrates how users may operate large public displays by means of a tablet's input capabilities. Users connect to a public display through an according tablet application which enables them to transfer media data to the public display's desktop or operate through a video portal. Upon creation of a video portal, the portal's

[5]http://www.microsoft.com/download/en/details.aspx?id=11029 (Apr. '14)

Figure 4. Example application: Public Display Toucher.

position and size can be adjusted through performing three finger multi-touch gestures. The public display can be controlled by means of single touches on the tablet which are translated to mouse clicks on the public display's user interface. Furthermore, key input on the tablet's virtual keyboard are put through to the public display and translated into regular key events. By this means, the tablet takes over the public display's mouse and keyboard allowing users to operate the public display's desktop, for instance to start applications, perform mouse clicks, or enter text. Based on this basic functionality, multi-touch enabled applications may be started on the public display which may be controlled further with the tablet. Just as with the MediaBrowser, development of the application mainly focused on user interface related logic. In addition, the application for the public display included logic for translating key messages from tablet devices into Microsoft Windows key events.

CHALLENGES FOR MDE FRAMEWORKS

When engineering a framework for the MDEs in focus of this paper, questions arise such as how to design a framework to support different platforms without implementing, managing and developing the whole framework for each platform separately, or how to structure and distribute responsibilities for a reasonable architecture, or how to manage the participating devices and applications in case of multiple different MDE applications running in the same physical MDE?

We address such questions regarding architecture, design, and implementation by first identifying essential requirements on the MDE framework in question and then presenting our approach. The following requirements are also considered challenges to tackle within the engineering process:

1. *Heterogeneity of platforms.* From a technical point of view, a big challenge for a framework is to support different heterogeneous device platforms. For each platform, the framework's functionalities have to be implemented based on platform specific development requirements. For example, each platform requires developers to use a specific programming language, such as Java for Google Android, C# for Microsoft Surface, or Objective-C for Apple iOS. Moreover, each platform provides access to the functionality through different APIs, packages and methods.

   Supporting different device platforms is not only reasonable for commercial development, but also for scientific research in case of distributing the framework or framework-based applications to fellow researchers who may not necessarily use the same device platforms.

2. *Efficiency and latency.* A framework must provide efficiency and low latency for network transfers and for framework logic. In particular, video portals require fast packet transfers and fast processing of the video stream in order to enable low latency. The lower the latency, the more responsive an application appears, which directly affects user experience [2].

3. *Flexible device management.* Finding and managing available devices must support MDE scenarios, where devices take part in an ad-hoc manner and may vanish suddenly. Devices have to identify themselves to each other and approve or deny connection requests as well as handle connections from multiple devices in parallel.

4. *Sensor support.* Nowadays devices are richly equipped with sensors, such as touch sensor, accelerometer, compass, or gyroscope. In order to offer novel interaction experiences, such sensors are often integrated into interaction with MDE applications. Therefore, a framework has to provide the support and infrastructure to retrieve, transport, process, or consume the sensor data.

DESIGN OF ENVIRONS

Environs is a software framework designed to aid development of distributed applications for MDEs with support for nowadays heterogeneous device platforms. Developers of those applications are given a set of self-contained platform specific libraries of which they include the library targeting their device's platform. In the current development state, Environs supports the platforms Microsoft Windows, Google Android, and Apple iOS. All libraries provide a consistent API across all platforms to custom applications for accessing the functionality of the framework.

Environs' functionality was designed to be implementation agnostic to the application logic layer which means that applications don't have to care about how to detect other devices or transfer files to them. Applications only need to invoke calls of the framework's API which can succeed or fail. The framework's functionalities so far include device and environment management, management of connections to other devices, transfer of files or binary data, communication between application instances by text or binary messages, real-time streaming of touch contacts to other devices and conducting touch

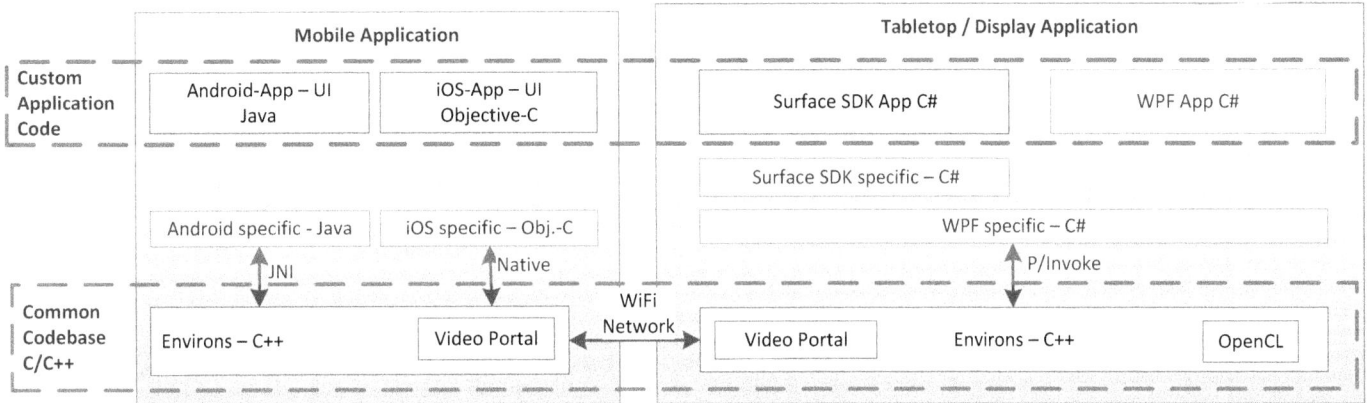

Figure 5. Environs libraries' code distribution.

events on destination devices, real-time streaming of sensor data to other devices, and real-time streaming of customizable high resolution video portals.

Code Distribution

Each library is comprised of a native component written in C/C++ and a platform specific component developed in the particular platform language, that is either C#, Java or Objective-C as outlined in Figure 5. Most part of the libraries, that is the aforementioned functionalities including image processing and video encoding, or gesture recognizers, share the same source code. This *common code base* is developed as portable C/C++-code and compiled as native component in order to *benefit from reduced development time*. This code distribution architecture addresses the *challenge (1)* and allows for the majority of the framework to be developed on the common code base for all platform specific libraries, for instance adding new or extending functionalities, modifying transport protocols, or debugging. In order to add support for a new platform, a platform specific API layer has to be written that connects the common code base with custom application logic.

Overall, the common code base drastically minimizes the development cost required for maintenance and development whilst supporting heterogeneous device platforms. In addition, native code provides rich opportunities to realize high performance implementations and low latency optimizations, for example in terms of memory management, platform optimizations, or direct access to hardware components which addresses the *challenge (2)*. The platform specific component of the libraries, that is the tiny slices above the common code base in Figure 5, primarily implements a consistent framework API across platforms supporting quick and easy integration into custom applications. Custom application logic (located at the top level in Figure 5) simply add the framework library and access MDE functionalities through the framework API. This code layer distribution best suits the needs of the engineering process for interactive applications supporting heterogeneous MDEs.

Concept of Environs' Environments

The Environs framework enables multiple logically separated application environments to coexist within the same physical MDE as sketched in Figure 6. Each application environ-

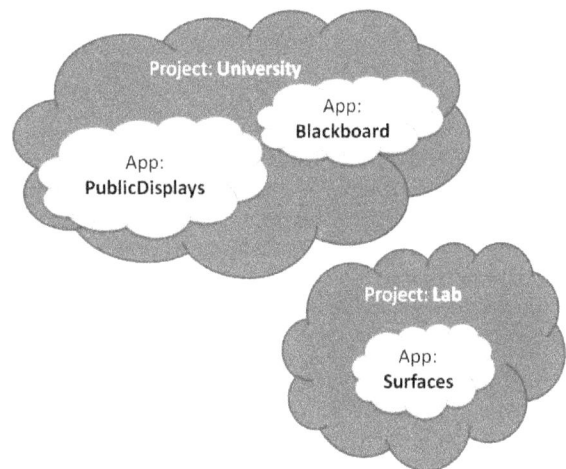

Figure 6. Multiple application environments distinguished by project/application names.

ment is identified by a project name and an application name which allows scenarios where, for example, multiple different Environs-enabled applications run on a tabletop display while the framework guarantees that each application sees and interacts only with other corresponding applications running within the same MDE. This logical separation helps the application logic of custom applications in communication with other application instances because different applications potentially communicate with disparate communication protocols. For example, a tablet application that exchange videos or images with a tabletop display does not need to connect to a public display application in the same MDE that runs a blackboard application.

Each application can request to see and communicate only with applications either with matching project and application

Figure 7. Device IDs in application environments.

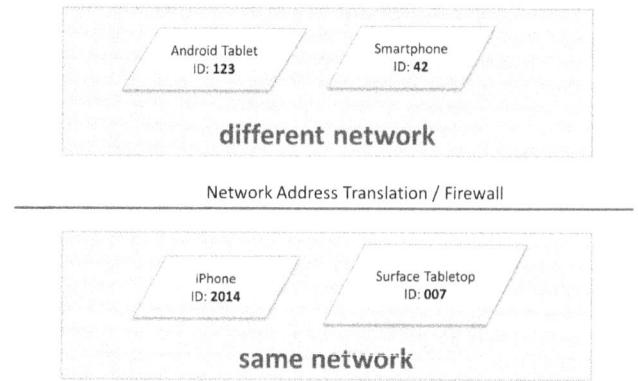

Figure 8. Supported network scenarios.

name, or with matching project name. The additional project name enables hybrid applications that provide the functionality of multiple different applications together and therefore needs to see application instances of all application names within the same project. In order to identify devices within an application environment, each device is assigned an ID (numeric 32 bit value) as sketched in Figure 7. This ID must only be unique within an application environment, that is the same device may use a different ID for a different application environment. The concrete assignment or partitioning of IDs can be chosen application dependent. For example, IDs lower than 1000 are assigned to tabletops and IDs greater than 1000 are assigned to mobile devices.

FRAMEWORK COMPONENTS

The Environs framework includes the following main components: (1) API/core component; (2) device and application management (mediator component); (3) network connectivity, communication and data transfer (network component); (4) touch event/sensor data handling which also includes gesture recognizer modules.

The API component (1) represents the linchpin for custom applications to access the framework functionality. It receives API calls from custom applications, translates them to commands, manages and delegates them to appropriate framework components, and informs the caller about results of its call, whereby results of longer lasting tasks are asynchronously notified to the caller. Each component mutually makes use of the services of the other components if appropriate. For example, the touch/sensor component makes use of the network component to send its data to destination applications. In addition to that, we implemented a subcomponent for streaming of video portals which also makes use of the services of the main components. For example, the network component is used to transfer stream packets to other devices. The following sections provide a description of each component.

Mediator Component

An essential requirement to realize distributed MDE applications is to detect corresponding application instances and its associated details for network connectivity within MDEs where application instances appear or vanish in an ad-hoc

manner. The mediator component is responsible for those tasks and addresses the *challenge (3)* by providing a list of currently available application instances. This list covers application instances for the following two scenarios as sketched in Figure 8: (1) the devices are in the same network and are able to contact each other directly; (2) a device is located in a different network and is not directly accessible. One example for the latter case is when mobile devices are connected to a wireless private network provided by a NAT[6] router whilst the corresponding large static display is connected to a different network provided by a LAN. Such scenarios often occur in research labs where multiple wireless private networks for dedicated projects or applications coexist.

Devices in the same Network
The mediator component in each application instance employs broadcast messages to maintain a list of all available application instances within the same network. Broadcast messages are received by every device on the same network. Therefore, they suit well to exchange application instance IDs with each other. An application instance ID contains the device ID, the project / application name and connectivity details. Upon start of the mediator instance, a greet ID message is broadcasted to the network to tell other instances about the existence and availability of the application. Every mediator instance that receives a greet message broadcasts its own ID message to inform the availability of itself, thus update the alive status to other mediator instances. On exit of the mediator instance, a bye ID message is broadcasted to the network in order to tell other mediator instances about the absence of itself.

Devices in different Networks
In order to support environments where an MDE is comprised of multiple private networks which have no direct route to each other but have routing to external addresses through NAT, the mediator component builds on a mediator server instance which all devices have access to. This setup is optional and only required for connections across different networks. Mediator instances of applications can register at a mediator

---

[6]Network Address Translation

server instance which maintains a list of registered application instances with their according application ID. This list is retrieved by the application's mediator instance and augments the list of available application instances with those not directly available. Furthermore, the mediator server instance helps application instances connect each other across different networks by means of the mechanisms STUNT[7] for TCP and STUN[8] for UDP.

Network Component

The network component is responsible for establishing connections to other devices and transferring messages and files or data buffers between devices. It is designed to support interactive systems through selectively distributing the data to be sent to appropriate transport channels. The most important requirement of responsive interactive applications is that the communication of custom application logic with other application instances (e.g. status updates, commands or requests) must not be delayed as best as possible. Furthermore, real-time data such as touch events or video stream packets have to be transferred as fast as possible without affecting the application logic's communication. Therefore, the network component operate with different transport channels as described in the following section. In preparation for establishing connections, the network component interacts with the mediator component to retrieve connection details for the mediator scenario (1) or to employ the mediator server instance's service to initiate STUNT/STUN channels in case of the mediator scenario (2).

Connections between Devices

Upon successful connection with a device, the network component has established the following channels: (1) TCP main channel; (2) TCP bulk data channel; (3) UDP interactive channel. The first channel (1) serves as communication channel for custom application logic as well as framework communication with other framework instances, for example to start/stop a video portal or handshake options for the video portal. The transfer of large files or data buffers potentially takes more time and would induce lag and wait times on communication of the application logic if conducted over the main channel. Therefore, such transfers are handled over the bulk data channel (2) to ensure responsiveness of the interactive application. The UDP data channel (3) is used for touch events and sensor data due to the timely constraints of such kind of data regarding interactivity. For example, users would not notice missing intermediate touch events during a touch gesture or missing intermediate compass values when rotating a tablet. However, they severely notice the lag in visualization of the effect of such events. For example, if touch events are delayed due to retransmissions of past touch events, then their happening as well as the according visualization occurs timely disrupted on the destination.

In addition to the three channels, a fourth portal channel is established on demand for a video portal. Applications can choose which transport protocol (TCP/UDP) the portal channel shall use. This additional channel is required because of

[7]RFC5382 http://tools.ietf.org/search/rfc5382
[8]RFC5392 http://tools.ietf.org/search/rfc5389

the real-time character and amount of data of video portals where the receiver is typically flooded with stream packets. Therefore, those data would disturb and negatively affect the other channels.

Handshake

Upon successful connection of the main channel (1), the devices exchange their capabilities, such as device type (tablet, smartphone, tabletop, display, etc.), screen dimensions in pixels, display density in dpi, support for video formats, availability of sensors, or socket buffer sizes. Those capabilities are autonomously detected by the framework and used to optimize the transport channels or to automatically derive parameters. For instance, if the custom application logic has not specified the size of the video portal on a tabletop, then the video portal's size is calculated to match the area that the device covers on the tabletop surface by means of pixel and dpi values.

Touch/Sensor Component

The touch/sensor component is responsible for putting through received events to the platform specific layer as fast as possible where the events are further handled depending on the particular platform. For instance, on tabletop systems, touch events are injected into the touch system and thereby appear as regular touch events. The second responsibility of the this component is to keep the event states consistent, that is to compensate for missing events due to packet drops or to drop old events that were outrun by newer events. For this purpose, each exchanged event carries an incremental sequence number and the current touch/sensor state is transmitted once every second. Both help the component detect missing or outdated packets. This mechanism is the same as employed in the TUIO protocol[9].

Furthermore, this component supports gesture recognizer plug-ins which are feed with the current event states on each change of the event states. If the plug-in has recognized a gesture, then a plug-in defined gesture string is put through to the platform specific layer which may consume the gesture event or pass it on to the custom application logic. Based on this infrastructure, we have implemented a recognizer plug-in that enables three finger touch gestures for scaling the video portal's size (pinch gesture) or moving the video portal's position (pan gesture) on the tabletop surface.

Smart Portal

In order to enable video portals, we have implemented a sub-component called *Smart Portal* which was designed to provide a high quality, high resolution video stream optimized for low latency. *Smart Portal* replicates part of a source window, such as the application visualization of an interactive tabletop, to the application window of a mobile device. The framework automatically renders the video stream to the window background of an application window specified by the user application. Thereby, developers can build portal applications as regular applications taking advantage of operating system widgets without the inclusion of additional external

[9]http://www.tuio.org/

stand-alone applications. The following design elements of the subcomponent are decisive contributions to achieve low latency and high resolution portals:

1. *Video compression* is used to minimize latency induced by network transport. *Smart Portal* employs the high efficiency video codec H.264 enabled through the opensource implementation libx264[10] based on the encoding profile "superfast/zerolatency".

   This library was natively compiled for all platforms and used for encoding and decoding. However, software decoding is only used as a fall-back case. The framework on mobile devices makes use of hardware decoding if available, which unburdens the CPU from video decoding while application and framework logic fully benefits from the CPU.

2. *GPU acceleration*: Virtually all nowadays graphic cards support scientific computation by means of the standardized OpenCL[11] API. For this reason, computational intensive preprocessings of the video stream's source images are performed on the GPU for which we developed optimized OpenCL kernels.

Real-time GPU Pipeline

Creation of the source portal stream includes several image processing steps such as comparison of subsequent frames, rotation by a given angle, bilinear scaling, and image format conversion from RGB to YUV. Comparison of subsequent frames is highly recommended and help reduce the system load by skipping all remaining filters in case of equality. Bilinear scaling is required since *Smart Portal* supports arbitrary portal source sizes which need to be scaled to the desired video stream resolution. Rotation by a given angle is a requirement for tabletop surfaces since mobile devices may be placed arbitrarily oriented on the tabletop. Finally, format conversion is a requirement for the H.264 encoding process.

All of the image processing tasks are moved from CPU to GPU because of two reasons. First, most of the time modern GPUs have only little workload caused by rendering the application user interface. Second, modern GPUs have multiple computing units where each unit can run a multitude of work items ($>= 256$) in parallel and extremely fast, thus process much more pixels of an image in parallel and much faster than the CPU.

Thereby, disburden the CPU results in preserved computing resources for the benefit of application and framework logic which further reduce system latency.

Scalability

In particular, this solution scales much better with increasing number of portals computed in parallel because of the available GPU computing units, where the GPU exploit the available units in parallel. In contrast, workload of the CPU increases with each additional portal resulting in potentially added latency or drop of frames.

---

[10]http://www.videolan.org/developers/x264.html (Apr. '14)

[11]http://www.khronos.org/opencl (Apr. '14)

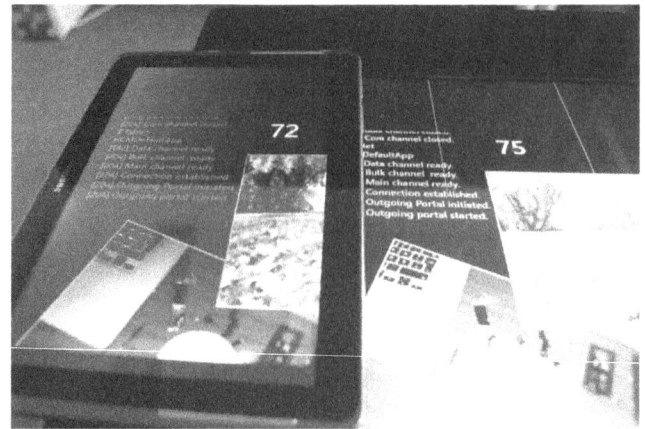

Figure 9. Latency measure of a portal that covers the tablet's physical size on the surface.

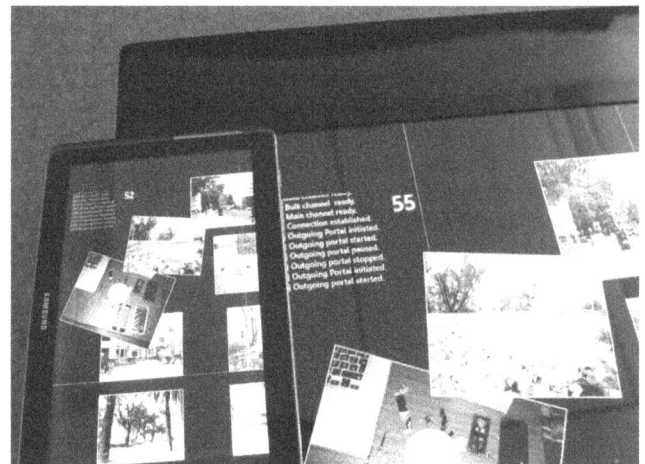

Figure 10. Latency measure of a high resolution portal source.

Latency

We roughly measured the latencies of our portal approach by means of a simple technique wherein we superimposed the portal's source with a number that increased with every frame at 30 fps. This number is then photographed in the way that the portal's source and the portal's destination are on the same picture, see Figure 9. Based on the difference of the numbers and the frame rate of 30 fps, we determined the latencies shown in Table 1 for a Microsoft PixelSense 2.0 device and a Samsung Galaxy Tab 2.

Table 1. Latencies at 30 frames per second ($\pm 16ms$).

Video stream size	Min. (ms)	Median (ms)	Max. (ms)
294 x 454	66.6	99.9	133.2
844 x 1080	99.9	133.2	166.5

Table 1 lists latencies of a TCP portal for two video stream resolutions, i.e. 294x454 (pixels of the surface covered by the tablet's physical size, see Figure 9) and 844x1080 (full height of the surface tabletop, see Figure 10). For each row in the table, we took at least 30 pictures in sequence and determined the median, the lowest, and the highest latency. The average latencies are between 100ms and 133ms which we consider low for such a complex MDE system. The difference between the video stream sizes are 33.3ms on average, which gives a strong indication that the main part of the latency was induced by network transport. Smaller video stream resolutions yield fewer video data to be transmitted which in turn can be displayed earlier on the portal destination. Therefore, the results revealed possibilities for further latency improvements through network optimizations.

FUTURE WORK

Environs is currently used to build MDE applications employing video portals in order to conduct research on appropriate interaction techniques and user interfaces. The further development of the framework includes distributing Environs[12] to fellow researchers and get feedback on the framework's concepts and functionality. We hope that our framework will help advance and conduct research for portal interaction within MDEs.

The code distribution of Environs allows for easy extension for further platforms, such as Linux, Apple MacOS, or Microsoft Windows Phone. Hence, we plan to add platform specific API layers for those platforms on demand.

CONCLUSION

Developing interactive video portal MDE applications requires engineering of essential functionality, such as device and environment management, reliable and responsive network communication, or enabling video portals. Considering nowadays heterogeneous device platforms, implementing those functionality for each platform can be elaborate and error prone. This paper addresses these issues by means of a multi-platform software framework that helps developers and designers focus on application and presentation logic. Engineering a framework for the targeted MDE application domain is quite challenging and rise questions in terms of architecture and design.

We have presented the Environs framework as an approach to tackle the engineering issues and described details which answer questions that arise within the engineering process. The framework's code distribution reduces the resources required to develop and maintain the framework while allowing the framework to exploit platform specific optimizations or adaptations. Our approach shows how to cope with multiple coexisting applications within the same physical MDE through the concept of application environments, how to realize high resolution video portals, or how to subdivide framework functionalities to components in order to enable interactive and responsive applications.

While this paper emphasized on MDEs with tabletop surfaces, the presented example applications demonstrate the general use of Environs also for other kinds of devices, such as large public displays. The examples also proved the usefulness of Environs and the concepts behind.

ACKNOWLEDGMENTS
The work described in this paper is co-funded by OC-Trust (FOR 1085) of the DFG.

---

[12] http://hcm-lab.de/environs

REFERENCES

1. Ajaj, R., Jacquemin, C., and Vernier, F. Rvdt: a design space for multiple input devices, multiple views and multiple display surfaces combination. In *Proceedings of the 2009 international conference on Multimodal interfaces*, ICMI-MLMI '09, ACM (New York, NY, USA, 2009), 269–276.

2. Anderson, G., Doherty, R., and Ganapathy, S. User perception of touch screen latency. In *Design, User Experience, and Usability. Theory, Methods, Tools and Practice*, A. Marcus, Ed., vol. 6769 of *Lecture Notes in Computer Science*, Springer Berlin Heidelberg (2011), 195–202.

3. Baudisch, P., Good, N., and Stewart, P. Focus plus context screens: combining display technology with visualization techniques. In *Proceedings of the 14th annual ACM symposium on User interface software and technology*, UIST '01, ACM (New York, NY, USA, 2001), 31–40.

4. Bérard, F., and Blanch, R. Two touch system latency estimators: High accuracy and low overhead. In *Proceedings of the 2013 ACM International Conference on Interactive Tabletops and Surfaces*, ITS '13, ACM (New York, NY, USA, 2013), 241–250.

5. Bezerianos, A., and Balakrishnan, R. View and space management on large displays. *IEEE Comput. Graph. Appl. 25*, 4 (July 2005), 34–43.

6. Bier, E. A., Stone, M. C., Pier, K., Buxton, W., and DeRose, T. D. Toolglass and magic lenses: the see-through interface. In *Proceedings of the 20th annual conference on Computer graphics and interactive techniques*, SIGGRAPH '93, ACM (New York, NY, USA, 1993), 73–80.

7. Cheng, K., Li, J., and Müller-Tomfelde, C. Supporting interaction and collaboration on large displays using tablet devices. In *Proceedings of the International Working Conference on Advanced Visual Interfaces*, AVI '12, ACM (New York, NY, USA, 2012), 774–775.

8. Dippon, A., Wiedermann, N., and Klinker, G. Seamless integration of mobile devices into interactive surface environments. In *Proceedings of the 2012 ACM international conference on Interactive tabletops and surfaces*, ITS '12, ACM (New York, NY, USA, 2012), 331–334.

9. Grubert, J., Morrison, A., Munz, H., and Reitmayr, G. Playing it real: magic lens and static peephole interfaces for games in a public space. In *Proceedings of the 14th international conference on Human-computer interaction with mobile devices and services*, MobileHCI '12, ACM (New York, NY, USA, 2012), 231–240.

10. Henze, N., and Boll, S. Evaluation of an off-screen visualization for magic lens and dynamic peephole

interfaces. In *Proceedings of the 12th international conference on Human computer interaction with mobile devices and services*, MobileHCI '10, ACM (New York, NY, USA, 2010), 191–194.

11. Hinckley, K., and Wigdor, D. *Input Technologies and Techniques.*

12. Holmquist, L. E., Sanneblad, J., and Gaye, L. Total recall: in-place viewing of captured whiteboard annotations. In *CHI '03 Extended Abstracts on Human Factors in Computing Systems*, CHI EA '03, ACM (New York, NY, USA, 2003), 980–981.

13. Jetter, H.-C., Dachselt, R., Reiterer, H., Quigley, A., Benyon, D., and Haller, M. Blended interaction: envisioning future collaborative interactive spaces. In *CHI '13 Extended Abstracts on Human Factors in Computing Systems*, CHI EA '13, ACM (New York, NY, USA, 2013), 3271–3274.

14. Jota, R., Ng, A., Dietz, P., and Wigdor, D. How fast is fast enough?: a study of the effects of latency in direct-touch pointing tasks. In *Proceedings of the SIGCHI Conference on Human Factors in Computing Systems*, CHI '13, ACM (New York, NY, USA, 2013), 2291–2300.

15. Kaaresoja, T., and Brewster, S. Feedback is... late: measuring multimodal delays in mobile device touchscreen interaction. In *International Conference on Multimodal Interfaces and the Workshop on Machine Learning for Multimodal Interaction*, ICMI-MLMI '10, ACM (New York, NY, USA, 2010), 2:1–2:8.

16. MacKenzie, I. S., and Ware, C. Lag as a determinant of human performance in interactive systems. In *Proceedings of the INTERACT '93 and CHI '93 Conference on Human Factors in Computing Systems*, CHI '93, ACM (New York, NY, USA, 1993), 488–493.

17. McGrath, W., Bowman, B., McCallum, D., Hincapié-Ramos, J. D., Elmqvist, N., and Irani, P. Branch-explore-merge: facilitating real-time revision control in collaborative visual exploration. In *Proceedings of the 2012 ACM international conference on Interactive tabletops and surfaces*, ITS '12, ACM (New York, NY, USA, 2012), 235–244.

18. Miller, R. B. Response time in man-computer conversational transactions. In *Proceedings of the December 9-11, 1968, fall joint computer conference, part I*, AFIPS '68 (Fall, part I), ACM (New York, NY, USA, 1968), 267–277.

19. Nacenta, M. *Cross-display object movement in multi-display environments*. PhD thesis, University of Saskatchewan, http://library2.usask.ca/theses/available/etd-01062010-123426/, 2009.

20. Ng, A., Lepinski, J., Wigdor, D., Sanders, S., and Dietz, P. Designing for low-latency direct-touch input. In *Proceedings of the 25th annual ACM symposium on*

User interface software and technology, UIST '12, ACM (New York, NY, USA, 2012), 453–464.

21. Rohs, M., Essl, G., Schöning, J., Naumann, A., Schleicher, R., and Krüger, A. Impact of item density on magic lens interactions. In *Proceedings of the 11th International Conference on Human-Computer Interaction with Mobile Devices and Services*, MobileHCI '09, ACM (New York, NY, USA, 2009), 38:1–38:4.

22. Seyed, T., Burns, C., Costa Sousa, M., and Maurer, F. From small screens to big displays: understanding interaction in multi-display environments. In *Proceedings of the companion publication of the 2013 international conference on Intelligent user interfaces companion*, IUI '13 Companion, ACM (New York, NY, USA, 2013), 33–36.

23. Seyed, T., Burns, C., Costa Sousa, M., Maurer, F., and Tang, A. Eliciting usable gestures for multi-display environments. In *Proceedings of the 2012 ACM international conference on Interactive tabletops and surfaces*, ITS '12, ACM (New York, NY, USA, 2012), 41–50.

24. Spindler, M., Stellmach, S., and Dachselt, R. Paperlens: advanced magic lens interaction above the tabletop. In *Proceedings of the ACM International Conference on Interactive Tabletops and Surfaces*, ITS '09, ACM (New York, NY, USA, 2009), 69–76.

25. Tsao, C.-L., Kakumanu, S., and Sivakumar, R. Smartvnc: an effective remote computing solution for smartphones. In *Proceedings of the 17th annual international conference on Mobile computing and networking*, MobiCom '11, ACM (New York, NY, USA, 2011), 13–24.

26. Voida, S., Tobiasz, M., Stromer, J., Isenberg, P., and Carpendale, S. Getting practical with interactive tabletop displays: designing for dense data, "fat fingers," diverse interactions, and face-to-face collaboration. ITS '09, ACM (New York, NY, USA, 2009), 109–116.

27. Wallace, J., Ha, V., Ziola, R., and Inkpen, K. Swordfish: User tailored workspaces in multi-display environments. In *CHI '06 Extended Abstracts on Human Factors in Computing Systems*, CHI EA '06, ACM (New York, NY, USA, 2006), 1487–1492.

28. Wilson, A. D., and Benko, H. Combining multiple depth cameras and projectors for interactions on, above and between surfaces. In *Proceedings of the 23nd annual ACM symposium on User interface software and technology*, UIST '10, ACM (New York, NY, USA, 2010), 273–282.

29. Yee, K.-P. Peephole displays: pen interaction on spatially aware handheld computers. In *Proceedings of the SIGCHI Conference on Human Factors in Computing Systems*, CHI '03, ACM (New York, NY, USA, 2003), 1–8.

User Interface Distribution in Multi-Device and Multi-User Environments with Dynamically Migrating Engines

Luca Frosini
HIIS Laboratory – ISTI-CNR
Via G. Moruzzi, 1
56124 Pisa (Italy)
luca.frosini@isti.cnr.it
+39 050 621 2602

Fabio Paternò
HIIS Laboratory – ISTI-CNR
Via G. Moruzzi, 1
56124 Pisa (Italy)
fabio.paterno@isti.cnr.it
+39 050 621 3066

ABSTRACT
In this paper we present a framework and associated run-time support for flexible user interface distribution in multi-device and multi-user environments. It supports distribution across dynamic sets of devices, and does not require the use of a fixed server. The distribution updates are processed taking in account device types and user roles. We also report on three example applications and a validation of the presented framework.

Author Keywords
Multi-device User Interfaces, Development Tools, Distributed and Migratory User Interfaces.

ACM Classification Keywords
H.5 Information Interfaces and Presentation; H.5.2 User Interfaces, H.5.3 Group and Organization Interfaces.

INTRODUCTION
In the last decade a wide variety of interactive devices have penetrated the mass market, and people spend more and more time using them. This has made it possible to create many environments where people spend a long time interacting with various devices sequentially or in parallel [4].

In order to better exploit such technological offer often people would like to better use multiple devices while interacting with their applications, for example to dynamically move components of their interactive applications across different devices with various interaction resources.

Unfortunately, the development of multi-device user interfaces is limited by current interaction development toolkits, which are still designed assuming to support the development of user interfaces for single devices without providing support for multi-device access. At the research

level some frameworks for multi-device user interfaces have been proposed but usually their support has been limited to specific contexts and applications, and thus their adoption has been rather limited.

The framework we present provides developers with an API that can be exploited both in Web and Java applications in order to obtain more easily application user interfaces (UIs) that can be dynamically distributed and/or migrated in multi-device and multi-user environments. The framework also allows dynamically creating multiple simultaneous sessions for applications used by groups of devices where the UI is distributed. Furthermore, it does not require a fixed server to manage the distribution. The elements of the UI can be distributed by specifying specific device(s), group(s) of devices, specific user(s), and groups of users according to roles.

In the paper, after discussion of related work we provide a description of the architecture exploited by our framework, the main concepts that characterize it, and the associated possible commands. We then describe three multi-device applications developed with it that have different requirements and discuss its generality and performance. Lastly, we draw some conclusions and provide indications for future work.

RELATED WORK
Distributed User Interface (DUI) is a topic that has been addressed from various viewpoints. The main aspects of user interface distribution are indicated in [1]: *What* can be distributed, *When* the elements can be distributed, *Who* can distribute and *Where* they can be distributed. Other important aspects of distributed user interface are *Portability*, *Decomposability*, *Simultaneity* and *Continuity*. These, as argued by Peñalver et al. [9], are needed properties to be guaranteed in a DUI and our framework aims to address them.

Furthermore, distributing user interfaces without constraints can result in an unusable user interface as argued by Luyten et al. [2]. A label distributed in a device and the correspondent input field in a different one is a simple example of unusable user interface. In order to address such issue we provide the possibility of specifying what elements can be distributed.

One contribution in this area provides a proposal for a peer-to-peer solution [3]. One issue in this regard is the lack of an explicit component able to maintain the state of the distribution at any time. In our solution we provide such component, which can be located and moved to any device involved in the distribution.

Another contribution [6]proposes a collaborative environment for the distribution of applications useful to support some tasks. A framework to orchestrate the spanning of a web-based UI over many different screens has been proposed by Hartmann et al.[7]. In contrast, our framework focuses on the distribution of user interfaces in multi-user and multi-device contexts in such a way as to limit the impact in the application code in order to also easily obtain distributed user interfaces in existing single device applications. A platform supporting distributed application user interfaces on interactive large public and personal mobile device screens has been proposed [8]. Our proposal is based on a similar session concept, though it also enables creating shared sessions amongst mobile and fixed devices.

A catalogue of distribution primitives to orchestrate DUI screens has been proposed [5]. In our proposal we use two simple commands maintaining the same expressivity. This decreases the time for developers to learn the framework and facilitates code reusability.

Fisher et all [10] describe general challenges for P2P DUI development in terms of design, architecture, and implementation but they do not provide a framework for the development of distributed user interfaces.

While previous work [11] has considered the use of model-based languages for supporting distributed user interfaces, in this work we have aimed to identify a solution with good performance that can be exploited in various applications domains. Thus, we have considered previous research [12] and report on a novel solution that is more flexible in terms of management of the distribution state, with the ability to exploit dynamic sets of interactive devices, and report on a validation in terms of applications developed, performance, and analysis of the impact on the code.

THE ARCHITECTURE OF THE FRAMEWORK

Our framework is logically composed of a library and runtime support. The library is used by the developers to introduce UI distribution in their applications. The runtime support can run on a dedicated server or in one of the devices participating in the distribution.

Figure 1 shows the logical components of the framework and its run-time support. There are two main blocks: Engine side and Client side.

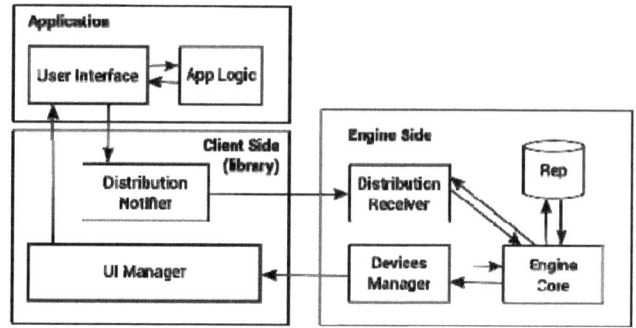

Figure 1. Overview of the framework architecture.

The Engine side is the runtime support and is responsible for managing the requests of distribution changes, processing them, and calculating the new distribution state.

The *Engine* is able to maintain the *Current State* of Distribution, which allows devices to join a distribution session at any time and sets their UIs in the proper state. The distribution state is mainly based on the concept of UI elements State. We have identified three states: *Invisible* (element is not visible at all), *Disabled* (visible but not reactive to user actions, e.g. a button that does not react to the users' clicks) and *Enabled* (visible and reactive to the associated user-generated events). Thus, it is possible to define a simple relation across the states, through which each state adds some aspect to the previous one (disabled adds visibility to the invisible elements; enabled adds reactivity to the disabled elements).

The *Client Side* library represents the component responsible of sending distribution change requests to the engine, and receiving updates of changes to apply on the managed UI. On the client side there is a *UI Manager* that receives and processes the notifications of the distribution updates arriving from the engine. The *UI Manager* invokes a callback function in order to apply the received update..

The callback is triggered in response to a distribution update received from the engine (because of a state change or a value change of a UI element). The framework provides some standard behavior for each change. Moreover, the framework provides the possibility of specifying personalized behavior to apply when a distribution change occurs. For example, the default callback for an *ASSIGN Notification* to set an element to invisible simply makes the element no longer visible without any additional effect. If the developer wants to use a fading effect when this occurs, he can register a specific callback for this purpose.

Figure 1 also shows the application part which uses the framework client side.

Please note that the *Client Side* library does not make any distribution choice, instead such changes depend on the application. In the application any policy can be implemented.

Authentication Process

When a device wants to take part in the distribution it has to subscribe to the engine. The device sends its own capabilities and credentials to the engine. Using the supplied credentials the engine decides whether to allow the device to take part in a session. Furthermore, according to the supplied capabilities the engine inserts the device in one or more groups. The groups are used in the distribution to target devices with similar capabilities.

Once the device is allowed to take part in a session, the engine sends information regarding what UI elements should be shown to the user. We refer to this information as the *Distribution State* (as explained in the next section).

A device (if it has proper credentials) can subscribe to a distribution session at any time. Each device receives from the engine the distributed UI consistent with the other devices, and in the same situation as if it had subscribed at the beginning of the session.

During the session life the device can send updates of the UI distribution to the engine or receive notifications by the engine of updates made by other devices.

Any communication made by the device to the engine is accepted by the latter only if the device has enough rights.

Distribution State

The framework is based on the concept of distribution state, which indicates what UI elements are associated with each device and their state. Indeed, the framework allows developers to assign three basic states to the user interface elements: enabled, disabled (which means visible but not reactive to events), and invisible. We can express the relations: *Enabled > Disabled > Invisible*

At any time the distribution state of a UI is known by the engine.

The state changes dynamically under the effect of updates generated by clients and elaborated by the engine.

The component that knows the distribution state is not in a fixed server but can be in any device involved in the distribution, even in a mobile device.

When the engine receives an update it performs these main operations:

- Validate the request;
- Calculate the new *Distribution State*;
- Calculate which devices have to be updated;
- Inform involved devices of changes in their UIs.

Devices categorization (Target)

The framework exploits two concepts (*Type* and *Role*) to address the devices involved in the distribution.

Type

The type concept is associated with a set of device capabilities. The possible types are not static but they can vary depending on the application.

When a device subscribes to the distribution it provides its capabilities and the engine assigns one or more types to the devices. The *Type* is used by the engine and by other devices to address a group of devices without the need to know devices ID.

In many cases we can find that some types are a subset of another. For example a Laptop is a sub-type of PC because requires all the capabilities of PC plus a Battery. We can argue that the PC type is broader (or at least equal) to the Laptop type. All Laptop devices will also be considered PC devices but not vice versa. In this case we can say that PC > Laptop. Two sets are not comparable if one is not a superset of the other.

The possibility of comparing different types is important when the engine receives a distribution update: first of all to calculate the new *Distribution State* (reducing it); secondly to avoid sending unneeded updates to devices.

The reduction of the types enumerated in the state (when possible) implies a more efficient calculation for managing states.

Role

The role concept is related to the type of tasks carried out by the user using a device in the distributed application and is independent of the device type.

In order to exploit the distribution support the user authenticates through an identity certificate, which contains information regarding the user role. The details regarding how certificates are issued, verified and implemented are beyond the scope of this paper.

The Distribution API

The framework supports an API with two commands (from clients to engine) to perform distribution changes. The first (*ASSIGN Command*) is used to change the devices that can display or allow manipulation by the user of a certain element in the UI. The second (*Feedback Command*) informs devices of a change in the value of an element. Examples of the feedback that can be provided is that of the values of an input field, the selected tabs in a tab container, the center and the zoom values of an image which can be panned or zoomed.

ASSIGN Command

The parameters of the ASSIGN command are:

- *What*: identifies an interface part, typically the ID of the element or the container of elements that has to be distributed.

- *Target*: specifies the devices that should receive it, they are indicated by type(s), role(s) or identifier(s).

- *Basic State Level*: identifies the new state levels for the elements indicated in What for the devices specified in Target.

Feedback Command

The parameters of the Feedback command are:

- What: identifies an interface part, typically the ID of the element or the container of elements to be considered.

- Data: indicates the new value for the element identified by What that will be sent to all the devices with a State Level > Invisible

These commands flow from client to engine. Once the engine has elaborated them it will generate a corresponding command flowing from the engine to the involved clients. We will refer to them as Notification commands.

ASSIGN Notification

This is the engine's *ASSIGN Command* response. Because the notification is sent directly to the device, the target is implicit and for this reason it is omitted.

- *What*: identifies an interface part, typically the ID of the element or the container of elements that has to be distributed.

- *Basic State Level*: identifies the new state levels for the elements indicated in What for the devices considered.

Feedback Notification

This is the engine's Feedback command response and has the same content and signature:

- What: identifies an interface part, typically the ID of the element or the container of elements to be considered.

- Data: indicates the new value for the element identified by What that will be sent to all the devices with a *Basic State Level > Invisible.*

Distribution Orchestration

The framework has been designed in order to support different sessions for the same application. Depending on their role users can:

- Create new sessions;

- Subscribe to an existing session;

- Leave a session;

- Subscribe to all sessions;

- Unsubscribe from all sessions;

- Send ASSIGN command to distribute an element;

- Send Feedback command to change the data value of an element.

- Manage the devices subscribed to a session.

When a device subscribes successfully to the distribution environment it receives the *Current State* of the UI. The *Current State* is communicated through an array of *ASSIGN Notification* and *Feedback Notification* containing all the information needed by the client to update its own UI.

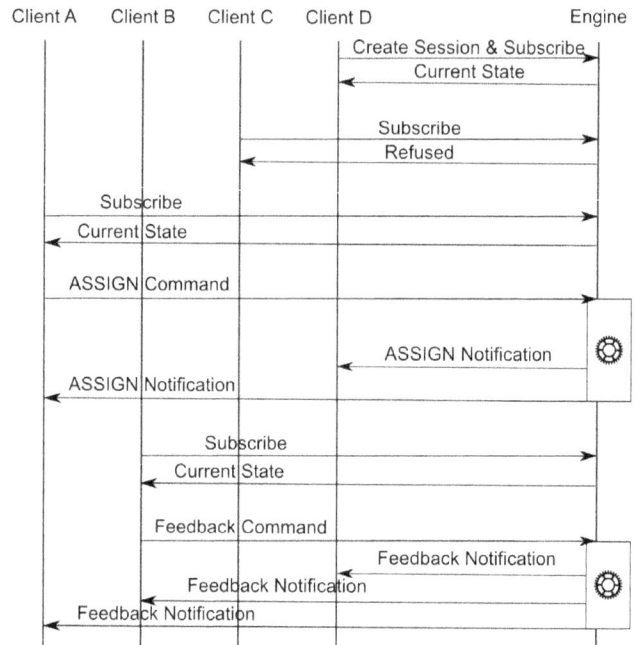

Figure 2. Sequence Diagram describing examples of subscription requests (accepted and refused) and commands sent by multiple devices.

Figure 2 shows a sequence diagram describing an example of interactions between the engine and four different clients that subscribe and then send distribution updates. Client D creates a session and subscribes itself. After that client C tries to subscribe but the request is refused by the engine because it does not provide the necessary credentials. Client A instead subscribes successfully and then sends an *ASSIGN command*. The engine calculates the new state and sends the corresponding notification to the involved devices. This is repeated by client B, which after a successful subscription sends a *Feedback Command*.

A device can request to be part of all the possible sessions (if this is allowed by the configuration parameters of the application). Only when the device with the relevant rights activates it then it can be actually part of a specific session. When a device is removed from a session then it gets back in a waiting list for participating in another session.

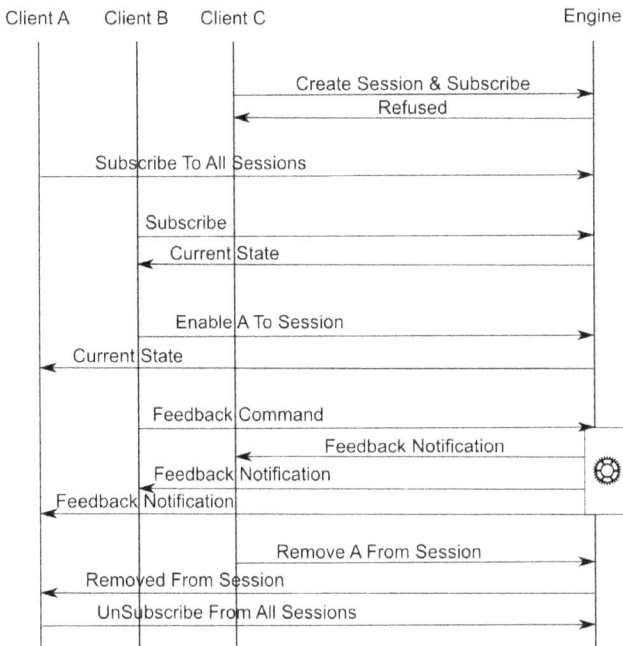

Figure 3. Sequence Diagram describing an example subscription and all related requests.

Figure 3 shows a sequence diagram describing an example of subscription to all session from a client (A) and then client (B) enables it a specific session.

A device that has subscribed to a session then receives all the relevant UI updates. When the clients receive the updates they apply them according to their UI element types.

The distribution of all the standard UI elements supported by Web and Android user interfaces is provided for through an extension mechanism using callbacks. This is useful in case the developers want to customize how the corresponding state is updated, or to achieve specific effects in updating the state (e.g. introducing a fading effect when an image disappears).

Distribution State Representation in the Engine

For each distributable element of the UI a JSON document is created and memorized in a document-oriented database (CouchDB). When the *Engine* receives an *ASSIGN Command* for a UI element, the groups indicated in the *Target* parameter are compared with groups associated to each *Basic State* of the element. The element states are updated taking in account any relations existing among groups. Let us suppose that a button is *Invisible* for the *Smartphone* devices and an *ASSIGN Command* to set the button to *Disabled* for *Mobile* devices arrives at the *Engine*. If we suppose that the *Mobile* type includes the *Smartphone* type then the *Smartphone* type is no longer associated with the *Invisible* state, and the *Mobile* type is associated with the *Disabled* state for the button.

Analyzing more in detail how the state is maintained, we can see that for each user interface element there is an indication of the corresponding targets for each of the three possible basic states (Figure 4 shows an example). The table contains an assigned sequential number for each possible target. This sequential number is incremented by the engine each time it performs a state update. Thus, these numbers define a temporal order between the elements of the distribution state table.

For example, by analysing the state presented in Figure 4 it is possible to understand that for the element with *TabHost* id, the *Mobile* devices visualize it but they cannot interact with it since they are associated with the *Disabled* state (and are associated with number 2), while all the other devices visualize the element and can interact with it.

Furthermore, all the devices associated with users with the *Admin* role visualize and can interact with *TabHost* even if the device is *Mobile*. In fact, the number for the *Admin* role (5) is higher than the Mobile one (2) and this means that the corresponding state change occurred afterwards, and is thus the currently dominant one.

```
{
    "_id": "TabHost",
    "type": "element",
    "Enabled": {
        "types": {"ALL":0},
        "roles": {"Admin": 5},
        "devices": {}
    },
    "Disabled": {
        "types": {"Mobile":2},
        "roles": {},
        "devices": {}
    },
    "Invisible": {
        "types": {},
        "roles": {},
        "devices": {}
    },
    "data": {
        "position": 0
    },
    "count": 6
}
```

Figure 4. Distribution State representation of a UI element.

Moving the Engine

As we mentioned the Engine can be moved dynamically. For this reason the framework provides an API to move the *Distribution State*.

If the engine has to be moved from one device to another, the receiver device invokes the *MoveEngine Command* in the current *Engine*. This command contains as parameter the URL where the new *Engine* will be available. If the requester has sufficient rights to become the new *Engine*, the current one serializes the *Distribution State* and sends it to the requester device. The *Distribution State* is sent to the new *Engine* in a notification called *Distribution State*

Notification. Please note that this is not the *Current State* (which contains only the State for a Device) but the full *Distribution State*.

Then, the old *Engine* stops processing other requests from devices and sends an *EngineMoved Notification* (with the URL of the new *Engine*) to the devices already subscribed to the session. If a device wants to continue to participate in the distribution, it must subscribe to the new *Engine*. The callback associated with the client for the *EngineMoved Notification* is already implemented for subscription to the new *Engine* and developers need do nothing unless they want to personalize the behavior.

APPLICATIONS

In order to verify the suitability of the framework we have used it in the design and development of three applications that needed distributed user interfaces in three different contexts of use.

Museum Guide

One application aimed to improve the user experience during a museum visit. So, we considered a single user application able to exploit mobile devices in conjunction with a public display in an indoor environment. The museum has some large public displays, which allow visitors to access relevant multimedia content. When users are near the large screen they can use the smartphone to select the content shown in it. For example, the visitors can select and display some high-resolution images of artworks that for some reasons (e.g. security, or art preservation issues) cannot be viewed from a short distance.

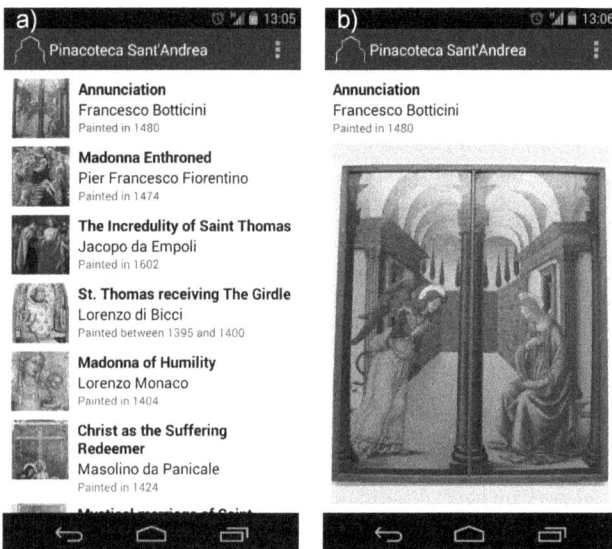

Figure 5. User interface of museum Android application. The one on the left (a) shows the artwork list and the one on the right (b) shows the artwork picture draggable and zoomable.

In addition, it is possible to access graphical information regarding the available artworks, such as maps indicating where the artwork was located before arriving at the museum, sketches of the artwork made by the artists, when available, and video guide introducing the opera.

When started the application on the large display side (implemented using the web version of the framework) immediately subscribes to all the existing sessions through the framework.

Users can launch the application through Android devices, which immediately create and subscribe to one session. When they want to access the large screen they use the smartphone's camera to scan the QR code with the ID of the large screen, which is used to add it to the session and then allow interaction.

On the smartphone it is possible to access the artworks list and select one artwork of interest through touch (Figure 5a). The device will generate a *Feedback Command* containing the URI of the image and default zoom and center for the image.

Then the users can perform pan and zoom through their smartphone in order to control what is visualized in the large screen (Figure 5b).

Each time a user zooms or pans the image on the mobile a *Feedback Command* with the new center and zoom level is sent to the *Engine*. When the large screen receives the *Feedback Notification* it will apply it. On the large screen a personalized callback is used to correctly apply the new zoom and center.

The data value of the *Feedback Command* and *Notification* have the following structure:

data : {

      URI: "VALUE",

      zoom: 0,

      center : [960.0,540.0]

}

Using the menu (Figure 5b top-right corner) is possible to show in the large screen one of the tabs (white background bottom center in 6a and 6b) which contains the extra content of the artwork.

Selecting one of the menu options, an ASSIGN Command with the id of the selected element (tab on large screen) is generated. The Basic State Level will be Disabled and the target will be the large screen ID. When it receives the Feedback Notification, the large screen will show the tab. When the user returns to the image, an ASSIGN Command to set the tab to Invisible will be generated. The large screen implements its own callback to perform the desired behavior.

a)

b)

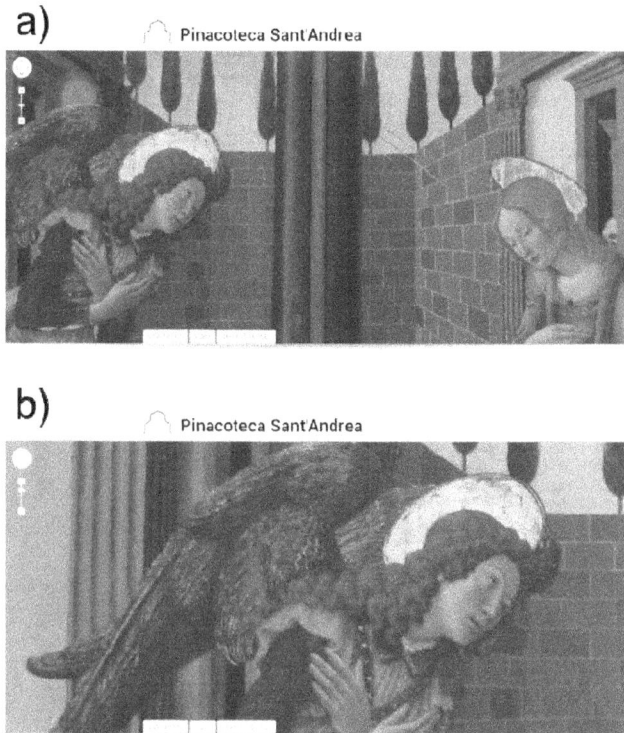

Figure 6. User interface of large display application. 7a (above) shows a lower level of zoom than the 7b (below) and a different center position.

a)

b)

Figure 7. User interface of Android city mobile guide. The image above (a) is the guide version and the one below (b) is the tourist version.

Once the users have accessed an artwork, they can continue the navigation to other items or release the large screen. In any case, after some time without user interaction there is a timeout event that allows the release of the large screen from that session, which occurs also if the user starts to interact with another large screen.

City Guide

The second application is a city mobile guide support for groups of visitors. So, it is an example of a multi-user, multi-device application for outdoor environments.

The application supports guides accompanying groups of visitors who can have either tablets or smartphones. The application shows information supporting the mobile visit. The application version associated with the guide role allows them to select the content to show in the version of the tourist role.

Thus, the user interface elements are in the *Enabled* state for the guide while they can be *Disabled* or even *Invisible* for the tourists. The guide can interactively change the states for the elements shown in the tourist's user interfaces.

The guide has the rights to create and subscribe to a session while the tourists can only subscribe to the session created by the guide. This is achieved through the certificate mechanism previously introduced, which allows the environment to provide different rights depending on the user's role.

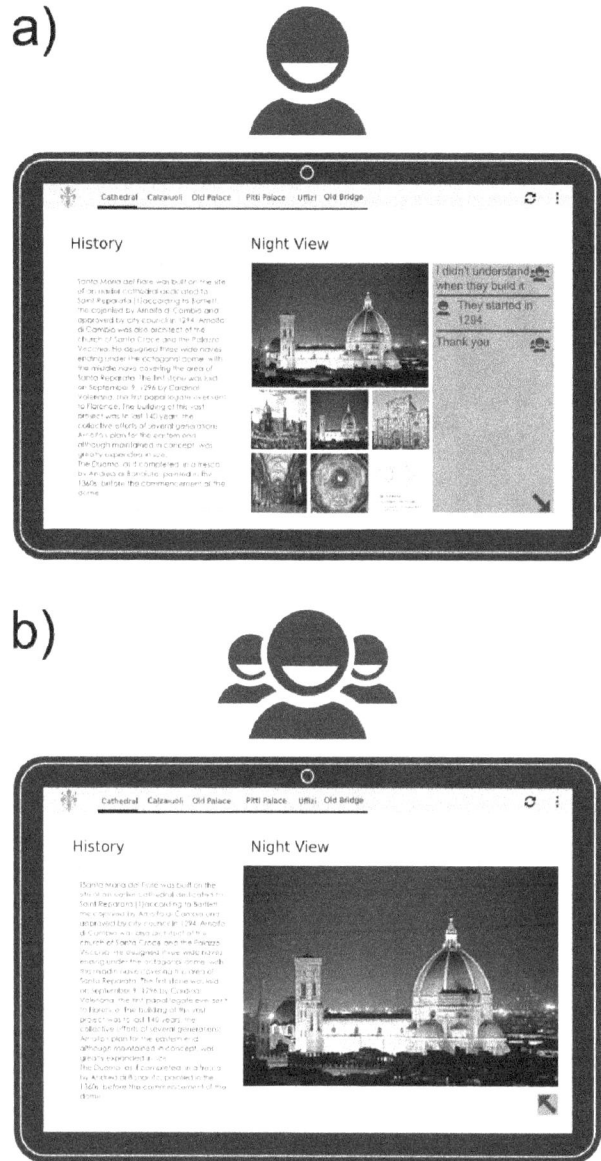

Figure 8a shows the city guide application. The guide can select the different images to be shown to tourists. The big image (element with id *FeaturedImage*) is visible to tourists and enabled to guide. The thumbnails block is enabled to guide and invisible to tourist. Tapping the thumbnail the guide change the *FeaturedImage*. Thus, a *Feedback Command* is sent to the *Engine* containing the URI of the image to be shown.

Crossword Game

The last application is a crossword game that allows multiple users to participate in solving a puzzle with the support of a PC or a WebTV.

Users subscribe to the session through their mobile devices and are thereby able to enter words in the crosswords. Each time that a user enters a word then it is shown on all the other users' devices.

When a user insert a word a *FeedbackCommand* is generated so all the other involved devices will be updated about the solved word.

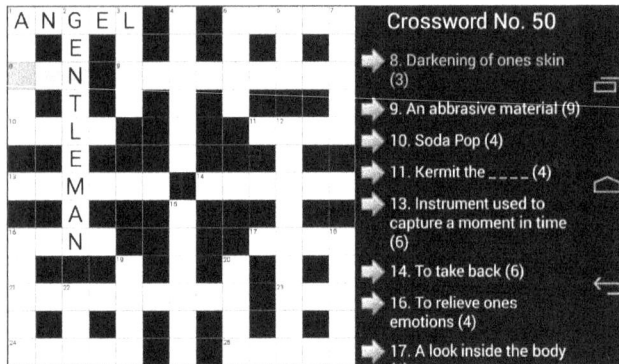

Figure 8. User interface of Android crossword application.

Each question is considered an element of the interface and *FeedbackCommand* is used intensively when:

* A user enter a solution;
* The entered solution conflicts with an intersecting word;
* A user suggests a solution to other participant.

The data value has the following structure.

data : {

        value: "VALUE",

        proposed: [proposed1, proposed2],

        discarded : [discarded1, discarded2]

}

Every time a user enters a solution the typed value is inserted in value field. When a user is not sure about a solution but wants to try to suggest it to other users the proposed word is inserted in proposed field and a *FeedbackCommand* is sent.

Furthermore, the user has the possibility to discard a value or a proposed solution. In the default modality all the users have all words elements to be solved in in enable mode.

The device which creates the session is the only one which can distribute the elements using *ASSING Command*. All the others can only send *Feedback Command*.

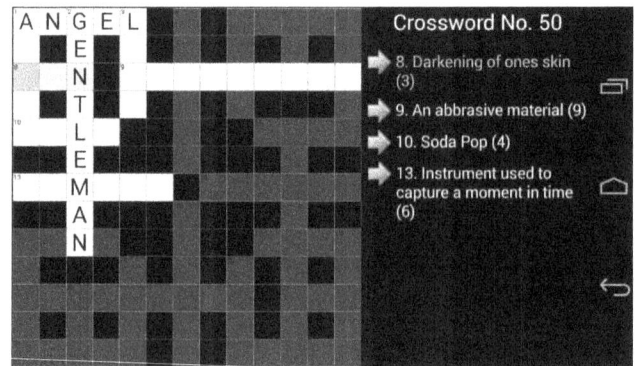

Figure 9. User interface of Android crossword application with hidden questions.

This allows the session creator to switch from default to a version where each user only sees a set of random questions. The creator can redistribute parts to each player with two options:

* with timeout
* manually

In the timeout version the questions are redistributed each time the configurable timeout is triggered. This is performed by the session creator client sending a list of *ASSIGN Command* to the *Engine*. In the second one, it is the user who creates the session that manually triggers the event, the distribution logic of the random questions is completely in the application, no choice is made by the *Engine*.

Figure 8 shows a screenshot of crossword application where all the questions are available to all users. Figure 9 shows instead a screenshot were only 1, 8, 9, 10 and 10 across words and 1, 2, 3 down words are enabled and all the rest are invisible.

To implement this game we used personalized versions of callback both for *ASSIGN Notification* and *Feedback Notification* associated to question elements.

IMPACT FOR DEVELOPERS

In this section we provide a concrete description of the support provided by the framework for the developers, showing how it requires limited number of code instructions.

Indeed, if developers want to start using the framework in order to include a device in the distribution environment using the standard callback functions they just need to write about 40 lines of code. The Android version is shown in Figure 10. With such code the corresponding device will receive all the relevant distribution change notifications.

```
private void subscribe() throws Exception {
    DistributionClientManager.setApplicationID("APP-ID");
    DistributionClientManager.setSessionID("SESSION-ID");

    distribution = DistributionClientManager.getInstance();
    distribution.setActivityRID(this, R.id.class);

    UUID webSocketKey = UUID.randomUUID();

    List<ClientConnector> clientConnectors = new ArrayList<ClientConnector>();
    clientConnectors.add(new WebSocketClientConnector(webSocketKey));

    List<Feature> features = new ArrayList<Feature>();
    features.add(new Feature("FEATURE 1"));
    features.add(new Feature("FEATURE 2"));
    features.add(new Feature("FEATURE 3"));

    String name = AndroidUtility.getDeviceName();
    String id = AndroidUtility.getDeviceID();

    Device device = new Device(name, id, clientConnectors, features);
    distribution.setRuntimeDevice(device);

    WebSocketEngineConnector engineConnector = new WebSocketEngineConnector(
            webSocketKey, webSocketURL, new SocketOpenCallBack() {
                @Override
                public void call() {
                    subscribeDevice();
                }
            }
    );
    distribution.setEngineConnector(engineConnector);

}

private void subscribeDevice() {
    try {
        distribution.subscribeDevice();
    } catch (Exception e) {
        logger.e(String.format("Error while subscribing device : %s",
                e.getLocalizedMessage()));
    }
}
```

Figure 10. Example of Java code for Android used to subscribe a device to a session.

In Figure 10 the Android code to subscribe to a session is shown. In the first two rows the identified of application and the session is set. A Distribution Client Manager (the Java class wich coordinates all the distribution operations) is instantiated. The client register itself to the istance of DistributionClientManager, with name, id and the list of the capabilities (Feature class) thata the Engine will use to associate one or more *Type* to the Device.

The invocation of sucription is made using the *distribution.subscribe()*; instruction.

The client is using a WebSocket to send command to the Engine and viceversa for the Engine to send Notification, for this reason we can recognized WebSocketEngineConnetor and WebSocketClientConnector. This is an implementation issue out of the scope of this paper

Furthermore, with just 10 more rows of code they can manage the user actions that generate a distribution update to send to the engine. Figure 11 shows an example of code written in JavaScript for the management of Web tabs. The code shows an example of callbacks for *ASSIGN* (*tabHostUIUpdate*) and *Feedback* (*tabHostFeedback*) *Notifications*. These callbacks have to be registered with the *UIManager*.

```
function tabHostFeedback(connector, feedback){
    console.log(feedback);
    var selector = connector.getClientSelector(feedback);
    var position = feedback.data.position;
    console.log("Tab to select : " + position);
    var disabled = jQuery("#TabHost").isDisabled(position);
    var visible = jQuery("#TabHost").isVisible(position);
    if(visible){
        if(disabled){
            jQuery("#TabHost").enableTab(position);
        }
        jQuery(selector).tabs({ active : feedback.data.position });
        if(disabled){
            jQuery("#TabHost").disableTab(position);
        }
    }
}

function tabHostUIUpdate(connector, uiupdate){
    console.log(uiupdate);
    var position = parseInt(uiupdate.what.id.substring(3)) - 1 ;
    var visible = uiupdate.level > 0;
    var enabled = uiupdate.level > 1;
    if(visible){
        jQuery("#TabHost").enableTab(position);
        if(!enabled){
            jQuery("#TabHost").disableTab(position);
        }
    }else{
        jQuery("#TabHost").disableTab(position, true);
    }
}
```

Figure 11. Example of JavaScript code of callback used to manage a *TabHost*.

VALIDATION

Expressivity

In some interviews developers unfamiliar with distributed UI stated a preference for a limited number of commands for managing distribution. Thus, this was an initial design requirement for our framework. Despite the simplification we aimed to preserve the command expressivity in such a way to be able to provide the same possibilities as presented in previous work [5]. For example, the DISPLAY operation in [5] can be achieved with the ASSIGN command of state level > Invisible; conversely, an UNDISPLAY can be obtained with a state level = Invisible. The MOVE operation can be achieved using an ASSIGN command of state level to Invisible for the elements in the source device and an ASSIGN command of state level to Enabled in the target device.

The REPLACE operation can be achieved by the composition of an *ASSIGN Command* of state level = *Invisible* to the element to be replaced and with an *ASSIGN Command* of state level to *Enabled* to the replacing element.

The MERGE command can be achieved using an *ASSIGN Command* of state level to *Enabled* to the device where we want to merge.

The SEPARATE command can be obtained by using an *ASSIGN Command* of state level to *Invisible* for the elements in the device where the UI is being separated and an *ASSIGN Command* of state level to *Enabled* in the device the element is going to appear on.

Performance

In order to assess the performance of our environment we have focused on the engine performance, and we have measured on average the number of commands it received from the clients during a session, and the minimum, maximum, average, and variance of the time taken to process them. In the processing time we included both that required to calculate the new distribution state but also that required to notify the involved devices of the distribution change.

The results were calculated considering 18 sessions of the city guide application involving three devices gathered during a user test. This application mainly uses the Feedback command because it mainly supports a kind of co-browsing across multiple devices. The average number of commands per session was 287. The minimum amount of time to elaborate a request was 236 msec and the maximum was 661 msec. The average time was 296.46 msec and the standard deviation is 50.11.

With the applications and their informal use we have learnt that the framework processing time is sufficiently short to avoid creating particular usability issues.

CONCLUSIONS AND FUTURE WORK

We have presented a framework and run-time support for enabling cross-device interaction. The client side part is currently available for Android and Web-based applications, and we plan to provide a version for iOS as well.

A number of multi-device user interface applications have been designed and developed through it. We have also shown how the impact of the framework in the application code is limited. In terms of performance we have reported the results of a first study, which are encouraging.

The three applications show that the framework can be used in different domains and in different environments: single or multi-user applications; indoor or outdoor environments; mobile and stationary devices.

Future work will be dedicated to introducing more flexible mechanisms for selecting user interface elements, security, and dynamic device allocation across multiple sessions.

ACKNOWLEDGMENTS

We thank the IUDSM (Distributed User Interfaces and Mobile Security) Project (funded by Regione Toscana, CNR-ISTI and IIT, and Softec)[1] for supporting this work, and Zeno Amerini (Softect) for useful discussions on the topics of the paper.

REFERENCES

1. Demeure, A., Sottet, J.-S., Calvary, G., Coutaz, J., Ganneau, V. and Vanderdonckt, J. The 4C Reference Model for Distributed User Interfaces. ICAS (2008), 1-10.

2. Luyten, K., Van den Bergh, J., Vandervelpen, C. and Coninx, K. Designing distributed user interfaces for ambient intelligent environments using models and simulations. Computers & Graphics (2006), 702-713.

3. Melchior, J., Grolaux, D., Vanderdonckt, J. and Van Roy, P. A toolkit for peer-to-peer distributed user interfaces: concepts, implementation, and applications. In *Proc.* EICS 2009, 69-78.

4. Google. The new multi-screen world: Understanding cross-platform consumer behavior. Technical report, August 2012. http://www.google.com/think/research-studies/the-new-multi-screen-world-study.html

5. Melchior, J., Grolaux, D., Vanderdonckt, J. and Van Roy, P. A model-based approach for distributed user interfaces. In *Proc.* EICS 2011, 11-20.

6. Bardram, J., Gueddana, S., Houben, S. and Nielsen, S. ReticularSpaces: activity-based computing support for physically distributed and collaborative smart spaces. In *Proc.* CHI 2012, 2845-2854.

7. Hartmann, B., Beaudouin-Lafon, M. and Mackay, W. E. HydraScope: creating multi-surface meta-applications through view synchronization and input multiplexing. In *Proc.* PerDis 2013, 43-48.

8. Hosio, S., Jurmu, M., Kukka, H., Riekki, J. and Ojala, T. Supporting distributed private and public user interfaces in urban environments. In *Proc.* HotMobile 2010, 25-30.

9. A. Peñalver, E. Lazcorreta, J. J. López, F. Botella, and J. A. Gallud. 2012. Schema driven distributed user interface generation. In *Proc.* Interacción 2012.

10. Fisher, E.R., Badam, S. K. and Elmqvist, N. Designing peer-to-peer distributed user interfaces: Case studies on building distributed applications. International Journal of Human-Computer Studies. 2013.

11. M. Manca, F. Paternò: Extending MARIA to Support Distributed User Interfaces. Distributed User Interfaces 2011: 33-40

12. L. Frosini, M. Manca, F. Paternò: A framework for the development of distributed interactive applications. EICS 2013: 249-254

---

[1] http://hiis.isti.cnr.it/IUDSM/index_en.html

XDKinect: Development Framework for Cross-Device Interaction using Kinect

Michael Nebeling, Elena Teunissen, Maria Husmann and Moira C. Norrie

Department of Computer Science, ETH Zurich

CH-8092 Zurich, Switzerland

{nebeling,husmann,norrie}@inf.ethz.ch, telena@student.ethz.ch

ABSTRACT

Interactive systems set in multi-device environments continue to attract increasing attention, prompting researchers to experiment with emerging technologies. This paper presents XDKinect—a lightweight framework that facilitates development of cross-device applications using Kinect to mediate user interactions. The main benefits of XDKinect include its simplicity, adaptability and extensibility based on a flexible client-server architecture. Our framework features a time-based API to handle full-body interactions, a multi-modal API to capture gesture and speech commands, an API to utilise proxemic awareness information, a cross-device communication API, and a settings API to optimise for particular application requirements. A study with developers was conducted to investigate the potential of these features in terms of ease of use, effectiveness and possible use in the future. We show several example applications of XDKinect, as well as discussing advantages and limitations of our framework as revealed by our user study and experiments.

Author Keywords

Kinect; development framework; cross-device applications.

ACM Classification Keywords

H.5.2 User Interfaces: Input devices and strategies

INTRODUCTION

The flexibility and complexity imposed by multi-device environments often requires experimentation with alternative, sometimes radically different, user interface designs. Our goal is to exploit the potential of Microsoft Kinect[1] for experimentation with different forms of multi-modal interaction involving multiple devices and users. Kinect's RGB camera, 3D depth sensors and high-quality audio capture are valuable for augmenting target applications with support for multi-modal input. Its relatively cheap price and increased popularity make Kinect attractive to be explored for multi-device

---

[1] http://www.kinectforwindows.org

application development, in particular, in settings that previously required complex hardware and software setups [1, 16].

This paper presents XDKinect, a user interface development toolkit that uses Kinect to mediate interactions between multiple devices and users. XDKinect is characterised by three main aspects: (1) lightweight support for cross-platform, multi-device development based on native web technologies with which many developers are already familiar, (2) a flexible client-server architecture enabling a variety of multi-device ecosystems around Kinect, (3) useful programming abstractions from low-level details of Kinect's standard SDK.

First, our goal is to provide a lightweight toolkit for easy and rapid development of multi-device applications using Kinect as an intermediator. Currently, a wide range of skill sets and experience with many different platforms, languages and technologies are required for implementations to achieve compatibility with many types of devices. We promote a web-based approach that seems promising to reach across device boundaries as it, not only enables applications to run on the wide range of web-enabled devices available today, but also allows developers to leverage their knowledge of web standards. This is in contrast to approaches that promote new models and languages to support multi-device development [13]. These approaches often tie in with certain programming paradigms (e.g. model-based [8], object-oriented [4], data-oriented [2]), impose multiple abstraction levels, or require proprietary languages for programming and specification, all of which seems to work against widespread adoption.

The second important aspect of XDKinect is its flexible client-server architecture. The core logic of XDKinect applications can be shared and distributed between one or multiple clients and a server used for hosting Kinect. This special role of the server enables many different multi-device scenarios around Kinect. Supported operating systems and platforms include Android, iOS and Windows. Given that the Kinect SDK is only available for Windows, the XDKinect server currently requires Windows. However, XDKinect clients can be any web-enabled device with support for modern web browsers. This includes the whole range from mobile devices such as smartphones and tablets (e.g. Android phones, Apple iDevices), over laptops and desktops, to tabletops (e.g. Microsoft PixelSense) and interactive walls.

Third, XDKinect affords useful abstractions from Kinect's standard SDK. Specifically, it provides a settings API to op-

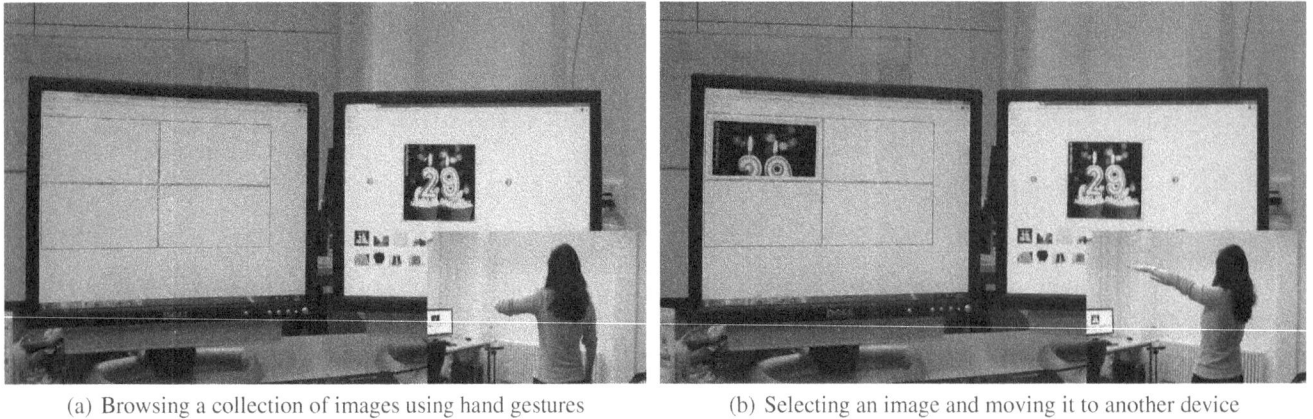

(a) Browsing a collection of images using hand gestures   (b) Selecting an image and moving it to another device

Figure 1. Scrapbook application using XDKinect for whole-body gesture-based cross-device interaction

timise for particular application requirements, a time-based API to query and constrain Kinect streaming data, a multimodal API for gesture and speech recognition, and APIs for inter-client communication to implement cross-device sessions involving multiple, distributed clients [11] as well as for proxemic interaction [1].

To demonstrate the potential of XDKinect, we present two applications created using our framework. A first example application is Scrapbook shown in Figure 1. Here, a user can browse through a collection of images on one device using hand gestures and pull selected ones over to another device for additional tasks. In a second application, we show how XDKinect can also take cues from the user's position and adapt the displayed content to fit either into personal or ambient interaction modality [16]. Moreover, collaborative interaction is feasible since input from more than one user and device can be distinguished using XDKinect.

This paper is organised as follows. We begin in the next section with a discussion of related work. The key features of XDKinect and its architecture are then presented together with our implementation. This is followed by a description of the two sample applications developed using XDKinect. We then present our study conducted with 12 developers to assess its ease of use and effectiveness for building cross-device applications. Finally, we compare XDKinect with other solutions and discuss limitations as well as future work.

BACKGROUND
Our work relates to three streams of research: proxemic and ambient interaction, multi-device user interfaces and in-browser Kinect applications.

Proxemic and Ambient Interaction
Research in proxemic interaction investigates spatial relationships between users and objects, taking cues from distance, orientation, movement and identity to study interaction behaviour of users and devices in their immediate environment. Ballendat et al. [1] extended Hall's proxemic theory by adding notions of fine-grained sensing of nearby people and devices, mediating between implicit and explicit interaction, and distinguishing between four discrete proxemic zones. These principles were incorporated into a framework,

which they illustrated using the scenario of a Proxemic Media Player. Later, they developed the Proximity Toolkit [6] that gathers data from various tracking devices, making it available through an event-driven, object-oriented API. Relationships between entities can be observed and closely investigated using a visual monitoring tool. Finally, GroupTogether [7] augments proxemic principles with theories of F-formation and micro-mobility. The former investigates physical arrangements of a small group of people engaged in a focused conversation, while the latter considers the impact of re-orienting and re-positioning physical devices on information sharing techniques. Combining these two aspects, new techniques of cross-device interaction with emphasis on fluid and smooth communication can be designed. For instance, tilting a device by a small angle may trigger an information sharing process with other devices within proximity.

Similar ideas for proxemic interaction were also proposed in [16], conceptualising design principles for developing a shareable, public and private Interactive Ambient Display. The principles include visualising the data in a calm, aesthetically pleasing manner, naturally revealing meaning and functionality, supporting short-duration fluid interaction, and promoting shared use while combining public and personal information. Based on these principles, an interaction framework was developed with support for four continuous phases with fluid inter-phase transitions: ambient display, implicit interaction, subtle interaction and personal interaction.

XDKinect builds on these works, implementing the core ideas in a web-based toolkit with the goal of providing lightweight technical tools for rapidly developing and experimenting with new forms of cross-device interaction in multi-device environments. While previous works focused on the types of applications and interaction techniques that could be supported if there were such technologies, our main goal is to enable developers with varying programming experience to implement such applications given technologies such as Kinect.

Multi-Device User Interfaces
A logical framework to alleviate development of multi-device applications with distributed user interfaces was presented in [13]. Their work identifies several design dimensions to help

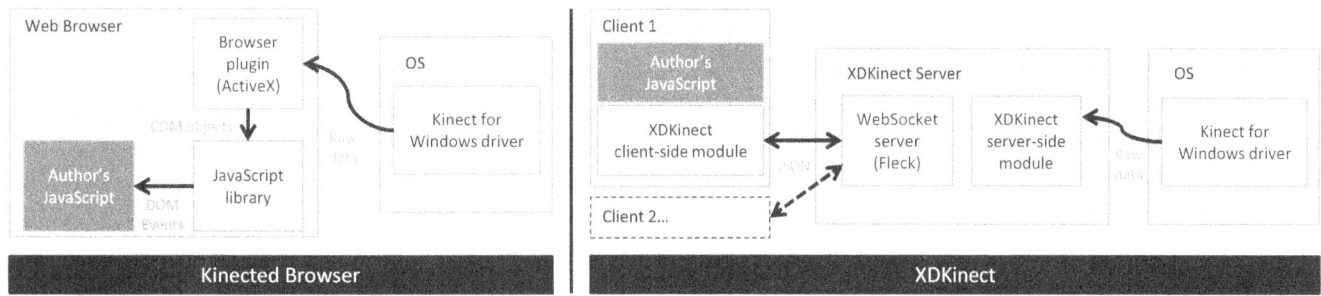

Figure 2. XDKinect's client-server architecture compared to the typical way of using a web browser plugin to access Kinect data directly

researchers and developers better analyse and evaluate current solutions. It provides an extensive overview of a wide range of various strategies in cross-platform development including abstract user interface representations, distribution and migration between multiple devices and users. As such, it offers a systematic classification of an assortment of design decisions and their shortcomings, serving as a valuable starting point into research about multi-device environments.

Many different approaches have been explored with object-oriented frameworks such as ZOIL [4], data-oriented frameworks such as Shared Substance [2] and model-based frameworks such as [8]. In a recent paper [11], we presented our ongoing work on a platform facilitating design and evaluation of cross-device applications both at the data model and user interface level. The paper introduces the notion of cross-device sessions that link the concepts of user, device and information. Developers can specify different scenarios of information sharing, where devices and sessions can be paired flexibly, allowing completely independent interactions, shared interactions, or arbitrary mixtures thereof. XDKinect implements a simplified version of this session concept for cross-device communication and keeping track of participating devices and users.

In-Browser Kinect Applications

Several attempts have been made to make Kinect available from within web browsers. Common to libraries such as Kinected Browser [5], KinectJS[2] and DepthJS[3] is that they extend the familiar JavaScript DOM event model with custom events to support processing of Kinect's skeletal tracking and raw data streams (audio, colour, depth and infrared) directly in the browser. While this is one of the initial challenges we also had to address in developing XDKinect, these solutions are limited to single-device scenarios and only certain browsers. Also, tight integration with the browser requires that the Kinect is connected to the same computer on which the client is running. These factors taken together considerably limit the types of applications that can be created and the settings in which they can be deployed and tested.

XDKINECT

The aim of XDKinect is to facilitate development of cross-device interfaces and interaction techniques that can cater for a wide range of applications and use scenarios. A crucial

step in designing a general and useful framework was to experiment with different concepts and architectural designs to support the development process. To do so, we created several applications to assess Kinect's capabilities and recognise the most common requirements. We present some examples in the following sections.

XDKinect's architecture was developed in several iterations. Initially, the main idea was to provide a shorthand method to access Kinect data from within the browser. We also wanted to base the project on existing frameworks, KinectJS and DepthJS. Sadly, however, these are no longer maintained and incompatible with current browser versions. As we started to experiment with our own Kinect framework in several related projects, the number of architectural concerns grew with the need to support different requirements. For example, some applications such as a simple gestural controller for Power-Point presentations only required Kinect's skeleton tracking, while another one with the goal of supporting web browsing using Kinect for gesture and speech input required additional Kinect data streams. In March 2013, Microsoft released a new version of the Kinect SDK[4], which was after we had started working on the XDKinect project. A novel set of features was provided with KinectInteraction, an extension that incorporates gesture-based tracking of a user's primary interactive hand allowing grip and press gestures to be detected. KinectInteractions rely on another tracking method that requires an additional Kinect data stream. Evolutions like this drove us to pay particular attention to the design of XDKinect's architecture so that any component could be adapted and extended to include new features with little effort.

Figure 2 shows XDKinect's final architecture and how it compares to previous solutions. Although based on a client-server model, XDKinect breaks from the traditional roles in that the server is not primarily used to host and manage the content, but to host and control the Kinect. Our architecture is different from existing solutions as it enables scenarios in which the Kinect is not directly connected to the client computer. This includes cross-device interaction involving multiple distributed clients, which is possible based on a single Kinect server. The cost of this indirection is kept minimal as XDKinect is highly configurable and implements several mechanisms to reduce client or server-side processing as required and manage with the bandwidth while controlling what kinds of data are processed and transferred.

---

[2]http://kinect.childnodes.com
[3]http://depthjs.media.mit.edu

[4]http://www.microsoft.com/en-us/kinectforwindows/develop/new.aspx

Feature	Examples	Description
settings	XDKinect.settings({ maxUsers: 2, joints: ['leftHand', 'rightHand'] });	Set tracked skeleton limit and selected joints to be tracked
skeleton	XDKinect.on('skeleton', function(skeleton) { console.log("distance: "+skeleton.joints.spine.z); });	Register callback for new skeleton frames
gesture	XDKinect.on('gesture', { 'leftGrip', 'rightGrip' }, function(skeleton, gesture) { console.log("gesture recognized: "+gesture); });	Register callback for gesture events of interactive hand
speech	XDKinect.on('speech', { 'Kinect on', 'Kinect off' }, function(term) { console.log(term); });	Register callback for speech commands
distance	XDKinect.on('distanceFar', function() { console.log("ambient zone"); });	Register callback for 4 or more metres distance from Kinect
users	XDKinect.on('userJoined', function(skeleton) { console.log("Welcome, user "+skeleton.trackingId); });	Register callback for new recognised user
message	XDKinect.message('ambient', 'hello', JSON);	Send hello message with JSON data object to ambient display
	XDKinect.on('hello', function(client, data) { console.log("received "+data+" from client "+client); });	Register callback for hello message from main display

Figure 3. XDKinect's features with code examples

The client and server-side components both employ an event-driven design. Based on this architecture, XDKinect supports two different ways of accessing Kinect data. First, similar to Kinected Browser [5], a low-level approach is supported by providing direct access to Kinect's data streams. For example, XDKinect provides an event to capture skeleton coordinates from the server (Figure 3). The event is fired whenever a new Kinect skeleton frame is available. To receive skeleton data, developers only need to subscribe to the event by declaring a callback function. At the same time, however, we also support high-level access similar to KinectJS and DepthJS, with which it is possible to fire custom events for more complex actions composed of multiple low-level events that may be generated on either the client or the server side.

In the following, we discuss the key concepts and how they are encapsulated in XDKinect's APIs (cf. Figure 3).

Time-based API
To support low-level access, XDKinect generalises the central concept of a touch history used in jQMultiTouch [10] to different interaction modalities in that XDKinect maintains internally a history for each Kinect data stream. For example, XDKinect collects joints coordinates for each tracked user from the skeleton stream. New Kinect skeleton events are generated at a rate of 30 frames per second. Every incoming Kinect skeleton object is pushed into a buffer, while the oldest entries are deleted. Here, the default storage duration amounts to 4.5 seconds (135 frames per tracked user). This is sufficient for many applications relying on skeletal tracking, but we will later describe how it can be configured both client and server-side. Possible applications include hand-as-cursor tracking, custom gesture detection, and various statistics to deduce user behaviour. A sample joints coordinates history object is shown in Listing 1.

```
[{trackingId: 148, timestamp: 1374225394869, rightHand:
    {x : 0, y: 0.1, z: 0.2}},
{trackingId: 148, timestamp: 1374225395678, rightHand: {x
    : 0.3, y: -0.15, z: 0.25}}]
```

Listing 1. Sample history object; only right hand is tracked

Similar to jQMultiTouch, developers are able to segment, query and constrain the history easily, e.g. to seek a certain frame, extract a portion of the history, filter by skeleton, look

for selected joints, and evaluate it based on thresholds. Listing 2 shows a simple example for flick-hand gestures.

```
XDKinect.on("skeleton", function(skeleton) {
  var hand = skeleton.joints[hand], handRef =
      XDKinect.skeletonHistory({ skeleton: skeleton,
      time: '0..300', joints: ['leftHand', 'rightHand']
      }).last().joints[hand], deltaX = hand.x-handRef.x,
      deltaY = hand.y-handRef.y;
  if (Math.abs(deltaX) >= 0.4 && Math.abs(deltaY) <=
      0.075) {
    if (deltaX < 0) {
      console.log(hand+" flick-left");
    } else {
      console.log(hand+" flick-right")
    }
  } });
```

Listing 2. History usage for left/right-hand flick gestures

Additionally, the colour stream can be buffered either at 30 frames per second with 640x480 RGB colour bitmaps or at 12 frames with 1280x960 pixels. The depth and infrared streams are represented in specific image formats at 30 frames with 640x480 pixels, while audio is available in 16-bit PCM format, sampled at 16 kHz. Similar to the skeleton stream, these raw data streams can be segmented, constrained and, using additional libraries, further processed, e.g. looking for certain speech commands in the audio stream.

Multi-modal API
As mentioned above, XDKinect also offers a high-level API to register for, and react on, recognised gesture and speech commands from the server. XDKinect deduces high-level events from the skeleton, interaction and audio streams. While Kinect's skeletal tracking does not include hand tracking, KinectInteraction can detect hand gestures such as grip, grip release and press, and can discern between the right and the left hand of one or two users. The audio stream can be processed using speech recognition software. Kinect's default speech recognition service, Microsoft.Speech[5], was specifically optimised for the Kinect hardware. It can detect speech commands specified in W3C speech recognition grammar[6]. XDKinect application developers do not have to worry about the specifics and differences of these Kinect-internal APIs. Rather, clients only need to subscribe for the desired gesture and speech commands and will be notified automatically as these are recognised (cf. Figure 3).

Proxemic API
Based on Kinect's skeleton stream, another feature of XD-Kinect is distinguishing different proxemic parameters such as near and far distances between users and Kinect or between users themselves [1]. XDKinect allows developers to divide Kinect's field of view into multiple interaction zones and trigger events based on distance thresholds. Applications may use this information to support transition from one mode into another similar to [16]. XDKinect also supports a simple form of multiple user tracking. Whenever a user enters or leaves Kinect's field of view, XDKinect triggers a corresponding event. User identification is performed on the basis of the Kinect skeleton IDs (cf. Figure 3).

---

[5] http://msdn.microsoft.com/en-us/library/jj127857
[6] http://www.w3.org/TR/speech-grammar

Cross-Device Communication API

While the features discussed so far rely on Kinect, XDKinect adds an inter-client communication mechanism based on instant messaging to enable cross-device interaction in real-time. Information can be exchanged and shared between any clients registered in the system. Each new client only needs to connect to the server to be able to communicate with other clients. Clients can pass information along and share state through XDKinect's internal messaging service that was inspired by [14], but was adapted to the web environment by using web sockets and JSON for data exchange. We experimented with different JSON formats to find a good compromise between readability and traceability, which are important for debugging, and processing time required for encoding/decoding.

XDKinect is scalable to support a large number of clients. First, each client runs independently from the others and may only subscribe for information from the server. By default, interactions performed with one client have no impact on others. In order to be able to accept messages from other clients, a listener for this type of event is required (Figure 3). An important principle is the notion of active and passive clients. While active clients continuously receive Kinect data, passive clients do not. For example, while the main display is alert and awaits interaction, a secondary, passive display could be in sleeping mode since it first requires shared content from the main display. All clients can be explicitly set to active/passive mode by the developer. This contributes to a boost in performance, decreasing the overhead by cutting information flow. Passive clients can be configured to automatically "wake up" upon a message receipt from another client.

Note that it is also possible to run one or more XDKinect clients and the XDKinect server locally so that it is sufficient to use a multi-monitor setup on a single device.

XDKinect was specifically designed for cross-device application development. While the cross-device support is therefore an essential part of the framework, it is implemented as a module following good principles of software design. As a result, developers may choose to extend or even replace this component without having to touch other parts of the framework. It is also the case that not all XDKinect applications must make use of the cross-device communication API and, as mentioned above, clients can work independently.

Settings API

One of XDKinect's key features is the facility to configure the server so that only data relevant for subscribed events is processed and transferred to clients. Furthermore, many parameters serve the goal of increasing the system's overall performance. For example, developers may switch Kinect's tracking (default/near), choose a skeleton selection strategy (track the closest/most active skeletons) and specify the maximum number of users to be tracked[7].

In order to receive information, clients must connect and first instruct the server by providing an individual configuration,

such as active/passive status, joints to be tracked, gestures to be recognised, speech grammar, and any additional XD-Kinect events. Based on the information desired by clients, the server configures the Kinect and filters the event histories to only send back relevant data. While clients also have the possibility to change Kinect settings dynamically at run-time, some changes may cause a delay or may even require Kinect to be reset at run-time. For example, switching Kinect tracking mode and reloading grammar for speech recognition exhibits a seconds-long delay. XDKinect tries to avoid such interruptions as much as possible by aggregating individual client configurations on the server side.

IMPLEMENTATION

XDKinect is implemented in C# on the server and in JavaScript/jQuery[8] on the client side. The main purpose of the server application is to pre-process Kinect data and transfer it to each client as specified by that client's individual configuration. The server logic can be separated into four main components responsible for 1) configuring Kinect, 2) the handling of Kinect streams, 3) history keeping and filtering, and 4) inter-client messaging. The client-side module parses and dispatches messages from the server and other clients. It exposes the Kinect data to the developer through XDKinect's client-side APIs. Communication between the server and clients, and between clients, is based on the Web-Socket protocol. Note that web sockets offer full duplex bidirectional communication with much less overhead than traditional HTTP-based methods. XDKinect relies on Fleck[9], an open-source web socket server in C# to transmit data to, and between, subscribed clients. All data, server-side notifications as well as inter-client messages, are exchanged via a common JSON format.

Kinect's skeleton stream is the primary source of information, as it offers not only joint coordinates, but distance metrics and multiple user tracking is also deduced from it. Essentially, the server maintains a list of tracked skeletons and· checks it for users that joined or left by comparing the Kinect skeleton IDs each time a new frame arrives. If there are any changes, all subscribed clients are notified. Analogously, any client subscribed for distance change notification receives a message when a user's z skeleton coordinate is smaller or larger than specified thresholds. Accordingly, the interaction stream and audio stream are watched for gesture and speech commands. Whenever a command is recognised, the server compares the recognition results with the criteria set by any of the clients. Should a match occur, the corresponding client is notified. Cross-device communication is implemented using the same mechanism. The server listens for message events from clients. Once such an event is received, the server parses the message and forwards it to the target client.

XDKinect can be extended on both the client and the server side with little programming effort. For example, when the new KinectInteractions came out, we linked the library to the server, registered the interaction stream in XDKinect, and specified a new event handler. Likewise, the client side was

---

[7]Note that current Kinect hardware can recognise up to six users and fully track 20 joints of up to two skeletons.

[8]http://jquery.com
[9]https://github.com/statianzo/Fleck

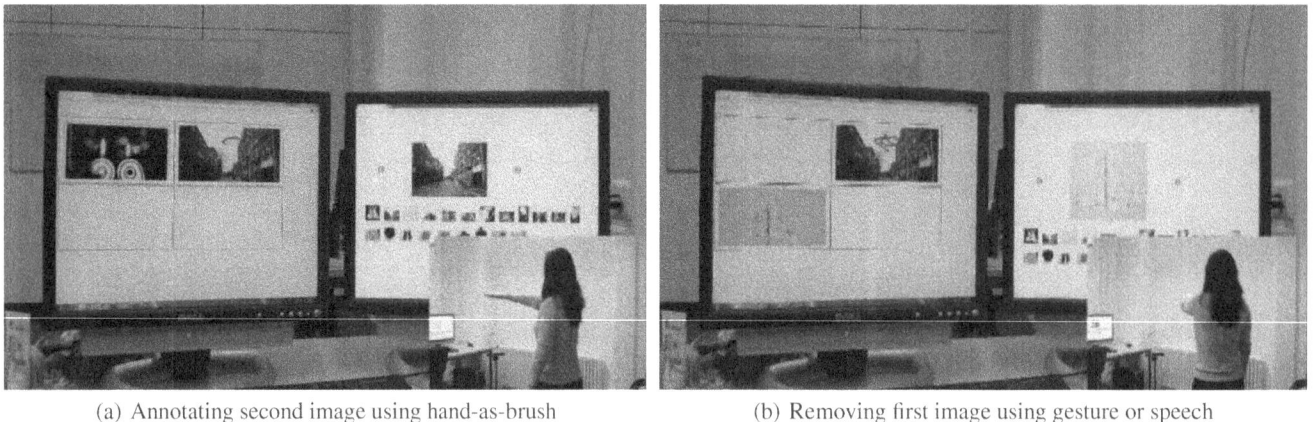

(a) Annotating second image using hand-as-brush   (b) Removing first image using gesture or speech

Figure 4. Scrapbook application using XDKinect for whole-body gesture-based cross-device interaction (cont.)

extended with a new event listener. It is also easily possible to integrate client-side gesture libraries such as $1 recogniser [17], e.g. to support stroke-based gestures such as circle-hand. This requires a mapping from 3D space to 2D, e.g. by only considering x and y coordinates.

APPLICATIONS

In this section, we present two sample applications based on XDKinect. The first application, the Scrapbook mentioned in the introduction, was produced with an early version of XDKinect. The idea of Scrapbook is to browse through and collect images from a large photo collection, e.g. photos of places visited on a holiday, to put together an album. The second application, Fotobook, is similar in idea, but makes more advanced use of XDKinect's features as it reacts to multiple users and distinguishes different interaction zones.

Scrapbook

A web designer, Leia, searches for a collection of pictures for a customer's website. She stands in front of a large display and browses through the image gallery by swiping left or right to go to the next or previous item (cf. Figure 1(a)). One of the images catches her attention. Leia extends her arms and, in one swishing motion, pulls the image to be copied to the Scrapbook display (cf. Figure 1(b)). Satisfied with the result, Leia continues browsing for more pictures. Another one seems to satisfy her demands, and so she drags it over as well. Yet, there is something about that image that disturbs her. Deciding to fix it, Leia makes a graphical note on it using her right hand as a brush (Figure 4(a)). For some time, Leia continues browsing through the gallery and buffering pictures on the Scrapbook. Suddenly she changes her mind about the very first image and decides to remove it from the storage by saying "delete one" (Figure 4(b)).

The early version of XDKinect offered only parts of the time-based and multi-modal APIs. Support for flick hand gestures and the pick-and-drop metaphor [15] was added by tracking the user's arm movements, comparing their actions against a set of templates on the client side, and evaluating against the respective joints' coordinates tracked over time. The beginning of the settings API was already implemented, enabling

developers to register only for selected joints. Speech recognition was available, but not yet dynamically configurable as all commands still had to be hard-coded on the server side. The cross-device communication API was close to the final version except for some wrapper functions.

Fotobook

Fotobook is based on the final version of XDKinect and exploits all available APIs. As before, we illustrate its usage by means of a sample scenario. A professional photographer, Luke, receives a last-minute call by a customer to do a web photo album for one of his recent shoots. While he could also look up the project on his main computer, Luke immediately looks at his wall-sized display. Usually in an ambient mode, the display exhibits an image slideshow to demo his work to visiting clients, and no direct interaction is possible (Figure 5(a)). However, as he walks towards it, the display detects his presence and switches into a personal interaction mode [16] (Figure 5(b)). Luke browses through the images by using his hand as a cursor [9]. Hovering over images that look promising, he quickly performs a push gesture in the air [9] to select images for the photo album. As he is still not quite happy with the album page's design, he again marks some of the images and rotates them by performing a mid-air circle gesture. Furthermore, he adds shadow and polaroid effects to the images using additional speech commands. Meanwhile, dinner time approaches, and Luke's friend, Han, comes over just as Luke performs a pick-and-drop interaction [15] to move the content to the main display. When Han enters the interaction zone, the ambient display flickers shortly to announce the presence of another user [1]. Han likes Luke's first design, but suggests adding a background image to the photo album page. He, too, selects an image from the interactive display to "copy" it to the main display. The system notices that Han, not Luke, performs this action, and places the image in a temp area. To finish the design, Luke picks it up and sets it as background.

In this scenario, the use of most XDKinect APIs comes together to realise interaction techniques known from related work [1, 9, 15, 16]. For example, the time-based and multi-modal APIs are used for the gesture and speech commands similar to Scrapbook, but in this case also employing Kinect-

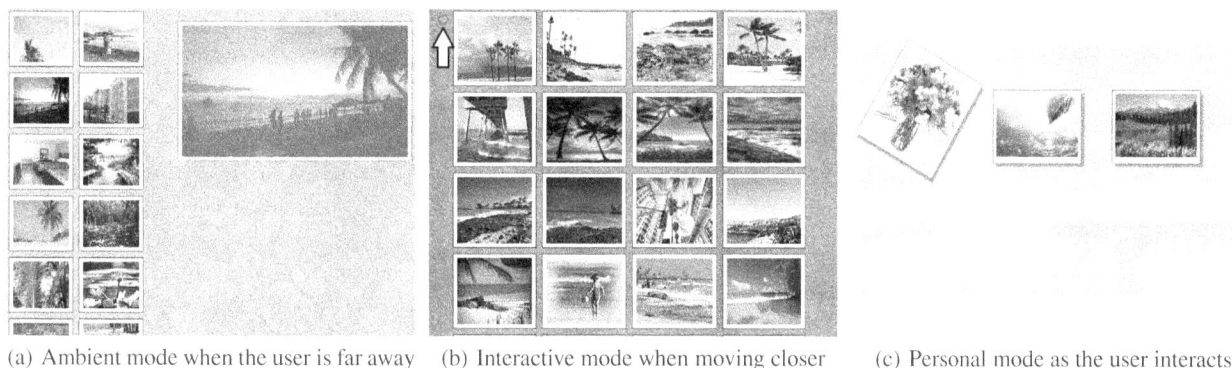

(a) Ambient mode when the user is far away   (b) Interactive mode when moving closer   (c) Personal mode as the user interacts

Figure 5. Fotobook application using XDKinect with support for hand-as-cursor interaction and different interaction zones

Interaction's built-in press gesture to select images. In addition, the cursor's position is calculated by mapping Kinect skeleton coordinates into browser screen coordinates every time a new Kinect frame arrives. The proxemic API is used to switch between the ambient and interactive modes depending on whether a user is closer or farther than 2 metres from the display. Moreover, the system noticed the arrival of a new user, Han, by receiving information about another tracked skeleton associated with a new ID. As a result, it switches to an edit mode in which changes first have to be confirmed by Luke, the owner of the photo album.

EVALUATION

We conducted a user study to examine XDKinect's development experience. Following Olsen's guidelines [12], the goal of our evaluation is to demonstrate "reduced solution viscosity" and "ease of combination" by making use of XD-Kinect's various APIs as well as showing the potential to empower new users. The main task assigned to participants was to develop a simple cross-device application based on Fotobook from the previous section. The application consisted of two XDKinect clients—an ambient display showing an image gallery and another display to which the selected images would be copied (Figure 6). Users should be able to move a cursor with their hand and select images by performing a push or a grip gesture. A magnified version of that image would be transferred onto the main display. Users could then use speech to tag the selected image. The recognised text would be shown on an HTML5 canvas on the main display. Moreover, the ambient display should react to proximity of the user, switching from passive mode when users stand further away to interactive mode as they come closer. At the same time, the main display should show a notification when users join and leave the Kinect sensor's field of view.

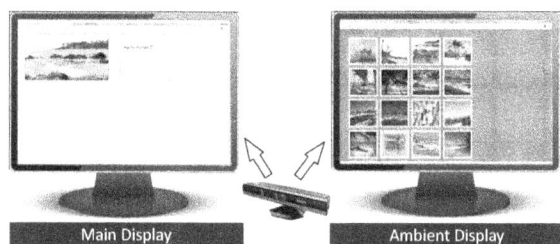

Figure 6. Study setup and target XDKinect application

Method

The study itself comprised 5 programming tasks, leading step-by-step to the fully-fledged XDKinect application just described. To give participants sufficient time to experience development using XDKinect, the study was anticipated to last around 1 hour. Each participant generally worked alone and was free to adjourn at any moment without completing all tasks. The tasks were carefully chosen to encompass every interaction dimension offered by XDKinect. For example, moving the cursor required skeletal tracking and management of the time-based API. The multi-modal API was reflected in the press/grip gestures for image selection as well as in speech recognition results being displayed on the canvas. Inter-client messaging was required to handle and sync interactions across the displays. The settings API was thoroughly exploited as well, as participants had to set and adjust many parameters including joints to be tracked, gestures to be recognised, proximity to the display, and speech grammar.

The study procedure was as follows. First, participants were given a short motivation about XDKinect and were introduced to the study setup. A background questionnaire then collected demographic information. In particular, they were asked to state their prior knowledge of Kinect—both as a user and developer—as well as rating their general web development, interaction design, and JavaScript/jQuery programming experience. For the rest of the study, participants worked mostly autonomously under our supervision. We supplied participants with a cheatsheet giving an overview of XDKinect's APIs, configuration options, and all supported events. All participants were provided with the same skeleton code in which they had to fill in the gaps. To focus the development process on XDKinect's features, we provided auxiliary functions to avoid implementing XDKinect-unrelated functionalities such as moving the cursor by translating the position using HTML, CSS and JavaScript. Once participants indicated that they were done, they completed a post-study questionnaire, asking them to express agreement with different statements on a 5-point Likert scale (1 = Strongly Disagree, 5 = Strongly Agree).

We recruited 12 participants (1 female) with a general background in computer science. Ages ranged from 24 to 39 years with a median of 28. Half of them had prior experience using Kinect and the other half did not. On a 7-point

	Background	Ease of Use								Time	Future Use
	Kinect	Kinect SDK	JS/jQuery	Skeleton	Gesture	Speech	Distance	Multi-User	Cross-Device	mins.	
P1	✓									55	
P3	✓									50	
P5	✓									55	
P7	✓									60	
P11	✓									45	
P12	✓									25	
P2										65	
P4										35	
P6										30	
P8										40	
P9										45	
P10										60	
Mean		1.92	3.42	4.42	4.33	4.82	4.50	4.82	4.67	47.08	4.33
Median		1	4	5	4.5	5	5	5	5	47.5	4

Table 1. Results from our study with 12 developers (first 6 had previous Kinect experience)

scale from 1 = Novice to 7 = Expert, participants reported on average medium web development ($mode = 3$), interaction design ($mode = 3$) and JS/jQuery programming experience ($mode = 5$). While some did have programming experience with the Kinect SDK, the overall rating was low ($mode = 1$).

Table 1 gives an overview of the participants' skills and their ratings. We discuss the results and our observations below.

Results

All participants were able to complete all tasks with almost no help from us. The minimum completion time amounted to 25 minutes, while the maximum completion time was 65 minutes ($mean = 47.5$, $sd = 12.5$).

In the post-study questionnaire, participants rated ease of use and effectiveness of XDKinect in different areas including skeletal tracking, gesture support and speech support, proxemic awareness, multiple users tracking, and cross-device communication. Table 1 shows mean and median ratings for ease of use. The ratings for effectiveness were very similar. All in all, the received feedback was very positive.

We analysed which current concepts and interaction dimensions had the most potential for improvement in terms of both ease of use and effectiveness. For this, we considered the lowest marks for all criteria. Speech recognition and multiple users tracking received the best marks—no one awarded a lesser grade than a 4 out of 5. Skeletal tracking, gesture and distance support also fared fairly well with a neutral 3 being the lowest mark. Cross-device communication was considered the least effective with a 1 by one participant, but was still considered easy to use with the lowest rating of 4. Although based on the principles described in [14], which were argued to be powerful and effective for many applications, some participants felt that our initial support for cross-device sessions [11] using instant messaging might be too simple.

We also compared median ease of use and effectiveness ratings between participants with and without prior knowledge of Kinect. Participants without previous experience awarded very high marks, resulting in the maximum median grade of 5 for all aspects. Participants who had at least used Kinect for gaming or development were slightly less generous, but still provided ratings in the range of 4 to 5.

We wondered to what extent users would want to use XD-Kinect in the future considering their previous background knowledge and the XDKinect development experience. Most participants were positive about this and, independent of previous Kinect experience, provided mostly high ratings between 4 and 5.

Apart from these ratings, participants were also asked to comment and make suggestions on future versions of XDKinect. Whilst not everyone provided additional feedback, the received comments were helpful for the overall assessment and identifying current drawbacks. The written feedback was analysed, grouped and ordered by frequency as in Table 2.

Comment	Count
Easy to use	5
More built-in gestures	3
Ability to define custom gestures	3
Documentation is too concise	2
Visual notification when Kinect detects the user	1
Server-side GUI to disable certain streams	1

Table 2. Users' comments and feedback

In summary, the overall feedback from the study was very promising. Both ease of use and effectiveness were consistently rated very high. In particular, 5 out of 12 participants praised XDKinect for its ease of use. The initial documentation was sufficient for all participants to complete all tasks. Still, there is room for improvement. The main criticism was the limited gesture support for both built-in gestures and the ability to define custom gestures. Currently, XDKinect only supports KinectInteraction gestures from the official Microsoft Kinect SDK. Given the flexible architecture and support for extensibility of XDKinect, gesture support could be enriched in two ways. First, the server-side could be extended with built-in gestures based on advanced gesture recognition algorithms for static and dynamic template matching and pattern recognition. Second, the client-side could be extended using simpler techniques similar to the $1-family of stroke recognisers [17]. Both support using custom templates.

CONCLUSION

In this paper, we presented XDKinect, a lightweight toolkit that facilitates the development of cross-device applications using Kinect to track interactions and respond accordingly.

The framework is adaptable to different application requirements and can be extended on both the client and the server side. XDKinect uses an event-driven architecture, where clients subscribe for information required from the server connected to a Kinect. We approached the task of developing XDKinect by re-implementing several example applications described in the literature, and also extending them with features to enable cross-device interaction, and attempting to eliminate the major technical challenges that developers currently encounter while building such applications.

Discussion

Despite the availability of several frameworks and open-source projects such as Kinected Browser [5], KinectJS and DepthJS, the idea of using whole-body gesture and speech commands as primary user input is still rarely implemented in existing applications. We argued that there are several issues and generally believe that there is a need for better experimentation methods and tools. One of the strongest features of XDKinect is its simplicity. As our study demonstrated, users found XDKinect's APIs intuitive and easy to use. Since XDKinect directly builds on web technologies, developers will benefit from existing experience in web languages and tools and be able to rapidly design and develop interactive cross-device applications. As Kinect is at the core of our framework, a number of new input dimensions are available to XDKinect applications that may better describe the use context in terms of users, devices and the environment.

Existing frameworks served as a source of inspiration for XDKinect. For example, [1] exploiting facets of proxemic interaction prompted us to introduce the stand-by and inter-active zones for the ambient display scenario, where XDKinect takes cues from the user's distance to Kinect. Moreover, cross-device interaction techniques can be implemented with only little effort due to the flexible architecture and message-exchange protocol. We assessed the role of XDKinect in the context of existing research. Table 3 presents key concepts, available features and supported interaction dimensions of selected projects extracted from the papers and proof-of-concept implementations if available. However, our idea was not to prove that one solution is better than the other. Rather, we wanted to review and compare available frameworks. This means that if a certain feature is not supported by a framework, the lack thereof may not necessarily be considered a shortcoming. Moreover, while they share many principles and concerns, it is difficult to perform a direct comparison between each solution in terms of power and expressiveness and the types of applications that can be constructed. For example, frameworks such as Proxemic Media Player [1] and Interactive Ambient Displays [16] require special motion tracking hardware, whereas Kinected Browser [5] and XDKinect use Kinect as primary interaction medium.

An 'x' stands for a supported feature (partial or complete), while '–' denotes the absence of a feature. All listed frameworks support interaction for more than one user. Device-to-device awareness, i.e. knowledge about identity, position and orientation of other devices in the environment, is best supported by proxemic interaction frameworks. Only a small set

	cross-device comm.	device-device aware.	gesture	speech	distance	orientation	identity	motion	multi-user
XDKinect	x	x	x	x	x	–	x	–	x
Kinected Browser [5]	–	–	x	x	–	–	x	–	x
jQMultiTouch [10]	–	–	x	–	–	–	–	–	x
Shared Substance [2]	x	x	x	–	–	–	x	–	x
GroupTogether [7]	x	x	–	–	x	x	x	–	x
Interact. Ambient Dis. [16]	–	–	x	–	x	x	x	x	x
Proximity Toolkit [6]	x	x	–	–	x	x	x	x	x
Proxemic Media Player [1]	–	x	–	–	x	x	x	x	x

Table 3. Main features of XDKinect and other frameworks

of frameworks support cross-device communication similar to XDKinect. Also, the combination of supporting both gesture and speech input still seems to be a relatively rare feature, as it is incorporated only in XDKinect and Kinected Browser. However, both support only a subset of user-related proxemic interaction principles compared to Proximity Toolkit and GroupTogether. These applications make use of advanced motion tracking systems or multiple Kinects and can thus react on velocity and acceleration of user movement. They also leverage user identity for personalisation and safeguarding as in the Proxemic Media Player. Enhancing XDKinect with a richer proxemic API would in principle be possible and allow for a number of exciting use scenarios, but is currently constrained by the technical limitations of Kinect.

Limitations and Future Work

While XDKinect offers a solid base for a variety of cross-device interactive applications, a number of restrictions apply. Several limitations of the implementation stem from the underlying Kinect hardware and utilised libraries. First, gesture recognition currently manifests in a high rate of false positives. For example, a half-open hand is often interpreted as a grip gesture. Second, XDKinect does not support a dictation mechanism for speech recognition, so the vocabulary to be recognised must be conveyed to the application in advance. As mentioned previously, the multi-modal API relies on the Microsoft.Speech library. Its counterpart, the System.Speech library, permits free text dictation. However, using System.Speech in conjunction with Kinect SDK results in error prone recognition, since only Microsoft.Speech API possesses a language pack specifically calibrated for Kinect hardware characteristics. A further restriction of XDKinect is the ability to track only two people in detail. One possible solution for this shortcoming would be to extend the server-side to receive data from two Kinect sensors, but these then need to be positioned at a specific angle to avoid interference, which may be in conflict with intended interaction zones.

Other limitations concern features that XDKinect's APIs currently lack. As pointed out in the user study, XDKinect offers only a restricted set of built-in gestures and no API for defining custom gestures. To alleviate this shortcoming, the server-side module could be extended to recognise a set of popular gestures, such as swipe, zoom or clap hands, while the client-side component could be extended with an interface for user-defined gestures. In the future, we plan to incorporate solutions from other Kinect research, e.g. for more efficient multi-modal input in speech and gesture interfaces [3], into the framework. In principle, any technique based on the standard Kinect SDK could be integrated with XDKinect. Additionally, our proxemic API could be extended to accommodate modalities suggested by [1]. The new Kinect sensor to be released in the near future appears to provide sufficient data required for determining user and device orientation and measuring velocity and acceleration.

In summary, despite some limitations, XDKinect is already able to support a rich set of cross-device interactive applications exploiting a variety of user and device interaction dimensions. The immediate future work comprises systematic performance evaluations and collecting more user feedback to continue improving the development experience. To this end, we have started to embed XDKinect in several student and research projects with promising initial results.

Acknowledgements

We thank the anonymous study participants for their time and feedback. Special thanks to Alexander Huber and David Ott for their support in developing and evaluating XDKinect.

REFERENCES

1. Ballendat, T., Marquardt, N., and Greenberg, S. Proxemic interaction: designing for a proximity and orientation-aware environment. In *Proc. ITS* (2010).

2. Gjerlufsen, T., Klokmose, C. N., Eagan, J., Pillias, C., and Beaudouin-Lafon, M. Shared Substance: Developing Flexible Multi-Surface Applications. In *Proc. CHI* (2011).

3. Hoste, L., and Signer, B. SpeeG2: A Speech- and Gesture-based Interface for Efficient Controller-free Text Entry. In *Proc. ICMI* (2013).

4. Jetter, H.-C., Zöllner, M., Gerken, J., and Reiterer, H. Design and Implementation of Post-WIMP Distributed User Interfaces with ZOIL. *IJHCI* (2012).

5. Liebling, D. J., and Morris, M. R. Kinected Browser: Depth Camera Interaction for the Web. In *Proc. ITS* (2012).

6. Marquardt, N., Diaz-Marino, R., Boring, S., and Greenberg, S. The proximity toolkit: prototyping proxemic interactions in ubiquitous computing ecologies. In *Proc. UIST* (2011).

7. Marquardt, N., Hinckley, K., and Greenberg, S. Cross-device interaction via micro-mobility and f-formations. In *Proc. UIST* (2012).

8. Melchior, J., Vanderdonckt, J., and Roy, P. V. A Model-Based Approach for Distributed User Interfaces. In *Proc. EICS* (2011).

9. Morris, M. R. Web on the Wall: Insights from a Multimodal Interaction Elicitation Study. In *Proc. ITS* (2012).

10. Nebeling, M., and Norrie, M. C. jQMultiTouch: Lightweight Toolkit and Development Framework for Multi-touch/Multi-device Web Interfaces. In *Proc. EICS* (2012).

11. Nebeling, M., Zimmerli, C., Husmann, M., Simmen, D., and Norrie, M. C. Information Concepts for Cross-Device Applications. In *Proc. DUI@EICS* (2013).

12. Olsen Jr., D. R. Evaluating User Interface Systems Research. In *Proc. UIST* (2007).

13. Paternò, F., and Santoro, C. A Logical Framework for Multi-Device User Interfaces. In *Proc. EICS* (2012).

14. Pierce, J. S., and Nichols, J. An Infrastructure for Extending Applications' User Experiences Across Multiple Personal Devices. In *Proc. UIST* (2008).

15. Rekimoto, J. Pick-and-Drop: A Direct Manipulation Technique for Multiple Computer Environments. In *Proc. UIST* (1997), 31–39.

16. Vogel, D., and Balakrishnan, R. Interactive Public Ambient Displays: Transitioning from Implicit to Explicit, Public to Personal, Interaction with Multiple Users. In *Proc. UIST* (2004).

17. Wobbrock, J. O., Wilson, A. D., and Li, Y. Gestures without Libraries, Toolkits or Training: A $1 Recognizer for User Interface Prototypes. In *Proc. UIST* (2007).

Interaction Design Patterns for Coherent and Re-usable Shape Specifications of Human–Robot Collaboration

Tina Mioch, Wietse Ledegang, Rosie Paulissen, Mark A. Neerincx, Jurriaan van Diggelen

TNO

Kampweg 5, 3769 DE Soesterberg, The Netherlands

{tina.mioch, wietse.ledegang, rosie.paulissen, mark.neerincx, jurriaan.vandiggelen}@tno.nl

ABSTRACT

Sharing and re-using design knowledge is a challenge for the diverse multi-disciplinary research and development teams that work on complex and highly automated systems. For this purpose, a situated Cognitive Engineering (sCE) methodology was proposed that specifies and assesses the functional user requirements with their design rationale in a coherent and concise way. This paper presents this approach for the development of human-robot collaboration, focusing on a recently added component: the application of interaction design patterns to capture and share design knowledge on the shape of the human-robot interaction (i.e., the communication level). The sCE case study in the urban search and rescue domain provided the specification and assessment of functions and shape of a team-awareness display. Twenty fire fighters participated as operator of a ground or aerial robot, in several realistic earth quake scenarios to assess the functions and shapes of this display in different settings. It showed that the functions (i.e., the task level requirements and rationale) were valid, while the shape (communication level) was (yet) suboptimal. Based on this evaluation result, a design improvement on the communication level has been proposed without the need to adjust the task-level design solution.

Author Keywords

Cognitive engineering; Interaction design patterns; Human-robot collaboration.

ACM Classification Keywords

H.5.2 User Interfaces: Evaluation/Methodology

INTRODUCTION

Urban search and rescue (USAR) missions are very stressful and consist of high-demand tasks, as the layout of the situation is often uncertain and dangerous situations can easily arise. Requirements may change during the development- and the application phase. This makes an iterative design process necessary, with continuous enhancements and evaluations, involving end-users and human factors experts. When developing personalized support systems for the USAR team, the social, cognitive, and affective state of the team members need to be taken into account. A common way to address the complexity of developing such systems is to use a cognitive engineering approach (We refer to Norman [16] and Vicente [23] for an overview).

In the NIFTi and TRADR project[1], we develop systems to improve human-robot cooperation in the USAR domain. Robots are part of the USAR team, share a common goal with their human team members, and have their own capabilities and responsibilities. This means they function as full-fledged team members. Yearly evaluations in a realistic environment with end-users are executed to be able to make sure the robots are built to be used in the context of the USAR domain by the eventual end-users.

When developing these kinds of systems, an iterative development process is necessary. After each cycle, the user requirements the system needs to fulfill are revisited, leading to validations and refinements. So far, the acquisition, specification and validation of requirements have been mainly focused on the functional level. However, the actual shape (i.e., the "look, feel and hearing" in the human-technology communication) of these functions affects their effectiveness substantially. Design specifications and assessments should therefore explicitly address both the functional and communication level [15]. In general, the cognitive engineering methodology should clearly distinguish two levels of specification, the function (or task) and shape (or communication) level, and explicating the design rationale on both levels. So far, a re-usable specification of the shape, with explicit and coherent relations to functional requirements and their design rationale, is lacking. This leads to the following research question:

- How to specify and evaluate the communication level of human-robot collaboration in a situated cognitive engineering methodology that already provides a sound task level specification and evaluation?

In this paper, we present a methodology for situated cognitive engineering, focusing on the application of reusable interaction design patterns for specifying and assessing the shape of human-robot interaction (i.e., the communication level). We

---

[1] www.nifti.eu, www.tradr-project.eu

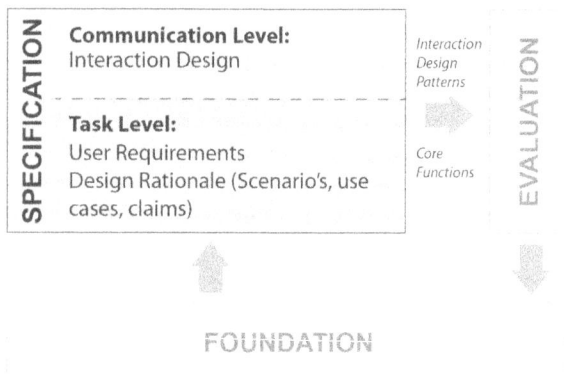

Figure 1. sCE design process.

demonstrate how the methodology is applied for the development of human-robot cooperation in the urban search and rescue domain, including the evaluation of the human-robot collaboration at the task and the communication-level.

SITUATED COGNITIVE ENGINEERING METHODOLOGY

The situated Cognitive Engineering (sCE) methodology is an iterative human-centered development process, aiming at an incremental development of advanced technology [14]. It consists of an iterative process of generation, evaluation, and refinement, and is based on earlier views on Cognitive Engineering (e.g., [11]). Figure 1 shows the general structure of the sCE methodology, consisting of three components: the foundation entails operational, human factors, and technological analyses to derive a sound and practical design rationale, the specification and maintenance of the requirements baseline, and the evaluation by means of simulation or a prototype, to validate and refine the requirements baseline. In the first component, foundational knowledge is described to identify actors, objectives, and contexts of the system and the (task) environment. This paper focuses on the second component, distinguishing two levels of specification: the task and communication level [15]. We choose for a minimal approach to keep the specification concise, whereas others propose more extensive abstraction levels (e.g., the four levels of the Unifying Reference Framework: task and concepts, abstract user interface, concrete user interface and final user interface, [4]).

Task level

The task level specification consists of the construction and maintenance of the requirements baseline, and the general design rationale that consists of the core functions, claims, and scenarios & use cases. The *core functions* are derived from the analyses of the first component. For each core function, one or more testable *claims* on its operational effects have to be specified; such a claim can be assessed unambiguously in the evaluation process. Both positive and negative claims can be specified. Furthermore, for each core function, one or more *requirements* have to be specified for the future system (i.e., what the system must do). *Use cases* describe the general behavioural requirements for software systems, and have

a specific specification format. According to the methodology, each use case should explicitly refer to one or more requirements and each requirement to one or more claims.

The requirements baseline can subsequently be justified according to its associated (task-level) claims. So far, the sCE methodology focused on the design and evaluation of the functional or task-level aspects of human-technology collaboration. This includes the mapping of situated user goals, information needs, and support needs to (adaptive) technology functions, information provisions and dialogue acts [15]. In this way, the system's functions and information provision are specified or assessed (i.e., the task level, such as user fit, work context and information needs conformance). However, human-robot collaboration should also be established well at the communication level, such as consistency, feedback and mode awareness, interaction load and user control [15].

Communication level

For the control of the functions and the presentation of the information, we propose to use so-called *interaction design patterns*, providing the designer a structured format to capture and share design knowledge for a recurring problem in a specific context with a common language for multidisciplinary teams. Similar to the justification of requirements via (task-level) claims, the interaction design patterns are justified via so-called (communication-level) premises.

Interaction design patterns have recently received considerable attention in the field of human computer interaction as a means for developing and communicating design knowledge to support good design [5]. Design patterns can be defined as follows: a pattern describes a problem that occurs over and over again in our environment, and then describes the core of the solution to that problem, in such a way that you can use this solution a million times over, without ever doing it the same way twice [1]. Or in other words, a pattern provides a structured format to capture and share design knowledge. It describes the core (key invariants) of a good design solution to a recurring problem in a specific context [5]. A pattern language includes a collection of such patterns organized in a meaningful way.

Alexander's [1] philosophy of constructive, coherent and meaningful design in architecture, inspired the development of pattern languages in many other domains and application fields. These include, for example, Software Design Patterns [7] in the field of software engineering, Activity Patterns in the field of activity and ethnographic research, User Interface Design Patterns [17, 22], Interaction Design Patterns [3] and Design Patterns for sociality in human-robot interaction [12] in the field of Human-Computer Interaction.

In general, patterns provide practice-based solutions accompanied by a theoretical account. Design patterns emerge from 'best practices', specifying solutions of how a problem can be solved. Theory is necessary for the justification of a chosen design patterns. Theory can provide the rationale (e.g. a theoretical account) of why the solution works in a specific context, and what trade-offs are involved [5].

COMMUNICATION LEVEL

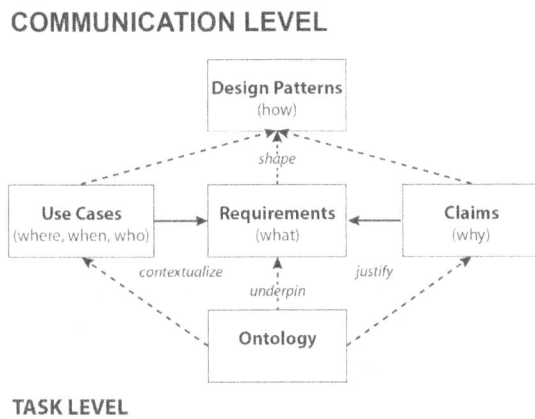

Figure 2. The sCE specification model.

Furthermore, a design pattern should show examples of successful implementation in applications. These examples play an important role in the validation of patterns. Successful implementation in applications in practice provides empirical evidence for the pattern's validity. Design Patterns have to deal with the dynamic aspects of an interaction, which could be represented, for example, by exemplifying storyboards [3].

Patterns can include different levels of scale and abstraction, varying from a general overview of the problem to specific characteristics for the solution.

Alexander's [1] patterns contain a unique name, the patterns context (including relation to other patterns), description of the design problem, design solution, how to implement the solution, rationale of why the design solution is good and in what context the pattern can be applied. Dearden and Finlay [5] argue in their review that the discussion about a universal pattern format is still ongoing. We propose to integrate interaction design patterns into current functional specifications of use cases, user requirements and claims. As a complement, they should cover the embodiment (shape) of the requirements within the given context of the use cases. Therefore, we propose it should (at least) consist of title and ranking, the design problem (what, interaction intention), the context (related use case), the design rationale (why does it work, trade-offs, premises), the design solution (how), the related patterns (at the same/different level of scale and abstraction, other context), and examples.

For an overview on how design patterns fit into the specification phase of the sCE methodology, please see Figure 2.

EXAMPLE DESIGN FOR HUMAN-ROBOT COOPERATION IN USAR MISSIONS

In the following, we will describe how behaviours and functions for a human-robot cooperation system are translated into reusable interaction design patterns at the communication level. To do this, we give an example specification of each step in the sCE methodology. We first shortly outline the theoretical foundation to establish the design rationale, followed by the specification of requirements, claims, and a suggestion for a concrete human-robot design example in the urban search and rescue domain. This design example is then improved as a first step towards a generic design pattern.

Foundation

Operational demands

After a disaster, robots can be needed for a safe and conscientious reconnaissance of the area. The scenario that has been specified with the end-users in the NIFTi project is an earthquake site, in which the rescue team's goal is to safely extract victims. It is suspected that several people are still alive in the area. The team needs to perform reconnaissance of the area, and identify and triage victims.

Human factors knowledge

Developing adequate situation awareness proves to be difficult during the reconnaissance, recover, and rescue operations of human-robot teams in disaster areas. Robot operators spend up to 60% of their time attempting to establish and maintain situation awareness, leaving little time for the operation of the robot or the visual search for victims. In addition to the need for cognitive load reduction, there is a clear need of theoretically and empirically founded, design proposals for integrated, context-sensitive situation maps [9, 10]. In addition, team awareness needs to be supported. In the NIFTi project, the team consists of at least two robotic team members (UGV, Unmanned Ground Vehicle, and UAV, Unmanned Aerial Vehicle), and 4 human team members (UGV-operator, UAV-operator, in-field rescuer, and mission commander). All these actors can be sources of valuable information to the professionals that work in this environment, but forwarding all information to everybody will cause unmanageable overload and interruption.

Technological innovation

All team members have access to the team awareness display. The team awareness system is tailored to support teams of professionals in their complex task environments [6]. Such environments are characterized by a large number of humans, networked computing devices, sensors, and possibly robots working together. All these actors can be sources of valuable information to the professionals that work in this environment, but forwarding all information to everybody will cause unmanageable overload and interruptions. To make optimal use of the vast amounts of digitally stored information we need a system that delivers the Right Message at the Right Moment in the Right Modality, or $(RM)^3$ [20].

Such a system could be based on a set of extendible OWL ontologies which specify the formats in which information can be represented and shared.

In addition, the envisioned system can pro-actively send information to a user, but a user can also request information. By allowing a user to express his or her information needs, the system can return appropriate pieces of existing information, or even actively create new relevant information (e.g. by asking other users or sensors to share information).

The system adapts its information supply to its user. For example, people in different roles receive information that fits

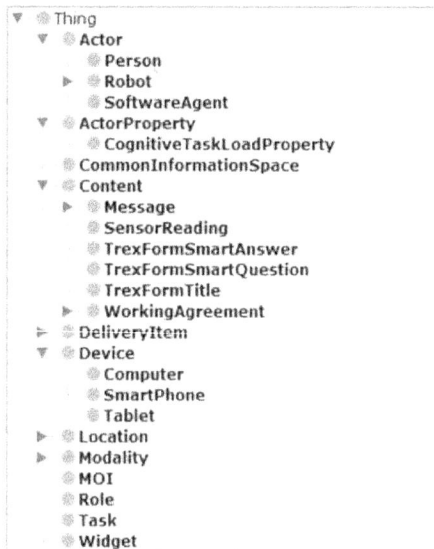

Figure 3. Part of the NIFTi Ontology.

Step nr.	Description	Requ.nr.
1	In-field rescuer hears victim scream, it appears to come from no-go area.	
2	In-field rescuer adds SUSPECTED victim to team awareness display and adds 'smart question'.	R048, R097
3	The Mission commander sees the SUSPECTED victim on the team awareness display, and gives the UGV operator command to investigate the victim.	
4	UGV-operator has a look at the current information and the 'smart question' concerning victim in no-go area.	R098
5	UGV-operator indicates waypoint and UGV proceeds to area.	R085

Table 1. Example use case for in-field rescuer and UGV cooperation.

their task description, people at a certain location receive information which is relevant for that location, and people with a high cognitive task load receive less information because they are assumed to have less information processing capacity.

The system supports multiple devices, such as visual displays (e.g. stationary computers, tablet computers, surface tables, smart phones), auditory devices (e.g. headphones), or tactile devices (e.g. a tactile vest). This means that the system must be capable of choosing the most appropriate interface, depending on type of information and the user.

The information that is shared between users can be facts, i.e. information describing the current situation. Another type of information is policies (information that describes the conditions under which collaboration takes place). An example of a policy is a no-go area. Such a policy may have its origin in a mutual working agreement, an order from the commanding officer, or a law. Policy-monitoring agents ensure that appropriate action is taken when the user breaks a policy, e.g. by notifying the user, or by preventing access.

Specification
Ontology
In information science, an ontology is defined as a specification of a conceptualization [8]. It describes the terms and

Requ.nr.	Name	Description	Step nr.
R097	Identifying and adding information needs.	The NIFTi system shall present up-to-date and combined overviews of available and missing information that infield rescuers and robot operators can adjust and complement (e.g., frames for victim's status that can be edited in a structured way).	Step 2
R098	Communicating information needs.	When a need for a specific information object has been identified (i.e., a "known unknown"), the NIFTi system shall notify the appropriate team member who can acquire this information (e.g., based on location and capabilities).	Step 4

Table 2. Example of a specification of requirements.

Claim nr.	C006
Name	Improvement of shared situation awareness
Description	Each team member has insight in the tasks, plans, and capabilities of the other team members. This also includes that 'unknowns' are made explicit, and that the 'right' team member knows (according to his capabilities) that there is still some information missing.
Positive	The team members can see the plans and tasks of the robot, which increases the trust in the system [trust questionnaire]. More optimal task distribution possible, as team members can see which 'unknowns' fit their capabilities [performance: time it takes for a user to act on new 'unknowns'?].
Negative	Having access to a team display in which a lot of team information is presented might lead to too much information, which leads to a higher workload to process the information. [workload questionnaire; heart rate and GSR measurement when processing the information]; [usability questionnaire on system]
Relations	R097, R098

Table 3. Example of a specification of a claim.

concepts and relations that are used in a certain domain. As argued in [19], ontologies are used for a variety of purposes:

- Communication between people with different needs and viewpoints arising from their different context. Domain knowledge of the fire fighters can be shared with a multi-discplinary team, supporting common and consistent understanding.

- Inter-operability between systems (e.g. databases using the same database schema's). Human-robot systems consist of many components which can have dedicated (sometimes temporarily) databases.

- System engineering benefits:

  - Re-usability. A shared understanding is the basis of the formal encoding of the important entities in a computer.

  - Automatic verification. A formally specified ontology can be used to automatically detect inconsistencies, serving as a verification of the domain analysis (e.g., for the identification of a fire or triage of a victim).

  - Specification. A shared understanding can assist the process of identifying requirements and defining a specification in IT system design.

Based on literature research, the scenario analyses and discussions with NIFTi end-users, we formulated an ontology for the human-robot collaboration in the NIFTi-project. A part of the NIFTi ontology is presented in Figure 3.

Use Case

The use cases provide a (formal) contextualization (conditions, scope) in which the requirements are applicable (*when* the requirements apply). For a simplified example of the specification of a use case, see Table 1.

Requirements

The requirements describe *what* the system shall do. For a simplified example, see Table 2.

Claims

The claims provide the justification behind the requirements (i.e., *why* the requirement is important). Claims should always refer to evaluation methods or tools (such as performance time measurements and user questionnaires). For a brief example, see Table 3.

Interaction Design Patterns

The interaction design patterns provide a (formal) description of the shape of the requirements, as shown in Figure 2. The specification of the design patterns is explained below.

Name The name of the design pattern should provide a meaningful description that indicates the essence of the pattern.

Ranking The ranking should indicate the validity of the patterns premise. It can help the reader to distinguish early pattern ideas from patterns confirmed in practice [3].

Design problem The design problem describes the design problem in terms of the interaction intention (the effect on the user and/or user interaction with the system and/or other parties). The intention of an interaction can be extracted from the user requirements.

Use case, requirement, claim Here, the corresponding use case, requirements, and claim should be specified.

Context The context describes the characteristics of the tasks, the users, and the environment for which the pattern can be applied. This should provide the designer insight in when the design pattern can be used, and when the design pattern is less suitable. The use cases already provide the situational factors (e.g., dialogue partner(s), physical and social context, interaction platform, and dialogue context) that influence the design solution (specific embodiment of the dialogue). The design pattern should only list the contextual characteristics that determine in what situation the design solution can be applied.

Design solution The design solution provides a concrete description of the solution for the design problem. This encompasses the specific shape of the dialogue by describing what characteristics express the intended interaction within the given context, e.g., which verbal and non-verbal communication should be used, which dialogue rules should be followed. Only the core of the solution should be described, references to other relevant patterns can be used.

Design pattern level According to Woods [24], interface design can be assessed at different levels: workspace, views,

forms, fragments, atoms and pixels, where each of these levels builds on the design decisions of the level below it. Accordingly, we describe Interaction Design Patterns at these levels of abstraction, although especially the high-levels are more useful to describe generally applicable and reusable design patterns. Furthermore, patterns at different levels of abstraction can be related in a hierarchical way, e.g., a general high-level pattern describes the sharing and handling of (un)knowns, while a lower level child-pattern covers the specifics for interactions on a mobile phone, tablet or touch table.

Design rationale The rationale provides insight in how the design pattern works, why it works and how it is based on underlying principles and mechanisms. It provides a convincing argumentation on the effects of the chosen design solution, including trade-offs. It includes premises that may need empirical validation.

Examples The examples should show successful uses of the pattern (e.g., best practices). It shows how the pattern can manifest itself differently in various 'real-life' applications.

Related patterns Links to any related patterns should be mentioned here. For example, a parent pattern (similar interaction intention, higher in the abstraction hierarchy), sister pattern (similar interaction intention, same abstraction level) and/or other relating patterns (different interaction intention, but in another way related to context and/or product characteristics of the design solution).

For the NIFTi team awareness system, the following two example Interaction Design Patterns are worked out: Explicit unknowns and Area policies. It must be noted that the two examples both consist of a set of individual interaction design patterns that together form the total design solution.

1. Explicit unknowns (for a screenshot of the design, see Figure 4). In the NIFTi team awareness system, users have the possibility to identify information that is unknown or indirectly submit a request for information to others.

   (a) Raise an explicit unknown
   (b) Notification that an Explicit Unknown is raised, based on relevant stakeholder and priority (specified in Table 4)
   (c) Answering an Explicit Unknown
   (d) Notification that the Explicit Unknown is answered

2. Area policies (for a screenshot of the design, see Figure 5). In the NIFTi team awareness system, an area with a specific policy (e.g. no-go area) can be defined and visualized on the digital map, while its policy will be enforced to in-field users of the system.

   (a) Creation of an Area Policy
   (b) Visualization of an Area Policy
   (c) Enforcement of an Area Policy

In Table 4, the interaction design pattern is worked out for 'Notification that an Explicit Unknown is raised, based on relevant stakeholder and priority'. Note that the interaction design pattern worked out in Table 4 does not concern the total Explicit Unknown design solution, but only a subset.

Title	Notification that an Explicit Unknown is raised, based on relevant stakeholder and priority
Ranking	1b
Design problem (what)	Make other relevant stakeholder aware of required information that is missing, its location and priority
Use case (context, use when)	Person1 finds a victim and creates a new victim icon at the specific location on the map display. But, because he cannot (completely) fill the required information fields, he raises an Explicit Unknown to make other people aware of the information need. Since the information request concerns an important triage, a medic is notified with high priority.
Requirement	- Identifying and adding information needs - Communicating information needs
Claim	- Improvement of shared situation awareness
Design solution (how)	- An explicit unknown is visualized with a question-mark icon, which is presented both at the relevant information field and at the specific location on the map. - If an explicit unknown is relevant to the user the question-mark icon on the map display is colored red. If the explicit unknown is relevant to other stakeholders, the icon is colored grey. - If an explicit unknown is relevant to the user and has high priority the icon is enlarged, compared to the normal icon size.
Design rationale (why, premises)	By showing the explicit unknown with a recognizable and dedicated element of information at a specific location on the map, it becomes clear where there is a request for information, to whom it applies, and what is the level of priority.
Design pattern level (workspace, views, forms, fragments, atoms, pixels)	Forms
Example, files, selected	
Related patterns	1a - Raise an explicit unknown 1c - Answering an Explicit Unknown 1d - Notification that the Explicit Unknown is answered

Table 4. Interaction Design Pattern for '1b - Notification that an Explicit Unknown is raised, based on relevant user and priority'

EVALUATION

Setup of evaluation
An evaluation has been conducted, in which a realistic team task in the urban search and rescue domain was executed by fire fighters in cooperation with robots. Each participant performed the experiment once, either in the role of the robot (UGV or UAV) operator, mission commander, or as an infield rescuer. There were 5 runs, with 20 participants. The participants were mostly male professional fire fighters (with the exception of one female fire fighter).

Task
The participants were asked to execute the following scenario: An earthquake occurred. The buildings in the area have

Figure 4. Explicit unknowns.

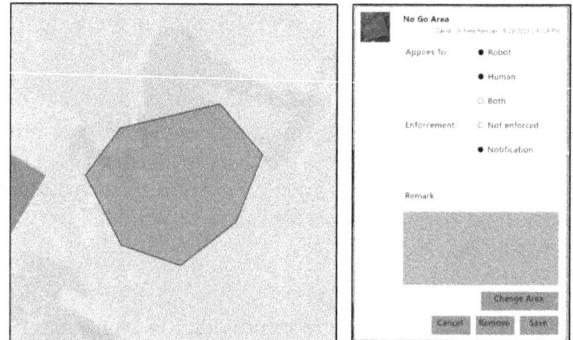

Figure 5. Area policies.

collapsed. One of the building has been a hospital, with suspected radioactive material present. Also, it is suspected that several people are still in the area, probably alive. Human victims need to be found as fast as possible, and the situation needs to be evaluated.

The scenario was a team reconnaissance task; the team consisted of an unmanned ground vehicle (UGV), the operator of the UGV, an infield rescuer, a mission commander, an unmanned aerial vehicle (UAV), and the operator of the UAV.

For the validation of the design patterns, eighteen of the twenty expert users (UGV and UAV operators, mission commanders, and in-field rescuers) answered a questionnaire on the interaction design patterns 'Explicit Unkowns' and 'Area Policy' of the team awareness system. In the questionnaire, statements were rated with 5-point rating scales (fully disagree to fully agree) on both task and communication levels.

Materials
In the evaluation, two robots were used: an unmanned ground vehicle (UGV) and an unmanned aerial vehicle (UAV), see Figure 6. For more details on the specification, see [18]. The UGV, see Figure 6, is a custom-made robot for situational assessment during the early phases of a disaster response [2]. The operator of the robot has access to a variety of information sources, in a multi-screen multimodal user interface set-up. The views include UGV Operator Control Unit (OCU [13]), and tactical views for team-level situation awareness (the team awareness display [21]). The infield rescuer also had the possibility to add information to the team-level situation awareness tool, by means of a tablet, see Figure 7. In addition, the robot operator was asked to fill in the experienced workload at that moment into a PDA.

RESULTS

Figure 6. The UGV and UAV in the scenario.

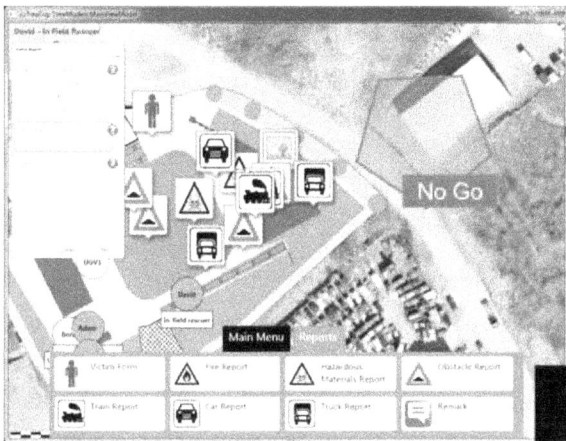

Figure 7. Screenshot of team awareness display.

The subjective evaluation aimed to assess the validity of the team awareness design specifications on 'Explicit Unknown' and 'Area Policy'. In the evaluation, 18 subjects rated statements on the task- and communication level design specifications with an ordinal 5-point Likert-scale (1 - fully disagree to 5 - fully agree). A design specification is assumed to be acceptable for ratings above neutral (rating above 3). Whereas all average ratings were between 2.8 and 3.8, here only the most noticeable deviations from average will be highlighted.

Explicit Unknown

Task level The results on 'Explicit Unknowns' indicated that 11 out of 18 subjects rated the task level being acceptable. More specifically, 11 out of 18 subjects rated the task level acceptable on the fact that 'unknowns' can be made explicit by raising an information request. For only 5 out of 18 subjects it was clear enough where attention was drawn when help was needed, enhancing their mental picture of the situation (task level).

Communication level The communication level of the design solution was rated acceptable by 12 out of 18 subjects. More specifically, 11 out of 18 subjects rated the communication level above 3 regarding the fact that an 'explicit unknown' can intuitively be raised with the question-mark button next to the relevant information field. For only 5 out of 18 subjects

it was clear enough that the color of the question-mark symbol indicated who is responsible to answer on the information request.

Area Policy

Task level The results on 'Area Policy' indicated that 10 out of 18 subjects rated the task level being acceptable. More specifically, 11 out of 18 subjects rated the task level acceptable on the fact that a working agreement can be indicated explicitly on the map to share with team members. Only 7 out of 18 subjects rated above 3 on both the understanding how working agreements can be overruled whenever necessary, and on the type of enforcement and to whom it applies.

Communication level The communication level of the design solution was rated acceptable by 12 out of 18 subjects. More specifically, 11 out of 18 subjects appreciated that a pop-up notification indicates that a working agreement area has been reached.

It must be noted that the three UAV operators, who had less time to familiarize with the system for their highly dynamic task, rated both design solutions overall lower than the other users. For both design solutions, only 1 out of 3 subjects rated the task- and communication level being acceptable.

DISCUSSION AND CONCLUSION

This paper presented a study on cognitive engineering and the integration of communication level specifications into a "functional" requirements baseline. In general, this approach provided concise and delimited specifications, which are traceable in the prototype and, consequently, distinctive in the evaluation. Componentes to maintain or improve could be well-identified in a user evaluations. More specifically, design specifications at a task level could be validated, while the evaluation showed sub-optimal results because of a moderate communication level.

So-called Interaction Design Patterns proved to provide a useful language to specify the communication level, complementary to the task level design specification. This can be illustrated with an example from the team awareness design specification validation on Explicit Unknowns. It is observed that on the one hand users appreciate that an 'unknown' can be made explicit by raising an information request to a responsible team member (task-level). On the other hand, the color use of the question-mark symbol, indicating who is responsible to answer an information request (communication), is not clear enough. In this example it is clear that the design specification on functionality level satisfies, while an iterative improvement on the communication level may be required. A suggested design improvement is to extend the visualization of the Explicit Unknown icon on the map with source- and destination information (see Figure 8), which obviously requires validation.

Interaction Design Patterns are complementary to the traditional task level design specification, and therefore facilitate a more specific validation of design specifications by splitting task level and communication level. It facilitates the validation of interaction design solutions, because clear components are constructed for evaluation, based on 'premises', dis-

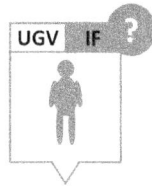

Figure 8. Suggested Design improvement for the 'explicit unknown' icon. A source- and destination information is added to make it clearer who is responsible for answering an information request.

tinguishing the communication-level effectiveness from the task-level effectiveness (i.e., 'claims'). It benefits from the structured format to capture and share design knowledge. In this respect, the gap between validation and design specification with a differentiation of functional and communication level can be narrowed. Furthermore, in this way, we are developing a library of (validated) interaction design patterns for human-robot collaboration that will be shared, re-used and further developed in other projects (e.g., from the NIFTi-project to the TRADR-project that focuses on persistent human-robot team performance during all disaster response phases).

During the NIFTI project, both the method of situated Cognitive Engineering (sCE) and the sCE tool (www.scetool.nl), developed within TNO, have been improved and extended. It allows designers to generate and test interaction shapes in an structured way, aiming at concise and coherent specifications that can be easily shared, refined and re-used. The Specification phase of the sCE tool has been extended to allow documentation of the Interaction Design Patterns such that incrementally a validated Design Pattern Library can be built for future projects in which interaction aspects play an important role.

ACKNOWLEDGMENTS

This research is supported by the EU FP7 ICT Programmes, Project 247870 (NIFTi) and Project 609763 (TRADR). We would like to thank the fire fighters of FDDo (Dortmund, Germany) and of Prato, Italy, for their support.

REFERENCES

1. Alexander, C., Ishikawa, S., and Silverstein, M. *A Pattern Language: Towns, Buildings, Construction.* Center for Environmental Structure Berkeley, Calif: Center for Environmental Structure series. Oxford University Press, USA, 1977.

2. Balmer, P., Lê, H., and Terrien, G.and Tomatis, N. Platform specification and design. Tech. Rep. Public Deliverable DR 6.1.1, EU FP7 NIFTi / ICT-247870, 2010.

3. Borchers, J. O. A pattern approach to interaction design. *AI & SOCIETY 15*, 4 (2001), 359–376.

4. Calvary, G., Coutaz, J., Thevenin, D., Limbourg, Q., Bouillon, L., and Vanderdonckt, J. A unifying reference framework for multi-target user interfaces. *Interacting with Computers 15*, 3 (jun 2003), 289–308.

5. Dearden, A., and Finlay, J. Pattern languages in hci: A critical review. *Human–computer interaction 21*, 1 (2006), 49–102.

6. Diggelen, J. v., and Neerincx, M. A. Electronic partners that diagnose, guide and mediate space crew's social, cognitive and affective processes. In *Proceedings of Measuring Behaviour* (2010), 73–76.

7. Gamma, E., Helm, R., Johnson, R., and Vlissides, J. Design patterns: Elements of reusable object-oriented software. *Addinson-Wesley Longman Inc* (1995).

8. Gruber, T. R., et al. A translation approach to portable ontology specifications. *Knowledge acquisition 5*, 2 (1993), 199–220.

9. Gunawan, L. T., Alers, H., Brinkman, W., and Neerincx, M. A. Distributed collaborative situation-map making for disaster response. *Interacting with Computers 23*, 4 (2011), 308–316.

10. Gunawan, L. T., Fitrianie, S., Yang, Z., Brinkman, W., and Neerincx, M. A. Travelthrough: A participatory-based guidance system for traveling through disaster areas. In *Proceeding of Computer Human Interaction, CHI 2012* (Austin, Texas, USA, May 2012), 241–250.

11. Hollnagel, E., and Woods, D. D. Cognitive systems engineering: new wine in new bottles. *Int. J. Man-Mach. Stud. 18*, 6 (June 1983), 583–600.

12. Kahn, P. H., Freier, N. G., Kanda, T., Ishiguro, H., Ruckert, J. H., Severson, R. L., and Kane, S. K. Design patterns for sociality in human-robot interaction. In *Proceedings of the 3rd ACM/IEEE international conference on Human robot interaction*, ACM (2008), 97–104.

13. Larochelle, B., Kruijff, G., Smets, N., Mioch, T., and Groenewegen, P. Establishing human situation awareness using a multi-modal operator control unit in an urban search & rescue human-robot team. In *RO-MAN, 2011 IEEE*, IEEE (2011), 229–234.

14. Neerincx, M., and Lindenberg, J. Situated cognitive engineering for complex task environments. In *Naturalistic Decision Making and Macrocognition*, J. M. C. Schraagen, L. Militello, T. Ormerod, , and R. Lipshitz, Eds. Aldershot, UK: Ashgate, 2008.

15. Neerincx, M. A. Situated cognitive engineering for crew support in space. *Personal Ubiquitous Computing 15*, 5 (June 2011), 445–456.

16. Norman, D. A. Cognitive engineering. In *User centered system design; new perspectives on human-computer interaction*, D. A. Norman and S. W. Draper, Eds. L. Erlbaum Associates Inc., 1986, 31–61.

17. Tidwell, J. *Designing interfaces.* O'Reilly, 2010.

18. Tretyakov, V., Winzer, J., and Worst, R. Platform manufacturing and sensor integration (uav). Tech. Rep. Public Deliverable DR 6.1.2b, EU FP7 NIFTi / ICT-247870, 2011.

19. Uschold, M., Gruninger, M., et al. Ontologies: Principles, methods and applications. *Knowledge engineering review 11*, 2 (1996), 93–136.

20. van Diggelen, J., Grootjen, M., Ubink, E. M., van Zomeren, M., and Smets, N. J. Content-based design and implementation of ambient intelligence applications. In *Ambient Intelligence-Software and Applications*. Springer International Publishing, 2013, 1–8.

21. van Diggelen, J., van Drimmelen, K., Heuvelink, A., Kerbusch, P. J., Neerincx, M. A., van Trijp, S., Ubink, E. M., and van der Vecht, B. Mutual empowerment in mobile soldier support. *Journal of Battlefield Technology 15*, 1 (2012), 11.

22. Van Welie, M., Van Der Veer, G. C., and Eliëns, A. Patterns as tools for user interface design. In *Tools for Working with Guidelines*, C. Farenc and J. Vanderdonckt, Eds. Springer, 2001, 313–324.

23. Vicente, K. J. *Cognitive Work Analysis: Toward Safe, Productive, and Healthy Computer-Based Work.* Lawrence Erlbaum Associates, New Jersey, April 1999.

24. Woods, D. D. The theory and practice of representation design in the computer medium (ver 4.2). Tech. rep., Cognitive Systems Engineering Laboratory, The Ohio State University, 1997.

Multi-Models-Based Engineering of Collaborative Systems: Application to Collision Avoidance Operations for Spacecraft

Célia Martinie, Eric Barboni, David Navarre, Philippe Palanque, Racim Fahssi
ICS-IRIT, University of Toulouse
118, route de Narbonne
F-31062, Toulouse, France
{lastname}@irit.fr

Erwann Poupart, Eliane Cubero-Castan
CNES
Centre Spatial de Toulouse
18, avenue Edouard Belin
F-31401 Toulouse Cedex 9, France
{Firstname.Lastname}@cnes.fr

ABSTRACT

The work presented in this paper is based on a synergistic approach [1] integrating models of operators' tasks (described using the HAMSTERS notation) with models of the interactive system (described using the ICO notation) they are using. This synergistic approach makes it possible to bring together two usually independent (but complementary) representations of the same world. Even though supported by modeling and simulation tools, previous work in this area was rather theoretic focusing on concepts and principles in order to articulate this synergistic use of the models. The current article extends this line of research to address groupware applications. These extensions are performed on HAMSTERS notation in order to describe activities involving multiple users dealing with information flow, knowledge they are required to master and communication protocol (synchronous or asynchronous). Other extensions are performed on PetShop tool (supporting the ICO notation) in order to model and execute local and distant groupware applications. These extensions have been brought together by a more complex synergistic module bringing the two views together. Lastly, these extensions have been used for the modelling, design, and construction of a groupware system dedicated to collision avoidance of spacecraft with space debris. This case study is used to assess the applicability of the contributions and to identify paths for future work.

Author Keywords

Task and interactive systems models, CSCW, groupware, space systems.

ACM Classification Keywords

D.2.2 [Software] Design Tools and Techniques - *Computer-*

aided software engineering (CASE), H.5.3 Group and Organization Interfaces.

INTRODUCTION

The evolution of computer use from one computer for several persons to many computers for one person could have been the end of multi-user computing. However, the widespread of internet and the rise of social computing has demonstrated that dealing with single user applications is nowadays part of history. Designing interactive systems thus requires most of the time to need to address the needs of group of users involved in common tasks for which the communication, cooperation and production is mediated by computers. Despite this undeniable situation, most of the research contributions in the area of interactive systems engineering still focus on single user applications. This is easily understandable as multi-users application are far more difficult to build than single user ones. This difficulty comes from different sources:

- The difficulty to gather and understand the requirements as well as the need of the users;

- The difficulties to address the required communication infrastructures in order to allow both synchronous and asynchronous communication between the users;

- The difficulty to ensure usability of these applications that are used jointly by different users (with different characteristics and needs) and under different environmental conditions (time zones, seasons, light, sound, …);

- The difficulty to ensure the reliability of these computing systems involving underlying communication mechanisms, networks…

This paper aims at proposing a model-based approach for the design of usable and reliable collaborative applications.

To address the usability issue we propose a notation for describing collaborative task i.e. tasks having group of users trying to achieve common goals. This notation extends current models such as GTA [25] or CTT [18]. As for CTT, which the most mature notation in that domain, extensions refine further the task types (see section 3), adds explicit representation of information and knowledge required for performing the tasks and does not require the construction of an "artificial" task model describing the collaboration.

To address reliability, we propose the use of the ICO formalism and its related tool PetShop extended in order to edit and execute models of interactive distributed applications. This work takes advantage of previous work done with ICO notation to formally specify distributed applications over Corba middleware [2]. Following the philosophy presented in [1] we propose also a synergistic approach integrating models of operators' tasks (described using the extended HAMSTERS notation) with models of the interactive system (described using the ICO notation).

These various elements are successively presented in the paper. This presentation is followed by the description of the application of the approach on a real life case study from the space domain. This case study consisted in designing and modeling a collaborative collision avoidance management application for the CNES (French Space Government Agency) Orbit Computation Center. Current existing and in use applications are not supported by dedicated tools for collaboration. They are distributed over many time zones, involve multi-national teams and aim at forecasting and avoiding collisions between spacecraft and space debris.

RELATED WORK
In the field of Computer Supported Cooperative Work (CSCW) and groupware, many contributions deal with classification and properties of groupware applications [20], but also with guidelines about how to design and evaluate the usability of such applications [6]. Another thread of work addresses user interfaces, interaction techniques and underlying computer-based tools for supporting collaborative activities [23].

The engineering of groupware applications is also represented amongst the scientifics contributions. For example, Jakobsen et al. propose a collaborative development environment for software development [11] while Bates et al. propose an applicative framework for integrating collaborative functionalities [3]. Wu and Graham [26] propose an architectural design framework for software architectures of collaborative applications based on the concept of workspace while Greenberg et al. [22] propose a toolkit for the construction of real-time groupware.

Model-based approaches for engineering groupware applications can be of several types. Workflow approaches such as YAWL [24] target at describing and simulating workflow activities systems and subsystems while some recent approaches such as BPEL4People try to take into account user's activities [10]. Task-model based approaches target at describing collaborative activities involving group of users collaborating to achieve a common goal [25] [18] [12]. UML-based and tool supported approaches have also

been proposed [8] to support development of collaborative applications. However, while the firstly mentioned contributions focus on user interface and interaction techniques and the later ones on workflows and activities of group of users, none of them propose a solution to bring those two worlds together and address in one single framework these two threads of work that are required to develop usable groupware. Indeed, while efficiency of interaction can be addressed through user interface design, the effectiveness of communication tools and interaction techniques can only be addressed by exhaustive representation of tasks to be performed by collaborating users.

AN INTEGRATED ENVIRONMENT SUPPORTING THE CO-EXECUTION OF TASKS AND GROUPWARE
We propose a synergistic use of task and system models for ensuring consistency, coherence and conformance between collaborative activities and their associated distributed user interfaces and applications. In order to reach this research goal, several extensions that have been made to an existing framework previously introduced in [1]. The presented framework and tool suite is composed of:

- A modeling and software development environment for interactive systems (Petshop).

- A modeling and simulation CASE tool for engineering user tasks (HAMSTERS).

- A synergistic module for linking system behavioral models and user task model, which then enables their co-execution (Synergistic module).

Petshop extensions
The very early versions of Petshop tool followed a Corba approach to handle communication between models [2]. Naming Service and Interface Repository were mandatory parts of Corba to make communication possible. But as Corba implies a time consuming workflow (IDL compilation, IDL registration), the Naming Service and Interface Repository were centralized and then the prototyping activities were complex.

As Petshop is Java based, we naturally studied Java RMI in order to reduce the compilation phase (as it was embedded in Java). However, the centralized registration issues remained. In order to ease deployment and more flexibility, the communication layer was updated to follow a peer to peer approach, where each Petshop instance is serving models they run. The proposed implementation uses the Ivy bus. The Ivy protocol[1] was initially designed for broadcasting text messages using regular expressions (regex) for prototyping Air Traffic Control applications. As the approach is using regex, it makes possible to deploy lightweight clients on separate computers. Those separate

---

[1] http://www.eei.cena.fr/products/ivy/documentation/

computers are not able to detect some specifics messages on the bus, which makes it possible to log workflows without polluting the client computers. One of the main advantages of the Ivy approach is that its adoption didn't require modifying the ICO notation which was originally designed for describing systems as a set of cooperating instances of classes (independent from their location).

HAMSTERS extensions

The HAMSTERS notation and CASE tool has been introduced in 2010 in order to provide support for task-system integration at the tool level [1]. Since then, this tool and notation has been refined several times in order to provide support for:

- Automation design. The notation has been extended to help with the analysis of function allocation between human and system thanks to the refinement of cognitive tasks into analysis and decision subtypes of cognitive tasks according to the Parasuraman model of human information processing [13].

- Structuring a large number and complex set of tasks introducing the mechanism of subroutines [16].

- Precise description of knowledge, information and objects required and manipulated [15] in order to accomplish tasks.

These elements are necessary to describe collaborative activities but they are not sufficient. Hereafter are the extensions we propose in order to deal with groupware.

Adding notation elements to describe collaborative activities
Collaborative work is performed by several persons, each one having a role in the achievement of common goals. The concept of role we are using is the same as the one used in [18] and [25]. Figure 1 illustrates the structure of a HAMSTERS project with several roles, each of them having associated task models structured according to the

mechanism of subroutines introduced in [16]. In the same way, we also integrate the concept of actor [25] in the HAMSTERS notation and tool.

Collaborative work can be described at different abstraction levels: at the group level and at the individual level. A group task is a set of task that a group has to carry out in order to achieve a common goal [17], whereas a cooperative task is an individual task performed by a person in order to contribute to the achievement of the common goal [21].

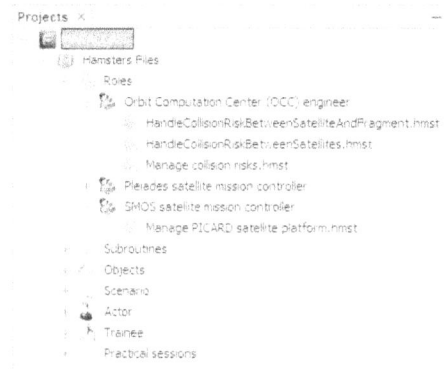

Figure 1. Structure of a HAMSTERS project

In order to be able to describe group tasks, we introduce several new task types illustrated in Figure 2 (in the last right column). These group tasks provide support for describing high level activities that a group of person have to accomplish:

- An abstract group task is a task that can be decomposed into user, system, interactive and collaborative tasks.

- A group (of users) task is task that can be decomposed in user and collaborative user tasks.

- An interactive group task can be decomposed in interactive and collaborative interactive tasks.

		Abstract	Input	Output	I/O	Processing	Group
Abstract			Not applicable	Not applicable	Not applicable	Not applicable	
User	Indiv.						
	Coop.						
Interactive	Indiv.					Not applicable	
	Coop.					Not applicable	
System							

Figure 2. Task types in HAMSTERS

• A system group task can be decomposed in system tasks.

The refinement of group tasks into low-level activities needs fine-grain task types to describe individual and cooperative tasks that have to be performed in order to contribute to the group activities. As individual task types were already available within HAMSTERS, we then introduce cooperative tasks, illustrated in Figure 2. A cooperative task is a task related to a role and accomplished in correlation with another cooperative task that relates to a different role. A cooperative task may be of various types within the user and interactive main family types.

Cooperative tasks may be performed within various space-time constraints (local/distant, synchronous/asynchronous) [7]. These constraints can be described with notation elements illustrated in Figure 3.

	Local	Distant
Synchronous	 Cooperative input task	 Cooperative input task
Asynchronous	 Cooperative input task	 Cooperative input task

Figure 3. Elements of notation related to space-time constraints

Cooperative task may be dedicated to one or more of the following type of collaborative activities: production, coordination, communication. It is then possible to associate one or more properties amongst this set. For example, Figure 4 a) shows that one task is dedicated to coordination whereas Figure 4 b) shows that the task is dedicated to both coordination and communication.

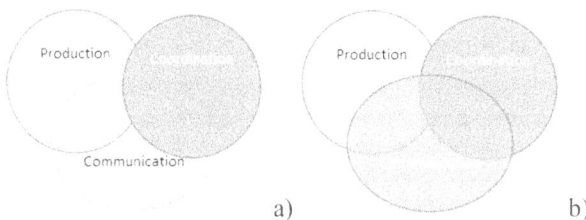

Figure 4. Example of cooperative task properties from a "functional clover" [9]

Adding edition and simulation capabilities

Several functionalities have been added to HAMSTERS CASE tool[2] in order to support the edition and simulation of tasks models describing collaborative activities:

• At the edition level, a mechanism to link cooperative tasks across task models belonging to different roles (by mean of contextual menu appearing after a right click on a cooperative task and proposing the list of available cooperative tasks in the other task models belonging to the other roles, as illustrated in Figure 5).

---

[2] http://www.irit.fr/recherches/ICS/softwares/hamsters/

• At the simulation level, a mechanism to enable the execution of several models belonging to different roles.

HAMSTERS make it possible to structure users' activities belonging to one role in several tasks models edit several task models. The association between cooperative tasks of different roles is not made across an additional task model (as for example the cooperative task model in CTTe [18]) but it is achieved via an internal correspondence table in the tool.

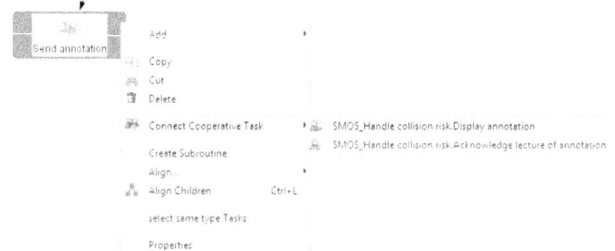

Figure 5. Defining correspondence of cooperative tasks of 2 task models representing different roles

Synergistic module extensions

The synergistic module has been improved for both design time editing of correspondences and runtime simulation to support collaborative activity modelling and simulation.

Design time

To support collaborative simulation, the editing of correspondences requires three main improvements w.r.t what have been previously done [1]:

• Allowing the use of several task models instead of a unique one.

• Allowing the use of several collaborative ICO models instead of models concerning a local instance of the application.

• Taking into account cooperative input and output tasks, additionally to input and output tasks previously used.

Runtime

The two main improvements for the runtime use of models concern the task driven simulation as it mainly requires the use of HAMSTERS:

• We added means to select the HAMSTERS role involved in the simulation.

• An important improvement is about the value selection for task objects: executing an input task may requires to select a particular set of values that may be found within the PetShop data set or that may be provided by the user (for instance feeding in a text box). These values are thus used to control the PetShop execution of a transition.

Architecture of the extended environment

As stated in [1], the integration of the tools relies on specific API provided by both HAMSTERS and PetShop. In this section we present how the whole tool suite has been improved to handle synergistic execution.

As described in the previous sections, the two main specificities introduced by this new approach are:

- HAMSTERS allows the editing and simulation of several roles described using several task models.

- PetShop allows the editing and execution of several distributed ICO models.

The goal of the tool suite is thus improved in order to allow the specification of a distributed user application and the related user activities. The whole interactive system may be considered as a set of pairs of single users and single user application with communications means supported by both the applications and the users. Making these two parts of a pair correspond requires identifying points of connection for both design time and runtime:

- From each tasks specification we extract the set of interactive tasks and cooperative interactive tasks (for both input and output) representing a set of manipulations that can be performed by the users on the system and outputs from the system to the users.

- From each ICO specification we extract the activation and rendering function that may be seen as the set of inputs and outputs of the system model.

Design time architecture
The principle of editing the correspondences between the models of one pair {role, system} is to put together interactive and cooperative interactive input tasks (from the task models) with system inputs (from the system models) and system outputs (from the system models) with interactive and cooperative interactive output tasks (from the task models). Setting up this correspondence may show inconsistencies between the task and system models such as interactive tasks not supported by the system or rendering information not useful for the task performance. The correspondence editing process is presented on Figure 6 where each tool feeds the correspondence editor with information from the API in order to notify it with modifications are done both in the task model and in the system model.

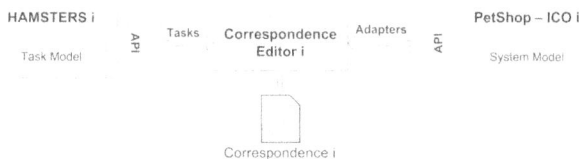

Figure 6. Design time architecture of the tool suite.

This process that produces a correspondence is repeated for each pair on the entire system. Each pair is being put into correspondence separately producing a set of independent correspondences. These dependencies totally rely on the connection of task tree leaves (both input and output

cooperative tasks). These elementary tasks are performed on the local system (represented by a set of ICO models). The separation of the correspondences relies on the fact that each part of the distributed system is modelled by a set of independent ICOs, connected by communication means (method calls) supported at runtime by the Ivy bus.

As the correspondence editing goal is to put together user activities and interactive features, this correspondence is only possible with the finest grain item of both descriptions.

Runtime architecture
Our framework allows the co-execution of task and system models controlled by both the execution of the system model and the execution of the task model as shown in Figure 7 (where the correspondences are those produced by the process described by Figure 6).

Figure 7 highlights the two ways communication within each pair {task, system} allowed by the services embedded within the two following APIs:

- Between HAMSTERS and the Simulation Controller: On one side HAMSTERS notifies changes in the current scenario to the Simulation. On the other side the Simulation Controller is able to ask to perform the corresponding task (according to the correspondence provided by the Correspondence editor), simulating the user action.

- Between PetShop and the Simulation Controller: on one side the PetShop interpreter notifies the Simulation Controller the evolution of the current execution of the system model (notifications come from both rendering and activation functions). On the other side, the Simulation Controller fires the corresponding activation adapter (according to the correspondence provided by the Correspondence editor) simulating the user action.

Such as in [1] such architecture allows a two ways simulation controlled by the system execution or controlled by the task simulation. The principle of the simulation is the same as in our previous work:

- When driven by the tasks, building a scenario using HAMSTERS is translated by the Simulation Controller into user actions within PetShop (a sequence of transition firing).

- When driven by the system execution, user actions are directly linked to the corresponding tasks from the task model and the user's action on the user interface of the application change the current state of the task model simulation.

The task driven simulation introduces the data correspondence. This correspondence is built on runtime capabilities of the two tools HAMSTERS and PetShop:

- HAMSTERS provides the description of objects, information and knowledge required and manipulated in order to accomplish tasks.

- PetShop, by describing data structure and data flow of the system, provides the set of data manipulated at any moment by any actions (firing of transitions).

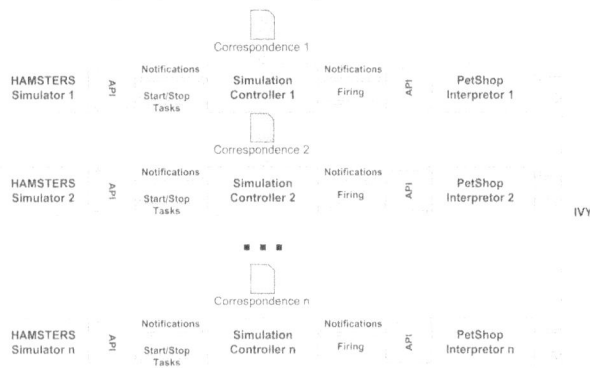

Figure 7. Runtime architecture of the tool suite

It is thus possible for any couple (*task, event handler*) within the correspondence description to match system data and the required objects for the task performance. An example of such data matching is provided by the case study (see next section). The originality of this work relies on the distribution of the system. The choice made to handle this distribution (as illustrated by Figure 7) is to use the communication means offered by PetShop (thanks to the Ivy software bus). The distribution is thus fully supported by the system side of the specification as it requires concrete data communication that should be out of the scope of task modelling.

EXAMPLE FROM A LARGE CASE STUDY

The proposed tool suite has been used to design and develop a prototype of groupware application belonging to the space ground segment category of applications. This study has been led in the context of a Research and Technology project funded by the French Space Government Agency (CNES). MARACCASS stands for Models and Architectures for the Resilience and Adaptability of Collaborative Collision Avoidance System for Spacecraft and aims at studying methods, techniques and tools to design and develop collaborative applications. This project is particularly targeting groupware for the management of collision avoidance between satellites and space objects. In this section, we present illustrative extracts from the case study which are relevant to highlight the key points of the contribution.

Management of collision risks between space objects and satellites

CNES and various other international agencies have to cope with the increasing number of space fragments, which are a threat to on-going satellite missions. Collision avoidance management is a collaborative, cross-team, and international activity. Amongst the national and international organizations, two main types of teams can be distinguished: the space observation teams and the satellite mission teams. The observation teams, thanks to various

equipment's and tools are gathering information about space objects and their trajectories (past, present, future). The mission teams focus on one particular space object (usually a satellite) and are monitoring and controlling the space object they are in charge of and its operations. If the observation team detects a collision risk between a satellite and a space object, it contacts and alerts the mission team in charge of the satellite.

Roles and main goals to manage collision risks

In this case study, we take the example of the collaboration between the CNES team in charge of monitoring space objects (called the Orbit Computation Center or OCC) and the SMOS[3] satellite mission team. In order to collaboratively manage a collision risk, the teams are assisted with several non-integrated software tools: individual software tools to analyze probability of collision and traditional communication tools (email and telephone) to coordinate and communicate about the risk.

Preliminary work before high-fidelity prototyping phase

The first phase of the project has consisted in analyzing current activity with the production of corresponding task models. Then, we proposed several low-fidelity prototypes for a new groupware application to support collaborative activities of collision risk management. These low-fidelity prototypes take into consideration groupware principles [7] but also contributions about design considerations for collaborative visual analytics [9]. We then produced task and system models from low-fidelity prototypes that had been validated with operational teams.

In the next paragraphs we present extracts from models and from the high-fidelity groupware prototypes that highlight how the proposed framework has been applied to develop a high-fidelity prototype of the collaborative application for collision risk management. In these extracts, we will focus on the collaborative asynchronous activities related to posting annotations (OCC engineer role) and consulting these annotations (SMOS controller role) in the corresponding remote applications. Figure 8 and Figure 9 presents screenshots of the two remote applications dedicated to collaborative management of collision risks. Figure 8 presents the application dedicated to OCC engineers (with a larger set of functionalities such as deep probabilistic calculus and Conjunction Summary Messages creation and edition). In the presented screenshot, a popup window is opened in order to let the OCC engineer edit an annotation. Figure 9 presents the application dedicated to the mission controllers with a reduced set of functionalities. Its main purpose is to provide situation awareness about the collision risks related to the mission and communication and coordination support. In the presented screenshot, an

---

[3] http://smsc.cnes.fr/SMOS/index.htm

annotation is displayed (pined to the table) to the attention of the SMOS mission controller.

Figure 8. Screenshot of the Hi-Fi prototype for collision risks management dedicated to OCC engineers

Figure 9. Screenshot of the Hi-Fi prototype for collision risks awareness dedicated to SMOS mission engineers

Task models

In this section, extracts of the task models illustrate the HAMSTERS extensions and especially how the new cooperative task types have been applied to support the development of the groupware Hi-Fi prototype.

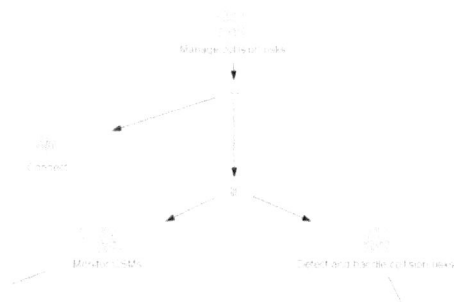

Figure 10. Extract of the highest level task model for the OCC activities (OCC engineer role)

Orbit Computation Center (OCC) engineers
Figure 10 presents an extract from the set of activities that have to be performed by the expert engineer on duty from the Orbit Computation Center to monitor and manage collision risks.

Figure 11 presents an extract from the set of activities performed once a collision risk has been detected for the SMOS satellite mission. In particular, it shows the sequence of activities led when the SMOS mission controller was not available for a live communication. The OCC engineer first creates an annotation ("Create annotation" input tasks), then positions the annotation (iterative task "Move annotation") until the position is adequate ("Fix annotation position" input task). The OCC engineer then edits the annotation (input task "Edit annotation"), decides to send the annotation (cognitive decision task "Decide to send annotation") and then send the annotation (cooperative asynchronous task "Send annotation").

Figure 11. Extract of the task model "Handle collision risk between satellite and fragment" for the OCC engineer role

SMOS command and control room controllers and engineers
Figure 12 presents an extract from the set of activities that have to be performed by the SMOS controller when warned by the OCC engineer.

Figure 12. Extract of the highest level task model for the SMOS mission activities

Figure 14 presents an extract from the set of activities performed once a collision risk has been detected. In particular, this set of activities is cooperative and bound to the above presented set of activities for the OCC engineer role. Once the OCC engineer has sent an annotation, it is displayed in the SMOS remote application (cooperative output task "Display new annotation"). When the SMOS mission controller will be available for consulting the application, s/he detects and acknowledges reception of the annotation (cooperative input asynchronous task "Acknowledge lecture of annotation"). S/he then analyzes the reported risk and may delete the annotation (cooperative input task "Delete annotation").

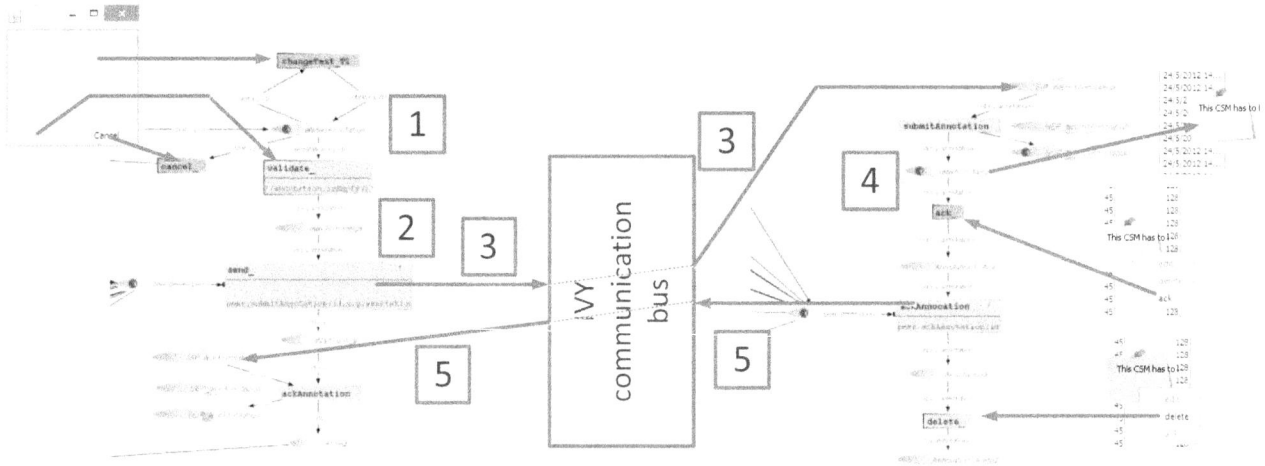

Figure 13. ICO modelling of the two remote applications COO (left part) and SMOS (right part)

ICO modelling of the collaborative application to manage collision risks

Figure 13 illustrates an excerpt of the connected models of the two remote applications OCC (left part of the figure) and SMOS (right part of the figure). The two excerpt of the models presented here describe how the editing of an annotation is performed on the OCC side and how it is sent and acknowledged back on the SMOS side. In both case, a snapshot of the dedicated graphical part is provided. These models behave as follows:

1. When in editing mode (a token is put in place EditedAnnotation at the top of the left part of Figure 13), it is possible to edit the text of the annotation using the edition window (see left part of Figure 13). It results in a state change (by the firing of transition changeText_, changing the marking of place EditedAnnotation with the new text) or it is possible to validate or cancel the editing (where button OK fires the transition validate_ and button CANCEL the transition cancel_).

2. When validated (cancellation producing a return to the initial state) a token is put in place newAnnotation, the created annotation is sent to the peer application (SMOS) by the remote invocation peer.submitAnnotation(…).

3. The communication bus Ivy then sends this method call to the ICO SMOS model (a token is put in the service input port of the corresponding method, the place SIP_SubmitAnnotation on the top of the right part of Figure 13).

4. The firing of the following transition submitAnnotation puts a token in place newAnnotation making the transition ack_ available (which is translated into activating the corresponding menu item within the popup menu show on the right part of Figure 13).

5. Using the menu item ack results in setting a token in place AnnotationToAck which thus allows the firing of transition ackAnnotation. The firing of this transition results in the remote method peer.ackAnnotation(…)

invocation (on the bottom of the left part of the figure) and finally makes the transition delete_ fireable (the corresponding menu item becoming enabled).

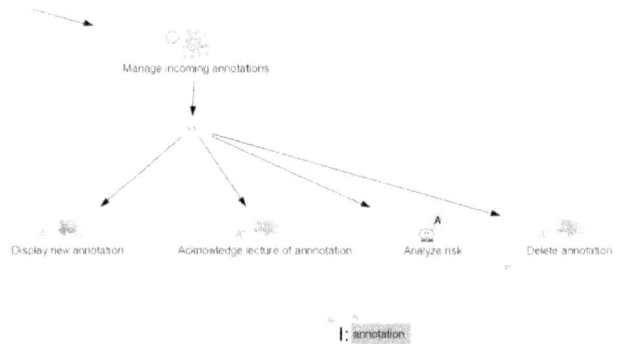

Figure 14. Extract of the task model "Handle collision risk" for the SMOS mission controller role

Distributed co-execution between tasks and applications

Figure 15 illustrates two remotes instances of the tool suite presented in this paper, connected using the Ivy communication bus. The left part (resp. the right part) corresponds to the editing of the OCC (resp. SMOS) models. The left-hand part of the figure shows the project structure of the tool suite (i.e. a set of modules of the NetBeans IDE[4]). This tool may be divided into four parts:

- The top part is a set of classical IDE menu bars and tool bars buttons.

- The left part provides means to navigate amongst the project files (java sources, ICO, HAMSTERS and correspondence models).

- The right part shows properties of the sources or models (bottom part) and tools to modify the currently selected model (on the top part a specific toolbox appears

---

[4] https://netbeans.org/features/index.html

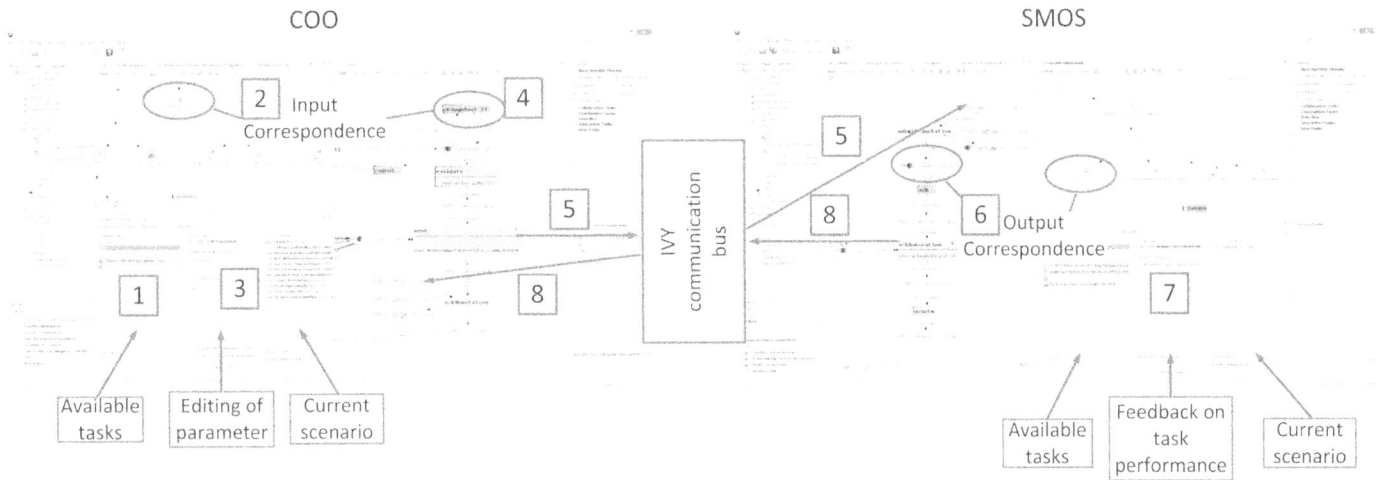

Figure 15. Illustration of the collaborative co-execution using two instances of the tool suite

depending on the king of the selected model (HAMSTERS or PetShop).

- The center part allows the editing and execution control of both the sources and models. The layout of this part is fully reconfigurable as illustrated by the layout difference of the left and right part of the figure.

To illustrate the synergistic exploitation of both the system and task models, we use the models presented in the previous sections, following the same scenario as used for the ICO models presentation (editing of an annotation). As the correspondence editing between system and task models are a simple table editing and was already presented in [1], we only focus here on the task driven simulation with a special focus on the cooperative activities.

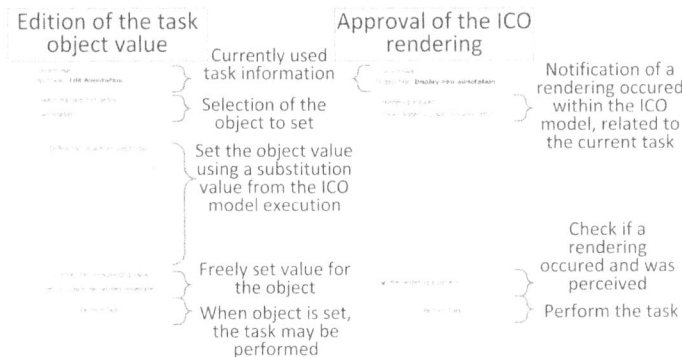

Figure 16. Detailed view on task-system related data.

Following the eight numbered steps presented on the figure, the behavior of the task driven simulation is the following one:

1. A set of available tasks is provided by the HAMSTERS environment that is selectable within the associated list box.

2. The selected task is connected to a transition by the correspondence editing.

3. As the tasks requires an object (see task Edit Annotation in Figure 11 in Task models section of the case study), a dedicated panel is available (see the left part of Figure 16 for a zoomed snapshot of this part of the tool), providing means to select values built from the data (system side) of the running ICO model, related to the transition connected to the task. It is also possible to manually provide a value using the bottom text field of this panel (see bottom right part of Figure 16).

4. When set, the selected value is sent to the ICO model by sending an event (such as graphical part would have done it).

5. Such as in the step 3 of Figure 13 (the scenario described in the ICO models section), an invocation is performed on the remote application.

6. When a token enters a place within the ICO model, a rendering may occur and this rendering may be related to an output HAMSTERS task, using the output correspondence edition.

7. When an output task is selected, a dedicated panel appears at the bottom of the tool, showing whether a rendering occurs and if it corresponds to an output correspondence (Figure 16 shows a detailed view of this panel). In this panel it is possible to indicate if the rendering was effectively correct and perceive (for log purpose).

8. Finally, such as in step 5 of Figure 13 (the scenario described in the ICO models section), an invocation is performed back on the remote application.

CONCLUSIONS AND FUTURE WORK

This paper has proposed a tool supported approach for bridging the gap between tasks and system views in the design of multi-user interactive systems. To this end we have briefly introduced extensions to the notation called HAMSTERS for the description of multi-users tasks models. These extensions allow the production of very detailed description of collaborative tasks beyond the expressive power of other task notations. This expressive power has allowed us to embed this notation within a synergistic framework where collaborative task models are connected to the interactive parts of a distributed system.

Through the application of the approach on a real life case study (that was carried out over the 3 years lifespan of the project) we have demonstrated the validity of the approach in the context of space critical systems. However, this validation has only demonstrated that the notations are able to describe multi-user activities and interactive systems and that they were able to scale enough to describe a real life application. We have not presented in this paper all the work that has been carried out around the definition of the user interfaces, the interaction techniques and the communication and collaboration functionalities. This work has been performed using a User Centered Design approach based on low-fidelity and high-fidelity prototypes.

The work presented here belongs to a longer term research program targeting at the design of resilient interactive systems using model-based approaches. Future work targets at exploiting this approach, to propose model-based usability evaluation of multi-user interactive systems extending the approach proposed for mono-user ones in [4]. We will also build on this model-based work to identify function allocations between operators and interactive systems to design more usable and reliable automation for critical systems.

ACKNOWLEDGMENTS
This work was partly sponsored by CNES R&T MARACCASS. We would like to thank the OCC team and in particular Jean-Claude Agnèse and François Laporte.

REFERENCES
1. Barboni E., Ladry J-F., Navarre D., Palanque P. and Winckler M. Beyond modeling: an integrated environment supporting co-execution of tasks and systems models. EICS'10, 165-174.
2. Bastide, R., Palanque, P., Sy, O., Navarre, D. Formal specification of CORBA services: experience and lessons learned. In Proc. of OOPSLA 2000, 105-117.
3. Bates, J.; Spiteri, M.D.; Halls, D.; Bacon, J. Integrating real-world and computer-supported collaboration in the presence of mobility. In Proc. 7th IEEE Int. Workshops on Enabling Technologies: Infrastructure for Collaborative Enterprises, 1998, 256-261.
4. Bernhaupt R., Navarre D., Palanque P., Winckler M. Model-Based Evaluation: A New Way to Support Usability Evaluation of Multimodal Interactive Applications. Maturing Usability: Quality in Software, Interaction and Quality. Springer Verlag, April 2007.
5. Calvary, G., Coutaz, J., Nigay, L. From single-user architectural design to PAC*: a generic software architecture model for CSCW. In Proc. of CHI '97. ACM, NY, USA, 242-249.
6. Cockburn, A., Jones, S. Four principles for groupware design. Interacting with Computers. IJHCI, 7(2), 1995, 195-210.
7. Ellis C. A., Gibbs S. J., Rein G., Groupware: some issues and experiences, Comm. of the ACM, v.34 n.1, p.39-58, Jan. 1991.
8. Giraldo, W.J., Molina, A.I., Collazos, C.A., Ortega, M., Redondo, M. A Model Based Approach for GUI Development in Groupware Systems. In Groupware: Design, Implementation, and Use, LNCS, Vol. 5411. Springer-Verlag, Berlin, Heidelberg, 324-339.
9. Heer; J., Agrawala, M. 2007. Design Considerations for Collaborative Visual Analytics. Proc. of IEEE Symp. on Visual Analytics Science and Technology (VAST '07). IEEE Computer Society, 171-178.
10. Holanda, J. Merseguer, G. Cordeiro, and A. Serra. Performance evaluation of web services orchestrated with ws-bpel4people. Int. Journal of Computer Networks Communications, 2:18, 11/2010
11. Jakobsen M.R., Fernandez R., Czerwinski M., Inkpen K., Kulyk O.A., Robertson G.G. WIPDash: Work Item and People Dashboard for Software Development Teams. INTERACT 2009, pp.791-804.
12. Jourde F., Laurillau Y. & Nigay L. 2010. COMM notation for specifying collaborative and multimodal interactive systems. In Proc. of EICS '10. ACM, New York, NY, USA, 125-134.
13. Martinie C., Palanque P., Barboni E., Ragosta M. Task-Model Based Assessment of Automation Levels: Application to Space Ground Segments. Proc. of the IEEE SMC, Anchorage, 2011.
14. Martinie C., Palanque P., Navarre D., Winckler M. and Poupart E. Model-Based Training: An Approach Supporting Operability of Critical Interactive Systems: Application to Satellite Ground Segments. Proc. of EICS 2011, pp. 141-151, ACM DL.
15. Martinie, C., Palanque, P., Ragosta, M and Fahssi, R. Extending Procedural Task Models by Explicit and Systematic Integration of Objects, Knowledge and Information, ECCE 2013, 23-33.
16. Martinie, C.; Palanque, P. A. and Winckler, M. (2011): Structuring and Composition Mechanisms to Address Scalability Issues in Task Models. Proc. INTERACT (3) p. 589-609.
17. McGrath J. E. Groups: Interaction and Performance. Prentice Hall, Inc., Englewood Cliffs, 1984.
18. Mori, G., Paternò, F., Santoro C. 2002. CTTE: support for developing and analyzing task models for interactive system design. IEEE Trans. Softw. Eng. 28, 8 (August 2002), 797-813.
19. Paternò F., Ballardin G.: RemUSINE: a bridge between empirical and model-based evaluation when evaluators and users are distant. Interacting with Computers 13(2): 229-251 (2000)
20. Rama, J., Bishop, J. A survey and comparison of CSCW groupware applications. In Proc. of SAICSIT '06, 2006, Republic of South Africa, 198-205.
21. Roschelle, J., & Teasley, S. D. (1995). The construction of shared knowledge in collaborative problem solving. In C. E. O'Malley (Ed.), Computer-supported collaborative learning (pp. 69-197).
22. Roseman M, Greenberg S: Building Real-Time Groupware with GroupKit, a Groupware Toolkit. ACM Trans. Comput.-Hum. Interact. 3(1): 66-106 (1996).
23. Sun, A., Sun, C. Xpointer: an x-ray telepointer for relaxed-space-time wysiwis and unconstrained collaborative 3d design systems. In Proc. of CSCW '13. ACM, NY, USA, 729-740.
24. Van der Aalst, W.M.P, ter Hofstede, A.H.M. YAWL: Yet Another Workflow Language. Information Systems, 30(4):245-275, 2005.
25. Van der Veer, G. C., Lenting, V. F., Bergevoet, B. A. GTA: Groupware Task Analysis - modeling complexity. Acta Psychologica, 91, (1996), 297-322.
26. Wu, J., Graham, N. T. C: Toward Quality-Centered Design of Groupware Architectures. EHCI/DS-VIS 2007, 339-355.

The EICS 2014 Doctoral Consortium

Laurence Nigay
Univ. Grenoble Alpes, LIG
CNRS, LIG, F-38000 Grenoble, France
laurence.nigay@imag.fr

Kris Luyten
Hasselt University - tUL -iMinds
Expertise Centre for Digital Media, Belgium
kris.luyten@uhasselt.be

ABSTRACT
In this short extended abstract, we present the doctoral consortium of the Engineering Interactive Computing Systems (EICS) 2014 Symposium. Our goal is to make the doctoral consortium a useful event with a maximum benefit for the participants by having a dedicated event the day before the conference as well as the opportunity to present their on-going doctoral work to a wider audience during the conference.

ACM Classification Keywords
H.5.m. Information interfaces and presentation (e.g., HCI): Miscellaneous. D2.m Software Engineering: Miscellaneous.

PARTICIPATION IN THE DOCTORAL CONSORTIUM
Doctoral Consortium submissions typically present a PhD thesis topic motivated by aims and goals, supported by some work in-progress and present original, sound, and well-founded results in order to address a well-defined problem.

The motivation of the Doctoral Consortium is to foster PhD students in the field of Engineering Interactive Computing Systems (EICS) by offering them the opportunity to receive feedback about their research by more senior colleagues with similar research interests.

The Doctoral Consortium is a closed event, the day before the conference, in which a selected group of doctoral candidates present their research to each other and to a panel of advisors. Each presentation follows the same structure highlighting the addressed research questions, the method and initial results. The presentations are kept short on purpose to force focus on the key issues. In addition to the presentations, discussion between the participants is encouraged: each participant is playing a supporting/opposing role to another participant, by identifying positive or negative points on the doctoral research of another participant. The goal is to become better acquainted with one another, be part of the EICS community and reflect on her/his own research in the larger context of EICS.

A further goal is to better link the Doctoral Consortium to the main conference, by providing the participants with the opportunity to present their work to all the EICS 2014 attendees during a dedicated session at the conference. This session is organized on the first day of the conference so that participants can have the opportunity to further discuss their work with colleagues during the entire conference. The presentation is accompanied with a poster that will be on display during the entire conference.

LIST OF PARTICIPANTS
This year seven doctoral candidates are selected for the Doctoral Consortium. The students range from being in the initial stages of their doctoral research planning, to the final stages of dissertation completion.

The set of seven participants of this year cover a wide variety of EICS topics and application domains. Two sessions structure the Doctoral Consortium:

* *HCI and Model-Driven Engineering*: this session includes research involving model-based approaches. Examples of models include task models, UI models, context models as well as user models.

* *Large, Complex and Critical System*s: this session is dedicated to research on engineering interactive large complex and critical systems. To do so different research axes are adopted from collaborative annotation, visual interactive support, formal specification to incident investigation methodology.

The accepted PhD students to the Doctoral Consortium are:

Ragaad AlTarawneh (University of Kaiserslautern, Germany) presenting *Visual Interactive Support For Understanding Structural and Behavioral Aspects of Complex Systems*.

Amjad Hawash (Sapienza University, Rome, Italy) presenting *Introducing Groups to an Annotation System: Design Perspective*

Huayi Huang (Queen Mary, University of London, UK) presenting *Two Analytical Approaches To Support Patient Safety Incident Investigation Methodology*.

Yucheng Jin (Fortiss GmbH, institute associated with the Technical University of Munich, Germany) presenting *Generating Model-Based User Interfaces for the Connected Appliances*.

Eyfrosyni (Effie) Karuzaki (University of Crete, Greece) presenting *Automatic Assembly of Adaptive User Interfaces: Models, Architectures, Services and Applications.*

Mathias Kühn (University of Rostock, Germany) presenting *A Model-Based Approach for Specifications of User Interface Behavior.*

Vincent Lecrubier (ONERA – DTIM, Toulouse, France) presenting *A Formal Language for Critical Embedded User Interfaces.*

ORGANIZERS BACKGROUND

Laurence Nigay is a full Professor in Computer Science at Université Joseph Fourier (UJF, Grenoble 1). She is the director of the Engineering Human-Computer Interaction (EHCI) research group of the Grenoble Informatics Laboratory (LIG). From 1998-2004, she was vice-chair of the IFIP working group WG 2.7/13.4 "User Interface Engineering". She was advisor or co-advisor of 14 students who defended their theses: 8 of them are currently professors, lecturers or CNRS researchers. She is currently advising or co-advising 5 students. More on her research can be found at http://iihm.imag.fr/nigay/

Kris Luyten is an associated professor in Computer Science at Hasselt University in Belgium and member of the HCI lab of the iMinds research institute Expertise Centre for Digital Media. He was full paper co-chair for both EICS 2011 and EICS 2013. He was advisor or co-advisor of 7 students who defended their theses and is currently advising or co-advising 7 students. More on his research can be found at http://research.edm.uhasselt.be/kris

ACKNOWLEDGEMENTS

The organizers would like to thank the committee of advisors for their contribution to the Doctoral Consortium.

A Domain-Specific Textual Language for Rapid Prototyping of Multimodal Interactive Systems

Fredy Cuenca, Jan Van den Bergh, Kris Luyten, Karin Coninx

Hasselt University - tUL - iMinds

Expertise Centre for Digital Media, Diepenbeek, Belgium

{fredy.cuencalucero,jan.vandenbergh,kris.luyten,karin.coninx}@uhasselt.be

ABSTRACT

There are currently toolkits that allow the specification of executable multimodal human-machine interaction models. Some provide domain-specific visual languages with which a broad range of interactions can be modeled but at the expense of bulky diagrams. Others instead, interpret concise specifications written in existing textual languages even though their non-specialized notations prevent the productivity improvement achievable through domain-specific ones.

We propose a domain-specific textual language and its supporting toolkit; they both overcome the shortcomings of the existing approaches while retaining their strengths. The language provides notations and constructs specially tailored to compactly declare the event patterns raised during the execution of multimodal commands. The toolkit detects the occurrence of these patterns and invokes the functionality of a back-end system in response.

Author Keywords

Multimodal systems; composite events; declarative languages.

ACM Classification Keywords

H.5.m. Information Interfaces and Presentation (e.g. HCI): Miscellaneous

INTRODUCTION

Multimodal systems can process commands that are conveyed through a wide variety of modalities (e.g. speech, gestures, gaze, etc.) in a coordinated manner. They expand computing to accommodate to a broader spectrum of people and more adverse usage conditions than in the past [19]. However, their implementation comes with a cost: existing commercial frameworks (.NET, Java) cannot separate the concerns of event handling and event detection for multimodal systems as well as they did for traditional WIMP systems.

Whereas traditional systems respond to simple, single action commands (e.g. mouse clicks and keystrokes), multimodal

systems must respond to a series of coordinated user actions that are to be regarded as a single command, a multimodal command. For those multimodal systems implemented with commercial frameworks, the execution of multimodal commands will lead to a series of event notifications that a multimodal system must process separately but without ever neglecting their interdependence. The implementation of a mechanism for detecting meaningful event patterns -hereafter called composite events- greatly complicates the creation of multimodal systems.

To ease this problem, the HCI community has proposed toolkits that support the specification and detection of composite events. Some of them provide domain-specific visual languages [3, 7, 6, 17, 8] that enable modeling a wide variety of composite events. However, these specifications easily degenerate into complex diagrams for relatively simple commands such as the *put-that-there* [5]. Other toolkits can interpret textual specifications [1, 15, 24, 13] made in some existing languages, e.g. XML or CLIPS, not specialized for multimodal systems. But the generality of these languages prevents the productivity improvement associated with the use of domain-specific ones [16].

Our research seeks to explore the potential of a distinct type of modeling language -one that combines the distinguishing features of mainstream approaches: the domain-specificity and the textual notation. The former offer substantial gains in expressiveness and ease of use, with corresponding gains in productivity and reduced maintenance costs [16]. The latter leads to concise, easy-to-scan specifications [12].

This paper presents a language that allows defining a broad range of composite events for its subsequent detection by a toolkit. This can acknowledge the partial detection of composite events through multimodal output, and react to their full detection by sending requests to a back-end system. The toolkit is ideal for rapid prototyping: the ease of editing composite events that can be attached with feedback messages allows quick iteration over different interaction techniques while the application-specific code remains unaltered at the back-end side.

Many of our ideas will be illustrated by the *put-that-there* system because (1) it requires integrating both simultaneous and sequential multimodal inputs, and (2) it can serve as a benchmark so that readers can compare different languages.

Algorithm 1 Oversimplified version of the put-that-there system

---

1: **boolean** $bPut, bThat, bThere, bClick1, bClick2$ ▷ Variables capturing external information
2: **datetime** $dPut, dThat, dThere, dClick1, dClick2$
3: **int** $x1, y1, x2, y2$

4: **procedure** SPEECHRECOGNIZED(e)   ▷ Detection of speech inputs
5:     **if** $e.Text =$ 'put' **then** $bPut \leftarrow true, dPut \leftarrow Now()$
6:     **if** $e.Text =$ 'that' **then** $bThat \leftarrow true, dThat \leftarrow Now()$
7:     **if** $e.Text =$ 'there' **then** $bThere \leftarrow true, dThere \leftarrow Now()$
8:     **if** $hasPutThatThereOcurred()$ **then** $putThatThere(x1, y1, x2, y2)$

9: **procedure** MOUSECLICK(e)   ▷ Detection of mouse clicks
10:     **if** $dClick1$ is null **then** $x1 \leftarrow e.X, y1 \leftarrow e.Y, dClick1 \leftarrow Now()$
11:     **else** $x2 \leftarrow e.X, y2 \leftarrow e.Y, dClick2 \leftarrow Now()$
12:     **if** $hasPutThatThereOcurred()$ **then** $putThatThere(x1, y1, x2, y2)$

13: **procedure** HASPUTTHATTHEREOCURRED()   ▷ Detection of the put-that-there event
14:     **if** $bPut$ & $bThat$ & $bThere$ & $bClick1$ & $bClick2$ **then**
15:       **if** $(tThat - tPut).Milliseconds < 500$ & $(tThere - tThat).Milliseconds < 500$ **then**
16:         PUTTHATTHERE($x1, y1, x2, y2$)

17: **procedure** PUTTHATTHERE($x1, y1, x2, y2$)   ▷ Handler of the put-that-there event
18:     **for all** $o \in Controls$ **do**
19:       **if** $o.contains(x1, y1)$ **then** $o.Location = new\ Point(x2, y2)$

PUT-THAT-THERE: A MOTIVATING EXAMPLE

In order to highlight the difficulties encountered when developing multimodal systems with commercial frameworks, we will discuss the implementation of the well-known *put-that-there* [2] multimodal command. This allows a user to move a virtual object from its original position to a new one by uttering the sentence *'put that there'*. The user must utter the pronouns *'that'* and *'there'* while simultaneously clicking on the target object and its intended position respectively.

A simple desktop-version of the aforementioned system requires a Windows form with colored buttons on it (Figure 3a), a library for speech recognition, and the variables and subroutines outlined in Algorithm 1.

Most parts of the pseudo-code shown in Algorithm 1 aim at detecting whether the user has already issued a multimodal command: Boolean variables (line **1**) are used to check the occurrence of relevant events; datetime variables (line **2**), to timestamp the event notifications; and a dedicated subroutine (line **13**), to combine the information carried by these variables in order to verify whether the arrival of speech inputs and mouse clicks matches with the expected order of receipt. Only one subroutine (line **17**) implements the computation required to move the target object; the others are in charge of detecting the occurrence of an specific event pattern.

Variables such as those in lines **1** and **2**, and subroutines such as those in lines **4**, **9** and **13** are not individual peculiarities of the case being studied. Similar members will always be needed to implement two inherent functions of every multimodal system: the recognition and fusion of multimodal

natural input [19]. On one hand, the recognition of inputs involves transforming the information captured by input devices into variables (as in procedures SPEECHRECOGNIZED and MOUSECLICK). On the other hand, the fusion of inputs entails combining the information scattered among the aforementioned variables, which requires at least one dedicated subroutine (as procedure HASPUTTHATTHEREOCURRED).

The proposed language and its supporting toolkit will allow programmers to dispense the majority of the program outlined above. Since the toolkit can detect composite events, like the stream *'put that* (click) *there* (click)', the application-specific functionality encoded in the PUT-THATTHERE method will suffice to create a running system.

WORKFLOW OVERVIEW

The presented toolkit allows defining composite events, attaching them with partial feedback messages, and choosing the methods that will handle these events. Although the handlers have to be coded in a back-end application, they can be referenced from the toolkit.

Figure 1 gives an overview of the steps needed to define a composite event. In step ①, one specifies its constituent events and how these are temporally related with one another, as well as the signature of the subroutine that will be launched upon the detection of the composite event. Once this is done, one can check the composite event expression for correct syntax. This verification causes the generation of a finite state machine (step ②) that will be subsequently used for event tracking, i.e. each well-defined composite event has a reciprocal finite state machine-based representation. Optionally,

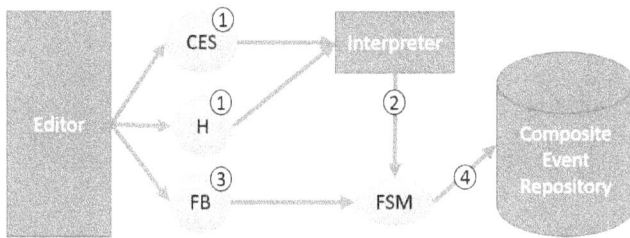

Figure 1: Components involved in the specification of composite events (CES), their handling subroutines (H), and their feedback annotations (FB).

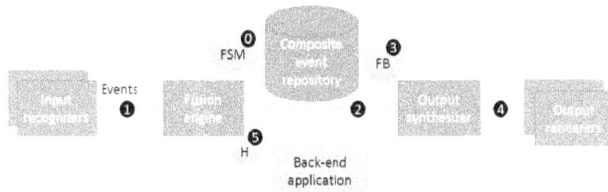

Figure 2: Components involved in the evaluation of composite events through interactive simulation.

one can then annotate the finite state machine with intermediate feedback mechanisms (step ③), after which the composite event is saved (step ④). The toolkit offers the possibility to evaluate the adequacy of a composite event by means of interactive simulation. This evaluation gives one the opportunity to experience the toolkit's recognition speed and rate at runtime, thus guiding modality allocation.

In simulation mode (see Figure 2), the user inputs will be perceived through a set of software recognizers incorporated in the toolkit. In the current implementation, these can sense speech inputs, mouse gestures, mouse inputs, keystrokes, and internally-generated timeout events. The input events are sent to a component called fusion engine (❶). This engine is in charge of detecting the occurrence of composite events, in which case it will activate the functionality of a back-end application (❺). The toolkit can provide intermediate feedback so that its user can be constantly aware of whether it is correctly detecting his/her inputs. In this case, the output synthesizer is notified (❷). Partial feedback is provided by different output renderers (❹), based on the feedback annotations (❸) that were attached to the finite state machine-based representation of the composite event.

COMPOSITE EVENT DEFINITION LANGUAGE
This section begins by explaining the underlying concept behind the composite event definition language we are proposing. It then shows the operators that permit constructing composite events in a declarative manner. Finally, the syntax required to specify event parameters is exposed and illustrated.

Composite Events
Existing commercial frameworks (.NET, Java) can notify about the occurrence of a large, predefined set of simple user events e.g. mouse clicks, keyboard presses, and menu selections. These events are considered to happen in a moment of time. Their instantaneous occurrence earned them the name -in this article at least- of atomic events.

In contrast, composite events occur over a time interval. They are series of related happenings with a unifying meaning, e.g. saying *'zoom here'* while circling on a map. A composite event is composed of several atomic events; it occurs whenever its constituent events occur in a particular order. The definition of a composite event with the proposed language requires declaring the atomic events that comprise it and the relations among them. These relations are specified through predefined event operators.

Event Operators
The operators to be presented were defined after surveying a wide assortment of graphical toolkits for prototyping multimodal systems [4]. These have been widely used to specify multimodal human-machine interaction with executable visual models. We have factored out significant features of these visual languages into a compact textual notation. The resulting operators resemble those successfully used in the field of active databases [21] to specify event-patterns.

Let A and B be two events (atomic or composite). The event operators of the proposed language, in increasing order of precedence, are:

- *FOLLOWED BY* (;): This binary operator is denoted with a semicolon. The utterance $A; B$ indicates the toolkit to notify the occurrence of a composite event whenever the event B occurs after A.

- *OR* (|): This binary operator is denoted with a pipe. The utterance $A|B$ indicates the toolkit to notify the occurrence of a composite event whenever either of A and B occurs.

- *AND* (+): This binary operator is denoted with a plus. The utterance $A + B$ indicates the toolkit to notify the occurrence of a composite event whenever A and B occur simultaneously –read within a short time span. We use (customizable) time thresholds to consider the fact that even when the end user tries to perform simultaneous actions, there may be a short delay between them [18].

- *ITERATION* (∗): This unary operator is denoted with an asterisk. The utterance B^* makes the toolkit aware that zero or more occurrences of the event B can be part of a larger composite event.

Parentheses can also be used to alter the pre-established precedence, i.e. to explicitly indicate the terms that have to be evaluated first. For instance, the expressions $A; B|C$ and $(A; B)|C$ have different meanings: the former will be triggered upon the detection of event A followed by either B or C; the latter may be trigger after the consecutive occurrence of A and B, or alternatively upon the detection of C.

Being notified about the ocurrence of a predefined sequence of events may not be enough to determine an appropriate system's response. Specific information about these events may also be required. Such information is accumulated in the parameters of the composite events.

Composite Event Parameters

The parameters of a composite event are variables that store the information carried by its constituent events.

In the proposed language, composite event parameters must go accompanied by an atomic event and within angular brackets ($\langle$, $\rangle$). Not all atomic events need to have associated parameters, e.g. the detection of the voice command *print* may be enough to produce an appropiate system response.

The semantics of the parameters depend on its associated atomic event and are predefined, e.g. the event key down may be defined with one associated parameter to store the character on the key pressed if necessary. The names of the event parameters must be character strings starting with a letter; their types do not have to be explicitly declared.

To clarify matters, the composite event that will be triggered because of the *put-that-there* command can be specified as follows:

$$putThatThere \quad = \quad \begin{array}{l} speech.put\,; \\ speech.that + mouse.click\langle x1, y1\rangle\,; \\ speech.there + mouse.click\langle x2, y2\rangle \end{array} \quad (1)$$

This utterance indicates the toolkit to store the position of the first and second click in the variables $x1$ and $y1$, and $x2$ and $y2$ respectively. These variables will be set at runtime as the user issues the *put-that-there* multimodal command. They will permit to determine the target object and its intended position respectively.

Continuing with (1), the atomic event *mouse.click* is predefined in the grammar of the proposed language whereas the speech inputs are dynamically incorporated. Atomic events *speech.put*, *speech.that*, and *speech.there* are recognized as such, because they belong to the alphabet of the speech recognition grammar that the toolkit reads at startup.

The presence of parameters stems from the fact that their values may be needed by the handling subroutines. For instance, the composite event defined in (1) makes it possible to bind it to the PUTTHATTHERE($x1, y1, x2, y2$) method of Algorithm 1. Indeed, the toolkit to be presented in the next section allows establishing this binding.

TOOLKIT USAGE

The proposed toolkit launches one subroutine every time a composite event is detected. The handling subroutines have to be implemented -with no support from the toolkit- in a back-end application. This is a prerequisite to creating multimodal prototypes with our toolkit.

Coding the composite event handlers

The handlers to be invoked upon the detection of a composite event must be coded in a different environment, Microsoft Visual Studio, with a .NET programming language, e.g. C#, Visual Basic.

For instance, to execute a system supporting the *put-that-there* command, both an application containing a windows form with colored buttons on it (Figure 3a), and the PUT-THATTHERE method (line **17** of Algorithm 1) are needed. Since the toolkit performs voice recognition and mouse hooking, no speech recognition libraries or mouse events handlers need to be implemented in the back-end application whose path must be specified in the toolkit's configuration file.

Defining and binding a composite event

Whereas a composite event has to be defined by typing in the toolkit text editor (Figure 3a, CES), its handling subroutine has to be selected from a list (Figure 3b, ③). The text editor offers syntax highlighting, auto completion popups, and function call tips. These features aim at reducing typos, and facilitating the editing and readability of the text. The list of handlers is loaded at startup when the toolkit reads the location of the back-end application from the configuration file. Unlike coding the event handlers, defining composite events requires little programming skills.

Syntax checking a composite event

The syntax of a composite event definition must be verified (Figure 3b, ②) before registering it in the repository (Figure 3b, CER). Each well-defined composite event will be automatically transformed into a semantically equivalent finite state machine (Figure 3b, STM) that the toolkit will use at runtime for event tracking. For ease of exposition, we will not directly refer to the finite state machine but to its graphical form: the state diagram. The nodes of this diagram represent the states the toolkit may be in during event tracking; its arrows indicate the state transitions to be caused upon the detection of atomic events; and its overall topology reflects the temporal constraints among the atomic events.

Attaching feedback to a composite event

Multimodal commands may involve long series of actions. Thus, it may be desirable for the end user to be progressively notified about whether his/her actions are being correctly detected. This acknowledgment may prevent end users from frustration: no one wants to realize that his/her commands were misinterpreted after few seconds of system inaction.

Toolkit users can attach partial feedback to the nodes of the state diagram representing a composite event. For instance, in Figure 3b, FB, the toolkit is configured to synthesize the utterances *'what?'*, *'where?'* and *'done!'* after the detection of *'put'*, *'that'* (click), and *'there'*(click) respectively.

Transforming user-defined text messages into synthesized voice is not the only way to provide feedback. The toolkit can also be configured to play audio files, to show mouse gesture trails, and/or to display the progression of a timeout event through a progress bar.

Evaluating a composite event

In simulation mode, the toolkit user can convey a myriad of inputs in order to evaluate the adequacy (e.g. to test recognition speed) of a composite event. The progressive recognition of a composite event will be reflected in its reciprocal state diagram-based representation.

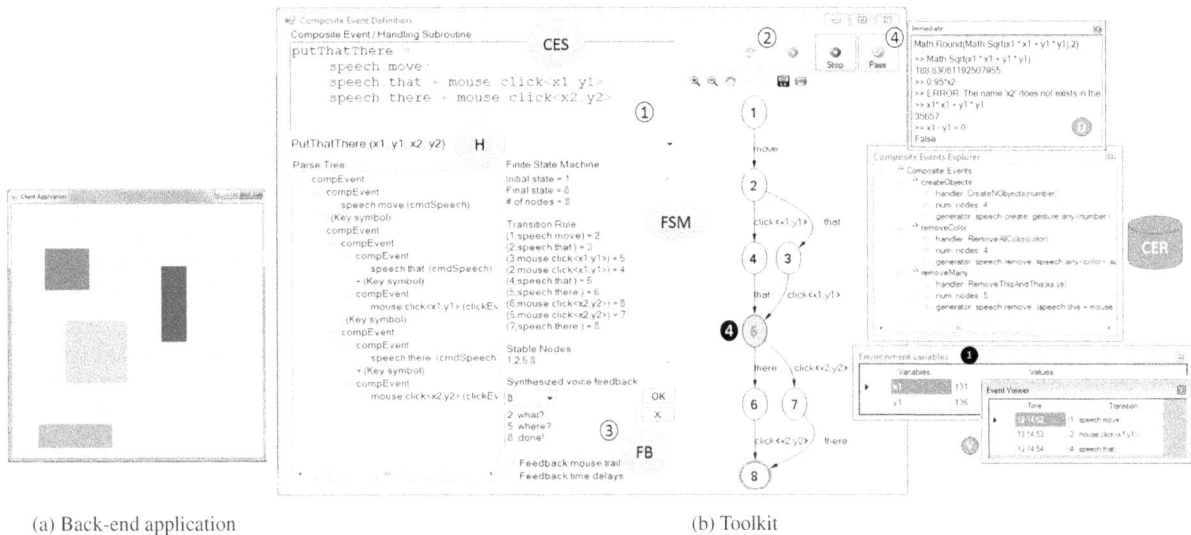

(a) Back-end application　　　　　　　　　　　　(b) Toolkit

Figure 3: The application that handles the composite events (a) and the current version of the toolkit (b) during a simulation of the put-that-there composite event. The toolkit in (b) is annotated with some of the labels from Figure 1 and Figure 2.

Simulations start with the toolkit in the initial state, labeled as 1, meaning that it is ready to sense the external environment. Subsequently, it will change its state as atomic events occur. The new state after a transition is determined by the arrow indicating the name of the triggering event. Eventually, the toolkit will reach its final state, depicted as a double circle, meaning that it has detected the occurrence of the composite event under evaluation. In that moment, a handling subroutine will be launched and the toolkit will go back to the initial state waiting for the next composite event. All toolkit state transitions are graphically reflected in the state diagram, i.e. the current toolkit state is always highlighted (Figure 3b, ❹).

The animated state diagram leads to a quick identification of input recognition problems (when the toolkit becomes stagnant in a particular state). There are also other debugging tools enabling more precise analyses. The variable browser (Figure 3b, ❶) is a window showing the event parameters values; it is updated in each state transition. The interactive debugger (Figure 3b, D) is a scratchpad window in which C# statements involving the event parameters can be evaluated on the fly. The event viewer (Figure 3b, V) shows the happenings detected during the simulation along with their timestamps. Through these tools, for instance, we observed that after 35 executions of the *put-that-there* command, this was detected without fail 68.5% of the times. Mouse clicks, and inputs *'that'* and *'there'* were missed in 2, 6, and 3 occasions respectively. When receiveing partial feedback as in Figure 3b, the recognition rate increased to 94.2%.

Based on the simulation and up to the toolkit user's criteria, the evaluated composite event may be discarded, modified for re-evaluation, or registered into the toolkit. Then, he/she can repeat the process for other composite events. A dedicated window will show all those composite events registered in the toolkit (Figure 3b, CER).

Testing the final prototype

Once the toolkit user has registered all the composite events the intended prototype has to handle, this is ready for end user testing. In this phase, the end user will freely interact with the prototype, i.e. composite events will be triggered in arbitrary order. Unlike simulations, the animated state diagram will not be shown to the end user.

In the final prototype, every multimodal command starts with a pre-defined reset action (like Google Glass [9] commands are activated by first saying *'O.K. Glass'*). In this way, we guarantee that multimodal commands will be issued one at a time. The reset action also allows users to cancel their multimodal command executions at any time. This design decision, however, comes with a cost: the toolkit cannot support the prototyping of multi-user applications since these must handle several commands simultaneously.

EXPLOITING ADVANCED LANGUAGE FEATURES

This section shows how to use the toolkit to exploit language features that were not required by the *put-that-there* example.

Aside from the *put-that-there*, the studied application (Figure 3a) also supports other multimodal commands that allow the creation and deletion of arbitrary sets of objects. The simplicity of this application should not mislead the reader's judgement to underestimate the applicability of the proposed toolkit. Clearly, the same multimodal commands that can be detected during the manipulation of this simple application can also be detected for a more sophisticated one. We expect the reader to focus on the toolkit's functionalities, and distinguish them from the application's functionalities. The implementation of the latter is independent of our tools.

Variable events

End users can remove all the objects of a specific color by uttering a sentence like *'take the green out'*. This required implementing a subroutine $removeAllColor(string\ color)$

-with the obvious functionality- in the back-end application, and using the toolkit to define it as the handler of the event:

$$removeColor \quad = \quad speech.take;$$
$$speech.any\langle color\rangle;$$
$$speech.out$$

The keyword any causes the toolkit to consume an input event that is not accurately declared. In the example, unlike '$take$' and 'out', the declaration of the second speech input is rather flexible: it can be any word. Its textual form will be used to set the variable $color$.

The speech recognition grammar includes the words 'take', 'out', and several color names, but not the article 'the', which it is ignored by the toolkit.

Equivalent events

End users can create, from one to nine, objects on the canvas of the application. The number of objects to be created can be specified by means of speech or mouse gesture. This was done by implementing the said functionality into a subroutine, $createNObjects(int\ N)$, and binding it to the composite event:

$$createObjects \quad = \quad speech.create;$$
$$speech.any\langle N\rangle \mid gesture.any\langle N\rangle;$$
$$speech.objects$$

The operator '$\mid$' allows end users the possibility to pronounce the number of objects to be created (e.g. by saying '$three$'), or to write it down with a mouse gesture (e.g. by drawing the symbol '3'). In any case the result will be the same: the execution of $createNObjects(N)$ with $N = 3$. Thus, the disjunctive operator allows the definition of robust multimodal commands.

The matching templates of the digits one to nine are stored in xml files in a specific directory. For commands involving mouse gestures, the toolkit can be conveniently configured to show the mouse trail; this is possible through the controls shown in Figure 3b, FB.

Arbitrarily long events

End users can remove an arbitrary number of objects from the canvas of the application. The objects to be removed must be pointed with the mouse. The input stream '$remove\ this$ (click) $and\ this$ (click) now' is an example of how the said functionality can be activated.

This interaction technique was implemented by coding the method $removeThisAndThis(int\ xs[\ ], int\ ys[\ ])$ -with the obvious functionality- and defining it as the handler of the composite event:

$$removeMany \quad = \quad speech.remove;$$
$$speech.this + mouse.click\langle x[\ ], y[\ ]\rangle;$$
$$(speech.and;$$
$$speech.this + mouse.click\langle x[\ ], y[\ ]\rangle)^{*};$$
$$speech.now$$

The toolkit will treat variables x and y, included in the definition of $removeMany$, as arrays because of the brackets that come upon. At runtime, every time a click is detected, the mouse coordinates are inserted at the end of the arrays $x[\ ]$ and $y[\ ]$ that will eventually be passed as parameters to the $removeThisAndThis$ method.

Timeout events

The toolkit can be configured to detect single, double, and triple clicks that can lead to a different computation in the back-end application. To this end, the following composite event must be defined:

$$manyClicks \quad = \quad mouse.click\langle xs[\ ], ys[\ ]\rangle;$$
$$(mouse.click\langle xs[\ ], ys[\ ]\rangle;$$
$$mouse.click\langle xs[\ ], ys[\ ]\rangle \mid delay\text{-}250$$
$$) \mid delay\text{-}250$$

The keyword $delay$ serves to define a timeout event. The number that comes upon the hyphen ('-') indicates the number of milliseconds after which the timeout event is thrown. In the previous expression, no more than 250 milliseconds can elapse between two consecutive clicks when issuing double or triple clicks.

A subroutine $nClicks(int\ xs[\ ], int\ ys[\ ])$ implements different responses to the single, double, and triple click detection. The number of clicks is disclosed from the size of the arrays $xs[\ ]$ and $ys[\ ]$ passed as parameters.

TOOLKIT IMPLEMENTATION

This section will describe the main libraries and algorithms used to implement the proposed toolkit. This was developed in C# the same as the back-end application described in the previous sections.

Third-party software components

The toolkit text editor is the control ScintillaNET [22]. Its API makes it simple to benefit from advanced text editing and syntax highlighting. Both the grammar specification of our language and the parsing of its utterances were implemented by invoking the Irony library [14]. The state diagrams used during the simulations are controlled through MSAGL [10]. Reflection libraries are used to inspect the methods of the back-end application and to invoke them upon the detection of composite events.

Voice recognition is implemented through the System.Speech namespaces in the Microsoft .NET Framework; mouse gestures are identified by the 1$ recognizer [25]; and mouse actions and keystrokes are intercepted through hook procedures. As to the synthesizers, speech generation is implemented by the System.Speech namespaces; and the visibility of the mouse trails is controlled through the Windows API.

Verifying the validity of composite events

The grammar defining the proposed composite event definition language can be seen in (2).

The nonterminal symbols, $\langle compEvt\rangle$ and $\langle atomEvt\rangle$, refer to composite and atomic events respectively; $\langle pName\rangle$ defines the syntax of the event parameter names and is expressed as a regular expression. As to the terminal symbols, some of them, e.g. $mouse.click$, are predefined by the toolkit; others, e.g. $speech.put$, are incorporated at startup while the toolkit reads the speech recognition grammar file.

$$
\begin{aligned}
\langle compEvt \rangle &\rightarrow \langle atomEvt \rangle \\
\langle compEvt \rangle &\rightarrow \langle compEvt \rangle^{*} \\
\langle compEvt \rangle &\rightarrow \langle compEvt \rangle \ ; \ \langle compEvt \rangle \\
\langle compEvt \rangle &\rightarrow \langle compEvt \rangle \ | \ \langle compEvt \rangle \\
\langle compEvt \rangle &\rightarrow \langle compEvt \rangle \ + \ \langle compEvt \rangle \\
\langle atomEvt \rangle &\rightarrow \ mouse.click \\
& \quad | \ mouse.click \langle pName, pName \rangle \qquad (2)\\
& \quad | \ mouse.move \langle pName, pName \rangle \\
& \quad | \ speech.any \langle pName \rangle \\
& \quad | \ speech.put \\
& \quad | \quad \dots \\
& \quad | \ (\ \langle compEvt \rangle \ ) \\
\langle pName \rangle &\rightarrow \ [a\text{-}zA\text{-}Z][a\text{-}zA\text{-}Z0\text{-}9]^{*}
\end{aligned}
$$

The correct syntax of each string specifying a composite event is verified against this grammar. Such syntactic analysis may have two results: the string does not belong to the language in which case an error message is thrown, or it is well formed in which case a parse tree is returned.

Transforming composite events into finite state machines

The parse tree of a well-defined composite event will be transformed into an state diagram by the function $createStateDiagram$ (Algorithm 2). This transforms the tree whose root node is passed as an argument into an state diagram, which is then returned as output. Hence, the state diagram representing a composite event E can be obtained by invoking $createStateDiagram(rt)$ -where rt is the root node of the tree obtained from parsing E.

The base case of the recursive Algorithm 2 occurs when its argument is a node with a single child. Such nodes represent atomic events and have trivial transformations, e.g. the smallest graph of Figure 4a represents the atomic event $e3$. The recursive cases involve intermixing small state diagrams obtained from transforming fragments of the parse tree. Each operator defines a different way to intermix state diagrams.

When two composite events are linked by a 'FOLLOWED BY' operator, the toolkit concatenates its reciprocal state diagrams (Figure 4b). When two composite events are connected by the disjunctive operator 'OR', the toolkit creates a new state diagram by overlaying the initial and final states of its graphical counterparts (Figure 4c). Two composite events connected by the conjunctive operator 'AND' causes the creation of a state diagram whose paths between its initial and final nodes are the permutations of all the events contained in their reciprocal state diagrams (Figure 4d). Finally, a single composite event followed by the 'ITERATION' operator causes the alteration of its parallel state diagram: the ingoing arcs of its final state will be redirected to its initial state (Figure 4e).

Events consumption policy

When entering simulation mode, the input recognizers are activated so that the toolkit can embark on event tracking. Every time an event occurs, the toolkit checks whether it was expected, i.e. whether its name is annotated in some outgoing arc of the node representing the current toolkit state. In the affirmative case, the toolkit moves to another state and sets the event parameters values associated with this transition. Otherwise, the toolkit state remains the same. In both cases, the triggering event will be consumed and no longer available for processing.

End user testing adds a layer of complexity. Here, the toolkit must handle several composite events occurring in arbitrary order. However, since our approach requires multimodal commands to be executed one at a time, identifying the multimodal command under execution will reduce the problem to the simulation case. This identification is achieved from the first event detected after the reset action.

Handling parallel inputs

When a composite event is transformed into its reciprocal state diagram, its nodes are automatically classified into: stable/unstable. The toolkit uses these unstable nodes to handle parallel input. Visits to unstable nodes cannot last longer than a threshold time set in the toolkit's configuration file.

For instance, during the detection of the *put-that-there* command, the toolkit entrance to states 3 or 4 (Figure 3b) will cause the activation of a timer ensuring fast transitions to state 5. If the timer expires the toolkit will go back to state 2, the last visited stable state. This prevents long delays between speech inputs and mouse clicks, i.e. end users are enforced to issue them simultaneously.

Unstable states appear when events are connected by the 'AND' operator. All the intermediate nodes of the graph returned by PERMUTE($sd1$, $sd2$) will be classified as unstable states, e.g. all nodes except for 1 and B in Figure 4d. When the toolkit steps back from an unstable to the last visited stable state, the variables set during this interim are rolled back.

RELATED WORK

There are currently toolkits that allow specifying the composite events characterizing multimodal human-machine interaction. These can be classified into two groups:

Toolkits providing domain-specific visual languages

MEngine [3] offers a graphical editor that allows users to depict composite events as state diagrams. It can combine gestures and speech inputs but its models grow too quickly when dealing with simultaneity. To correctly model simultaneous events, many possibilities must be considered, e.g. deictic terms can precede pointing or vice versa during speak-and-point selection. Our toolkit protects its users from this state explosion through the automatic generation of state diagrams.

NiMMiT [6] was a visual language used to specify multimodal interactions in the context of virtual environments. Its notation allows grouping sets of simultaneous events but not successions of related events. Another NiMMiT issue is that the parameter values of a triggering event, e.g. mouse cursor position, have to be captured by the back-end system. Thus, sequentially multimodal interactions lead to bulky diagrams. In our language, large series of sequential events can be regarded as a single composite event through the FOLLOWED BY operator. Moreover, the parameter values are captured and stored by our toolkit until the back-end system is invoked.

ICO [17] allows formal descriptions of multimodal interactive systems. It has been successfully applied in the field

---

Algorithm 2 Transforms (a fragment of) a parse tree into a state diagram

---

procedure CREATESTATEDIAGRAM($node$)   ▷ $node$ is the root of the (sub)tree to be transformed

    if $isAtomic(node.children[1])$ **then**
        return TRIVIALSD(node.children[1])

    else if $isComposite(node.children[1])$ & $node.children[2] =$ '$*$' **then**
        $sd1 \leftarrow createStateDiagram(node.children[1])$
        return LOOP(sd1)

    else if $isComposite(node.children[1])$ & $node.children[2] =$ ';' & $isComposite(node.children[3])$ **then**
        $sd1 \leftarrow createStateDiagram(node.children[1])$
        $sd2 \leftarrow createStateDiagram(node.children[3])$
        return CONCATENATE(sd1, sd2)

    else if $isComposite(node.children[1])$ & $node.children[2] =$ '|' & $isComposite(node.children[3])$ **then**
        $sd1 \leftarrow createStateDiagram(node.children[1])$
        $sd2 \leftarrow createStateDiagram(node.children[3])$
        return OVERLAY(sd1, sd2)

    else if $isComposite(node.children[1])$ & $node.children[2] =$ '+' & $isComposite(node.children[3])$ **then**
        $sd1 \leftarrow createStateDiagram(node.children[1])$
        $sd2 \leftarrow createStateDiagram(node.children[3])$
        return PERMUTE(sd1, sd2)

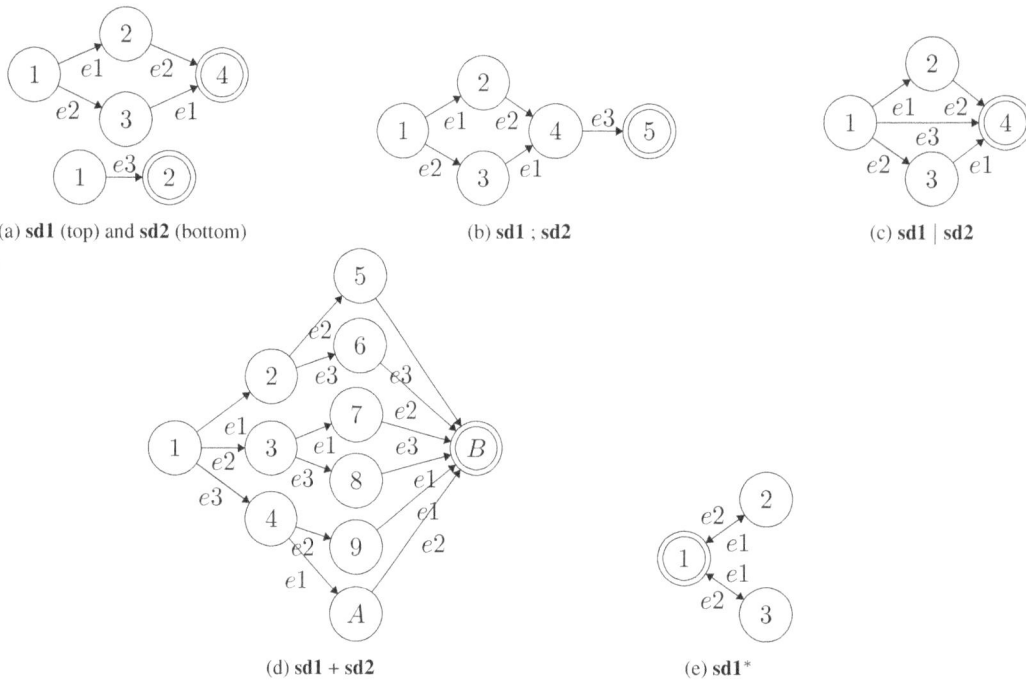

Figure 4: The effect of the operators as applied on two state machines specified in (a): (b) **CONCATENATE(sd1, sd2)**. (c) **OVERLAY(sd1, sd2)**. (d) **PERMUTE(sd1, sd2)** and (e) **LOOP(sd1)**.

of safety-critical systems. Both simultaneous and sequential user actions can be specified through the depiction of Petri nets-based models. But the correct understanding of these models is not a simple task: it requires a solid command of the transition rule of Petri nets. In contrast, our notation maps directly to the problem domain without need of specialized knowledge beyond multimodal interaction.

The visual models of HephaisTK [8] include symbols to group simultaneous and successive events. However, it can only group fixed-length sequences of events. Besides that, event parameters have to be specified in a separate file. In our language instead, an arbitrarily long sequence of events can be regarded as one composite event through the ITERATION operator. Our specifications also include event parameters.

Additional graphical toolkits were described in [4].

Toolkits exploiting ready-made textual languages
Mudra [13] interprets CLIPS-based specifications. Composite events are defined by declaring a set of rules that will be verified against a fact base. Facts are inserted as user events are detected. The satisfaction of a rule indicates the occurrence of a composite event. Unlike our toolkit, Mudra offers multi-user support.

MIML [1], XISL [15], and UsiXML [24] are XML-based languages aimed at describing multimodal interfaces. MIML describes interfaces in three layers: interaction, tasks and platform. XISL allows describing the user operations and system actions separated from XML contents. It offers constructs to describe sequential, parallel, alternative, and coordinated use of modalities. UsiXML can shape the user interface of any interactive application including multimodal ones. With UsiXML, the user interfaces can be described in a way that preserves the design independently from peculiar characteristics of physical computing platform. The proponents of these languages also offer toolkits that transform their specifications into concrete interfaces.

For each of these toolkits, its users must pay for the verboseness of its underlying language. Both CLIPS and XML programs contain a high number of pair-delimiter symbols. The commands, facts, and arguments, which are essential elements in CLIPS programs, must be enclosed between parentheses. This leads to expressions with excessive pairings as the comparison between our specification, shown in (1), and the one in [13, p. 5] attests. Likewise, the editing of XML documents is riddled with tag pairs. The use of pair-delimiter symbols is not only tedious, but also a potent source of slips since it is not uncommon for the pairing to go wrong [11].

DISCUSSION
As mentioned above, previous research has focused on two classes of executable multimodal human-machine interaction models. In this paper, we elaborate on a new approach to multimodal interaction modeling through the use of a domain-specific textual language. We decided to implement an specialized language because domain-specificity can lead to substantial gains in expressiveness and ease of use [16]. With the textual notation, we looked for compact specifications.

Our language certainly leads to compact specifications as the comparison of our *put-that-there* definition (1) against the six models shown in [5, p. 5], [13, p. 5], [3, p. 2], and [20, p .4] suggests. More precisely, the physical space occupied by the enclosing boxes of the aforementioned models ranges from 22.8 (HephaisTK) to 60.8 cm^2 (NiMMiT) whereas our specification only requires 9.0 cm^2. If we consider that the visual specification of HephaisTK is incomplete (parameters are set in another file), the second briefer specification would be the one of Mudra (25.4 cm^2). In this comparison, all models were printed to have similar readability. Although these results cannot be generalized, they serve as an indicator of the conciseness of our language. The benefits of a concise notation should not be underestimated: the less material to be scanned, the higher the proportion of it that can be held in working memory, and the lower the disruption caused by frequent searches through the model [11].

The expected gains in expressiveness were also observed. When counting the minimal number of subroutines required to implement the examples previously described, we found that this can be reduced by a range of 33% to 60% when using the toolkit. For instance, without using the toolkit, we needed five procedures to create a standalone C# *put-that-there* application: the four shown in Algorithm 1 plus the $InitializeComponent$ method required when building windows forms. When using the toolkit, we only needed a back-end C# system with two methods: PUTTHATTHERE and $InitializeComponent$.

It must be emphasized that our approach does not rely on the low frequency at which the speech inputs or mouse clicks, used in the examples, are normally generated. The toolkit can also handle high throughput of events. For instance, mouse movements, which may be raised around 100 times per second, can be processed by using the $mouse.move\langle x[\,], y[\,]\rangle^*$ pattern in unimodal commands such as the *drag and drop*. Then, extending the toolkit so that it can support other devices generating high throughput data streams, e.g. laser pointers or accelerometers, would not challenge our approach.

FUTURE WORK
We will investigate the usability of our toolkit via user studies. This includes measuring the time and programming workload required to define multimodal interfaces in both our toolkit and a commercial framework.

A manageable issue that we will address in future work is that the toolkit only invokes the external back-end application upon the full detection of a composite event. This can be a problem when specifying interactions that require application-dependent intermediate feedback, e.g. when the selected object in the *put-that-there* has to be highlighted. To redress this problem, we plan to modify the system structure so that the handling subroutines can be bound not to the state diagrams but to their nodes.

At this point, our toolkit can only handle one multimodal command execution at a time, which precludes multi-user applications. We will evaluate the feasibility of using UML state machines [23, Chapter 15]. In theory, treating composite events as the orthogonal regions of a UML state machine would permit modeling simultaneous execution of multimodal commands.

CONCLUSION

The detection of multimodal commands requires a supervisory mechanism for detecting event patterns. In order to free programmers from implementing such mechanism, the HCI community has proposed many toolkits seeking to ease this problem. Some toolkits provide domain-specific visual languages in which the composite events to be detected must be specified. Other toolkits interpret specifications performed in a ready-made textual language like XML or CLIPS.

We have proposed a composite event definition language that combines the distinguishing features of these dominant approaches: the domain-specificity and the textual notation. The former offers gains in expressiveness and ease of use; the latter leads to compact specifications. The language allows defining composite events for their subsequent detection by a toolkit. This transforms user-defined composite events into finite state machines enhanced with parameterized events and unstable nodes. The partial detection of a composite event can be acknowledged through multimodal output; its full detection causes the invocation of handles in a back-end system.

REFERENCES

1. Araki, M., and Tachibana, K. Multimodal dialog description language for rapid system development. In *Proceedings of the 7th SIGdial Workshop on Discourse and Dialogue* (2006), 109–116.

2. Bolt, R. Put-that-there: Voice and gesture at the graphics interface. In *Proceedings of the 7th annual conference on computer graphics and interactive techniques (SIGGRAPH' 80)*, ACM (1980).

3. Bourguet, M. A toolkit for creating and testing multimodal interface designs. In *Proceedings of UIST'02* (2002), 29–30.

4. Cuenca, F., Coninx, K., Luyten, K., and Vanacken, D. Graphical Toolkits for Rapid Prototyping of Multimodal Systems: A Survey. *Interacting with Computers* (2014).

5. Cuenca, F., Vanacken, D., Coninx, K., and Luyten, K. Assessing the support provided by a toolkit for rapid prototyping of multimodal systems. In *Proceedings of the 5th ACM SIGCHI symposium on Engineering interactive computing systems (EICS'13)*, ACM (2013), 307–312.

6. De Boeck, J., Vanacken, D., Raymaekers, C., and Coninx, K. High level modeling of multimodal interaction techniques using NiMMiT. *Journal of Virtual Reality and Broadcasting 4*, 2 (2007).

7. Dragicevic, P., and Fekete, J. Support for input adaptability in the icon toolkit. In *Proceedings of the 6th International Conference on Multimodal Interfaces (ICMI'04)*, ACM (2004), 212–219.

8. Dumas, B., Lalanne, D., and Ingold, R. Description Languages for Multimodal Interaction: A Set of Guidelines and its Illustration with SMUIML. *Journal of multimodal user interfaces 3*, 3 (2010), 237–247.

9. Google Glass. http://www.google.com/glass/start/.

10. Microsoft Glee. http://research.microsoft.com/en-us/projects/msagl/.

11. Green, T., and Petre, M. Usability analysis of visual programming environments: a cognitive dimensions framework. *Journal of Visual Languages & Computing 7*, 2 (1996), 131–174.

12. Green, T. R., and Petre, M. When visual programs are harder to read than textual programs. In *In Human-Computer Interaction: Tasks and Organisation, Proceedings of ECCE-6 (6th European Conference on Cognitive Ergonomics)*, ACM (1992).

13. Hoste, L., Dumas, B., and Signer, B. Mudra: a unified multimodal interaction framework. In *Proceedings of the 13th international conference on multimodal interfaces (ICMI'11)*, ACM (2011), 97–104.

14. Irony. http://irony.codeplex.com/.

15. Katsurada, K., Nakamura, Y., Yamada, H., and Nitta, T. Xisl: A language for describing multimodal interaction scenarios. In *Proceedings of the 5th International Conference on Multimodal Interfaces (ICMI 2003)* (2003), 281–284.

16. Mernik, M., Heering, J., and Sloane, A. When and how to develop domain-specific languages. *ACM Computing Surveys (CSUR) 37*, 4 (2005), 316–344.

17. Navarre, D., Palanque, P., Ladry, J., and Barboni, E. ICOs: A Model-Based User Interface Description Technique dedicated to Interactive Systems Addressing Usability, Reliability and Scalability. *ACM Transactions on Computer-Human Interaction 16*, 4 (2009).

18. Oviatt, S. Ten myths of multimodal interaction. *Communications of the ACM 42*, 11 (1999), 74–81.

19. Oviatt, S. Multimodal interfaces. In *The Human Computer Interaction Handbook: Fundamentals, Evolving technologies and Emerging Applications* (2003).

20. Palanque, P., and Schyn, A. A model-based approach for engineering multimodal interactive systems. In *INTERACT* (2003).

21. Paton, N., and Daz, O. Active database systems. *ACM Computing Surveys 31*, 1 (1999), 63–103.

22. ScintillaNET. http://scintillanet.codeplex.com/.

23. UML State Machines. http://www.omg.org/spec/UML/2.4.1/Superstructure/.

24. UsiXML. http://www.usixml.org/.

25. Wobbrock, J., Wilson, A., and Li, Y. Gestures without libraries, toolkits or training: a $1 recognizer for user interface prototypes. In *Proceedings of the 20th annual ACM symposium on User interface software and technology (UIST'07)*, ACM (2007), 159–168.

Metadata Type System: Integrate Presentation, Data Models and Extraction to Enable Exploratory Browsing Interfaces

Yin Qu, Andruid Kerne, Nic Lupfer, Rhema Linder and Ajit Jain

Interface Ecology Lab, Texas A&M University

College Station, TX, USA

yin, andruid, nic, rhema, ajit@ecologylab.net

ABSTRACT

Exploratory browsing involves encountering new information during open-ended tasks. Disorientation and digression are problems that arise, as the user repeatedly loses context while clicking hyperlinks. To maintain context, exploratory browsing interfaces must present multiple web pages at once.

Design of exploratory browsing interfaces must address the limits of display and human working memory. Our approach is based on expandable metadata summaries. Prior semantic web exploration tools represent documents as metadata, but often depend on semantic web formats and datasets assembled in advance. They do not support dynamically encountered information from popular web sites. Optimizing presentation of metadata summaries for particular types of documents is important as a further means for reducing the cognitive load of rapidly browsing across many documents.

To address these issues, we develop a metadata type system as the basis for building exploratory browsing interfaces that maintain context. The type system leverages constructs from object-oriented programming languages. We integrate data models, extraction rules, and presentation semantics in types to operationalize type specific dynamic metadata extraction and rich presentation. Using the type system, we built the Metadata In-Context Expander (MICE) interface as a proof of concept. A study, in which students engaged in exploring prior work, showed that MICE's metadata summaries help users maintain context during exploratory browsing.

Author Keywords

Dynamic Metadata; Exploratory Browsing; Type Systems

ACM Classification Keywords

H.5.2 Information interfaces and presentation: User Interfaces: Graphical user interfaces.

INTRODUCTION

Browsing is a fundamental World Wide Web (WWW) activity [33]. According to Marchionini and Shneiderman, "browsing is an exploratory, information-seeking strategy that depends

on serendipity" [32]. By *exploratory browsing*, we mean browsing when the task is open-ended and the user is unfamiliar with the information space. Exploratory browsing is key to *berrypicking* [3], the iterative process in which the user encounters new information, and her understanding and information needs evolve. Browsing and search are complementary strategies for exploring information [32]. In *exploratory search* [46], users engaged in learning and investigation iteratively refine information needs. While this paper directly addresses exploratory browsing, its implications also impact exploratory search.

Users lose context while browsing, as new information is encountered [16]. Interlinked pages are shown in separate viewports, leading to *disorientation* [10], the problem of not knowing where you are or how to return to an encountered page in a network of information, and *digression* [17], the problem of going off track amidst many open windows or tabs. Disorientation and digression can grow acute during exploratory browsing. To counter, we design new interfaces that maintain context for the user during exploratory browsing.

Engineering exploratory browsing interfaces that maintain context requires building mechanisms for dynamically presenting trails [9] of linked documents. Since display and the user's cognitive resources, such as working memory [11], are limited, the interface must present documents as summaries, to reduce display space and cognitive load. Typically, summaries refer to manually or algorithmically extracted texts that reveal the chief points or substance of a document.

The present research hypothesizes that *metadata* – a data structure that describes a document – can function as a valuable form of summary. Many popular, useful web sites do not directly publish metadata. Thus, mechanisms for extracting metadata from ordinary web pages are required. Further, exploratory browsing involves encountering heterogeneous types of information, each of which is best represented with particular data models, layouts, and styles. The interface must dynamically derive and present metadata summaries particular to encountered information types at runtime, to reduce the cognitive load of browsing chains of linked information.

The present research operationalizes a metadata type system to address challenges of dynamically summarizing and presenting heterogeneous documents as expandable metadata in a unified context, to enable exploratory browsing across diverse websites. The type system integrates object-oriented mechanisms for describing: (1) *data models* of underlying

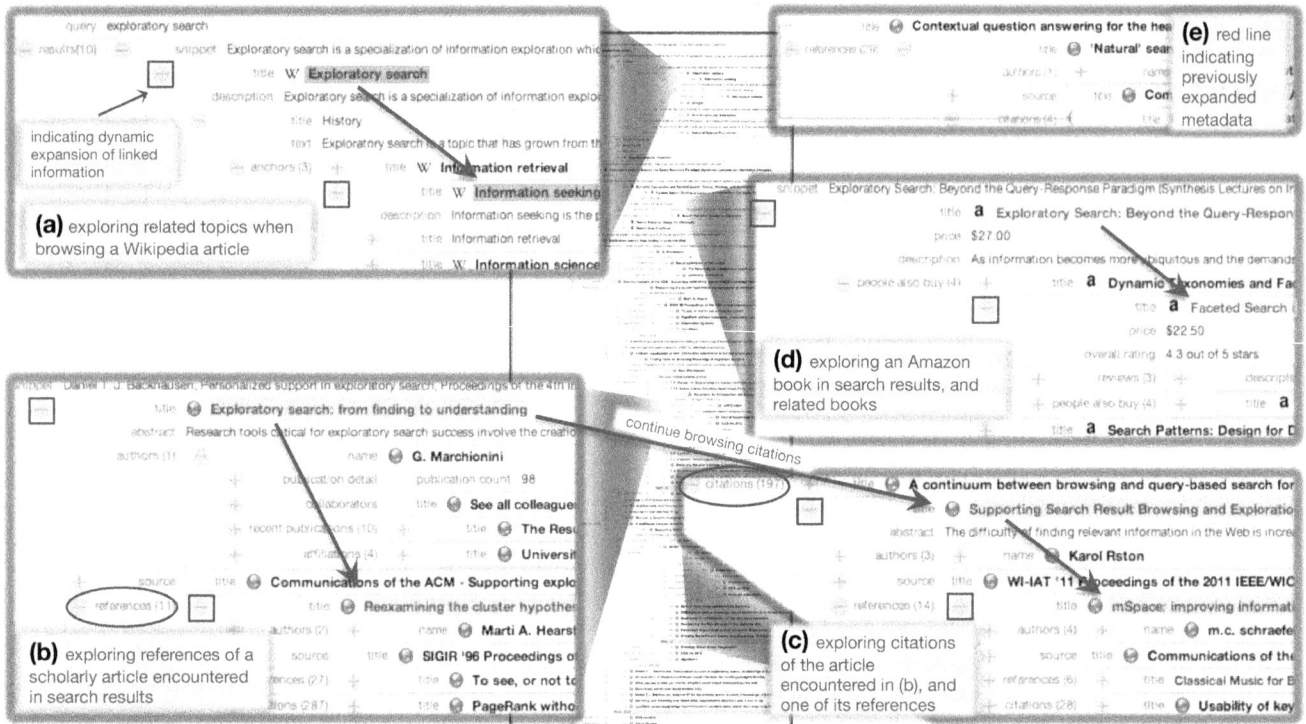

Figure 1: An overview of Mia's exploratory browsing with MICE. Snippets show close-up views of her session. Arrows denote browsing linked information.

metadata schemas; (2) *extraction rules* for deriving metadata summaries from particular web pages, using appropriate data models; and (3) *presentation semantics* to guide usable display of metadata summaries. When the user explores a web page in context, the runtime dynamically assigns the optimal metadata type, instantiates typed metadata summary objects, extracts metadata from the page to populate the instances, and passes appropriate semantics to the interface, along with instances, for type-specific presentation. The interface makes relationships between linked documents visible.

Our contributions include:

1. Demonstrating, in exploratory browsing, the unique value of metadata as a form for document summaries.

2. Integrating data models with extraction rules and presentation semantics for rich, usable presentation of metadata summaries that helps mitigate cognitive load.

3. Supporting heterogeneous information types through document subtype polymorphism, which promotes reuse.

4. Supporting encountering new information as needed for exploratory browsing and berrypicking, by dynamically binding documents, types, extraction, and presentation.

5. Making metadata available from popular web sites, such as Amazon, ACM Digital Library, and search engines.

Using the metadata type system, we built an **example** dynamic exploratory browsing interface, the Metadata In-Context Expander (MICE) (Figure 1) [24]. The visual appearance of MICE looks like a typical XML or RDF visu-

alizer, but goes beyond by supporting dynamic acquisition, presentation, and exploration of new information.

We begin this paper with an exploratory browsing scenario that motivates development of the interface and type system, followed by a discussion of related work. Next, we use the scenario to contextualize an explanation of how the metadata type system enables exploratory browsing interfaces, such as MICE. We then present a user study in which computer science students browse and explore scholarly articles for prior work search and project ideation. The results show how MICE supports exploratory browsing in context. We finish by deriving implications for engineering exploratory browsing interfaces, and drawing conclusions.

SCENARIO: EXPLORATORY BROWSING WITH MICE

Mia is a computer science student who wants to conceptualize a research project about exploratory search. She starts by searching Google for "exploratory search". MICE presents search results in an expandable list. Each result is presented as a snippet followed by a collapsed document with only the title visible. Mia notices that the title shown in MICE is clickable, like the title links Google would present. She clicks on the plus button to expand the collapsed document in the first result, which is a Wikipedia article [47]. Information from that document is accessed in real time, converted to metadata summary, and presented in MICE (Figure 1a).

The metadata summary of the Wikipedia article introduces the concept of exploratory search, including its history, research challenges, and major researchers. Related topics are linked. Some linked topics are new to Mia. With MICE,

Mia can easily expand linked topics, bringing metadata about them into the current context (Figure 1a). Further related topics are again linked as expandable metadata. Using this recursive information expansion, she explores topics, such as "information seeking", "faceted search", and "information foraging". She can still see the central topic, exploratory search, at the top, which helps her maintain focus without being disoriented by Wikipedia's many links. After a period of exploration in Wikipedia, she collapses these related topics in MICE and returns to the search results.

Wikipedia provides a good overview, but Mia wants to dig deeper. From the search results, she expands a scholarly article [31] from the ACM Digital Library. MICE extracts metadata for that article, including authors, abstract, references, and citations, and presents it in a concise form (Figure 1b).

Mia expands that article's references in MICE, seeking prior work it builds upon. She sees an interesting article [20] (Figure 1b) about exploring information, in which the user starts with a broad query and uses clustering to gradually refine the scope of information to explore [12]. She finds this idea inspiring. Another reference [32] distinguishes two different strategies for finding information: search and browsing. Mia keeps chaining references, discovering a seminal survey on experiential problems in hypertext [10], e.g., the cognitive load of seeing enormous amounts of information and maintaining context. By exploring prior work, Mia expands her understanding of the roots of research in this field.

With this understanding, Mia seeks new work in this field. She goes back to a scholarly article encountered in the search results, and expands its citations (Figure 1c). MICE shows 10 citations at a time, out of 197. Mia clicks on a button at the end of the list to reveal the next 10. She expands a title that catches her eye: [35] (Figure 1c). It discusses an interesting idea of applying zoomable user interfaces to clustering-based exploration. From the references of this article, she notices another one [27] by one of the major researchers introduced in the Wikipedia article. She expands it (Figure 1c).

As Mia continues exploring, she encounters information from sources including CiteSeerX, Google Books, and Amazon (on which she orders books on exploratory search and faceted search, Figure 1d). MICE supports her exploration process by showing rich, useful metadata summaries of browsed documents, and iteratively bringing linked information into context on click. When she encounters a previously expanded document, MICE displays a red line on hover, leading her to the previous occurrence (Figure 1e). Over an extended period of non-linear exploratory browsing, Mia learns a lot about the topic, including motivation, prior work, critiques, and new directions. Synthesizing what she learns, Mia conceptualizes a project about software architecture that supports multiple paradigms of exploratory browsing and search interfaces.

RELATED WORK
The metadata type system and exploratory browsing interface relate to prior work on the Semantic Web, metadata extraction, and exploration. It differentiates from them in making metadata available from popular web sites, extracting meta-

data of multiple types from heterogeneous sources, and supporting exploratory browsing with new information.

Metadata on the Web
The Semantic Web [2] effort develops standards and techniques to represent, query, and process metadata. RDF [42] is the primary information model. It represents metadata as *triples*, each consisting of a subject, a predicate, and an object. RDF can describe complex, interlinked metadata and relationships. However, many useful web sites and services, e.g. Google Search, Amazon, ACM Digital Library, and Twitter, do not publish RDF. RDF-S [43] and OWL [44] are Semantic Web technologies that specify metadata schemas using RDF. The focus is on inference rather than presentation. In consideration of contemporary web programming practice, we observe that presently out of the 10604 APIs indexed by `http://programmableweb.com`, only 74 use RDF. Thus, the Semantic Web representation of types and data seems unpopular with web developers. This problem is not new [1].

Microdata [45] embeds metadata into HTML pages using attributes denoting types and properties, making it easier for websites to publish formal semantics. Major search engines have been collaborating on a set of standard semantic types described in microdata, at `http://schema.org`. However, like RDF, many useful web sites, including Amazon and the ACM Digital Library, do not publish microdata.

Extracting Metadata
To overcome the scarcity of metadata on the web, prior systems extract metadata, for the user to collect and view.

Web Summaries [14] is a browser extension that allows users to create extraction patterns, extract metadata from web pages, and see collected metadata in different views. In a 10-week study [15], extracted metadata was found useful for both transient and long-term user tasks. Users liked a functionality called that takes a hyperlink on a page, extracts metadata from the destination page, and brings it into the context of the current page. They valued directly accessing linked metadata from within an initial context.

Piggy Bank [23] extracts metadata from web pages using a browser extension, stores it in an RDF database, and provides a faceted browsing interface. Exhibit [21] allows the user to publish metadata in a special JSON-based format in a faceted interface. Presentation is templated and customizable.

Marmite [48] and Vegemite [30] let end users create browser based metadata extraction scripts, or *mashups*. However, studies showed that users without programming skills experienced difficulty in authoring mashups. Thus, the applicability of these tools to general, unskilled users is unclear.

Clui [34] provides a browser plugin for users to collect metadata from the browser, represented with types called "webits". The type system lacks inheritance or polymorphism, and so is limited.

The present metadata type system actively extracts metadata from regular web pages. Different from scrapers that extract individual metadata records from open browser windows, the type system supports extensibility by enabling developers to reuse data models and presentation semantics, through an object-oriented programming language, as well as to reuse types, such as scholarly article, across different information sources. Further, this research addresses presenting *linked* metadata in one context. while making relationships visible, to support exploratory browsing.

Exploring Metadata

mSpace is a faceted browser for exploring a fixed repository of knowledge in the form of a metadata collection [27]. The user can re-order facets (dimensions) to re-organize presentation. When the user hovers over a facet label, mSpace shows associated snippets extracted from documentsl, bringing limited information into context. mSpace requires the knowledge to be encoded in RDF in advance [39], preventing exploratory browsing of newly encountered information.

CS AKTive Space presents a UK Computer Science research metadata collection [18]. The interface displays search results in a faceted list, supporting column sorting and preview cues, like mSpace. When the user selects a research group, person, or publication, details are shown beneath the faceted list, in the same page, maintaining context. However, only one detailed item can be shown at a time. Metadata is collected through *ad hoc* programs translating data to RDF, called *mediators*. They have been used "predominantly for large, comparatively static data sources" and "high-value data sources of general interest to the community" to populate the system with enough data, implying a scarcity of RDF data in the domain. Since knowledge acquisition precedes interaction, the ability for serendipitous browsing and exploration is limited. The system only addresses information in one domain, not an open-ended set of heterogeneous sources.

PGV [13] visualizes interconnected metadata in RDF as a graph; nodes are entities and edges are relationships. The user can expands linked nodes incrementally. The Atom Interface [37] improves visual presentation of such a graph using circles. X3S [40] reconstructs RDF query results in XML, which is further transformed to HTML styled with CSS for presentation. These interfaces operate on prepared RDF datasets, and thus do not support open exploratory browsing.

Tabulator [5] is a generic browser for linked RDF data. Its outliner mode shows metadata in a manner similar to MICE. Tabulator supports serendipitous browsing, differentiating from prior RDF interfaces. It is more generic. When the user expands a field, and the field is a link to another metadata record, it actively deferences the link and shows connected metadata in the same context. The authors emphasized such serendipity, since it supports "re-use of information in ways that are unforeseen by the publisher, and often unexpected by the consumer". However, Tabulator's scope is limited by the scarcity of RDF data on the web. The absence of type-based presentation semantics leaves issues of metadata's cognitive load un-addressed.

Parallax [22] enables "set-based browsing". The user starts with a set of metadata records, connected by facets. However, when browsing across facets, direct presentation of con-

text is lost. The user views metadata linked to the current set in a new viewport. To ameliorate, Parallax maintains a linear trail of previously browsed sets. However, browsing and exploration processes may not be linear [29] [19]. Parallax works with a prepared dataset, available at `freebase.com`. Users thus cannot explore live information outside the prepared dataset, such as ACM Digital Library papers.

METADATA TYPE SYSTEM

Building upon the open source *meta-metadata* language and architecture [28], we develop a metadata type system to support exploratory browsing interfaces such as MICE. The type system addresses representing documents as metadata, dynamic metadata extraction, and presenting linked, heterogeneous metadata. We use the above scenario to contextualize our presentation of the metadata type system.

Figure 2 presents a procedural overview of the metadata type system. When the user encounters a document, the type system automatically selects the most appropriate type and binds it to the document. Data models and extraction rules specified by the type enable dynamic metadata derivation from the document. Then, the extracted metadata instance and the type, including presentation semantics, are sent to the interface. The interface dynamically binds data models and presentation semantics with extracted metadata and generates customized visual elements to present heterogeneous metadata in context.

Representing Documents as Metadata

Limits in human cognition form the basis of a need to concisely and consistently represent documents. In Mia's exploratory browsing session, she encounters diverse documents, such as articles, author profiles, and books. Some documents contain nested structures, such as a long list of citations. Presenting original documents with all the information in one context could overwhelm, since working memory is limited [11]. To mitigate this, the present research summarizes documents as *metadata*. Nested structures, such as citation lists, are broken down into constituent sub-objects, which the user can collapse and expand to focus use of attention and display. Figure 1b shows metadata for a scholarly article, e.g., title, authors, and references.

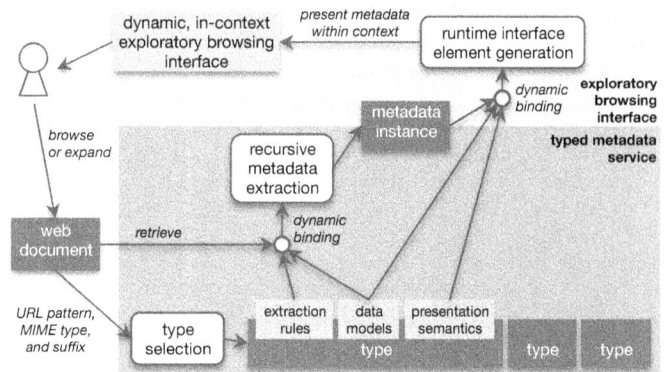

Figure 2: Metadata type system: procedural view.

The present metadata type system specifies types in code blocks called *wrappers*. Figure 3 shows example wrappers used in Mia's scenario. Wrapper `creative_work` specifies a common type for creative work, which includes *fields* such as `year`, `references`, and `rating`. The type system supports three kinds of fields. (1) A *scalar field* defines a typed slot for scalars – values conveniently represented as a string. For example, field `year` in wrapper `creative_work` specifies a slot for an integer. (2) A *composite field*, such as `rich_media` in wrapper `creative_work`, defines a slot for an instance of a specified `type`. (3) A *collection field* defines a slot for a set of instances of a common type specified by `child_type`. In wrapper `creative_work`, field `references` specifies a reference list in which each reference must be an instance of `document` (or its subtypes by *polymorphism*, which we will explain later), and field `citations` specifies a citation list in which each citation is an instance of `creative_work`. A collection field can also hold a set of scalar values. Composite and collection fields can represent relationships between linked metadata, as `references` and `citations` do.

The type system supports *inheritance*, denoted by attribute `extends`, for reusing and extending types. For instance, as a form of creative work, we derive a type, `scholarly_article`, that inherits from `creative_work`, adding new fields such as `source` and `keywords` (Figure 3). Wrapper `acm_portal` further subtypes `scholarly_article` to extract metadata in the general scholarly article data model from a specific source (the ACM Digital Library). A common practice is to define a data model in a base type and use it for source-specific extraction in subtypes. The type system defines a common base type, `document`, for general web pages, which includes a `title`, a `location` (the URL), and a `description`.

The present metadata type system further enables representation of real world semantics involving multiple inheritance. We use *mixins* [8], which enable non-hierarchical incorporation of structures from another type without explicit inheritance to address this issue, achieving type flexibility on par to that of Freebase [6].

Extracting Heterogeneous Metadata From Documents

A major difficulty with representing documents as metadata is that many popular, useful web sites do not publish metadata. The metadata type system addresses this by actively extracting metadata of heterogeneous types from regular HTML pages published by these sites.

The extraction process begins when the user encounters a document. In Mia's case, when she clicks on the plus button to expand the encountered ACM Digital Library article, MICE makes a request to an underlying typed metadata service to extract metadata for that article. Since Mia could encounter many types of documents, the service needs to select the wrapper appropriate for the requested document. This is enabled by matching URL or mime-type features using *selectors* defined in wrappers. In Figure 3, the wrapper `acm_portal` specifies a selector for ACM Digital Library articles, with a URL pattern as the feature. Once matched, the wrapper associated with a selector is bound to the document for extraction.

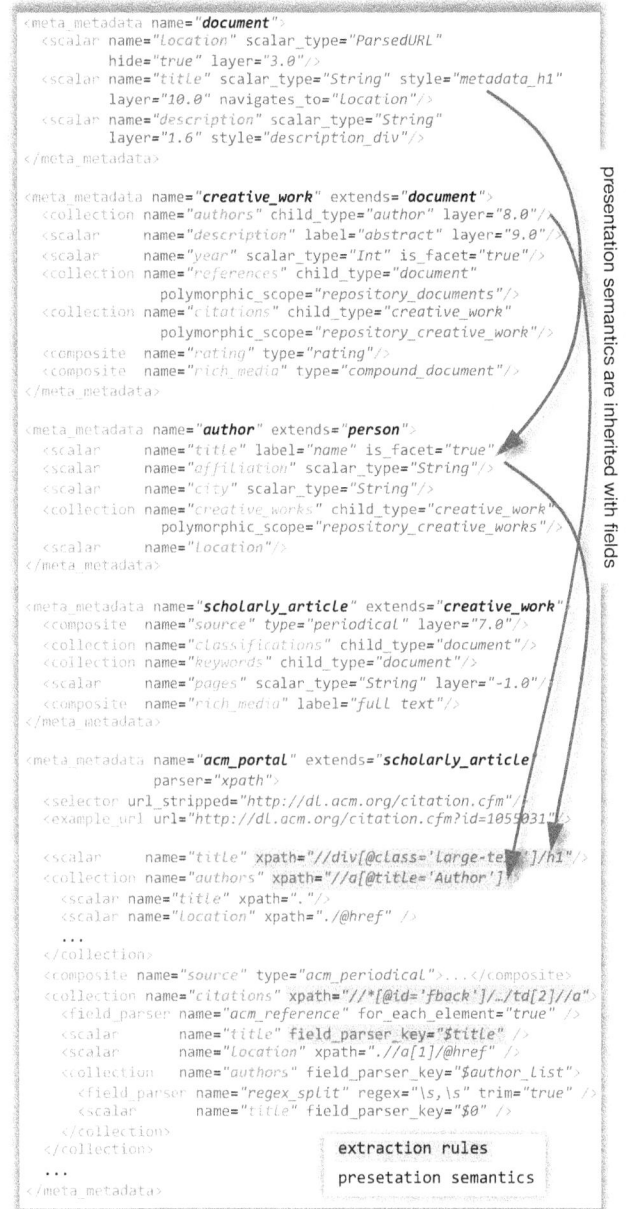

Figure 3: Type inheritance and referencing in example meta-metadata wrappers from Mia's scenario.

After binding the wrapper `acm_portal` with Mia's encountered article, the runtime uses *extraction rules* integrated with data model fields to extract metadata from the document. Extraction rules can include (1) XPaths which operate on the HTML DOM tree, (2) names that directly map to elements in XML or JSON documents, (3) regular expressions for pattern matching and filtering, and (4) *field parsers* for injecting algorithms to parse strings in special formats. Figure 3 shows example extraction rules (XPaths and a field parser) for extracting article metadata from ACM Digital Library articles.

Algorithmically, the extraction process first instantiates an empty metadata object of the selected type, then populates the instantiated metadata object with extracted information

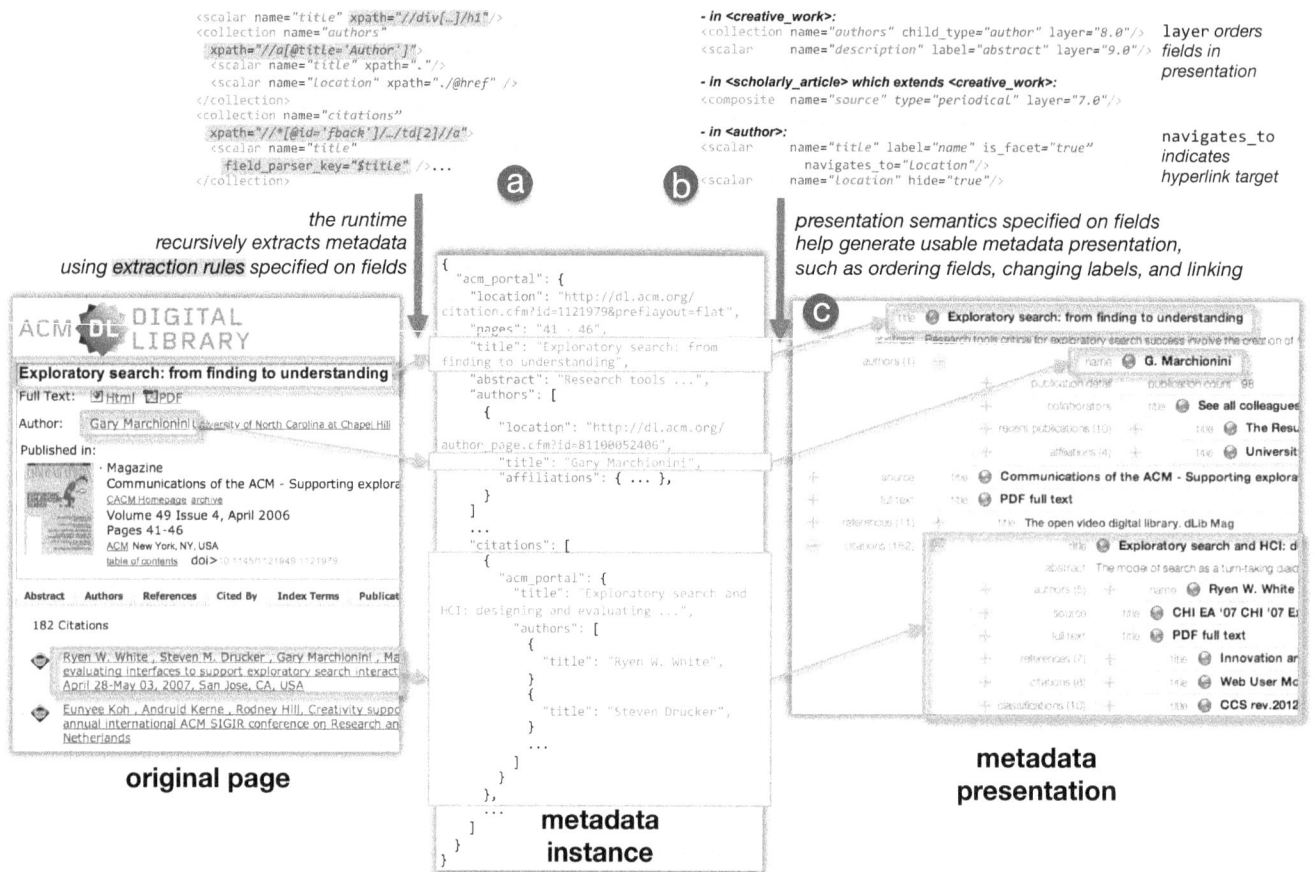

Figure 4: Metadata type system: semantic view. Types drive extraction from the source web page. The type is then joined with the resulting instance (seen as JSON), to drive presentation.

by iterating over data model fields. For each field, the integrated extraction rules are used to acquire information from the document (Figure 4a). For a scalar field, the extracted representation, a string, is converted into a value of the specified scalar type, such as integer or URL. For a composite or collection field, the process recursively instantiates and populates sub-object(s), using contextual DOM node(s) located by the extraction rule specified in the declaration of the encompassing composite or collection field.

In Figure 4a, the XPath on `citations` matches a list of contextual nodes, each of which corresponds to an anchored, formatted citation string (framed in the figure) in the original page. Formatted citation strings are parsed into key-value pairs, such as authors, title, and publication venue, using a field parser for ACM reference formats. Values are then assigned to the fields of a nested `creative_work` sub-object, such as `title` and `authors`, by `field_parser_key`. The anchor destination of a citation is extracted using a relative XPath and bound to the sub-field `location`, making the citation sub-object a pointer to linked metadata. Recursively extracting sub-objects is key to supporting nested or linked metadata, and experiences such as collapsing, and expanding details. The integration of data models and extraction rules enables this practical, field-by-field, recursive algorithm to derive rich metadata for heterogeneous types.

Heterogeneous Metadata and Presentation Semantics

In her task, Mia explores Wikipedia articles, research papers, and Amazon books. For Wikipedia articles, she follows links embedded in paragraphs to related concepts. For research papers, she uses references, citations, and authors to chain to related significant research. For Amazon books, she reads reviews to get others' opinions. Exploratory browsing involves encountering metadata of heterogeneous types. Each type may require *rich* presentation tailored to its specific structures and relationships, to make good use of the user's attention.

The metadata type system uses *presentation semantics* to address this heterogeneity. Integrated with data model fields, presentation semantics specify how a particular field in a particular type should be presented. Presentation semantics reference CSS classes to situate the details of presentation in abstractions, such as `metadata_h1`, separating low-level details and parameters, such as fonts, where designers can customize them. We developed a set of simple, yet effective presentation semantics, including hiding, ordering, positioning, collapsing, expanding, hyperlinking, concatenating, and changing labels for fields. In Figure 4b, `layer` decides the order of fields in presentation, and `navigates_to` specifies hyperlinking the field to a destination indicated by another field.

Presentation semantics can be inherited along with data model fields, and overridden as needed, promoting reuse. For example, `layer` specifications in wrapper `scholarly_article` will be inherited by subtypes such as `ieee_xplorer` and `acm_portal`, if not explicitly overridden. Thus, the field order specified in the base type `scholarly_article` will automatically apply to metadata extracted from any of these digital libraries.

Interfaces can render the same presentation semantics in different, yet consistent ways, to meet situated needs. The example, MICE, provides a default hierarchical HTML5 rendering, which will be explained in the next section.

Recursive Expansion of Heterogeneous Metadata

Being able to navigate to linked information with one click is crucial for web usability. By providing previously unanticipated information that evolves the user's understanding and information needs, links function as the basis for exploratory browsing and berrypicking. Mia encounters links that lead to new information, such as related concepts, names of recognized researchers, citations, and books that people also buy. Exploratory browsing interfaces must support such encounters with linked information, while maintaining context.

The example, MICE, uses *recursive expansion of heterogeneous metadata* to address this. A link, such as a citation, is initially presented as an abridged metadata object, with only the title; a plus button indicates further information. When the user clicks the plus button, MICE calls the underlying typed metadata service to extract detailed metadata from the linked document. After extraction, the service sends extracted metadata and the corresponding wrapper back to MICE, for presentation. Upon receipt, MICE recursively binds data model fields with extracted metadata values, and then iterates over these fields to generate HTML5 elements for presentation. Interface generation uses presentation semantics to customize display for each particular type, including sorting fields, hiding or changing labels, and hyperlinking.

For example, in Figure 4c, the scalar field `title` is presented as a header, anchored to the source ACM Digital Library page, as specified by `navigates_to`. The fields `authors` and `citations` are presented as lists of nested or linked metadata, initially with 10 items and a "show more" button. On expansion, the generated HTML5 elements are injected, replacing the abridged form with a detailed presentation. A sub-object whose `location` field points to a linked document, such as a citation, can be further expanded, which will recursively trigger the information expansion process.

The whole process of selecting the appropriate type, extracting metadata from the document, and presenting metadata with customized visual elements is dynamic, that is, executed in real time as the user encounters the document. Thus, the interface is able to dynamically present heterogeneous information as metadata that can be conveniently collapsed or expanded to the user in real time, while addressing characteristics of particular types.

Document Subtype Polymorphism

In programming languages, *subtype polymorphism* allows for general functions to operate on instances of different subtypes of a common type, enabling different behaviors at runtime and promoting reuse. In the metadata type system, *document subtype polymorphism* is a key to addressing heterogeneous information types and sources. The runtime provides general functions, such as metadata extraction and presentation, which operate on the general base type `document`. The type system and runtime then *polymorphically* operate on subtypes of `document`, such as `scholarly_article` and `amazon_product`, to extract heterogeneous metadata with different structures and contents, and consistently display them with rich presentation. This polymorphism is operationalized by dynamic bindings of documents to types integrating data models, extraction rules, and presentation semantics, and the invocation of extraction and presentation functions (Figure 2).

The type system comes with a wrapper repository [25] addressing a range of information types, including books, movies, patents, products, hotels, social media, and searches. As new polymorphic document subtypes are introduced, exploratory browsing interfaces building upon the type system, such as MICE, immediately support them.

USER STUDY

We designed and conducted a 2x2 within-subjects experiment to validate our hypotheses that: (1) metadata will serve as an effective form of summary, and (2) dynamic exploratory browsing interfaces like MICE will support exploratory browsing tasks better than a typical web browser. In the task context, students from an information retrieval class used *citation chaining*, the process of following references, citations, and authors for exploratory browsing, to conceptualize a project for the class. Independent variables we manipulated were *initial document set* and *interface*, each with two conditions. The instructor picked two topics for initial document set: *query log* and *PageRank*. Each initial set consisted of 7 scholarly articles from ACM Digital Library, IEEE, or CiteSeerX. The experiment interface condition uses MICE for exploratory browsing, while the control interface condition uses a regular web browser and hyperlinks.

We recruited 8 undergraduate (1 female, 7 male) and 5 graduate (all male) students who were taking or had taken the class. None of them, nor the instructor of the class, was affiliated with our lab. The study process for each participant consisted of a survey (5 min), an introductory video (5 min), two sessions of exploratory browsing (25 min x2) with different initial document set and interface conditions, and a survey (5 min). Conditions were counterbalanced. In each session, the participant spent 5 min on an interface tutorial video before engaging in exploratory browsing with papers. Participants used CiteULike to collect interesting papers in all conditions.

We recorded browser interactions and collected articles. A two way ANOVA shows students spent significantly less time directly browsing digital library web pages when using the MICE interface: .83 minutes compared to 16.43 minutes for the control ($p < .001$). This indicates that though the students could browse the original digital library web pages from MICE, they overwhelmingly did not need to, since metadata summaries presented by MICE were sufficient for them to perform the task. There was no significant difference in the number of collected papers between conditions.

The questionnaire asked participants about their experiences with both interfaces, gathering Likert scale quantitative and open-ended qualitative data. The Likert scale ranges from -4 (strongly preferring control interface) to 4 (strongly preferring MICE). Participants rated MICE better than the control in all four dimensions of experience. A single sample one-tailed t-test with $\alpha = .95$ and $\mu < 0$ as the alternative hypothesis showed statistical significance for each (Table 1).

Qualitative data analysis depicts aspects of user experience:

1) *Concise representation.* Users reported the concise representation of metadata summaries helped them browse while citation chaining:

> u8: [MICE] provides a much better method to chain documents by saving space and condensing the data for users to read and skim through.

> u12: The compactness of the UI makes it easier to go through a chain without losing track of where you started.

2) *Less digression.* Users said that the control interface often left them confused about how they got there:

> u3: With the web page [control] method, I quickly got off topic and had to keep multiple tabs open.

> u6: [MICE] better shows how papers are related and shows how I got to them.

> u2: [MICE] allowed me to traverse through documents while seeing where I was in relation to my past clicks. Whereas the [control] method required me to click the 'back' button anytime I wanted to backtrack on links.

> u4: Seeing how papers reference each other was much simpler in the tree view, as opposed to relying on memory and wondering how I got to the current paper from where I started.

3) *Supports comparison.* MICE supported knowledge formation that users thought would be missed while using the control interface:

> u7: It is easier to see all the surrounding papers, the ones cited by the paper, referenced by the paper, and the surrounding citations.

> u3: MICE definitely gave much more useful information than did the web page [control] method. Each factoid linked directly to other papers that shared some similarity through that particular fact.

4) *Integrated view mitigating disorientation.* Students found MICE's integrated view to be valuable and useful. Student u7 found MICE's visualization of cycles helped him understand which papers he had already seen.

> u10 : With MICE, I was able to see more diverse papers in the same viewing space, ... I discovered even more interesting papers from other topics. With the [control] method, interesting papers were more narrow in topic. I had to navigate further to find the next set of interesting papers.

> u1: MICE seemed quicker. I like using tabs for doing broad searches like this, but being able to see all the relations on one screen is very useful.

> u7: The red line linking the same paper... [helps you] see what papers you have already looked at.

Qualitative data further confirm that metadata works as a form of document summary. The concise representation of metadata summaries helped students read large amount of information and rely less on visual memory. Relationships

Question	Rating μ	p
(interesting) Which method helps you better find interesting papers along the citation chain?	1.46	.009
(overview) Which method helps give you a better sense of the referred or cited papers, before you actually read the paper?	1.70	.002
(overall) Which method do you prefer to use, overall?	1.46	.007
(citations) Which method is easier to use for citation chaining?	2.70	< .001

Table 1: Mean user ratings on a scale from -4 (strongly preferring control interface) to 4 (strongly preferring MICE), and t-test statistics.

between previously and newly browsed papers were visible through metadata fields, helping students keep their browsing sessions on track.

Overall, MICE helped students understand context, browse related papers, and build knowledge through citation chaining. Participants preferred MICE for the exploratory browsing task. The time they spent in MICE instead of in the control interface shows that the metadata effectively summarizes digital library entries. The results show that the present interface supports exploratory browsing, while maintaining context for the user.

DISCUSSION

We need to discover new methods for making the world's vast, growing information resources more valuable to humanity. Consistently structured metadata representations of widely-used web documents enable summarization, usable presentation, and exploratory browsing experiences that maintain context. From our experiences with the metadata type system and the MICE interface, we derive implications for designing and engineering exploratory browsing and search interfaces supporting open-ended tasks:

Use metadata to represent summaries of web documents. Metadata summaries provide unique value to users browsing large collections of documents. Fields can function as facets, facilitating tasks that involve quick scanning, filtering, and comparison of multiple items, such as sorting products by price or finding most cited papers. Hierarchically nested structures enable collapse and expansion of details, helping users to better allocate their limited attention and make sense of information at different levels of abstraction. Representing linked metadata is an expandable field, in which the field name represents the relationship, helps users form mental models of citation chains, and so to acquire new knowledge.

In the study, participants with MICE spent 2 orders of magnitude less time (.84 vs. 16.43 min on average) viewing digital library pages, showing that metadata provided by MICE effectively summarized the source documents for the exploratory browsing task. While MICE presents metadata in a table-like structure, other interfaces can use different layouts driven by the same underlying metadata types.

Usable presentation of metadata summaries requires clearly presenting abundant details on the wild web, while managing redundancy and noise. Real world metadata is full of details and cross-references. Abundant details reveal the inherent complexity of the world. Details support various contextualized and personalized user tasks. Tufte wrote: "Detail cumulates into larger coherent structures ... To clarify, add detail." [41] Abundant details, when properly arranged, make full use of human capabilities of processing information, reduce the need of visual memory for switching contexts [41], and thus are essential to usable presentation of metadata summaries. In the MICE study, details such as references and citations, which are often absent in prior approaches to metadata summaries [14] [36], enable citation chaining.

On the other hand, inevitable redundancy and noise in real world metadata distract users' inherently limited cognition. The more information that is presented, the more cognition is consumed [38]. Presentation semantics can focus metadata displays toward usability. For example, DOIs [26] and URLs [4] of browsed papers are more useful to the machine than the user. Presentation semantics thus guide the dynamic exploratory browsing interface to avoid direct display of this information to the user, while using it as the destination of a hyperlink on the title field.

Integrate the meta-information of data models, extraction rules, presentation semantics, and type selectors to drive effective, usable metadata summary experiences. To provide value to the user, data models alone are not sufficient. Individual metadata summaries must be extracted and usably presented. Metadata data models, extraction, and presentation are inherently intertwined in user experiences. Integrating meta-information of data models, type selection, extraction, and presentation provides a general method for generating rich presentation. The structures of abundant details are expressed through metadata types, providing for consistency and variation, while enabling management of redundancy and noise. Extraction rules recursively acquire pieces of information from the DOM to form typed metadata instances. Presentation semantics enable hiding, relabeling, reordering, emphasizing, hyperlinking, expanding, collapsing, and concatenating fields, to generate type-specific rich presentations, addressing diverse use cases from the ACM Digital Library to Amazon and beyond.

The integrative metadata type system, with inheritance, helps scale metadata extraction and presentation to many information sources and types. The selector mechanism automatically picks the optimal type for each encountered document. This is essential for expanding serendipitously encountered metadata. Exploratory browsing interfaces, like MICE, operate on the base type of document, while using integrated types to drive presentation. For development and maintenance, the type system supports reuse and overriding of data model fields, extraction rules, and presentation semantics through inheritance [7].

Operate on popular and useful web information. Popular websites are, inherently, repositories of information that matters to people. The Semantic Web approach assumes that they will be published using standards for machine-understandable, linked data. Based on this assumption, many Semantic Web applications treat metadata as the result of pre-processing performed in advance. SPARQL queries then retrieve metadata for presentation. Alas, many useful web sites publish only semi-structured HTML, with human-oriented markup and styles, rather than RDF, OWL, or microdata. While a WWW 2007 paper articulated the need to connect semantic web and Web 2.0 approaches [1], `programmableweb.com` shows that six years later, RDF plays a role in less than 1% of registered APIs.

The present research enables extraction and presentation of metadata from a wide range of popular and useful web sites. This is important for building interfaces that provide immediate value to users by supporting everyday scenarios. Working with popular and useful web sites also enables investigation of *real world* use cases, which leads to holistic, deep understanding of people's practices with web information, especially semantics. This is crucial for driving research into the design and engineering of interactive information systems.

CONCLUSION

Based on object-oriented programming concepts and constructs such as inheritance, polymorphism, and dynamic dispatch, this research develops a novel approach to engineering usable exploratory browsing interfaces working with heterogeneous web semantics. Types integrate metadata data models, extraction, and presentation. Seemingly contrary to common practices of separating concerns, this integration is demanded by how these aspects of exploratory browsing are inherently connected in vital user experiences. Integrative metadata types operationalize dynamic exploratory browsing interfaces by enabling recursive extraction and usable presentation of heterogeneous metadata summaries from diverse sources.

The example exploratory browsing interface, MICE, enables browsing summaries of web pages through linked metadata, which can be dynamically expanded. The dynamic nature of such interfaces is essential to exploratory browsing. When the user serendipitously seeks to explore new information encountered through links, the interface dynamically expands, using types to customize metadata derivation and presentation. Further, newly published information can be dynamically incorporated. Thus, the metadata type system fundamentally differs from technologies that only operate on datasets assembled in advance.

The custom presentation semantics specified in types, such as ordering, formatting, hiding, and hyperlinking field values, enable type-specific emphasis that can mitigate the cognitive load inherent in browsing large amounts of information. The type system and MICE constitute a practical method for building web-scale dynamic exploratory interfaces. Study participants found MICE's concise presentation of linked metadata usable and valuable for exploratory browsing.

Disorientation and digression constitute deep rooted problems in popular user experiences of web browsing. A solution to this is to present summaries of multiple documents in a continuous space, maintaining context. Metadata summary representations produced by the type system enable reduced, yet expandable presentation of web pages. Presentation semantics enable the user to browse original web pages, as needed. Study participants found that MICE helped reduce disorientation and digression by displaying metadata in one context and making relationships visible, including to previously encountered information.

Dynamic interfaces based on the metadata type system have the potential to transform browsing experiences with web information for a wide range of open-ended, exploratory tasks. Exploratory browsing interfaces can be embedded into HTML pages to transform passive hyperlinks, enriching diverse, integral, 21st century information experiences, including digital libraries, shopping, social networks, messaging services, email clients, and newspapers. Our open source implementations of the type system and MICE [25] have the potential to facilitate the engagement of research, open source, and industry communities in engineering new interactive systems in diverse domains for exploratory browsing and search.

The metadata type system enables a new family of dynamic interfaces that help users browse the WWW. Support for exploratory browsing while maintaining context will be valuable in many sensemaking and berrypicking tasks. Future research can incorporate these techniques with query input and history to develop new support for exploratory search.

REFERENCES

1. Ankolekar, A., et al. The two cultures: mashing up web 2.0 and the semantic web. In *Proc of WWW* (2007), 825–834.

2. Antoniou, G., and van Harmelen, F. *A Semantic Web Primer*. The MIT Press, 2004.

3. Bates, M. The design of browsing and berrypicking techniques for the online search interface. *Online review 13*, 5 (1989), 407–424.

4. Berners-Lee, T. RFC 1738: Uniform resource locators (URL). *RFC* (1994).

5. Berners-Lee, T., et al. Tabulator: Exploring and analyzing linked data on the semantic web. In *Proc SWUI* (2006).

6. Bollacker, K., et al. Freebase: a collaboratively created graph database for structuring human knowledge. In *Proc. of SIGMOD* (2008).

7. Booch, G., et al. *Object Oriented Analysis & Design with Application*, 3 ed. Addison-Wesley, 2007.

8. Bracha, G., and Cook, W. Mixin-based inheritance. In *Proc OOPSLA/ECOOP* (1990).

9. Bush, V., and Wang, J. As we may think. *Atlantic Monthly 176* (1945).

10. Conklin, J. Hypertext: an introduction and survey. *Computer 20*, 9 (1987), 17–41.

11. Cowan, N. The magical number 4 in short-term memory: A reconsideration of mental storage capacity. *Behavioral and Brain Sciences 24*, 1 (2001), 87–114.

12. Cutting, D. R., et al. Scatter/gather: a cluster-based approach to browsing large document collections. In *Proc. of ACM SIGIR* (1992).

13. Deligiannidis, L., et al. RDF data exploration and visualization. In *Proc. of CIMS*, ACM (New York, NY, USA, 2007), 39–46.

14. Dontcheva, M., et al. Summarizing personal web browsing sessions. In *Proc UIST* (2006).

15. Dontcheva, M., et al. Experiences with content extraction from the web. In *Proc UIST* (2008).

16. Edwards, D. M., and Hardman, L. Lost in hyperspace: cognitive mapping and navigation in a hypertext environment. In *Hypertext: theory into practice*. Intellect Books, Exeter, UK, 1999, 90–105.

17. Foss, C. L. Detecting lost users: Empirical studies on browsing hypertext. Tech. rep., 1989.

18. Glaser, H., et al. CS AKTive Space: building a semantic web application. In *Proc. of ESWS*, Springer Verlag (2004), 417–432.

19. Greenberg, S., and Cockburn, A. Getting back to back: alternate behaviors for a web browser's back button. In *Proc HFWEB* (2002).

20. Hearst, M. A., and Pedersen, J. O. Reexamining the cluster hypothesis: scatter/gather on retrieval results. In *Proc. of ACM SIGIR* (1996).

21. Huynh, D., et al. Exhibit: lightweight structured data publishing. In *Proc. of WWW* (2007).

22. Huynh, D. F., and Karger, D. Parallax and companion: set-based browsing for the data web. In *Proc WWW*, ACM (2009).

23. Huynh, D. F., Mazzocchi, S., and Karger, D. Piggy bank: Experience the semantic web inside your web browser. In *Proc. of ISWC* (2005).

24. Interface Ecology Lab. Metadata In-Context Expander (MICE) Demo. `http://ecologylab.net/mice`.

25. Interface Ecology Lab. An open source metadata type system implementation. `https://github.com/ecologylab/BigSemantics/wiki`.

26. International DOI Foundation. The digital object identifier system. `http://www.doi.org/`.

27. Karam, M., et al. mSpace: interaction design for user-determined, adaptable domain exploration in hypermedia. In *Proc. of AH* (2003).

28. Kerne, A., et al. Meta-metadata: a metadata semantics language for collection representation applications. In *Proc. of CIKM* (2010).

29. Klemmer, S. R., et al. Where do web sites come from?: capturing and interacting with design history. In *Proc CHI* (2002), 1–8.

30. Lin, J., et al. End-user programming of mashups with vegemite. In *Proc. of IUI*, ACM (New York, NY, USA, 2009), 97–106.

31. Marchionini, G. Exploratory search: from finding to understanding. *CACM 49*, 4 (2006), 41–46.

32. Marchionini, G., and Shneiderman, B. Finding facts vs. browsing knowledge in hypertext systems. *Computer 21*, 1 (1988), 70–80.

33. McAleese, R. Navigation and browsing in hypertext. *Hypertext: theory into practice* (1989), 6–44.

34. Pham, H., et al. Clui: a platform for handles to rich objects. In *Proc. of UIST*, ACM (New York, NY, USA, 2012), 177–188.

35. Rástočný, K., et al. Supporting search result browsing and exploration via cluster-based views and zoom-based navigation. In *Proc. WI-IAT*, vol. 3 (2011).

36. Roy Rosenzweig Center for History and New Media. Zotero. `http://zotero.org`.

37. Samp, K., et al. Atom interface - a novel interface for exploring and browsing semantic space. In *Proc SWUI at CHI* (2008).

38. Simon, H. A. Designing organizations for an information-rich world. *Computers, communications, and the public interest 72* (1971), 37.

39. Smith, D. A. *Exploratory and faceted browsing, over heterogeneous and cross-domain data sources*. PhD thesis, U of Southampton, 2011.

40. Stegemann, T., et al. Interactive construction of semantic widgets for visualizing semantic web data. In *Proc. EICS* (2012), 157–162.

41. Tufte, E. *Envisioning Information*. Graphics Press, 1990.

42. W3C. RDF primer. Tech. rep., 2004.

43. W3C. RDF vocabulary description language 1.0: RDF schema. Tech. rep., 2004.

44. W3C. OWL2 web ontology language document overview. Tech. rep., 2009.

45. W3C. HTML5: A vocabulary and associated apis for html and xhtml. Tech. rep., 2012.

46. White, R. W., Kules, B., Drucker, S. M., and schraefel, m. Supporting exploratory search, intro to special issue. *CACM 49*, 4 (Apr. 2006).

47. Wikipedia editors. Exploratory search. `http://en.wikipedia.org/wiki/Exploratory_search`.

48. Wong, J., and Hong, J. I. Making mashups with Marmite: Towards end-user programming for the web. In *Proc. CHI*, ACM (2007).

Towards a Behavior-Oriented Specification and Testing Language for Multimodal Applications

Marc Hesenius
marc.hesenius@paluno.uni-due.de

Tobias Griebe
tobias.griebe@paluno.uni-due.de

Volker Gruhn
volker.gruhn@paluno.uni-due.de

paluno - The Ruhr Institute for Software Technology
University of Duisburg-Essen
Gerlingstr. 16, 45127 Essen, Germany

ABSTRACT

Initiated by the ubiquity of mobile devices, human computer interaction has evolved beyond the classic PCs' mouse and keyboard setup. Smartphones and tablets introduced new interaction modalities to the mass market and created the need for specialized software engineering methods. While more and more powerful SDKs are released to develop interactive applications, specifying user interaction is still ambiguous and error-prone, causing software defects as well as misunderstandings and frustration among project team members and stakeholders. We present an approach addressing this problems by demonstrating how to incorporate multimodal interaction into user acceptance tests written in near-natural language using Gherkin and formal gesture descriptions.

Author Keywords

Software Engineering; Multimodal User Interfaces; Specification;

ACM Classification Keywords

D.2.1. Software Engineering: Requirements/Specifications; H.5.2. User Interfaces

INTRODUCTION

Mobile devices triggered an immense paradigm shift in Human Computer Interaction (HCI) – touch screens evolved into a common and everyday tool. Equipped with several sensors, mobile devices also offer a wide range of additional interaction modalities like motion gestures or speech input, allowing users to choose their preferred interaction style. We furthermore can observe how more and more mobile interaction modalities are making their way back to the desktop PC: the latest releases of Apple's OS X support several touch gestures on a trackpad and parts of Microsoft's Windows 8 are specifically tailored for touch screens. New motion gesture toolkits like Microsoft's Kinect or the Leap Motion Controller allow for completely new ways of interaction.

The new interaction modalities allow to satisfy a new quality criterium for applications that emerged in recent years. Software must not only function as expected and look good, it must also *feel good* and provide a satisfying User Experience (UX). Unfortunately, UX is a rather fuzzy term and cannot be easily defined. Recent research shows that it is very specific to each user, context-dependent and based on the interaction with the application [11].

UX has become an important factor for an application's economic success and therefore must be taken into account in all stages of development. As a consequence, an interaction concept should be discussed and defined before development begins. It also enforces the necessity of thoroughly testing an application's User Interface (UI). Users will judge the application first of all by its interface as it provides the only means of interaction accessible to them.

Unfortunately, UI specification and testing are hard to achieve nowadays. Typically, specification documents suffer from the ambiguity of natural language, causing misunderstandings between involved stakeholders. Developers and testers alike are in danger of misinterpreting what requirements engineers and UI designers defined, leading to additional workload when errors have to be corrected.

Thoroughly testing an application's UI is a tedious and time-consuming process. Unfortunately, due to the lack of adequate test automation technology, most UI tests are manual work, meaning that certain functionality is called over and over again – a highly repetitive and error-prone approach. Developers dedicate up to 90% of the total development effort test the developed application [13].

Both problems – communication between stakeholders and automated application testing – are addressed by Behavior-Driven Development (BDD) techniques, but recent interaction modalities are not supported in typical BDD frameworks. BDD centres around a set of *User Acceptance Tests* specifying the application's behavior. The implementation can be validated with suitable test automation technology against the specification. Gherkin is a Domain Specific Language (DSL) for this purpose using a near-natural language syntax.

We demonstrate an approach to incorporate multimodal interaction in Gherkin-based user acceptance tests. We aim to elaborate basic ideas in order to create a multimodal specification language, which can be read and written by tech-

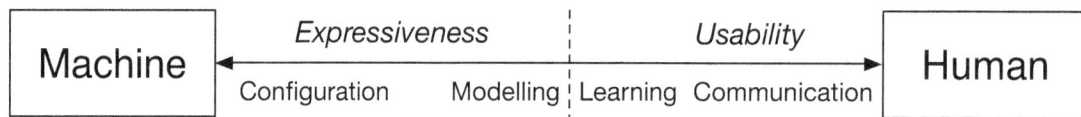

Figure 1. Purposes of multimodal specification languages [4]

nical as well as non-technical project team members and be used for automated UI tests. Specification languages for interactive systems can serve a wide range of purposes – from system configuration to human communication [4]. Our approach is strictly directed at human communication and cannot be used to configure applications (the main goal of related projects). In Fig. 1, our approach can be placed in the middle of the right side.

The next section introduces the basics of BDD and the DSL Gherkin, the underlying technologies used. We will then present a set of requirements for our multimodal specification language, followed by the language definition itself. We evaluate our approach with a first prototype of an automated test system capable of processing user acceptance tests for gesture-intensive mobile applications. Finally, we analyse related work, conclude the paper and present future research.

BEHAVIOR DRIVEN DEVELOPMENT

To overcome the communication gaps between stakeholders in software projects, BDD was developed as an evolution of Test-Driven Development (TDD). While TDD focuses on writing tests to verify correctness of the program before starting development, the basic element of software testing – the *Unit Test* – is typically a piece of software itself, forcing testers to attain certain programming skills. Therefore, it leaves test creation to technically skilled members of the project team.

BDD-practitioners use *User Acceptance Tests* to describe the system's behavior. The BDD-framework Cucumber[1] introduced Gherkin, a DSL specifically created for this purpose. Gherkin's outstanding trait is its near-natural language syntax, making it easily understandable and writable for project team members with different technical backgrounds. User acceptance tests focus on what the user does and how the system reacts; they describe a system's behavior from a user's point of view. A complete set of user acceptance tests corresponds to an overall description of all possible user-system interactions.

```
1 Scenario: Activation of push services
2 Given my app is running
3 Then the "GameMain" activity should be open
4    And the view with id "push-ind" should
         not be visible
5 When I touch the "Activate Push" button
6 Then the view with id "push-ind" should be
         visible
```
Listing 1. Example of a BDD user acceptance test for an Android application expressed in Gherkin.

The example in Listing 1 demonstrates the power of the BDD approach. The script can be understood by all project stakeholders due to the near-natural language approach and, with a suitable framework (e.g. Calabash[2] for mobile applications), can be used for automating application UI tests. User acceptance tests therefore become *executable specifications* instead of mere test descriptions [14].

Suitable test automation tools should mimic the user and must be configured to perform the same actions as human users would. There should be no difference between the automated test case execution and a human user's input. The necessary information is delivered within the script – line 5 in Listing 1 defines the user's action and line 6 how the system should respond. While a variety of BDD frameworks capable of executing user acceptance tests exist and are actively used, none covers the necessary functionality to include modern interaction modalities (e.g. touch/motion gestures, voice commands). Instead, they are restricted to classic Point'n'Click (PnC) interaction – a flaw caused by the lack of suitable specification languages leading to the aforementioned problems (misunderstanding between project members and the necessity of manual tests).

SPECIFICATION LANGUAGE REQUIREMENTS

A language to specify multimodal interaction must adhere to two important rules. First, descriptions for different interaction modalities must be allowed. While some modalities share common traits, others might differ. Second, different forms of multimodality must be supported. In order to extend Gherkin with corresponding capabilities, we need taxonomies to categorize (a) the various interaction modalities according to common traits and (b) different multimodality types. Finally, a set of new keywords is necessary. These should not interfere with the existing language definition.

We aim to allow all project team members to understand and create specifications, hence a common language easy to read and write is necessary. Gherkin is a suitable candidate due to its near-natural language approach: its syntax does not require deeper technical understanding.

Interaction specification must be integrated directly into user acceptance tests as a means to specify applications and to allow automated processing by UI testing frameworks. To avoid misunderstandings, interactions must be specified as precise as possible – a suitable task for formal description techniques. Unfortunately, heavy use of interaction formalization will disturb Gherkin's near-natural language style, hence a common path between exact formalization and natural language description must be found.

---

[1] http://cukes.info/

[2] http://calaba.sh

Summarized, a suitable specification language must meet the following requirements:

1. Human-readability for technical as well as non-technical stakeholders. This includes the addition of suitable new keywords.

2. A taxonomy to distinguish different kinds of interaction and multimodality, leading to additional keywords and parameters to specify and define interaction using different modalities.

3. Formal descriptions of interaction modalities.

Human-readability

This requirement is basically given by Gherkin but must not be violated by any extension, including the definition of additional keywords. Gherkin defines a couple of keywords[3] for step definitions: 'Given', 'When', 'Then', 'And' and 'But', partly used in the example in Listing 1. These mainly support readability – Gherkin allows to mask them with an asterisk, making the use a matter of personal style. However, as we will be introducing new keywords when defining our language, masking keywords will disturb readability.

We furthermore aim to not reuse existing keywords; they have a predefined meaning and could lead to problems in testing framework implementations. As a consequence, we need to create our own set of keywords for the taxonomies defined in the next section. For most cases, no problems should arise as Gherkin itself does not define any specific keywords for modern interaction modalities, but e.g. 'and' cannot be used to combine any kind of input. It must also be noted that Gherkin-based frameworks might introduce own keywords, hence conflicts are possible.

Taxonomies for Multimodal Interaction

In order to define the basics of our specification language, we use a simple taxonomy to categorize different modalities. We aim to infer necessary keywords and define common attributes. However, each modality might need individual semantics. This taxonomy is by no means complete and just serves our purposes; other works might be more detailed.

We distinguish three main categories:

Point'n'Click (PnC) describes any interaction with UI elements such as buttons and refers to classic WIMP[4] interfaces. Despite all advances in HCI, PnC is still the prevalent interaction paradigm. UI elements typically ship with common interaction methods, e.g. `onPress` for buttons.

Gestures include all modalities allowing for two- or three-dimensional movement. These include touch gestures on a flat surface as well as movements with a device, e.g. a smartphone, moving certain body parts, e.g. in front of a Kinect or using the Leap Motion Controller, or using a remote control like the WiiMote. Although touch gestures and PnC are closely related – on e.g. mobile devices buttons are touched

or sliders moved with a finger – PnC is more focused on the element that is interacted with. Specification of e.g. a slider movement would most likely be stated as *moving the slider* and not *performing a gesture on the slider*.

Audio interaction describes all modalities using audio signals, with voice commands being the most common technique.

Furthermore, we need to distinguish different types of multimodality. We adapt Coutaz & Caelen's separation in *exclusive* and *synergic* multimodality [2] and add *sequential* multimodality.

Exclusive Multimodality describes systems that allow for different but interchangeable modalities. Users can choose between various modalities to achieve the same goals but cannot use them in combination. For example, users might use either the 'Back' button or a swipe gesture in a web browser to go backward in the browsing history.

Synergic Multimodality allows to combine modalities, e.g. touching an object on the screen and uttering a voice command. The resulting interaction is a bit fuzzy – users do not speak exactly in the very same moment they touch the screen. The different inputs' order is unclear: users might first touch the screen and then speak or vice versa.

Sequential Multimodality describes sequences of interaction occurring one after another in a predefined order. For example, a question mark consists of two gestures – a semicircle followed by a connected downward line and a separate dot.

Formal Interaction Description

Several approaches to formally describe user interaction have been developed in recent years, especially for multi-touch-gestures. A suitable formalization technique should fit nicely into Gherkin's near-natural language syntax.

Proton [9, 10] uses Regular Expressions (RegEx) to describe gestures, strictly corresponding to the finger's movements. A sequence starting with a D (down), followed by several Ms (move) and operators, and ending with a U (up) denotes a gesture. Fingers are identified with indices and custom attributes can be used to parameterise gestures. Complex gestures result in complex RegEx – a problem the authors address by providing a tool to visually design gestures and create the corresponding RegEx.

GISpL [6] describes gestures in a JSON-format and is not limited to multi-touch applications. A set of executable features and customisable screen regions defines a gesture, which may also include attributes like the movement direction or number of fingers used. GISpL is human-readable as it uses JSON, but requires some technical background due to the use of e.g. vectors.

GeForMT [7, 8] uses a basic grammar of atomic gestures; complex gestures are created by combining atomic gestures with operators. Movement directions can be added using a compass notation. Its very simple, grammar-based approach is easily understandable for non-technical users, but lacks the capability to add custom attributes like movement velocity.

---

[3] A basic yet incomplete Gherkin BNF grammar can be found here: `https://github.com/cucumber/gherkin/wiki/BNF`
[4] windows, icons, menus, pointer

SPECIFICATION LANGUAGE

Language Definition

Human-readability

Gherkin's near-natural language approach satisfies this requirement, hence no additional work is necessary. Any extensions must fit into this requirement.

Include taxonomies

We will reuse the keywords predefined by Gherkin and not change their meaning. For PnC interaction, we add no further keywords at this stage of development; existing frameworks like the aforementioned Calabash typically define them.

To indicate the use of gestural interaction, we use the keywords 'perform gesture', followed by a formal expression describing the gesture and defining its type, e.g. touch or movement with the device.

Audio interaction is denoted by the keyword 'say' followed by a string as speech recognition is the most common technique.

To differentiate between types of multimodality, we add 'while' (synergic multimodality), 'or' (exclusive multimodality) and 'followed by' (sequential multimodality). Although 'and' would be a better fit for synergic multimodality as it emphasises the use of combined modalities, it is already used by Gherkin, hence we settle for an alternative.

Include formal interaction description

Of the different techniques to formally specify gestural interaction, especially GeForMT is interesting due to its minimalistic, grammar-based approach. Its expressions are simple and concise and the basics can be easily explained and understood. Listing 2 shows how nicely GeForMT fits into Gherkin user acceptance tests.

```
1 Scenario: Activation of push services
2 Given my app is running
3 Then the "GameMain" activity should be open
4 Then the view with id "push-ind" should not
      be visible
5 When I perform gesture "1F(CIRCLE_N_CW,
      LINE_N,LINE_E)"
6 Then the view with id "push-ind" should be
      visible
```

Listing 2.   Example of a BDD user acceptance test for an Android application expressed in Gherkin with a GeForMT expression describing a touch gesture.

The GeForMT expression in line 5 describes the gesture visualised in Fig. 2. It consists of three atomic parts: a clockwise circle ending in the north (CIRCLE_N_CW), a line to the to north (LINE_N) and another to the east (LINE_E). These elements should be performed without leaving the screen. The initial 1F indicates that one finger is to be used.

GeForMT, however, is focused on 2D multi-touch gestures. As we aim to include any gestural input, an extension into 3D space is necessary. Furthermore, the gesture source must be added. We prefix GeForMT expressions with e.g. *TOUCH* to indicate multi-touch input (as demonstrated in line 6 of Listing 3) or *DEVICE* to indicate device motion.

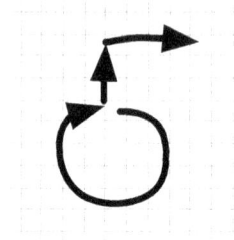

Figure 2. The gesture used in Listing 2.

Example

We demonstrate how our specification language can be applied by specifying a scenario from Bolt's famous *Put That There* [1] application, a first example for combining different input channels. In Bolt's basic setup, a user sitting in a chair could point to an object on the screen and say 'put that' to mark it, then point somewhere else and say 'there', making the system place the marked object at the desired position. We take the scenario to a mobile application running on Android as shown in Fig. 3, hence the user should touch the screen instead of pointing to it.

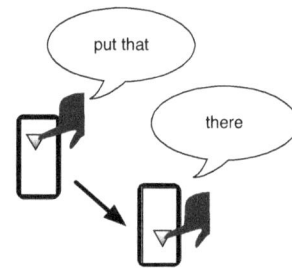

Figure 3. *Put That There* on a mobile device.

First, we want users to hold a finger on an object. In GeForMT, this can be simply expressed by 1F(HOLD(object)). We have to add the touch input information, hence TOUCH_1F(HOLD(object)) is used. Additionally, users say 'put that', so the application knows what the desired object is and what to do with it. According to our taxonomy, this is synergic multimodality, as the command is built on two different input modalities. We therefore combine a gesture with spoken language, leading to the following Gherkin step linked by the keyword 'while':

```
When I perform gesture "TOUCH_1F(
    HOLD(object))"
  While I say "put that"
```

The second part of the scenario, placing the desired object somewhere else, is very similar. Notice how the expression does not reference the object instance anymore to indicate holding somewhere on the canvas. Users can touch the screen and say 'there':

```
When I perform gesture "TOUCH_1F(HOLD)"
  While I say "there"
```

Listing 3 shows how *Put That There* can be expressed using our extension to Gherkin. Notice how the specification is precise due to the integrated formal interaction specification yet easy to read due to the near-natural language approach.

```
1 Scenario: Put That There
2 Given my app is running
3 Then the "Main" activity should be open
4 When I perform gesture "TOUCH_1F(HOLD(
     object))"
5    While I say "put that"
6 Followed By I perform gesture "TOUCH_1F(
     HOLD)"
7    While I say "there"
8 Then the object should appear at this
     position
```

Listing 3. Bolt's *Put-That-There* as a BDD user acceptance test expressed in Gherkin. Instead of pointing, touching on a surface is used additionally to voice commands.

EVALUATION & DISCUSSION

We extended the aforementioned Calabash, a BDD framework for mobile applications, by integrating touch gestures described as GeForMT expressions to demonstrate our approach. Calabash allows to automatically run Gherkin user acceptance tests on mobile devices. We chose Calabash's Android flavor and added a *gesture generator* capable of translating the GeForMT expression into a sequence of touch events and injecting them into the Application Under Test (AUT). We aimed to demonstrate that the AUT itself cannot distinguish whether it is controlled by the test automation system or a human user, hence both can be seen as equivalent.

Figure 4. Gestures used when searching for "STO"

We defined a user acceptance test for *Google Gesture Search*[5], an application allowing users to search for different information on an Android device by *writing* characters on the touch screen. A search for 'STO' would yield the *Google Play Store* app as a result; the necessary gestures are displayed in Fig. 4 (Google Gesture Search treats the angular shape as a 'T').

```
1 Feature: Google Gesture Search Test
2 Scenario: Gesture Test 01
3 Given my app is running
4 When I perform gesture "1F(SEMICIRCLE_S_CCW
     ,SEMICIRCLE_S_CW)"
5 Followed by I perform gesture "1F(LINE_N,
     LINE_E)"
6 Followed by I perform gesture "1F(
     CIRCLE_N_CW)"
7 Then I see the text "Play Store"
```

Listing 4. User acceptance test used to search for 'STO' in Google Gesture Search

---

[5]https://play.google.com/store/apps/details?id=com.google.android.apps.gesturesearch

Listing 4 demonstrates how a user acceptance test in Gherkin for the described search looks like. Although our prototype is currently limited to touch gestures (hence the missing TOUCH-prefix) and does not allow for the simulation of e.g. voice commands or synergic multimodality (both a matter of future work), it already demonstrates the benefits of our approach. The specification is concise as well as precise, can be understood by non-technical project team members and automatically evaluated against the implemented application.

However, for automated UI testing, additional information might be necessary. In the *Put That There* example, testing frameworks need to know where e.g. selected objects are located and where they should be placed, hence coordinates or the like have to be added. Additional information however might clutter the specification with details only relevant to a certain stage of the overall development process, leading to two common problems: *Incidental Details* and *Bored Stakeholders* [14]. Being used to source code, developers are typically trained to filter out certain details, but non-technical stakeholders might find themselves overwhelmed with additional information. As a consequence, they might loose interest in working with user acceptance tests, and stakeholder participation is an important factor in BDD. Additional details must be hidden, maybe in enhancing information layers for certain project team members.

A closely related pitfall is the use of GeForMT respectively interaction formalization in general. How interaction is described might be a matter of personal taste, and the formal specification might as well be hidden behind a more natural-language-oriented syntax. As GeForMT is based on various atomic gestures and a set of operators used to compose complex gestures, these could be translated into natural language representations – an approach integrating much nicer into Gherkin.

RELATED WORK

To the best of our knowledge, related research mainly deals with frameworks providing powerful *configuration* capabilities, specifically targeting application developers – the left side in Fig. 1. The projects aim to create description languages used to minimize programming efforts. While this is a valid approach and a desirable goal, our focus differs and takes non-technical project team members into account. As a consequence, we focus on describing the system's behavior from a user's perspective and validating the developed application automatically against the specification – we do not aim to automate application configuration.

Several configuration-oriented specification languages have been developed in recent years, mainly using XML as a description language. One example is SMUIML, created by Dumas et al. [4], which specifies interaction as a set of recognisers, triggers, actions and dialogs. As it is specifically aimed at developers to support application implementation, it can be used in conjunction with our approach by deriving the necessary components from our specifications. SMUIML has been used in different frameworks and projects, e.g. by Cutugno et al. in a framework for multimodal mobile applications [3].

Another family of specification languages aims to support developers with visual tools for modelling multimodal applications. For the aforementioned SMUIML, Dumas et al. recently presented a graphical editor [5].

Peissner et al. presented MyUI [12], a framework for creating adaptive UIs from abstract descriptions based on multimodal design patterns. They aim to automatically create different UIs that are adapted to user-specific preferences. The authors use *Abstract Application Interaction Models* (AAIMs), an extension to UML state charts, to create abstract models of the application without any interaction details. Instead, they describe possible functions users can call and leave interaction details to later implementation of the different UI variations derived from the abstract description.

CONCLUSION & FUTURE WORK

We proposed an extension to the Gherkin language used in BDD user acceptance tests to specify a system's behavior, allowing to include different interaction modalities by using formal interaction description techniques. We demonstrated a prototype implementation for touch-based interaction using the formal gesture description language GeForMT. We furthermore extended Calabash to process our modified Gherkin user acceptance tests and translate the described gestures into a sequence of touch events injected into the AUT.

The first implementation showed promising results. Our gesture generator simulated the gestures described in our Gherkin scripts as expected. By incorporating more interaction modalities, we expect our approach to simplify interactive application development and testing by supporting development teams in creating executable user acceptance tests using near-natural language specifications.

For future work, the implementation of additional interaction modalities remains. Although our current work focuses on mobile applications, with the increasing distribution of new interaction modalities in classic desktop PCs, other environments and modalities are interesting for future research. Furthermore, the integration of context parameters such as GPS coordinates is of interest.

REFERENCES

1. Bolt, R. A. Put-that-there: Voice and gesture at the graphics interface. In *Proceedings of the 7th Annual Conference on Computer Graphics and Interactive Techniques*, SIGGRAPH '80, ACM (New York, NY, USA, 1980), 262–270.

2. Coutaz, J., and Caelen, J. A taxonomy for multimedia and multimodal user interfaces. In *Proceedings of the ERCIM Workshop on User Interfaces and Multimedia*, ACM (1991), 143–147.

3. Cutugno, F., Leano, V. A., Rinaldi, R., and Mignini, G. Multimodal framework for mobile interaction. In

Proceedings of the International Working Conference on Advanced Visual Interfaces, AVI '12 (2012), 197–203.

4. Dumas, B., Lalanne, D., and Ingold, R. Description languages for multimodal interaction: a set of guidelines and its illustration with SMUIML. *Journal on Multimodal User Interfaces 3*, 3 (2010), 237–247.

5. Dumas, B., Signer, B., and Lalanne, D. A graphical editor for the SMUIML multimodal user interaction description language. *Science of Computer Programming* (2013).

6. Echtler, F., and Butz, A. Gispl: Gestures made easy. In *Proceedings of the Sixth International Conference on Tangible, Embedded and Embodied Interaction*, TEI '12, ACM (2012), 233–240.

7. Kammer, D., Henkens, D., Henzen, C., and Groh, R. Gesture formalization for multitouch. *Software: Practice and Experience* (2013).

8. Kammer, D., Wojdziak, J., Keck, M., Groh, R., and Taranko, S. Towards a formalization of multi-touch gestures. In *Proceedings of ITS'10*, ACM Press (2010), 49.

9. Kin, K., Hartmann, B., DeRose, T., and Agrawala, M. Proton++: A customizable declarative multitouch framework. In *Proceedings of the 25th Annual ACM Symposium on User Interface Software and Technology*, UIST '12, ACM (2012), 477–486.

10. Kin, K., Hartmann, B., DeRose, T., and Agrawala, M. Proton: Multitouch gestures as regular expressions. In *Proceedings of the SIGCHI Conference on Human Factors in Computing Systems*, CHI '12, ACM (2012), 2885–2894.

11. Law, E. L.-C., Roto, V., Hassenzahl, M., Vermeeren, A. P., and Kort, J. Understanding, scoping and defining user experience: a survey approach. In *Proceedings of the SIGCHI Conference on Human Factors in Computing Systems*, ACM Press (2009), 719.

12. Peissner, M., Häbe, D., Janssen, D., and Sellner, T. Myui: Generating accessible user interfaces from multimodal design patterns. In *Proceedings of the 4th ACM SIGCHI Symposium on Engineering Interactive Computing Systems*, EICS '12, ACM (New York, NY, USA, 2012), 81–90.

13. Tassey, G. The Economic Impacts of Inadequate Infrastructure for Software Testing. Tech. rep., National Institute of Standards and Technology, 2002.

14. Wynne, M., and Hellesoy, A. *The Cucumber Book: Behaviour-Driven Development for Testers and Developers*. Pragmatic Bookshelf, 2012.

WiFi Proximity Detection in Mobile Web Applications

Clemens Nylandsted Klokmose[1,2]   Matthias Korn[3,1,2]   Henrik Blunck[2]
clemens@cs.au.dk   korn@iupui.edu   blunck@cs.au.dk

[1]Center for Participatory IT, Aarhus University, DK-8200 Aarhus N, Denmark
[2]Department of Computer Science, Aarhus University, DK-8200 Aarhus N, Denmark
[3]School of Informatics and Computing, Indiana University, IUPUI, Indianapolis, IN 46202, USA

ABSTRACT

We present a technique for enabling WiFi proximity detection in mobile web applications based on proximity-adaptive HTTP responses (PAHR). The technique requires zero installation on the client and is client platform independent. Our reference implementation ProxiMagic is low-cost and provides robust and responsive interactivity based on proximity detection. We demonstrate the technique's applicability through a real-world example application deployed during a month-long participatory art exhibition. We document the reliability and suitability of the simple proximity detection employed in ProxiMagic through a controlled experiment.

Author Keywords

WiFi proximity detection; context-awareness; HTTP; mobile web applications; mobile devices; zero installation.

ACM Classification Keywords

H.5.m. Information Interfaces and Presentation (e.g., HCI): Miscellaneous

INTRODUCTION

In our research we study how IT can enable participation in activities in and around a local space. In a recent interdisciplinary research project we explored how we could let visitors of an art exhibition participate in the curatorial activity of describing and interpreting the exhibited artworks using their personal mobile devices [11]. A central goal in the project was to minimize the effort required for the occasional visitor to participate in the collaborative writing and reading activity. This lead to four design requirements: (1) Visitors should be able to edit the curatorial text of an artwork they are standing in front of from their personal device with minimal or no navigation required on their part—i.e., navigating from one artwork to another should happen *automagically* as one moves around in the physical space of the gallery. Hence, the system should reliably detect when a user device is within 2-4 meters of an artwork. (2) Because visitors may only ever visit the exhibition once, they should be able to participate without having to install any software on their personal devices

and requirements for bootstrapping (e.g., configuring the device) should be minimal. (3) Visitors with a wide variety of devices and operating systems should be able to participate. (4) The needed hardware infrastructure in the space should be cheap and based on off-the-shelf components to fit a meager institutional budget. We believe that these requirements of zero install, minimal navigation, platform independence, and low cost apply not only to art exhibitions, but to various kinds of public and semi-public spaces that are sought to be augmented with an interactive digital layer accessed from personal devices.

We realize these requirements through our novel technique based on *proximity-adaptive HTTP responses* (PAHR) and present our reference implementation *ProxiMagic*. In brief, the technique adapts the response to an HTTP request to a local web server based on clients' proximity to points of interest in the local space. These points of interest are instrumented with sensing nodes that continuously report proximity data to the web server. Hence, the client needs nothing but a wireless network interface and a standard web browser.

We report insights from one of only few real-world uses of WiFi positioning [7] as a means for engineering novel interactive systems in physical spaces. While the literature on WiFi positioning has high-accuracy absolute positioning as the ultimate goal [10], we demonstrate that simple, low accuracy proximity detection is adequate for building a novel interactive system.

RELATED WORK

Location-awareness has been part of the early ubiquitous computing vision and prototypes, where it commonly requires custom software (or even hardware) on the client side. The ParcTab system was designed around an IR-based local area network that could identify the room the user was in and deliver relevant content in the user interface [15]. The Cyberguide, aiming at a design for a virtual tour guide, combined indoor IR-based proximity detection with outdoor GPS tracking to provide access to services and content related to a location [2]. Both the ParcTab and Cyberguide relied on custom client software. GUIDE was similarly developed as an intelligent tourist guide [5]. It provided outdoor proximity detection not through GPS but with the help of several WiFi base stations. GUIDE in fact employed location-aware web content delivery, however, using a customized web-browser capable of navigating web content based on proximity data from the WiFi base stations. Today, outdoor positioning has become a standard feature of modern mobile devices, and the W3C Geolocation API [12] allows access to location information in the web browser. They do not, however, support indoor positioning.

Apple's Bluetooth Low Energy (BLE)-based[1] iBeacon[2] is a promising technology for proximity detection. iBeacon relies on low-cost signal emitting beacons, that can be placed at points of interest in a local space such as a museum or a mall. The Proximity Profile of Bluetooth 4.0 (PXP 1.0)[3] allows one device to detect whether another device is within a close physical range. As in our approach, physical proximity is estimated using the radio receiver's RSSI value, which has no absolute calibration of distances. The iBeacon technology is currently only available from within an (iOS 7 or Android 4.3) app on a device supporting Bluetooth 4.0. Hence, (as of now) it does neither meet our requirement of platform-independence nor of zero install on the client device. Moreover, there is no mention yet of enabling access to the iBeacon API from the web browser. Lastly, concerning backward compatibility, iBeacon does not support devices without Bluetooth 4.0, whereas our approach transparently works with any WiFi-enabled device with a web browser.

There exists a multitude of indoor positioning techniques that provide absolute positioning to varying degrees of accuracy. These techniques are based on, e.g., infrared [14], ultrasound [16], WiFi fingerprinting [3], Bluetooth [1], GSM fingerprinting [13], or even GPS [6]. Proximity to points of interest (POIs) can be inferred as an intermediate result from WiFi fingerprinting, even if sensing nodes do not align with the POIs [9]. However, fingerprinting requires a costly initial collection phase in order to establish a database of signal strength readings for later comparison; furthermore, this phase has to be repeated whenever the environment or the sensing node setup changes [3, 8]. In contrast, our technique relies on instrumenting all POIs with cheap sensing nodes. This strategy adds to the physical deployment complexity, but provides good proximity-detection accuracy even without fingerprinting— and thus avoids costly calibration or collection procedures.

TECHNIQUE

In order to provide *proximity-adaptive HTTP responses* (PAHR), a web server looks up the proximity of requesting devices on a given wireless network to a number of points-of-interest, and adapts the responses accordingly. PAHR thus enables to, e.g., serve information about the POI that a device is closest to (e.g., the closest artwork in our art exhibition case). PAHR requires that the web server can map the client IP in the header of the HTTP request to information about the proximity of the device to the relevant POIs. Based on this proximity information, PAHR then allows to either switch between different static web pages, or to dynamically update the content of a webpage through AJAX.

In our realization of PAHR, we instrument POIs with dedicated sensing nodes, (low-cost) credit card-sized single-board computers equipped with a WiFi adapter running in passive mode. 802.11 packet capturing on a given WiFi network is employed on the sensing nodes to detect the presence of wireless devices and their communication with wireless access points.

Based on the packet capturing (filtered by network), the sensing nodes continuously report the *received signal strength indicator*

---

[1] http://www.bluetooth.com/Pages/low-energy.aspx

[2] http://support.apple.com/kb/HT6048

[3] https://www.bluetooth.org/docman/handlers/downloaddoc.ashx?doc_id=239392

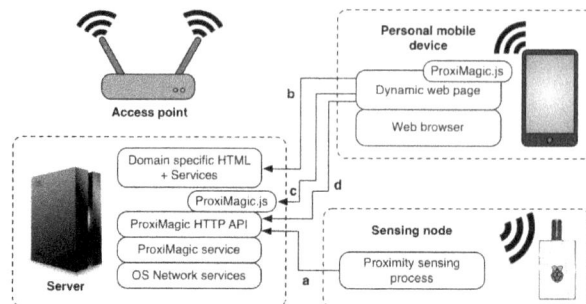

Figure 1. Components of ProxiMagic.

(RSSI) from each of the detected devices to the web server as tuples in the form of: `{sensingNodeID: int, readings: list({clientMAC: string, rssi: int})}`. The web server stores a mapping of the MAC addresses of all (detected) wireless devices on the network and their measured signal strengths at all the sensing nodes. This mapping is used when a device on the local network makes an HTTP request to the web server: The web server can extract the client IP from the HTTP request header, and through an address resolution protocol request on the local network (using `arp` on Unix-like operating systems) map it to the MAC address of the device. Based on a configured global signal strength threshold that signifies being in proximity, the server then produces a list of received signal strengths at all sensing nodes to the given device and uses this information to adapt its response. This means that the web server can provide, e.g., a basic HTTP API to retrieve the list of proximity information for a client to all points-of-interest, or the server can simply redirect HTTP requests based on proximity.

REFERENCE IMPLEMENTATION

ProxiMagic[4] is our reference implementation of a PAHR-based system. Figure 1 shows the interaction between the components involved: **a)** The sensing node continuously posts proximity data to the web service. **b)** A client loads the dynamic web page which **c)** also loads the client side ProxiMagic API *ProxiMagic.js*. **d)** Through the ProxiMagic client side javascript library, the dynamic web page requests the nearest objects of interests, resulting in an operating system request on the web server to map the IP of the client to a MAC address, and finally returning the proximity information to the client.

A requirement for ProxiMagic was that the hardware should be *low-cost* and off-the-shelf. Hence, the sensing nodes were built using the US$35 single-board computer Raspberry Pi (model B) running Raspian (Wheezy release). The Raspberry Pi were equipped with a ~US$15 D-Link DWA-140 (Rev b3) USB wireless network card. For monitoring the wireless network we used the open source packet capturing tool *Airodump-ng* (ver. 1.1).[5] While not interested in the actual data transmitted on the wireless network, we were interested in knowing the origin and destination of a given packet which we could extract using Airodump-ng. The sensing nodes ran a small Java process parsing and filtering the output of Airodump-ng, and posting it to the ProxiMagic web service.

---

[4] Download at http://proximagic.projects.cavi.au.dk/

[5] http://www.aircrack-ng.org/doku.php?id=airodump-ng

The ProxiMagic web service was implemented in PHP on an Apache web server running on Ubuntu Linux. We used the *arp* implementation provided by Ubuntu to perform the MAC-to-IP address lookup. The web service provided a simple HTTP API for the sensing nodes to post their data, and for web clients to retrieve proximity information to points-of-interest. The web service additionally served a client side Javascript library enabling the client to subscribe to proximity events (by polling the web service). The server can furthermore host and serve application-specific web content, which it did in our example application described below. However, the content does not have to be served from the same machine. On the client side the proximity information can, e.g., be used to dynamically load new content in an iFrame based on proximity events (which is what we did).

STRENGTHS AND LIMITATIONS

The strength and novelty of PAHR is the provision of proximity-based services i) on all WiFi-enabled devices capable of communicating through the HTTP protocol, and ii) without the need to install non-standard software on client devices.

Since we do not rely on an installed app, we have little control over the wireless network card on the device—i.e., we cannot keep the WiFi card from powering down on inactivity. As a result, we can only obtain proximity information when the device is generating network traffic. Therefore, the proposed technique can be considered to be *on demand*, and would not support, e.g., push notifications of proximity when the device is sleeping or otherwise not communicating (as promised, e.g., by Apple's iBeacon).

PAHR relies on the server being able to maintain a mapping between the IP addresses of requesting devices and their MAC addresses. In our reference implementation this requires the server to be on the same IP subnet as the clients for it to make the address resolution protocol request. In a more complex network infrastructure, this problem could be overcome by delegating ARP requests to the sensing nodes. However, this strategy would require at least one sensing node on each IP subnet of the network where there are points of interest. The ProxiMagic implementation is currently limited to a wireless network comprised of a single access point. It is possible to support larger wireless networks with multiple access points on different channels. This would, however, increase the latency of the proximity detection significantly as the sensing nodes would have to hop between channels. While in our deployments the sensing nodes have been connected to the wired network for communication with the web server, we have successfully tested wireless sensing nodes being both connected and monitoring the same wireless network with a single WiFi adapter. However, this limits the possibility for channel hopping even further.

ProxiMagic requires that each POI is instrumented with a sensing node. In the light of the recently announced iBeacons, this seems to be an approach adopted by industry as well. It is furthermore important to note that our proximity detection is based on received signal strength indicators (RSSI). Hence, it is only an approximate value and cannot be mapped to a metric distance without more sophisticated triangulation between sensing nodes. In effect, this means that a threshold RSSI indicating proximity (as we use) will result in different actual distances from device to device and other environmental conditions.

REAL-WORLD APPLICATION EXAMPLE

ProxiMagic was developed and deployed as part of the system Local Area Artworks (LAA) in a month-long participatory art exhibition in a contemporary art gallery in Denmark. LAA was designed to engage visitors of the exhibition in collaboratively writing descriptions and interpretations of displayed artworks using their own personal devices. Description panels next to artworks with text traditionally written by curators were replaced with digital panels in the form of framed iPads, and visitors could collaboratively edit the texts on the panels from their personal devices if they were in proximity of the artworks.

LAA was an interdisciplinary project. During the exhibition the use of the system was studied in the wild through observations, interviews, and logging (initial findings can be found in [11]). Throughout the deployment period of LAA, 141 unique devices were tracked by our sensing nodes, and 118 (84%) also communicated with the web server. On average, 5.4 unique devices interacted with the system per day with a peak of 34 different devices on the opening night. Three iPod Touch were available for borrowing at the cash desk, and these were responsible for 44% of the logged activity in the system. One of our goals with LAA was to minimize the burden put on the *occasional* visitor in the form of avoiding installation on personal devices and complex navigation tasks. Hence our requirements for zero installation and 'automagic' navigation.

ProxiMagic was used to let visitors interact with specific artworks without the need to manually connect to them (e.g., through scanning QR codes) or to select them in the interface. Instead, people could navigate the gallery space with their feet and ProxiMagic would take care to automatically show the artwork they were closest to. In addition to the ProxiMagic base layer, LAA contained an application layer to enable location-based collaborative writing about specific artworks in the gallery space. The application layer was based on a modified EtherPad[6] installation, which is a web-based collaborative writing engine. An EtherPad view was used both on the personal devices and the digital panels. This enabled that the text on the digital panels updated live when the visitors edited it on their devices, which emphasized the co-located use. Furthermore, the digital panels displayed a row of dots indicating how many devices were in proximity of it and how many of those were actively editing (colored if actively editing, grey if not).

Visitors connected their own personal device (or a borrowed device) to an open wireless network. This wireless network did not provide Internet access, and all HTTP requests were redirected to our web server on the local network. Hence, when visitors opened a URL in a browser on their phone, they would automatically be redirected to our web-based system. If they moved into proximity of a panel (within 2 to 4 meters), ProxiMagic would redirect the browser to an editable version of the text for the particular artwork.

Members of the audience could only participate actively by being there, by being in close physical proximity of an artwork. Once they moved out of proximity of the art piece, they were no longer able to edit the texts. Moving to another artwork automatically redirected to the respective editable text. Moving out of proximity

---

[6]`http://etherpad.org`

of any panel, visitors were presented with a floor plan of the art gallery indicating the locations of the panels.

Deployment Experiences. To our surprise, the visitors we observed and interviewed did not explicitly question nor, even when directly asked, reflect upon in which way the artworks were 'served' to them. For the users, it seemed natural to move around the space and thereby be navigated to different artworks on your personal device; it just worked. However, they did experience some ambiguities in our proximity detection that fundamentally underlie all radio-based approaches [4]. We found that people employed their own strategies to work around and compensate for the way proximity was defined and detected. Due to our proximity being an approximate measure, users did not know when they were within proximity at any given point (i.e., in which zones they could move around freely). Hence, they tested this out themselves by moving back and forth and observing changes on the interface. For example, users adapted when they did not get the content they expected by moving around or by holding their phones closer to the panel. Some visitors had to go really close with their device to a given point-of-interest, almost touching it. As our experiment below shows, varying power of the WiFi radios across devices, the users' orientation and their grasp of the device are to blame.

While our approach was zero install, it was not zero setup. Visitors were required to connect to a specific wireless network and navigate to an arbitrary page in the browser. The latter seemed hard to grasp, hence we ended up instructing visitors to navigate to a fictional URL. Not all visitors were comfortable with changing network settings on their devices, and hence required assistance from the staff. However, even non-tech savvy visitors grasped the logic of having to connect to the local wireless network of the exhibition space to participate in the discussions from their personal device.

EVALUATION OF PROXIMITY DETECTION

In the following, we demonstrate that the proposed simplistic technique for proximity detection reliably detects devices within a 2-4 meter radius of a POI—across a wide variety of mobile user devices and conditions, per our design requirements.

Setup. We conducted a series of 13 controlled experiments in a small sports hall (16x16 meters) with one sensing node and one user moving for ca. 3 minutes while carrying a mobile device. For the experiments we used variants of the following *default conditions*: using an iPod Touch running iOS 6.1.3 as user device, grasping it naturally, always facing the sensing node, and stop-walking (i.e., step—2s stop—step) along a fixed path that is visualized in Figure 2 (left). Each of the 12 experiment variants deviated from the default conditions in exactly one of the following 4 aspects:

- user device of various form factors and platforms: a Samsung Galaxy Nexus GT-i9250 running Android 4.3; an iPad 3 running iOS 7.0.2; and a late 2010 MacBook Air running Mac OS X 10.8.5
- orientation of the user: always facing away; facing right; and facing left
- the device-holding type: grasping with two fingers only; shielding with two hands; in-hand, arm pointing downward; and in pocket

- moving freely in the hall: walking; and running

As sensing node we used a Raspberry Pi, equipped with a D-Link DWA-140 WiFi antenna, placed at 2m distance from the center of the hall's south wall. The sensing node posted signal strengths from user devices at ca. 10Hz to a web server for data logging. We obtained ground truth of the user's location, and thus of her distance to the sensing node, via a floor-mounted Leuze ROD4-50 Plus laser scanner that was co-located with the sensing node. The scanner scanned in an angle space of 180 degrees for objects near the floor (e.g., feet) with an angular resolution of 0.35 degrees and a frequency of 10Hz. Each reading posted to the server from a sensing node was logged with the last reading from the laser scanner. Additionally, video of the experiments was recorded.

ProxiMagic is designed to detect proximity events, i.e., to detect when the user comes closer (or moves further away) than a prescribed distance. This proximity zone is associated with a pre-configured received signal strength indicator (RSSI) threshold. This threshold is experimentally established in order to approximate a metric proximity zone, e.g., of 4 meter radius around the sensing node. In the following, we evaluate ProxiMagic's accuracy for *several* proximity radii in order to gain statistical insights. To be able to do so, we produced a complete mapping m between between distance and signal strength. We chose to derive this mapping via using a simple regression scheme and solely on the basis of data from the default condition experiment. We decided against using more experimental data—and thus against learning a (potentially better fitting) mapping—foremost in order to evaluate and illustrate two features of the proposed technique: i) that it does not require time-consuming calibration procedures, and ii) that it provides reasonable results even when the real-world use conditions vary in terms of devices, grasp, and orientation.

Results. For illustration purposes, Figure 2 (left) plots the signal strength measurements for the stop-walk experiment, as obtained by the Pi for the default condition at their respective ground truth locations. Complementing, Figure 2 (right) illustrates the distances measured by the laser scanner (blue) compared to the distances as obtained through the mapping m of the measured signal strengths (green). This mapping thus allows us to systematically compute (and to statistically analyze) the recorded *distance errors* coming with the RSSI-estimated distances, i.e., how much these differ from the actual ground truth distances in our experiments. As an example, the figure furthermore illustrates, in orange, the RSSI-based estimates of whether or not the user is within a 4m proximity zone. It can be seen that the signal strength fluctuations can cause a local oscillation of the proximity detection result. In order to fight such 'flickering', smoothing techniques can be applied—at the expense, though, of a delayed detection: To obtain the smoother detection in Figure 2 (red), simple Kalman-filtering was applied.

Table 1 lists observed distance errors, averaged over each experiment's measurements. The overall error levels of, e.g., 2.64m on average across the four used devices, are higher than those usually provided by dedicated and more costly positioning systems. Nonetheless, the results suggest that ProxiMagic is suitable for its intended purpose—as illustrated by Figure 2 (right): The absolute error of 1.95m translates here to a responsive and almost always accurate proximity detection. Errors are also given differentiated

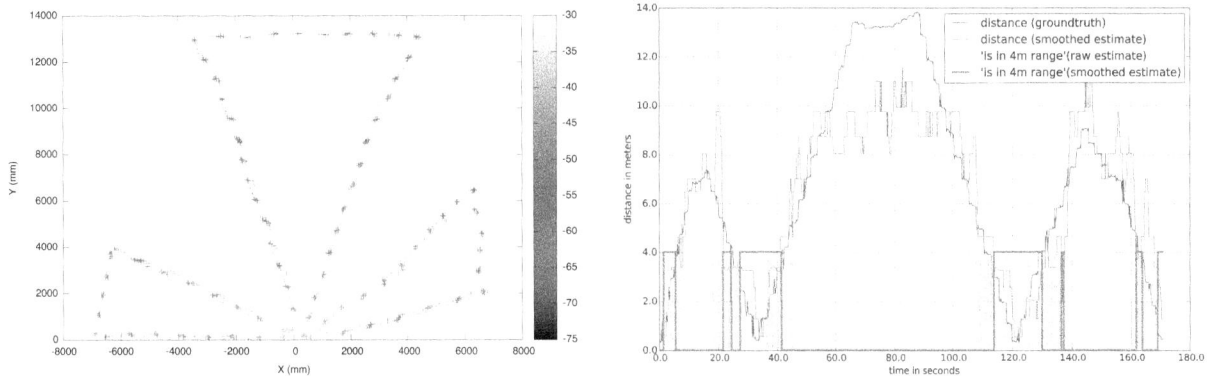

Figure 2. Measurements and results from the experiment with default conditions over time. Left: Ground truth in mm along X and Y, and signal strength on a color scale. Right: The distance to the user device, the signal-strength-based estimate of it; and whether the user is estimated to be in a 4m radius around the Pi.

	default	user device			user orientation			grasp				free-form	
		Galaxy Nexus	iPad	MB Air	facing away	facing right	facing left	minimal grasp	2-hand shielding	pointing down	in-pocket	running	walking
distance error (m)	1.95	2.69	2.81	3.14	3.62	2.50	2.39	2.57	5.23	2.54	2.93	2.07	2.72
distance error at ~2m	1.34	1.32	1.12	1.68	5.52	2.53	1.53	2.20	7.46	1.25	3.16	1.94	3.01
distance error at ~4m	1.72	1.77	1.68	2.19	4.57	1.92	1.83	2.92	6.77	1.81	2.64	2.00	2.96
distance error at ~6m	1.72	1.97	2.37	2.34	3.28	1.82	1.95	2.56	5.69	2.52	2.33	2.18	2.74

Table 1. Accuracy results for default conditions (grasping an iPod naturally, while constantly facing the wall with the Pi, and moving along a default path) and variations of it. Errors are given for all measurements, and specifically for those obtained at ranges around 2, 4, and 6m, respectively.

for individual user proximity ranges, i.e., for when the user's actual distance is close to (i.e., between $2/3$ and $3/2$ of) a proximity threshold of 2, 4, and 6 meter, respectively. The absolute error levels are similar across all of these three ranges; this implies that the relative error (i.e., relative to the user's actual distance) is higher for shorter distances. On this basis, we argue that the accuracy levels obtained can be deemed acceptable for use scenarios requiring coarser proximity thresholds, e.g., for our art exhibition case. However, the accuracy levels obtained for close-range proximity prohibit precise detection of fine-grained proximity changes within arm's length, e.g., for supporting gestures.

Table 1 furthermore provides evidence that the proposed technique provides generalizable results—and that it does not require a tuning of the technique to the wide range of device types or device grasps: The error levels for all four devices used, and also for the investigated device grasps are similar. An exception from this are the high error levels for the condition of the '2-hand shielding' grasp of the device—which lead to a overestimation of the user's distance. A similar shielding effect is observable for when the user is facing away from the sensing node. In contrast to the hand-shielding, a facing away can be expected in real-world use scenarios. Here, the overestimation though aids the proposed technique, since it prevents it from reporting proximity events when facing away, that is, when the user is most likely not actually approaching the POI in question.

Potential accuracy improvements. The results listed in Table 1 were obtained by smoothing signal strength measurements over $\Delta t = 0.5s$—which reduced distance errors by on average 15%. As discussed using Figure 2, a larger time window Δt leads to delayed proximity event reporting. Thus, a trade-off between distance error and responsiveness has to be made in dependence

of the use scenario, and on the proximity distances relevant to it. While for larger distances the distance error may be more crucial, we argue that responsiveness becomes more critical for near proximity use cases: e.g., if immediate and fluid interactions with the approached object of interest should be supported. Another potential means for improving proximity detection accuracy is to observe for a time window Δt not only the average signal strength, but also its trend—indicating whether the user is approaching and/or turning towards a sensing node. It remains to be evaluated how the results given here generalize to other, e.g., larger or more secluded environments and to more complex WiFi setups. To this end, we produced results as in Table 1 using an alternative signal strength to distance mapping m' with data from another environment (a large office building complex) and using other devices; the obtained errors were only insignificantly higher on average than those given in Table 1. Finally, the accuracy gains achievable when utilizing costlier sensing nodes, specifically costlier antennas remain to be explored.

DISCUSSION

The experiment and deployment are limited to what extent they demonstrate scalability in terms of significantly more users or sensing nodes. There are a number of parameters impacting performance that could be evaluated experimentally such as the density of sensing nodes, their placement in relation to the layout of the room, the maximum amount of detectable wireless transmitters, and the density of people in a room. However, our experimental evaluation and our experiences from the real-world deployment show that it is feasible to use WiFi proximity detection as an interaction technique.

The opaqueness of the actual proximity distance to the users turned out to be an interesting property in the LAA deployment. Given the nature of our technique, we could not make a direct metric definition of proximity, e.g., draw a line on the floor where our defined zone of proximity would be. In effect, this meant that our users could not build up expectations regarding accuracy and rather tested in a playful manner how the proximity detection worked for a given art piece and their particular device. If proximity zones are, however, defined at a very close distance to support close-range interaction (e.g., under 1m), then the accuracy of the proximity detection becomes more important.

Since our technique is network-based (i.e., proximity detection is handled exclusively on sensing nodes and server) and mobile devices are monitored passively, the user has no control over being located beyond turning off their WiFi or stopping to communicate with our server. On the other hand, our technique does not employ continuous tracking and does not rely on storing historical data beyond a couple of seconds to compute trailing averages. Furthermore, monitoring the wireless traffic has the aim to explicitly provide a service to the user based on the proximity detection.

CONCLUSION AND FUTURE WORK

In this paper we have presented a technique based on *proximity-adaptive HTTP responses* to bring WiFi proximity detection to web applications without having to install non-standard software on the client device. Through ProxiMagic we have demonstrated that PAHR can be realized with low-cost hardware and providing adequate proximity detection even with a simplistic proximity detection scheme. Local Area Artworks demonstrates the real-world applicability of the technique, and motivates the need for zero-install proximity detection.

There are numerous potential application domains that could make use of anchoring a digital layer to a physical space at certain points of interest. This includes located information, discussions or advertisements. But it also includes access to physical resources, whether to control the servo of nearby window blinds or to diagnose a piece of equipment on the factory floor. In the future, we seek to integrate the technique into i) a whiteboard capture system that allows mobile access to captured content of different whiteboards by being in the respective room, into ii) a system for the public library to provide section-specific information but also localized discussions and literature recommendations, and into iii) multi-surface environments where the technique could allow the pairing of mobile devices to stationary surfaces in order to act as remote input devices or to transfer content between devices.

ACKNOWLEDGMENTS

This work is funded by the Center for Participatory IT at Aarhus University, and by the Danish Council for Strategic Research through the EcoSense project. We thank Janus Bager Kristensen and Rolf Bagge from the Center for Advanced Visualization and Interaction (CAVI) at Aarhus University for being instrumental in the development and testing of ProxiMagic. We thank Anna Maria Polli for observations and interviews, and Kunsthal Aarhus for their cooperation in the project.

REFERENCES

1. Aalto, L., Göthlin, N., Korhonen, J., and Ojala, T. Bluetooth and WAP push based location-aware mobile advertising system. In *Proc. MobiSys 2004*, ACM Press (2004), 49–58.

2. Abowd, G. D., Atkeson, C. G., Hong, J., Long, S., Kooper, R., and Pinkerton, M. Cyberguide: A mobile context-aware tour guide. *Wireless Networks 3*, 5 (1997), 421–433.

3. Bahl, P., and Padmanabhan, V. RADAR: An in-building RF-based user location and tracking system. In *Proc. INFOCOM 2000*, vol. 2, IEEE (2000), 775–784.

4. Benford, S., Crabtree, A., Flintham, M., Drozd, A., Anastasi, R., Paxton, M., Tandavanitj, N., Adams, M., and Row-Farr, J. Can you see me now? *ACM Transactions on Computer-Human Interaction 13*, 1 (2006), 100–133.

5. Cheverst, K., Davies, N., Mitchell, K., Friday, A., and Efstratiou, C. Developing a context-aware electronic tourist guide: some issues and experiences. In *Proc. CHI 2000*, ACM Press (2000), 17–24.

6. Kjærgaard, M. B., Blunck, H., Godsk, T., Toftkjær, T., Christensen, D., and Grønbæk, K. Indoor positioning using GPS revisited. In *Proc. Pervasive 2010*, Springer (2010), 38–56.

7. Kjærgaard, M. B., Krarup, M. V., Stisen, A., Prentow, T. S., Blunck, H., Grønbæk, K., and Jensen, C. S. Indoor positioning using wi-fi – how well is the problem understood? In *Proc. Indoor Positioning and Indoor Navigation (IPIN 2013)*, IEEE (2013).

8. Kjærgaard, M. B., Treu, G., Ruppel, P., and Küpper, A. Efficient indoor proximity and separation detection for location fingerprinting. In *Proc. MOBILWARE 2008*, ICST (2007), 1:1–1:8.

9. Krumm, J., and Hinckley, K. The NearMe wireless proximity server. In *Proc. UbiComp 2004*, Springer (2004), 283–300.

10. Liu, H., Darabi, H., Banerjee, P., and Liu, J. Survey of wireless indoor positioning techniques and systems. *IEEE Transactions on Systems, Man, and Cybernetics, Part C: Applications and Reviews 37*, 6 (2007), 1067–1080.

11. Polli, A. M., Korn, M., and Klokmose, C. N. Local Area Artworks: Collaborative art interpretation on-site. In *Adjunct Proc. UbiComp 2013*, ACM Press (2013), 79–82.

12. Popescu, A. Geolocation api specification. *World Wide Web Consortium, Candidate Recommendation CR-geolocation-API-20100907* (2010).

13. Varshavsky, A., de Lara, E., Hightower, J., LaMarca, A., and Otsason, V. GSM indoor localization. *Pervasive and Mobile Computing 3*, 6 (2007), 698–720.

14. Want, R., Hopper, A., Falcão, V., and Gibbons, J. The active badge location system. *ACM Transactions on Information Systems 10*, 1 (1992), 91–102.

15. Want, R., Schilit, B. N., Adams, N. I., Gold, R., Petersen, K., Goldberg, D., Ellis, J. R., and Weiser, M. An overview of the PARCTAB ubiquitous computing experiment. *IEEE Personal Communications 2*, 6 (1995), 28–43.

16. Ward, A., Jones, A., and Hopper, A. A new location technique for the active office. *IEEE Personal Communications 4*, 5 (1997), 42–47.

Model-Driven Tools for Medical Device Selection

Judy Bowen
The University of Waikato
New Zealand
jbowen@waikato.ac.nz

Annika Hinze
The University of Waikato
New Zealand
hinze@waikato.ac.nz

Selina Reid
The University of Waikato
New Zealand
sjg32@students.waikato.ac.nz

ABSTRACT

Safety-critical medical devices are used in hospitals and medical facilities throughout the world, and are relied upon to function correctly and be usable so as not to endanger patients. While such devices are often designed for specific use-cases in specific locations, in reality they may be used in a much wider range of contexts. In addition, the proliferation of these devices within a single environment means that selecting the most appropriate device for a specific task is not always straightforward. In this paper, we consider ways of modelling the context of use of medical devices and how such models may be used to support tools which provide medical personnel with assistance in making decisions about which devices to use in which circumstances.

Author Keywords

Formal concept analysis; ontology; medical devices

ACM Classification Keywords

H.1.2 User/Machine Systems: Human factors; I.2.4 Knowledge Representation: Formalisms and methods

General Terms

Human Factors, Reliability, Design

INTRODUCTION

The U.S. Department of Health and Human Services' division on Food and Drug Administration (FDA) released a report in 2000, that identifies as a potential hazard the *use of medical devices in multiple contexts which are not fully understood* [18]. In this paper, we consider ways of modelling the context of use of medical devices and how such models may be used to support tools for medical personnel. We further aim to develop such a tool that provides support to medical practitioners when selecting the appropriate device for a given situation. Failure to identify the appropriate device might not result in single catastrophic events but rather be one contributing factor in a system of moderate complexity, which on their own may appear trivial but in combination can become deadly [1].

In previous work [8], we described how we used an ontology to model information about medical devices and their context of use. We employed the Protégé tool to support the ontology and then used the in-built reasoning with the SWRL language. This allowed us to deduce information about the appropriateness of using particular devices in particular locations and situations. The aim was to find ways of supporting medical practitioners and decision makers who typically have a variety of devices available to them, which are used in many different locations with their own particular contexts.

We found that we were able to achieve our initial goal of deriving useful information from the ontology, allowing us to answer questions of the form "Should device A be used in location X?" It was clear, however, that the ontology tool, Protégé, and the reasoning language, SWRL, while useful for our purposes, were not suitable as a mechanism for supporting medical practitioners in their daily working lives. It would not be appropriate to expect them to be able to update the ontology with new information as it arose (through the addition of a new device or a new location of use) or to use the reasoner in the way that we had to infer the required information.

Our next step then was to consider how to make this reasoning easily accessible, and how to support the addition (and if necessary, removal) of information. Our ultimate goal is to create a tool which uses the ontology (or some other model) as the basis for this. This paper reports on our research into developing a tool for selecting medical devices for an expected context of use that is *suitable for health care practitioners*.

We identified a number of steps required to achieve this goal.

1. **Methodology analysis** Firstly, more work is required to understand whether or not the Protégé tool and SWRL reasoner are the most appropriate tools for visualising and reasoning about the ontology as well as providing the relevant data for our medic tool. Initial research, therefore, focussed on examining other modelling approaches as well as initial experiments of writing software to interact with Protégé.

2. **Ethnographic Studies** The second step will gain a more thorough understanding both of the data we are modelling and the requirements of the users. This involves studies within environments of use of the medical devices and requirements gathering from relevant medical personnel. It has been previously observed that even minor mismatches between intended use and actual practice may lead to major safety issues [6, 5]. It is therefore essential for us to obtain a clear picture of the actual practice of the devices in a hospital setting.

3. **Prototype development** The third step is the design and development of the initial prototypes of our proposed tool and studies to investigate its usefulness and appropriateness in the required domain.

This paper describes the development of formal concept analysis and lattices as an alternative way of viewing the ontology (step 1), and the development and testing of the medic tool prototype (step 3). The process of gathering further information about the domain itself (to populate the models) is still ongoing – an outline can be found in [7]. Here we describe those parts of Step 2 that relate to requirements gathering from users.

The remainder of the paper is structured as follows: The background section introduces the project context and our original ontology example for the use of syringe pumps. Next we critically evaluate the methodological approach taken in this project so far and discuss alternative options for modelling and for ontology data management and reasoning. In particular, we explore alternatives to Protégé and SWRL as methods for managing the ontology and reasoning. We then introduce initial prototypes for a new tool that gives access to the ontology data and reasoning to medics. Following this we describe the results of our initial user study carried out on the prototype. Then we discuss our proposed approach to identifying relevant parameters to consider within the context descriptions. Finally we present a discussion of the contribution of this work, and show how it fits into the larger picture of worldwide research into medical devices, and then present our conclusions and a summary of future work.

BACKGROUND

In this section, we provide a brief recap of the original motivation for our work and the research already undertaken. Our initial work had looked at ways of using an ontology to reason about the usability of interactive medical devices in differing locations and situations of use. It was driven by an understanding that when using devices such as syringe and infusion pumps, which are not context-aware, there are situations of use that require the user to act differently in order to successfully interact with the device.

Safety and medical devices

The World Health Organisation defines patient safety as "the absence of preventable harm to a patient during the process of health care" [26]. Currently, in developed countries as many as one in 10 patients is harmed while receiving hospital care. The chance of being harmed during heath care is one in 300 while the chance of being harmed during air travel is one in 1 000 000 [26]. A summary of issues of patient safety problems in the American Health Care system is given in [21]. Zhang et al. observe that "human errors in medical device use account for a large portion of medical errors. Most of these errors are due to inappropriate designs for user interactions" [27]. A number of errors due to mixups, as well as malfunctions and mal-use of devices (syringe pumps, infusion pumps and epi-pens) are reported by Cohen [15], who stresses the need to focus on human factors in device design.

The ECRI Institute[1] recently released their predictions for the top 10 health technology hazards for 2014 [16]. The list includes the following three items and their respective ranking:

1. Alarm hazards,

8. Risks to pediatric patients from "adult" technologies,

9. Robotic surgery complications due to insufficient training.

The ECRI reports that a Sentinel Event Alert was issued after 98 alarm related events had been reported in the USA over a three-and-a-half year period resulting in death for 80 patients and permanent loss of function for 13 others [16]. All three health hazards listed above fall into the category of potential problems which may be identified within our models and subsequently by our proposed medic tool.

Project context

Figure 1 provides an overview of the elements of this project as a whole.

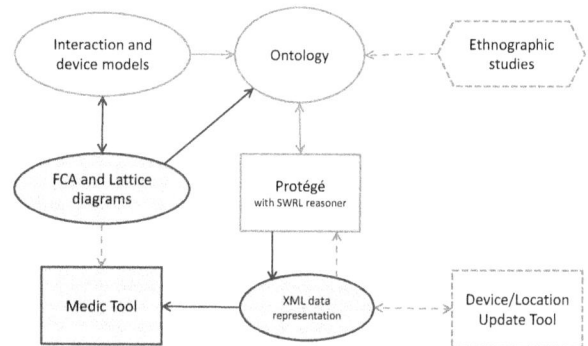

Figure 1. Proposed Software Solution

The elements shaded in green represent the work done previously (reported in [8]): we developed an ontology from the device and interaction models, and used the Protégé tool with its SWRL reasoner to determine where conflicts arise.

The blue elements represent the outputs reported in this paper. As Protégé was found to not be appropriate for use by medical personnel, we aimed for developing a tool that allows medics to identify possible safety issues when using medical devices in a given patient context. This 'medic tool' uses as input an XML representation of the ontology data and the reasoner output. We also explored alternatives to reasoning in Protégé by using Formal Concept Analysis (FCA).

The gray elements with dashed outlines represent currently ongoing and next stages of our work (discussed later). The update tool is conceptually part of the medical tool but has been decoupled into a separate software as we assume that different medical and technical personnel will be performing the tasks of updating and feeding location information. This will be verified through further user studies.

_____
[1]formally the Emergency Care Research Institute

Ontology for Syringe example

Our initial research originally focussed on one example device: a modal interactive medical syringe pump, which is used in multiple situations. A syringe pump is a small battery-powered device which delivers the contents of a syringe to a patient via an intravenous line over a set period of time. Medical settings can include different wards within a hospital, outdoor and mobile settings (including road ambulances and medical emergency helicopters), home environments and many others. These have a variety of different properties which can effect the ability to interact with different medical devices. These properties can include physical and environmental aspects such as lighting levels, noise levels *etc.* but also include diverse aspects such as patient/practitioner ratios, stress levels, rate of patient turnover *etc.* which may be harder to quantify. Our intention is to include these diverse and subtle properties within our modelling as well as the physical properties.

Although in this paper we continue to use the simplified example of a pump with a single interactive element (audible alarm) and the use of this pump within a helicopter with situations of excessive noise, this is done for convenience of explanation only. The larger real-world examples typically consist of a number of different factors that must be considered, for example a paediatric patient requires medication whilst being transported first to a medical facility and then whilst moving between several different areas within that hospital where additional medical procedures will also be performed. Both the chosen modelling approach, and the subsequent medic tool must be able to support the more complex, real-world examples.

The medical device itself is the same irrespective of where it is being used. A medical practitioner using this device in a helicopter needs to be aware that they will not hear the audible alarm of the device if it is activated due to the noise of the helicopter and the noise-cancelling headphones they are wearing. Although this is in some sense an 'obvious' example, it represents the pattern of information and inference we are interested in, where properties of a device and its interaction may be compromised by elements of the environment in which it is being used. Many more relevant properties exist and elements of the environment also include aspects such as staff training, patient types *etc.* Determining these is part of the ongoing work described under Step 2 in the introduction.

We first developed an ontology using classifications of elements in our domain, such as medical devices, their components, situations, and the relationships between these classes. Reasoning over this ontology in Protégé allowed us to identify available devices and gave a list of devices that were inferred to be affected by a current situation.

This first example of modelling the contextual factors for our small example was successful and enabled us to generate warnings based on rules for relationships between attributes of devices and locations. However, we wanted to ensure that our models could also capture the more detailed and harder to quantify properties described above, we explore the modelling alternatives next.

METHODOLOGY ALTERNATIVES

The results from the ontology modelling and reasoning could provide two possible outcomes: it may indicate that medical practitioners need different training or instructions for devices depending on where they are being used, or it may suggest that some devices are more appropriate than others for use in certain locations or situations.

The tool we propose, and describe later in this paper, supports both of these elements. It will provide information to users to assist with the selection of appropriate devices, and by including information about relevant training of medical personnel also assist in ensuring that a person is appropriately trained both on the device itself and the device in the context it is going to be used.

Our initial experiments, however, focussed on developing the medic tool using the ontology as described within Protégé as the basis, as discussed next.

Experimenting with the Protégé and Outputs

We began by developing a 'proof of concept' tool with the aim of showing that we could use either the API provided by Protégé, or the XML data representation which it exports for an ontology as a means of providing the required data for a reasoning tool. The Protégé-OWL API is an open-source Java library [2] which provides classes and methods to load and save OWL files (the ontology format), to query and manipulate OWL data models, and to perform reasoning. In addition, Protégé can export an ontology as an OWL-formatted XML file which contains all of the reasoning data in addition to the object knowledge. The API provides methods to parse this file to get the data from the relevant tags (which initially was the data we needed to populate the location and device information) and to perform reasoning using the rules encoded in the XML file.

The aim was for lists of devices and locations to be populated from the information in the ontology and for the result of a check operation to similarly be defined by the reasoning of the ontology. We then planned a second step, which was to investigate whether or not we could add new devices and locations into the tool and then have this new information added to the ontology.

This initial tool allowed us to replicate the reasoning of our simple example described earlier, but using simple drop down menus and choice buttons to perform the interaction. The final experiment for this tool was to try and add new information to the ontology. The use case was that a new device has been procured, or a new location of use has been identified, and this information needs to be added to the tool and the ontology so that it can be reasoned about. For this experiment, we used a sample data file (containing only the information required) which could be read by the tool, and this then edited the OWL-XML file, which in turn updated the ontology when reloaded into Protégé.

While this initial experiment showed that it was possible to work with the ontology data in the manner we required, it

---

[2] `http://protege.stanford.edu/plugins/owl/api/`

highlighted the fact that further thought needed to be given to the input and updating of new data. We can assume that new devices will be modelled in the same way as the existing devices (functional and interaction models). This means that when updating the medic tool with this new information an update to its underlying data is a more appropriate choice to achieve this (rather than requiring the user to provide this data). For new locations, however, it was determined that a separate process from the medic tool was required as it is unlikely to be a feature required by the same users of our medic tool who are using it to provide device selection support, this is discussed further in future work.

We now wanted to move on to developing a more sophisticated tool, however, in light of some new considerations that our proof-of-concept tool had raised, we first revisited the ontology modelling within Protégé to consider other options.

Experimenting with the Ontology Model

One of the conclusions from our previous work was that while an ontology could be used to support the sort of knowledge we required, it was not certain that Protégé was the best tool to perform either the reasoning, or to provide the data inputs needed by the tool for medical practitioners. The medical devices themselves are already modelled (using a combination of interaction models [9] and functional models), which provides one of the inputs to the ontology. It is important to ensure, therefore, that the information within the ontology is consistent with these models. One of the disadvantages of using an ontology is that it is difficult to provide proof that the knowledge represented is in fact correct or consistent with other models or that it even correctly describes the domain being modelled. Our goal in this next stage of the work was to consider the following questions:

1. Is an ontology the most appropriate mechanism for describing the device and context information?

2. Is the Protégé tool in combination with SWRL the best choice for reasoning about the information?

3. Are the outputs of Protégé the best way of providing data input to our new medic tool?

4. What is the best way of adding new information to the knowledge base?

Our initial investigations focussed on the knowledge modelling and alternatives to ontologies as a means to both model and reason about the information.

Classification trees: We began by looking at classification trees [11], which use a graph structure to show the outcomes of decisions. They use a branching method, so that each node down the tree represents a test on an attribute while each edge represents possible choices from that node. Traditionally, the leaf nodes of a classification tree represent the class to which each of the above decisions applies. This appeared to be a promising solution as for each domain we could identify which factors (or decisions) are true or false for a given object – so we could determine where conflicts exist, *e.g.*, between devices and locations. However, once we began modelling

examples of a non-trivial size (several devices with a number of different factors and conflicting relationships), we found that the trees we were creating contained multiple replicated subtrees and that while the leaf nodes (decisions) of the tree had unique and readable paths, the structures were inefficient and grew exponentially as new attributes were added. Figure 2 shows part of the classification tree for an example of modelling just two locations which makes this problem clear.

Bigraphs: We next looked at using bigraphs [4] which is a graphical representation that uses two forms of graph (hence bi-graph) together to represent a given problem. One of the graphs is a place graph which is a tree structure containing no cycles, while the other graph is a link graph that can be used to show the relationships between members of the place graph. The very nature of a bigraph is that they are designed to relate objects from the place graph to each other using hyperedges in the link graph which seemed a fitting solution to our modelling problem. In addition, existing research into using bigraphs to model context-aware systems [4] added credence to bigraphs as a viable solution. Figure 3 shows an example of a bigraph model of a single device and location and their conflicting relationship.

The two main problems we encountered when using bigraphs were the lack of a single defined semantics and the lack of tool support, which meant that the overhead in producing the models, and then using them for our medic tool, will be too high. Nevertheless we remain interested in bigraphs as a useful solution within this domain even though they are not practical for our current requirements, and in other work we are investigating their use within the wider context of our research.

Formal Concept Analysis: Before continuing with our research in this area, we returned again to our questions given above, and with the additional knowledge from our modelling experiments concluded that in answer to Question 1, the combination of our initial research (described in [8]) along with these new investigations suggested that the ontology was still the best approach. What we in fact needed was a better way of managing the ontology rather than a replacement. With this in mind, we focussed our attention on formal concept analysis (FCA), which is a theory of data analysis used to identify conceptual structures among data sets, along with a method of deriving a formalised ontology or a concept hierarchy from a set of objects and their individual attributes. A formal context is simply a table that represents the binary relations between objects and their attributes; this can then be translated into a lattice diagram which provides a visual representation of the relations between objects and their attributes, which is formally devised ensuring correctness. There are also tools available to translate a formal context into a lattice diagram (for example Lattice Miner).[3]

FCA is an appropriate solution as it enables us to support the structuring of our data by means of concept lattices and provides mechanisms for visualisation, navigation and analysis of the generated ontology [14, 25]. It is also possible to generate relationships and model context simply by filling in a

---

[3]available from **http://lattice-miner.sourceforge.net/**

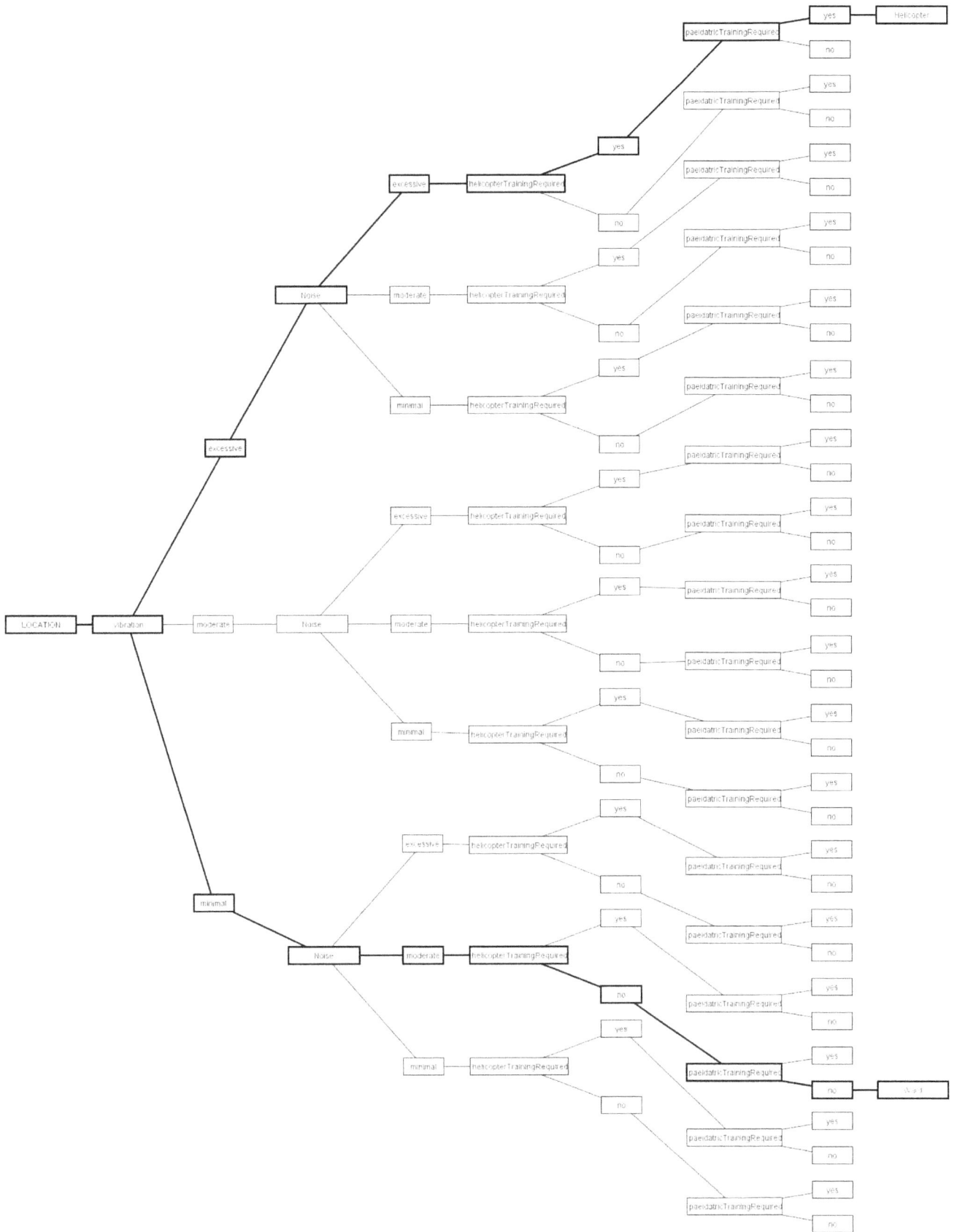

Figure 2. Partial Classification Tree for Two Locations

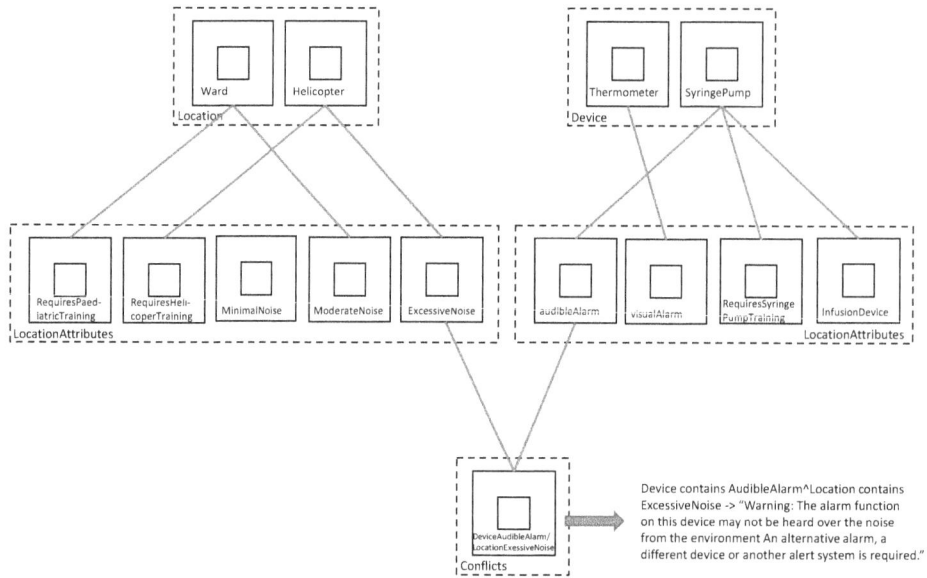

Figure 3. Bigraph for Two Devices in Two Locations

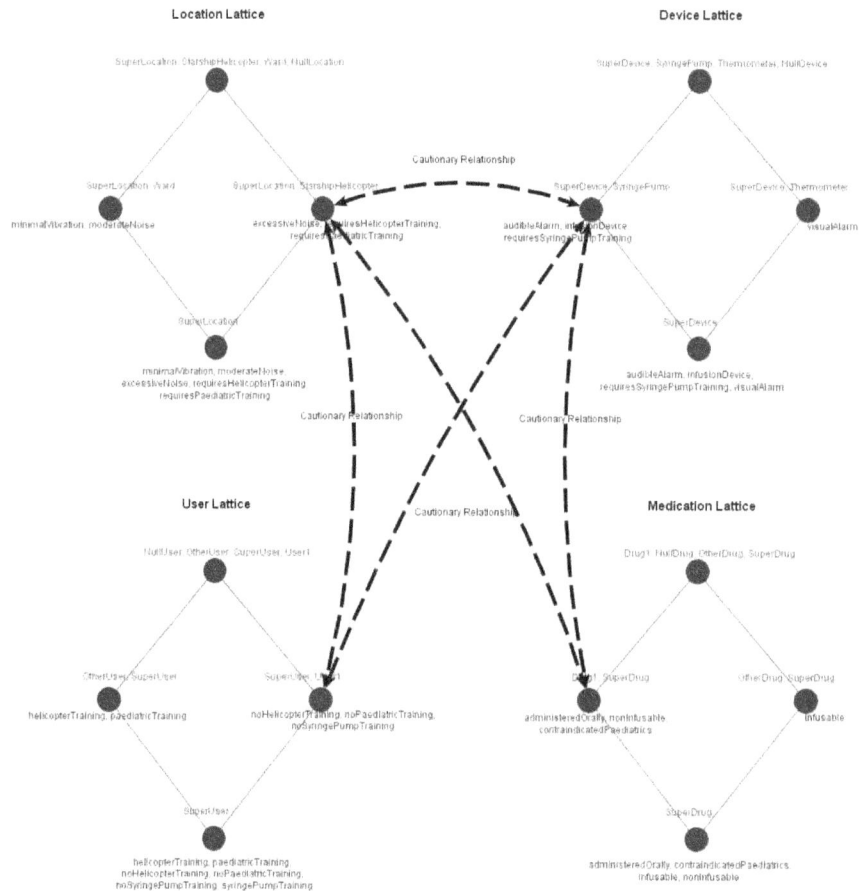

Figure 4. Lattice of Relationships

Original setup [8]	Proof of concept	Medic tool support
Interaction model and workflow		

Compare and Contrast		
+ reasoning about relationships	+ reasoning about relationships	+ reasoning about relationships
+ ontology for easy knowledge integration	+ ontology for easy knowledge integration	+ ontology export/import for easy knowledge integration
– original ontology design has to be correct (no verification)	– original ontology design has to be correct (no verification)	+ verification of correctness of ontology
– inconsistent data will not be identified	– no option to identify inconsistency	+ verification of consistency of data
– decision support only via complex Protégé interface	+ simple decision support	+ medic-specific decision support (tablet interface)
– update only via experts (Protégé interface)	– no easy update via decision tool	+ easy input and update of relationships
		– further update option planned as separate tool

Table 1. Comparison of our previous research with the two approaches discussed earlier.

formal context table, suggesting it might be a solution to the problem of supporting medical staff in adding new knowledge to the ontology. While there is still more work to be done on considering the relationship between FCA and our interaction models, our current investigations suggest that it will enhance our ontology in Protégé both for managing the ontology data, reasoning about that data and enabling the addition of new data (answering Questions 2, 3 and 4 above).

As an example, we can produce a lattice diagram for each of the required domains within the ontology (for example locations, devices, medical users and medications) and then these lattices are traversed to search for cautionary combinations or combinations requiring warnings or alternate actions. Figure 4 shows the lattice diagram for a set of relations for a device, location, user and medication.

There are several plug-ins for Protégé that add FCA capabilities, for example FCAView Tab [20] which enables users to visualise ontologies as formal contexts and lattices, and OntoComP [2] which uses FCA attribute exploration to extend ontologies and check for completeness. The existence of such tools supports our combined use of FCA and ontologies within Protégé and the ability to easily create similar plug-ins and export data provides the ability to use these as the basis for our medic tool.

Our new approach then is to start by creating a formal context and lattice (using a tool such as Lattice Miner) and use this as the basis for deriving the ontology. We then use FCA to reason about the ontology and the knowledge (to infer the required relationships between the objects in the ontology). The ontology data in its lattice form is used to provide the data for the medic tool.

Comparison of approaches

Table 1 offers a comparative overview of our previous approach [8], and the two improvements discussed here. The top part shows the workflow as experts and medics interact with each tool. In our original work, both experts and medics had to interact via the Protégé interface, which is of extremely limited use for medics. The Proof-of-concept implementation shows that it is possible to give simple tool support for medics based on complex ontology data. However, the interface was of limited capabilities.

The Medic tool we designed for the full application has a range of additional features appropriate for medics. The lower part of the table shows a comparison of advantages (black text labelled '+') and disadvantages (blue text labelled '-') of each approach. These are summaries of the arguments we outline throughout the paper. The second part of the paper focusses on our exploration of the medic tool, its requirement analysis and several stages of a user study of the interface design.

With a clearer understanding of the strengths and weaknesses of our modelling options, and a decision to remain with ontologies supported by formal concept analysis, the next step was to begin the development of the tool which would be used to support decision making based on the rules encoded in the ontology. The focus of the rest of the paper is on the development of the front-end and user interface of the tool which will use the ontology data to populate the data and rules of the back-end.

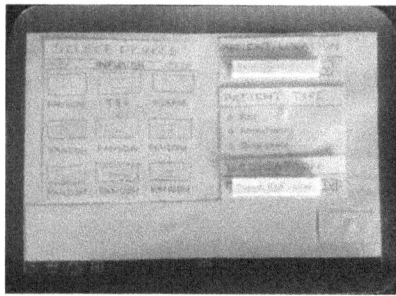

Figure 5. Prototype of Initial Screen   Figure 6. Prototype after making selections   Figure 7. Prototype with 'Do Not Continue'

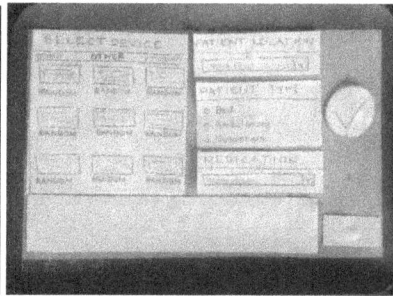

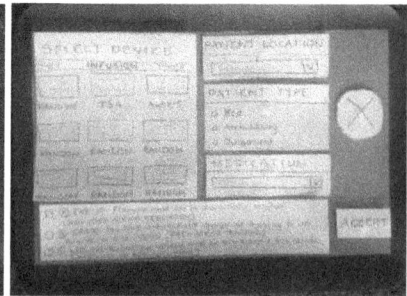

INITIAL PROTOTYPES FOR THE MEDIC TOOL

Initial requirements were gathered following discussions with medical personnel who are actively involved with using medical devices in different areas within our local hospital and who are required to make decisions around suitability of devices for different patients. It is already clear from these early investigations that the choices made regarding the devices to use and the interacting with and monitoring of these devices are affected by an enormous range of factors which include (but are not limited to) the atmosphere within given locations, medication being delivered, type of patients *etc.* In the neo-natal ward for example, premature babies all require an umbilical IV set up upon admission but subsequently some have single-line infusion pumps whereas others have double-line pumps depending on additional medication requirements. Some medications require continuous infusion such that attending to warning alarms that infusions are coming to an end is a critical activity, whereas for other medications these can be ignored and attended to when time permits. Conversely in the oncology out-patient department every effort is made to deal with alarms as soon as they occur to endeavour to keep the noise (and subsequent patient stress levels) to a minimum.

As medical personnel are frequently moving around within their environment, we decided to design the tool for a mobile device (in particular, Android tablet devices). Based on our initial findings, we explored mechanisms for conveying information to medics in these different environments. We adapted a traffic-light approach [3] to support the three different levels of information provided by the tool – ok to continue, warning that additional considerations must be acknowledged and not safe to continue. From here we developed our initial prototypes, and we then began experimenting with implementing these on an Android tablet (to see which parts of our proposed designs were effective and practical) which led to the revised prototypes shown in Figures 5, 6 and 7.

USER STUDY OF PROTOTYPE

A user study was carried out to perform an initial evaluation of the paper prototypes described above. The twelve participants in the study were primarily not medical personnel (although some were) as at this stage we were interested in general software usability issues rather than problems relating specifically to the use of the tool by medical personnel. These will be studied once we have an implemented prototype. We provide an overview of the study and subsequent

development here (full details of the tool and user evaluation to appear elsewhere).

The evaluation focussed on uncovering usability problems, determining task-level user satisfaction, and identification of possible user errors. The participant tasks were devised to allow us to determine that there were no significant usability problems with the design (which would prevent them from completing the tasks), that the users understood the concepts as presented by the tool (both required inputs and information outputs) and that there was sufficient error-prevention with the design.

The evaluation study design consisted of a persona (that of an agency nurse) which was presented to the participants to adopt along with three typical scenarios of use for the tool. The participants were given instructions to guide them through the the task of entering the required information for each of the tasks, and then asked to interpret the output from the tool. For example, scenario one and its associated questions is:

> You have been assigned to a bed-bound patient in the paediatric ward (Ward 17) who is a boy of 9 suffering from multiple trauma injuries. He requires the delivery of antibiotics intravenously and you have been asked to use the Alaris infusion pump to perform this task.
>
> Step 1: Use the prototype to select the medical device you would use
> Step 2: Use the prototype to select the patient location
> Step 3: Use the prototype to select the type of patient you are treating
> Step 4: Use the prototype to select the medication you intend to administer to your patient
> Step 5: Use the "check" button to determine if it is safe to continue
>
> Q1: Why do you think the background colour changed?
> Q2: Do you know what the symbol on the right-hand-side of the screen symbolises?

As the participants performed the tasks for each of the scenarios, they were observed to identify errors, corrections and confusion. They were also encouraged to "think aloud" and verbalise what they were doing at each step to further help identify any mismatches between the system's behaviour and their understanding.

The most significant finding from the study was that selecting "Patient Type" proved confusing and difficult. Two thirds of participants during Scenario 1 and all but one participant in Scenario 2 experienced difficulties with this concept, in Scenario 3 one third of participants failed to select anything. Closer examination of this suggests that the problem lies in the overlap of concepts being captured within this – firstly there is the practical aspect of whether or not a patient can actually move independently (are they bed bound or ambulatory), then there is another dimension relating to the permanence of their current location (are they in bed and staying there or are they an outpatient who will be leaving the premises at some point). This needs to be reconsidered in relation to the relevance of these two dimensions and what effect each has on the decision outcomes.

More positively, however, the use of the combination of colours, icons and messages to convey information was understood by all participants and all were able to complete all of the tasks without difficulty (apart from the issue described above) and with minor error rates. Requirement to acknowledge warning messages prior to continuing was missed by a third of participants across all tasks, however in discussion they all felt that deactivating the "Accept" button until these items have been checked would have prevented this. Figure 8 shows the next iteration of the prototype at a higher fidelity developed following the study.

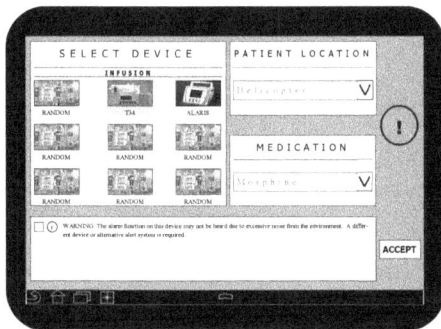

Figure 8. Refined Prototype of Warning Screen

With having developed this strong foundation for our medic tool prototype, the next step is now to implement the prototype application for Android tablet device and to carry out user testing with medical personnel. The next section discusses the impact of our current results on the project plan, while the following section places our work in the context of existing research.

IDENTIFYING THE PARAMETERS

Until now the locations and situational factors we have been working with have been limited to small-scale toy examples (such as the audible device in a helicopter) or to a subset or real-world issues. From our initial investigations into requirements we identify two categories of situational factors in which we are interested:

Tangible factors – which includes things such as noise, lighting levels, practitioner/patient ratios *etc.* which can be measured and compared against a scale of ideal values;

Intangible factors – which include such things as stress-levels, level of emergency *etc.* which are much harder to quantify.

In order to progress further and be certain that our models are indeed capable of capturing all of the elements we need to

describe, we must perform a number of studies to investigate these. These studies will comprise of activities such as:

- Surveys of the environment – to determine all possible locations within the hospital where medical devices as well as all possible devices currently being used, *etc.*;

- Ethnographic studies – to fully understand both the tangible and intangible factors that should be recorded;

- Further interviews with medical practitioners – to develop our understanding of appropriate tools which can support them in their work.

A more detailed description of these can be found in [7]. In addition, the increased understanding of the real-world factors and user needs will allow us to refine the tool we are developing so that it focusses on the important attributes in the most appropriate manner. At the moment our prototype tool aims to cover several different elements within our problem domain (such as understanding which device to use in a particular location, which drugs can be used with particular types of patients *etc.*) and we may find that these need to be separated into several different tools.

DISCUSSION

There is a large body of current academic research focussing on the development and use of safety-critical medical devices worldwide. Academic research around the world by groups such as CHI+MED *etc.* can be loosely categorised into the following areas (with the caveat that there are obviously overlaps between this categories):

- Ethnographic studies of use of devices in practice - for example [19, 24]

- Analysis of usability and design considerations of devices in the lab - for example [22, 13]

- Formal modelling of devices to consider functionality and interaction - for example [23, 12, 10]

In addition, regulatory bodies such as the The U.S. Department of Health and Human Services' division on Food and Drug Administration (FDA) and healthcare technology foundations such as Association for the Advancement of Medical Instrumentation (AAMI)[4] are continually working to develop standards, guidelines, regulatory processes *etc.* to ensure the safety of design and use of medical devices such as those described here.

The work we have described here complements all of these approaches by adding in the dimension of context of use, in a way (via formal models and reasoning) which enables it to be integrated into the work of others, such as the examples given above. One of our proposed next steps relates directly to the gathering of contextual information via ethnographic studies, clearly this will be informed by the existing work done as part of the CHI+MED project [17] (some examples above) and we would hope that our results will also help inform their future work. Whilst we are not considering the design of new

---

[4]http://www.aami.org/

medical devices within this current work, we must certainly take on board lessons learned in the design of the medic tool (as it will itself be a tool used in a medical situation) such that it reflects the best practice knowledge being developed by Thimbleby *et al.* Finally the importance of formal modelling, both of devices and their contexts of use is central to our work and we continue to be informed and motivated by the existing work in this domain.

CONCLUSIONS AND FUTURE WORK

In this paper, we have described our new approach for modelling contexts of use of medical devices, and using this information to support medical personnel in selecting appropriate devices. We have also described our initial work on developing the medic tool. The new approach provides additional benefits (over and above the existing benefits described in previous work) of ensuring the correctness of the ontology, having a more sound reasoning process and, in future, an easier way to update and add information. The medic tool is currently under development and the next iteration of a higher fidelity prototype will shortly undergo user testing.

The next steps for this research are the completion of ethnographic studies within our local hospital (who provide the domain examples for our work) and further investigation of using FCA and lattice miner as the basis of a tool which enables medical personnel to add to the location and context data. Our work fits into a larger worldwide picture of ensuring safety in the use of medical devices and, as such, provides a valuable contribution to this domain.

REFERENCES

1. Alan F Merry, C. S. W. Medication error in new zealand-time to act. *Journal of the New Zealand Medical Association 121*, 1272 (April 2008).

2. Baader, F., Ganter, B., Sertkaya, B., and Sattler, U. Completing description logic knowledge bases using formal concept analysis. In *In Proceedings of IJCAI 2007*, AAAI Press (2007), 230–235.

3. Bardram, J. E., and Nørskov, N. A context-aware patient safety system for the operating room. In *Proc. Int. Conf. on Ubiquitous Computing*, UbiComp '08 (2008), 272–281.

4. Birkedal, L., Debois, S., Elsborg, E., Hildebrandt, T., and Niss, H. Bigraphical models of context-aware systems. Tech. rep., IT University of Copenhagen, 2005.

5. Blandford, A., Buchanan, G., Curzon, P., Furniss, D., and Thimbleby, H. Who's looking? Invisible problems with interactive medical devices. In *Proc. Int. Workshop on Interactive Systems in Healthcare*, ACM SIGCHI (2010), 9–12.

6. Blandford, A., Cauchi, A., and *et al.*, P. C. Comparing actual practice and user manuals: A case study based on programmable infusion pumps. In *Proc. ACM SIGCHI Symp. on Engineering Interactive Computing Systems (EICS)*, ACM (2011), 59–64.

7. Bowen, J., Cunningham, S. J., Hinze, A., Jung, D., and Reeves, S. Eliciting usage contexts of safety-critical medical devices. In *SmartHealth'13, 5th International Workshop on Smart Healthcare and Social Therapy at OZCHI 2013. Available as a working paper from: http://researchcommons.waikato.ac.nz/handle/10289/6* (November 2013).

8. Bowen, J., and Hinze, A. Using ontologies to reason about the usability of interactive medical devices in multiple situations of use. In *Proc. ACM SIGCHI Symp. on Engineering Interactive Computing Systems (EICS)*, ACM (2012), 247–256.

9. Bowen, J., and Reeves, S. Formal models for user interface design artefacts. *Innovations in Systems and Software Engineering 4*, 2 (2008), 125–141.

10. Bowen, J., and Reeves, S. Modelling safety properties of interactive medical systems. In *EICS* (2013), 91–100.

11. Breiman, L., Friedman, J. H., Olshen, R. A., and Stone, C. J. *Classification and Regression Trees.* Chapman & Hall, New York, NY, 1984.

12. Campos, J. C., and Harrison, M. D. Modelling and analysing the interactive behaviour of an infusion pump. *ECEASST 45* (2011).

13. Cauchi, A. Using differential formal analysis for dependable number entry. In *EICS* (2013), 155–158.

14. Cimiano, P., Hotho, A., Stumme, G., and Tane, J. Conceptual knowledge processing with formal concept analysis and ontologies. In *Concept Lattices, Int. Conf. on Formal Concept Analysis, ICFCA 2004*, vol. 2961, Springer (2004), 189–207.

15. Cohen, M. R. *Medication Errors.* American Pharmacists Association, Washington, DC, 2007.

16. ECRI Institute. Top 10 health technology hazards for 2014. *Health Devices* (November 2013).

17. Engineering and Physical Sciences Research Council. CHI+MED: Multidisciplinary computer-human interaction research for the design and safe use of interactive medical devices, EPSRC reference: EP/G059063/1, 2011.

18. FDA. Medical device use-safety: Incorporating human factors engineering into risk management. Tech. rep., U.S. Department of Health and Human Services Food and Drug Administration, Center for Devices and Radiological Health, July 2000. Guidance for Industry and FDA Premarket and Design Control Reviewers.

19. Furniss, D., O'Kane, A. A., Randell, R., Taneva, S., Mentis, H. M., and Blandford, A. HCI fieldwork in healthcare: creating a graduate guidebook. In *CHI Extended Abstracts* (2013), 3203–3206.

20. Jiang, G., Ogasawara, K., Nishimoto, N., Endoh, A., and Sakurai, T. Caview tab: A concept-oriented view generation tool for clinical data using formal concept analysis. In *Proceedings of 8th International Protégé Conference, Madrid, Spain* (2005).

21. Kohn, L., Corrigan, J., and Donaldson, M., Eds. *To err is human: building a safer health system. A report of the committee on Quality of Health Care in America, Institute of Medicine.* National Academy Press, 2000.

22. Masci, P., Ruksenas, R., Oladimeji, P., Cauchi, A., Gimblett, A., Li, K. Y., Curzon, P., and Thimbleby, H. W. On formalising interactive number entry on infusion pumps. *ECEASST 45* (2011).

23. Masci, P., Rukšėnas, R., Oladimeji, P., Cauchi, A., Gimblett, A., Li, Y., Curzon, P., and Thimbleby, H. The benefits of formalising design guidelines: A case study on the predictability of drug infusion pumps. *Innovations in Systems and Software Engineering, Springer-Verlag London* (2013).

24. Noble, P., and Blandford, A. You can't touch this: Potential perils of patient interaction with clinical medical devices. In *INTERACT (2)* (2013), 395–402.

25. Obitko, M., Snsel, V., and Smid, J. Ontology design with formal concept analysis. In *CLA*, V. Snsel and R. Belohlvek, Eds., vol. 110 of *CEUR Workshop Proceedings*, CEUR-WS.org (2004).

26. Organisation, W. H. What is patient safety? online WHO information available at http://www.who.int/patientsafety/about/en/.

27. Zhang, J., Patel, V. L., Johnson, T. R., Chung, P., and Turley, J. P. Evaluating and predicting patient safety for medical devices with integral information technology. In *Advances in Patient Safety: From Research to Implementation (Volume 2)*. Agency for Healthcare Research and Quality (US), Rockville (MD), 2005.

Predicting Task Execution Times by Deriving Enhanced Cognitive Models from User Interface Development Models

Michael Quade[1]
michael.quade@dai-labor.de

Marc Halbrügge[2]
marc.halbruegge@telekom.de

Klaus-Peter Engelbrecht[2]
klaus-peter.engelbrecht@telekom.de

Sahin Albayrak[1]
sahin.albayrak@dai-labor.de

Sebastian Möller[2]
sebastian.moeller@telekom.de

[1]DAI-Labor
Technische Universität Berlin
Ernst-Reuter-Platz 7, 10587, Berlin

[2]Quality and Usability Lab
Technische Universität Berlin
Ernst-Reuter-Platz 7, 10587, Berlin

ABSTRACT

Adaptive user interfaces (UI) offer the opportunity to adapt to changes in the context, but this also poses the challenge of evaluating the usability of many different versions of the resulting UI. Consequently, usability evaluations tend to become very complex and time-consuming. We describe an approach that combines model-based usability evaluation with development models of adaptive UIs. In particular, we present how a cognitive user behavior model can be created automatically from UI development models and thus save time and costs when predicting task execution times. With the help of two usability studies, we show that the resulting predictions can be further improved by using information encoded in the UI development models.

Author Keywords

HCI; Model-Based Development; Automated Usability Evaluation; User Behavior Model; Simulation

ACM Classification Keywords

H.5.2 Information Interfaces and Presentation (e.g. HCI): User Interfaces

INTRODUCTION

One of the major challenges of today's user interface (UI) development is to ensure the usability of UIs when adapting to context changes. A common goal is to develop *plastic* UIs [4], which adapt to context changes while preserving certain usability properties within a predefined range. To do so, proposed properties for *plasticity*, such as observability and predictability [8], need to be expressed by a human designer at development time in a quantifiable way and require to be monitored and maintained during runtime of the application.

Another approach to achieve the goals of plastic UIs is conducting usability evaluations at development time. Usually,

the best way is carrying out tests with real users; e.g. by applying *Think Aloud* [18]. Additionally, experts can check the application's UI and interaction logic against predefined criteria; e.g. by performing a *Cognitive Walkthrough* [21] or a *Heuristic Evaluation* [18]. Carrying out any of these methods is a time consuming and expensive task. This is particularly true for UIs that adapt to users or contextual parameters because different users and context conditions need to be analyzed. Since this is impractical, applying automated usability evaluation (AUE) methods is promising [9].

AUE methods that simulate user actions are based on models of the user and the system [9]. Thus, it is possible to draw on a vast body of research dealing with *model-based evaluation* [14]. In general, model-based evaluation specifies a formal framework for applying established knowledge about how users interact with computers in a design situation. Therefore, it has similarities with expert evaluation methods. However, due to the formal nature of the framework, it is principally suitable for automation.

In this paper, we apply model-based evaluation at development time in order to address the challenges of complexity and time consumption for usability evaluations of adaptive UIs. In particular, we show how model-based evaluation is performed automatically based on runtime UI models conforming to the CAMELEON reference framework [4]. The framework structures the development process for plastic UIs during model-based UI development (MBUID). Most notably, UI development models are categorized into *task models*, modality-independent *abstract UI models* (AUI), modality-specific *concrete UI models* (CUI) and platform-specific *final UI models* (FUI). Even though most MBUID approaches differ in detail, their generic structure and development processes can be aligned to CAMELEON; e.g. approaches based on the UsiXML description language [15].

A main benefit is that by using these UI development models in a model-based evaluation approach, different stages of the prototypes and adaptation variants can be evaluated without creating system models in the required evaluation method and thus saving time and costs. Furthermore, we show that such UI development models contain valuable information about the UI which is used to render more precise evaluation results without further intervention of usability experts.

The remainder of this paper is structured as follows. Below, we give an overview of related work and lead over to the description of our approach. After that, we introduce a pilot usability study and derive our findings in order to enhance our approach. We then evaluate this enhanced approach with a second usability study and discuss the results before we present a general discussion and final conclusions.

RELATED WORK

In this section, current work in the domain of MBUID is presented and we refer to how usability evaluations are introduced to the process. After that, we present benefits from model-based evaluation methods and automated tools.

Model-based UI Development and Usability Evaluations

A generic overview of potential combinations and the placement of usability evaluation methods within MBUID is presented in [1]. In general, the access to the application's task model allows calculating all potential task sequences and therefore enables using the task models for usability evaluation purposes as described e.g. in [19]. Specifically, by simulating different task performances, it becomes possible to detect potential pitfalls regarding the structure of the interaction process and to compare different variants.

The approach proposed in [7] uses MatLab to describe the system model and UsiXML to describe the UI in order to check early prototypes against a set of usability related rules and to predict human performance using a cognitive architecture. While first results have been promising, the approach does not cover an integration of UsiXML with the system model and the cognitive architecture and therefore does not cover automation for providing the evaluation models.

The TERESA authoring tool [17] supports the user-centric development of interactive applications based on UI models that are derived from task models using the ConcurTaskTree (CTT) notation [19]. TERESA allows for an early evaluation of the interaction flow by simulating the task tree and thus enables detecting possible dead ends or unreachable states.

The Multi Access Service Platform (MASP) [3] is a runtime framework for adaptive UI models. The MASP is based on executable models for multimodal UIs focusing on the domain of smart environments. MASP UIs are defined as sets of models compatible with CAMELEON. A main feature of the MASP is that the models are interconnected via mappings and can be held at runtime in order to dynamically derive the final UI; i.e. the models are executed at runtime. By this means, modifications to the models are reflected in the UI and actions on the UI lead to changes in the underlying models. During creation and testing of the task models, the MASP Task Tree Editor (MTTE) is used which is based on the CTT Editor [19]. The MTTE assists in defining the task hierarchy by structuring tasks according to their (temporal) relationships. Further, the MTTE can be used to simulate task flows by hand in order to check if all scenarios are covered.

Model-based Usability Evaluation and AUE Tools

Traditionally, model-based evaluation has been focused on execution time for routine tasks performed by skilled users.

As Kieras [14] points out, trying to explain purely cognitive tasks is complex and usually requires to understand the involved processes, whereas routine tasks mainly consist of perceptual and motor activities, which can be modeled more generally and are related to UI design. Task execution time is a popular instrumental measure to quantify efficiency as one criterion of usability. As argued by [14], the execution time of routine tasks is closely related to the number of perceptual and motor steps: a routine task involving less such steps can be performed more quickly. At the same time, a UI allowing to perform the same task with fewer steps will likely be simpler and thus more usable [14]. To encounter concerns about the models' validity, guidelines for dealing with uncertainty in the predictions have been defined, especially for the case that one of several designs is to be pursued further [14].

The GOMS approach for analytical modeling uses models of *goals*, *operators*, *methods* and *selection* rules [5]. In a GOMS model, *goals* are used to represent the direction of interaction. In order to model how a human user would achieve these goals, *operators* are being performed on a perceptual, cognitive or motor-act level. Execution times are bound to these operators in order to predict overall task execution times for expert users. Furthermore, *methods* describe sequences of operators in order to achieve sub-goals. Finally, *selection* rules are applied if more than one method can be used to achieve a goal. An overview of methods from the GOMS family with different application areas is given in [11].

The Keystroke-Level Model (KLM) is a simplified approach of GOMS for modeling human performance with an interactive application [5]. The focus of this analytical modeling method is to predict the interaction time of expert users for specific tasks. Larger tasks can be divided into smaller unit tasks. These unit tasks can further be subdivided into an acquisition phase and an execution phase. For the execution phase of each unit task, an expert writes down the method to perform the task and counts the keystrokes involved. By adding up the allocated times for these actions, the overall execution time can be predicted.

ACT-R [2] is a cognitive architecture which incorporates various theories about human information processing and has been applied to the analysis of HCI. While ACT-R implements the limits of human information processing (such as restricted working memory), it allows for parallel processing in some cases, making ACT-R models very powerful but complex compared to other approaches. Due to this complexity, usually it is only applied by experts in research.

Based on the aforementioned approaches, CogTool [12] was developed in order to simplify model-based evaluation and make it accessible to developers with less psychological expertise. It is based on a compilation approach which produces ACT-R models from KLM sequences. The KLM model is automatically generated from a user interaction demonstration which the designer performs on a storyboard of the UI. This storyboard consists of screenshots or mockups and needs to be created for each evaluation. User actions are then translated to perceptual and motor operators like *look-at* and *point*. *Think* operators that represent mental activity of the user are automatically added at every decision point. The resulting model is compiled together with information from the storyboard into an ACT-R model which is used to predict task execution times. Initial work in applying CogTool to further interaction devices is described in [13]. While the results are promising, comparisons with real user tests also revealed that changes to the underlying KLM model need to be made in order to cope with specific domains [13].

To sum up, model-based evaluation can only make predictions on the basis of what is known about the user. Since some aspects of the users' interaction behavior, and in particular their judgments about the system (e.g. user satisfaction), cannot be anticipated by an analyst or a formal method, today's methods are not able to fully substitute evaluations with real users and experts. Instead, model-based methods should be used complementary to expert or user-based evaluations; e.g. to make early decisions between design alternatives or when user tests are too costly or too hard to apply.

PREDICTING TASK EXECUTION TIMES BY COMBINING UI DEVELOPMENT MODELS AND AUE TOOLS

When applying AUE to the development of model-based adaptive UIs, there are specific requirements that need to be addressed [23]. Basically, this involves making information about the application, the context of use, the user, and the task accessible to the specific AUE approach. In previous work, main benefits of combining MBUID with model-based evaluation were highlighted which lie in reducing the complexity and costs for applying AUE [22].

A specific approach, which deploys UI development models of the previously introduced MASP framework [3] to a model-based usability evaluation approach, has been introduced in [22]. The work in this paper builds on top of that basic approach and adds further integration of the UI development models and thus more automation to the evaluation process. However, we do not only address this extended automation but also demonstrate how specific requirements of an AUE tool can be covered by information from the UI development models in order to gain improved results.

Below, we give a short summary of the MASP framework models in order to better present required extensions to the architecture which are introduced in the following sections:

The Task Model defines the interaction flow between user and application. Interaction tasks define direct actions by the user and application tasks define application logic that is executed without user actions.

The User Interface Models are specified independently from modalities and devices on the level of the AUI model, while modality-specific definitions of the CUI models exist in parallel at runtime and are connected to the final UI on the specific devices.

The Domain Model serves as a dynamic storage for domain information. Relevant for rendering the UI is that this information is used to dynamically link domain data to UI elements for input and output.

The Context Model holds sensor and device data in order to reflect on the environment, user, and interaction devices.

Enhanced Model-based Architecture for Predicting Task Execution Times

As introduced in [22], for our combined approach we chose to apply CogTool as an AUE tool for predicting task execution times. The main reason for this decision is that CogTool is widely used and the underlying ACT-R concepts are sufficiently validated. In order to apply an evaluation with CogTool, representations of all visited UI elements from each UI screen that is on a demonstrated interaction path are required. For this reason, the task model of the application does not suffice alone. This is due to the fact that the evaluation with CogTool relies heavily on the interaction logic of the application in combination with UI surface information, such as type, label, size and position of UI elements (see [23]). Consequently, the approach needs to provide means for deriving this UI information and – as equally important – a simulation component to extract required interaction paths. For this purpose a module was implemented that transforms UI information from the AUI and FUI models of the current UI screen and provides this to a user model for simulating interaction. The resulting interaction traces are then compiled to ACT-R using CogTool and can be analyzed further. Figure 1 gives an overview of the processes and participating models which are described in the remainder of this section.

Converting UI Information and Performing Interaction

In a first step, all UI elements from a given UI screen and their relevant attributes for an evaluation using CogTool are identified. The intermediate model *UI Element Information* from Figure 1 is used to provide this information from each UI element. During this process, we make use of the task models that are being executed in the MASP. We build a subset of the enabled tasks by filtering only tasks that are actually presented on the screen - the presentation task set (PTS). Each task of the PTS also links to an AUI element that has a FUI representation on the current UI screen. Consequently, all required FUI elements are then collected by following the mappings from AUI elements to FUI representations in the runtime platform (see upper left of Figure 1).

For the case studies of this paper, a concept was applied which uses expressions in the AUI models in order to map AUI elements with their corresponding HTML elements (on the FUI level). These mappings from AUI to FUI were implemented using descriptive paths to the location of the specific HTML element in predefined templates. By following these mappings, the required interconnection from task and AUI models to FUI elements is accessed during runtime. Hence, this concept provides up-to-date information of the UI screen as it is at any given point of time on any available interaction device and for any adaptation variant of the UI. The required attributes are then transformed to the aforementioned *UI Element Information* (arrows 1a and 1b in Figure 1).

During simulation the *User Model* is initialized with *User Task Knowledge* which consists of a list of labels that need to be interacted with in order to reach a specified goal state. This

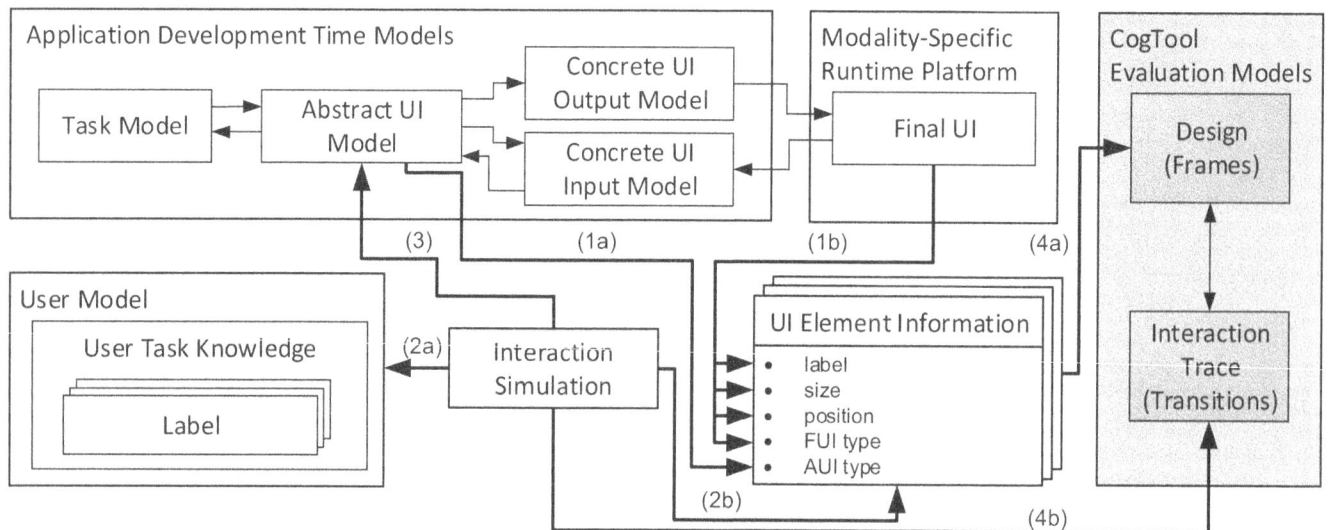

Figure 1. Integrated architecture with interconnections between UI development and runtime models (white) and intermediate models required for simulation (light gray) and evaluation (dark gray). Bold lines indicate processes and thin lines depict mappings and exchange between the models.

process is controlled by the *Interaction Simulation* component which accesses the *User Task Knowledge* and compares it to the labels from the *UI Element Information* of the current UI screen (arrows 2a and 2b in Figure 1). The definition of this knowledge matches the approach of CogTool to evaluate expert interaction tasks that are pre-defined by the developer and is used for the evaluation of the user studies in the following sections. A more detailed description how the labels are compared and alternative ways to retrieve required information for the *User Task Knowledge* are presented in [22].

When the current *User Task Knowledge* matches the label of a *UI Element Information*, an interaction on that specific element is simulated. This interaction is then performed on the corresponding AUI element which activates the next task set of the application (arrow 3 in Figure 1). By this means, the follow-up UI screen is triggered, which is evaluated accordingly until the goal-state is achieved; i.e. all labels from the *User Task Knowledge* are matched.

In the last step, each set of *UI Element Information* from the current UI screen and the simulated interaction are transformed to specific CogTool models - *Frames* that are interlinked by *Transitions* (arrows 4a and 4b in Figure 1). By this means an interaction trace is created and evaluated automatically in order to predict the task execution time. Additionally, the whole interaction process can also be validated using internal analysis methods and views of CogTool.

Below, we describe a pilot usability study that was conducted with a prototypical application of the MASP in order to gain first results from real user interactions that we used as a basis for enhancing and evaluating the described approach later on.

COGNITIVE USER MODEL
In order to test whether automatically generated cognitive user models can inform the usability engineering process, we conducted a usability study with a MASP based cooking assistant (CA, see Figure 2). The CA consists of several UI

screens and allows searching for recipes depending on attributes like calorie intake and type of dish. After having selected a recipe, the user can check the needed ingredients against the contents of the storage cabinet and – if applicable – generate a shopping list. The actual preparation of the selected recipe is performed using a step by step guide.

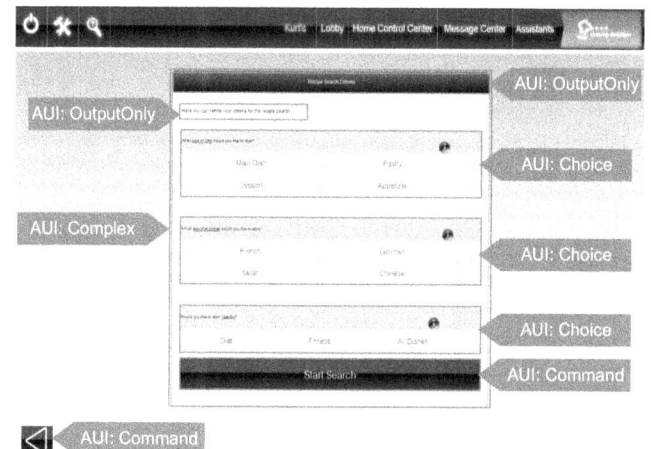

Figure 2. Screenshot of the English version of the cooking assistant with annotated AUI elements and their types.

Pilot Usability Study
The usability test presented here focused on the task of finding a recipe and took place in May 2013. Ten subjects (40% female; M_{age}=29, SD_{age}=12) were recruited mainly off campus. The CA was presented on a 19" (48.3 cm) touch screen with a 4:3 ratio mounted on a wall cupboard above the kitchen sink (see Figure 3). We recorded the interactions of the subjects with the user interface while they completed five simple tasks, e.g. "Search for German main dishes and select lamb chops".[1] All subjects had worked with the recipe finder and

---
[1]The full instructions are available for download at http://www.tu-berlin.de/?id=135088

the touch screen in a previous part of the experiment so that they could be considered adequately trained.[2] Task instructions were given verbally, user actions were logged by the MASP and additionally recorded on video to be able to identify system errors or misinterpreted user actions (see placement of camera in Figure 3). The video recordings and system logs were synchronized using ELAN [26], which was also used to annotate user interaction errors, such as wrong and unrecognized clicks, as well as system response times, starts and ends of individual trials.

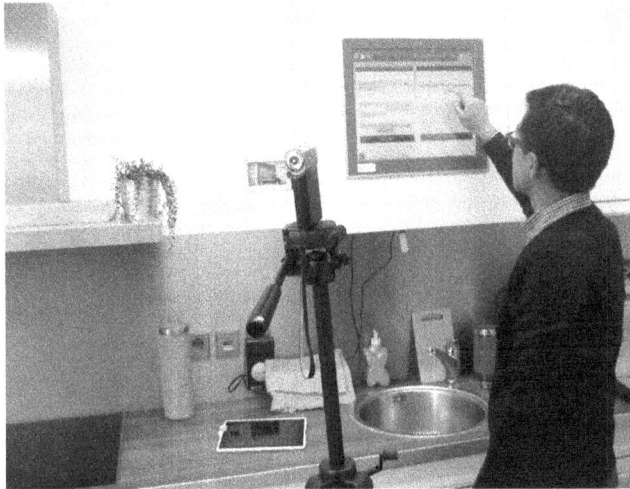

Figure 3. Experimental setup with the cooking assistant on the mounted touch screen for the pilot study conducted in May 2013.

Results

Average task execution times and number of errors per task are presented in Table 1. The relatively high number of errors is most probably caused by the six-year-old touch screen used during the experiment which suffered from a substandard input detection compared to current devices. As described above, these errors were extracted from video and log recordings. Errors are especially important to us, because CogTool, which is part of our combined approach, aims at predicting task completion times for expert users in error free conditions. For the comparison between our data and a Cog-Tool model to be meaningful, we have to discard all erroneous trials beforehand. In case of the pilot study, this yields only one to four observations per task – too few for statistical analysis.

Task / Recipe	Steps	time (s)		errors	
		M	SD	M	SD
1 Lamb Chops	5	10.7	2.3	1.7	1.3
2 Roast Apples	5	8.7	2.4	1.0	.8
3 Panna Cotta	6	11.4	6.3	.4	.5
4 [Group size]	4	3.8	1.5	.8	1.1
5 Chicken Breasts	14	32.6	8.0	3.9	1.3

Table 1. Task completion times and error rates from the pilot study.

---

[2] The experiment was embedded in a larger evaluation study. We only report the relevant parts here.

In order to get as much information as possible from the experiment, we rejected complete tasks as subject of the analysis and went for times between pairs of clicks instead. If for example a task consisted of five clicks, and an error happened between click 2 and 3, we removed everything between 2 and 3, and used only the remaining three steps (1 to 2, 3 to 4 and 4 to 5).

Next we developed a classification for the different types of clicks. The class of a click should be related to the time a user needs to perform it. The simplest and fastest one should be repeated clicks on the same UI element. We will call this type *same button* in the following. The other extreme are clicks on buttons that are not part of the same UI screen, i.e. a new page must be loaded before the second click can be performed. We denote this as *new screen*. The remaining clicks are performed on the same form, but on different buttons. The buttons of the cooking assistant's user interface are grouped semantically, e.g. there is a button group called "Regional Dishes" with individual buttons for "French", "German", "Italian", and "Chinese" (see Figure 2). We decided to differentiate between clicks within and across those groups and finally obtained four types of click pairs, ordered by semantic and also physical proximity: *same button* (repeated clicks); other button in the *same group*; other button in an*other group*; other button on a later displayed *new screen*.

In total we observed 447 single clicks during the experiment, of which 78 (17%) had to be discarded due to hardware (mainly touch screen) errors. The remaining clicks formed 218 valid pairs of clicks that could be divided into the four categories above. The time interval between clicks is significantly different depending on type (linear mixed model [20] with subject as random factor, $F_{3,205} = 19.9, p < .01$).

Visual examination of the data indicated the presence of extreme outliers (up to 10 seconds between clicks), most probably caused by the inclusion of erroneous trials in the analysis. We therefore based any further examination on robust statistics like 20% trimmed means [25].

Automatically Generated Cognitive User Model

Main goal of the initial study presented above was to show that automatically generated cognitive user models can provide useful information to system developers and designers. As a baseline, we exported the task information contained within the MASP UI models to CogTool as explained in the previous section (see also Figure 1). CogTool bases its predictions on the Keystroke-Level Model, estimating the motor time needed to perform a click by Fitts' Law [6] and placing generic *think* operators (1.2 s) at every decision point (i.e. between clicks). This basic approach yields already moderate fits, but cannot really differentiate between all of the click types (see CogTool "Ootb" out of the box predictions, ■ in Figure 4). The goodness-of-fit statistics given in Table 2 indicate significant room for improvement. CogTool out of the box predictions are especially off the mark in the *same group* and *new screen* conditions. In the following part, we examine these conditions in more detail. We provide theoretical explanations for the mismatch between model and observed data and derive a revised cognitive user model. At the same time, we demonstrate how the cognitive user model benefits from information contained within the development models.

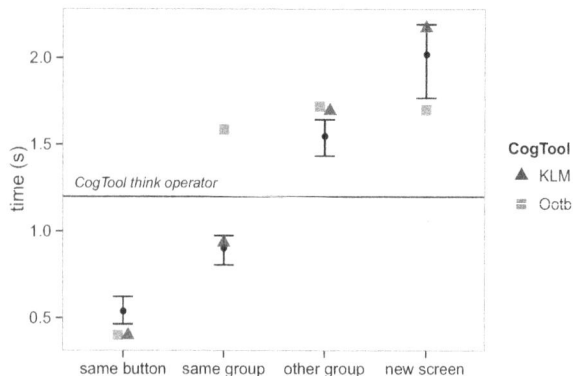

Figure 4. Average times between clicks on different elements on the user interface for the pilot study. Circles denote 20% trimmed means, lines bootstrapped 95% confidence intervals (10000 repetitions).

Hypothesis I: Units of Mental Processing

The first observation worth discussing is the difference between the *same group* and *other group* clicks (see Figure 4). Buttons in the same semantic group are also physically closer to each other; therefore it should need less time to move the finger from one to another. But is this explanation sufficient? Fitts' Law provides well-researched predictions for the time the user needs for finger pointing movements. In our case, Fitts' index of difficulty is close to 1 bit within a group and raises up to 3 bit across groups. Even when using a comparatively high coefficient of 150 ms/bit, Fitts' Law only predicts a difference of 300 ms between *same group* and *other group* clicks. This is much less than the 640 ms that we measured; hence we have to reject Fitts' Law as a single explanation.

In addition, the absolute time between clicks within the same group in the pilot study was approximately 900 ms. If the premise of a generic 1.2 s *think* operator before every click holds, this would not be possible. We concluded that the basic CogTool model does not sufficiently match our data and decided to augment the model using additional rules and heuristics from the literature [10] and structural information of the user interface from the MASP user interface models [22].

The original formulation of the Keystroke-Level Model formed the basis for the revised cognitive model. Card, Moran, and Newell present several rules for the placement of *think* operators. In principle, those rules are already incorporated in CogTool, but some cannot be applied automatically, i.e. without human *interpretation* of the user interface in question. The rule that is most important for the given experiment is rule 2, which says that if several actions belong to a cognitive unit, only one *think* is to be placed in front of the first one. This rule definitely applies to the *same button* condition, where one button is clicked a fixed number of times in a row. A more interesting case is the *same group* condition which indicates consecutive clicks within a group of buttons belonging to the same concept, e.g. changing the type of dish

from "appetizer" to "dessert". In terms of cognition, this task can be solved using a single chunk of memory that represents the target type of dish ("dessert"), and thus no *think* operator is to be assigned to the *same group* condition. This also fits well with the empirical mean being noticeably smaller than the 1.2 s *think* time.

A main benefit of the described approach is that such cognitive units can be automatically extracted from the UI development models. As described above, we make use of the mappings between the runtime FUI elements and the AUI model. An example is presented in Figure 2, which depicts a screenshot of the recipe finder dialogue with additionally annotated types of the corresponding AUI element. While the overall container has the abstract type *Complex*, it consists of several further AUI elements which directly relate to a specific task, namely *OutputOnly* for presenting text or graphics, *Command* to trigger application actions and *Choice* for presenting elements from which to choose. FUI elements of the same semantic group, such as the nationalities of the dishes, are modeled using the same AUI element, which is of the type *Choice*. Thus, they are also grouped by their semantics on the level of the AUI model. Consequently, the specific AUI element of each FUI element is queried during conversion to CogTool. In case several FUI elements share the same AUI element (besides *Complex* container elements), they are considered to be a cognitive unit and the generation of the CogTool model is altered by removing *think* steps prior to consecutive interactions on FUI elements from the same AUI element.

Hypothesis II: System Response Times

Another property of the Keystroke-Level Model that we can take advantage from is the inclusion of system response times. Navigation from one UI screen to another took approximately 500 ms on the hardware setup used in the pilot study, which is comparable to the difference between the *other group* and *new screen* click types. Following the original KLM rules, system response times that occur in parallel to *think* operators are only taken into account to the extent that they *exceed* the think time, i.e. a frozen system does block mouse and keyboard input, but does not block the mental preparation of the user [5, p. 263]. CogTool applies this rule out of the box, and as the 500 ms screen loading time is shorter than the 1.2 s *think* operator, CogTool does not predict the difference between the *other group* and the *new screen* conditions (see Figure 4).

We decided to deviate from the original rules here. When Card et al. formulated the Keystroke-Level Model, their users were solving tasks like typing commands into line-oriented text editors from the pre-graphical-user-interface era. Using the system response time for the memory retrieval of the next command to be executed makes perfectly sense in this scenario. Our graphical interface and selection of tasks are sufficiently different to call for a gentle refinement of the KLM. The biggest change is that the main bulk of user actions is no longer (blindly) typing on a physical keyboard, but finger-tapping on dynamic visual elements on the screen. While memory retrieval still plays an important role in this scenario, searching the screen for the next button to press should be at least equally so. And as visual search is not possible when the graphical objects to be searched are not yet presented to the user, this kind of preparation for the next physical action *is* being delayed by a system response if this is accompanied by the screen being blank. We therefore decided to add the blank time to our cognitive model in the *new screen* condition.

Comparable measures have been taken by other researchers before, e.g. while applying the KLM to handheld devices [16]. There, system response times that are not shadowable by *think* operators were introduced by adding bogus widgets to the system mockups. As it is our goal to get rid of mockups and use real applications instead, we did not follow this direction.

Due to the fact that system response times may vary between different platforms and devices, these need to be measured or estimated once. However, here MBUID approaches that rely on executable models benefit from the fact that the evaluation of the models is actually directly combined with testing the real application. This specifically allows measuring and including system response times into the conversion process of the interaction traces. After each simulated user interaction it is checked whether the presentation task set has changed. If so, it can be assumed that a new UI screen was rendered. In this case the system response time is automatically added in sequence with a *think* operator because users cannot perceive information from the following UI screen until its rendering is finished. If the presentation task did not change, the system response time is added conforming to the CogTool implementation and might be shadowed by a parallel *think* operator. To sum up, task and AUI model are used to check on changes in the UI and to alter the cognitive user model.

Hypothesis III: Monitoring
What remains is the 360 ms difference between the *same button* and *same group* click types. Clicking the same button repeatedly does not incorporate movements of the forearm, moving the finger to another button of the same group does. Therefore we expect a difference between the two types. The movement time can be predicted using Fitts' Law, but again, this does not give sufficiently big estimates. We propose a monitoring hypothesis to fill this gap: Given the bad reliability of the touch screen, we assume that our subjects monitored whether their physical tap on the screen yielded a correct system response (i.e. a visible change of the displayed button). The time that this additional monitoring step needs consists of the time the systems needs to display a change and the time the user needs to notice this change. This system time is about 300 ms for our device. CogTool can be used to predict the time the user needs to encode and notice the change.

During conversion to CogTool the system response time (see Hypothesis II) and an additional *look-at* operator are added automatically in order to model a user monitoring if the desired action is reflected in the GUI. For this purpose, the FUI type of the UI element is queried and, in case it is an interaction on a UI element that can be toggled; e.g. radio buttons and checkboxes, the cognitive model is altered accordingly.

Model Fit
Predictions of CogTool out of the box (■, labeled "Ootb") and our augmented CogTool model (▲, labeled "KLM") are displayed in Figure 4. For both models, we computed several goodness-of-fit statistics, namely the coefficient of determination (R^2), the root mean squared error (RMSE), the maximum likely scaled difference (MLSD, [24]) and the maximum relative error (max diff). We based the comparisons on 20% trimmed means and bootstrapped confidence intervals. The results are reported in Table 2.

Model	R^2	RMSE	MLSD	max diff
CogTool Ootb	.597	0.39 s	4.6	75.9%
CogTool KLM	.995	0.13 s	1.4	25.3%

Table 2. Goodness-of-fit of the two cognitive models for the pilot study. Statistics are based on 20% trimmed means of the time intervals between the clicks of the users.

CogTool promises prediction "within 20% of the actual performance" out of the box [12]. We could not achieve this in the pilot study, the results are nevertheless promising. Especially the CogTool KLM model obtained a R^2 close to the maximum possible value of 1. The MLSD of 1.4 indicates that the measured differences between the model and the empirical trimmed means are very close to the amount of uncertainty in the data. The model therefore cannot be refined much more without taking the risk of overfitting.

Discussion
We showed that semi-automated predictions of task execution times based on UI development models are possible. On top of that, we identified properties of the MASP UI models behind our interface that we could use for further improvements of the cognitive user model. The goodness-of-fit that we achieved without parameter tuning is very promising. The use of few and very selective tasks and the small number of subjects put the validity of the cognitive user model into question, though. Thus, further analyses based on independent empirical test data are necessary.

Using CogTool for click by click analyses instead of predicting task execution times could be criticized as atypical application or even unfair towards CogTool. The 1.2 s *think* operator time used in CogTool is estimated from empirical data, and as Card et al. state, these operators for mental activity vary strongly within and across subjects. This means that the horizontal line labeled "CogTool think operator" in Figure 4 should not be considered a strong cut-off, but rather demarks a somewhat blurry transition area. When applying KLM to full tasks, the variance within think times should partially average out, i.e. a model with moderate fit on click level can still achieve good fit on task level. As the empirical basis of the pilot study is too weak for this kind of analysis, we decided to perform a second experiment.

EVALUATION
In order to test the validity of the cognitive model that we developed on the basis of the empirical data of the pilot study, we conducted a validation study with new subjects and additional user tasks. The study took place in November 2013,

12 subjects were recruited mainly from within the research groups of the authors (17% female; M_{age}=28.8, SD_{age}=2.4). In order to achieve a higher coverage of the cooking assistant's functionality, each subject completed 34 individual tasks. The presentation of the user interface was moved from the wall-mounted touch screen to a personal computer with integrated 27" (68.6 cm) touch screen with a 16:10 ratio. This was done both to reduce error rates compared to the first experiment and to test whether the model generalizes well to new devices due to adaptation of the UI caused by a different aspect ratio and size of screen. The latter question is of high importance for automated usability evaluation of plastic UIs that are developed without knowing on which devices they will later be used [22].

Besides the changes in subject group, physical device and task selection, we closely followed the experimental design of the previous study. User actions were again logged by the MASP and recorded on video. In the same way, system response times, start times and end times of the individual tasks were annotated using ELAN [26].

Results
We recorded a total of 180 minutes of video footage, about six times the amount of the pilot study. For being able to compare the results with the previous experiment, we conducted an analysis on the click-to-click level first. We observed a total of 1930 pairs of clicks that can be divided into the classification given above. Means and confidence intervals for these are given in Figure 5. The differences found in the pilot study are qualitatively replicated in the second study. We observed an overall increase in speed, though. The average time between clicks decreased from 1.41 s to 1.04 s between the experiments (linear mixed model [20], additional factors: click type as fixed and subject as random effect, $F_{1,20} = 55.5, p < .01$).

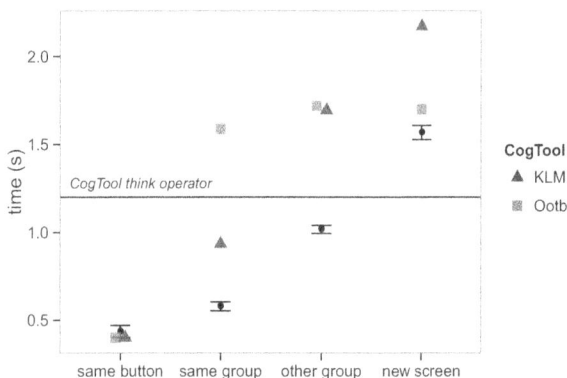

Figure 5. Average times between clicks on different elements on the user interface for the validation study. Circles denote 20% trimmed means, lines bootstrapped 95% confidence intervals (10000 repetitions).

For examining the generalizability of our cognitive model, we used the unchanged models from the previous study and computed predictions for the tasks of the new one. Goodness-of-fit statistics are given in Table 3. While the correlations es-

pecially between the KLM model and the data are still near to perfect, RMSE and relative difference degraded substantially.

CogTool Ootb	R^2	RMSE	MLSD	max diff
pairs of clicks	.425	0.61 s	20.0	173.9%
complete tasks	.735	3.32 s	8.4	104.0%
CogTool KLM	R^2	RMSE	MLSD	max diff
pairs of clicks	.927	0.47 s	13.8	66.0%
complete tasks	.965	2.77 s	8.4	70.9%

Table 3. Goodness-of-fit of the two cognitive user models for the validation study. Statistics are based on 20% trimmed means and bootstrapped confidence intervals (10000 repetitions).

Due to the higher number of subjects, tasks and fewer errors, we could extend our analysis to the execution times of complete tasks instead of single clicks. Task completion times are a much more natural measurement than clicks and are also the level of analysis originally used by the Keystroke-Level Model and hence CogTool. We grouped the 34 tasks into seven categories by the total number of steps per task and by how many of these were *same group* and *new screen* type of clicks as those were the critical conditions in the first study. Average completion times and model predictions per category are given in Figure 6, goodness-of-fit statistics in Table 3.

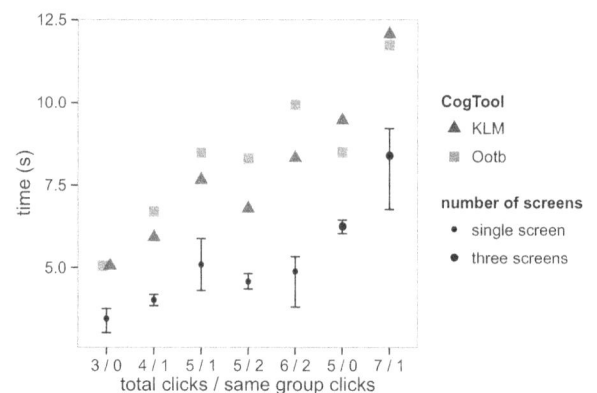

Figure 6. Average task completion times for the validation study. Circles denote 20% trimmed means, lines bootstrapped 95% confidence intervals (10000 repetitions).

Discussion
The results of the validation study are qualitatively similar to the first study, but we also found big quantitative differences. The overall gain in click speed between the experiments could be accounted to differences in subject selection, device used, length of the experiment and so on. As all of these variables are confounded; we can neither confirm nor reject any of them as influence factors.

What is more important is the degree of generalization of our cognitive model to the changed situation. The goodness-of-fit of the model to the new data is an important indication of the usefulness of our approach to automated usability evaluation in general. We will get back to this line of thought in the general discussion below and only discuss the evidence here.

Of the fit statistics that we applied, RMSE and maximum relative difference are most sensitive to overall shifts in the data, whereas the determination coefficient R^2 neglects these and identifies changed relations between (classes of) observations. R^2 being very high in our case means that especially the KLM model describes the differences between the identified types of clicks very well. RMSE, scaled difference (MLSD) and relative difference on the other hand clearly show that our predictions miss the actual task completion times.

One promising result is that the modified KLM model still yields substantially higher fits than CogTool out of the box in the second study (see Table 3). This provides backing for the validity of the hypotheses that we derived from the results of the first study. The goodness-of-fit computed on task completion times being comparable to the one computed on click level also hints at the robustness of our approach.

Finally the most general question: Does the relatively bad fit put the KLM that formed the theoretical basis of our user model into question? Looking at Figure 5 shows that nearly all clicks moved below that 1.2 s *think* operator time in the validation study. This could be taken as evidence for the general inappropriateness of such an operator. While being correct in itself, this argumentation misses the heuristic nature of the KLM. As Card et al. pointed out, users differ a lot in how they mentally encode a task, and higher levels of user expertise can be modeled by placing fewer *think* operators for the same task [5, p. 265]. Taken together with the highly selective group of participants in the second study, this can explain the apparent disappearance of mental preparation times.

GENERAL DISCUSSION

With the help of information from UI development models and an AUE tool (CogTool) we have created a cognitive user model that yields very good fits to data from a usability study conducted in parallel. We validated the model with data from a second experiment where the task domain was kept constant, but user group and physical device were varied, thereby testing generalization to new contexts of use. While the cognitive model was able to predict time differences between the new tasks of the second experiment very well, we also observed an overall shift in task completion time that was not anticipated by the model. We can conclude that the model provides a good basis to compare different UI adaptation variants, or to predict the efficiency of a UI for frequently vs. rarely used functions. Especially in the domain of smart home environments, specific recurring functions are used quite often and profit from an efficient interaction. In addition, the validation study shows that adding information from UI development models significantly improves the goodness-of-fit of the cognitive user model.

Compared to further model-based evaluation approaches that focus on evaluations of task models (e.g. [19]), our integrated approach also uses AUI and FUI information and thus allows creating richer cognitive models. Especially, exact button positions (and their labels for matching purposes) can be used for optimized predictions using Fitts' Law [6] without requiring data from real user tests. It needs to be remarked that compared to approaches that focus on exhaustive task model evaluations, the degree of simulation is currently limited to predefined interactions. So, our approach presents a complementary evaluation with a focus on detailed execution time predictions. But specifically this focus provides benefits when evaluating plastic UIs because task execution times are a quantifiable criterion of usability. When adapting the UI to a different context, the automatically predicted execution time, whether annotated during development or predicted during runtime, can e.g. serve as a hard constraint to exclude adaptations or to prefer a specific variant over others.

Specifically for the domain of model-based evaluation, our approach presents a benefit that is highly important. Modeling the system usually requires a significant part of the modeling effort [14]. Thus, connecting the user model to the real system and still using information from the development models simplifies model-based evaluation greatly. Finally, we showed that an additional benefit lies in a better placement of *think* operators which, otherwise, would require case-specific expert knowledge.

Possible areas of application arise, when taking a look at current challenges in MBUID. On the one hand, our approach provides a tool that can predict efficiency across different contexts of use and thus can be included in developing and maintaining plastic UIs. On the other hand, usability regression testing can be included into the development cycle after each iteration step, starting with early prototypes. The described approach could also be used to add automation to existing solutions [1]. Finally, the applied methods to gain information from UI templates in combination with dynamic CSS and JavaScript even allows automated extraction of UI information in the current trend of *responsive design*.

CONCLUSIONS

In this paper we have presented an approach for automatic generation of cognitive user models in order to predict task execution times during model-based UI development. The process strongly benefits from information available in the UI development models which we used to create better cognitive models without requiring further intervention by usability experts. The described approach does not require extensive knowledge in the usability domain in order to be introduced to evaluation cycles during the development process. Typical areas of application arise when there is a need to compare different design decisions or alternative adaptations such as when creating plastic user interfaces. Even if usability experts are available, they can base their work on the automatically created CogTool models, sparing them from the laborious creation of UI mockups and storyboards.

Acknowledgement: We gratefully acknowledge financial support from the German Research Foundation (DFG) for the project "Automatische Usability-Evaluierung modellbasierter Interaktionssysteme für Ambient Assisted Living" (AL-561/13-1).

REFERENCES

1. Abrahão, S., Iborra, E., and Vanderdonckt, J. Usability evaluation of user interfaces generated with a model-driven architecture tool. In *Maturing Usability*, Human-Computer Interaction Series, Springer London (2008), 3–32.

2. Anderson, J. R., Bothell, D., Byrne, M. D., Douglass, S., Lebiere, C., and Qin, Y. An integrated theory of the mind. *Psychological review 111*, 4 (2004), 1036–1060.

3. Blumendorf, M., Lehmann, G., and Albayrak, S. Bridging models and systems at runtime to build adaptive user interfaces. In *Proceedings of the 2Nd ACM SIGCHI Symposium on Engineering Interactive Computing Systems*, EICS '10, ACM (New York, NY, USA, 2010), 9–18.

4. Calvary, G., Coutaz, J., Thevenin, D., Limbourg, Q., Bouillon, L., and Vanderdonckt, J. A unifying reference framework for multi-target user interfaces. *Interacting with Computers 15*, 3 (2003), 289–308.

5. Card, S. K., Moran, T. P., and Newell, A. *The Psychology of Human-Computer Interaction*. Erlbaum Associates, Hillsdale, New Jersey, 1983.

6. Fitts, P. M. The information capacity of the human motor system in controlling the amplitude of movement. *Journal of Experimental Psychology 47*, 6 (1954), 381–391.

7. González-Calleros, J. M., Osterloh, J. P., Feil, R., and Lüdtke, A. Automated ui evaluation based on a cognitive architecture and usixml. *Science of Computer Programming Journal In Press* (05 2013).

8. Gram, C., and Cockton, G., Eds. *Design principles for interactive software*. Chapman & Hall, Ltd., London, UK, 1997.

9. Ivory, M. Y., and Hearst, M. A. The state of the art in automating usability evaluation of user interfaces. *ACM Comput. Surv. 33*, 4 (2001), 470–516.

10. John, B. E., and Jastrzembski, T. S. Exploration of costs and benefits of predictive human performance modeling for design. In *Proceedings of the 10th International Conference on Cognitive Modeling, Philadelphia, PA* (2010), 115–120.

11. John, B. E., and Kieras, D. E. The goms family of user interface analysis techniques: Comparison and contrast. *ACM Trans. Comput.-Hum. Interact. 3*, 4 (1996), 320–351.

12. John, B. E., and Salvucci, D. D. Multipurpose prototypes for assessing user interfaces in pervasive computing systems. *Pervasive Computing, IEEE 4*, 4 (2005), 27–34.

13. John, B. E., and Suzuki, S. Toward cognitive modeling for predicting usability. In *Human-Computer Interaction. New Trends*, J. Jacko, Ed., vol. 5610 of *Lecture Notes in Computer Science*. Springer Berlin / Heidelberg, 2009, 267–276.

14. Kieras, D. Model-based evaluation. In *The human-computer interaction handbook: fundamentals, evolving technologies and emerging applications*, A. Sears and J. A. Jacko, Eds. Lawrence Erlbaum Associates, Mahwaw, NJ, 2007.

15. Limbourg, Q., Vanderdonckt, J., Michotte, B., Bouillon, L., and López-Jaquero, V. Usixml: A language supporting multi-path development of user interfaces. In *Engineering Human Computer Interaction and Interactive Systems*, R. Bastide, P. Palanque, and J. Roth, Eds., vol. 3425 of *Lecture Notes in Computer Science*. Springer-Verlag, Berlin, Heidelberg, 2005, 200–220.

16. Luo, L., and John, B. E. Predicting task execution time on handheld devices using the keystroke-level model. In *Extended Abstracts Proceedings of the 2005 Conference on Human Factors in Computing Systems*, G. C. van der Veer and C. Gale, Eds., ACM (Portland, OR, 2005), 1605–1608.

17. Mori, G., Paternò, F., and Santoro, C. Design and development of multidevice user interfaces through multiple logical descriptions. *IEEE Trans. Softw. Eng. 30*, 8 (2004), 507–520.

18. Nielsen, J. *Usability Engineering*. Morgan Kaufmann Publishers Inc., San Francisco, CA, USA, 1993.

19. Paternò, F. Model-based tools for pervasive usability. *Interacting with Computers 17*, 3 (2005), 291–315.

20. Pinheiro, J., Bates, D., DebRoy, S., Sarkar, D., and R Core Team. *nlme: Linear and Nonlinear Mixed Effects Models*, 2013. R package version 3.1-113.

21. Polson, P. G., Lewis, C., Rieman, J., and Wharton, C. Cognitive walkthroughs: a method for theory-based evaluation of user interfaces. *International Journal of Man-Machine Studies 36*, 5 (1992), 741 – 773.

22. Quade, M., Lehmann, G., Engelbrecht, K.-P., Roscher, D., and Albayrak, S. Automated usability evaluation of model-based adaptive user interfaces for users with special and specific needs by simulating user interaction. In *User Modeling and Adaptation for Daily Routines*, E. Martín, P. A. Haya, and R. M. Carro, Eds., HumanComputer Interaction Series. Springer, London, 2013, 219–247.

23. Quade, M., Rieger, A., and Albayrak, S. Requirements for applying simulation-based automated usability evaluation to model-based adaptive user interfaces for smart environments. In *Distributed, Ambient, and Pervasive Interactions*, N. Streitz and C. Stephanidis, Eds., vol. 8028 of *Lecture Notes in Computer Science*. Springer, Berlin, 2013, 235–244.

24. Stewart, T. C., and West, R. L. Testing for equivalence: a methodology for computational cognitive modelling. *Journal of Artificial General Intelligence 2*, 2 (2010), 69–87.

25. Wilcox, R. R. Comparing medians: An overview plus new results on dealing with heavy-tailed distributions. *The Journal of experimental education 73*, 3 (2005), 249–263.

26. Wittenburg, P., Brugman, H., Russel, A., Klassmann, A., and Sloetjes, H. ELAN: a professional framework for multimodality research. In *Proceedings of LREC*, vol. 2006 (2006).

Considering Task Pre-Conditions
in Model-based User Interface Design and Generation

Marco Manca, Fabio Paternò, Carmen Santoro, Lucio Davide Spano
CNR-ISTI, HIIS Laboratory
Via Moruzzi 1, 56124 Pisa, Italy
{marco.manca, fabio.paterno, carmen.santoro, lucio.davide.spano@isti.cnr.it}

ABSTRACT
Deriving meaningful and consistent user interface implementations from task models is not trivial because of the large gap in terms of abstraction. This paper focuses on how to handle task preconditions in the design and generation process, an issue which has not adequately been addressed in previous work. We present a solution that is able to manage the information related to task pre-conditions at the various possible abstraction levels. The paper also reports on some example applications that show the generality of the solution and how it can be exploited in various cases.

Author Keywords
Task models, Model-based User Interface Design, User Interface Generation

ACM Classification Keywords
H.5.m. Information interfaces and presentation (e.g., HCI): Miscellaneous.

INTRODUCTION
Task models have been widely investigated in the literature, since they provide a structured representation of how different activities should be carried out for reaching users' goals. They are popular for their high-level description that can be understood by people without programming background and therefore can be used for communicating between the different actors involved in the design and development process: designers, developers and users.

According to the CAMELEON Reference Framework [2] there are four abstraction levels in model based-design and generation: task models, abstract user interfaces, concrete user interfaces and implementations. Thus, when generating from task models it is possible to go through all of them for progressively refining the interactive application

description. Over time the notations for task models have become more expressive in order to be able to describe more complex sets of activities. However, this increase in expressiveness raises new challenges for model-based user interface design and generation. In this paper, we show how some of such challenges can be addressed. In particular, we show how to handle pre-conditions expressed in task models both in the task model analysis phase and when refining them through the various abstraction levels. We describe our solution by considering ConcurTaskTrees (CTT) [7], a widely known notation for task models, and show how we have designed the solution's implementation in the analysis environment and in the refinement process. The corresponding user interface can be derived through the abstract user interface (AUI) and the concrete user interface (CUI) abstraction levels. We consider the MARIA language [8] for such abstraction levels.

In the paper, after discussing related work, we describe the method that we have designed and implemented for managing the pre-conditions information across the various abstraction levels. We then describe some example applications showing how such new features can be exploited in various cases, and lastly we draw some conclusions with indications for future work.

RELATED WORK
Many tools and notations based on hierarchical descriptions and different sets of operators exist for describing task models. A comparison is available in [9]. Most of them include the possibility to specify conditions on the task execution, but often this specification is limited to natural language, in order to reduce the modelling complexity. Examples of such approach can be found in both research (e.g. UsiXML [4] and Hamsters [5]) and commercial tools (e.g. IBM Information Architecture Workbench [3]). They include a *precondition* and/or a *postcondition* for the task execution, which are defined as strings. This approach does not allow manipulating the condition definition while generating code or other models from the task description.

Other modelling approaches select a structured representation of pre- and post-conditions, describing them through Boolean predicates to be checked on the domain objects manipulated by tasks. The cost of having a more complex representation is balanced by the possibility of enabling tool support for model checking during definition and simulation. For instance, the KMADe [1] tool supports model checking, while AMBOSS [3] simulates different scenarios allowing the designer to indicate interactively whether a condition is satisfied or not. Thus, there is a lack of tools able to manage preconditions in task models, in the user interface design and generation process, and in this paper we present a solution to cover this gap.

HANDLING PRECONDITIONS AT THE VARIOUS ABSTRACTION LEVELS

The design and implementation of interactive applications starting with task models and involving preconditions can go through various steps:

- Specification of task models, including task preconditions;

- Analysis of the dynamic behavior of the task model with preconditions through the interactive simulator, which allows designers to enter values associated with the data defining the preconditions as well.

- In the case of service-based applications, it is possible to bind Web service operations and corresponding tasks. Bindings are then exploited at runtime (by the generated application) to dynamically get values for the user interface objects that are considered when checking the preconditions.

- Identification of Presentation Task Sets (which are sets of tasks associated with the presentations in the user interface logical descriptions), with the support of some heuristics to merge them [8];

- Generation of the corresponding logical UI descriptions at the abstract and/or concrete level;

- Generation of the corresponding Final UI (FUI) implementation.

In this refinement process it is important to identify tasks that are mutually exclusive because of their preconditions. This happens when the preconditions associated to these tasks involve shared variables that assume different values: according to the values that are taken, either one task or the other is enabled. Consequently, the mutually exclusive tasks will be associated with different user interface presentations that correspond to the different cases. For example, if the precondition is associated with the user's role then depending on it (associated with the preconditions) different user interfaces should be enabled.

In the refinement process, we exploit two concepts: *Presentation Task Sets* (PTSs) [8] and *conditional connections*. Tasks enabled over the same period of time according to the temporal constraints indicated in the task model are grouped into PTSs. The latter are automatically calculated through an algorithm that takes as input the formal semantics of the temporal operators of the CTT

notation and a task model. In the transformation into an abstract or concrete user interface each PTS corresponds to a presentation. In order to avoid fragmented user interfaces some PTSs can be merged according to heuristics [8]. Navigating from a resulting presentation to another is described through connections, which are defined by the interface element activating the navigation and the target presentation. Conditional connections are a particular type of connection: they model cases where moving from a presentation to another is triggered only if the specified condition is verified. Therefore, the approach proposed to appropriately support task preconditions in the logical description of UIs is first to include mutually exclusive tasks in distinct PTSs, and when deriving the corresponding logical user interface description, set a conditional connection able to support moving to a presentation or another according to the value of the variable associated with the precondition. In the following we analyse more in detail the steps of the approach proposed and how to consider task pre-conditions in each of them.

Task Model Specification

In this step the designer should specify tasks, their temporal relationships, objects manipulated by tasks and possible task preconditions. A task precondition indicates what must be verified before the task is carried out. Mutually exclusive preconditions on two (or more) tasks indicate that the associated tasks cannot be enabled at the same time, for instance the preconditions involve some Boolean expression or a comparison with numbers having a value higher/equal/less than another, or a comparison between strings, etc. Thus, they indicate that the tasks cannot be enabled at the same time simply because they are associated with (pre)conditions that cannot hold at the same time.

Preconditions in Interactive Task Model Simulation

In order to analyse how the task model behaviour varies depending on the values associated with the objects defining the preconditions it is possible to use the interactive simulator. CTTE [6] provides an interactive simulator, useful for checking the task model against usage scenarios. The simulator highlights the leaf task nodes that can be executed at a given time, considering the temporal relationships among them (defined in the model). The user can simulate the performance of a task by double-clicking its icon. After that, the simulator updates the set of enabled tasks.

We have extended the existing simulator for supporting pre- and post-conditions and analyse their impact on the dynamic behaviour of the tasks. We added a panel for controlling the dynamic state of task objects. Different scenarios can be supported by specifying different object values exploited by the preconditions. The designer can modify the values before each simulation step, through the interface shown in Figure 1. The panel shows each object's name, its type (e.g. string, integer etc.), the current value (which can be interactively modified) and the list of tasks that manipulate the object. In each step, the simulator updates the list of enabled tasks, disabling those that have preconditions that are not satisfied by the current object values. In addition, it prompts the user when one or more post-conditions are not verified after the execution of a task. In this way, designers can verify the correspondence between the model and different usage scenarios.

Filter Objects   None

Name	Type	Value	Owner
Login	String	bob	Insert user data
Password	String	passwd	Insert user data
Role	String	administrator	Check User Data Insert content
loggedIn	Boolean	☑ true	Insert user data Check User Data

Figure 1: Task model simulator interface for objects

Generation of PTS

PTSs are sets of elementary tasks enabled in the same period of time and associated with a given presentation when transforming the task model into an abstract or concrete user interface specification. PTSs are identified taking into account temporal relationships between tasks [8]. For instance, if two tasks are composed by the choice operator, they are both enabled at the same time, therefore they should belong to the same PTS. However, preconditions have an impact on the PTS definition. For instance, two tasks composed by the choice operator are both enabled and they should belong to the same PTS. However, if both tasks have a precondition involving the same object and these preconditions are mutually exclusive, then the tasks cannot belong to the same PTS because they cannot be enabled at the same time. Thus, we had to extend the rules to identify PTSs with the following rule:

a) if in the task model there are two (or more) sibling tasks composed through a choice relationship, and

b) these tasks share one (or more than one) object, and

c) these tasks have mutually exclusive preconditions involving one (or more than one) shared task object

then such tasks should be included in distinct PTSs.

Application of heuristics for PTSs processing

After having generated PTSs according to the semantics of the temporal operators, the designer can apply some heuristics to merge two or more PTSs.

This is done in order to avoid generation of fragmented user interfaces with many presentations with little content. The heuristics that are currently supported are the following:

- If two (or more) PTSs differ by only one element and their elements are at the same level composed by an enabling operator, they can be joined together.

- If a PTS is composed of just one element, it can be included within another superset that contains such element.

- If two (or more) PTSs share most elements, they can be unified in order not to duplicate elements that are already available in another presentation.

- If there is an exchange of information between two tasks, they can be put in the same PTS in order to highlight such relation.

The automatic support guarantees that tasks having mutually exclusive preconditions involving the same objects are kept in distinct PTSs even *after applying such heuristics*. In the tool, if the generated PTSs contain tasks with mutually exclusive preconditions, they are not merged (i.e. the application of heuristics has no effect on the PTSs), otherwise they are merged according to the above heuristics.

Generation of Abstract and Concrete User Interfaces

In this step for each PTS a presentation is created together with connections to enable navigation to/from other presentations. The type of connection that is created between two presentations depends on whether the target PTS contains a task with preconditions. On the one hand, if a target PTS does not contain tasks with preconditions then an elementary connection is created in the source PTS. On the other hand, if a target PTS contains tasks with preconditions, then a conditional connection is created in the presentation corresponding to the source PTS. The condition in the connection is associated to the expression defined in the precondition.

Generation of the Final User Interface

In this step the automatic support generates the UI final code supporting what was specified in the more abstract UI descriptions. For instance, it generates appropriate code for supporting conditional connections amongst various presentations. In particular, the final code generated enables the UI to move to the target presentation only if the condition contained in the conditional connection is verified. In next sections we detail how the conditional connections are implemented.

Dynamic association of precondition values

At run-time the actual values for the objects used in the precondition can be received in various ways. In some cases the values can be entered by the user. In other cases, in order to associate data values with preconditions it is useful to exploit bindings between the application tasks and the operations specified in the Web services, which should implement the tasks. Out tool allows designers to specify such bindings at design time, and then they will be exploited at runtime by the generated application to get actual values for the precondition parameters and then check the precondition validity. An illustrative example showing how the binding phase works with the support of the tool is provided in the next section.

EXAMPLE APPLICATIONS

We present three examples that show the broad impact that task models with preconditions can have and the associated issues that we have solved.

Content Management System Access

In this section we show an example application to demonstrate how we manage task model preconditions during the generation process involving first Presentation Task Sets, then AUI/CUI and finally the FUI.

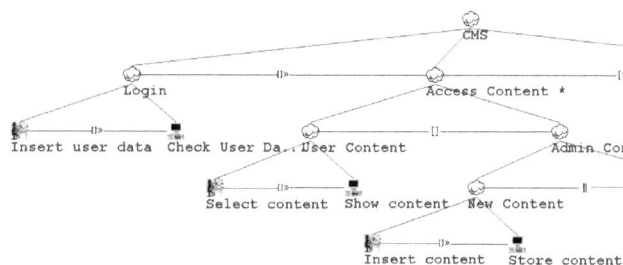

Figure 2: Content Management System example

Figure 2 shows an excerpt of the task model of a Content Management System (CMS) that allows publishing, editing and modifying the content in a Web application.

This model contains different tasks, such as '*Select Content*', '*Insert Content*', that can be performed depending on the user role. These tasks are composed by the choice operator and are enabled after the 'Check User Data' task has been performed.

Two (or more) tasks composed by a choice operator usually are enabled at the same time, but in this case only one task can be enabled at a given time, and the choice depends on the precondition expressed in the task properties.

In particular, the first of the considered tasks describes the possibility for people with the 'user' role to select an article and read it. The other one models the activity to insert content for users with the administrator role. Both tasks contain a pre-condition that describes when they can be enabled. The precondition concerns the same task object, but the values are different and mutually exclusive. For this reason, these two tasks cannot belong to the same Presentation Task Set and during the generation process should be placed in different PTSs. Also during the heuristics application process, even if one of the tasks could be merged with another, they are kept in distinct PTSs.

At run-time the interactive application needs a Web service that given the user data returns the user role. For this reason, a binding between the 'Check User Data' task and the

corresponding Web Service operation should be specified at design time. For this purpose, our tool allows designers to interactively select a task and an operation of the analysed Web services, which can be automatically imported. Once this binding has been created, the tool shows input and output parameters of the operation along with the corresponding tasks, which should provide the input parameters and receive the output ones (see Figure 3). Such tasks are automatically identified through an analysis of the task model [8], the association can be modified by the designer if something is wrong. In order to manage the preconditions, we have introduced in the tool the possibility to automatically identify whether an output parameter of the Web service corresponds to a data object used in a precondition. In this case, the tool allows the designer to specify for which values of the output parameter the precondition is true in each of the tasks associated with it.

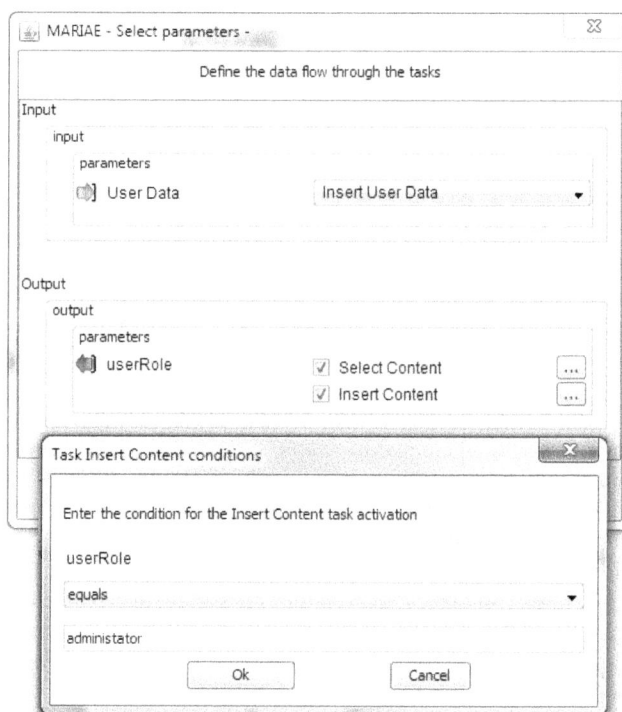

Figure 3: Example of binding between a task and a web service operation

In more detail, we assume to use a Web service implementing the login operation that, according to a username and a password, returns a string indicating the user's role (e.g. "administrator" or "user"), if the login is successful. The relevant excerpt of the related task model is shown in Figure 2. The *Insert Content* interactive task is available only for administrators. Therefore, it contains a precondition checking if the role task object is equal to "administrator". It is possible to bind a task in the model and an operation in the web service through the following steps: 1) importing a description of the web service operation (specifying its URL), 2) connecting a system task with a web service operation (in our example the Check User Data task and the login operation), 3) specifying which interactive task provides the input values for the operation (Insert User Data) and 4) specifying which tasks receives the operation output, connecting the returned values and the task objects (Figure 3). In our case, the string returned by the login operation is therefore connected with the role task object. The binding allows the generator to exploit the web service result at runtime in order to check the precondition. For this purpose the designer should have indicated which value is associated for each of the two tasks. Figure 3 shows the case in which the designer selects the administrator value for the Insert Content task.

Three PTSs are generated from the tasks considered: the first one contains 'Insert User Data' and 'Check user Data' tasks and the other two contain one task with one precondition each. Consequently, the automatic support generates one presentation for each PTS. Since there are PTSs containing tasks with preconditions, then in the first presentation one conditional connection containing two target presentations is generated in the MARIA description (see Figure 4): these presentations are those generated from the PTSs with preconditions. The values of the 'data reference' attribute are associated with the data model element containing the user role value, and are those entered during the binding operation described before.

```
<connections>
  <conditional_conn interactor_id="P1_Check_User_Data">
    <target presentation_to_load="Show_Content_Presentation">
      <condition
        data_reference="data:[ns1_checkUserData/userRole==user]"/>
    </target>
    <target presentation_to_load="Insert_Content_Presentation">
      <condition
        data_reference="data:[ns1_checkUserData/userRole==administrator]"/>
    </target>
  </conditional_conn>
</connections>
```

Figure 4: Conditional Connection Example

For the implementation, the tool generates a JSP page in which, when an action is triggered, the value of the first operand expressed in the data reference (stored in a session field) is compared to the second operand contained in the data reference attribute (*user or administrator*). If the value is equal to one of the two values, then the JSP page transfers the control to the corresponding presentation (see **Figure 5**).

```
if(session.getAttribute("ns1_checkUserData/userRole")
    .equals("user") {
    pageContext.forward("Show_Content_Presentation.jsp");
} else
    if(session.getAttribute("ns1_checkUserData/userRole")
    .equals("administrator") {
    pageContext.forward("Insert_Content_Presentation.jsp");
}
```

Figure 5: Implementation of the example conditional connection

Educational Application
The second example we present is a task model that describes an Educational Application that, after a login task, permits

displaying the student timetable, subscribe/unsubscribe course and other tasks that are omitted for the sake of brevity.

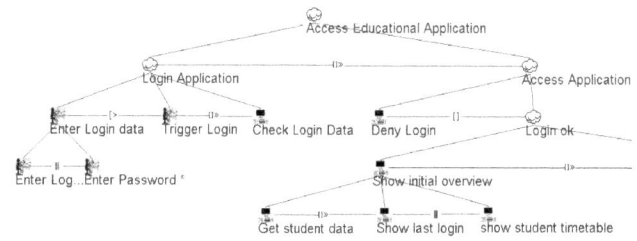

Figure 6: Educational Application Task Model

Figure 6 shows an excerpt of the task model: after performing the 'Check Login Data' there are two tasks enabled, 'Deny Login' and 'Get Student Data', since they are composed by the choice operator. These two tasks model activities that cannot be performed at the same time: the first one should be enabled if the login operation fails and the second one only if the login task has success. For this reason the designers have to specify a precondition that models the possibility to perform tasks only if the login service returns the Boolean value true. 'Deny Login' and 'Get Student Data' tasks share the same task object named *logged_in*, however the preconditions involve the same object but the values are mutually exclusive: the first task is enabled if the object logged_in is false and the second is enabled only if the object is true. For the reasons explained before these two tasks have to be placed in different PTSs and consequently in different presentations.

Figure 7 shows the generated user interface: when the login is successful, user's information and the student's timetable will be shown, otherwise the user will be redirected to an error page.

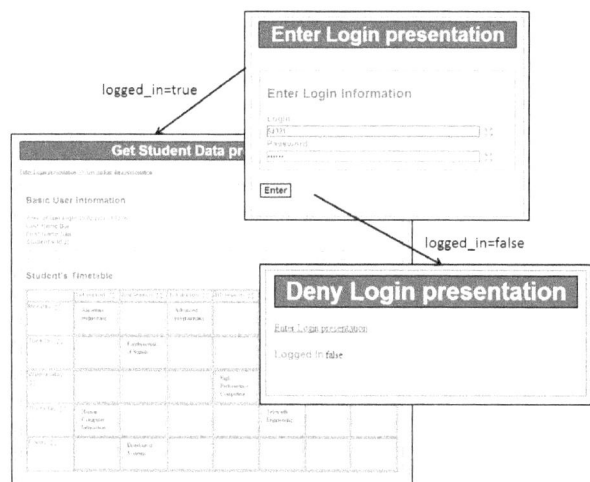

Figure 7: The User Interface generated

ATM Application
Figure 8 shows an example of an excerpt of an ATM task model. The bank's customers can *Enable Access* to the ATM (insert cart and then inset pin) and after they can *Withdraw*

Cash, Deposit Cash, Get Information and finally *Close the access. Withdraw Cash* is an abstract task and its sub-tasks describe the activities necessary to complete the withdrawal: *Select Withdraw, Show Possible Amount, Decide Amount, Select Amount, Check Amount* and *Check Cash.*

The task *Check Amount* is decomposed into two sub-tasks (*Provide Cash* and *Amount not valid*) that cannot be performed at the same time. Indeed, two preconditions are needed: the first one specifies that *Provide Cash* can be executed only if the amount is greater than zero, the other one states that *Amount not valid* is enabled if the amount is equal to zero. The preconditions share the same object (amount) and cannot be satisfied simultaneously, then the respective tasks are placed in different PTSs (and, accordingly in different presentations).

CONCLUSIONS AND FUTURE WORK

We have presented a method to handle task preconditions in the model-based user interface design and generation process, an aspect that has not adequately been addressed in previous work. Our solution is able to manage the information about task pre-conditions at various abstraction levels. A set of example applications has been considered in the paper to show how the approach works and demonstrates the effectiveness of the method in various cases.

Future work will be dedicated to a study involving several designers and developers applying our solution in various case studies in order to analyse its expressiveness and usability.

REFERENCES

1. Caffiau, S., Scapin, D., Girard, P., Baron, M., and Jambon, F. Increasing the expressive power of task analysis: Systematic comparison and empirical assessment of tool-supported task models. *Interacting with Computers 22*, 6 (2010), 569–593.

2. Calvary, G., Coutaz, J., Bouillon, L., Florins, M., Limbourg, Q., Marucci, L., Paternò, F., Santoro, C., Souchon, N., Thevenin, D., Vanderdonckt, J., 2002. The CAMELEON Reference Framework, Deliverable 1.1, CAMELEON Project, http://giove.isti.cnr.it/projects/cameleon/pdf/CAMELE ON%20D1.1RefFramework.pdf.

3. Giese, M., Mistrzyk, T., Pfau, A., Szwillus, G., and von Detten, M. AMBOSS: A task modeling approach for safety-critical systems. In *Engineering Interactive Systems*. Springer, 2008, 98–109.IBM. IBM Information Architecture Workbench. http://www14.software.ibm.com/webapp/download/pre config.jsp?id=2009-09-02+13%3A57%3A13.416731R&S_TACT=&S_CMP=

4. Limbourg, Q., Vanderdonckt, J., Michotte, B., Bouillon, L., and López-Jaquero, V. Usixml: A language supporting multi-path development of user interfaces. *Engineering Human Computer Interaction and Interactive Systems*, (2005), 200–220.

5. Martinie C., Palanque P., Winckler M.: Structuring and Composition Mechanisms to Address Scalability Issues in Task Models. INTERACT (3) 2011: 589-609

6. Mori G., Paternò F., Santoro C., "CTTE: Support for Developing and Analysing Task Models for Interactive System Design", IEEE Transactions on Software Engineering, pp.797-813, August 2002 (Vol. 28, No. 8), IEEE Press.

7. Paternò, F., 2000. Model-Based Design and Evaluation of Interactive Applications. Springer Verlag.

8. Paternò, F., Santoro, C., Spano, L.D.,: Engineering the Authoring of Usable Service Front Ends. Journal of Systems and Software 84(10): 1806-1822 (2011)

9. Paternò, F., Santoro, C., Spano, L.D., and Ragget, D. (eds). MBUI-Task Models. 2012. http://www.w3.org/TR/2012/WD-task-models-20120802/.

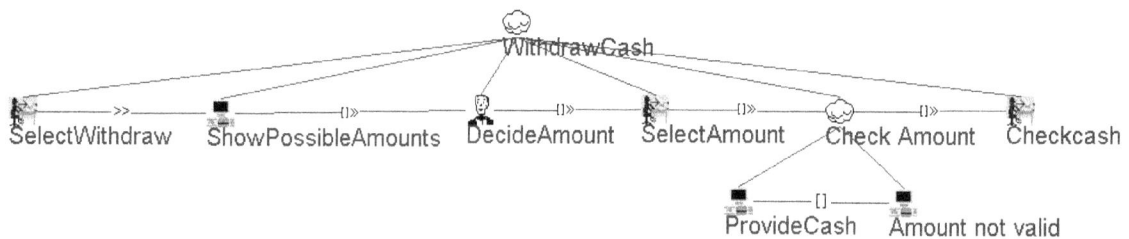

Figure 8: The ATM task model

Generating Code Skeletons for Individual Media Elements in Model-driven Development of Interactive Systems

Andreas Pleuss
Lero, University of Limerick, Ireland
andreas.pleuss@lero.ie

ABSTRACT
Model-driven approaches for interactive systems development usually generate User Interfaces (UIs) composed of standard widgets. However, in practice, high quality UIs can require individual media elements such as interactive graphics or animations. However, while a model-driven approach can provide various benefits – e.g., reduced complexity or multi-platform development – individual media elements are usually designed by specific experts using visual authoring tools. One solution to resolve this conflict is generating code skeletons which can be directly processed and filled out in visual authoring tools. This paper discusses how such skeletons need to be structured to provide best possible support on the one hand for a model-driven process and on the other hand for the media design in authoring tools.

Author Keywords
User Interface Engineering; Model-Driven Development; Code Generation; Rich User Interfaces; Multimedia

ACM Classification Keywords
D.2.2 Software Engineering: Design Tools and Techniques—*User interfaces*; H.5.2 Information Interfaces and Presentation: User Interfaces—*Theory and methods*

INTRODUCTION
Model-driven development (*MDD*) [12] can provide significant benefits for software development. Models (e.g., domain-specific languages) raise the level of abstraction resulting in advantages such as reduced cognitive complexity, better communication, and (depending on the approach) e.g., support for multiple target platforms, devices, or usage contexts. Model transformations automatically generate code from the models resulting in increased efficiency, reuse of expert knowledge encoded in the transformation, and enforced compliance to the model. Various approaches have proposed concepts for MDD of User Interfaces [3, 4]. However, while

MDD has become established in some domains (e.g., embedded systems development), automated generation of User Interfaces (UIs) is still challenging with respect to usability.

An important research issue is the individuality and richness of generated UIs [4]. Most MDD approaches so far restrict to UIs composed of standard widgets. However, integration of individual media elements (like graphics, animations, or 3D) can significantly improve UI quality, e.g., by increasing efficiency, providing more perceptual representations of complex information, or increasing entertainment value [2]. An example is the UI in "car configurator" online applications[1] provided by many car manufacturers which allow users to interactively configure their car and directly see the result as 2D and/or 3D graphics.

Some existing MDD approaches support specifying complex graphics or animations in a model [10, 9, 5]. However, complex individual media content is traditionally created by specific experts for media design (in the following referred to as *media designers*) using authoring tools such as Adobe Flash or Autodesk 3ds Max. Designing media elements within a model (instead of in authoring tools) can be complex and tedious and is hardly acceptable for most media designers in practice.

It is a common situation in MDD practice that not all parts of a system (e.g., complex behavior) can be specified within models with reasonable effort [12]. This is usually solved in MDD by generating *code skeletons* from the models that can be completed by developers with manually written custom code. This idea can also be applied to UIs [7]: From the UI models, code skeletons are generated which contain placeholders for complex media content that cannot be generated from the models. These placeholders are then filled out manually, e.g., using appropriate authoring tools. In this way the advantages of both worlds are combined: 1) MDD to generate most parts of the application and their interrelationships, and 2) usage of established visual authoring tools for professional, creative media design.

However, generating skeletons to be manually completed is challenging in practice. Experience in MDD has shown that code skeletons must be carefully structured to support *regenerating* code (e.g., after changes on the model) without loosing manually added content [12, 1]. On the other hand, complex media often have a complex *inner structure* (e.g. a

[1]c.g., http://www.porsche.com/uk/modelstart/

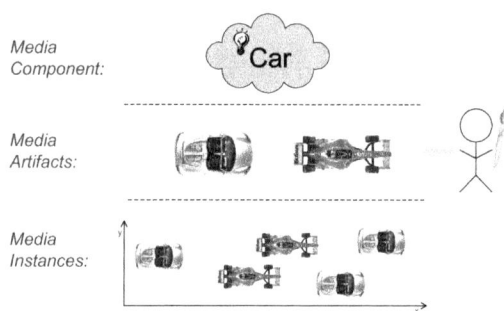

Figure 1. Abstraction layers for modeling media.

car in a car configurator consists of many parts) which has to be supported by the structure of the generated skeletons as well. These aspects have not been considered in existing work (e.g. [7]) so far.

This paper discusses structuring of code skeletons for complex media elements. It focuses on visual media such as graphics and animations. The paper is structured as follows: It first introduces modeling concepts for complex media based on existing work. The subsequent sections analyze requirements for structuring code skeletons, propose three solution alternatives, and discuss their pros and cons. Finally, an example implementation is discussed.

MODELING INTERACTIVE MULTIMEDIA APPLICATIONS
This section describes concepts for modeling media in interactive applications. An exemplary modeling approach used here is the *Multimedia Modeling Language (MML)* [8] which supports MDD of interactive multimedia applications. This paper focuses on the media aspect [6] only; for other parts of the application (e.g., application logic) please refer to [8].

MML provides the concept of *media components* to model media content. A media component has a *media type*, like text, image, graphics, audio, video, 2D animation (i.e., graphics changing over the time), or 3D. It encapsulates the actual media content together with some standard functionality to control and render (play) the content. This paper takes as an example a media component Car of type 2D animation. The remainder of this section introduces three concepts for modeling complex media: media-specific abstraction layers, inner structure, and multiple artifacts.

Abstraction Layers for Modeling Media
A media component (e.g., Car) is associated with some application logic (a *domain class*) specifying a car's properties and behavior in the application. There can be multiple *instances* of Car on the UI.

However, a media component is an abstract representation and has to be distinguished from the actual media content. For instance, there can be different types of cars like Porsche and Ferrari where the users can choose from. Those are called *media artifacts* in MML. In some cases the media artifacts could be partially unknown at development time, e.g., if they are loaded from an external database or created dynamically at runtime. Thus, MML uses the more abstract media components as main modeling concept and allows specifying the

concrete media artifacts at a later time in the development process. With respect to the scope of this paper we assume here that the media artifacts are known at design time and are to be created by a media designer.

Figure 1 shows how these different abstraction levels are distinguished in MML: the most abstract concept are the media components which can represent multiple artifacts with the same properties, roles, and behavior in the application. A media artifact "manifests" a media component and represents the concrete media content to be created by the media designer. Finally, there can be multiple instances of media components which can be of different artifacts. For instance, consider cars in a car racing game application: there can be various types of cars (media artifacts) and various car instances in a race.

Inner Structure of Media Components
In an interactive application, the inner structure of media components can be important for the application's behavior: First, the application logic can modify specific parts of a media component. For instance in a car configurator application, various parts of a car (e.g., wheels) might be interactively animated, replaced, or modified (e.g., their color). Second, specific parts of a media component might trigger events. For instance, the user should be able to click on a car's wheels to change them. In both cases the media designer has to design these parts in such a way that they can be accessed by the application logic (e.g., as independent graphical sub-objects with an identifying name by which they can be accessed). Thus, it should be possible to specify a media component's inner structure in the models as far as relevant for the application's behavior. (Parts not relevant for the application logic need not to be specified in the model as the detailed media design should be performed in authoring tools — not within models).

MML supports to specify the inner structure of media components in terms of *media parts*. A media part has a type depending on the type of media component it belongs to. For instance, a 3D graphic can consist of 3D objects (i.e., geometries), transformations, lights, etc., while 2D animations consist of graphical objects called *sub-animations*.

An instance of a media part within a media component is called an *inner property*. Inner properties are structured in a tree hierarchy (like in most 2D and 3D formats). Modification of a parent node in the hierarchy modifies also all its children (e.g., if a wheel turns, its rim turns as well).

Let's consider as example a 2D animation of a car used in a car configurator application as shown in the lower right corner of Figure 2. Let's assume the car configurator allows the user to select between different types of *wheels* (Sport19in, Turbo20in) and two types of *mirrors* (Standard, Sport) and the color of the *rims*. In addition, the *wheels* and the *door* are animated.

The main part of Figure 2 shows the corresponding MML model. It specifies a 2D animation Car which has an inner property for each element that need to be accessed by the application logic (frontwheel, backwheel, door, and mirror). As

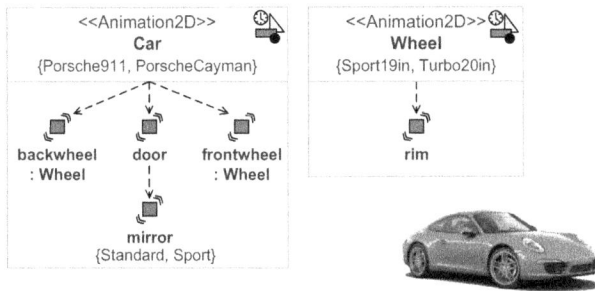

Figure 2. MML model showing two media components and a resulting example implementation.

wheel is reused multiple times it is defined as a media component of its own (Wheel).

In MML, inner properties that instantiate a reusable media part (e.g., another media component) need to be explicitly typed using the ':' notation (here frontwheel : Wheel and backwheel : Wheel). Otherwise the inner property is implicitly associated with an individual media part (which by convention has the same name as the inner property). For instance, door and mirror are instances of implicit (non-reusable) media parts Door and Mirror.

Artifacts

As explained above, a media artifact defines the concrete (here: visual) representations of a media component. Media artifacts are specified in the model denoted in curly brackets. For instance the model in Figure 2 specifies two media artifacts for the media component Car (Porsche911 and PorscheCayman) and two for Wheel (Sport19in, Turbo20in). Of course, all (implicit) media parts (e.g., Door) need to have a concrete visual representation as well (called *part artifact*). By default, there is one part artifact *for each* media artifact it belongs to, i.e., there is one door for Porsche911 and one for PorscheCayman (named as Porsche911_Door and PorscheCayman_Door in the generated code by convention).

It is also possible to explicitly specify part artifacts. In the example, there are two different variants of mirror: Standard style and Sport style. By default this means again that each of these variants is designed separately *for each* media artifact (resulting in four part artifacts Porsche911_Mirror_Standard, Porsche911_Mirror_Sport, PorscheCayman_Mirror_Standard, and PorscheCayman_Mirror_Sport).

REQUIREMENTS FOR STRUCTURING SKELETONS

This section analyzes the requirements for generating code skeletons for media components. The implementation of a media component consists of two main parts: 1) the media document (e.g., a Flash or X3D document) containing the media content and 2) associated program code (e.g., Action-Script for Flash or Java for X3D). The program code has to realize the media component's behavior and to provide an interface to inner properties.

While there are various ways how to structure the skeletons, the structure should be chosen carefully as it strongly influences the utility of the generated skeletons. Voelter [11] de-

scribes best practices for MDD. Three of them are particularly relevant for generating code skeletons and need to be considered for our purpose:

R1: *Separation of Generated Code.* The best practice "Don't modify generated code" [11] claims the need to clearly separate generated and manually written code. If generated and manually written code are interwoven (e.g., contained in the same class file) it is difficult to throw away previously generated code after changes have been made to the models. This leads to "sediments", like code generated previously for model elements which no longer exist (see [11]). A common way to implement this separation is the *Generation Gap* pattern [11, 1] which means that generated code is put into an abstract superclass which has to be implemented by manually written code. In this way the generated code can be thrown away and re-generated after each change on the model without the risk of unintended loss of manually written code. Other ways are, e.g., usage of delegation, reflection, or aspect-oriented programming [11].

R2: *Support for Completion.* The best practice "Control manually written code" [11] describes the need to support the developer to fill out all generated stubs. Ideally, the developer is supported by a list of open issues displayed in the IDE. This can be easily achieved when using the Generation Gap pattern (see above) as IDEs like Eclipse notify the developer if abstract methods have not been implemented yet. Another way is to generate constraints to be validated by constraint checkers within the IDE.

R3: *Prevent Violations.* The best practice "Make the code true to the model" [11] claims that the structure of the generated code should prevent violations of the model. For instance, if a model specifies component relationships, the manual code must not add any additional relationships not specified in the model. This can be achieved, e.g., by structuring the generated code so that other components are not (or hardly) accessible from the manually written code.

In addition to these general requirements there is another media-specific requirement:

R4: *Support Media Design.* While a good and modular structure of the generated skeletons according to the best practices above is desirable, the structure must not limit the media designer in the design of the media content.

STRUCTURING MEDIA SKELETONS

In particular, two challenges need to be addressed which result from the abstraction in the models:

C1: *A media component represents multiple artifacts.* As a media component is manifested by multiple media artifacts, there needs to be a media document for each media artifact. However, as it should be possible to load artifacts dynamically at runtime it must be possible for the application logic to handle them all in the same way, i.e., as a single type (representing the media component).

C2: *Inserting children into the inner structure.* The model specifies the inner structure of media components only as far as relevant for the application logic. The final media content designed by the media designer can consist of much more parts (not accessible from the application logic). This can also mean that the media designer wants to insert parts into the inner structure generated from the model. For instance, the break discs, which are partially visible through the wheels, might be inserted by the designer as parent nodes of the wheels.

The remainder of this section shows three alternative solutions and discusses their pros and cons with respect to the requirements from the previous section. For explanation purpose a very simplified model of a media component Car is used now (Figure 3) with just two inner properties door and mirror and one artifact Porsche.

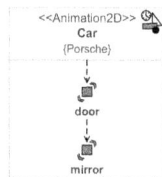

Figure 3. Simplified example model to illustrate the solution alternatives.

Solution 1: High Modularity

Figure 4 shows the first solution. It consists of a class Car which is associated with a media document with the same name. The media document is a generated skeleton containing placeholders for the inner properties as specified in the model. The class makes those inner properties accessible to other classes (e.g., providing them as public class properties). Multiple artifacts (see C1 above) are handled by the operation loadArtifact() which dynamically loads content into the Car document skeleton. The media designer has to provide (fill out) a media document for each part artifact. The generated class Car and the generated document skeleton Car remain untouched, i.e. must not be manually edited. (If desired, class Car can be extended with custom operations by creating a subclass.)

Separation of generated code (see R1 above): This solution provides a very good separation as the media component's inner structure is defined in the generated media document skeleton Car which must not be edited. The documents provided by the media designer can be freely designed and do not have to follow any specific structure themselves.

Support for completion (R2): Usually, there is no automated way to enforce that the media designer fills out all required artifacts. However, there will be a runtime error if the class

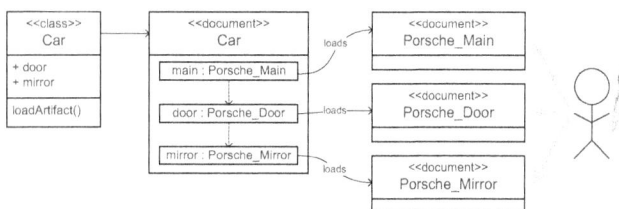

Figure 4. Solution 1: High Modularity.

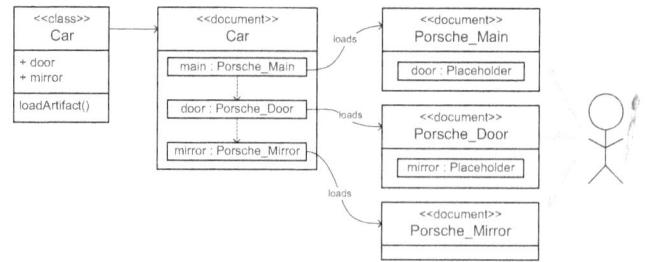

Figure 5. Solution 2: High Modularity & Extended Design Support.

Car cannot find an artifact to be loaded. One way to support the media designer is to generate some dummy content into all artifacts to be filled out. The media designer has to replace this dummy content with own content. A search for this dummy content (e.g., by its name) over all documents provides all artifacts not edited by the media designer yet.

Prevent violations (R3): As the generated class Car loads other documents according to the inner structure defined in the model, the structure cannot be violated by the documents provided by the media designer.

Support for Media Design (R4): This solution causes three limitations for the media designer: 1) As the overall Car document is composed at runtime, the media designer cannot see the result directly in the authoring tool. 2) It is difficult for the media designer to specify the spatial location of a child within its parent (e.g., the x- and y-coordinate of the mirror within the door) as this can only be specified within the child as relative position and the result becomes visible only after Car is composed at runtime. 3) There is no support to insert children that have not been specified in the model into the document hierarchy (see C2 above).

Solution 2: High Modularity & Extended Design Support

In contrast to solution 1, this solution (Figure 5) enables the media designer to influence the inner structure within the authoring tool: Each artifact which has children contains a specific placeholder (visualized, e.g., as simple rectangle shape with some explaining text) for each child. This placeholder has to be left empty by the designer; it is only used to indicate the position and relative size of the children within its parent. The media designer can do this easily in the authoring tool by moving (and/or resizing) the placeholder shape. Each placeholder instance is named with the name of the child it represents. When the class Car loads an artifacts for an inner properties it searches for the corresponding placeholder and replaces it with the loaded content.

Separation of generated code (R1): The degree of separation is a bit lower than in solution 1 as the media designer has to deal directly with the generated placeholders and must not delete them. However, the overall inner structure is still kept separately in the generated document Car.

Support for completion (R2) & Prevent violations (R3): Same as solution 1 above.

Support for Media Design (R4): This solution resolves the limitation 2) from solution 1 as the media designer can use

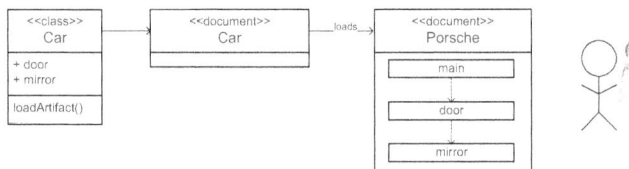

Figure 6. Solution 3: High Support for Media Design.

the placeholder to specify the spatial position, size and rotation of a child (relative to its parent) within the authoring tool. Limitation 3) is resolved to some extent as the placeholder can be moved into another media part that should be inserted into the hierarchy. However, this has still limitations. For instance, it is not easily possible to specify for multiple wheels that *each* wheel should have a break disc as parent node. Also limitation 1) from above still remains, i.e. the designer still cannot see the overall result directly in the authoring tool. Moreover, the media designer now has to take care of the placeholder.

Solution 3: High Support for Media Design

With this solution (Figure 6), the document Car acts only as a placeholder for media artifacts, while the inner structure defined in the model is under full control of the media designer. In this way the media designer has full flexibility and can view the result directly in the authoring tool. The class Car searches at runtime for the inner properties defined in the model using reflection, e.g., by crawling through the loaded artifacts and searching for graphical objects named door, mirror, etc.

Separation of generated code (R1): The separation is low as the media designer directly edits the documents containing the generated inner structure. However, still the class Car has the final control over the inner structure.

Support for completion (R2): Same as solution 1 and 2.

Prevent violations (R3): Now violations are detected at runtime only (if the class Car cannot find an inner property which has been specified in the model).

Support for Media Design (R4): This solution provides very good support for the media design as the designer sees the results directly in the authoring tool at design time and has full control over all children and their location. However, children must be named as defined in the model to be found by the class Car.

IMPLEMENTATION

This section discusses an implementation for the proposed solutions. The example implementation platform used here is Adobe Flash Professional as it is a well established authoring tool frequently used by professional designers in practice.

Flash applications consist of *Flash documents* (FLA files) and program code in *ActionScript* (AS files). Flash documents contain the media content, in particular, graphics and animations. Reusable graphics and animations are called *MovieClips* which can be instantiated either directly on the UI or within other MovieClips (i.e., as children).

Figure 7. Generated folder structure for the example from Figure 2.

ActionScript (AS) is an object-oriented language and each class is kept in separate AS file. A MovieClip can be connected to an AS class. Each MovieClip instance can then be accessed from AS code as an instance of this class which allows manipulating the MovieClip's properties such as location, size, rotation, and contained child MovieClip instances.

The code generation in this paper is implemented using model transformations written in the Atlas Transformation Language (ATL)[2]. A difficulty arises from the fact that FLA file format is a proprietary binary format and cannot easily be generated. However, the Flash authoring tool supports extensions written in JSFL (JavaScript Flash Language). JSFL enables to automate actions in the authoring tool and to automatically create Flash documents similar to the way HTML documents can be created with JavaScript. Hence, to create Flash documents from MML models, JSFL files are generated and then executed in the Flash authoring tool [7]. AS files are in text format and can be generated directly.

Figure 7 shows the generated folder structure resulting from applying solution 2 (see previous section) to the example from Figure 2. The generated code is structured into different folders according to the Generation Gap pattern (see R1) as discussed in [1][3]. The folder structure is explained in the following.

The folder src contains (manually) written library classes for reuse. This could be, for instance, a general base class for media components specifying the basic behavior that is common to all media components. With respect to the scope of this paper, the only reusable library element relevant here is a MovieClip Placeholder used to implement solution 2.

The folder src-man contains the documents to be filled out manually by the media designer. They are generated only once as a starting point for the media designer but will never be overwritten or removed by the code generator. As described in solution 2, there is a FLA file for each media artifact and each part artifact. Each of these FLA files contains initially some dummy graphics (to be replaced by the media designer) and an instance of the MovieClip Placeholder for each child.

The folder src-gen contains generated content only and can be thrown away and re-generated every time the model has

---

[2] https://www.eclipse.org/atl/
[3] [1] describes multiple variants how to structure folders; only the first one, "Generate Once", is discussed here for simplicity.

changed. There is a FLA file and an AS class for each media component. The FLA files contains an empty MovieClip connected to the AS class. The AS class represents the "interface" of the media component; in particular, its inner properties as class properties. As explained in solution 2, the AS class loads the artifacts (from the folder src-man) and composes the media component by replacing placeholders with loaded content. Finally, if a media component or one of its properties can be represented by different artifacts, the AS class needs to provide methods to select between them (e.g., set a car's wheels to either Sport19in or Turbo20in).

The folder tests contains AS classes to support developers in testing the application and to indicate open developer tasks. There is a test class for each media component that enables to directly instantiate the media component and the different combinations of artifacts, view the results, and get notified about missing elements. In addition, an AS class searches in src-man for dummy content that has not been replaced yet to indicate open tasks for the media designer.

As explained above, Figure 7 shows the result for solution 2. In case of solution 1, the only difference is that Placeholder.fla is omitted as solution 1 does not use the concept of placeholders. In case of solution 3, the FLA files for media parts are omitted in addition as there are only FLA files for the media components themselves.

Based on the proposed structure, the content in src-gen can be thrown away and re-generated each time the model changes. In addition, the consequences for the manually written content in src-man are as follows: *Adding* model elements has only consequences on src-man in case of adding a part artifact or media artifact; a new corresponding FLA document is then generated to be filled out by the media designer. *Removing* model elements has no effect on src-man; obsolete elements will just be no longer loaded by the re-generated code in src-gen. *Modifying* the inner structure of a media component has no effect either; the artifacts from src-man will just be composed differently. *Renaming* model elements will have the same result as removing an element and adding a new one. In this case, src-man needs to be manually updated by renaming artifacts that should be kept. A solution how to reduce this effort can be found in [1].

In case of solution 2, adding, removing or moving inner properties is trickier as the placeholders need to be adapted. In this case, the code generator needs to update the placeholders within the files in src-man. This is basically possible with JSFL without deleting other content. However, when removing or moving an inner property, the information about the previous placeholder (location and size) gets lost and needs to be manually restored if the model change should be reverted.

SUMMARY AND CONCLUSIONS

This paper has shown three solution alternatives to generate code skeletons for complex media content within model-driven development of interactive systems. Each of them has its pros and cons and, as the paper shows, there is not a single solution that fits every need. Solution 1 and 2 enforce compliance with the models but result in some increased complexity

of media design while solution 3 provides full flexibility to the media designer but requires executing (generated) tests to ensure compliance with the models. Solution 2 provides more advanced support for media design than solution 1 but a less strict separation between generated and manually written content. It depends on the specific project and the developer's priorities which solution fits best.

Future work needs to extend the implementation to other platforms, aim for developer feedback, and further investigate integration of MDD and visual design.

Acknowledgements

This work was supported, in part, by Science Foundation Ireland grant 10/CE/I1855 to Lero — The Irish Software Engineering Research Centre (http://www.lero.ie).

REFERENCES

1. Behrens, H. Generation gap pattern, 2009.
   `http://heikobehrens.net/2009/04/23/generation-gap-pattern/`.

2. Hoogeveen, M. Towards a theory of the effectiveness of multimedia systems. *International Journal of Human Computer Interaction 9*, 2 (1997), 151–168.

3. Hussmann, H., Meixner, G., and Zuehlke, D., Eds. *Model-Driven Development of Advanced User Interfaces*. Springer, 2011.

4. Meixner, G., Patern, F., and Vanderdonckt, J. Past, present, and future of model-based user interface development. *i-com 10*, 3 (2011), 2–11.

5. Mirlacher, T., Palanque, P., and Bernhaupt, R. Engineering animations in user interfaces. In *EICS 2012*, ACM (2012), 111–120.

6. Pleuss, A., Botterweck, G., and Hussmann, H. Modeling advanced concepts of interactive multimedia applications. In *VL/HCC 2009*, IEEE (2009), 31–38.

7. Pleuss, A., and Hussmann, H. Integrating authoring tools into model-driven development of interactive multimedia applications. In *HCI Int. 2007*, Springer (2007), 1168–1177.

8. Pleuss, A., and Hussmann, H. Model-driven development of interactive multimedia applications with MML. In Hussmann et al. [3], 199–218.

9. Strobl, T., and Minas, M. Specifying and generating editing environments for interactive animated visual models. *ECEASST 29* (2010).

10. Vitzthum, A. SSIML/Behaviour: Designing behaviour and animation of graphical objects in virtual reality and multimedia applications. In *ISM'05*, IEEE (2005), 159–167.

11. Voelter, M. Md* best practices. *Journal of Object Technology 8*, 6 (2009), 79–102.

12. Voelter, M., Benz, S., Dietrich, C., Engelmann, B., Helander, M., Kats, L., Visser, E., and Wachsmuth, G. *DSL Engineering: Designing, Implementing and Using Domain-specific Languages*. CreateSpace, 2013.

A Domain-Specific Model-Based Design Approach for End-User Developers

Anke Dittmar, Mathias Kühn, and Peter Forbrig

University of Rostock, Department of Computer Science

Albert-Einstein-Straße 22

D-18051 Rostock

[anke.dittmar|mathias.kuehn|peter.forbrig]@uni-rostock.de

ABSTRACT

The paper investigates model-based design (MBD) ideas for supporting end-user developers in creating mobile data collection tools. End-user developers cannot assumed to be able (or willing) to specify formal task models as they are common in MBD approaches. They use their knowledge about domain objects and general task characteristics to specify constraints on the execution of tasks. The paper shows that the restriction to specific task domains makes it possible to tailor the underlying meta-models and transformation rules accordingly and to provide end-users with convenient tool support. In particular, dialog models and their stepwise enrichment and refinement are considered in the paper. General implications of the suggested ideas for MBD are discussed. The proposed approach is implemented using the Eclipse Modeling Framework and a case study demonstrates the applicability of the approach.

Author Keywords

Model-based design of user interfaces; end-user developers; model-driven engineering; dialog models; state charts.

ACM Classification Keywords

H.5.m. Information interfaces and presentation (e.g., HCI): Miscellaneous.

INTRODUCTION

In model-based design of user interfaces (MBD), different perspectives of the design problem are captured in models at different levels of abstraction. This includes, for example, the description of the task structure and the context of users, the presentation and the dialog structure of the user interface, and the platform [5]. The design process typically starts at the task and domain level to inform user-centered design decisions. Myers et al. [8] point out that

MBD has not been widely applied in practice and explain two possible reasons for this. First, the connection between models and the final user interface (UI) is sometimes difficult to understand and to control, and second, the generated UIs are generally not as good as UIs that are created with conventional programming techniques. However, the authors also acknowledge the increasing interest in MBD approaches in order to reduce the development efforts for the growing variety of platforms, devices, and programming tools [8]. Additionally, the emergence of Model-Driven Engineering (MDE) has given new impulses to MBD methods, techniques and tools. In particular, there is advanced support for model transformations [14].

The quality of model-based UIs depends to a large extent on the richness of the underlying meta-models and on the applied transformation rules. Research in this area has shown that a universal model-based approach is difficult to achieve. Therefore, the paper investigates model-based design ideas for a specific task domain and a specific group of developers: end-user developers are supported in creating mobile data collection tools. This restriction allows to make more assumptions on transformation processes, on models, and on user interfaces to be generated. In particular, it is possible to deal with dialog models at different levels of abstraction and to include data models of applications. In the paper, dialog models are represented by state charts that allow to specify the behavior of interactive data collection tools at a conceptual level. Their stepwise extension and refinement is controlled by explicit transformation rules as it is already common in existing MBD approaches for user interface structures (presentation model). These rules apply, for example, knowledge about navigation patterns in user interfaces [15]. In the suggested approach, abstract and concrete state charts control the coupling of abstract and concrete UI models respectively to the data model of the application, and thus, support a more holistic generation process. The ideas are implemented using the Eclipse Modeling Framework (EMF) with meta-models captured by Ecore models and transformation rules specified in the ATLAS transformation language (ATL).

The paper first gives an overview of existing MBD methods, techniques, and general-purpose meta-models for UIs. It is argued that the constraints of domain-specific meta-models facilitate the transformation process and increase the quality of generated domain-specific applications ('less is more'). This is demonstrated at the example of mobile data collections in an end-user development context. After a short introduction of the domain appropriate meta-models and their mappings are discussed. The paper especially concentrates on the role of dialog models, their stepwise enrichment and refinement. A case study validates the approach throughout the paper. Finally, general implications of the paper for model-based design are discussed.

BACKGROUND AND RELATED WORK

MBD provides a systematic way to develop user interfaces and looks back on a history of more than 20 years. In early approaches, the focus was on discussing appropriate abstractions and models for UIs and on finding mappings between these models. In [16], task models, domain models, and user models are mentioned as common high-level models describing user goals as well as means and constraints to achieve them. Presentation and dialog models specify the structure and behavior of user interfaces. Other models mentioned in the literature are, e.g., platform models capturing technical constraints [5] and context models [2]. Mechanisms for creating and refining models can be classified in three categories: model derivation, model linking, model composition [16]. There is, for example, extensive work on (semi-)automatically deriving presentation and dialog models from task models which are assumed to be in a formal notation such as the CTT-notation (Concur Task Trees) [11,16,10,4].

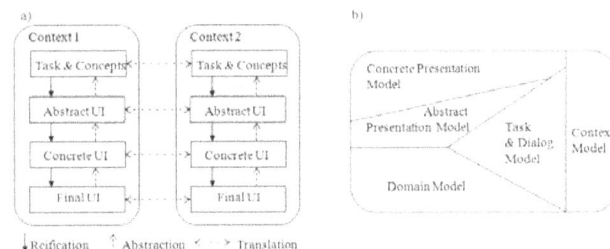

Figure 1. a) Cameleon Reference Framework [2], b) Reference frame for comparing which models and which relationships between models are used in different MBD approaches [2].

Mobile devices, multi-platform UIs or distributed UIs are only some technological advances that have slightly changed the focus of MBD research to better cope with challenges such as context-sensitivity, adaptivity, or consistency between multiple versions [5,11]. This is also reflected in the Cameleon Reference Framework depicted in Figure 1a), which emphasizes the distinction between different abstraction levels and supports ideas of MDE [2] to facilitate software engineering activities such as model reuse and re-engineering. This implies that formal meta-models for the models and transformations of the framework have to be developed as done, e.g., by UsiXML

[17]. In [14] and many other approaches, the applicability of MDE techniques in UI design is demonstrated.

What becomes evident from Figure 1b) is the fact that a stepwise concretization of the dialog component of a user interface is less supported in many MBD approaches. While there is a distinction between abstract and concrete presentation models, dialog models are not even clearly distinguished from task models. In this paper, some ideas for a stepwise enrichment and refinement are considered, but for a restricted application domain.

While the above mentioned work deals with general-purpose methods, techniques, and notations to systematically develop user interfaces, the domain-specific application of model-driven design ideas is reported, e.g., in [6,13]. Here, meta-models can be tailored to the particular needs of the domain. In [9], MBD is recommended as a means to allow end-user developers to create and modify programs. According to [12], end-user developers should be provided with a domain-specific visual language and should be able to focus on user-dependent properties, whereas software engineers should focus on quality or maintenance properties of the product. As it is shown in the paper, MBD approaches help to implement these goals.

THE DOMAIN: MOBILE DATA COLLECTION TOOLS

Mobile data collection tools (MDC tools) are interactive systems that allow in-situ data collections. One well-known application area are research methods like the Experience Sampling Method (see in [1]), but other application scenarios can be developed. For example, a teacher could ask her young students to plant cress and log its growth on a daily basis. The collected data (e.g. pictures, audio comments, texts) could be used by the teacher to support the students' collaborative reflection of good living conditions for the plant.

The use of MDC tools is typically very context specific and their need may arise temporarily from the work situation. In this paper, a model-based approach is applied to enable end users, such as researchers and teachers in the above mentioned usage scenarios, to develop MDC tools according to their actual needs. In the following, we refer to these end-user developers as *questioners* and to the users of their MDC tools as *respondents*. Questioners are concerned with the design of mobile data collection processes, with the distribution of developed MDC tools, and with the collection and analysis of in-situ data. Respondents have to install the MDC tool and to enter and submit their data. The focus of the paper is on supporting the questioners' design of MDC tools and on the model-based generation of corresponding user interfaces for mobile devices.

Assumptions on Task and Domain Descriptions

Questioners can neither be assumed to be familiar with technical details of different mobile devices and implementation languages nor with formal specification techniques (e.g., formal tasks models like CTT-models [11]). In their conceptual design of mobile inquiries, they make use of well-known survey question types such as single choice and multiple choice questions. They may be interested in encouraging respondents to submit multimedia data of the current situation. Questioners also know about the importance of the order of questions to guide respondents in their answering process. Other means to frame the completion and submission process are, for example, optional questions, optional or obligatory submissions, enabling resubmission, different types of deadlines (e.g., fixed date, time period), different modes to access submission details (e.g., submission time, name of respondent), and different modes to answer to questions (e.g., in sequential or arbitrary order). We refer to such features as task characteristics.

Illustrative Example

The case study that is considered throughout the paper concerns a biology field trip of a school class. The teacher may want to create a mobile inquiry with three groups of questions.

Group1: Document a dominant plant in grassland.
1. Take a picture of the plant. <Image input>
2. Choose to describe in more detail:
   <single choice: Leaves/Blossoms>
3. <if in 2. Leaves was chosen:> How is the margin of the leaves shaped?
   <single choice: Smooth/Lobed/Toothed/free text>
4. <if in 2. Blossoms was chosen:> How are the petals shaped?
   <single choice: Tube/Bell/Trumpet/free text>
5. <optional question> Measure the height of the plant. <text input>

Group 2: Document a tree in open forest.
1. Take a picture of the tree. <Image input>
2. How are the veins of the leaves composed? ...

Group 3: Document a plant in bog ...

In addition, the questioner constrains the students' completion of the mobile form by following task characteristics.

- *Obligatory submission for all students.*
- *Completion of the mobile form can be paused.*
- *Groups can be answered in arbitrary order and given answers are editable.*
- *Questions of one group have to be answered in sequential order.*

MODEL-BASED GENERATION OF MDC TOOLS

Figure 2 shows that the generation of data collection applications is guided by the already mentioned CAMELEON Reference Framework [3]. Four different levels of UI specifications are distinguished: task & domain level, abstract UI level (AUI), concrete UI level (CUI), and the final UI (FUI). In addition, a data model is derived from

the task and domain model, which does not need to be further refined in this case. The suggested approach has been implemented by MDE techniques (Ecore meta-models and ATL transformation rules [7]) in order to release end-user developers from the tasks of UI designers and software engineers. Several points are specific to our approach and will be explained in more detail in the following sections.

- Meta-models and transformation rules for the models and transformations in Figure 2 are not general-purpose but geared towards the requirements of the specific task domain.
- There is no single task specification. Tasks and temporal constraints between sub-tasks are partly encoded by task domain objects and partly by task characteristics.
- There is more emphasis on a stepwise enrichment and refinement of dialog models than in most existing approaches.

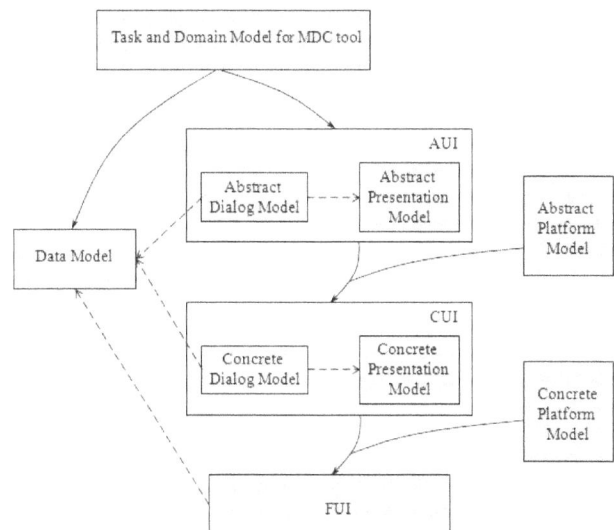

Figure 2: Models used to produce a MDC tool. Dashed lines refer to links between models, solid lines depict model transformations.

Task and Domain Meta-Model

The Ecore class model in Figure 3 captures general domain knowledge about surveys as well as possible expectations on mobile forms and on how respondents have to complete them. Class `MobileForm` is the anchor of all data collection related specifications. Mobile forms are assumed to have a simple structure: a sequence of questions or question groups. To each question, a template is assigned to define the respondents' way to answer it. It is also distinguished between independent, dependent, and adapted dependent questions. A dependent question has to be answered if a certain condition is fulfilled (e.g., a previous question was answered in a certain way). Adapted dependent questions and their answer templates are constructed from previous answers.

Possible paths to answer the questions of a mobile form are not only defined by their specified sequence and the question types that were used, but they are also influenced by those attributes of classes `MobileForm`, `FormElement`, and `Group` that describe additional task characteristics discussed in the previous section.

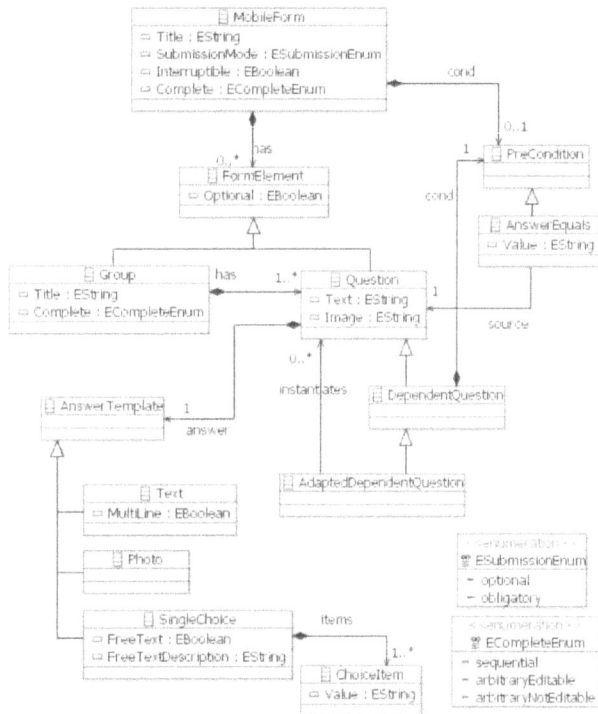

Figure 3: Main part of the Task and Domain Meta-Model for MDC tools.

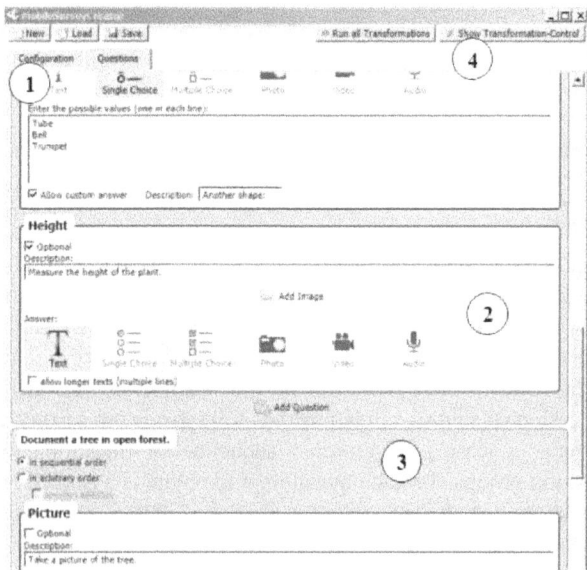

Figure 4: Part of the task and domain model of the case study created by the questioner with the graphical editor.

Tool Support for Questioners

Figure 4 depicts a prototypical front end providing questioners with a graphical task and domain model editor to conveniently specify their MDC tools at a conceptual level. The editor is tailored to the meta-model in Figure 3. Global task characteristics can be specified in the configuration part (1). Questions (2) and groups (3) can be added to the conceptual structure of a mobile form, their position in the sequence can be changed, and they can be removed from the form. The questioner has also to select relevant platform models from a predefined set (4), and then, all other models are generated on the basis of the underlying Ecore meta-models and ATL transformation rules as selectively described below.

Transformation to Abstract System Models

In the first transformation phase, abstract system models are produced from the conceptual task and domain model. Again, the corresponding meta-models are specific to the task domain (see Figure 6). The derivation of the data structure of MDC tools (data models) is straightforward. As for presentation models, questions and question groups are mapped to AUI (sub-)containers (class `VContainer`), and answer types of questions are mapped to corresponding objects of `VDataInputAction` sub-classes.

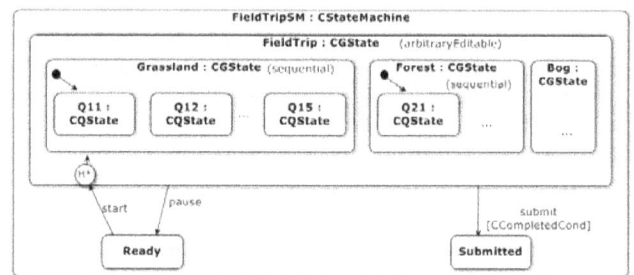

Figure 5: Underspecified state chart for the case study.

Abstract dialog models are represented by *underspecified state charts*. Two specific state types are specified in the meta-model of Figure 6. Questions from the task and domain model are mapped to objects of class `CQState`. They represent composite states which are described at the AUI level as 'black boxes' and have to be *refined* at the CUI level. Question groups are mapped to objects of class `CGState`. Such composite states contain sub-states of type `CQState`, but are underspecified with respect to the transitions between these sub-states. Figure 5 partly shows the underspecified state chart that has been derived in the illustrative example. Here, transitions and events `start`, `pause`, and `submit` have been created from the specified global task characteristics (obligatory submission, completion process can be interrupted).

Each state in the dialog model is linked with a container element from the presentation model and with a question or group element form the data model. Events refer to the presentation of actions in the presentation model, conditions

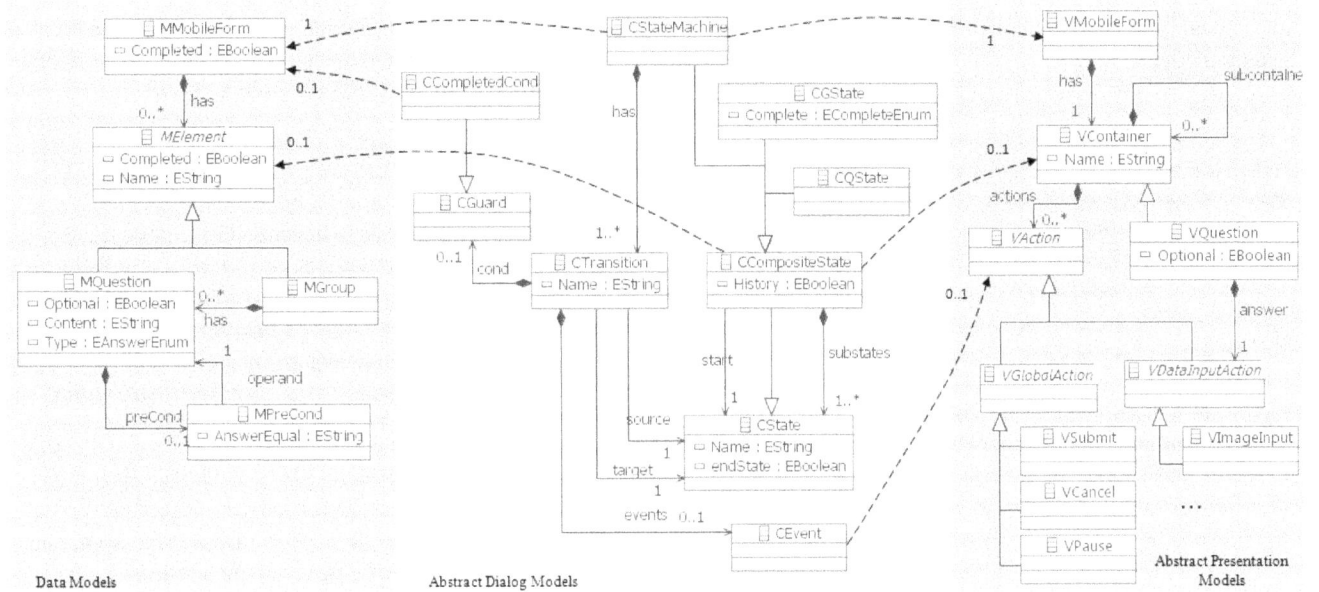

Figure 6: Parts of the abstract level meta-models with their interrelations.

in a state chart depend from the data model. AUI models are consciously left underspecified because they only consider the task environment but not the constraints arising from the platforms in use.

Transformation to CUI Models

Underspecified state charts are completed in the second transformation phase from AUI models and abstract platform models to CUI model. In our context, an abstract platform model describes a set of (physical) platforms that can be treated equally regarding the concrete UI design. Screen size and resolution are such important platform characteristics [6]. Screen designs for devices with small-size displays and low resolution typically differ from screen designs for high-resolution devices, and this also constrains the design of the navigation structure of the application. Therefore, conceptual dialog structures cannot be fully defined until the CUI level.

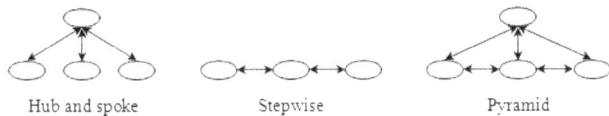

Figure 7: Navigation patterns for mobile applications [15].

In our approach, transformation rules make use of UI design patterns to derive the overall navigation structure of concrete dialog models. Figure 7 depicts some basic navigation patterns from [15] that can be adapted or composed to multi-level structures. Figure 8 and Figure 9 show the overall navigation structure of two possible concrete dialog models in our example. As to be seen, both solutions adapt the pyramid-pattern to meet the requirements of the CGStates (groups can be completed in arbitrary order, the questions of one group in sequential order).

In the first solution, each question of the mobile form is mapped to a separate screen in the related concrete presentation model and corresponding `next`-transitions are inserted. In the second solution, all questions of a group are presented on the same screen.

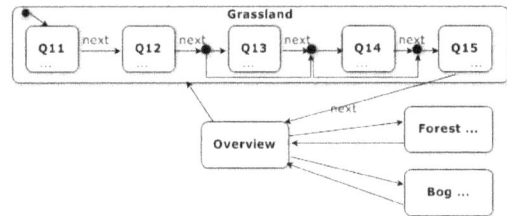

Figure 8: Navigation structure for small-size, low-resolution displays in the case study.

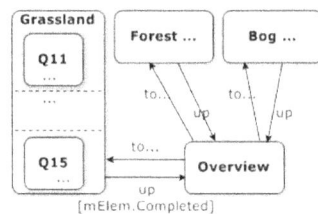

Figure 9: Navigation structure for higher resolutions.

The refinement of states which represent questions (`CQState` objects) is determined by the question type, certain task characteristics and it's embedding into the overall navigation structure. Figure 10 illustrates the refinement of AUI states for dependent and optional questions with editable answers. Events from the abstract dialog model are specialized now: data input events are derived from the answer template, the ignore event is needed for optional questions, and there are different navigation events such as 'back' and 'next'. Preconditions of dependent questions are mapped to guards of transitions which refer to the data model.

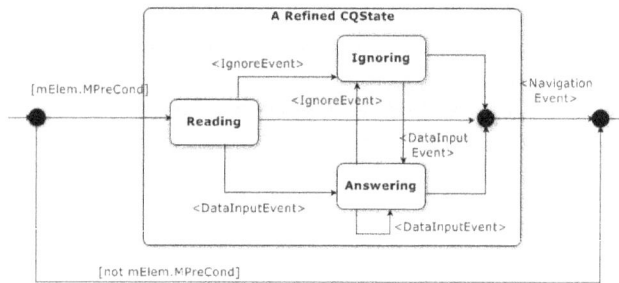

Figure 10: A refinement for a CQState object representing a dependent and optional question with editable answer.

Figure 11: Generated FUIs a) according to Figure 8, and b) according to Figure 9.

DISCUSSION AND CONCLUSIONS

Based on the example of mobile data collection tools, the paper has shown that MBD approaches offer useful means to develop domain-specific end-user developer tools. But moreover, the considered needs of end-user developers and presented solutions encourage to reconsider, in general, the following two aspects of MBD. First, task models typically describe constraints on task execution as temporal relations between sub-tasks. Existing approaches rarely take into consideration that domain objects can already encode understandings of such temporal constraints and that there is seldom one monolithic unified task description from which, for example, a presentation model can be derived. Second, while there is a fair amount of work on the stepwise refinement of presentation models, there is relatively little work on a stepwise refinement of dialog models. In this paper, underspecified state charts represent abstract dialog models. They are refined by transformations. This was possible for a specific application domain, but we have not examined yet whether the idea can be generalized. In future work, we want to further investigate both the above mentioned problems.

ACKNOWLEDGMENTS

We thank Florian Binder for his contribution to the implementation of the end-user developer front end.

REFERENCES

1. Batalas, N., and Markopoulos, P. Considerations for computerized in situ data collection platforms. In *Proc. of EICS '12*, ACM (2012), 231–236.

2. den Bergh, J. V., and Coninx, K. Model-based design of context-sensitive interactive applications: a discussion of notations. In *Proc. TAMODIA '04* (2004), 43-50.

3. Calvary, G., Coutaz, J., Thevenin, D., Limbourg, Q., Bouillon, L. and Vanderdonckt, J. A Unifying Reference Framework for Multi-Target User Interfaces. In *Interacting with Computers*, Vol. 15(3) (2003), 289-308.

4. Dittmar, A., Forbrig, P. The Influence of Improved Task Models on Dialogues. In *Proc. of CADUI'04* (2004).

5. Eisenstein, J., Vanderdonckt, J. and Puerta A. Applying model-based techniques to the development of UIs for mobile computers. In *Proc. of IUI '01*. ACM (2001).

6. Fogli, D., and Provenza, L. P. A meta-design approach to the development of e-government services. J. Vis. Lang. Comput. 23, 2 (2012), 47-62.

7. http://www.eclipse.org/modeling/emf, http://www.eclipse.org/atl/

8. Myers, B., Hudson, S.E. and Pausch, R. Past, present, and future of user interface software tools. In *ACM Trans. Computer-Human Interaction*, 7(1) (2000), 3-28.

9. Lieberman, H., Paterno, F., and Wulf, V., Eds. End-User Development. Kluwer/ Springer, 2006.

10. Luyten, K., Clerckx, T., Coninx, K., and Vanderdonckt, J. Derivation of a Dialog Model from a Task Model by Activity Chain Extraction. In *Proc. of DSVIS'03* (2003), 203-217.

11. Paterno, F. and Santoro, C. One model, many interfaces. In *Proc. CADUI 2002, Vol 3* (2002), 143-154.

12. Pérez, F., Valderas, P., and Fons, J. Towards the involvement of end-users within model-driven development. In *Proc.of IS-EUD'11* (2011), 258-263.

13. Pleuss, A., Wollny, S., and Botterweck, G. Model-driven development and evolution of customized user interfaces. In *Proc. of EICS* (2013), 13-22.

14. Sottet, J.-S., Calvary, G., Coutaz, J., and Favre, J.-M. A model-driven engineering approach for the usability of plastic user interfaces. In *Proc. of EIS '08*, Springer (2008), 140–157.

15. Tidwell, J. *Designing Interfaces*. O'Reilly Media, 2010.

16. Vanderdonckt, J., Limbourg, Q., and Florins, M. Deriving the Navigational Structure of a User Interface. In *Proc. of INTERACT'03* (2003), 455-462.

17. Vanderdonckt, J., Limbourg, Q., Michotte, B., Bouillon, L., Trevisan, D., Florins, M.: UsiXML: a User Interface Description Language for Specifying Multimodal User Interfaces. In: *Proc. W3C Workshop on Multimodal Interaction WMI'2004* (2004).

Consolidating Diverse User Profiles Based on the Profile Models of Adaptive Systems

Effie Karuzaki[1], Anthony Savidis[1,2]
{karuzaki, as}@ics.forth.gr
[1]Institute of Computer Science, FORTH, Greece
[2]Department of Computer Science, University of Crete, Greece

ABSTRACT

Profile-based adaptivity is an important ingredient of interactive systems. Today, although users keep many profiles in different applications, adaptive systems still request them explicitly. While lingua franca methods on profiles are suggested, unless standardized, they are hardly deployed by different vendors. We present an approach to *consolidate diverse user profiles* based on a profile model that is *supplied as input*. The latter is instantiated in our Gandalf system, where user profiles from various sources are aggregated, merged and mapped to *any given model*, by also preserving private user attributes. No common models for profiles are assumed, neither any shared models across adaptive systems are prescribed. Our method uses a thesaurus service, while it proposes lightweight rules for structure matching and conflict resolution to accompany the input profile model. Gandalf is under implementation as a web service, and allows adaptive systems to hook custom pre- and post- processing logic on profiles using JavaScript.

Author Keywords

User Profiles; Profile-Based Adaptivity; Profile Consolidation; Adaptive Interactive Systems.

ACM Classification Keywords

H.5.2 [*User Interfaces*]: Theory and methods

INTRODUCTION

Nowadays, users are involved in various diverse-purpose applications and activities, many of which are interested in keeping a set of personal information packed as profiles, to achieve better adaptation and personalization. Since our lives are teemed with social media, blogs, shopping sites etc., our personal information is all around the internet. However, we still need to re-create our profiles every time we wish to use a new service or application that wants to adapt to our needs. Existing profile information can also be

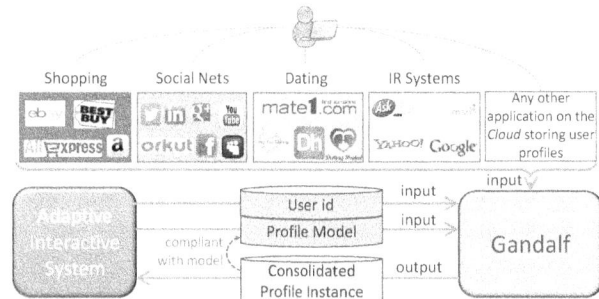

Figure 1: The idea of consolidating diverse user profiles based on a given profile model

used for better personalization in recommender systems, in addition to existing learning techniques which are based on user clicks, searches, previous buys etc. to solve the "cold start" issues. For example, an online music store should be able to allow recommendations based on user's likes on Facebook instead of trying to deduce users' tastes only from previous music searches. Another example applies to recommender systems and search engines, which could also use publicly available profile information to better adapt their suggestions to their clients.

One of the reasons why this isn't happening today, is because currently there is no way for applications to gather profile information from diverse distributed profile providers and merge them into a single user profile compatible with *their own models*. Our work is based on this idea outlined under Figure 1. Exploiting multiple existing user profiles from diverse resources may also give an important boost to user interaction experience, since adaptation mechanisms would have more information about user interests, tastes and needs. In this direction, many profile consolidation techniques have been proposed in the literature, most of which make use of user models. However, since every application has different needs, it develops its own user model and follows different consolidation rules. Overall, the challenges raised here are: (i) Can we collect and consolidate user profiles from several distributed resources while preserving user privacy? (ii) How can we merge the retrieved profiles into a single one without imposing a universal user model? (iii) How can the inconsistencies met in the various user profiles be resolved and finally, (iv) How can the consolidated profile reflect any profile model provided by adaptive systems?

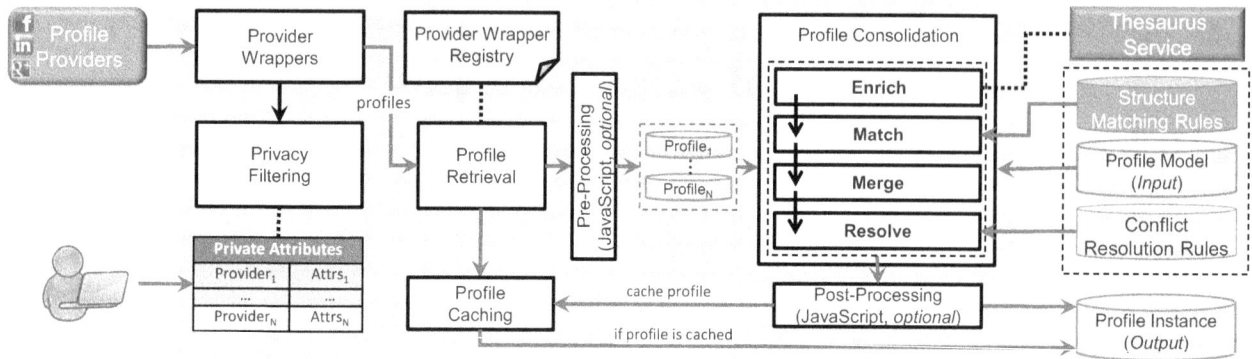

Figure 2: The Gandalf system architecture

Contributions

We propose an approach for collecting and merging user profile information from multiple providers into a single user profile, maintaining the following properties: (i) Profile providers are distributed and completely independent of each other; (ii) No assumptions are made about the vocabulary and the profile structure each provider uses; (iii) The retrieved profiles are consolidated and combined into a single user profile reflecting any given user profile model supplied as input to the system with consolidated profiles cached for later use; (iv) The consolidation steps can be refined via scripting; (v) Inconsistencies regarding the type and the values of attributes retrieved across the different profiles are resolved with configurable application-specific rules; and (vi) End-users maintain control over which of their personal information are retrieved from each profile provider.

SYSTEM OVERVIEW

The software architecture of the Gandalf system is illustrated under Figure 2. The system retrieves user profile data from a list of registered providers based on the end-user id. It also receives a target profile model to convert these profiles into, and a set of structure-matching and conflict-resolution rules. These rules are deployed along with a thesaurus service to consolidate the retrieved profiles into a single one which reflects the given model. To this end, the following components are distinguished:

- *Provider wrappers*, enlisted in a component registry, being the communication bridges between our system and the various profile providers.

- *Privacy filtering*, enabling user control over which information can be retrieved by the provider wrappers.

- *Profile retrieval*, which, given a user id, checks if it can find a previously cached combined profile for that user conforming to the given model. If found, it is returned, otherwise a new aggregation process is initiated.

- *Profile caching* for the consolidated profiles to avoid repeating the overall process.

- *Profile consolidation* of all retrieved user profiles into a single profile according to the given profile model.

After retrieving the user profiles from the providers, and just before profile consolidation, we provide an optional hook for developers to perform custom *pre-processing* on the retrieved profiles via JavaScript code. A similar hook is also provided just after the end of the consolidation process, to enable *post-processing* of the consolidated profile output. Finally, we allow the client adaptive system to substitute any or all of the designated consolidation steps (see Figure 2) with custom components.

RETRIEVING PROFILES

According to [8], all distributed user profiles on the Web represent different facets of the user and therefore their aggregation provides a more comprehensive picture of a person's profile.

Provider Wrappers

Any third-party profile provider service can be deployed, once a respective provider wrapper component is registered into our system. Since every provider has its own profile structure and control API, a wrapper is required to effectively bridge it with our system. Wrappers, being aware of the corresponding provider API and structure, retrieve user information and hand it over to our system in JavaScript Object Notation (JSON) format. Provider wrappers implement a common API for (i) reporting the profile attributes that can be retrieved from the corresponding provider, (ii) providing type and format information for every profile attribute (e.g. dates can be provided as MM/DD/YY); (iii) retrieving all, or a subset of the available profile attributes and (iv) constructing a JSON file representing the information collected. The *provider wrapper registry* keeps a list of profile provider ids, URLs and their wrappers. Every time our system needs to retrieve profile information for a given user id, the registered wrappers are used to communicate with the corresponding providers and receive the requested profile.

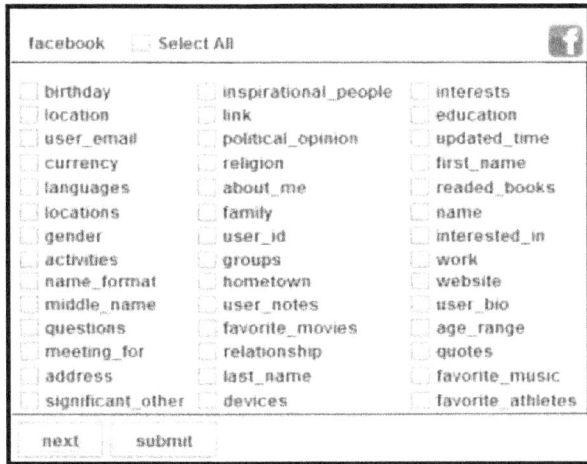

Figure 4: Privacy filtering dialogue for Facebook

Privacy Filtering

When it comes to personal profile information, users are often skeptical about the information they share. Thus, it is important to provide a mechanism to enable user control over the attributes retrieved from each provider. To this end, provider wrappers offer a list with the available profile attributes in each provider. The privacy filtering module dynamically composes a dialog for each provider based on that list, requesting user's agreement on the attributes to be retrieved. Figure 4 shows the privacy filtering dialogue for the Facebook profile provider. Next, if required by the provider, users should explicitly log in with their original accounts and grant access to our system.

Profile Caching

Practically, the profile retrieval and consolidation process may become a time-consuming process when many and elaborate profiles are involved. However, users do not change their profiles that often, and new profile providers are rarely added. Based on these remarks, we included a caching module to directly retrieve previously consolidated and stored profiles when possible. To assert that the cached profiles is up-to-date, we keep the following information for each cache entry: (i) the user id; (ii) the providers used and (iii) a creation timestamp for the stored profile. Given a user id, the system firstly checks the cache for a stored profile. If found, and *the available providers are exactly the same as the cached ones* and *the cache creation timestamp is newer than the modification date of all profiles from the providers*, then the cached profile is up-to-date and thus directly used. Otherwise, the cache entry is discarded.

PROFILE CONSOLIDATION

After any optional application-defined profile pre-processing, the profiles are ready for consolidation. Each provider may adopt a different naming policy for profile attributes and a custom hierarchical profile structure. In this context, the target is to detect which profile attributes essentially refer to the same profile model attribute, and compile a single profile out of them without losing valuable information. To this end, two solutions have been proposed in the literature: (i) impose a common profile model that all providers should adopt for their user profiles; and (ii) suggest a standard profile model that all adaptive systems should adopt. Both cases promote the notion of standardized profile models, or a lingua franca on user

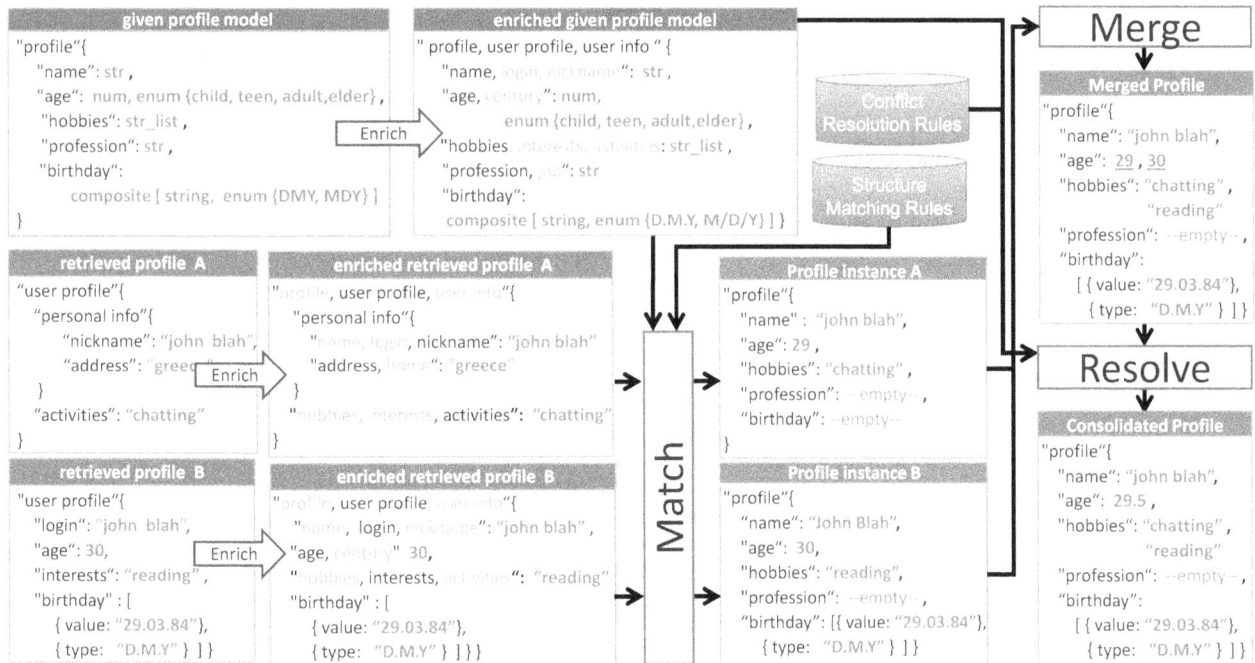

Figure 3: Outline of the steps involved in the profile consolidation process

models. While the latter is technically sound, past experience shows that such standardization activities tend to be very slow and rarely conclude. Also, in the future, profile providers and adaptive systems may require important extensions or updates on profiles and models, thus rendering any standardized models impractical.

Our approach imposes no common profile models among providers and adaptive systems, shifting away from the *one model to rule them all* philosophy. Adaptive systems should choose their own profile models which will be supplied as input to a system capable of consolidating the diverse user profiles into a single profile complying with the *given profile model*. For the definition of input profile models we adopted a popular data interchange format being JSON, with a few string tags reserved for basic data types, such as *num, enum* and *str*. In order to map the retrieved user profiles to the given model, we also require a set of rules for structure matching and conflict resolution. The overall consolidation process has four steps, being enrich, match, merge and resolve, and is illustrated in Figure 3. The enrich step mainly introduces synonyms to the field names. Then, the match step maps the attributes of the enriched profiles to the enriched model, while applying structure matching rules. Profile attributes that are not met in the model are discarded, while model attributes not met in profiles are left empty. The outcome of this step is instances of the input profile model. The next step is merging, where a single user profile is produced by aggregating all profile instances. Finally, the resolve step applies conflict resolution rules on attribute values of the consolidated profile.

Enriching Profiles

As mentioned earlier, the retrieved profiles may use different names for essentially the same user attributes. For

Table 1: The grammar for structure rules and examples

S   → *(Name Rule+)+*
Rule   → *ItemList '.' Name | Name*
ItemList → *ItemList '.' Item | Item*
Item   → *Name |* '*' *|* '?' *|* '[' *Name* ']' *| Nums*
Name   → **ident | quoted_string**
Nums   → **number** *| Range*
Range   → '(' *Border* '..' *Border* ')'
Border   → **number** *| ε*

Examples:

```
height
      height
      personal.*.height
      "personal info".*.height
"home address"
      address
      home.*.address
      *.family.*.address
"color blind"
      abilities.*."color blind"
      personal.*."color blind"
```

instance, the attribute relating to *address* may be named as "address", "location", "home" etc., with variations in case sensitivity. Therefore, we utilize a thesaurus service, which will produce a list of synonyms for attribute names. Many of such services are freely available online, e.g. at *thesaurus.altervista.org*. The idea is to enrich the attribute names in the input profile model and in the retrieved profiles with their synonyms, resulting into multi-named attributes. Figure 3 illustrates this process on the left part, where the profile model and the retrieved profiles are enriched to contain extra names (shown in blue typeface). Adaptive systems may substitute the thesaurus service, as well as the whole enrichment process by explicitly supplying custom JavaScript code to carry out these tasks.

Matching Attributes

This step compares every enriched profile with the enriched model to find multi-name attributes matching in at least one of their names. Any profile attribute with no respective attribute matching in the model is discarded, while the rest are selected as potential matches meaning they probably map to a model attribute.

To confirm a match, the attribute paths between the profile and the model should also match, since even attributes with identical names can have different semantics across profiles. For instance, attribute *name* under a *personal-info* node is completely different from the same attribute under a *pet-info* node. The path of an attribute in its profile is denoted via dotted names, e.g. *personal-info.name* is *name* attribute inside parent attribute *personal-info*. In this context, we have designed a grammar to define alternative acceptable paths for the profile model attributes. Such definitions are called *structure rules*, and they are optional. If no structure rules are applied our system only seeks for exact matching of attribute paths.

Structure rules are textual contain multiple *<attribute, rules>* definitions. Table 1 depicts the grammar and provides a few examples: The first one regards the model attribute *height*, and associates it with three rules; the first rule matches the height attribute when found as top-level, while the next two rules match it when found in any depth inside the subtree descending of a top-level node named *personal* and *personal info* respectively. The second example displays similar rules for the attribute *home address*. Here, the third rule indicates that it can be matched to any attribute named *address* as long as it is descendant of a node *family*, found anywhere in the profile.

Structure rules are applied on top of the enriched profiles, meaning that we match all names of an attribute found in a rule path. If, using structure rules, a profile attribute matches the profile model, we take the attribute value from the profile and add the respective attribute in the profile instance. Once the matching process finishes, we have one profile instance for each profile retrieved from the providers, all complying with the input profile model.

Figure 3 shows the input and output of the matching procedure. The matching step can be substituted with a custom implementation in JavaScript.

Merging Profile Instances and Resolving Conflicts

In this step, all profile instances have to be merged together. This is straightforward since all instances have the same attribute names and follow the same structure. All the values of the same attributes across profile instances are collected, resulting into multi-value attributes (see Figure 3, merged profile). Sometimes, the values of the same attribute across different profile instances can be in different domains. For example, for the attribute *height*, some profiles may define it as a numeric value measured in *cm*, while others may carry enumerated values (e.g. *short*, *average*, *tall*). To effectively collect such diverse attribute values and allow the profile model to encompass all of them, we support multiple-type attributes as part of the profile model. This is an important extension which enables the addressing of such scenarios of attribute domain variations which are common in profiles coming from different providers. Adaptive systems are able to define multi-type attributes in their profile models if they can handle them. We provide a grammar through which attribute types are expressed in the input models, illustrated in Table 2 (to part, *ATypes* non-terminal).

The conflict resolution step aims to eliminate multi-values of attributes with filtering rules, while also preserving the types defined in the profile model. In case multiple values

Table 2: (i) attribute types; (ii) conflict resolution rules

ATypes → *Type* [',' *Type*]*
Type → '**num**' *OptTag* | '**bool**' | '**str**' *OptTag* | *Enum* | '**str_list**'
Enum → '**enum**' '{' **string** [',' **string**]* '}'
OptTag → ε | ':' (*Enum* | **string**)

CRules → ([*Attr*] *Type Res*)*
Attr → **ident** ['.' **ident**] *
Res → **avg** | **vote** | **union** | **max** | **min** | **recent** | **script string**

are identical and already match the type defined in the input model, resolution is trivial. For example, for the values of *age* attribute being {20, 20, 20} with type ***num*** in the input model, the user age in the consolidated profile is {20}. Thus conflicts occur when for an attribute there is variation with respect to their *value* (e.g. age: {10, 10, 12}), *type* (e.g. number or enumerated) or the optional *tag* (see Table 2, *CRules* non-terminal).

To resolve tag conflicts, we offer the *script* policy, with a JavaScript source text supplying a custom conflict resolution function. The latter is usable for cases like *height* attribute with *cm* or *ft* tags, or for *date* formatted as *dd/mm/yy* or *mm-dd-yy*, and all other cases with such alternative value formats. Table 2 contains the grammar for describing such rules. We allow adaptive systems to provide the resolution policies for their profile model since

resolution is applied on the profile domain. If the attribute name is not provided, generic rules are defined for all values of the same type. The *Type* parameter refers to the attribute's acceptable types while *Res* selects the actual policy from a list of alternatives. To give an example of their usage, consider the following rules:

age **num average**
age **enum vote**

And the model:

age: **num, enum{child, teen, adult}**

If the values met across the profiles are:

age **{10, 20, teen, teen, adult }**

Then the numeric values are averaged and the enumerated ones use a voting scheme (2 *teen* votes against 1 *adult* vote), leading to the following consolidated profile:

age: **[num: 15, enum{teen}]**

RELATED WORK

Although a lot of research has been presented for matching user profiles across several networks, little work has focused on merging these profiles to reflect any given model. Most authors propose the use of common models among profile providers and consumers. In the context of semantic web, the FOAF (Friend of a friend) ontology has been proposed for describing persons, their activities and their relationships to other people in a uniform manner. Although it is a relatively simple use-case and standard, FOAF has had limited adoption on the web [1]. Golbeck and Rothstein in [2] used FOAF along with Semantic Web Reasoning techniques to show that a significant percentage of profiles found in social networks, belong to the same users, and thus can be merged. To identify such profiles, they describe them using the FOAF:person class and use the Inverse Functional Property (IFP), which connects an instance to a unique identifier. Raad et al. [3] follow a different approach by providing a suitable matching framework able to consider all the user profile's attributes. In their work, profiles are also described in FOAF; however users can tag some attributes as more important and assign a different similarity measure to each of them for resolving possible conflicts. Orlandi et al. describe their methodology in [4] for extracting, aggregating and representing user profiles, focusing on user interests. Firstly they create application-dependent profiles from information retrieved from social networks, then they transform these profiles into FOAF ones and finally they merge them while giving higher weight to recurring interests found. A more recent work, presented by Veen [5] gathers all the user information from social networks, compares it to detect differences and propose a solution for every detected inconsistency. Moreover, standard formats are used to translate properties gathered from several networks. Authors still need to find a method for comparing profile attributes for detecting similarities (e.g. word, Word and work all differ by one letter, however the latter is irrelevant to the former two). Virtual User Modelling and Simulation Standardisation project cluster [6] proposes that the lack of common definitions makes different user models incompatible to each other and define a common vocabulary to avoid confusion among relative terms and user characteristics. Bettini and Riboni in [7] present a patent-pending approach for merging generic user and context profiles retrieved from users, network providers and operator providers to adapt internet services. In contrast to the aforementioned approaches, user profiles are provided explicitly and conflicts are resolved based on priorities given by the developers.

DISCUSSION

Gandalf is being developed as part of an ongoing research on user interface adaptivity using distributed user profiles. Common models previously suggested in the literature seem to be a pretty good solution when comes to consolidating and merging multiple user profiles. However, we are not sure that a single user model can cover the needs of *every* future adaptive system. A lot of different user models have already been proposed across applications, indicating that a standardized profile model cannot cover all application demands. In this vain, we proposed a system that receives as input the adaptive application's model, collects user profiles from different distributed providers, matches them to the input profile model and merges them into a single user profile reflecting this model. To this end, our system needs to be aware of some of the model semantics, and be able to apply the provided structure and conflict resolution rules.

This poses the limit for client adaptive applications to use the JSON format along with the textual keywords we provide to define their models, and use the provided grammars for defining the structure rules and the conflict resolution rules. These inevitable limitations are relatively small compared to using a single common model. However they may be a problem for adaptive applications whose models cannot be covered by our propositions or need different consolidation algorithms to be applied to the retrieved profiles. In these cases, our system features (i) an optional preprocessing step over the retrieved profiles before the consolidation procedure starts, (ii) substitution of any or all of the four stages of the consolidation process with custom components provided by the client adaptive system and (iii) an optional post-processing step over the final consolidated profile to enable fine-tuning of the output profile. The proposed idea can also be applied for context profiles, where location services, network providers, user devices and several sensors can be utilized as providers.

SUMMARY AND CONCLUSIONS

We have discussed the Gandalf system for retrieving multiple user profiles from existing providers and consolidating them into a single profile that matches a given model. The innovation of this work is that no standardized profile model is defined. Instead, we use the input model as a reference point for matching and merging all the others. The consolidation process is highly configurable via a set of structure matching and conflict resolution rules provided along with the model, defined by adaptive systems following their needs. Using a thesaurus service and a set of structure matching rules, we essentially map the retrieved profiles to the input profile model thus producing profile model instances. Next, we merge all them into a single user profile and use the conflict resolution rules to produce the final consolidated profile. We allow the overall consolidation process or any of its steps to be substituted by custom JavaScript components supplied by the client adaptive systems. Our approach is more generic and flexible than many existing propositions, since, it is the first system not relying on a standardized user model to achieve consolidation of multiple profiles. An initial prototype of the proposed system has been implemented, utilizing Facebook, LinkedIn and Google+ as profile providers. Once completed, it will be delivered as a web service, enabling adaptive applications to use it. We consider that our work will allow future adaptive systems exploit the available user-profile online assets, thus leading to better adaptation decisions.

ACKNOWLEDGMENTS

We thank Eleytherios Benisis, undergraduate student at the Computer Science Department of the University of Crete, for his contribution in the implementation of this work.

REFERENCES

1. http://en.wikipedia.org/wiki/FOAF_(ontology)

2. Golbeck, J., & Rothstein, M. Linking social networks on the web with FOAF: a semantic web case study. In AAAI'08 (pp. 1138–1143). AAAI Press (2008).

3. Raad, E., Chbeir, R., & Dipanda, A. User Profile Matching in Social Networks. In NBiS'10 pp. 297–304, (2010)

4. Orlandi, F., Breslin, J., & Passant, A. Aggregated, interoperable and multi-domain user profiles for the social web. SEMANTICS '12 p. 41 (2012).

5. Veen, H. van der. Merging User Profiles on Social Networks. 18th Twente Student Conference on IT January 25th, (2013)

6. Kaklanis, N, et al. An Interoperable and Inclusive User Modelling concept for Simulation and Adaptation. In Proceedings of the 20th UMAP (2012).

7. Bettini, C., & Riboni, D. Profile aggregation and policy evaluation for adaptive internet services. In MOBIQUITOUS 2004, pp. 290–298 (2014)

8. F. Abel, N. Henze, E. Herder, and D. Krause. Interweaving Public User Profiles on the Web. In User Modeling, Adaptation, and Personalization (2010)

Formal Modelling of Dynamic Instantiation of Input Devices and Interaction Techniques: Application to Multi-Touch Interactions

**Arnaud Hamon[1,2], Philippe Palanque[2], Martin Cronel[2], Raphaël André[1],
Eric Barboni[2], David Navarre[2]**

[1] AIRBUS Operations, 316 Route de Bayonne, 31060, Toulouse, France
[2] ICS-IRIT, University of Toulouse, 118 Route de Narbonne, F-31062, Toulouse, France
(hamon, palanque, silva, barboni)@ irit.fr, raphael.andre@airbus.com

ABSTRACT

Representing the behavior of multi-touch interactive systems in a complete, concise and non-ambiguous way is still a challenge for formal description techniques. Indeed, multi-touch interactive systems embed specific constraints that are either cumbersome or impossible to capture with classical formal description techniques. This is due to both the idiosyncratic nature of multi-touch technology (e.g. the fact that each finger represent an input device and that gestures are directly performed on the surface without an additional instrument) and the high dynamicity of interactions usually encountered in this kind of systems. This paper presents a formal description technique able to model multi-touch interactive systems. We focus the presentation on how to represent the dynamic instantiation of input devices (i.e. finger) and how they can then be exploited dynamically to offer a multiplicity of interaction techniques which are also dynamically instantiated.

Author Keywords

Multi-touch interactions, model-based approaches, formal description techniques

ACM Classification Keywords

D.2.2 [Software] Design Tools and Techniques - Computer-aided software engineering (CASE), H.5.2 [Information Interfaces]: User Interfaces - Interaction styles.

INTRODUCTION

Over the last decade the field of interactive systems engineering had to face multiple challenges at a pace never encountered before. Indeed, while new interaction techniques have been proposed on a regular basis by the research community (e.g. multimodal gesture+voice interactions by R. Bolt in [5], post-WIMP interactions such as [4] etc.) recent years have seen the adoption and deployment of such interaction techniques in many different types of systems. Together with this evolution of interaction techniques, the appearance and adoption of new input devices is also a significant change with respect to the past. Indeed, mass market computers remained for nearly 20 years equipped with standard mouse and keyboard while nowadays, one interacts with more sophisticated input devices such as multi-touch surfaces, Kinect, Wiimote, …

However, these new input devices and their associated interaction techniques have significantly increased the complexity the development of interactive systems. For instance, multimodal interaction techniques are now common both as input and output modalities. One of the most challenging examples is the one of multi-touch systems[1]. Indeed, even though some studies [4] show that they improve the bandwidth between the users and the system, they bring specific challenges such as handling dynamic management of input devices (the fingers) and their associated interaction techniques (including fusion and fission of input (e.g. input fusion for a pinch) as well as fusion and fission of rendering (e.g. output fusion for fingers clustering)).

This paper presents a formal description technique able to describe in a complete and unambiguous way the behavior of multi-touch systems. As it consists in extensions of previous work [9], we make explicit the changes that have been made to the ICO notation. We present the basic constructs of the extensions and how they can be applied on a simple example making particularly explicit how dynamic management of both input devices and interaction techniques are accounted for. This paper addresses more specifically multi-touch input devices and interaction techniques but the concepts are applicable to any interactive system where input devices are connected and disconnected at runtime and requiring reconfiguration of interaction techniques.

---

[1] We use in this paper multi-touch systems as a shortcut for interactive systems offering multi-touch interactions

MODELLING CHALLENGES DUE TO DYNAMIC ASPECTS OF MULTITOUCH SYSTEMS

In classical interactive systems, the set of input and output devices are identified at design time and the interaction techniques to be used for interacting with the application are based on this predefined set and also defined beforehand [3]. Multi-touch systems challenge this by requiring the capacity for handling input devices (i.e. fingers) that may appear and disappear dynamically while the interaction takes place.

In such context, when the interactive system is started input devices arc not present and thus not identified. Users' fingers are considered as input devices and are only detected as they touch (or get close enough to) the tactile surface. The input devices (fingers) detected at execution time need to be dynamically instantiated in order to be registered and listened to. While this can be easily managed using programming languages, such aspect is usually not addressed by modelling techniques as highlighted in the related work section (next section). While model-based approaches provide well identified benefits such as abstract description, possible reasoning about models, complete and unambiguous descriptions, in order to deal with multi-touch systems they have to address the following challenges:

→ Describe the dynamic management of input devices. This includes the description (inside models) of dynamic creation (instantiation) of input devices and the description of how many of them are present at any time. This management also requires the removal of the devices from the models when they are freed;

→ Make explicit in the models the connection between the hardware (input devices) and their software counterpart (i.e. device drivers and transducers as introduced in [6] and formalized in [1]);

→ Describe the set of states, the events produced and the event consumed by the device drivers and the transducers;

→ Describe the interaction techniques that have to handle references to dynamically instantiated models related to the input devices (drivers and transducers);

→ Describe how interaction techniques behavior evolves according to the addition and removal of input devices. Such capability is extremely demanding on the specification techniques requiring dynamic management of interaction techniques as demonstrated in [14].

→ Described fusion and fission of input and output within the interaction technique. Indeed, the use of multiple input devices (fingers) makes it possible for interaction designers to define very sophisticated interaction techniques making use of several fingers grouped together for instance. Such grouping requires fusions of events from the groups of fingers but also the fusion of output information to provide feedback to the users about the current state of recognition of the interaction.

For example, interaction techniques featuring a group of two fingers will require modifying the initial rendering of each finger's graphical feedback as in Figure 1-b). Figure 1-a) presents a graphical feedback of three fingers on a multi-touch application.

These challenges go beyond the ones brought by multimodal interactions identified in [13].

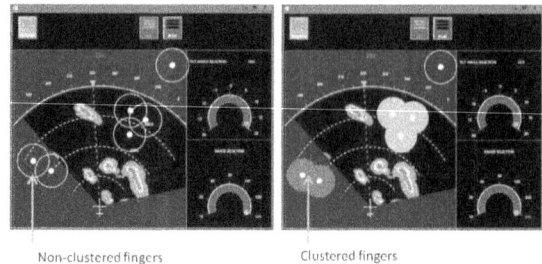

Non-clustered fingers   Clustered fingers

Figure 1- a) (left) 3 input device detected; b) (right) output of the clustering of two input devices (merged disks bottom left)

RELATED WORK

This section provides a succinct overview of the related work in the area of modelling techniques for multi-touch interactions. Table 1 summarizes this related work, structuring the comparison according to the criteria (represented as lines in the table) detailed below.

The first three characteristics deal with description of information in the models including namely "Data", "State", and "Events". There is no specific constraint related to multi-touch systems. Concurrent behavior representation is critical for multi-touch interactions due to the concurrent use of multiple fingers and hands this is why all the notations listed address this characteristic.

Time

Quantitative time between two consecutive model elements represents behavioral temporal evolutions related to a given amount of time (usually expressed in milliseconds). This is necessary for the modeling of the temporal windows in a fusion engine for multimodal interfaces, where events from several input devices are fused only if they are produced within a same time frame. Quantitative time over nonconsecutive elements was introduced in [18] for multi-mice double and fusion double click interactions.

Dynamic instantiation

As explained in the list of challenges in previous section, dynamic instantiation is a corner stone for modeling techniques for multi-touch interactions. Three types of dynamic instantiation have been identified, but only the last two ones are idiosyncratic to multi-touch interactions. In the multi-touch context, new fingers are detected during at execution time. Thus, the description language must be able to receive dynamically created objects. Supporting explicit representation of dynamic instantiation requires the description technique to be able to explicitly represent an unbounded number of states, as the newly created objects will by definition represent a new state for the system. Most of the time, this characteristic is handled by means of code and remains outside the description technique. In Petri nets [8] this is particularly easy to represent by the creation/destruction of tokens associated to the objects. This way, for instance, for each finger currently touching the multi-touch surface, a corresponding token will be set in a place of the Petri net.

Dynamicity has also to be addressed at operation time in order to cope with potential hardware failure reconfigurations of the interaction techniques might be required [14]. This requires a meta-level representation of interactions which can be dynamically selected at run-time. This is an important aspect to address if multi-touch interactions and is presented in a static way in [19].

Multimodality

These rows refer to the capability of a language to support the fusion and fission of several distinct modalities such as the combination of pen and multi-touch in [7]. Fusion engines have been a focal point of the research in the area of multimodal interactions and they are of prime importance as far as multi-touch interactions are concerned. Multi-touch interactions are by nature multi-modal and their design requires at least the same expressive power as the one of multimodal one (see [13] for a survey on these aspects).

		ConstraintJS [17]	GeForMT [10]	Gest It [14]	Proton++ [11]	ICO [c]
Data						
States						
Events						
Time	Quantitative between two consecutive model elements					
	Quantitative over non consecutive elements					
	Concurrent Behaviors					
Dynamic Instantiation	Widgets					
	Input devices					
	Reconfiguration of Interaction technique					
Multimodality: fusion of several input modalities						
Multimodality: fusion of several output modalities						

Yes   Partly   Code   No

Table 1 - Partial comparison of UIDLs

For all characteristics in Table 1, there are four possible values.

- **Yes** means that the characteristic is explicitly handled by the multi-touch description technique;
- **No** means that the characteristic is not explicitly handled (at least in the referred article);
- **Partly** means that the characteristic is not completely explicit;
- **Code** means that the characteristic is made explicit but only at the code level and is thus not a construct of the description language.

The notations referenced in Table 1 are not formal. We chose to highlight the fact that event non-formal notations, which are supposed to have a higher expressive power, do not handle dynamic instantiation for example.

THE EXTENDED ICO NOTATION

Based on the study of the related work and the dimensions described in [9], only the ICO notation allows the explicit modelling of all the multi-touch characteristics. However, extensive modelling of multi-touch systems has demonstrated the need for modifying the ICO notation in order to provide primitives for handling specificities of multi-touch systems. It is important to note that these primitives do not constitute extensions to the expressive power of ICOs but bring the formal description technique closer to what is needed to model multi-touch systems. This is why the proposed extensions contribute beyond ICOs as such extensions could be added to other notations, provided their expressive power is sufficient for modeling multi-touch systems.

Introduction

The ICO notation (Interactive Cooperative Objects) is a formal description technique devoted to specify interactive systems. Using high-level Petri nets [8] for dynamic behavior description, the notation also relies on object-oriented approach (dynamic instantiation, classification, encapsulation, inheritance and client/server relationships) to describe the structural or static aspects of systems. ICO notation objects are composed of four components: a cooperative object for the behavior description, a presentation part (i.e. Graphical Interface), and two functions (activation and rendering) describing the links between the cooperative object and the presentation part.

ICOs have been used for various types of multi-modal interfaces [12] and in particular for multi-touch [9]. This notation is also currently applied for formal specification in the fields of Air Traffic Control interactive applications [16], space command and control ground systems [19], or interactive military [2] or civil cockpits [1].

Informal description of dynamic instantiation

ICOs, due to their Petri nets underpinning, are particularly efficient to create and destroy elements when they are represented as tokens. As ICOs' tokens refer to objects or other ICOs, it is possible to use such high-level tokens to represent input devices such as fingers on a touchscreen. Such tokens refer to other ICO models describing the detailed behavior of the input device. For instance, Figure 3 presents the behavior of a finger both in terms of states (values for position, pressure, etc.) and events (e.g. update corresponding to move events).

The ICO model in Figure 2 describes how new input devices are instantiated and stored in a manager. The top-left transition in Figure 2 illustrates how new input devices can be added to an ICO model with the creation of a model of finger type (instruction finger=create Finger(touchinfo)). The newly created reference is then stored in a waiting place (called ToAddFinger) in order to be connected to an interaction technique in charge of handling the events that will be produced by the new device.

Handling events from dynamically instantiated sources

An ICO model may act as an event handler for events emitted by other models or java instances. The detailed description of these mechanisms is available in [20]. In addition, the different transition blocks of Figure 2 (top-left transition) are presented in Table 2.

Block	Field Name	Field Description
1: Name block	name	unique name, not necessary linked to the eventName
2 : Precondition block	precondition	boolean expression independent form the event but depending on marking
3 : Event block	eventName	name of the event the transition is linked to
	eventSource	the source of the event received
	eventParameters	The collection of the parameters of the received event
	eventCondition	boolean expression based on the eventParameters' values used for the firing
4 : Action block	action	an action

Table 2- Properties of the generic event transition

Formal description

Due to space constraints, the formal definition of the extensions are not given there but its denotational semantics is given in terms of "standard" ICOs as defined in [16].

DEMONSTRATING HANDLING OF INPUT DEVICES: AN SIMPLE EXAMPLE USING ICOS

This paragraph describes the ICO models used for the example presented Figure 1-b which handles dynamically referenced input devices.

Low-level transducer description

The model presented in Figure 2 is called a transducer as it is located (in terms of software architecture) in between the hardware devices and the interaction techniques. There could be a chain of such models handling events from the lower level (raw events or data from the hardware input devices) to high-level events as a double click (see [1] for more details on transducers).

The low-level transducer encapsulates the references towards the upper-level models of the handling mechanism such as FingerModels and the interaction technique ClusteringModel. The role of this low-level transducer is to forward events received from the hardware to low-level events in FingerModels (which model the fingers' behavior).

During the initialization, the low-level transducer instantiates the ClusteringModel through the createClustering transition and stores its reference in the ClusteringModel place. When the low-level transducer receives a "rawToucheventf_down" event from the hardware, the fingerInstantiation transition is fired, the event parameters (the touch id, and its other information's) are retrieved and used to dynamically instantiates a new instance of FingerModel. The addFingerToClustering transition then adds the FingerModel

reference to the cluster model. This is how the interaction technique is informed of the detection of new fingers. The low-level transducer then stores the reference of the FingerModel in the FingerPool place (which contains the list of all the detected fingers). When the transducer receives "rawToucheventf_update" (resp. "rawToucheventf_up") events from the hardware, the transition updatingFinger (resp. freeFinger) is then triggered and updates accordingly the proper FingerModel. These updates are provided using the communication mechanism of ICO services and not using events since the low-level transducer contains references toward the FingerModels and is able to send hardware events to the corresponding finger model.

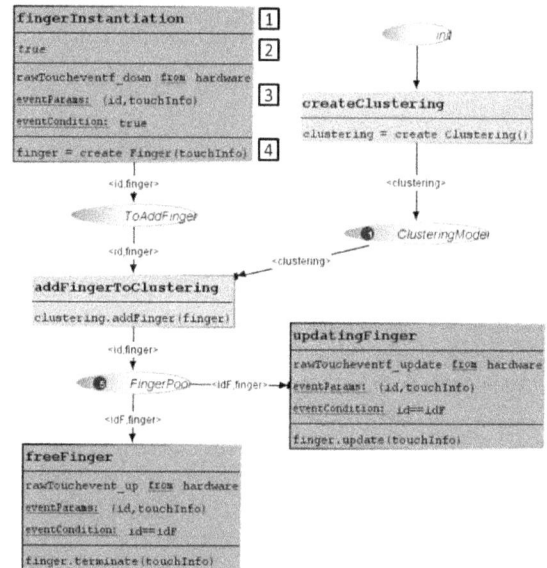

Figure 2 – Excerpt of the model of a low level transducer

Modelling touch fingers

Each time the low-level transducer receives an event corresponding to the detection of a finger on the hardware, it creates the model and links it with the interaction technique model(s). When the event received corresponds to an update of an already detected finger, the low-level transducer notified the corresponding finger model using the services "update". When the finger is removed from the hardware, the low-level transducer fires the transition freeFinger which destroys the corresponding FingerModel.

For readability purposes, the model presented in Figure 3 features a limited set of fingers properties: position and pressure. However, more complex finger models have been described offering various properties such as finger tilt angle, acceleration and direction of the movements.

Lastly, this finger model is an extensible model that can describe very complex behaviors. For example, if one needs to describe the behavior a finger input as in Proton++ [11], this can be done in a finger model as the one presented. Indeed this model specifies when the touch events are broadcasted and that such broadcasting can be controlled in order to match a sequential system sending user events every 30ms as in [11].

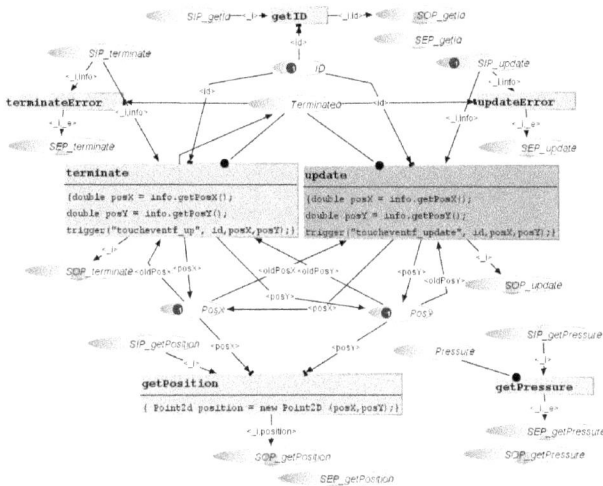

Figure 3 – Generic Model of Finger

Modelling the interaction technique "finger clustering"

This paragraph describes how the ICO notation handles interaction techniques including output fusion of information related to the reception of events produced by dynamically instantiated input devices (see Figure 4). In this example, the interaction technique model is in charge of pairing co-located input devices so they can be handled as a group of fingers. This corresponds to the interaction presented in Figure 1 where the right-hand side of the figure presents the rendering associated to the detection of a pair of fingers (bottom-left of the figure) while the other finger remains ungrouped. The model presented in Figure 4 is composed of a service (addFinger), two places (ListOfPairs storing the pairs of fingers and SingleFingersList storing the "single" fingers) and event-transitions to update the clustering according to the evolution of the position of fingers on the touchscreen. Each time a finger model is created (a new finger touches the screen), the low level transducer calls the "addFinger" service and a reference to a new finger model is set in place SingleFinger. When a finger from SingleFingerList (called finger1 for instance) moves close enough to another finger (e.g. finger2) in that place too, two cases are represented:

- finger2 is close enough of finger1 (condition in the event condition zone of transition cluster2Fingers is true) then transition cluster2Fingers is fired, finger1 and finger2 are removed from place SingleFingerList and a new token consisting of the pair (finger1, finger2) and their respective position is stored in place ListOfFingerPairs.

- finger2 is too far from finger1 (condition in the event condition zone of transition noClusterDetected is true) then that transition is fired and the new position of finger is updated.

When a pair is detected, the user interface should display graphically such dynamic grouping. This is defined by the rendering function associated to the interaction technique and

presented in Table 3. When two fingers are merged, the token referencing these two models are removed from SingleFingerList place which triggers the method hideFingerRendering for each model. This method hides the elementary rendering associated to each finger. When a pair is detected, both references are combined in a token added to place LisfOfFingerPairs which calls the method createPairedFingerRendering which displays the rendering associated to the two-finger cluster.

ObCS Node name	ObCS event	Rendering method
SingleFingerList	tokenAdded	showFingerRendering
SingleFingerList	tokenRemoved	hideFingerRendering
ListOfFingerPairs	tokenAdded	createPairedFingerRendering
ListOfFingerPairs	tokenRemoved	removePairedFingerRendering

Table 3 -Rendering functions of the interaction technique

It is important to note that output is thus connected to state changes in the models (which only occur when tokens are added to or removed from places) while input are event based and thus associated to transitions.

CONCLUSION

This paper has identified a set of challenges towards the production of complete and unambiguous specifications of multi-touch systems. The main issues deal with the dynamic instantiation of input devices and the dynamic reconfiguration of interaction techniques. We have highlighted the fact that such concerns have not previously encountered (at least at this large scale) when engineering interactive systems. This paper has presented a twofold way for addressing these issues:

- A layered software architecture made of communicating models which makes explicit a set of components and their inter-relations in order to address this dynamicity challenge;

- A formal description technique able to describe in a complete and unambiguous way such dynamic behaviors.

While the formal notation contribution is very specific to the work presented here, the layered architecture is independent from it and can be reused within any framework dealing with multi-touch interactions.

REFERENCES

1. Accot J., Chatty S., Maury S. & Palanque P. Formal Transducers: Models of Devices and Building Bricks for Highly Interactive Systems. DSVIS 1997, Springer Verlag, pp. 234-259.

2. Bastide R., Navarre D., Palanque P., Schyn A. & Dragicevic P. A Model-Based Approach for Real-Time Embedded Multimodal Systems in Military Aircrafts. Int. Conference on Multimodal Interfaces (ICMI'04), ACM DL, 10 pages.

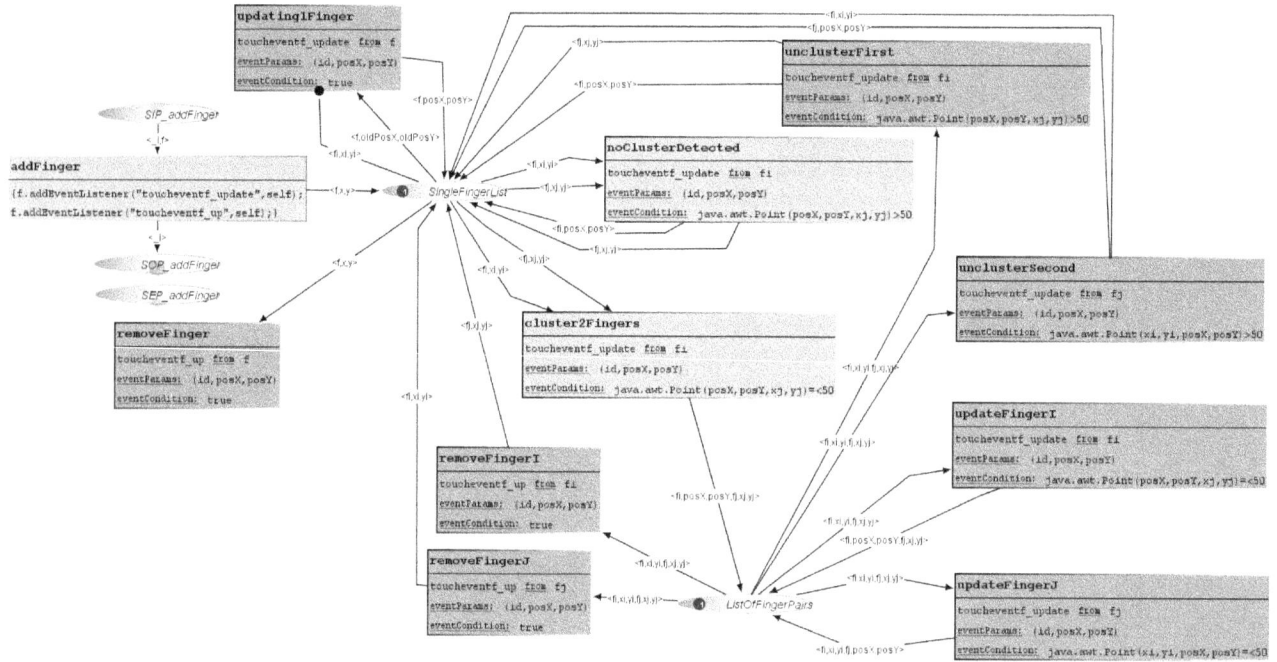

Figure 4 - Model of the interaction technique "finger clustering"

3. Bellik Y., Rebaï I., Machrouh E., Barzaj Y., Jacquet C., Pruvost G., Sansonnet J.-P.: Multimodal Interaction within Ambient Environments: An Exploratory Study. INTERACT (2) 2009: 89-92

4. Bi X., Grossman T., Matejka J., and Fitzmaurice G.: 2011. Magic desk: bringing multi-touch surfaces into desktop work. In Proceedings of the SIGCHI Conference on Human Factors in Computing Systems (CHI '11). ACM, New York, NY, USA, 2511-2520.

5. Bolt, R and Herranz, E. (1992). "Two-Handed Gesture in Multi-Modal Natural Dialog", Proceedings of the fifth annual ACM symposium on User interface software and technology, ACM Press, p 7-14

6. Buxton W. A three-state model of graphical input, IFIP TC 13 INTERACT'90, 1990, p. 449–456.

7. Frisch M., Heydekorn J., & Dachselt R. 2009. Investigating multi-touch and pen gestures for diagram editing on interactive surfaces. In Proc. of the ACM Int. Conf. on Interactive Tabletops and Surfaces (ITS '09). ACM, 149-156.

8. Genrich, H. J. 1991. Predicate/Transitions Nets. In High-Levels Petri Nets: Theory and Application. K. Jensen and G. Rozenberg, (Eds.), Springer Verlag (1991) pp. 3-43

9. Hamon A., Palanque P., Silva J-L., Deleris Y., & Barboni E. 2013. Formal description of multi-touch interactions.5th symp. on Engineering interactive computing systems (EICS '13). ACM, 207-216

10. Kammer D., Wojdziak J., Keck M., Groh R., & Taranko S. 2010. Towards a formalization of multi-touch gestures. ACM Int. Conf. on Interactive Tabletops and Surfaces (ITS '10)

11. Kenrick K., Björn H., DeRose T. & Maneesh A. 2012. Proton++: a customizable declarative multitouch framework. Proc. of ACM symposium on User interface software and technology (UIST '12). ACM, 477-486.

12. Ladry J-F., Navarre D., Palanque P. Formal description techniques to support the design, construction and evaluation of fusion engines for sure (safe, usable, reliable and evolvable) multimodal interfaces. ICMI 2009: 185-192

13. Lalanne D., Nigay L., Palanque P., Robinson P., Vanderdonckt J. & Ladry J-F. Fusion engines for multimodal input: a survey. ACM ICMI 2009: 153-160, ACM DL

14. Spano L-D., Cisternino A., Paternò F., Fenu G. GestIT: a declarative and compositional framework for multiplatform gesture definition. EICS 2013: 187-196

15. Navarre D., Palanque P, Basnyat S. A Formal Approach for User Interaction Reconfiguration of Safety Critical Interactive Systems. SAFECOMP 2008: 373-386

16. Navarre D., Palanque P., Ladry J-F. & Barboni E. ICOs: A model-based user interface description technique dedicated to interactive systems addressing usability, reliability and scalability. ACM Trans. Comput.-Hum. Interact., 16(4), 18:1–18:56. 2009

17. Oney S., Myers B., and Brandt J.. 2012. ConstraintJS: programming interactive behaviors for the web by integrating constraints and states. 25th ACM symp. on User interface software and technology (UIST '12). ACM, N-Y, 229-238.

18. Palanque P., Barboni E., Martinie De Almeida, Navarre D., Winckler M. A Tool Supported Model-based Approach for Engineering Usability Evaluation of Interaction Techniques. ACM (EICS 2011), Pisa, Italy.

19. Palanque P., Bernhaupt R., Navarre D., Ould M. & Winckler M. Supporting Usability Evaluation of Multimodal Man-Machine Interfaces for Space Ground Segment Applications Using Petri net Based Formal Specification. Ninth Int. Conference on Space Operations, Italy, June 18-22, 2006

20. Palanque P. & Schyn A. A Model-Based Approach for Engineering Multimodal Interactive Systems in INTERACT 2003, IFIP TC 13 conf. on HCI, 10 pages.

21. Songyang Lao, Xiangan Heng, Guohua Zhang, Yunxiang Ling, and Peng Wang. 2009. A gestural interaction design model for multi-touch displays. Proc. of the BCS HCI Conf. (BCS-HCI '09), 440-446

A Gestural Concrete User Interface in MARIA

Lucio Davide Spano
Department of Mathematics
and Computer Science,
University of Cagliari
Via Ospedale 72, 09124,
Cagliari, Italy
davide.spano@unica.it

Fabio Paternò
ISTI-CNR
Via G. Moruzzi 1
fabio.paterno@isti.cnr.it

Gianni Fenu
Department of Mathematics
and Computer Science,
University of Cagliari
Via Ospedale 72, 09124,
Cagliari, Italy
fenu@unica.it

ABSTRACT

In this paper, we describe a solution for engineering and modelling user interfaces for supporting input collected through gesture recognition hardware. We describe how we applied such approach by extending the MARIA UIDL, and how the modelling solution can be applied to other UI toolkits. In addition, we detail the model-to-code transformation for obtaining a running application through an example case study.

Author Keywords

Gestural interaction, Input and Interaction Technologies, Analysis Methods, Software architecture and engineering, User Interface design.

ACM Classification Keywords

H.5.m. Information Interfaces and Presentation (e.g. HCI): Miscellaneous

INTRODUCTION

Different gesture recognition devices are available on the market nowadays. They are more and more becoming popular not only in the entertaining field, but also for desktop applications (e.g. the Leap Motion or Microsoft Kinect). Most of the times, the interfaces exploiting such devices are created starting from different widget toolkits that do not support them natively. Developers are therefore required to create bridging code between UI toolkits and the libraries managing the input device. Such separation, while useful for reusing graphic controls also in gestural interfaces, forces developers to redefine functionalities that are usually supported by the underling toolkit, such as the pick correlation.

In this paper, we describe how we extended MARIA [9], a model-based user interface description language, in order to support gestural interaction, taking as starting point

the graphical desktop interface meta-model. We identified two problems shared with other UI toolkits: the implicit relationship between the pointing device and the pointer position and the lack of separation between the definition of gestures and their effects on the UI. We propose solutions to these problems, which can also be reused in other toolkits. In addition, we discuss a modelling technique for reusing the definition of platform-independent behaviour, which is useful for other modelling languages that exploit different abstraction levels in their definition.

RELATED WORK

The problem of a more effective integration of the gestures in both the design process and the structure of UI toolkits, has been addressed in [1]. They identified the different stakeholders involved in the design process and a set of extensions points for the currently available UI toolkits (in particular for pen-based interaction) applying an abstraction-level approach for modelling user interfaces, which is similar to the one we propose in this paper. They considered classifier-based gesture recognition, which is affected by a granularity problem: raising a single event when the gesture is completely recognized impedes the definition of intermediate feedback during the gesture performance.

In this paper, we consider a hierarchical modelling technique, which describes the gestures staring from a set of basic building blocks and creates complex ones, allowing intermediate feedback. Different work employ a similar representation with different formalisms like regular expressions [7, 6], Json [4] or Petri-Nets [3]. We adopted the approach described in [11, 12], which provides a description of gestures through the connection of ground terms related to the low-level events raised by the recognition devices, with a set of temporal operators defined through Petri-Nets and providing a set of compositional operators more expressive than regular expressions (see [12]). In this paper, we go beyond the gesture description, providing a solution for integrating it with the other aspects of existing UI toolkits.

Other approaches adopted in commercial UI toolkits, like e.g. the Kinect SDK, include a set of gestural widgets, containing a hard-coded gesture description, without any support for their composition (e.g. two gestures in sequence). In MARIA, the two aspects (graphic control and gesture definition) are completely decoupled.

BACKGROUND

MARIA [9] (Model-based lAnguage foR Interactive Applications) is a set of XML languages for defining UIs at different levels of abstractions, according to the CAMELEON [2] reference framework structure. The set includes an abstract language that has multiple refinements for the different interaction platform supported.

The Abstract User Interface (AUI) level describes a UI through the interaction semantics, without referring to a particular device capability, modality or implementation technology. In addition, the interface definition contains the behaviour and the description of the data types that are manipulated by the user interface. The data model is defined using the standard XML Schema Definition constructs.

A Concrete User Interface (CUI) in MARIA provides platform-dependent but implementation language independent details of a UI. A platform is a set of software and hardware interaction resources that characterize a given set of devices, such as desktop, mobile, vocal, multimodal etc. From the CUI different final user interfaces (FUI) can be derived and implemented with different technologies (e.g. web-based or standalone).

GESTURAL CONCRETE USER INTERFACE

In this section we describe the MARIA gestural CUI meta-model, providing a refinement of the AUI language and covering the modelling concepts needed by gestural interfaces. Conceptually, the meta-model should describe how the interface appears, how the user can provide input through the gesture-tracking device and how the interface reacts to such inputs. All these aspect are summarized by the following aspects:

1. The description of the interface layout
2. The description of the data provided by the device
3. The description of the gestures and the temporal relationships between them.
4. The description of the effects that the gestures have on the other parts of the interface.

The first point is related to the visual part of the gestural UI. Since MARIA already contains a desktop CUI definition (see [9] for additional details), we extended the graphic controls for supporting the gestural modality. This is a common starting point also for many UI toolkits: the definition of different graphic controls already exists, what is needed is the support for other input devices different from mouse and keyboard.

The second point covers the data received by the recognition device during the gesture performance. The data description needs to be independent from the actual programming language or development toolkit, a requirement for the compliance with the reference framework in [2].

The third point is related to the gesture description. We adopted the solution discussed in [11, 12], which allows describing gestures starting from a set of ground terms representing the device features (e.g. the joint position), which can be connected by means of different composition operators. This separates the gesture description from the UI behaviour, providing the possibility to reuse the gesture definition for different interfaces, and it can be adopted as solution also in other toolkits.

The forth point deals with two different aspects of the gestural UI model. The first one is how to model the visual feedback that the user has to receive during the gesture performance. The second aspect is the need to relate the definition of the UI behaviour at the abstract level and the recognition of the gestures at the concrete one in order to be compliant with the reification concept [2].

Interactors

The first problem for adapting the desktop interactors to the gestural modality is related to their selection mechanism. In all desktop toolkits, the user activates the interactors through a pointing device, whose movements are shown by the screen pointer. The mapping between the mouse position on the physical space and the pointer position on the screen space is not controlled by the UI developer. Instead, in a gestural interface, designers need to define such transformation. Indeed, it is possible to choose different ways for starting the interaction with a concrete UI object. For instance, we can provide a sequential navigation of the different objects represented on the screen through swipe gestures (a left-to-right swipe for selecting the next object and a right-to-left one for selecting the previous one) or the user may directly point with her hand the object to select.

When considering a gestural interaction, the usual selection process can be summarised as follows:

1. When the selection gesture is recognized (e.g. the swipe ends or the user points on object on the screen), the event-handler associated to the gesture recognition calculates which object has been selected through a pick correlation function.
2. After having identified the selected object, the application should provide feedback to the user. This can be done changing a visual property of the selected object (e.g. the border colour).
3. Finally, if the selected object has some behaviour associated to its selection, it must be executed.

All these steps are usually defined in the code activated by the gesture recognition, which is completely written by the application developer, without reusing any toolkit internal procedures such as the pick correlation, the event tunnelling or bubbling.

In MARIA, we extended the definition of the *Interactor Composition* elements (which represent groups of interactors) for easing the definition of such selection pattern: we exposed a property called *focusPoint* for specifying the pointing position. When the coordinates of a focus point are changed at runtime, the composition is responsible for the pick-correlation, either selecting a contained interactor or forwarding the notification to the nested compositions. With this protocol, the designer is no more in charge of defining the pick correlation between the point and the interactors, but it is possible to model different strategies for the interactor selection with the gestural modality.

It is worth pointing out that the same solution can be applied to UI toolkits and models different from MARIA, extending container elements (e.g. panels, windows etc.) with a focus point property, and to reuse their pick correlation algorithm, which has been already defined for reacting to mouse events.

Modelling device data

The device data modelling depends on the abstraction provided by the specific gesture tracking hardware. For instance, if we consider a multitouch screen, the device data can be modelled with the array of the 2D position of the on- screen touches (usually from 5 to 10).

If the device is able to track the entire skeleton (e.g. MS Kinect), the device data can be modelled with a structure containing the collection of the skeleton joint positions (a 3D point) and the joint orientation (a 3D vector). One instance of this data structure is available for each tracked user. It is possible to model similarly other tracking devices such as the Leap Motion, which provides the position and the orientation of the fingers, together with the orientation of the palm. The remote-based devices can be modelled through their position and orientation in the 3D space. Such data can be referenced in both event handlers and the modelling of the recognition constraints (detailed in the following section).

The changes on the device state are notified following the observer pattern (e.g. multitouch screens) or through streams returning frames at regular intervals (e.g. Kinect). Usually it is not sufficient to consider the current device state for modelling gestures, but we need to calculate differences between the current values and those received at previous notifications or frames. Our data representation contains also a history of the device state during the recognition. The runtime implementation of the model cannot obviously maintain the whole history, but it should maintain only the part that is necessary for the considered gesture model.

Gestures definition

In MARIA, at the AUI level the dialog model already contains elements for expressing the dynamic behaviour of a presentation. It defines the expected sequence (or sequences) of actions that are supported by the interface. We consider the temporal evolution of a gesture as a concrete example of such dialog model. Figure 1 shows the UML class diagram for the gesture model. At the AUI level, the *DialogModel* is associated to a *Presentation* and consists of different *DialogExpressions*. The *GestureExpression* refines such definition at the CUI level, introducing the modelling elements for the gestural interaction. In order to describe the temporal evolution

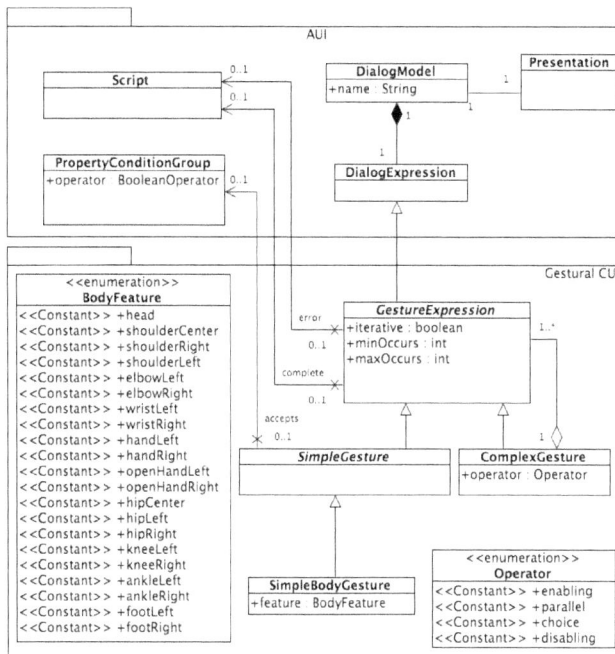

Figure 1. Full-body gesture model

of a gesture, we applied the composite pattern [5]: the gesture description starts from a set of *SimpleGestures* that can be composed in *ComplexGestures*.

A simple gesture recognises a change on a value that is tracked by the recognition device. Figure 1 shows its refinement for the values tracked by a full-body tracking device (e.g. MS Kinect), represented by the *BodyFeature* enumeration. Other devices can be added providing further refinements of the *SimpleGesture* class. In addition, the *SimpleGesture* instances may specify some constraints on such data change for e.g. calculating trajectories. In MARIA this is possible through the instances of the *PropertyConditionGroup* class, which represent Boolean predicates on i) the value of an interactor attribute, ii) the value of a data model element or iii) the result of the execution of an *ExternalFunction*, a functionality that is external to the definition of the UI model, such as a data source or a web service. The latter modelling element allows the reuse of the same predicate across different definitions. *ComplexGestures* are obtained connecting recursively other sub-gestures (either simple or complex) through a set of composition operators, the same used for modelling tasks in CTT [8].

In other UI toolkits it is possible to apply the same modelling solution by organizing the interface definition structure. The code that is responsible for recognizing the gesture must be separated from the code defining the UI behaviour. The simplest way is to use two different classes and to connect them using the observer pattern [5], notifying both the recognition success and error. In addition, there must be a composition mechanism for combining different gesture descriptions (e.g. a composite pattern [5]), specifying different relationships among the composed elements. The description model may be different from the one we propose in this paper and it may be more or less expressive, but the proposed approach allows isolating this aspect, with the advantage that possible changes in the description model (or even meta-model) would not affect the other UI parts (e.g. the behaviour).

Gesture effects

The hierarchical definition of the gesture model can be exploited in order to attach the UI behaviour to the entire gesture model and/or each one of its subparts, providing feedback not only at the end but also *during* the gesture performance. The UI can react to both the successful and the unsuccessful recognition. In this way, it is possible to define a "rollback" procedure for partially recognized gestures, which restores the UI state. This approach can lead to conflicts between different UI reactions when two different gestures in choice start with the same prefix. This is known as the selection ambiguity problem, and it has been discussed in [12].

In MARIA, the dynamic changes to the UI and to the data model state are defined through the *Script* class. It contains elements representing expressions and statements, which are able to define completely the UI behaviour at the abstract and/or the concrete level (see [9] for more information). In order to distinguish the behaviour associated to the successful recognition from the error management, we connected the generic *Gesture Expression* class with two instances of the *Script* class in Figure 1: the *complete* association defines the reaction to a successful recognition and *error* association defines how to recover a recognition failure.

In MARIA, the interface behaviour defined at the AUI level is inherited by concrete refinements. As we already discussed for the pick correlation problem, the designer may use different paradigms for both the interactor selection and activation. Therefore, the completion of a given gesture should be able not only to trigger the execution of some concrete-platform dependent behaviour, but also to activate the behaviour defined at the abstract level. The binding between the gestures and the abstract events cannot be derived implicitly as in the classical desktop interfaces, but the developer needs to define it explicitly. We rely on raising the abstract events inside the definition of the behaviour associated to a gesture expression in order to solve this problem. The meta-model contains the *Raise* element at the AUI level, which allows raising a specific event (either abstract or concrete) specifying the event name, the interactor identifier and the event arguments (if needed). Therefore, the schema for binding gestures to the abstract behaviour consists of the following steps: i) managing the changes that involve the concrete level (most of the times providing the intermediate feedback) and ii) raising the abstract event that the designer wants to trigger. We provide a modelling example for such binding with a sample application. This solution (including an explicit construct for redefining how the platform-independent behaviour can

be activated) can be employed also in other UI toolkits including an AUI level, in order to reuse the behaviour definition for different refinements.

Model to code transformation

A model to code transformation creates the FUI from a CUI definition, exploiting the following technologies:

- WPF as presentation layer
- C# for defining the application behaviour
- The GestIT library for gesture recognition [10, 12]
- The Kinect SDK for managing the sensing device.

The transformation process consists of two steps. The first one transforms the MARIA CUI mode into a XAML file, defining both the UI layout and the gesture description (GestIT provides the XAML tags for the gesture expression). The second step takes as input the same CUI and creates a C# file containing the definition of the application behaviour. Their combination defines the application completely, exploiting the C# partial class definition mechanism. Both transformations are defined using an XSLT, using plain text as output.

It is worth pointing out that the information regarding all the interface aspects (UI appearance and images, gestures and behaviour description) is contained in the CUI model. No other source is exploited for the generation.

SAMPLE APPLICATION

In this section we describe a sample gestural interface modelled in MARIA, a remote controller for a digital TV. The MARIAE tool supports the entire modelling process[1]. The application allows the user to watch a TV show, to change the current TV channel and to retrieve information on the program scheduling. It is organized as follows:

P1 The first presentation contains a video element for watching the TV show. It is connected with P2 through a hidden navigator, which can be activated through a wave gesture (using the greet the screen metaphor typical for Kinect applications).

P2 The second presentation contains two navigators: one pointing to the channel list and the other to the program schedule. The user points one of them with the open hand, and closes it for confirming the selection.

P3 The third presentation shows the channel list in a 3x3 grid. The user can select one element pointing at it and closing the hand or she can change the subset of visualized elements with a hand swipe from left to right (next 9 items) or from right to left (previous 9 items).

P4 The program schedule is shown using a tab container, including an element for each day of the week. The user can go back and forward among the tabs with a swipe gesture.

We start our discussion from the gesture description. In this interface we have three different gestures: wave (P1),

---

[1]The tool is available at http://giove.isti.cnr.it/tools/MARIAE/home

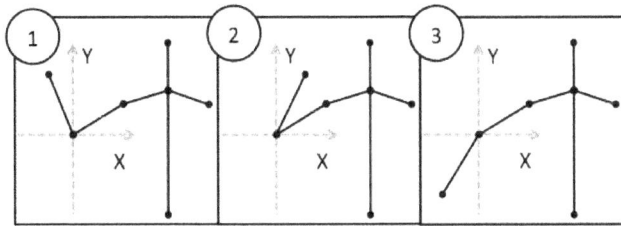

Figure 2. The wave gesture

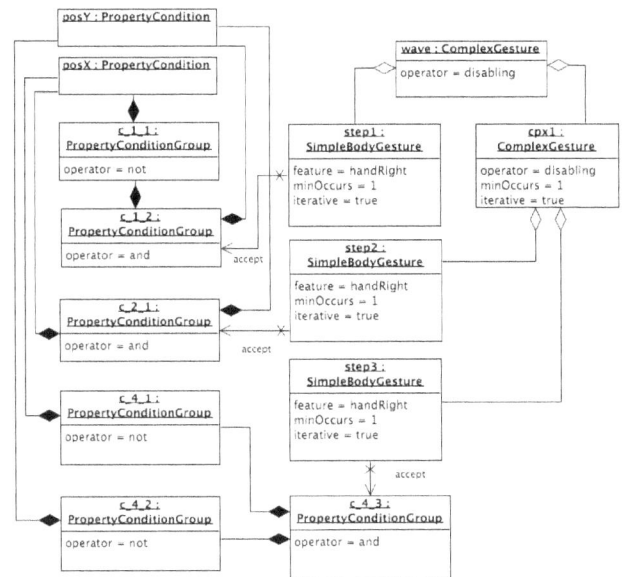

Figure 3. Wave gesture in MARIA

pointing (P2 and P3) and swipe (P3 and P4). Already in this simple example, the description of two gestures is referenced in more than one presentation. All gestures can be recognized tracking the position of the dominant hand. We assume here to be the right one (the definition for the left is symmetric).

The wave gesture can be defined considering three steps, visually represented in Figure 2. We set the origin of the coordinate system in the users elbow for simplicity in the description: the user starts her hand movement from the second quarter (positive Y and negative X values), then the hand goes in the first quarter (positive X and Y). This sequence must be performed at least once, but it can be repeated more than once. Eventually, the user lowers the hand (third quarter, negative X and Y).

In MARIA, we can model the wave gesture tracking the hand position, as defined in Figure 3. The three steps correspond to the *SimpleBodyGestures*, which differ for the hand positions they accept as valid (contained respectively in the second, first and third quarter of the coordinate system). Such conditions are defined by the accept property of each simple gesture, testing the positive sign of the x and y coordinates of the hand point (posX and posY instances). The conditions for the three steps are respectively $\overline{posX} \wedge posY$, $posX \wedge posY$ and $\overline{posX} \wedge \overline{posY}$. They are modelled by the *PropertyConditionGroup* instances in Figure 3.

The three simple gestures define each step in isolation. In order to define the entire gesture, we need to connect them through the composition operators, defining the *ComplexGesture* instance representing the wave gesture. During each step the hand moves iteratively (the iterative attribute in the *SimpleBodyGesture* instances) until it reaches a position valid for the next step, thus disabling the iteration. The first two steps must be recognized at least once, but they can be repeated an indefinite number of times (respectively the *minOccurs* and iterative attributes of the *cpx1* instance). The gesture is represented by the *wave* instance in Figure 3.

The other two gestures can be defined in a similar way. The pointing gesture consists of an iterative movement of the dominant hand, disabled by the hand closure. The swipe gesture simply consists in a rapid hand movement from left to right or from right to left. This can be modelled through an iterative movement of the dominant hand that maintaining a speed higher than a given threshold (defined in the *accept* property), which is disabled by a

hand movement below that speed. The UI behaviour can be attached to the *complete* and *error* properties of both simple and complex gestures, defining different instances of the *Script* class. In this way, it is possible to reuse the gesture definition in more than one presentation. For instance, the hand closure sub-component of the pointing gesture is associated with the function selection in P2 and with the channel selection in P3, while maintaining the same gesture definition. Since the same gesture can be used in different contexts, designers should include hints on the UI for helping the user in understanding which gestures are available and their effects. We analyse more in detail the definition of P3, in order to show a typical case where redefining the association between the screen pointer position and the physical device is needed. The interface for P3 is shown in Figure 4 (actually it is the result of the model-to-code transformation). The intermediate feedback (a blue border around the channel icon) is associated to the hand movement sub-component of the pointing gesture. The associated *Script* instance is responsible only to project the hand position in the device space on the screen plane (e.g. tracing a line), and to change the *focus point* property of the channel list grouping. The other operations (the pick correlation and the application of the focus styles to the selected element) are delegated to the grouping implementation, as usually happens for e.g. mouse hovering.

The last point we want to detail in this example is the mechanism for connecting the gesture effects and the behaviour inherited from the AUI level. The following actions can be defined at the abstract level in our application, since they are independent from the modality for triggering the interactor (e.g. mouse click, vocal command, gesture etc.) and their definition can be shared on different platforms:

P1 Navigation to P2
P2 Navigation to P3 or P4

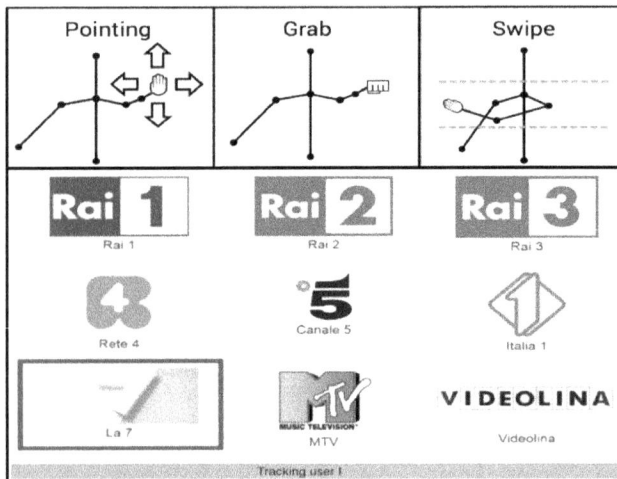

Figure 4. Channel selection interaction and presentation

P3 Changing the video stream (according to the selected channel) and going back to P1

P4 Navigation to P1

Considering the gestural modality, the user does not necessarily point an interactor before activating it: the activation may occur without a spatial correspondence between the gesture and the on screen representation of the interface. For instance, the wave gesture activates the navigation to P2, but the user does not select any link first. Therefore, in order to maintain the conformance to the different abstraction levels [2], we need to connect the completion of the wave gesture with the activation of the navigator between P1 and P2, inherited from the abstract level. In MARIA, this is possible through the *Raise* modelling element, which allows developers to explicitly request the UI runtime support to raise a specific event. In our case, the Script handling the completion of the wave gesture (specified in the complete property) contains a *Raise* element triggering the activation of the navigator between P1 and P2. After that, the UI support executes the event handler associated to the navigator, which has been defined at the abstract level.

CONCLUSION AND FUTURE WORK

n this paper we discussed a new Gestural Concrete User Interface we introduced in MARIA. Through the description of its meta-model, we identified a set of limitations that are common to different UI toolkits and we discussed the solutions we adopted in our modelling language, allowing the separation of four different aspects for defining a gestural UI (interface layout, device data, gesture description, gesture effects). Other modelling languages and toolkits, even with different formalisations of the different aspects, can adopt such organization. In addition, we reported on the model-to-code transformation and detailed the modelling approach through a concrete example.

In future work, we aim to extend the gestural CUI in order to support more interaction devices and to evaluate more in detail the expressiveness of the gesture description

model. In addition, we will enhance the tool support with a graphical notation for the gesture description, in order to study the impact of the proposed UI structuring on the design of real-world applications, providing a designer-centred evaluation of our modelling approach.

ACKNOWLEDGEMENTS
We gratefully acknowledge Sardinia Regional Government for the financial support (P.O.R. Sardegna F.S.E. Operational Programme of the Autonomous Region of Sardinia, European Social Fund 2007-2013 - Axis IV Human Resources, Objective l.3, Line of Activity l.3.1 "Avviso di chiamata per il finanziamento di Assegni di Ricerca".

REFERENCES
1. Beuvens, F., and Vanderdonckt, J. Designing Graphical User Interfaces Integrating Gestures. In *Proceedings of the 30th ACM International Conference on Design of Communication*, SIGDOC '12, ACM (New York, NY, USA, 2012), 313–322.
2. Calvary, G., Coutaz, J., Thevenin, D., Bouillon, L., Florins, M., Limbourg, Q., Souchon, N., Vanderdonckt, J., Marucci, L., Paternò, F., and Others. The CAMELEON reference framework. *Deliverable D 1* (2002).
3. Deshayes, R., Mens, T., and Palanque, P. A generic framework for executable gestural interaction models. In *Visual Languages and Human-Centric Computing (VL/HCC), 2013 IEEE Symposium on* (2013), 35–38.
4. Echtler, F., and Butz, A. GISpL: gestures made easy. In *Proceedings of the Sixth International Conference on Tangible, Embedded and Embodied Interaction*, TEI '12, ACM (New York, NY, USA, 2012), 233–240.
5. Gamma, E., Helm, R., Johnson, R., and Vlissides, J. *Design Patterns: Elements of Reusable Object-Oriented Software*. Addison-Wesley Professional Computing Series. Pearson Education, 1994.
6. Kin, K., Hartmann, B., DeRose, T., and Agrawala, M. Proton++ : A Customizable Declarative Multitouch Framework. In *Proceedings of the 25th annual ACM symposium on User interface software and technology (UIST 2012)*, ACM Press (Berkeley, California, USA, 2012), 477–486.
7. Kin, K., Hartmann, B., DeRose, T., and Agrawala, M. Proton: multitouch gestures as regular expressions. In *Proceedings of the 2012 ACM annual conference on Human Factors in Computing Systems (CHI 2012)*, ACM Press (Austin, Texas, USA, 2012), 2885–2894.
8. Paternò, F. *Model-based design and evaluation of interactive applications*. Springer Verlag, 2000.
9. Paternò, F., Santoro, C., and Spano, L. D. MARIA: A universal, declarative, multiple abstraction-level language for service-oriented applications in ubiquitous environments. *ACM Transaction on Computer Human Interaction 16*, 4 (2009), 19:1–19:30.
10. Spano, L. D. Developing Touchless Interfaces with GestIT. In *Ambient Intelligence*, F. Paternò, B. de Ruyter, P. Markopoulos, C. Santoro, E. van Loenen, and K. Luyten, Eds., vol. 7683 of *Lecture Notes in Computer Science*. Springer Berlin / Heidelberg, 2012, 433–438.
11. Spano, L. D., Cisternino, A., and Paternò, F. A Compositional Model for Gesture Definition. In *Proceedings of the 4th International Conference in Human-Centered Software Engineering (HCSE 2012)*, vol. 7623, LNCS, Springer (Tolouse, France, 2012), 34–52.
12. Spano, L. D., Cisternino, A., Paternò, F., and Fenu, G. Gestit: A declarative and compositional framework for multiplatform gesture definition. In *Proceedings of the 5th ACM SIGCHI Symposium on Engineering Interactive Computing Systems*, EICS '13, ACM (New York, NY, USA, 2013), 187–196.

Location Based Experience Design
for Mobile Augmented Reality

Anton Fedosov
Metaio GmbH
Hackerbrücke 6
Munich 80335 Germany
anton.fedosov@metaio.com

Stefan Misslinger
Metaio GmbH
Hackerbrücke 6
Munich 80335 Germany
stefan.misslinger@metaio.com

ABSTRACT

The main strength of Augmented Reality (AR) technology is the ability to immediately provide context in unfamiliar environments and experiences, representing digital virtual information that is associated with real world objects. AR has a proven record of commercial applications from tourism and entertainment industries to manufacturing and support services. In this work we are presenting a set of design decisions based on empirical observations for outdoor Augmented Reality. Present work led us to develop a consumer AR browser for mobile and wearable devices to be used in natural, uncontrolled settings.

Author Keywords

Point of interest; augmented reality; mobile; wearables; natural settings; information visualization.

ACM Classification Keywords

H.5.m. Information interfaces and presentation (e.g., HCI): Miscellaneous.

INTRODUCTION

Augmented Reality technology is a promising interactive paradigm to visualize information in real time in 3-D space [2]. Commercially available AR browsers present relevant location based information about world around us. Contemporary AR browsers present various points of interest (POI) – spatially registered virtual artifacts that describe in some way, and register to, an existing object [10]. There are several studies that elaborate on optimal layout of virtual annotations using image analysis [6] algorithms, dynamic adaptive representation [3], tackling the problem of visual clutter and information overload. Results, however, do not scale well in urban settings due to the substantial numbers, density and complexity of POI and their real world counterparts [8]. Additionally, ergonomic

EICS'14, June 17-20, 2014, Rome, Italy
ACM 978-1-4503-2725-1/14/06.
http://dx.doi.org/10.1145/2607023.2611449

factors such as device hand posture and sporadic nature of interaction with a personal mobile device or tablet have not been rigorously evaluated in the context of location based AR.

Our goal was to redesign the outdoor AR browser in such a way to encompass design considerations in Augmented Reality into seamless discovery and interaction experience with the world. We have taken a user-centered design approach, which consists of the four stages:

1. Need finding

2. Physical and conceptual design

3. Fast prototyping

4. Evaluation

Highly iterative design cycles helped us to prepare a new release of the Junaio application [7] that has accommodated the requirements of end-users. The application has been developed for smartphones and tablets and available for download through Apple App Store (iOS platform) and Google Play (Android platform). Through informal field experiments we have ensured that the proposed POI visualization concept is naturally incorporated for wearable computing platforms like the EPSON Moverio, Vuzix M-100 and Google Glass.

INTERACTION CONFLICTS

Augmented Reality browsers since inception have suffered from visual clutter and demanded high cognitive load. It is not uncommon that virtual artifacts representing POIs are positioned in such a way, that important details of the physical object are occluded. Hartmann et al. [4] emphasized that readability, unambiguity, aesthetics and frame-coherence are important user goals for placing computer generated dynamic content.

As depicted, (see Figure 1a) the information overload was an obvious issue in our previous implementation. Apart from literature review and peer critique from field experts that gave us necessary input to identify interaction conflicts, we have performed several opportunistic explorations, recruiting local users (14 male and 8 female participants with different level of expertise in location based AR) to identify shortcomings of an implementation of a former POI visualization system.

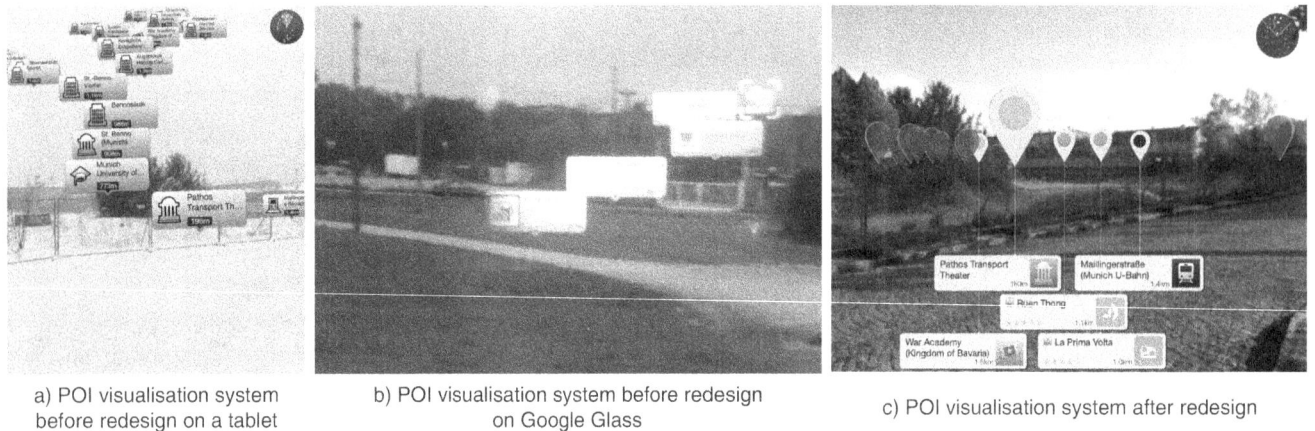

| a) POI visualisation system before redesign on a tablet | b) POI visualisation system before redesign on Google Glass | c) POI visualisation system after redesign |

Figure 1. POI visualization system before and after redesign on mobile and wearable devices.

We have found out that participants had some difficulties interacting with POIs that were not on the immediate line of sight. Also observed was that there is no clustering or grouping rules applied to a cluttered scene. On a wearable Google Glass device, due to an ambiguous placement of billboards and limited screen estate, the majority of participants had trouble reading descriptive information (see Figure 1b) about POI. Hand postures on the touch screen devices like smartphone and tablet [5] was not taken into consideration in order to quickly query additional information about interesting objects around user. We have observed that it is a very unnatural experience to hold a phone or a tablet in the mid-air for a significant amount of time that is often required in interactive Augmented Reality scenarios.

DESIGN CONSIDERATIONS

Our goal was to design a new effective and efficient interaction and visualization system that reduces information clutter for various device form factors. It was important for us to receive user feedback early in the design process to confirm whether it was worth proceeding to develop a new concept into a prototype application.

Interaction Type

We have developed several design alternatives that supports interaction between POI and user namely:

- "Classic" AR-browser view (see Figure 2a) where no touch interactions are necessary to discover new POIs. Upon user's spatial rotation, new POIs will be visible in a current viewport. We rely on a device's internal 6DOF sensor to analyze a user's pose.

- Split AR view with list view (see Figure 2b). This approach incorporates a vertical scrolling across annotations. Once user scrolls a list, newly selected annotation will be highlighted on radar, indicating user about its position with respect to the viewport.

- Split AR view with canvas view (see Figure 2c). This approach incorporates panning gesture across annotations. It bears the same discovery mechanism as a list view, but implements more natural mapping. Instead of scrolling top-down, it features left-right panning, prompting users to rotate the camera to discover additional digital information about surroundings.

We have asked 10 participants (4 males and 6 females) with extensive experience in the location based AR to evaluate our prototypes on smartphone or tablet device and fill the survey. Each participant has exercised every single concept three times with different data sets: Wikipedia entries, supermarket POIs and nearby restaurants. Our aim was to find out which concept provides more affordance, ease of use and effectiveness to find a desired point of interest. According to our observations we concluded that "Classic" AR view is the most effective approach to discover information in unknown environment around user. It performed the best in tests, where we ask to identify an object located in front of a user, as well as when user was asked to look for a specific object of interest in a surrounded area.

We observed that this concept is naturally adaptable to wearable devices since no additional input to discover POI is required. According to our informal user trials we identified no significant difference in effectiveness of finding annotated objects on touch and wearable displays in the location based Augmented Reality scenario. We have tested a prototype application of the proposed interaction type on such wearable computing platforms as Google Glass, EPSON Moverio and Vuzix M-100.

Visualization System

The new virtual representation of POI (see Figure 3) consists of three parts:

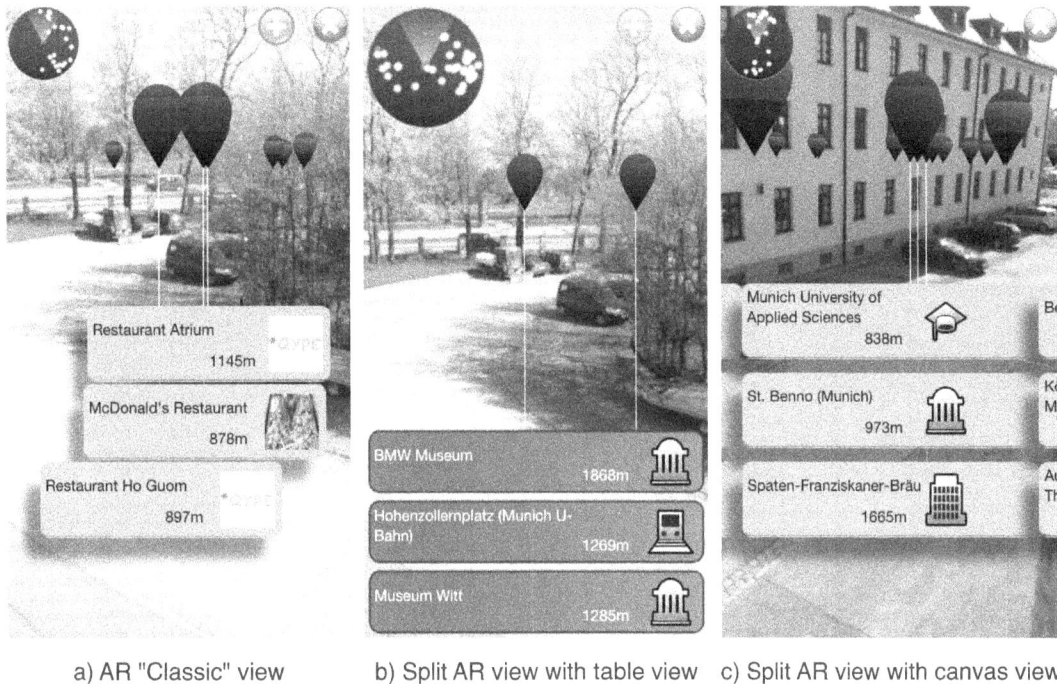

a) AR "Classic" view   b) Split AR view with table view   c) Split AR view with canvas view

Figure 2. Alternative designs exploring interactivity with a set of POIs.

- A pin: a 3-D model that has been designed with depth perception in mind, leveraging such monocular cues as occlusion, lighting and shading, curvilinear perspective, parallax effect, etc.

- An annotation: an interactive board that displays name, distance to and icon of the POI. The annotation is placed on the bottom of the screen to facilitate quick interaction with one handed and cradled mobile device use [5]. The annotation acts as a signifier to discover interactions with POI.

- A leader line that links a pin and an annotation to create a logical association.

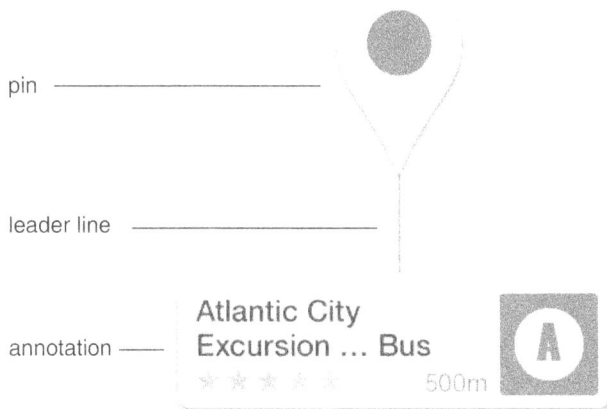

Figure 3. Virtual representation of the POI in detail.

Our approach maintains frame coherent POI, virtual elements rendered in such a way that a user can easily relate corresponding pieces of the POI. We have relied on AR view management requirements recommended in the literature [9] for building synthetic scenes:

- realism for better immersion
- transparency for improved perception
- motion parallax
- reduced clutter to prevent cognitive tunneling
- depth cues for improve estimation of a distance
- Gestalt laws

In order to stronger communicate a logical link between a 3-D pin and an annotation we have applied dynamic color-coding technique, matching a central circle of a pin to a closest average color of a user-defined thumbnail of a given annotation (see Figure 3). We have integrated a new level of abstraction for a displayed POI data set. There are focused (light textured) and unfocused (dark textured) POIs to make a clear visual statement and improve user focus during scene exploration (see Figure 1c).

Discovery Mechanism
We have explored an adaptive strategy to show POI visualizations on a screen. Those POIs that are closest to a center of a direction of a viewport will be displayed on screen first. Users can select an annotation board to query additional information about the POI. The boards are "sticky" to their pins, which create an illusion that an annotation follows a pin with a leader line. This is done to

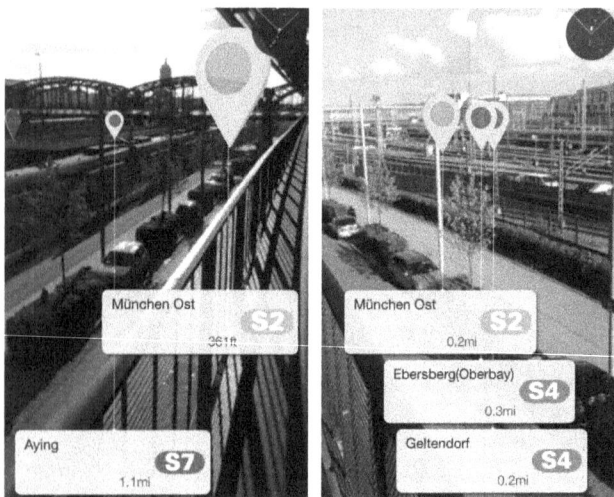

a) Train S2 arrives at the station   b) Train S2 leaves to the tunnel

Figure 4. Moving POI is being redrawn on the screen once it changes position.

increase dynamics of a scene. Once user changes viewport, by revolving clockwise (or counter-clockwise), another set of POIs will be selected to be shown on a screen according to the center rule described. The amount of annotations shown on a screen at once is limited and depends on a particular device screen estate. By enforcing this design constraint we attempted to reduce visual clutter problem.

In a scenario when user moves forward or backward along one direction, the current set of POIs presented on a screen will be redrawn once a device sensor registers new GPS position. A similar approach is applied when POI moves toward or away from the user: it will be redrawn with a appropriate scale factor once it changes position with respect to a viewport. Figure 4 illustrates this use case, where POI bears a real-time position of a suburban train S-Bahn.

FUTURE WORK

We would like to improve on computational cost (in time) needed to build custom POI visualizations for a given geo-referenced data set. A possible solution would be the creation of an authoring tool that incorporates logical links from these data sets to the AR browser. Currently it is fairly manual process to create AR visualizations for POIs. It could be accomplished through:

- Manually creating XML configuration file that contains all necessary information about set of POIs to be augmented.

- Dynamically creating POIs during runtime using Augmented Reality Experience Language (AREL) [1].

Among limitations of the Junaio AR browser we could outline the fact that it does not consider the altitude parameter of a POI. This is partially due to low accuracy of mobile device GPS data that contains altitude parameter. Sensor

fusion algorithms can be developed to reduce this inaccuracy to a reasonable value.

CONCLUSION

We have presented a new update of the Junaio AR browser [7] for smartphones, tablets and wearable devices. Design recommendations include elaborations of several empirical observations in outdoor Augmented Reality with location based services in unknown, uncontrolled environments. We are planning to show a demonstration of the Junaio application at the conference on iOS devices as well as on a wearable device running the Android platform. We believe that the presented interactive system brings some novel elements that can facilitate a discussion on building end-user location based Augmented Reality experiences.

ACKNOWLEDGMENTS

This work was supported in part by the German Federal Ministry of Economics and Technology (BMWi, reference number 01MS11020A, CRUMBS).

REFERENCES

1. Augmented Reality Experience Language. https://dev.metaio.com/arel/overview/

2. Azuma, R.T. The Survey of Augmented Reality. In Presence: Teleoperators and Virtual Environments 6, 4 (1997), 355-385.

3. Grasset, R., Langlotz, T., Kalkofen, D., Tatzgern, M., and Schmalstieg, D. Image-driven view management for augmented reality browsers. In *Proc. ISMAR 2012*. IEEE Computer Society (2012), 177-186.

4. Hartmann, K., Gotzelmann, T., Ali, K., and Strothotte, T. Metrics for functional and aesthetic label layouts. In *Proc. SG 2005*, 115–126.

5. How Do Users Really Hold Mobile Devices? http://uxmatters.com/mt/archives/2013/02/how-do-users-really-hold-mobile-devices.php

6. Kalkofen, D., Zollman, S., Schall, G., Reitmayr, G. and Schmalstieg, D. Adaptive visualization for outdoor AR displays. In *Proc. ISMAR 2009*, 19-23.

7. The Junaio Augmented Reality Browser. http://www.junaio.com

8. Yovcheva, Z., Buhalis, D., Gatzidis, C. and van Elzakker, C.P.J.M. Towards meaningful augmentation of the cityscape: new challenges for mobile GeoHCI. In *Proc. GeoHCI Workshop at CHI 2013*, 57-59.

9. Wegerich, A., Rotting, M. A context-aware adaptation system for spatial augmented reality. In *Proc. ICDHM 2011*. Springer-Verlag, Berlin (2011), 417-425.

10. Wither, J., DiVerdi, S., and Hollerer, T. Technical Section: Annotation in outdoor augmented reality. *Comput. Graph. 33, 6 (2009)*, 679-689.

AME: an Adaptive Modelling Environment as a Collaborative Modelling Tool

Alfonso García Frey, Jean-Sébastien Sottet and Alain Vagner

Public Research Center Henri Tudor

29 Avenue John F. Kennedy L-1855 Luxembourg

{alfonso.garcia, jean-sebastien.sottet, alain.vagner}@tudor.lu

ABSTRACT

The development of User Interfaces (UIs) is a complex task. Researches shown that one of the reasons is the lack of integrated views that often forces developers to implement suboptimal solutions. These integrated views refer to (1) the artifacts that are manipulated by the stakeholders during the UI development process and (2) how these artifacts relate to each other. To overcome the lack of integrated views in the context of model-based UI development this paper introduces AMEs, Adaptive Modelling Environments that support UI development by providing explicit representations of both the artifacts and their relations. A first prototype is depicted in a case study and illustrated with a video. Details of the architecture are provided.

Author Keywords

Human-Computer Interaction; Model-Driven Development; Multi-Stakeholders Engineering; User Interfaces; Tools; IDE; Collaborative Modelling;

ACM Classification Keywords

D.2.2 Software Engineering: Design Tools and Techniques; H.5.2 Information Interfaces & presentation: User Interfaces

INTRODUCTION AND PROBLEM STATEMENT

The development of User Interfaces "is a time-consuming and error-prone task" [29]. Approximately 50% of development resources are devoted to UI implementation tasks [23]. According to [28] one of the causes is "the lack of an integrated view" that "often forces developers to implement suboptimal solutions". This lack of integrated views affects not only how individuals work during the UI development process, but also how individuals collaborate in such process. A potential solution to overcome the lack of integrated views and thus, enhance individual and collaborative work [24] "is to develop more flexible tools". According to Schmidt [28] and Kimelman [19] these views should help individuals to understand how the artifacts they manipulate during the UI development

process are related to each other and, in consequence, provide a better comprehension of the UI development. Indeed, UI development teams are made of different stakeholder profiles, like usability specialists, designers, functional analysts and developers; suboptimal solutions often arise from communication and collaboration problems among the team.

The integrated views refer to (1) the artifacts that are manipulated by the stakeholders and (2) how these artifacts are related to each other. In the context of model-based UI development these artifacts are of very different natures. Examples of them are *ergonomic criteria* (e.g., cognitive workload, guidance) managed by usability experts, *widgets* and *wireframes* conceived by designers and *functions* programmed by the developers to implement the application behavior.

Most of the existing tools for UI development do not take into account the lack of integrated views neither for individual work nor for collaborative UI development. To this end, this paper provides an overview of AMEs, Adaptive Modelling Environments that aim at supporting both individual and collaborative work in order to improve UI development. AMEs are model-based for a number of reasons which are explained in the next section along with the related work. Afterwards, a first prototype of an AME is described through a case study. Details of the architecture are provided before the final conclusion and perspectives.

RELATED WORK

Model-Based approaches are suited for UI development for several reasons. First, a number of frameworks and languages [20, 25, 5] structure the way UIs are generated from models. Models are defined in [3] as "an artifact that conforms to a metamodel and that represents a given aspect of a system". Thus, thanks to this conformance relationship, models are successively transformed and combined using transformations to finally generate the code of the UI. Moreover, using model-based approaches for UI development provides a number of significant advantages like easier evolutions and reuse [17], dynamic adaptation to the context of use [8, 4], end-user programming [9], greater quality [10, 15, 22, 31] and automatic generation of support [14, 13] among others.

AMEs are model-based UIs themselves that aim to support collaborative modelling in the context of UI development. Indeed, previous research shown that collaborative modelling for one single type of models provides significant advantages

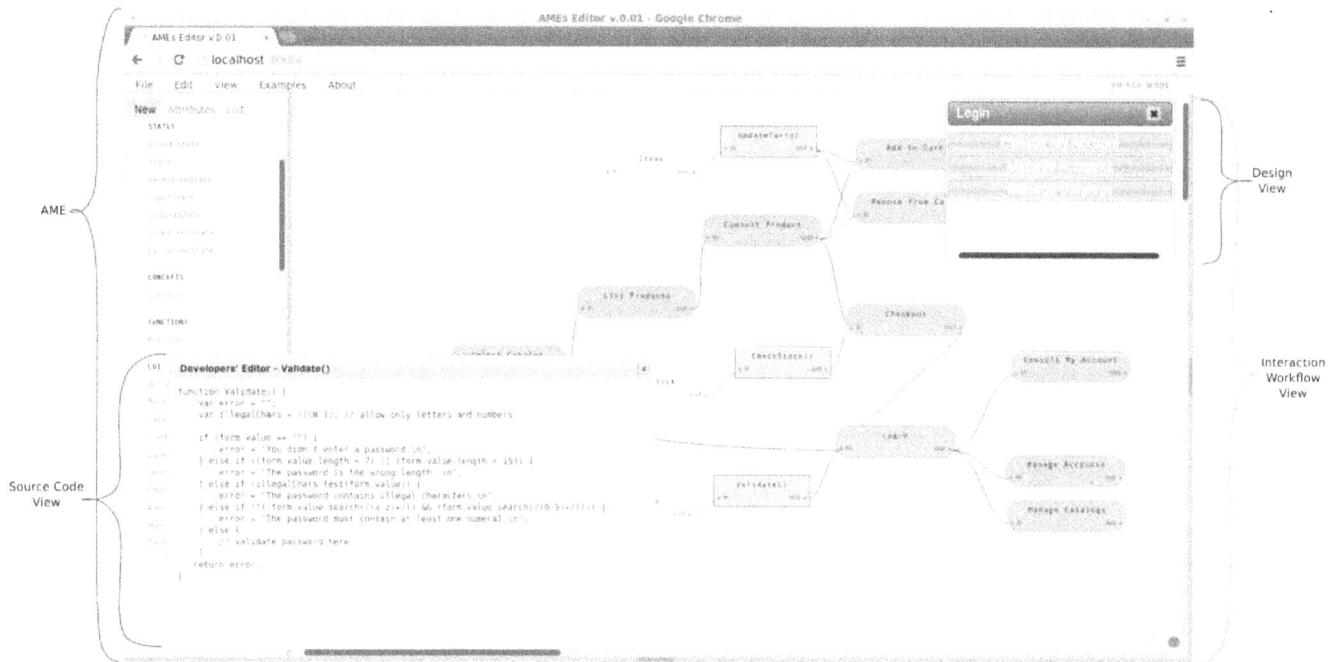

Figure 1. AME interactive online editor. The Interactive Workflow View enables stakeholders to (meta)model their artifacts. The figure shows a modelisation done by the *interaction designers* and the *functional analysts*. Inter-artifacts relationships are explicitly represented. The preview window corresponds to the highlighted container state named "Login". A video of the whole modeling process is available at https://www.youtube.com/watch?v=Mz_kSuraFe0&hd=1.

[11]. In consequence, providing support for multiple models should reiterate and possibly increase such benefits. However, collaborative modelling has been only lately considered, (e.g. in [18]). Existent collaborative environments such as Synergo [2], Space-Design [7], CoolModes [26] or Gambit [27] lack of integrated modelling views for multiple stakeholders or focus on a predefined set of models. On the contrary, our proposal does not fix neither the models nor their representations.

Most model-driven engineering tools[1] do not support collaborative modelling and when they do, collaboration is diluted into classical modelling editors without focusing on the relationships between different stakeholders' artifacts. Moreover, the models managed and generated by these tools are predefined at design-time whereas AME provides means for both (meta)modelling and importing existent (meta)models.

Most model-based UI development tools (Cedar Studio [1], MASP [4], Leonardi[2], GrafiXML [21], UsiComp [16], WebRatio [6], Xplain [12]) also lack of support for remote collaboration, integrated views, or have fixed (meta)models.

ADAPTIVE MODELLING ENVIRONMENTS
AMEs aim at supporting collaborative modelling of UIs in two ways. Firstly, providing stakeholders with specific views on their artifacts, represented with customizable representations. Secondly, providing views that make explicit the relationships between different stakeholders' artifacts. The combination of both is illustrated in the case study described next.

[1]http://wiki.eclipse.org/images/d/dc/Report.external.bvs.pdf
[2]http://www.leonardi-free.org

Case Study
The AME (figure 1) shows multiple integrated views of an online shopping website being developed. The shopping website provides several catalogues to the users, each of them containing a family of products. Once one or more products have been added to the cart (products can be either added or removed from the cart), users can checkout. To checkout or modify the account details, users are requested to login.

The figure shows four different views (three inside the AME plus the AME itself) addressing different stakeholders. These stakeholders are all involved in the co-design and co-development of the shopping website. These views and their stakeholders are depicted next.

1.- Interaction Workflow View
The Interaction Workflow View enables *interaction designers* to define the interaction workflow. The interaction workflow (already used by languages like IFML [6]) captures all the different workspaces (orange ovals) in which the UI is decomposed. The main workspace is the *Home website* from which users can navigate to *Select Catalogue*. From here, the products of the catalogue are available through the *List Products* workspace.

The interaction designer of the case study has a graphical design background and concentrates on page flow. The manipulated artifacts are thus the *workspaces* composing the interaction workflow of the website plus the *relationships* between them that enable navigation. Note that navigation from a workspace to another could eventually require external information. For instance, *Checkout* requires confirmation by the *CheckStock()* function. Other examples are saving the state of the application and updating information in the UI. These relationships are all examples of cases involving different stakeholders' artifacts (*workspaces* and *functions*). *Functional analysts* define these function signatures (blue boxes) that trigger functionality from the functional core.

2.- Source Code View

The source code view (bottom-left window, figure 1) enables *developers* to implement functional aspects previously identified by *functional analysts*. *Developers* are also involved in the interaction workflow to implement navigational relationships between workspaces. Regarding the chosen development methodology, *developers* can also discuss with *functional analysts* the relevance of defined functions and potential discrepancies between existing models and developments.

The artifact manipulated in this view is the *source code* implementing the function signatures that interface the functional core. This view in figure 1, opened by clicking the associated function, is showing the implementation of the validation function (blue box) used in the login workspace.

3.- Design View

The design view enables designers to have a first preview of the UI being designed. The preview is computed at runtime and updated according to stakeholders' actions. The preview provides designers with the benefits of rapid prototyping. This view is interactive but not directly modifiable.

4.- AME View

The AME is itself a view on the models of the application that enables for observation and modification by stakeholders. The left sidebar provides access to the (meta)models proposed by the AME or imported by the stakeholders. In case of imported (meta)models, default representations are used when no representation is provided.

Insights on the architecture and implementation of the AME are provided in the following section.

Architecture and Implementation

AME makes use of a set of metamodels as, for instance, a state-chart metamodel to capture the interaction workflow. The (meta)models are built with the Eclipse Modelling Framework (EMF) and finally persisted in a XML format on a model repository, so they can be later used and/or transformed according to users' actions and contexts.

AME has been designed as an online tool to maximize the collaboration possibilities, specially in non co-located environments. The AME front-end has been developed in JavaScript, HTML and CSS to provide fast run-time and multi-platform online interaction. The server side implements a modified MVC pattern described in figure 2.

The preview window corresponding to the design view in figure 1 is automatically updated every time a model is modified. The preview is generated with model-to-text transformations that produce the HTML excerpts used to update the view.

Importing custom (meta)models is supported with classical (meta)modelling exchange formats such as *Ecore* and *XMI*.

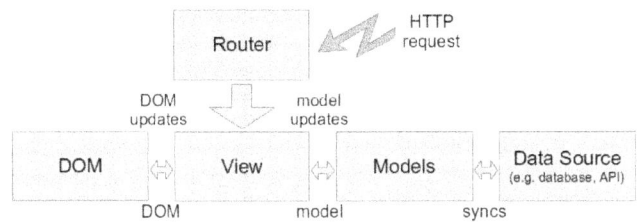

Figure 2. Modified MVC architecture of AME. URL routing, DOM events (e.g. mouse clicks) and Model events (e.g. attribute changes) trigger handling logic in the View. The handlers update the DOM and Models that may trigger additional events. Models are synced with data sources.

CONCLUSION AND PERSPECTIVES

This paper introduces AME, an Adaptive Modelling Environment that firstly, enables stakeholders to visualize and manipulate the metamodels, models and transformations, or any of their internal elements, that are relevant to their specific tasks in the context of model-based UI development; secondly, the AME should help stakeholders to understand the full stack of models by means of integrated views in which custom representations of the manipulated artifacts and their interconnections are displayed. An AME in the form of an online Integrated Development Environment -IDE- has been introduced. The AME has been depicted through a case study including four different stakeholders, each of them working with their own (meta)models. The architecture and implementation have been discussed.

Future work will use adequate evaluation techniques of the so called *groupware usability* to test the suitability of AMEs with real stakeholders and compare its performance against existing collaborative modelling tools. Remote collaboration and inclusion of visualization techniques for better interaction (as in as [30]) will be studied in future versions.

ACKNOWLEDGMENTS

This work has been supported by the Luxemburgish FNR MoDEL project (C12/IS/3977071).

REFERENCES

1. Akiki, P. A., Bandara, A. K., and Yu, Y. Cedar studio: An ide supporting adaptive model-driven user interfaces for enterprise applications. EICS'13, ACM (2013).

2. Avouris, N., Margaritis, M., and Komis, V. Modelling interaction during small-group synchronous problem solving activities: the synergo approach. In *Workshop on Designing Computational Models of Collaborative Learning Interaction, ITS'04*, Springer (2004).

3. Bézivin, J., Jouault, F., and Valduriez, P. On the need for megamodels. *Proc. of OOPSLA/GPCE: Best Practices for Model-Driven Software Development workshop, 19th Annual ACM Conf. on Object-Oriented Programming, Systems, Languages, and Applications* (2004).

4. Blumendorf, M., Feuerstack, S., and Albayrak, S. Multimodal user interaction in smart environments: Delivering distributed user interfaces. In *Constructing Ambient Intelligence*, vol. 11 of *Communications in Computer and Information Science*. Springer, 2008.

5. Botterweck, G. Multi front-end engineering. In *Model-Driven Development of Advanced User Interfaces*, vol. 340 of *Studies in Computational Intelligence*. Springer Berlin Heidelberg, 2011, 27–42.

6. Brambilla, M., and Fraternali, P. Large-scale model-driven engineering of web user interaction: The webml and webratio experience. *Science of Computer Programming* (2013).

7. Bravo, C., Duque, R., and Gallardo, J. A groupware system to support collaborative programming: Design and experiences. *J. Syst. Softw. 86*, 7 (July 2013).

8. Calvary, G., Coutaz, J., Thevenin, D., Limbourg, Q., Bouillon, L., and Vanderdonckt, J. A unifying reference framework for multi-target user interfaces. *Interacting with Computers 15*, 3 (2003).

9. Dittmar, A., García Frey, A., and Dupuy-Chessa, S. What can model-based ui design offer to end-user software engineering? In *Proc. of the 4th ACM SIGCHI Symposium on Engineering Interactive Computing Systems*, EICS'12, ACM (New York, 2012).

10. Fernandez, A., Insfran, E., and Abraho, S. Integrating a usability model into model-driven web development processes. In *Web Information Systems Engineering - WISE 2009*, vol. 5802. Springer, 2009, 497–510.

11. Gallardo, J., Molina, A. I., Bravo, C., Redondo, M. A., and Collazos, C. A. Groupware: Design, implementation and use. Springer, 2008, ch. Comparative Study of Tools for Collaborative Task Modelling: An Empirical and Heuristic-Based Evaluation, 340–355.

12. García Frey, A., Calvary, G., and Dupuy-Chessa, S. Xplain: an editor for building self-explanatory user interfaces by model-driven engineering. In *Proc. of the 2Nd ACM SIGCHI Symposium on Engineering Interactive Computing Systems* (2010).

13. García Frey, A., Calvary, G., and Dupuy-Chessa, S. Users need your models!: exploiting design models for explanations. In *BCS HCI*, British Computer Society (2012), 79–88.

14. García Frey, A., Calvary, G., Dupuy-Chessa, S., and Mandran, N. Model-based self-explanatory UIs for free, but are they valuable? In *INTERACT (3)*, vol. 8119 of *Lecture Notes in Computer Science*, Springer (2013).

15. García Frey, A., Céret, E., Dupuy-Chessa, S., and Calvary, G. Quimera: A quality metamodel to improve design rationale. In *Proc. of the 3rd ACM SIGCHI Symposium on Engineering Interactive Computing Systems*, EICS'11, ACM (2011), 265–270.

16. García Frey, A., Ceret, E., Dupuy-Chessa, S., Calvary, G., and Gabillon, Y. Usicomp: an extensible model-driven composer. In *Proc. of the 4th ACM SIGCHI Symposium on Engineering Interactive Computing Systems*, EICS'12 (2012), 263–268.

17. Hamid, B., Radermacher, A., Lanusse, A., Jouvray, C., Grard, S., and Terrier, F. Designing fault-tolerant component based applications with a model driven approach. In *Software Technologies for Embedded and Ubiquitous Systems*, vol. 5287. Springer, 2008.

18. Izquierdo, J. L. C., Cabot, J., Lopez-Fernandez, J. J., Cuadrado, J. S., Guerra, E., and Lara, J. Engaging end-users in the collaborative development of domain-specific modelling languages. In *Cooperative Design, Visualization, and Engineering*. Springer, 2013.

19. Kimelman, D., and Hirschman, K. A Spectrum of Flexibility-Lowering Barriers to Modeling Tool Adoption. In *ICSE 2011 Workshop on Flexible Modeling Tools* (2011).

20. Limbourg, Q., Vanderdonckt, J., Michotte, B., Bouillon, L., and López-Jaquero, V. Usixml: A language supporting multi-path development of user interfaces. In *Engineering Human Computer Interaction and Interactive Systems*, vol. 3425 of *Lecture Notes in Computer Science*. Springer, 2005, 200–220.

21. Michotte, B., and Vanderdonckt, J. GrafiXML, a multi-target user interface builder based on UsiXML. In *ICAS* (2008), 15–22.

22. Montecalvo, E., Vagner, A., and Gronier, G. Proposal of a usability-driven design process for model-based user interfaces. In *2nd Workshop on USIXML* (2011).

23. Myers, B. A., and Rosson, M. B. Survey on user interface programming. In *Proc. of the SIGCHI Conference on Human Factors in Computing Systems*, CHI'92, ACM (New York, 1992), 195–202.

24. Ossher, H., van der Hoek, A., Storey, M.-A., Grundy, J., Bellamy, R., and Petre, M. Workshop on flexible modeling tools, *flexitools11*. ICSE '11, ACM (2011).

25. Paternò, F., Santoro, C., and Spano, L. D. Maria: A universal, declarative, multiple abstraction-level language for service-oriented applications in ubiquitous environments. *TOCHI09 16*, 4 (Nov. 2009).

26. Pinkwart, N., Bollen, L., and Fuhlrott, E. Group-oriented modeling tools with heterogeneous semantics. In *ITS'02*, Springer (2002), 21–30.

27. Sangiorgi, U., and Vanderdonckt, J. Gambit: Addressing multi-platform collaborative sketching with html5. In *Proc. of the 4th ACM SIGCHI Symposium on Engineering Interactive Computing Systems*, EICS'12, ACM (New York, 2012), 257–262.

28. Schmidt, D. C. Guest editor's introduction: Model-driven engineering. *Computer 39*, 2 (2006).

29. Schramm, A., Preußner, A., Heinrich, M., and Vogel, L. Rapid ui development for enterprise applications: Combining manual and model-driven techniques. In *Proc. of the 13th International Conf. on Model Driven Engineering Languages and Systems: Part I*, MODELS'10, Springer (2010), 271–285.

30. Sottet, J., and Vagner, A. Defining domain specific transformations in human-computer interfaces development. In *2nd Conf. on Model-Driven Engineering for Software Developement, Modelsward'14* (2014).

31. Sottet, J.-S., Calvary, G., Coutaz, J., and Favre, J.-M. Engineering interactive systems. Springer, 2008, ch. A Model-Driven Engineering Approach for the Usability of Plastic User Interfaces, 140–157.

Metadata Enriched Visualization of Keywords in Context

Daniel Fischl
MODUL University Vienna
Am Kahlenberg 1, 1190 Vienna
daniel.fischl@modul.ac.at
+43 (1) 3203555 534

Arno Scharl
MODUL University Vienna
Am Kahlenberg 1, 1190 Vienna
arno.scharl@modul.ac.at
+43 (1) 3203555 500

ABSTRACT
This paper presents an interactive, synchronized and metadata enriched implementation of the Word Tree metaphor, which is an interactive visualization technique to show Keywords-in-Context (KWIC). Embedded into a Web intelligence platform focusing on climate change coverage, it provides users with a tool to better understand the usage of terms in large document collections. One of the novelties is the implementation of filters for the Word Tree, which shifts the focus of attention directly onto significant phrases, instead of punctuation or fill-words inherent to natural language usage.

Author Keywords
Algorithms; Design; Human Factors; Keywords in Context

ACM Classification Keywords
D.5.2 Graphical user interfaces (GUI); H.3.3: Information filtering; I.3.6: Interaction techniques

INTRODUCTION
If an analyst searches through the Internet for instances of a bank, product or any other items of interest, he or she will be confronted with a great amount of unstructured and unordered textual information to review. To help users achieve a better understanding of how terms or phrases are being used in articles and posts in different media (to which we will subsequently refer to as "documents"), and how they are perceived by these media, we make use and extend the functionality of the well-known Word Tree metaphor [5].

Our motivation, and subsequent use case for this work, is to better visualize the context of user-defined search terms inside the *Media Watch on Climate Change* [3] as shown in Figure 1, where the Word Tree is shown in the center part. Publicly available at www.ecoreserach.net/climate, the system collects documents from various news channels, social media platforms and the Web sites of NGOs and large cor-

porations. It allows users to query the document collection and uses multiple coordinated views [2] to display the results including various types of metadata – e.g., associated keywords, polarity (positive and negative sentiment), geographic location, etc.

WORD TREE VISUALIZATION
The Word Tree technique is a visual tool to show the different contexts in which certain terms appear. Its graph-based display facilitates the rapid exploration of search results and conveys a better understanding of how language is being used surrounding a certain topic. To generate the display, the system processes the list of concordances of the focus term and presents them in a structured manner. It complements other visualizations such as tag clouds and keyword graphs [3], which give a good overview of the main keywords, but do not reflect their usage context within specific sentences.

Unlike the original Word Tree [5], this work adopts a symmetrical approach [1] to directly visualize how the root of the tree, the search term, is embedded in the context. This allows representing the full sentence structures rather than fragments, which might leave out valuable information. The left part of the tree displays all sentence parts that occur before the search term (prefix tree), while the right part displays those that follow the search term (suffix tree). These branches to the left and to the right help users to spot repetition in contextual phrases that precede or follow the search term. The disadvantage of this symmetrical representation in comparison to the original version is that a link must be provided to show which sentence parts belong together. This is handled via mouse-over (see next Section).

Visual cues include different font sizes to indicate the frequency of phrases, and connecting lines to highlight typical sentence structures.

INTERACTIVE FEATURES
To explore the displayed information, the module provides several possibilities through interaction (the term "node" in this context refers to a specific word or phrase occurring multiple times, which is displayed between connecting lines):

- **Hovering** over a node highlights all connected sentences – only a single (complete) sentence in the case of leaf nodes, or all sentences containing the phrase

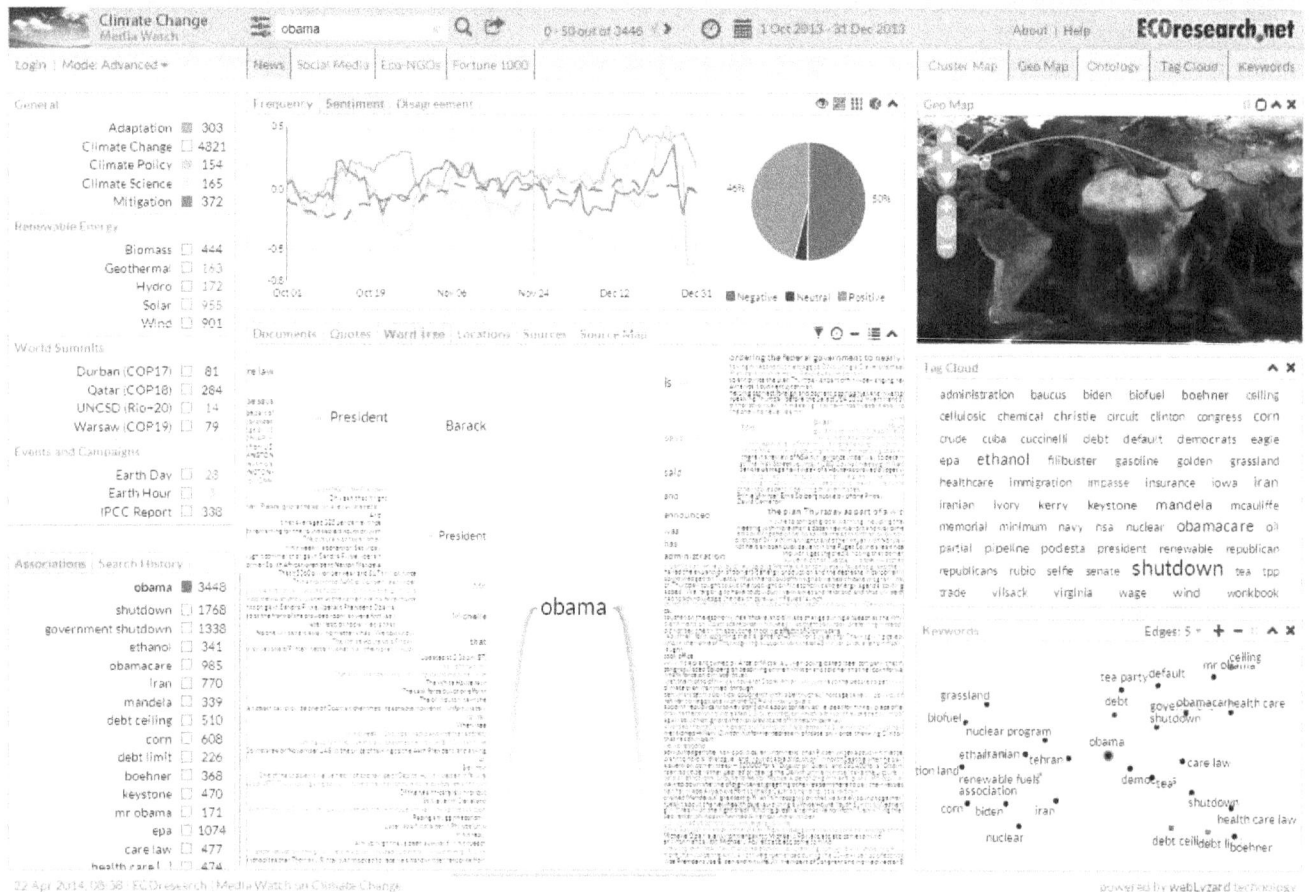

Figure 1: Screenshot of the Media Watch on Climate Change (www.ecoresearch.net/climate) with a Word Tree
that shows Anglo-American news media coverage on U.S. President Barack Obama in the fourth quarter of 2013

from the root to the hovered branch in the case of intermediate nodes.

- **Single clicking** on the *root node* (= terms matching the search query) displays alternative root terms, which can be used to create variations of the tree based on the same set of search results. This is useful when searching for multiple terms via complex queries or predefined topics.

- **Single clicking** on *any of the other words* reprocesses the shown data to create a new tree (the phrase from the previous root to the clicked word becomes the new root). This drill down operation limits the amount of information shown; e.g., to explore sub-branches of the tree containing specific phrases.

- **Double clicking** on any of the shown word triggers a new full-text search.

Filtering

Word Trees were initially conceptualized as tools for the lexical analysis of texts. One of the main goals of this work, however, is to help users gain quick insights into a collection of documents. This is done by providing them with a tool to see how, and in combination with which words, the

search term in the center of the tree is used in different contexts. Basically the original Word Tree is, by means of grouping, able to provide a structured view of the underlying text. Nevertheless, in order to understand the general message of a collection of texts, some characters and fill-words inherent to natural language use are not necessarily required. Since the original version treats each of those as a token when comparing phrases, a grouping which includes these might lessen the significance of the tree's overall structure. Therefore, we have implemented several possible filters, which adapt to the underlying data. A comparison of the different filter types is depicted in Figure 2, where each of the trees is based on the same data. Figure 2(a) shows the outcome of the original Word Tree algorithm. In all sub-figures, the newly gained groupings compared to the original version have been highlighted. For reasons of simplicity we only show the suffix-part of the tree. The exact differences will be further explained in the following subsections.

Filter punctuation

As seen in Figure 2(a), building the tree using the original method would lead to a grouping by comma, since several sentences contain the phrase "energy,". Our version of filtering by punctuation removes such groupings, which allows the algorithm to find groupings which have previously been obscured because of punctuation.

An example of a newly found grouping can be seen in Figure 2(b), where new groupings based on the words "like" and "is" have been found.

Filter stop-words
Based on the punctuation filter, we also provide a more restrictive filter, which filters not only punctuation marks, but also prevents groupings by a pre-defined list of stop-words.

Figure 2(c) shows the outcome of this approach, leading to a tree where additional groupings have been found, like "sustainable", "development" and "bills". Note that the cluster "is" has been removed, since it is considered a stop-word and therefore a grouping by it has been prevented.

Adaptive filtering
The results of an adaptive filter are presented in Figure 2(d). It is based on the previous two filters, but strips the text of punctuation or stop-words, only if a better grouping can be found without them. Otherwise, it maintains the original grouping.

Figure 2(d) shows that the same groupings were found as in the stop-word filtering process except for two groupings by "," and "is" – which are still smaller than the same groupings in Figure 2(a). This is because no superior solution could be found for the affected phrases.

Hierarchical Layers
To allow the users to focus on often occurring phrases, buttons to add and remove nodes have been provided. These buttons extend or trim the tree by either adding a hidden hierarchical layer of branches, or by removing the current set of leaf nodes. This allows users to hide single sentences which occur only once in the document collection and focus on the main tree structure by displaying only those phrases that have occurred multiple times.

This functionality, in combination with options to reduce the result set and drill-down into sub-branches allow users to focus on relevant data and sub-branches to gain further insights. An example of such a trimmed tree, where the first layer has been hidden, is shown in Figure 3.

Sentiment Display
The *Media Watch on Climate Change* computes a sentiment value for each sentence [4].

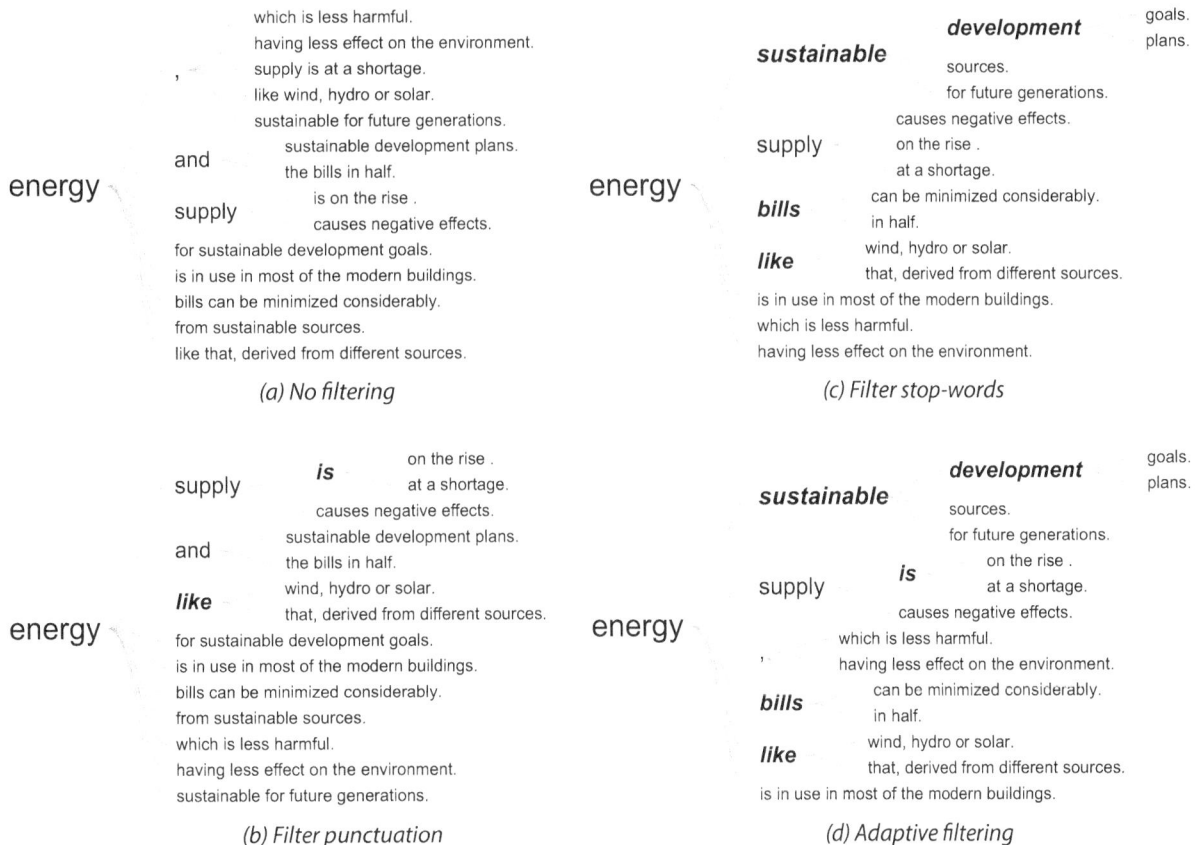

Figure 2: Comparison of different filtering techniques: (a) shows the original Word Tree structure, (b) filters groupings by punctuation (c) filters groupings by stop-words and (d) adapts the filtering by filtering only in the case of more favorable groupings

Intergovernmental	panel			but	
	report	on		is	expected to
		from		has	
		by		(IPCC)	
	of	the		report	
	effects	of	climate change	Leaders	
	human-induced			by	
	in			can	
	and			I	
	that			on	
	to			with	

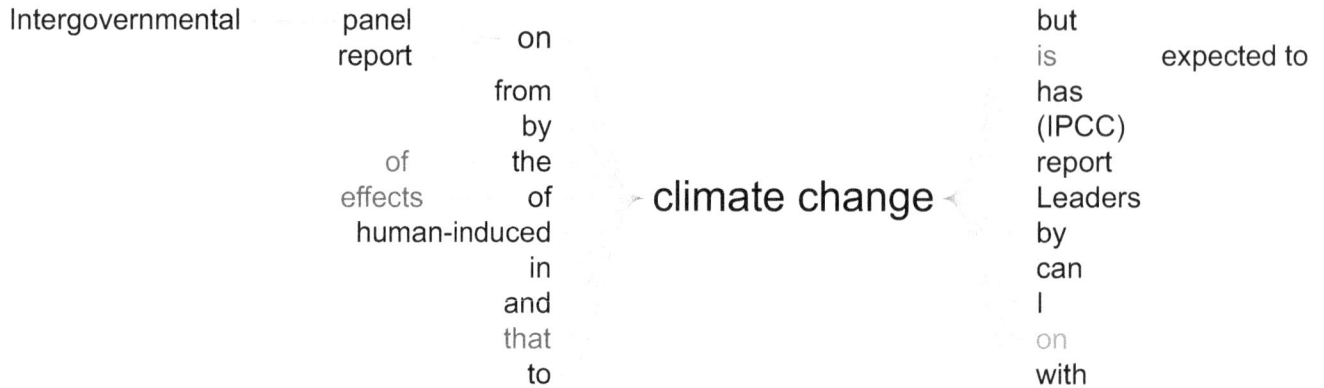

Figure 3: Example of the word tree with the root term "climate change" with the first layer (all leaf nodes) hidden and sentiment coloring active.

The system determines the ratio of positive and negative terms found in a document (based on a sentiment lexicon, an enumerative list of sentiment terms with indicators of their sentiment charges). It then uses this value as an indicator of overall polarity. The accuracy of this metric is further improved by considering linguistic features such as negations and intensifiers. The user has the option to enable color coding based on the distribution of these sentiment values. Each sentence is then colored in the range from red (negative) to black (neutral) to green (positive).

Intermediate nodes receive the average color of all their connected child nodes – this might result in neutral colors in the case of controversial phrases with a roughly similar number of positive and negative mentions.

CONCLUSION AND OUTLOOK

This paper presented the integration of the Word Tree concept into a news and social media aggregator focusing on the environmental domain, the *Media Watch on Climate Change* (www.ecoresearch.net/climate).

Adapted to the specific requirements of a multiple coordinated view interface, this implementation of the Word Tree metaphor offers a range of interaction possibilities to enable an effective and quick manipulation of the retrieved content, including filtering techniques to eliminate irrelevant terms and focus on the most significant information.

The display of additional metadata such as the color-coding of sentiment information helps users to quickly understanding the relevance of the various topics. All the required filtering is done in real time during the generation process, based on the retrieved set of search results. This one-pass generation eliminates the need for additional post- or pre-processing steps.

Future work will continue to explore Word Tree usage when exploring the large document collections within the *Media Watch on Climate Change*.

We will investigate the possibility of stripping the Word Tree of contextual information step-by-step until it transforms into a keyword-graph-like structure, where only the most important keywords remain, without additional context information. This could potentially facilitate the perception of information in the underlying data.

REFERENCES

[1] Culy, C. and Lyding, V. 2010. Double Tree: An Advanced KWIC Visualization for Expert Users. In *Proceedings of the 2010 14th Int'l Conference Information Visualisation* (IV '10). IEEE Press, Washington, DC, USA, 98-103.

[2] Hubmann-Haidvogel, A., Scharl, A. and Weichselbraun, A. 2009. Multiple Coordinated Views for Searching and Navigating Web Content Repositories. *Information Sciences,* 179, 12, 1813-1821.

[3] Scharl, A., Hubmann-Haidvogel, A., Sabou, M., Weichselbraun, A. and Lang, H.-P. (2013). "From Web Intelligence to Knowledge Co-Creation – A Platform to Analyze and Support Stakeholder Communication", *IEEE Internet Computing*, 17(5): 21-29.

[4] Weichselbraun, A., Gindl, S. and Scharl, A. (2013). "Extracting and Grounding Contextualized Sentiment Lexicons", *IEEE Intelligent Systems*, 28(2): 39-46.

[5] Wattenberg, M. and Viégas, F.B.. 2008. The Word Tree, an Interactive Visual Concordance. *IEEE Transactions on Visualization and Computer Graphics* 14, 6, 1221-1228.

IceTT: A Responsive Visualization for Task Models

Lucio Davide Spano
Department of Mathematics and Computer
Science, University of Cagliari
Via Ospedale 72, 09124, Cagliari, Italy
davide.spano@unica.it

Gianni Fenu
Department of Mathematics and Computer
Science, University of Cagliari
Via Ospedale 72, 09124, Cagliari, Italy
fenu@unica.it

ABSTRACT

Task models are useful for designers and domain experts in order to describe sequences of actions that need to be completed for reaching a user's goal. Their hierarchical structure is usually visualized through a tree representation that, for large models, is inclined to grow horizontally and reduces its readability. In this paper we introduce a visualization based on icicle graphs, which is able to adapt the tasks visualization to the screen width, suitable for displaying large models even on small screens.

Author Keywords

Task models; Visualization; Responsive Design;

ACM Classification Keywords

H.5.m. Information Interfaces and Presentation (e.g. HCI): Miscellaneous

INTRODUCTION AND MOTIVATION

Task models describe the sequence of actions that users need to complete in order to reach a specific goal. Given their simple and intuitive representation, task models have been used in multidisciplinary teams for communication purposes and in order persist a shared view of an interactive system. The most common graphical representation of a task model is a tree: the root node represents the entire application, and it is gradually detailed by its descendants, which are usually connected through a set of temporal operators (sequence, choice, concurrency etc.). Since the number of sub-tasks can be high in real world applications, task models often grow on the horizontal axis. In such cases, the model is difficult to read and understand, since the designer has to move the model visualization back and forth through the horizontal scrolling.

In this work we propose IceTT, a responsive visualization of task models, which is able to adapt to a given window width exploiting effectively the available space for including the model information. Such kind of visualization allows using different mobile devices, such as

EICS'14, Jun 17-20 2014, Rome, Italy
ACM 978-1-4503-2725-1/14/06.
http://dx.doi.org/10.1145/2607023.2611452

smartphones and tablets, in order to share and/or discuss task models. We provide a preliminary comparison between our visualization, CTTE [6], Hamsters [2] and K-MADe [3] on the same set of models, showing that IceTT is able to show more information on different small and medium standard screen resolutions.

RELATED WORK

Task models are usually built starting from a high-level description of the goal to accomplish (e.g. print a document), which is refined through different levels into a set of detailed actions. Such hierarchical description is suitable for being represented graphically with a tree. However, since task models describe not only the hierarchy among actions but also their temporal relationships, different techniques have been adopted for representing these aspects. In order to compare the proposed solution, we selected three public available representatives of three approaches, focusing on tools specifically designed for task modelling. We did not consider here more generic workflow or application flow visualizations (e.g. BPMN, Petri Nets, flow charts etc.).

The first group includes both the task description and the temporal relationships information inside the node representation, following the Hierarchical Task Analysis (HTA) [1] approach. This representation does not introduce additional nodes for the temporal operators, but the representation of a task requires more space. In this paper, the K-MADe [3] tool represents this group.

The second group we consider represents the temporal operators as nodes, including them as task siblings in the tree visualization. This group is represented by CTTE [6]. This kind of representation grows horizontally, since for task each sub-task we add to a given level, we have to add two nodes in the tree.

The third group represents the temporal operators through dedicated nodes, but they are on different levels with respect to the connected tasks. In this case, the tree is a bipartite graph, where tasks are always connected with operators and vice versa. The model representation grows vertically, since for refining a task we need to add two depth levels to the tree representation. In this paper, the Hamsters [2] tool represents this group.

THE PROPOSED VISUALIZATION

The IceTT task visualization has been designed in order to exploit the entire screen width, without exceeding

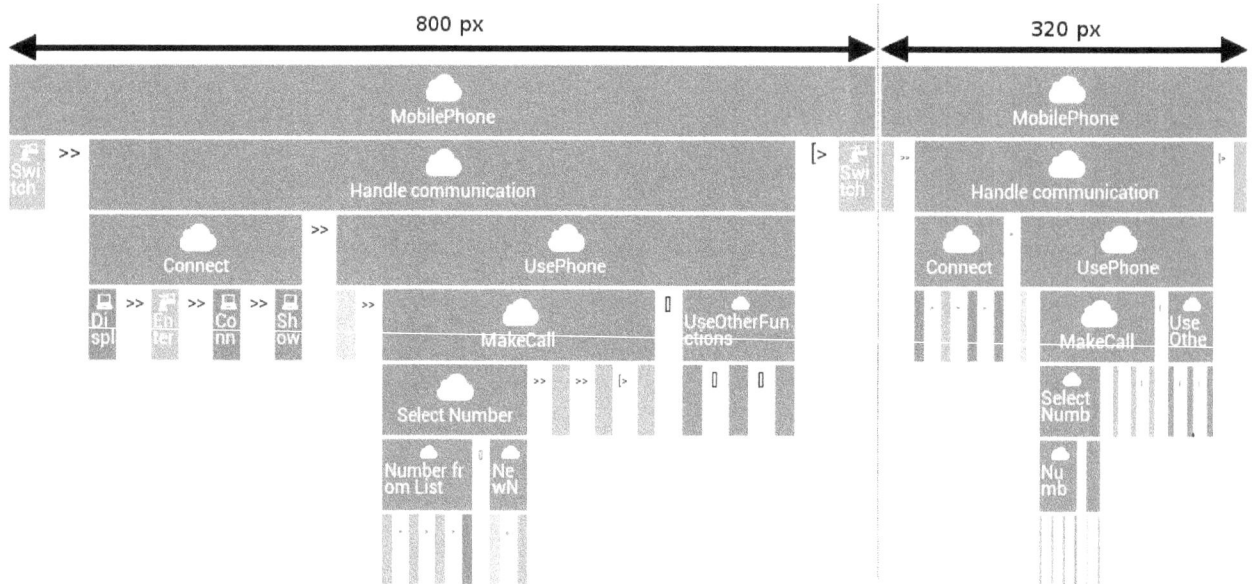

Figure 1. A sample task model, visualized in a window 800px (left part) and 320px wide (right part).

it. At the intermediate levels, the task visualization has different levels of detail, in order to adapt the displayed information to the width available. We selected an icicle plot visualization [5], with a vertical layout for fulfilling these requirements. It consists in a table-like hierarchical representation of the task model tree structure. We can summarize its properties as follows:

1. Each row in the diagram corresponds to an entire level of depth in the task tree. Therefore, all nodes at the same depth are painted in the same row.
2. The representation of a task node has the same height for all levels.
3. The root node fills the entire screen width.
4. The width allocated for a given task node is divided among its children in the next level.

The properties 3 and 4 guarantee that the task model visualization fills the entire window (or container width). The properties 1 and 2 have an impact on the model visualization height, which depends linearly on the task tree maximum depth, as happens for other tree-like representations. We created the visualization extending the Javacript Infovis Toolkit (JIT) in [4].

Figure 1 shows the IceTT visualization of a task model representing the interaction with a mobile phone. On the left part, the model is rendered in a window 800 pixels wide. In the right part, the same model is shown with a width of 320 pixels. As it is possible to see from the figure 1, the visualization does not exceed the window width. We differentiated the task categories [7] through both icons and colors:

- The *Abstract* tasks (used for grouping together task of different categories at the intermediate levels) are identified by a cloud icon and a sky-blue background
- The *Interactive* tasks (that involve both the system and the user) are identified by a human and a computer

icon connected with an arrow. The background color is green.
- The *System* tasks (that involve only the system) are identified by a computer icon and a red background.
- the *User* tasks (that involve only the human user) are identified by a human icon and an dark-yellow background.

The tool allows changing the color palette for solving accessibility issues.The composition operators are represented using the symbols defined in [7]. They express the temporal relationships between the different tasks ($\gg$ for sequential enabling, $[]$ for choice, $|||$ for concurrency, $|=|$ for order independence, $[>$ for disabling etc.).

In order to effectively distribute the space among tasks at the same depth level, the available space is divided among the children considering the number of leafs of their sub-trees. In the layout computation, we considered as children also the temporal operators, since we put their graphical representation between a task and its sibling, as happens in CTTE [6]. More precisely, we define a weight $w(n)$ for each node of the icicle graph (both tasks and temporal operators) in equation 1. C_n contains the children of a node n, while $deg(n)$ is the node degree.

$$w(n) = \begin{cases} 1 & \text{if } deg(n) = 0 \\ \sum_{m \in C_n} w(m) & \text{if } deg(n) > 0 \end{cases} \quad (1)$$

For instance, if we consider again the *Use Phone* task in figure 1, the layout function divides its space among five graphical elements: three tasks and two temporal operators. The first task (a user task represented with a dark yellow rectangle) and the two operators are leafs, therefore their weight is one. The *Make Call* and the *Use other functions* are the root of two different sub-trees, having respectively 16 and 5 leaf nodes and 17 and 5 as weight. Therefore, the *Make Call* task is wider than the other task and temporal operator representations: 17 times more than the sibling user task and about 3 times more than the *Use other functions* abstract task. The weight of *Use Phone* task is 25.

Such organization provides less space for representing tasks that are more deep in the hierarchy. Therefore, we used an incremental visualization of the task-related information, according to the available space. For each task, the visualized information in all tools is usually the category and the task name. The composition operators are usually represented through their symbols.

If we have very little space in width (less than 16 pixels), we show only a coloured rectangle for each task. This already provides information on the task existence and on its category. At higher widths, we show also the task name and icon. The visualization truncates the name if the available space is not enough for containing it entirely. In this way, even if the whole information on the task name is not present, the designer may recall it through its initial part. Finally, if there is enough space, the task name is visualized entirely and the icon is bigger.

For the composition operators we decrease the font size in order to draw its symbol in the available space. It the available space is not enough for displaying the symbol at the minimum font size (4pt), the operator is not shown.

Figure 1 shows an example of this incremental visualization technique. The *MobilePhone* task is the tree root, and it fits the entire visualization width. For this task, there is enough space and the name is visualized entirely, together with the icon and color assigned to the abstract category. For some tasks, such as the *Connect* children, it is not possible to include the entire name. The tool visualizes only the initial part (e.g. "Enter" for *Enter Pin*). For other tasks, the space is not enough even for displaying a small part of the task name. Therefore, the tool shows only a coloured rectangle indicating the presence of a task and its category. For instance, from the visualization in Figure 1, we know that the *Number from list* abstract task has four children, three interactive tasks and one system task. However, we have no information on their names.

The composition operators are visualized using different font sizes. At the higher levels they are bigger and more readable, while at lower levels they are more compact and less distinguishable. In Figure 1, the enabling symbol (≫) between the *Connect* and *Use Phone* task is more readable that the one between the children of the *Number from List* task.

Such layout technique has the drawback of hiding information for tasks at the lower levels, since the space is decomposed in width through the depth levels. Therefore, we added the possibility to select an intermediate task in the model and to set it as the root of the visualization, for focusing on a specific sub-tree. For instance, if we start from from the left part of Figure 1, the user may

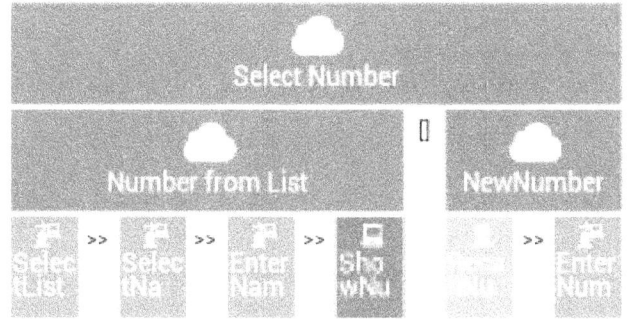

Figure 2. Enlarged visualization for intermediate tasks

Model	Description	Task	Dpt	Pts
Student	Access to student data	7	4	17
CMS	Content Management System	14	4	35
Museum	Virtual Museum	14	4	37
ATM	Automated Teller Machine	16	4	44
Phone	Mobile Phone	28	7	74
Nomadic	Nomadic Application	47	7	120

Table 1. Task models for the visualization comparison

click on the *Select Number* task. The IceTT tool enlarges its visualization and, through an animated transition, sets the selected task as the root of the icicle plot. The resulting visualization is shown in Figure 2. In order to going back to the parent task, the tool interface provides a level up button that can be used for navigating the task tree.

COMPARISON WITH EXISTING TOOLS

In this section, we provide a preliminary comparison between our tool and the visualization of three publicly available environments for modelling tasks: CTTE [6], Hamsters [2] and K-MADe [3], as motivated in the related work section. For the comparison, we considered a set of examples shipped with CTTE (we did not consider collaborative task models), which consists of six models. We re-created all models with all tools. In order to compare the different visualizations we defined a score for quantitatively summarize the visualized information. For each task, we assigned one point if the category is visible, one point if the task name is visualized (or partially visualized) and one point for each readable temporal operator. Such information is shown by all considered tools for each task. The set of models is summarised in Table 1. The "Task" column corresponds to the number of tasks in the model, the "Dpt" column to the maximum depth of the task tree, while "Pts" it the maximum visualization score.

We considered three different standard screen resolutions: QVGA (320x240), VGA (640x480), XGA (1024x768), aligning the root task to the top of the screen and centering it horizontally for calculating the scores. For each model and for each tool, we show in Figure 3 the percentage of the model information shown at the considered resolution. The data shows that the proposed visualization is able to effectively exploit the screen area. With small models it is able to visualize the entire model information already at low resolutions. With larger models, IceTT is able to visualize more information with respect to the other tools for all considered examples. In addition, IceTT consistently increases this advantage passing to higher resolutions. If we consider the QVGA resolution, IceTT is able to show the higher number of model attributes in all cases, except for the *Student* model, where CTTE performed better considering that it is particularly small. IceTT, Hamsters and K-MADe were able to maintain roughly constant the information visualized for all models. The percentages decrease with the growth of the models. In CTTE, the visualized information decreases with the growth of the model because of the horizontal expansion we discussed in the related work section. In particular for the *Nomadic* model, it was able to show only the root task. Passing from QVGA to VGA, IceTT is able to show all information for all models, except for the two largest models, outperforming the other tools on the entire test set. At this resolution, CTTE and Hamsters have a comparable performance, but CTTE is more efficient for the *Museum* and the *ATM* models.

Considering the XGA resolution, all tools are able to show most of the information for the first four models. K-MADe has a performance comparable with CTTE and Hamsters. IceTT is again able to consistently show more information with respect to the other tools. Considering the largest model (*Nomadic*), it is possible to see that only IceTT and K-MADe were able to increase the visualized information with respect to the VGA resolution, while for CTTE and Hamsters the difference is not relevant. However, IceTT was able to show the 66% of the information, while K-MADe only the 22%.

Considering this preliminary results, we can conclude that the proposed visualization has a good potential for representing task models of different sizes even on small screen resolutions. In addition, passing to medium and large screen resolutions, the visualization is able to exploit the space effectively for showing more information.

CONCLUSION AND FUTURE WORK

In this paper we introduced a task model visualization based on icicle plots [5]. The visualization is able to exploit the screen width and to adapt the visualization in order to maintain the model readable, even with low resolutions. We reported on a preliminary comparison against three existing, tools obtaining encouraging results. In the future, we aim to validate the visualization acceptance with the different stakeholders involved in task modelling (e.g. designers, domain experts etc.). In addition, we aim to extend the proposed approach also to other hierarchical models for user interface definition such as gestures and dialog models.

ACKNOLEDGMENTS

We gratefully acknowledge Sardinia Regional Government for the financial sup-port (P.O.R. Sardegna F.S.E. Operational Programme of the Autonomous Region of Sardinia, European Social Fund 2007-2013 - Axis IV Human Resources, Objective l.3, Line of Activity l.3.1 "Avviso di chiamata per il finanziamento di Assegni di Ricerca"

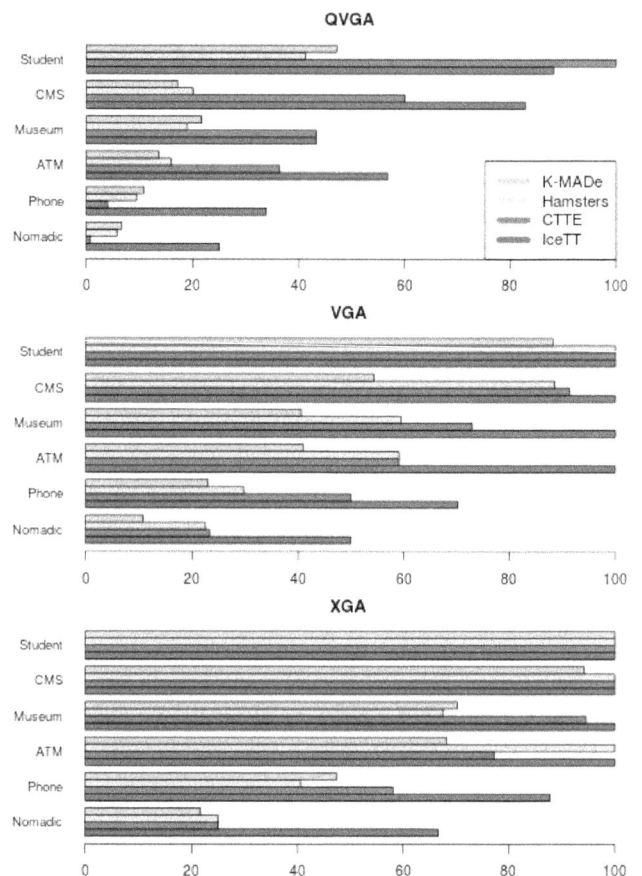

Figure 3. Percentage of task model information visualized at QVGA, VGA and XGA resolutions.

REFERENCES

1. Annett, J., Stanton, N. A., et al. *Task analysis.* 2000.

2. Barboni, E., Ladry, J.-F., Navarre, D., Palanque, P., and Winckler, M. Beyond modelling: An integrated environment supporting co-execution of tasks and systems models. In *Proceedings of the 2Nd ACM SIGCHI Symposium on Engineering Interactive Computing Systems*, EICS '10, ACM (New York, NY, USA, 2010), 165–174.

3. Caffiau, S., Scapin, D., Girard, P., Baron, M., and Jambon, F. Increasing the expressive power of task analysis: Systematic comparison and empirical assessment of tool-supported task models. *Interacting with Computers 22*, 6 (Nov. 2010), 569–593.

4. Garcia Belmonte, N. Javascript Infovis Toolkit `http://philogb.github.io/jit/index.html`. Accessed: 2014-04-09.

5. Kruskal, J. B., and Landwehr, J. M. Icicle plots: Better displays for hierarchical clustering. *The American Statistician 37*, 2 (1983), 162–168.

6. Mori, G., Paternò, F., and Santoro, C. Ctte: support for developing and analyzing task models for interactive system design. *Software Engineering, IEEE Transactions on 28*, 8 (2002), 797–813.

7. Paternò, F. *Model-based design and evaluation of interactive applications.* Springer Verlag, 2000.

ESSAVis++: An Interactive 2Dplus3D Visual Environment to Help Engineers in Understanding the Safety Aspects of Embedded Systems

Ragaad AlTarawneh[1], Jens Bauer[1], Shah Rukh Humayoun[1], Achim Ebert[1], Peter Liggesmeyer[2]

[1]Computer Graphics and HCI Group, [2]Software Engineering: Dependability Group

University of Kaiserslautern

Gottlieb-Daimler-Str. 67663 Kaiserslautern, Germany.

{tarawneh, j_bauer, humayoun, ebert, liggesmeyer}@cs.uni-kl.de

ABSTRACT

In this paper, we present demonstration of a 2Dplus3D visual interactive environment called **ESSAVis++**. It is an enhanced version of the ESSAVis platform and was designed to overcome the limitations of the previous version. Its goal is to facilitate the collaboration between different engineers and to lead to better understanding of the analyzing process of safety aspects in embedded systems. In this work, we provide an overview of ESSAVis++ platform and focus on the new modifications and the set of improvements that we added for providing the enhanced and intuitive visualization features to facilitate extracting important safety aspects about the underlying embedded system.

Author Keywords

Embedded Systems; Safety Aspects Visualization; Graphs visualization; Virtual Reality.

ACM Classification Keywords

C.3 [**SPECIAL-PURPOSE AND APPLICATION-BASED SYSTEMS**]: Real-time and embedded systems, I.3.7 [**Three-Dimensional Graphics and Realism**]: Virtual reality, I.6.8 [**Types of Simulation**]: Visual.

INTRODUCTION

In our application, we focus on helping the system engineers and safety experts in understanding the safety aspects of embedded systems. This is a critical task as nowadays, embedded systems are involved in many activities of our daily life. They are an essential part of many critical systems of our modern life like smart cards, cars, washing machines, robots, airplanes, etc. [8].

Normally, the complexity level of these systems is higher

EICS'14, Jun 17-20 2014, Rome, Italy
ACM 978-1-4503-2725-1/14/06.
http://dx.doi.org/10.1145/2607023.2611453

due to the fact that they consist of different sub-systems with different types (either hardware, software, or a set of interfaces). Due to this, analyzing the safety or the behavioral aspects of these systems is relatively a difficult task [6]. However, because of their usage in performing many of our daily life tasks there is a need to understand properly those critical situations that can affect these systems' safety and reliability levels. This understanding requires an intensive collaboration between different engineers and experts who design, implement, and maintain them.

Involvement of different engineers and experts having different backgrounds in the analyzing process means a difference not only in the used terms to describe the system status but also a difference in seeing the system from their own perspective. For example, *safety experts* are responsible for analyzing the failure relations between the system components, while *system engineers* are more interested in understanding the structural relations between the system components. Therefore, a platform is required for unifying the differences and bringing the participating parties (e.g., system engineers and safety experts) together for a better and accurate understanding of the safety and reliability aspects of these complex systems.

Targeting the above concern, we enhanced our previously developed interactive visual platform, called ESSAVis (Embedded Systems Safety Aspects Visualizer) [1, 4], to help different engineers and experts in collaborating together for analyzing the safety and reliability aspects of embedded systems. We call our enhanced tool **ESSAVis++**, as it provides all the functionalities of ESSAVis, and in addition includes many enhanced interaction options and visualizations to help the interested parties in understanding the safety and reliability aspects more clearly and accurately.

Compared to ESSAVis, few of the additional features provided by ESSAVis++ are: 1) explosion of the system 3D model using a slider bar, 2) using different graph layout techniques according to the situation for visualizing the safety abstract graph model rather than relying on just the orthogonal layout algorithm, 3) allowing users to navigate at different level of details on-demand in the target safety abstract graph representation through the expanding and contracting options attached to compound nodes, 4) additional interactive options to allow users changing the configuration of the scene on-demand, 5) allowing users to get additional information on-demand through a textual information box, and 6) visualizing software metrics information of the selected components.

These new features were driven as a result of a preliminary evaluation study of ESSAVis, conducted with domain experts who indicated some limitations of the platform. Results of that pilot study showed a promising acceptance ratio with high accuracy based on the designed test. However, in the open-ended questionnaires feedback almost all the participated engineers and experts demanded enhanced features to help them in gaining more insight about the underlying safety-scenario. Therefore, we revised the platform with the above-mentioned enhanced options and visualizations in order to provide clear and accurate understanding of the safety and reliability aspects.

THE ESSAVIS++ PLATFORM
In this section, we present ESSAVis++ overview and its capabilities in supporting the analysis of safety aspects of embedded systems while focusing on the new added units.

The key point about the ESSAVis++ platform is its ability of accepting different data sets and then integrating between them seamlessly. This principle is shown in Figure 1.

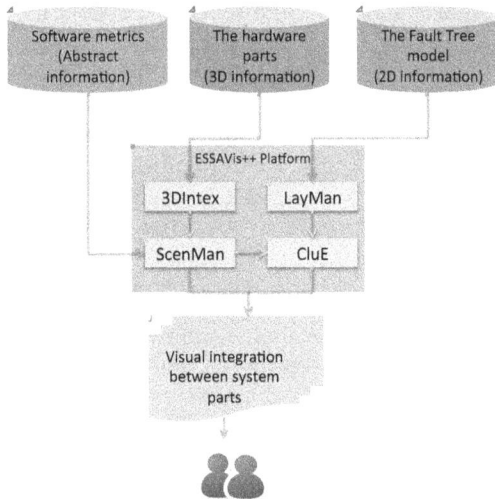

Figure 1. An overview of the possible data sets, acceptable by ESSAVis++.

After integrating the input data sets in different visual representations, ESSAVis++ allows users to interact with it through a number of interaction facilities. It provides two main views, i.e., the *abstract graph representation view* and the *system 3D model view* (see Figure 2), and combines them seamlessly for describing the safety status of the underlying embedded system. The abstract view represents the safety-scenario, which is modeled as a Component Fault Tree (CFT) model [6] of one of the possible failures in the

underlying embedded system. While the system 3D model view represents the geometry information of the underlying system to be analyzed.

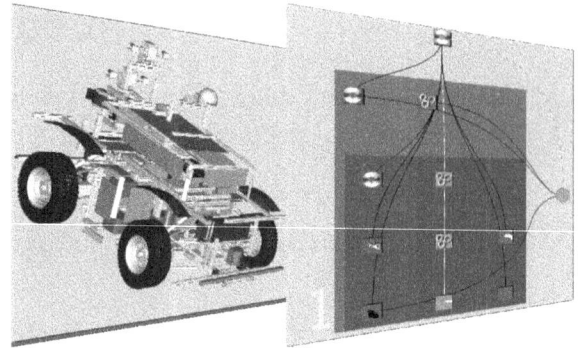

Figure 2. A snapshot showing ESSAVis++ two main views: the *abstract graph representation view* in the front layer (right-side of the figure), and the *system 3D model view* in the back layer (left-side of the figure)

Here, each view (i.e., the abstract view and the system 3D model view) represents the safety status from a different user group's perspective, e.g., system engineers feel more interest towards the system 3D model view while safety experts feels more interest towards the abstract view. The integration between these views helps them in collaborating with each other during the safety analysis process, as it allows them to understand the whole safety situation of the system, not only just from their own perspective, more easily and accurately.

For providing the enhanced interaction options and visual support, ESSAVis++ integrates tightly and seamlessly a set of new developed units. These extensions are useful for analyzing the underlying embedded system faster and more accurately. In the following, we focus on these newly added units and show the visual support and the interaction options provided by them.

The 3DintEX (3D interactive Explorer) Unit
ESSAVis++ uses the 3DintEX unit [2] to render the system 3D model. This unit parses the geometry of the CAD model and then renders it in the 3D world. This unit is also responsible for reducing the complexity of the CAD model in order to accelerate the rendering and the interaction steps. Additionally, it provides a number of interaction options for picking and selecting one or more components of the underlying system 3D model. Moreover, it provides the facility to expand the 3D model on-demand using the *explosion-slider* interaction facility. This option is triggered intuitively such that users can control the distance between the components in the CAD model on-demand. This is especially useful for the system engineers in picking one of the inside components to find further details about the picked component. In Figure 3, we show the exploded view of the system 3D model. The 3DintEx unit was built using the Vrui framework [7].

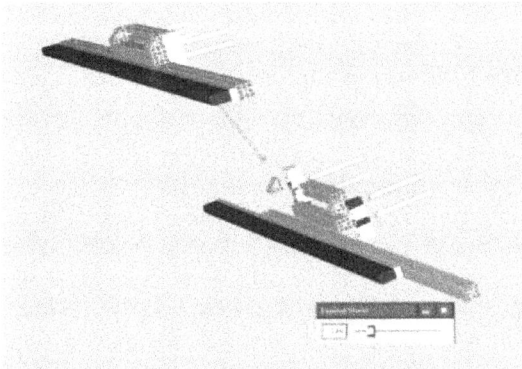

Figure 3. Interacting and exploding the system 3D model using the 3DintEx unit. The top-left side provides the original system 3D model, while the bottom-right side provides the exploded view of the system 3D model. The *explosion-slider* (in the bottom) is used to control the distance between system components.

The LayMan (Layout Manager) Unit

ESSAVis++ provides an abstract representation of the safety-scenario through the *LayMan* unit. This unit first parses the safety scenario modeled as a CFT model [6] and then arranges it on the designed data-structure. After this step, it converts the read data into a compound graph model where the system components are the graph nodes, the failure relations between these nodes are the adjacency relations in the graph model, and the structural relations between these nodes are the structural edges in the graph model. After building the graph model, LayMan uses one of the layout algorithms to calculate the graphical representation of the graph (see Figure 4). Rather than relying on only one layout algorithm, LayMan unit uses different layout algorithms [5] (e.g., the orthogonal layout algorithm, the Sugiyam layout algorithm, the Force-Directed layout algorithm, etc.) for the final graphical representation. It also uses the OGDF framework [9] for calculating the final graph representation.

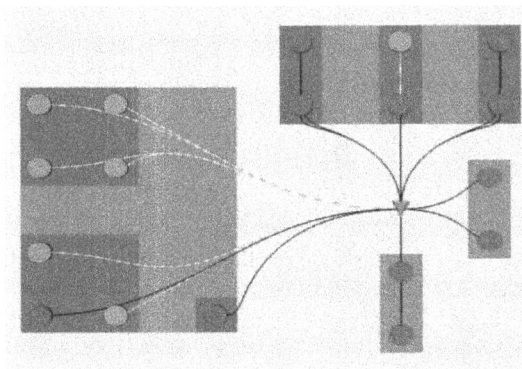

Figure 4. A snapshot showing the graph visualization of the safety-scenario produced by the LayMan unit.

The CluE (Cluster Expander) Unit

ESSAVis++ uses its CluE unit [3] to help users in navigating through the graph representation of the failure mechanism. In this regard, CluE provides the facility to users to expand or contract any of the compound nodes on-demand. The selected component is then expanded to show its internal structure, in addition to the failure relations between the sub-components inside it. This helps in navigating the failure mechanism structure in a way reflecting both, the structural and the failure relations in the graph view. This leads to keep the overall view of the graph and to show extra-level of details on-demand. This facility helps users in reserving the context information about the failure structure (see Figure 5).

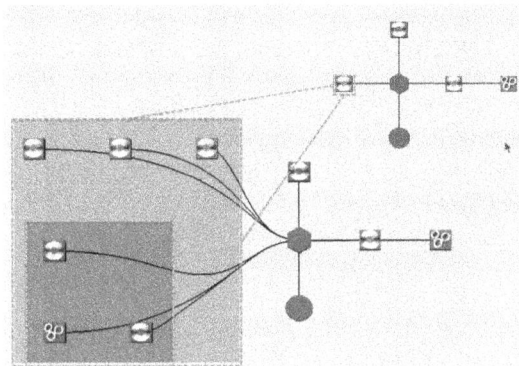

Figure 5. Illustrating the influence of CluE after expanding two nested compound nodes (on the left-bottom side) in the graph.

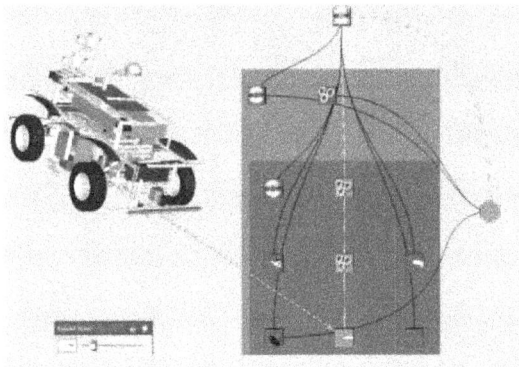

Figure 6. The two main views (i.e., the system 3D model and the abstract graph representation). Integration between two views is done by the SceneMan unit.

The SceneMan (Scene Manager) Unit

ESSAVis++ provides two main views (see Figure 6), the system 3D model and the abstract graph visualization of the system. In order to synchronize between these two views, ESSAVis++ uses SceneMan unit for connecting between them in such a way that if a user selects one node in the graph representation then the corresponding component in the system 3D model is also highlighted, as shown in Figure 6. This helps users in connecting between the two views such that on one hand they can find the location of the critical component from the abstract view to the actual system 3D model on-demand, while on the other hand they can find the failure relations of the selected component in the 3D model using the abstract view. This unit is also responsible for aligning the two views in the 3D space without extra-cluttering. Moreover, it provides different options to allow users to change the configuration of the scene on-demand.

The TextInfo (Textual Information) Unit

In order to extract information about any picked component from any of the two provided views, ESSAVis++ TextInfo unit provides a dialog box option to show the safety-information of the corresponding node (see Figure 7) on-demand. The displayed information includes the criticality value of the selected node, the parent node, and the node's name. The TextInfo unit also provides the facility of visualizing the software metric information embedded in the graph view of the failure mechanism (see Figure 8). This option helps system engineers and safety experts to highlight those software components that might be in a critical safety situation.

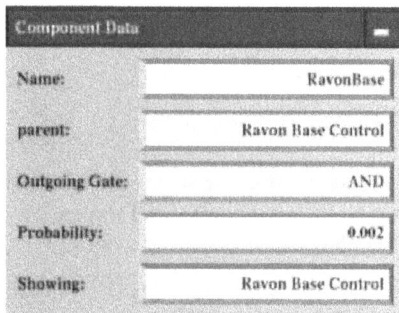

Figure 7. The information Box tool provides extra details about the selected component on-demand.

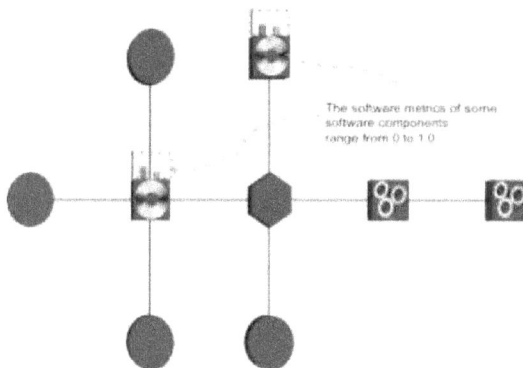

Figure 8. A snapshot showing the software metric information for the two selected software components.

CONCLUDING REMARKS

In this demo paper, we presented an interactive 2D*plus*3D visual platform called ESSAVis++ that helps different engineers and experts in collaborating together for understanding the failure mechanism of complex embedded systems efficiently and accurately. ESSAVis++ extends the ESSAVis [1, 4] platform; therefore, in this work we focused mainly on the enhanced features provided by the newly developed units.

In the conference, we provide a live demonstration of ESSAVis++ using the safety model and the 3D model of the RAVON [10] robot (Figure 2 and 6 show the 3D model of RAVON) for showing the different options provided by our platform.

The visitors of our platform demonstration learn about many aspects, such as: insights about designing and developing visual interactive tools for complex applications like embedded systems, how to integrate between different views of the same system from different perspectives, and how users from different backgrounds can collaborate through one common interactive visual environment. The ESSAVis++ demonstration open doors for further discussion on the challenges and possible improvements in designing and building of visual interfaces for such complex systems.

REFERENCES

1. AlTarawneh, R., Bauer, J., Humayoun, S. R., Ebert, A., and Liggesmeyer, P. Enhancing Understanding of Safety Aspects in Embedded Systems through an Interactive Visual Tool. *IUI Companion '14*. ACM, New York, NY, USA, 9-12, 2014.

2. AlTarawneh, R, Griesser, A., Bauer, J., Humayoun, S. R., and Ebert, A. Poster: 3DintEx -- A Tool to Explore Interactively the Structural and Behavioral Aspects of System Models in 3D Environments. *3DUI 2014*, IEEE, 141-142, 2014.

3. AlTarawneh, R, Schultz, J., Humayoun, S. R. CluE: An Algorithm for Expanding Clustered Graphs. *PacificVis 2014*, IEEE, 233-237, 2014.

4. AlTarawneh, R., Bauer, J., Keller, P., and Ebert, A. ESSAVis: A 2Dplus3D Visual Platform for Speeding Up the Maintenance Process of Embedded Systems. *BCS-HCI 2013*, British Computer Society, Article 43, 6 pages, 2013.

5. Herman, I., Melancon, G., and Marshall, M. S. Graph visualization and navigation in information visualization: A survey. *IEEE Trans on Visualization and Computer Graphics*, 6 (1), 24–43, 2000.

6. Kaiser, B., Liggesmeyer, P., and Mäckel, O. A new component concept for fault trees. *SCS '03* - Volume 33, Australia, 37-46, 2003.

7. Kreylos, O. Vrui: virtual reality toolkit. http://idav.ucdavis.edu/~okreylos/ResDev/Vrui/

8. Lee, E.A., and Seshia, S.A. Introduction to Embedded Systems, A Cyber-Physical Systems Approach. *Published by authors*, First Edition, ISBN 978-0-557-70857-4, 2011.

9. OGDF - Open Graph Drawing Framework, http://www.ogdf.net/

10. Proetzsch, M. Development Process for Complex Behavior-Based Robot Control Systems. *RRLab Dissertations*. Verlag Dr. Hut, 2010.

Implementing Widgets Using Sifteo Cubes for Visual Modelling on Tangible User Interfaces

Yves Rangoni, Valérie Maquil, Eric Tobias, Eric Ras
Public Research Center Henri Tudor
29 avenue JFK, Luxembourg-Kirchberg, Luxembourg
{firstname.lastname}@tudor.lu

ABSTRACT

Tangible user interfaces (TUI) have shown advantages for social and contextual interactions (e.g. collaboration). In this paper, we introduce active and reconfigurable tangibles that enhance the use of a TUI. We propose to design and implement different generic widgets, using Sifteo Cubes, based on a formal widget model. As a scenario, we used a BPMN2 collaborative business modelling task and put a focus on some widgets dedicated to this specific exercise. The use of Sifteo Cubes has been evaluated using this scenario by several participants in three case studies. The paper reports the results of these studies using a working prototype of the concepts presented in this paper.

Author Keywords

Widgets; Sifteo Cubes; Tangible User Interface; Tabletop; Design Science; Design Research

ACM Classification Keywords

H.5.m. Information Interfaces and Presentation (e.g. HCI): Miscellaneous

INTRODUCTION

Tangible user interfaces (TUI) provide new types of interactions combining physical artefacts with digital information in a common interactive space. The idea of TUIs is to make computer bits tangible and to allow users to grasp and manipulate them with their hands [1]. This concept has a number of advantages for social and contextual interactions, such as collaboration [9]. They blend digital information into a physical form [10], allowing the manipulation of the digital through natural, haptic interaction with the object which, by its construction and make, serves as a gateway to the information linked to it.

To date, literature proposes a large range of technical solutions to detect physical manipulations in order to interpret them as input for an application. Simultaneously, research

groups explored different kinds of application domains and evaluated the use of TUI in different contexts, such as urban planning, education, or entertainment.

Although experiments led to the discovery of a multitude of advantages, long-term case studies in real settings have highlighted an inherent problem of TUIs. With the increase in complexity of the application and the amount of functionalities, users are provided with a large number of physical objects that require extra effort to be organized within the workspace [13]. In this paper, we propose a new conceptual solution for interacting with digital information on a tangible tabletop. We describe a set of tangible widgets that use the Sifteo technology [17] in order to be reconfigurable over time. This allows the users, for each step of a selected collaborative work session, to choose the most important controls and to dynamically create widgets with different functionalities. Hence, the number of physical objects is reduced, whereas the support for simultaneous interactions during collaborative work can be maintained. At the same time, we expect the Sifteo cubes to incite interaction beyond the surface of a tabletop TUI [26].

We report on how these widgets have been designed and implemented in the context of collaborative business process modelling. A key aspect of our work is the use of a widget model as support for design and description of the different widgets. In our evaluation, we discuss the utility of reconfigurable widgets in the context of collaborative modelling session and reflect on the use of a formal widget model to design and describe tangible widgets.

RELATED WORK

In this paper, we propose to design active widgets through the use of two technologies: a tangible tabletop and interactive micro-computers. Similar implementations can be found, for example, in the work of Chang et al. [4] whose motivation is to build new biological systems by applying engineering principles (e.g. abstraction, modularity concepts) while using publicly accessible tools. They employed Sifteo Cubes [25] and the SUR40 tabletop from Microsoft to develop the concept of "BioBricks". The Sifteos make the tangibles active by supporting various gestures with objects, such as shaking, flipping, rotating, and neighbouring; typical work patterns of laboratory work.

Other attempts use different technologies, such as Touchbugs [18], Pico [21], or Ultra-Tangibles [15]. They aim to support physical actuation of tangibles on an interactive tabletop. The proposed physical objects use vibrating motors, electromagnets, or ultrasound-based air pressure waves to support autonomous motion across the tabletop surface.

This paper focuses on "everyday situation" of the majority of people who still work with standard computer systems [8], based on well-established technologies and following the philosophy of authors such as [28] on how to bring GUI paradigms on TUI. In our case, the tabletop is built by ourselves [14], driven by the ReacTIVision [11] framework, and the Sifteo Cubes are employed as well. Sifteo Cubes can be described as micro-computers embedded in small plastic cuboids of $4 \times 4 \times 2$ cm. This special physical design makes the cube more graspable [12] than a regular device such as a smartphone. On their top, they feature a 128×128 pixel colour display side. Their internal memory stores pictures and the source code of the application that is executing on the cube. In addition to being able to press the screen and use it as a button, the cubes possess MEMS sensors such as internal 3D-accelerometer which allows the detection of orientation and shaking. On the four smaller sides, the cubes come equipped with a proprietary near-field sensor which allows the detection of neighbouring cubes in close proximity. They are linked to a host computer and a total of six cubes can be continuously monitored. To find more technical details, one can refer to [16], the Sifteo Cubes prototype reveal called "Siftables" or [17] for a more up-to-date description.

Thanks to the use of reconfigurable and tangible objects works such as [6], where the authors propose a prototype for diagram editing on interactive surfaces using multi-touch and pen gesture, can be extended.

METHODOLOGY

In our context, the scientific body of knowledge for developing propositions for tangible widgets is rather limited since most design propositions are not decontextualised enough and rely on very specific applications and technologies used. This is also often the case where innovative solutions have to be designed [20]. This requires that we follow an iterative process with a strong interplay between both types of knowledge creation processes. As stated in [20] we follow a creative and collaborative learning process. Design propositions are iteratively built by combining practical with scientific knowledge.

The scenario of BPMN2 [19] modelling was selected as a concrete application where multiple stakeholders need to collaborate in order to integrate different perspectives in a shared model. Using inspirational material from pop-culture, science fiction, and fantasy, various metaphors have then been identified and used to conceptualise a large range of widgets allowing to create and modify a BPMN 2 model. These widgets were then iteratively selected, implemented, and evaluated with users in three different iterations, allowing to feed back the experience gains to the design of the widget model:

- The first iteration used paper mock-up substitutes to represent BPMN2 objects. Moreover, TUI interactions and feedback were simulated by staff members. This step showed us how users would react to the widgets and how

they would use them to manipulate digital content. It provided useful insights on the acceptance and comprehension of the proposed metaphors.

- The second iteration was played using a preliminary prototype of the TUI and scenario. During this step, several metaphors were refined and added.
- During the third iteration the final prototype was instantiated. The scenario could be fully re-enacted. During this session with the testers, the TUI proved to satisfy their expectation to a point where they went beyond the expected outcome and started exploring the limits of the widgets and their metaphors.

THE SCENARIO OF BUSINESS PROCESS MODELLING

According to Hevner et al. [7] it is essential that the design artefacts be evaluated in practice to demonstrate their utility. This paper aims to evaluate the proposed design artefacts in a custom scenario (Fig. 1) created in [27] as a collaborative modelling scenario on TUI using the Business Process Modeling and Notation 2 (BPMN 2) [3]. The scenario was created to investigate the possibility and benefits of moving a typically isolated one-man modelling activity into a collaborative, visual, and engaging environment. Thus, it provided a good scenario to evaluate the usability of Sifteo-based widgets in a collaborative environment.

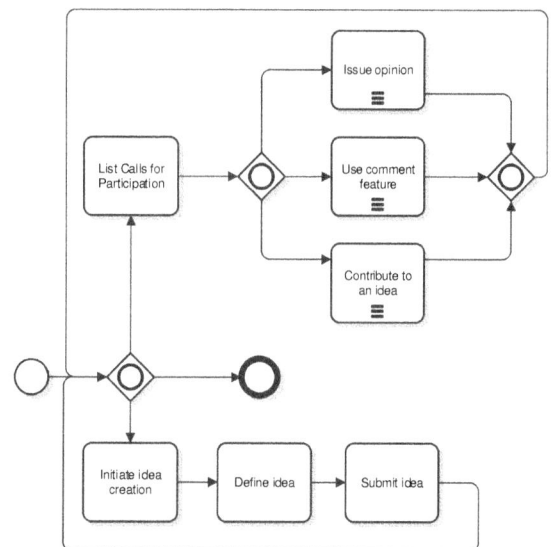

Figure 1. The BPMN2 model to be created in the scenario

DESIGN OF THE WIDGETS

The design of the widget was done with two constraints in mind: first, the widgets were to be designed with the scenario described in the previous section in mind; and second, the widgets had to be instances of a widget model proposed in [2] and formalised in [27]. The former constraint aimed at limiting the scope for the design as well as providing a concrete scenario in which to evaluate the metaphors and the widget design. The latter constraint was introduced to provide a common ground for all widgets and make them comparable and reusable. It also allowed collecting a first data set for evaluating the widget model down the line.

The widget model implements three design propositions: *Separation of Concerns*, *Design by Contract*, and *Atomic Interactions*. The model separates the physical nature of a widget from its behavioural aspects. As several Sifteo cubes will be used in the experimentation, it must be said that physical shape uniformity is clearly not necessarily an advantage. Their screen will be used as a way to reflect different digital functions or modes despite their common physical aspect. Indeed, the physical shape of a tangible user interface element is an important channel of communication between designer and user and it can greatly improve recognition, ergonomics and the directness of interaction [24, 5].

The behavioural aspects are referred to as: a) *WidgetStructure*, composed of one or more atomic *WidgetComponents*, and b) *WidgetBehaviour*. They use what the model calls an *Identity* to attribute functionality to the widget. The functionality is expressed through *Function* which maps *Action*(s) over optional *Effect*(s) to *EndPoint*(s). The *Identity* features a name which allows the widget's behaviour to be used consistently independent from the structural implementation. The same holds true for *Function* which allows referring to specific atomic concepts by name.

Due to the use of the Sifteo Cubes as common platform for all widgets, the *WidgetStructure* draws from the same pool of components. Only their instantiation varies as some widgets might not use all components or multiple instances of the same component. The Sifteo widgets feature:

- a display that shows the nature of the widget, in our case a simple label stating the widget's name;
- a screen to visualise the previously mentioned label;
- the plastic housing;
- a marker to allow the table to track the cube;
- an actuator which emulates a button push;
- and sensors to track the cube's orientation.

Together, these structural elements are referred to as the handle of the widget.

The Zoom widget

The Zoom widget (Fig. 2) is used to zoom in or out on the visualisation on the table surface or parts thereof. The widget uses: the screen visualising "Zoom", the plastic housing, and a uniquely identifiable marker. The rotation angle is captured by the TUI using the marker's transposition as a reference to infer the angle of rotation. The *Wid-*

Figure 2. Zoom widget

getBehaviour is given by its *Identity*, Zoom. The name adequately conveys the metaphor. The widget has three *Functions*. One to bind to a given zone (*Bind*) on the tabletop, one for removing the binding (*Unbind*), and one for mapping the *Action* of rotating the Sifteo Cube to the *Effect* of increasing or decreasing the zoom level depending on the direction of the rotation (*Zoom*). The affected *EndPoint* is the interface zone the Zoom is bound to. It is not uncommon for the name of the most prominent *Function* to be used to denote the *Identity*.

The Sword widget

The Sword widget (Fig. 3) is devoted to deleting scenario objects. The Sword uses the physical shell, the actuator, a specific marker, and two instances of the display. One is used to show its label while the second highlights the screen with a background colour. The widget also features a speaker, in our instance, the speaker of the tangible table. As

Figure 3. Sword widget

a metaphor of a real sword, the purpose is to cut a specific object with the Sword. When the Sword is moved over a component, it is deleted. To prevent any accidents, the widget must be activated/deactivated by pressing its display button. This toggles its internal state and the background colour of the display.In addition to the Bind and Unbind *Functions* mentioned above, the Sword features an Activate *Function* which modifies an internal state and changes the background colour of the display by mapping the *Action* of activating the actuator to the *Effect* of changing the colour. The *EndPoint* is in this case the display *WidgetComponent*. Lastly, a Cut *Function* maps the *Action* of swinging the sword to the *Effect* of deleting a model component and the *Effect* of playing a slashing sound to the *EndPoint* that the Sword was completely swung over.

The Annotation widget

Like the Link widget, the Annotation widget (Fig. 4) features two handles. It uses one physical shell, actuator, marker, and display (i.e. one Sifteo cube). The annotation widget is essential as the knowledge is built on-the-fly. To replace the keyboard to enter data, the widget uses a Wacom Intuos4 Wireless Tablet for on-line handwriting recognition

Figure 4. Writer widget

(Fig. 9). This widget is used by writing any string on the tablet to capture it. The Sifteo handle can then be used as a label maker: activating the widget will print the label onto any underlying BPMN2 component. Existing labels are overwritten. The Annotation widget can be used to label all BPMN2 objects. A discussion about the techniques implemented to tackle the recognition issues can be found in [23].

The Link widget

The Link widget (Fig. 5) is used to establish a connector between two BPMN2 objects. The Link uses two physical shells, two actuators, two unique markers, and both displays. Therefore, the widget uses two Sifteo Cubes. It is used by superposing each Sifteo with an existing BPMN2 component. A preview arrow, a BPMN2 connector, will form.

Figure 5. Link widget

To create the connector, an actuator must be activated. Once established, the Link widget can be removed.

Sporting two handles, the Link widget can bind to two interface zones at once. The Bind *Function* has an *Effect*, the preview arrow, which targets two *EndPoint*s. This *Function* specifies several pre-conditions such that the arrow is only displayed upon binding the second handle and removed when one is unbound. The Activate *Function* will make the connector permanent.

The Stamp widget

The Stamp widget (Fig. 6) is used to create BPMN2 scenario objects. The objects belong to a set of 4 symbols (Fig. 7). The Stamp uses the physical shell, the actuator, a unique marker, gyro sensor, and the display. The Stamp is a metaphor of the regular office stamp. It is used to first prime the stamp by taking on a specific BPMN2 from a dedicated interface area (Fig. 8). Then, the Stamp can be used to imprint the BPMN2 object any number of times on the tabletop which constitutes the modelling canvas.

Figure 6. Stamp widget

Figure 7. The four BPMN2 objects that can be assigned to the *Stamp* widget: *Activity, Start Event, End Event, Inclusive Gateway*

Figure 8. Assignation zone on the tangible table containing BPMN2 objects for use with the Stamp widget

In order to prevent any mishaps, after binding with an interface zone (Bind) the Stamp must be activated (Activate) to either take on a BPMN2 object or imprint an object. Two *Functions* model these separate intents. The first *Function* (Stamp) features preconditions that will only trigger when the Stamp is bound to the assignation zone while the second (Imprint) will only trigger when bound outside of that zone.

While the *Functions* have a different make, the first features an *Effect* which will change the label on the display to mirror the stamped BPMN2 object, both are triggered by the same *Action*. This is an example of how pre-conditions are used to decide which *Function* will execute. Hence, by this design choice, more than one action can execute. This allows for complex widgets to be easily and formally designed. The last *Function* of the Stamp widget allows it to clear the stamped BPMN2 object by shaking the cube (Shake). The gyro sensor will register the *Action* which is mapped to the *Effect*s of clearing the internal state and changing the display back to the original label. Similar to the Sword, the *EndPoint* is the display.

IMPLEMENTATION OF THE WIDGETS

To demonstrate the use of the widget model, we set up a tangible tabletop system, based on the well-known optical tracking framework ReacTIVision [11] where some improvements have been brought [22]. The tabletop surface area measures 95×120 cm, with an effective interactive area of 75×100 cm. A camera and a projector are placed underneath the table to detect objects and project onto the semi-translucent tabletop surface. The area below the table is flooded with infrared light reflected by the acrylic tabletop surface and objects on the surface. The light is captured by an infrared camera inside the table.

The Sifteo Cubes [25] are used as interactive fiducials. We wanted to make use of many embedded features: their independent display, their sensors and their ability to quickly react to any change, and also still being active even if they are used outside the tangible table.

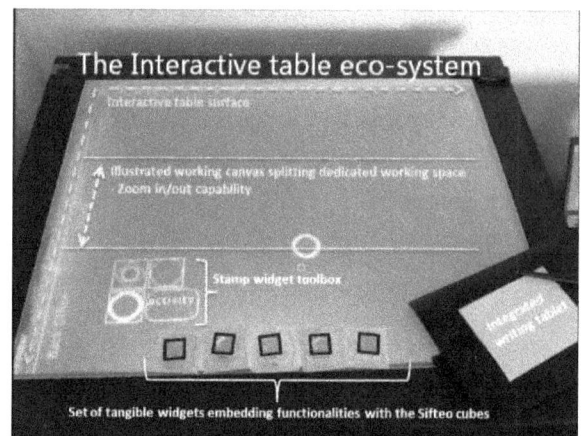

Figure 9. Overview of our tabletop using ReacTIVison and Sifteo Cubes

The tabletop TUI with ReacTIVison and the Sifteo Cubes are two independent devices. From a hardware point of view, plugging them together is straight forward. The solution consists in placing a fiducial on the bottom of each Sifteo cube. When a cube is put on the table surface, it becomes a tangible object. Thanks to the ReacTIVison framework, it can be localised on the table using x and y coordinates as well as its rotation angle (around the z axis). The tangible keep all features offered by its hardware instance making it possible to capture button presses, tilts, flips, shakes, and the proximity with other cubes. Moreover, it keeps its display capability so that the possibility to provide visual feedback to the users is greatly improved.

EVALUATION OF THE WIDGETS

We conducted several case studies based on a scenario of use. The goal of this scenario was to investigate and formulate a business process for submitting ideas, sharing them, asking for them to be peer-reviewed, and participate in help devising other co-worker's ideas (Fig. 1). The purpose of the case studies was to observe how the participants react and how they interact with the TUI while using widgets to solve the problem at hand. The process was modelled using BPMN2 [3].

A step-by-step scenario description has been handed out to the users. This scenario was split into small steps and resumed in a companion document that was distributed to the participants. In each step, the participants were asked to add one or more model entities, building the model from scratch. The participants used different widgets (*Zoom*, *Stamp*, *Chain*, *Link* and *Annotation Marker*) composed of one or more physical handles and appropriate graphical representation on the table surface:

- The *Stamp* widget is used with the stamp toolkit. The assignation zone exposes *start*, *end*, *activity*, and *gateway* elements of BPMN2. The binding between the handle and the BPMN element is highlighted using a red border when a handle is placed on top. Shaking will delete this binding;
- The *Sword* widget is used to delete one or multiple components, including connectors. It only deletes when active, this is shown by a red background on the widget;
- The *Link* widget is made of two handles. When they are placed on top of BPMN2 components, it will preview an arrow spanning between them. When either handle is activated, the arrow is imprinted onto the canvas;
- The *Annotation* widget has two handles: One handle selected the component to be annotated while a second handle, a Wacom Intuos4 PTK-540-WL Wireless Tablet (bottom-right on Fig. 9) was used to capture the writing of the users. When activated over an activity, the current text is overwritten with the recent stored text. If an activity is bound to the cube handle, entering new text will automatically overwrite the currently bound label. Shaking the cube handle will unbind it from the activity.

The three case studies were conducted along the development iterations of the widgets with three users each.

Case study 1: The first test session was played with a very early design of the widgets and no real prototype. The session was played using paper mock-ups for model elements as well as visual feedback from the widgets. The Sifteo Cubes were used to give the users the ability to express their opinion on the haptic dimension of the cubes and whether their use felt natural.

Case study 2: The second test session was played with an early prototype of the widgets. Most of the functionality was available and the Sifteo cube widgets were usable. The user's provided useful feedback about the use of Sifteo's and multiple widget instances. The feedback, for example, that the

use of the Sifteo's screen to show the widget instance by an image and the state of the widget by colour, was implemented in the third case study.

Case study 3: The third and final test session used the final prototype (Fig. 10). In addition to the widgets proposed for the second test phase, the Sword widget was implemented. Furthermore, the widgets provided visual feedback to the users and showed the identity and state of each widget.

Figure 10. Two users collaborating to create a link between two activities

The sessions were recorded on video to analyse the interaction afterwards. Further, qualitative feedback on the utility of the tool and ideas for future features was collected.

An analysis of the video material showed a few interesting insights. A typical collaboration pattern was to distribute work and share widgets between participants. For example, two users were each using one handle of the Link widget. This allowed them to proceed in a more efficient way to create the model. Interestingly, the two users hardly talked while performing these interactions. From this we can observe that the shared space supports exchange of information via body movement, gestures, and physical information in such a way, that, coupled with the intuitive nature of the widgets' functionality, talk is not necessary for coordination.

Due to the early stage of the prototype, the system showed some unintended characteristics. For instance, although the paper printouts of the fiducials were supposed to be stuck onto the Sifteo Cubes, they were loosely lying underneath. During the study, participants made use of this feature in two different situations. First, it allowed them to have a better look at the screen, or show the screen to another participant, by lifting the Sifteo from the table, but not moving the position of the widget (which is actually defined by the fiducial lying on the table). In another situation, the participants distributed the work concerning the use of one widget. One participant held the Sifteo to press the button, while the second one was moving the fiducial along the objects which needed to be deleted. This shows us, on one hand, that participants were able to collaborate in many different ways. On the other hand, it shows that, in contrast to static objects, the interaction area was increased. Sifteo Cubes were controlled outside the interactive surface of the tabletop (i.e. in the hand of a participant), thus allow interaction with the computer in a larger space than conventional, static objects.

Feedback of the studies was used to extend widgets or to develop new widgets (e.g. zoom to extend the canvas). They could be summarised into two types:

- Related to the scenario — Users asked for persistence of the model (i.e., saving the model), they asked for a template feature to reuse parts of the BPMN model, and they expressed the wish to use completed domain models outside of the TUI context.
- Related to the widgets — multimodal feedback was required while using the different widgets. Users asked for an editing of the created labels and rearranging model elements on the canvas. They expressed the need for a larger canvas and proposed ideas for new widgets.

CONCLUSION

This paper has proposed a set of tangible widgets for collaborative business process modelling on a tabletop. The widgets have been developed and evaluated in several iterations using design research methodology.

Our findings show that the reconfigurable widgets each allows to handle multiple controls, hence, provide means to increase the amount of features for an application. At the same time, typical collaborative work situations such as simultaneous interactions, were shown to be supported.

In addition, our results show that the use of interactive widgets allows to increase the area of interaction, thus, extends the hybridity of the user interface beyond the tabletop surface. Users were, for instance, activating objects while holding them in their hands.

ACKNOWLEDGMENTS

The present project is supported by the National Research Fund, Luxembourg and co-funded under the Marie Curie Actions of the European Commission (FP7-COFUND).

REFERENCES

1. Antle, A. N. The CTI framework: informing the design of tangible systems for children. In *International Conference on Tangible and Embedded Interaction*, ACM (New York, USA, 2007), 195–202.

2. Bicheler, P. A toolkit for table-based tangible widgets. Master's thesis, University of Luxembourg, 2012.

3. BPMN2. Business process modeling and notation version 2. www.omg.org/spec/BPMN/2.0, retrieved April 18, 2014.

4. Chang, K., Xu, W., Francisco, N., Valdes, C., Kincaid, R., and Shaer, O. Synflo: an interactive installation introducing synthetic biology concepts. In *International Conference on Interactive tabletops and surfaces*, ACM (New York, USA, 2012), 303–306.

5. Dourish, P. *Where the Action is: The Foundations of Embodied Interaction*. MIT Press, Cambridge, MA, USA, 2001.

6. Frisch, M., Heydekorn, J., and Dachselt, R. Diagram editing on interactive displays using multi-touch and pen gestures. In *International Conference on Diagrammatic Representation and Inference*, Springer-Verlag (Berlin, Heidelberg, 2010), 182–196.

7. Hevner, A. R., March, S. T., Park, J., and Ram, S. Design science in information systems research. *MIS Quarterly 28*, 1 (2004), 75–105.

8. Hurtienne, J., Israel, J. H., and Weber, K. Cooking up real world business applications combining physicality, digitality, and image schemas. In *International Conference on Tangible and Embedded Interaction*, ACM (New York, USA, 2008), 239–246.

9. Hurtienne, J., Weber, K., and Blessing, L. Prior experience and intuitive use: Image schemas in user centred design. In *Designing Inclusive Futures*, P. Langdon, J. Clarkson, and P. Robinson, Eds. Springer London, 2008, 107–116.

10. Ishii, H., and Ullmer, B. Tangible bits: Towards seamless integration between people, bits and atoms. In *Conference on Human Factors in Computing Systems*, CHI'97, ACM (1997), 234–241.

11. Kaltenbrunner, M., and Bencina, R. ReacTIVision. http://reactivision.sourceforge.net, retrieved April 18, 2014.

12. Karlesky, M., and Isbister, K. Fidget widgets: secondary playful interactions in support of primary serious tasks. In *Conference on Human Factors in Computing Systems Extended Abstracts*, ACM (New York, USA, 2013), 1149–1154.

13. Maquil, V. *The ColorTable : an interdisciplinary design process*. PhD thesis, Vienna University of Technology, 2010.

14. Maquil, V., and Ras, E. Collaborative problem solving with objects: Physical aspects of a tangible tabletop in technology-based assessment. In *From Research to Practice in the Design of Cooperative Systems: Results and Open Challenges*, J. Dugdale, C. Masclet, M. A. Grasso, J.-F. Boujut, and P. Hassanaly, Eds. Springer London, 2012, 153–166.

15. Marshall, M., Carter, T., Alexander, J., and Subramanian, S. Ultra-tangibles: creating movable tangible objects on interactive tables. In *Conference on Human Factors in Computing Systems*, ACM (New York, USA, 2012), 2185–2188.

16. Merrill, D., Kalanithi, J., and Maes, P. Siftables: towards sensor network user interfaces. In *International Conference on Tangible and embedded interaction*, ACM (New York, USA, 2007), 75–78.

17. Merrill, D., Sun, E., and Kalanithi, J. Sifteo cubes. In *Conference on Human Factors in Computing Systems Extended Abstracts*, ACM (New York, USA, 2012), 1015–1018.

18. Nowacka, D., Ladha, K., Hammerla, N. Y., Jackson, D., Ladha, C., Rukzio, E., and Olivier, P. Touchbugs: actuated tangibles on multi-touch tables. In *Conference on Human Factors in Computing Systems* (2013), 759–762.

19. OMG. Business Process Model and Notation. Specification, Version 2.0, Object Management Group, 2011.

20. Pascal, A., Thomas, C., and Romme, A. G. L. Developing a human-centred and science-based approach to design: The knowledge management platform project. *British Journal of Management 24*, 2 (2013), 264–280.

21. Patten, J., and Ishii, H. Mechanical constraints as computational constraints in tabletop tangible interfaces. In *Conference on Human factors in computing systems*, ACM Press (New York, USA, 2007), 809.

22. Rangoni, Y., and Ras, E. Benchmarking binarisation techniques for 2D fiducial marker tracking. In *International Conference on Pattern Recognition Applications and Methods* (2014).

23. Rangoni, Y., Ras, E., and Vajda, S. Using handwriting recognition modality in tangible user interface. In *International Workshop on Graphics Recognition* (2013).

24. Shaer, O., Leland, N., Calvillo-Gamez, E. H., and Jacob, R. J. K. The TAC paradigm: specifying tangible user interfaces. *Personal Ubiquitous Computing 8*, 5 (2004), 359–369.

25. Sifteo Inc. Sifteo - Intelligent Play. https://www.sifteo.com, retrieved April 18, 2014.

26. Sutcliffe, S. W., Ivkovic, Z., Flatla, D. R., Pavlovych, A., Stavness, I., and Gutwin, C. Improving digital handoff using the space above the table. In *Conference on Human Factors in Computing Systems*, ACM (New York, USA, 2013), 735–744.

27. Tobias, E. Visual Modelling of and on Tangible User Interfaces. Master's thesis, University of Luxembourg, 2012.

28. Ullmer, B., and Ishii, H. The metadesk: Models and prototypes for tangible user interfaces. In *Symposium on User Interface Software and Technology*, UIST '97, ACM (New York, USA, 1997), 223–232.

LoMAK: A Framework for Generating Locative Media Apps from KML files

Trien V. Do and Keith Cheverst
School of Computing and Communications
Lancaster University
{t.do, k.cheverst}@lancaster.ac.uk

Ian Gregory
Department of History
Lancaster University
i.gregory@lancaster.ac.uk

ABSTRACT

In this paper, we present the LoMAK framework which enables non-programmers (e.g., people working in the Digital Humanities, History, Geography, Geology and Archaeology areas) to generate locative media mobile apps from KML files, a format that these non-programmers are familiar with. The framework has two primary components: a *KML processor* web application and an Android mobile "player" app called *LoMAK player*. The *KML processor* parses KML files to: (1) extract points of interest (POI) and their associated media, (2) produce geo-fences for the POIs, and (3) render the PoIs and their geo-fences on a map. The framework also supports the editing of geo-fences, i.e., a new geo-fence can be drawn as a polygon. The POIs and their associated media and geo-fences are then saved as a *sharc* file on a server. The *LoMAK player* loads this *sharc* file to operate as a locative media application.

Author Keywords

Push-based; KML; Locative media; LBS; Geo-fences; Authoring tool; Framework.

ACM Classification Keywords

H.5.m. Information interfaces and presentation (e.g., HCI): Miscellaneous.

INTRODUCTION AND MOTIVATION

Locative media [2] mobile apps deliver relevant content to the user based on their current location. Designing and developing such apps often requires knowledge of different disciplines, e.g., Human-Computer Interaction, Software Engineer, and Interaction Design. The MediaScape framework [4] was introduced to enable non-programmers to design and develop locative media apps by simply drawing geo-fences and then associating media with these geo-fences.

Existing tools including both desktop applications, e.g., Google Earth, and mobile apps, e.g., FieldTrip GB (fieldtripgb.blogs.edina.ac.uk), allow the user to easily

associate media with locations then export these data to KML files. In this paper, we present the LoMAK framework which supports non-programmers (e.g., people working in the Digital Humanities, History, Geography and Archaeology areas) in generating locative media mobile apps from KML files, a format that these non-programmers are familiar with.

The motivation for this research derives from the involvement of the authors with two ongoing projects. The following subsections describe the projects in greater detail.

Shared Curation of Local History (SHARC)

The Wray PhotoDisplay [8] is a community photo display system which was co-designed with the residents of the village of Wray (a small village in the North West of England) using a technology probe [5] based approach (see Figure 1.a). One key co-design decision was to allow residents in the village to take ownership (including moderations) of their own content categories such as "Wray Flood", "Old Photos", etc. As of March 2014, 2635 photos (over 10 categories with 26 subcategories) have been uploaded to the PhotoDisplay. Photos of the "Old photos" category particularly relate to the local history of the village. Approximately, 80% of these photos are related to different historic locations in Wray. Most of these historic locations are landmarks (e.g., the Wray School). Comments can be added to photos and currently, 72% of them are associated with photos relating to the village's history.

The goal of the SHARC project is to explore other potential tools (e.g., mobile apps) to support the members of Wray in curating and sharing photos, stories, and narratives relating to local history. The shared content will be consumed by both residents (e.g., newcomers or children) and visitors.

In order to inform requirements for potential mobile tools, the authors had an interview with a local historian in Wray in July 2013. After the meeting, the historian took the authors for a 30-minute guided walk around the village. During the walk, the historian delivered an audio narrative which referred to six historic locations within the village. As the walk was unplanned, the authors recorded the narrative using a Dictaphone. Later, to obtain a GPS trace of the walk, one author came back and captured a trace of the guided walk using the My Tracks app (www.google.com/mobile/mytracks) on a smartphone. The trace was then exported to a KML file. Google Earth was then used to associate photos in the "Old photos" category with the six landmarks referred to in the historian's narrative (see Figure 1.b). One such photo is a photo of the Wray School landmark (see Figure 1.c).

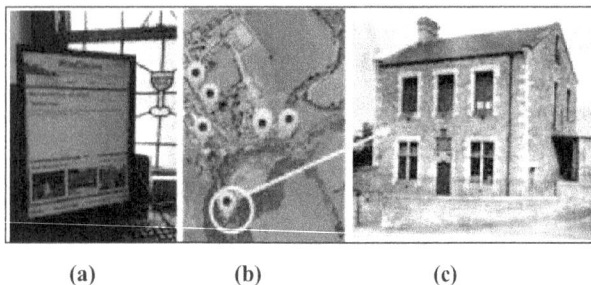

(a)   **(b)**   **(c)**

Figure 1. History related content in Wray village: a) the Wray PhotoDisplay deployed in the village pub, b) trace of a guided walk with 6 landmarks passed en-route highlighted, c) an old photo of the Wray School.

One avenue that the authors discussed with the historian was about developing a mobile push-based tool which will allow residents and visitors of Wray to experience his walk. For example, when a visitor is crossing the Wray School, the appropriate narrative (recorded from the local historian) would be automatically pushed and played to the visitor.

Streets of Mourning in the City of Lancaster (SoM)
The second project is concerned with commemorating casualties of the First World War. As part of the project, a webpage has been developed by researchers in Digital Humanities to show casualties from the city of Lancaster on the streets where they lived. An extract of the webpage is illustrated in Figure 2. Each shaded street contains one or more addresses of casualties. This mapping is stored in a KML file in order to enable it to be rendered on a webpage in a straightforward manner. A user can interact with the webpage by clicking on a street in order to be shown further details about casualties (e.g., house numbers, names of casualties, dates of death, ages).

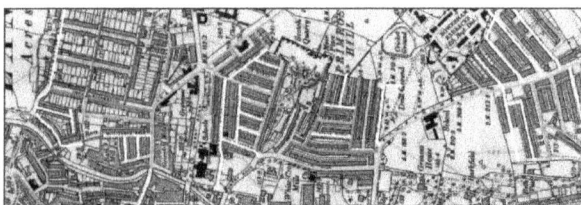

Figure 2. First World War casualties from Lancaster city.

The next step of the project is to create a mobile app which provides the user with a locative media experience. For example, when a person with interest in history walks into Windermere road, the mobile app would push information about casualties who used to live on the road.

The LoMAK Framework
The LoMAK framework has been designed to address the need for supporting non-programmers in generating locative media mobile apps from KML files. The framework has two primary components: a *KML processor* web application and

an Android mobile app called *LoMAK player*. The *KML processor* parses KML files to: (1) extract points of interest (POI) and their associated media, (2) produce geo-fences for the POIs, and (3) render the POIs and their geo-fences on a map. The framework also supports the editing of geo-fences, i.e., a new geo-fence can be drawn as a polygon. The POIs and their associated media and geo-fences are then saved as a *sharc* file (our own project file extension). The *LoMAK player* loads this *sharc* file to operate as a locative media app.

The remainder of this paper is structured as follows. In the next section we present background and related work. The design, development, and initial test of the LoMAK framework are then described. Finally, we present our conclusions and future work.

BACKGROUND AND RELATED WORK
Three areas of background and related work are applicable to the work presented in this paper, namely: locative media, associated development tools for non-programmers to design and create locative media apps, and KML.

Locative Media
A number of definitions of locative media are discussed in [2]. Recently, locative media has been put in a more social setting context: "The development of locative media applications is not simply about the physical location or social setting in which the interaction occurs, but rather about situating the media within the social setting of a community" [10]. An early example of a locative media system was the project "34 North 118 West" (34n118w.net). The system pushed audio narratives relating to places in Los Angeles when people passed by. GUIDE [1] pushed information about city landmarks to visitors of Lancaster city as the visitors approached (a pull-based version could also be used). Recently, with the growing of smartphone market, the number of locative media mobile apps has arisen from both research and commercial domains. However, the majority use a pull-based approach. Key considerations when designing a locative media app are as follows:

i.   When locative media should be pushed to the user: a previous study [1] suggested that media should only be pushed to the user where they can relate the media with physical locations around them.
ii. How to inform the user of the arrival of pushed media without requiring them to check their phones constantly: vibration alerts and notification sounds are candidate approached (e.g., [3]). The importance of supporting different notification sounds was also investigated in [1].
iii. How new media (e.g., an audio clip or screen graphic) should be presented to the user: *Back* and *Hold* approaches are described in [1]. With the *Back* approach, the latest media replace the previous. By contrast, with the *Hold* approach, media are pushed into a queue and the user interacts with the system in order to decide when to see the next media.

iv. How to address the issue of absent or limited data connectivity: caching media on a mobile device's local storage is employed in [1, 4, 6].

Tools to Design and Create Locative Media Apps

Previously, tools have been developed to support non-programmers in designing and creating locative media mobile apps. The most notable example is MediaScape [4], a framework which makes applications that delivery media in response to contextual cues such as the user's current location. The framework comprises three components: Mscape Maker, Mscape Tester, and Mscape Player. The Mscape Maker is a desktop authoring application which allows designers to design locative media by drawing geo-fences and associating media with these geo-fences. The designed media can be tested on the Mscape Tester which is another desktop application with a GPS simulator. Finally, the Mscape Player app loads the designed media to operate as a locative media app. MediaScape is still available for free download now. However, the Mscape Player was implemented for PDAs with Windows Mobile 2003 only.

Recently, the IVO [7] and 7Scene (7scenes.com) frameworks have been developed to provide similar functionality of MediaScape. These frameworks provide: (1) Web-based authoring tools for designers to create context-aware (e.g., location) applications by drawing geo-fences and associating geo-fences with media, and (2) iOS and Android mobile "player" apps for loading applications created by the authoring tools to operate as a locative media app. Both IVO and 7Scene are commercial products.

The LoMAK framework presented in this paper has been designed for the same goal of MediaScape, IVO, and 7Scene. However, unlike the aforementioned frameworks, LoMAK has the novel feature of exploiting KML files to automatically produce geo-fences and associate media with these geo-fences.

KML

Standing for Keyhole Markup Language, KML [11] is an XML notation for expressing geographic annotation and visualization. In short, a KML file describes a collection of geographic objects utilizing geometry elements (e.g., point, polyline, and polygon) and associates these objects with related media (e.g., text, images, audios, and videos). Media are often uploaded to a server then linked in KML documents. An excerpt of a KML file describing the Wray School in the SHARC project is shown in Figure 3, where the "Wray School" POI is represented by a single point. In the meanwhile, the streets in the SoM project are represented by polylines.

Being an open standard, KML is used by a wide range of users (e.g., architects, students, teachers, scientists, and organizations such as National Geographic and UNESCO) to display their rich sets of global data [11]. Numerous consumer and specialist applications can display KML files, including: Google Earth, Google Maps, ESRI ArcGIS Explorer, etc. One way of creating and editing a KML document is to use Google Earth. A number of mobile apps such as FieldTrip GB and Trip Journal (www.trip-journal.com), which enable the user to capture their routes, notes, photos, and videos, also allow the user to export these data to KML files.

```
<?xml version="1.0" encoding="UTF-8"?>
<kml xmlns="http://www.opengis.net/kml/2.2">
<Document>
<name>Cultural heritage related content in Wray</name>
<Placemark>
    <name>THE WRAY SCHOOL</name>
    <description>
    <![CDATA[<p>This is the XYZ school...</p>
    <p><img src="http://xyz.com/data/OldSchool.jpg"/></p>
    <p><img src="http://xyz.com/data/NewSchool.jpg"/></p>
    <audio controls autoplay>
        <source src="http://xyz.com/data/School.mp3"
        type="audio/mpeg"></audio>]]>
    </description>
    <Point>
        <coordinates>-2.6086,54.1013,0</coordinates>
    </Point>
</Placemark>
    ...
</Document>
</kml>
```

Defining a geographic object
Object's name
Describing associated media
Object's geometry type and coordinates

Figure 3. A KML excerpt describing the Wray School.

DESIGN OF LOMAK

The LoMAK framework comprises two components: the *KML processor* web application for authoring media and the *LoMAK player* mobile app for "playing" authored media. To avoid ambiguities, in the remainder of this paper, the term "designers" refers to people who will use the *KML processor* (e.g., members of the SoM project) and the term "consumers" refers to people who will use the *LoMAK player* (e.g., visitors and residents of Wray). The designers are required to have basic computer skills while the consumers should be familiar with using android apps on smartphones to fully exploit the *LoMAK player*'s features.

In order to use the LoMAK framework to design locative media, a designer is required to carry out three steps:

1. Load a KML file.
2. Optionally edit geo-fences and associated media of POIs extracted from the selected KML file.
3. Save POIs, geo-fences, and associated media to a *sharc* file on the KML processor's server.

To operate as a locative media app, the *LoMAK player* needs to load a *sharc* file. In the SHARC project, it is envisaged that visitors and residents can download the *LoMAK player* with a pre-loaded *sharc* file from the PhotoDisplay to their phones via Bluetooth or Wi-Fi while sitting in front of the PhotoDisplay in the village pub (see Figure 1.a). Conversely, in the SoM project, the tourist information center of Lancaster city can install the *LoMAK player* on smartphones and lend them to visitors. In other cases, consumers can browse and load available *sharc* files by selecting a menu (described later).

The following subsections describe the design of the LoMAK framework in detail.

The KML Processor Web Application

The *KML processor* contains a *task pane* and a *map view* (see Figure 4). The *task pane* enables designers to select a KML file and save designed media as a *sharc* file in a straightforward manner. To generate locative media apps, the *KML processor* needs to produce geo-fences for POIs. The results of this process need to be intuitive to the designers so they can preview and edit geo-fences and associated media. The *map view* is for these purposes.

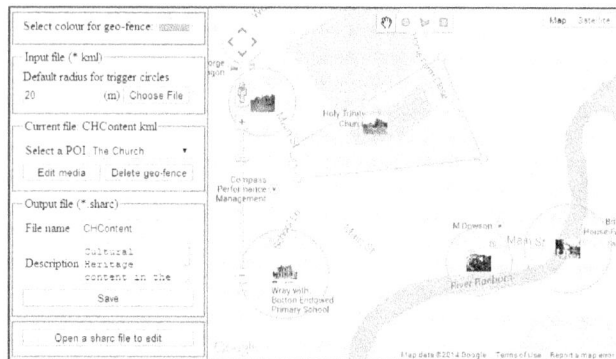

Figure 4. The *KML processor*'s user interface.

After loading a KML file, the *KML processor* parses its content. Each *Placemark* element (see Figure 3) is used to create a POI. The name, associated media, and coordinates of the POI are extracted from the *name, description*, and *coordinates* child elements of the *Placemark* element respectively. The names of all created POIs are then displayed in a dropdown list (see Figure 4). Next, the *KML processor* automatically produces geo-fences for these POIs. The *map view* presents the POIs and their geo-fences on a map. A POI can be represented by an image thumbnail if one of its associated media is an image or a video clip (an image can be extracted from the first frame of the video clip). A designer can click on a geo-fence to view its associated media.

One key challenge when designing the *KML processor* was how to automatically produce geo-fences for POIs. The current design creates geo-fences by using circles whose centers are at the coordinates of the POIs and radiuses are set in a textbox by designers before loading a KML file (see Figure 4). For example, when a POI is represented by a single point in a KML file (e.g., the Wray School in the SHARC project), this point is used as the center of the circle. If a POI is represented by other shapes (e.g., line, polyline, polygon) multiple circles are used. The centers of these circles are the vertices of the shapes. For example, in the SoM project, Windermere road in Figure 5 is represented by a line, so two circles are placed at the two end points of the line. When consumers reach these circles, media are pushed to them.

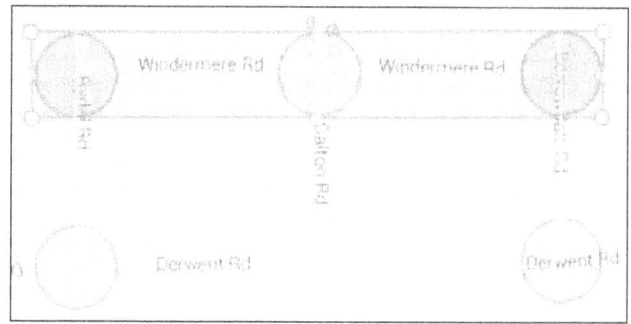

Figure 5. Roads are represented by lines/polylines.

It can be argued that if a POI is represented by a polygon in a KML file, the polygon should be used as a geo-fence. However, if so, media will not be pushed to consumers until they actually reach the POI. It is common that the consumers reach one of the vertices of a POI before other points of its boundary, therefore creating geo-fences as circles at these vertices will push media to the consumers when they view the POI from some distance away. In future work, algorithms to create geo-fences by drawing polygons around lines/polylines and expanding polygon boundaries of POIs will be investigated.

While geo-fences are highly automated, there will be occasions when designers will require a more sophisticated and manual approach to designing geo-fences. Therefore the *KML processor* allows the designers to edit geo-fences (e.g., editing boundaries of geo-fences, moving geo-fences to new locations, and adding new geo-fences). For example, in the SoM project, Windermere road in Figure 5 can also be accessed from Dalton road, so a designer can either add a new circle at the intersection of these two roads or draw a polygon around the road to define its geo-fence.

To add a new geo-fence for a POI, a designer first selects a POI from the dropdown list, e.g., *The Church* in Figure 4. By default, associated media of a new geo-fence are the media associated with the POI. However, the designer can edit the media by clicking on the "Edit media" button if s/he wants to push different media to consumers (e.g., photos taken from other perspectives of the POI). A simple HTML editor is employed for this editing task. Next, the designer can select the circle, polygon, or rectangle icons on the *drawing toolbar* at the top of the *map view* to start defining a new geo-fence as a circle, polygon, or rectangle respectively.

To select a geo-fence for editing, a designer simply needs to click on it. The designer can then move the geo-fence to a new location by dragging and dropping, edit its boundary by dragging and dropping its anchor points (see the polygon in Figure 4), or delete it by clicking on the "Delete geo-fence" button.

As illustrated in Figure 4, the *KML processor* enables designers to save all POIs, geo-fences, and associated media to *sharc* files on the server of the web application by clicking the "Save" button. When this button is clicked, Meta data about *sharc* files (e.g., filename, description, created date) are also stored in a database on the server.

The LoMAK Player Mobile App

The *LoMAK player* app has two primary components: a *map view* and a *menu system*. The menu system saves the screen real estate as it is only shown when consumers touch the menu button of a smartphone. The *map view* uses the whole screen to present POIs and geo-fences on a map (see Figure 6.a).

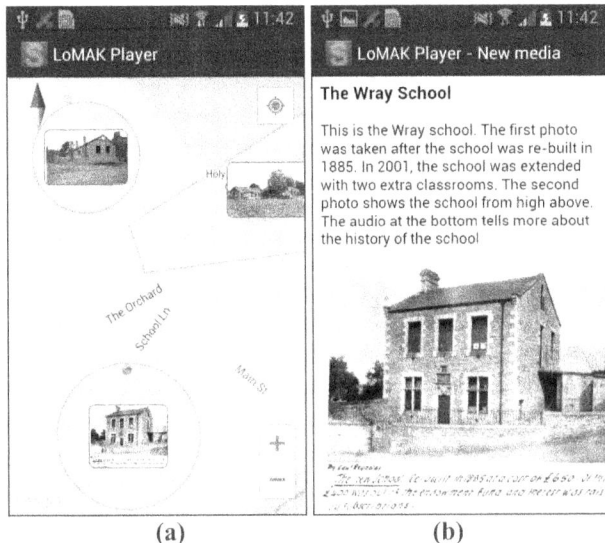

(a)   (b)

Figure 6. The *LoMAK player*: a) POIs and geo-fences on the *map view*, b) an example of media pushed to a consumer.

Consumers can customize their own preferences in a configurations form (see Figure 7). With the default configurations, when the menu item "Browse online *sharc files" is selected, the *LoMAK player* app connects to the server of the *KML processor* to retrieve and show the list of all available *sharc* files. Once a file on the list is chosen, the app downloads the file and all associated media (e.g., photos, audios, videos) to the smartphone in order to enable the app to function despite absent or limited data connectivity later. After loading the chosen *sharc* file, the *LoMAK player* displays its POIs and geo-fences on the *map view* (see Figure 6.a). The geo-fences are then registered to a *location tracking service* which runs in the background of the smartphone. This service regularly checks if the current position of a consumer is within any geo-fences. If the consumer is within a geo-fence, the app will examine the associated media of the geo-fence and will render the media (e.g., playing an audio file) if they have not been previously rendered. The *Back* approach is employed if there is more than one media pushed to the consumer. Figure 6.b is an example of media about the Wray School pushed to a consumer. As the service runs in the background, consumers can use other apps or leave their phones in the sleeping mode and do not need to check their phones constantly. Both vibration and notification sound can be used to inform the consumers about new media. The

LoMAK player can operate as an audio only guide if a consumer selects the "Push audio media only" option.

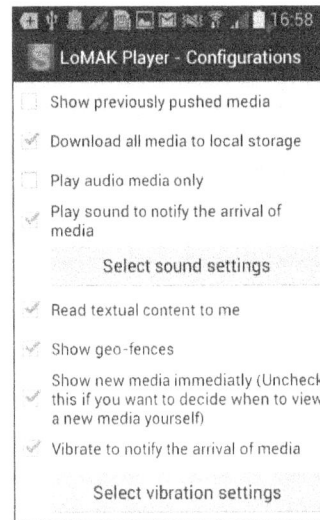

Figure 7. Configurations form.

IMPLEMENTATION

In general, any maps with open APIs (e.g., *Google Maps, OpenStreetMap*) can be used to implement the *map view* and to render POIs and geo-fences in the *KML processor* and *LoMAK player*. Although, *Google Maps* is currently employed, designers and consumers will be able to choose between *Google Maps* and *OpenStreetMap* later. The rest of this section summarizes the implementation of the *KML processor* and *LoMAK player*.

The KML Processor Web Application

The *KML processor* web application has been implemented with HTML/CSS and JavaScript for the front end and PHP with a MySQL database for the backend.

To extract POIs and their associated media in a KML file, JavaScript is used to parse the DOM tree of the KML file. The *Google Maps DrawingManager* class is employed to provide the *drawing toolbar* at the top of the *map view*. POIs, geo-fences, and their associated media are converted to a JSON object before being transferred to the server. The JSON object is then stored in a *sharc* file as a text file. Because JSON is an open standard and language-independent format, *sharc* files generated by the *KML processor* can be shared and reused in other projects. Metadata about the *sharc* file (e.g., name, description, created date) are inserted to a MySQL database.

The LoMAK Player Mobile App

The *LoMAK player* app has been implemented as an Android app. Its main user interface extends the *Activity* class while the *location tracking service* (see the Design of LoMAK section) extends the *Service* class. A standard Android *Webview* class is used to render media. Similar to a web browser, this *Webview* can render all types of media (e.g., text, images, audios, and videos) using built-in media controls of the Android OS. The *LoMAK player* retrieves data from the server via PHP webpages.

The *LoMAK player* is compatible with Android OS version 3.0 and newer. It has been tested with Samsung Galaxy Ace II, Samsung Galaxy S4, Google Nexus 5, and Google Nexus 7. Android was selected because as in October 2013, Android hit more than 80% the market share for smartphone shipments worldwide [12]. Another version of the *LoMAK player* for iOS will be developed in the future.

INITIAL TEST

The LoMAK framework has been initially tested with the KML files of the aforementioned projects and another *test case* which describes five landmarks on the campus of Lancaster University. With the SoM project, running on the Google Chrome browser on a Dell OptiPlex 9010, Intel® Core™ i7-3770 CPU @ 3.40 GHz, 6 GB RAM, the *KML processor* produced 1532 geo-fences for 258 POIs (streets) in less than 2 seconds. Its generated *sharc* file was less than 1MB. Other cases had much fewer POIs and geo-fences.

The *LoMAK player* has also been tested with the *test case* by an intern who was unfamiliar with the university and the app. The app was installed on a Samsung Galaxy Ace II. The *System Monitor* app on Android indicated that the *LoMAK player* used 0.0-0.5% CPU and 20-22 MB RAM. Initial feedback from the intern exposed two issues:

i. Media were not always pushed to the intern timely.
ii. Once, when a photo of a building was pushed to the intern, she could not relate the photo with any buildings around because the photo was taken from a different perspective.

These issues highlighted the need that designers should run the *KML processor* on a tablet to test and edit geo-fences and associated media in-situ in multiple iterations.

CONCLUSIONS AND FUTURE WORK

This paper has described LoMAK, a framework which allows non-programmers to design and create locative media apps. In comparison with other frameworks such as MediaScape, IVO, and 7Scene, the LoMAK framework is novel because it exploits geo-referenced media in existing KML files rather than requiring designers to define all geo-fences and associate media with these geo-fences. There are two scenarios which the framework will benefit designers:

i. According to [11], a number of individuals and organizations have used KML files to describe their rich sets of global data. They can use the LoMAK framework to create locative media mobile apps.
ii. One of the key requirements of designing locative media apps is that a designer should be able to create and associate media for a location when in-situ [9]. The LoMAK framework supports this. For example, the historian in the SHARC project can use an app such as FieldTrip GB in order to capture his narratives and

photos at historic locations in the village of Wray and comes home to export the data to a KML file which can then be used in the LOMAK framework.

In the near future, the LoMAK framework will be evaluated with the two aforementioned projects.

ACKNOWLEDGMENTS

This work was carried out as part of the EPSRC-funded SHARC project (EP/K015850/1).

REFERENCES

1. Cheverst, K., Mitchell, K., and Davies, N. Exploring Context-aware Information Push. *Personal and Ubiquitous Computing 6*, 4 (2002), 276-281.

2. Galloway, A. and Ward, M. Locative Media As Socialising And Spatializing Practice. *Leonardo electronic almanac 14*, 3 (2006).

3. Hornecker, E., Swindells, S., and Dunlop, M. A mobile guide for serendipitous exploration of cities. In *Proc. MobileHCI 2011,* ACM Press (2011), 557-562.

4. Hull, R., Ben, C., and Tom, M. Rapid Authoring of Mediascapes. In *Proc. UbiComp 2004,* Springer (2004), 125-142.

5. Hutchinson, H., Hansen, H., Roussel, N., et al. Technology probes: inspiring design for and with families. In *Proc. CHI 2003,* ACM Press (2003), 17-24.

6. Oppermann, L., Flintham, M., Reeves, S., et al. Lessons from touring a location-based experience. In Proc. *Pervasive 2011,* Springer (2011), 232-249.

7. Realinho, V., Dias, A.E., and Romão, T. Testing the Usability of a Platform for Rapid Development of Mobile Context-Aware Applications. *Proc. Interact 2011,* Springer (2011), 521-536.

8. Taylor, N. and Cheverst, K. Social interaction around a rural community photo display. *International Journal of Human-Computer Studies 67*, 12 (2009), 1037-1047.

9. Weal, M.J., Hornecker, E., Cruickshank, D.G., et al. Requirements for in-situ authoring of location based experiences. In *Proc. MobileHCI 2006,* ACM Press (2006), 121-128.

10. Willis, K.S. and Cheverst, K. Editorial: Special issue of international journal of human-computer studies locative media and communities. *International Journal of Human-Computer Studies 69*, 10 (2011), 615-617.

11. Request for comment on KML 2.2. http://www.opengeospatial.org/standards/requests/45

12. Android tops 81 percent of smartphone market share in Q3. http://www.engadget.com/2013/10/31/strategy-analytics-q3-2013-phone-share

The FrameSoC Software Architecture
for Multiple-View Trace Data Analysis

Generoso Pagano
INRIA
Grenoble, Rhône-Alpes
generoso.pagano@inria.fr

Vania Marangozova-Martin
UJF
Grenoble, Rhône-Alpes
vania.marangozova-martin@imag.fr

ABSTRACT

Trace analysis graphical user environments have to provide different views on trace data, in order to be effective in helping the comprehension of the traced application behavior. In this article we propose an open and modular software architecture, the FrameSoC workbench[1], which defines clear principles for view engineering and for view consistency management. The FrameSoC workbench has been successfully applied in real trace analysis use cases.

Author Keywords

Multiple-Views; User Interface; User Interaction; Ergonomics; Publish-Subscribe; Software Engineering; Execution Traces; Trace Management; Infrastructure.

ACM Classification Keywords

H.5.2 User Interface: Graphical user interfaces (GUI); D.2.5 Testing and Debugging: Tracing

INTRODUCTION

Execution trace analysis, though useful for debugging and performance evaluation of complex applications, is often a very difficult task. Indeed, traces are far from standard: they may contain huge amounts of information, which differ in their formatting, encoding and semantics. In this context, trace management and analysis tools are crucial in helping the developer manipulate and analyze the data conveniently and efficiently. A critical point of these tools is the provided graphical user environment.

Given the heterogeneity and the complexity of traces, there is no single data representation fitting all data manipulation requirements. As the user needs to investigate data using different perspectives and different levels of abstraction, the graphical environments needs to provide a multiple-view approach

to data representation. The different views have to compose a rich set that is intuitive to use and simple to understand. Indeed, the user should not be hindered by view heterogeneity and it should be simple to pass from one view to another. The different views should consistently represent trace data in accordance with the user attention focus and graphical elements selection. Moreover, the environment should not limit the user by imposing a fixed set of predefined views. The multiple-view management should be open and modular to allow for new view integration.

In this article we present the FrameSoC workbench, a multiple-view graphical user environment that responds to the above goals. Based on Eclipse[2], the workbench manages an extensible set of views for trace data manipulation. It defines the design principles for view engineering and manages view integration and correlation. It is provided as part of the FrameSoC trace management infrastructure [5], used in the domains of embedded and parallel systems.

The present article is structured as follows. First, we provide a user level description of the FrameSoC workbench, with a concrete example of interactive trace analysis. We then present the pursued goals and the workbench implementation. After discussing the related works, we finally conclude with our perspectives.

FRAMESOC FROM THE END-USER PERSPECTIVE

In the context of trace analysis, the role of the user is central. Even if the different analysis tools help the analysis process with more or less automatic methods, the analyst's knowledge about the traced application is often the key to understanding issues or hunting bugs. To exploit to the maximum extent the user's contribution to the analysis, the working graphical environment has to ease the interaction with data, supporting and guiding the user in creating his analysis workflow. In the ideal case, the environment combines intuitive interactions with efficient data analysis.

In this section, after a brief description of the graphical elements of our workbench, a real trace analysis use case is presented. We show how the user interaction is supported through an intuitive and effective workflow.

Overview of FrameSoC

Our workbench (Figure 1) is a desktop working environment offering trace management and analysis facilities. It contains

---

[1]We use the term *workbench* to designate an environment providing a common paradigm for the creation, management, and navigation of workspace resources (http://help.eclipse.org/juno/index.jsp?topic=/org.eclipse.platform.doc.user/concepts/concepts-2.htm).

[2]http://www.eclipse.org

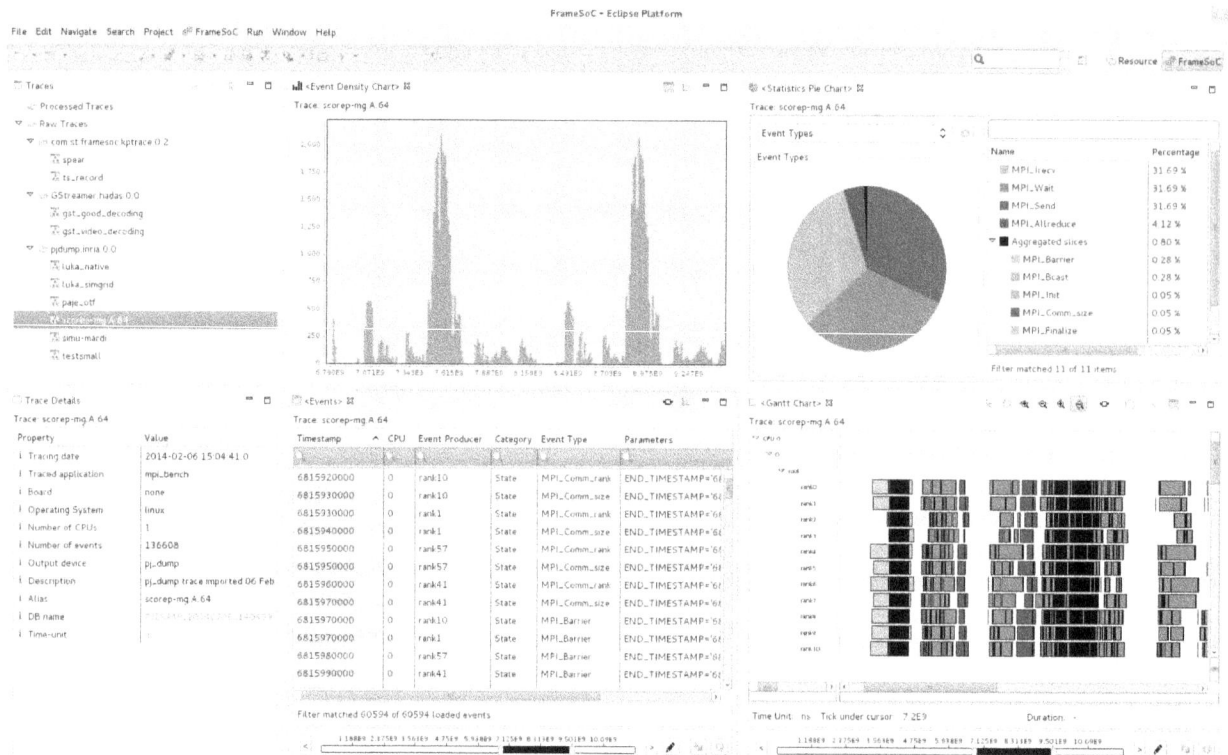

Figure 1: The FrameSoC Workbench

a custom menu, a toolbar of shortcuts and a set of custom views. The menu and the toolbar enable fast access to common functionalities, like configuring the system or importing a trace.

The views are logically grouped in two categories: management views (on the leftmost column) and analysis views (in the main workbench body). *Management views* include a trace browser and and a trace metadata viewer/editor. The first lists the available traces in the system, grouped by format, while the second shows the metadata of the currently selected trace(s). As the management views are global and provide the entry point for data analysis, they cannot be closed. They are located on the left, as typically done for workbench resources in all common Integrated Development Environments (IDE). *Analysis views* include an event density chart and a statistics pie-chart, on top, and a table of events and a Gantt chart, at the bottom. This default positioning has been chosen to have trace overviews on top and detailed trace views at the bottom. As the workbench allows for working with multiple traces, there can be an instance of analysis view per trace. The event density chart allows to zoom on a particular time region. With a simple click on a button, it is possible to represent this time region in the table or in the Gantt chart (the blackened part of both views indicate the time interval represented). Each of these two detailed views enable changing the time range and passing, with a click, to the sibling detailed view on the same range (*show in Gantt* and *show in Table* buttons). The different analysis views use the same

color code to refer to the same entities (e.g., a given event-type is represented with the same color in different views).

FrameSoC in Action

In the context of large scale complex environments, it is difficult to acquire meaningful traces. Indeed, on one hand, tracing such systems requires high technical expertise. On the other hand, confidentiality issues, as well as induced system perturbation, limit the access of tracing experiences in real production environments.

A promising alternative is to model real world environments and use simulation. However, simulation results cannot be trusted without a preliminary validation of the used simulation model. To do so, there is a need for comparing real world platform executions with their simulated versions [9].

To illustrate the functionalities of our workbench and show its support to interactive trace analysis, we use a real use case targeting the comparison of two traces. The first trace is issued by executing a parallel application on a real system containing 4 Graphics Processing Units (GPU). The second trace is obtained running the same application within the Simgrid[3] simulator. We call the first trace *native* and the second *simulated*.

The two traces, which are supposed to be similar, are completely different. For example, the native trace has more than 3 millions of events, while the simulated one has only about

---

[3]http://simgrid.gforge.inria.fr/

900 thousands of events. In our investigation, the goal is to understand what the simulator problem is and why simulation does not reflect the real system behavior.

We conduct our analysis using the well-known Shneiderman's mantra: overview first, zoom and filter, then details-on-demand [7]. We start by visualizing an overview of the two traces, using an event density chart per trace. The two views for the native and the simulated traces are given in Figure 2a and Figure 2b respectively. We set the same scale on both axis of both histograms, in order to enable an easy and consistent eye comparison between the two views.

(a) Native trace   (b) Simulated trace

Figure 2: Event-density chart

The comparison between the two density charts immediately shows that the simulated trace has much less events than the native one. Furthermore, in the case of the native trace, we observe two peaks, after about 24 s and 49 s. To inspect what is happening, we decide to focus on the small time interval around the first peak. We zoom on this interval on both views for both traces and trigger a more detailed view. Using the *show in Gantt* button, we open the Gantt-chart representation of this time interval for both traces, as shown in Figure 3 and Figure 4. In this type of representation, we have on the left the process hierarchy and on the right a timeline with states (colored rectangles) and communications (arrows).

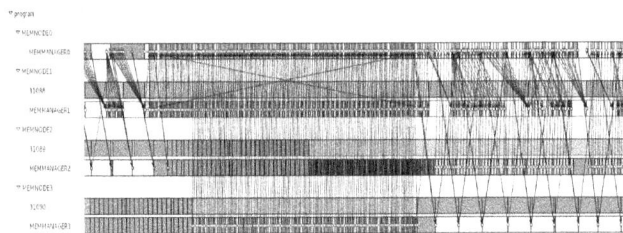

Figure 3: Native trace Gantt-chart representation of the trace interval centered on the first event peak (24 s)

The two Gantt charts are indeed completely different: in particular we note that the native one has a lot more communications among the different processes and a lot more state changes, mostly in the very central part of the time interval. However, it is difficult to compare, reason and gain some significant insight about the problem.

We try an alternative representation of the data concerning the central part of the time interval. We zoom some more on the native trace Gantt chart and, via the *show in Table* button, we pass to the table view (Figure 5). Inspecting the state transitions listed in the table makes us rapidly notice the repetition

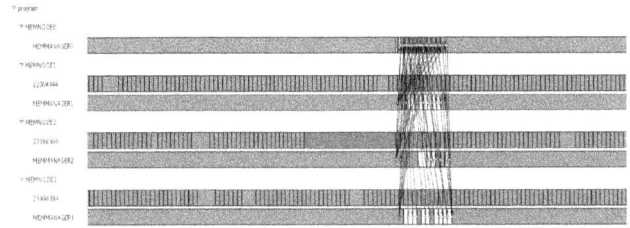

Figure 4: Simulated trace Gantt-chart representation of the trace interval centered on the point after 24 s of simulation

of a pattern, composed by the sequence of states *Allocating* and *Reclaiming*, highlighted in blue and red respectively. To verify whether this couple of memory management events is as significant to the whole trace, as to the selected interval, we come back to a higher level of abstraction view on the trace[4]. To do so, we use the event-type statistics pie chart for the native trace, shown in Figure 6a.

Figure 5: Detail of the native trace table view for a small time interval centered on the first event peak (24 s)

The pie-chart shows that the *Allocating* and *Reclaiming* events (always in blue and red) represent actually about 20% of all trace events. Opening the same view for the simulated trace (Figure 6b), we immediately notice that there is no blue, nor red. During the simulation the *Allocating* and *Reclaiming* events do not occur at all. This indicates that the problem is possibly related to the simulator memory management model. Indeed, we find that the simulator considers GPUs to have infinite memory therefore ignoring all RAM swapping operations. Removing this hypothesis and setting the GPU memory limits solves the problem.

---

[4]Doing this, we are actually starting a new iteration in the Shneiderman's mantra.

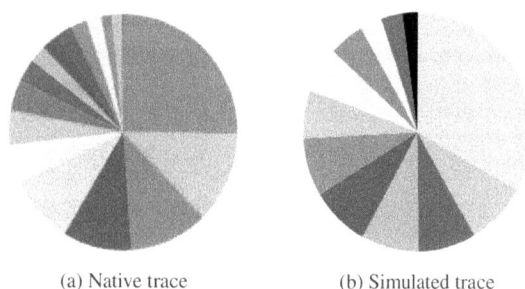

(a) Native trace   (b) Simulated trace

Figure 6: Event-type statistics pie-cart

It would have been difficult to find the problem without the user's knowledge of his application. However, the support provided by the analysis environment to simplify the interaction with data, is extremely valuable. Following a well-defined top-down analysis methodology and simply clicking or zooming with the mouse, simplifies the process of tracking the problem cause.

The presence of different views and the coordination among them is essential for obtaining this result. In fact, without the density chart overview, the zooming, the details in the Gantt and then the table, the analysis of the pie-charts would have been useless. Indeed, if we simply compare the pies, there are other than the memory management events which are in the native pie but not in the simulated one. On the other hand, finding the memory pattern by looking at all the data in the native table (which contains over 3 millions of events), without the refinement process done by using the density chart and the Gantt chart, would have been impossible.

FRAMESOC FROM THE SYSTEM PERSPECTIVE

Before describing the implementation details of FrameSoC, we discuss its general principles.

FrameSoC in a Nutshell

The FrameSoC architecture has pursued several goals concerning user interactions, multiple-view target behavior and development facilities.

From the *user interaction perspective*, our workbench focuses on a set of views which are intuitive to use and which support simple interactions for trace data analysis. The set of views is designed to be *open* in the sense that it is not predefined and allows for the integration of new types of views. The set is also *configurable* as it is possible to choose, among the available views, which ones to use in the working environment. A useful feature to take into account, especially when working with multiple traces, is the possibility to have multiple instances per type of view.

From the *view correlation perspective*, all views need to show consistent data representations. They should be able to represent the same trace data, during the same time interval and with the same color code. Moreover, view updates need to be correlated: when a user interacts with a view, the executed changes are consistently reflected in other views.

From the *development perspective*, our workbench facilitates the engineering and the integration of new types of view. It defines a global management architecture and provides predefined classes and interfaces to ensure the proper integration of newly developed views.

Figure 7 provides a high level vision of our workbench software architecture. The workbench is based on the design facilities provided by the Eclipse framework. The managed graphical views are provided as a packaged software module containing a set of Eclipse plugins. Views are managed through the Eclipse extension and extension point mechanism. In the Eclipse environment, extension points define the contracts between modules and are used for loose coupling. They may represent configuration information only or some code contribution. Extensions provide implementations for these contracts. The *management* views provided by our framework (the trace browser and the metadata viewer/editor) are managed as standard Eclipse views. On the contrary, the contribution of new *analysis* views for our environment is facilitated by our definition of a particular extension point. During a working session, the views implementing this specific extension point are managed using two mechanisms. At a lower level, we use a Publish-Subscribe architecture for flexible and scalable communication. Above this layer, we implement control entities to ensure consistent view correlation and take care of some performance issues.

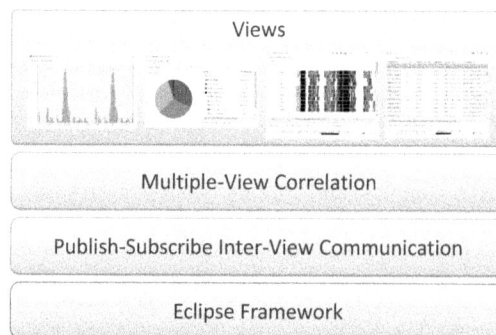

Figure 7: FrameSoC Workbench Software Architecture

Implementation Details

Publish-Subscribe Inter-View Communication

To support the correlation among views and achieve a global consistency in the analysis environment, we designed and implemented a simple communication mechanism based on the Publish-Subscribe messaging pattern [10]. The Publish-Subscribe architecture is based on the idea of decoupling message senders, called publishers, from message receivers, called subscribers. Messages are grouped in *topics*, so publishers can publish data for a given topic, without knowing the receivers of these data (if any). On the other hand, subscribers can subscribe to one or more topics, thus receiving all the data published on those topics, without explicitly naming or connecting to the publishers. This architecture achieves module separation, allowing for scalable systems that may grow incrementally with small development effort.

The FrameSoC Publish-Subscribe architecture is called the FrameSoC Bus. This bus enables message sending for a given topic and registering/unregistering to/from a given topic. The bus is physically implemented by a singleton, which offers the necessary `send(topic, data)`, `register(topic)`, `unregister(topic)` methods. Subscribers modules must implement a given interface, which provides the `handle(topic, data)` method. Message sending is synchronous, meaning that when a message is sent, all the handle methods of the subscribers are called sequentially. For this reason, if the handle methods are time consuming, it is preferable to ensure their execution by separate threads. Among the topics currently managed in the FrameSoC Bus there are, for example, the notification that a given analysis view has been selected or the notification that some trace metadata has been edited. The communications necessary to send the *show in Gantt* or *show in Table* requests also pass through this bus.

The FrameSoC Bus plays an additional role of a context container; i.e., it keeps relevant global information about the state of the working workbench. The corresponding data variables are stored in the singleton and can be consulted by all workbench components. Basically, the singleton provides `set` and `get` atomic methods for accessing these shared variables. An example of usage of this mechanism is the following. When a new analysis view is opened, in order to represent he necessary data, it needs to know which trace is selected in the trace browser view. It will consult the FrameSoC Bus, who has saved this contextual information when it has been broadcasted to the other components.

Multiple-View Correlation

To ensure view correlation and a consistent behavior among the different views, we implemented two main classes: `FramesocPart`, which is the base class of all FrameSoC analysis views, and `FramesocPartManager`, which is a singleton ensuring the coordinated behavior of the different analysis views.

The `FramesocPart` factorizes common behavior of analysis views and ensures proper management regarding the current working trace. It is, in particular, responsible for the following actions. It broadcasts on the FrameSoC Bus which trace has become active after a view has been given focus. It implements view highlighting in accordance with the currently selected trace. It implements the basic handling mechanisms for the events related to trace alias change, trace removal or generic trace metadata update. It ensures automatic unregistering from followed topics at view disposal. It defines the abstract method (to be specialized by the views) called by the framework to display a trace in the analysis view.

The `FramesocPart` class works in symbiosis with the `FramesocPartManager` singleton. The `FramesocPartManager` singleton manages the list of active data analysis views, is in charge of their creation, provides a naming service by generating unique view identifiers, and takes care of memory performance issues. When there is a workbench event requesting the activation of a given analysis view, the `FramesocPartManager` singleton verifies whether it should create a new instance or reuse an existing one. To this purpose, it listens the FrameSoC Bus and intercepts the topics supporting the *show in Gantt* and *show in Table* requests. Indeed, the `FramesocPartManager` guarantees the reuse of possible empty views, and it ensures that, for a given type of view, no more that a configurable number of instances is opened. Thus, the singleton ensures that the memory used for views is not wasted. Within the Eclipse framework, each type of view has an unique identifier. To have more instances for a given type of view, we have to provide a unique *secondary* identifier for that type of view. The `FramesocPartManager` singleton considers previously used secondary identifiers (stored by Eclipse in a configuration file) and generates unique ones using randomness (`UUID.randomUUID()`). The base `FramesocPart` class, on the other hand, ensures that, even if the view instance is opened through the Eclipse *Show View* menu (and not via the FrameSoC context menu in the trace browser), it acquires a valid secondary ID. This responds to the fact that, as for version 4.3.2, the Eclipse framework does not automatically set a valid secondary ID (it is `null`) when opening a view through the *Show View* menu.

Engineering of New Analysis Views

To enforce the modularity of the architecture and simplify the development process, the FrameSoC workbench defines an extension point to contribute a new trace analysis view to the system. The implementation of a new analysis view thus implies the development of a `FramesocPart` concrete class, to be included in a plugin extending this extension point.

This extension point defines all the information needed to create a view and place it in the correct position, display an item in the trace browser context menu to launch the view, and execute a given operation when such menu item is selected. More in detail, this extension point contains the following fields: `viewId`, the ID of the view provided, which must extend `FramesocPart`; `icon`, the icon to be displayed in the trace browser context menu; `launchCommand`, the ID of the command[5] opening this view; `position`, the position of the view in the FrameSoC perspective; `priority`, an integer representing the view priority regarding the positioning in the perspective and in the trace browser context menu, within a given position (as defined before).

Note that this extension point requires only a view ID and a command ID, but the plugin extending this extension point has to effectively provide extensions for the corresponding standard Eclipse extension points, namely `org.eclipse.ui.views` and `org.eclipse.ui.commands`, for those IDs. Note also that FrameSoC predefines some view IDs, to be used for views wanting to offer a service known to the system (e.g., a view able to show a Gantt chart or a table of events). This enables easy management of predefined functionalities (like the *show in Gantt* or *show in Table* requests), though not preventing the contribution of FrameSoC analysis views with custom IDs, but still respecting our extension point and extending `FramesocPart`.

---

[5]We refer here to the concept of *command* as defined by Eclipse.

RELATED WORK

Multiple-view management for data manipulation is a specific case for multi-modal interaction management [4]. However, multi-modal systems aim at using alternative interaction forms (e.g., speech or hand gestures) which is still a futurist idea in the context of application performance evaluation and debugging. Before focusing on these issues, trace management tools still need to identify the best ways of representing and manipulating trace data.

Multiple-view management for trace analysis is related to the larger research areas on scientific data visualization [8] and visual analytics [2]. While these focus on novel approaches for data visualization and analysis, our work is more interested in the mechanisms for flexible management of an evolutive set of views. Moreover, we put the focus on enhancing the interactions with "classical" data views.

There are numerous graphical environments targeting trace data analysis and manipulation. However, the set of available views is usually predefined and cannot be enriched. We can cite Vampir [3], an efficient trace analysis tool targeting parallel applications. Vampir is a commercial product and its view management is a closed black box. The approach is similar in the domain of embedded systems where proposed environments such as DS-5[6] or STWorkbench[7] target proprietary execution platforms and their corresponding traces. In the domain of operating systems, the LTTng Viewer[8] allows for manipulating kernel traces. It is an Eclipse-based open-source project and as such allows for view modification. However, this demands developer expertise with the global architecture and the source code of the whole tool. Some flexibility is offered in Aftermath[9] or Paraver[10], where the user may configure the data represented in the available views.

Publish-Subscribe [1] architectures have proven their value for multi-modal view development [6]. Since version 4, Eclipse and its Rich Client Platform programming model[11], propose an enhanced Publish-Subscribe mechanism. However, we still need to investigate how this mechanism may be combined with our management of a dynamic set of views. Also, we should evaluate the benefits and the drawbacks in terms of development complexity and performances.

CONCLUSIONS AND PERSPECTIVES

In this work, we presented the FrameSoC workbench, an open and modular software architecture simplifying the engineering of consistent multiple views for data trace analysis. Based on Eclipse, the FrameSoC workbench provides a rich set of different views on trace data, ensuring an intuitive interaction and simplifying the transition from one view to another. It also provides predefined classes and principles for view engineering and integration.

In addition to some immediate improvement ideas concerning data analysis and the corresponding views, we are interested in conceiving a diagnosis tool which can report on the different user interactions with the FrameSoC workbench. Not only this would be beneficial from the ergonomics point of view, but the information could be used as a reporting tool about executed trace analyses. Such reports could be used for defining a default data analysis workflow and automating some sequences of actions.

The FrameSoC workbench will be officially released in June 2014 as open-source software.

REFERENCES

1. Eugster, P. T., Felber, P. A., Guerraoui, R., and Kermarrec, A.-M. The many faces of publish/subscribe. *ACM Comput. Surv. 35*, 2 (June 2003), 114–131.

2. Fekete, J.-D. Visual analytics infrastructures: From data management to exploration. *Computer 46*, 7 (July 2013), 22–29.

3. Knüpfer, A., Brunst, H., Doleschal, J., Jurenz, M., Lieber, M., Mickler, H., Müller, M. S., and Nagel, W. E. The vampir performance analysis tool-set. In *Tools for High Performance Computing*. Springer Berlin Heidelberg, 2008, 139–155.

4. Oviatt, S. Ten myths of multimodal interaction. *Commun. ACM 42*, 11 (Nov. 1999), 74–81.

5. Pagano, G., Dosimont, D., Huard, G., Marangozova-Martin, V., and Vincent, J.-M. Trace Management and Analysis for Embedded Systems. In *Proceedings of the IEEE seventh International Symposium on Embedded Multicore SoCs (MCSoC-13)* (Tokyo, Japan, Sep 2013).

6. Shen, J., Shi, W., and Pantic, M. Hci^2 workbench: A development tool for multimodal human-computer interaction systems. In *Automatic Face Gesture Recognition and Workshops (FG 2011), 2011 IEEE International Conference on* (March 2011), 766–773.

7. Shneiderman, B. The eyes have it: A task by data type taxonomy for information visualizations. In *Proceedings of the 1996 IEEE Symposium on Visual Languages*, VL '96, IEEE Computer Society (Washington, DC, USA, 1996), 336–.

8. Simon, P. *The Visual Organization: Data Visualization, Big Data, and the Quest for Better Decisions*. Wiley and SAS Business Series. Wiley, 2014.

9. Stanisic, L., Thibault, S., Legrand, A., Videau, B., and Méhaut, J.-F. Modeling and Simulation of a Dynamic Task-Based Runtime System for Heterogeneous Multi-Core Architectures. Research Report RR-8509, INRIA, Mar. 2014.

10. Tarkoma, S. *Publish/subscribe systems: design and principles*. Wiley series in communications networking & distributed systems. Wiley, Chichester, West Sussex, 2012.

---

[6]http://ds.arm.com/

[7]http://stlinux.com/stworkbench/

[8]http://lttng.org/viewers

[9]http://openstream.info/aftermath

[10]www.bsc.es/computer-sciences/ performance- tools/paraver/

[11]https://wiki.eclipse.org/Eclipse4/RCP/Event_Model

PLACID: a Planner for Dynamically Composing User Interfaces Services
Problem Formalization and Solving

Yoann Gabillon
CRP - Gabriel Lippmann
41, Rue du Brill
L-4422 Belvaux, Luxembourg
gabillon@lippmann.lu

Gaelle Calvary
Univ. Grenoble Alpes, LIG
F-38000 Grenoble, France
CNRS, LIG, F-38000
Grenoble, France
gaelle.calvary@imag.fr

Humbert Fiorino
Univ. Grenoble Alpes, LIG
F-38000 Grenoble, France
CNRS, LIG, F-38000
Grenoble, France
humbert.fiorino@imag.fr

ABSTRACT
Dynamic Services Composition (DSC) aims at composing interactive systems from a set of available services corresponding to the available components. A component consists of a Functional Core and/or of a User Interface (UI) respectively providing computation and/or representation functions. In software engineering, a part of the literature focuses on the dynamic composition of computation services. Making the hypothesis that UI services can also be composed leads to a new research area in Human Computer Interaction: the dynamic composition of UI services. This paper presents two main contributions: the formalization of the problem and its solving by planning.

ACM Classification Keywords
H.5.2 User Interfaces: Ergonomics, Graphical user interfaces (GUI), Prototyping, User-centered design.

General Terms
Design, Human factors, Algorithms

Author Keywords
Dynamic composition, User Interface, UI service, UI composition, Formalization, Algorithm

INTRODUCTION
Dynamic Services Composition (DSC) aims at composing interactive systems at runtime from a set of available services so that to fulfil the user's goal. The DSC process can be decomposed into two steps: first, the plan composition, i.e., a selection and an ordering of the set of services that can be used for achieving the goal; secondly, the composition of the services according to the plan so that to produce the executable interactive system.

An interactive system consists of a Functional Core (FC) and of a User Interface (UI) [3]. In the same way, a distinction can

be done between computation and UI services like it is done in [16]. The computation services are provided by functional components containing controls and processes data that represent the domain concepts. The UI services are provided by UI components that contain perceivable behaviour of the system (such as buttons or labels). Making the hypothesis that UI services can be composed like functional services leads to a research area in Human Computer Interaction (HCI): the dynamic composition of UI services.

In Software Engineering (SE), a large part of the literature focuses on the dynamic composition of functional services. Either the UI services are considered as functional services, or the UIs are composed afterwards. However, in order to promote a user-centered dynamic composition, the UI services also need to be dynamically composed.

This paper presents two main contributions: the formalization of the problem and its solving by planning. Indeed, because dynamic composition needs Artificial Intelligence (AI), we investigate the automated algorithm concepts such as already used in DSC. This PLACID algorithm (PLACID stands for "PLAnner for dynamically Composing user Interfaces Descriptions") is used in the COMPOSE prototype that dynamically composes UIs from a plan in terms of UI services.

The paper starts with an overview of the background in DSC and UI design. Because, there is no approach that focuses on the dynamic composition of UI services in SE and HCI, we investigate the automated planning concepts in order to formalize the problem and to propose the PLACID algorithm. The feasibility of the approach is assessed in the COMPOSE prototype. The goal of this prototype is to dynamically generate a composed UI from the specification of the user's goal. The COMPOSE prototype uses a plan in terms of UI services computed by PLACID in order to produce a composed UI.

BACKGROUND
Services composition can be *static* or *dynamic* [1]. Static composition starts from a plan (composition schema) while dynamic composition computes a plan from a user's goal at runtime [1]. DSC is based on the hypothesis that each service can be seen as an action described by preconditions, postconditions and effects [18]. These actions are used to compute a plan according to the current context of use (properties concerning the *user*, his/her *platform* and *environment* [20]).

This section provides an overview of DSC principles in SE, and then identifies the specific needs of dynamic composition of UI services.

Software Engineering

Dynamic composition of services (web services) needs AI techniques to compute the plans. For example, Automated Planning [7] develops algorithms to achieve a goal from pre-existing actions. In SE, different approaches (AI techniques) have been investigated in order to compute a plan of services such as Situation calculus, Rules based planning, Theorem proving or Automated Planner [18].

Situation calculus. For example, [10] proposes to adapt the Golog language in order to automatically compute the plan that is a sequence of actions. Golog is a programming language that represents the changes or evolutions of situations, actions and objects. The user goal is expressed as first order predicates. The services are actions. Then, based on logical rules and constraints, the plan is computed at runtime.

Rules based planning. For example, [11] computes a composite service from composability rules to check whether two services can be composed or not. First, from high level descriptions, the set of possible compositions is described. Secondly, from composability rules, the high level descriptions are composed. Thirdly, the services are selected according to the descriptions in order to compute the plan.

Theorem proving. For example, [17] uses a Theorem prover. The available services and the user's goal are translated into first-order logic predicates. Then, the plan is computed by a Theorem prover from these predicates.

PDDL planner. For example, [8] uses a PDDL planner. Classically, a PDDL planner handles three inputs: a goal (e.g., "I need to go from my hotel to the doctor's office"), the initial state of the word (e.g., Victor is in Philadelphia) and a set of actions (e.g., travel by car). An action is defined by a precondition (a set of predicates to be true) and effects on the state of the world (e.g., the action "travel by car" from the Victor's hotel to the selected doctor, the effect will be that Victor will be at a doctors office). In turn, automated planning algorithms compute one plan (i.e., a sequence of actions) that achieves the goal.

HTN Planner. For example, [19] uses a HTN planner such as JShop. Hierarchical Task Network (HTN) [4] is a hierarchical approach to automated planning. In HTN, the dependency among actions can be given in the form of networks. In consequence, HTN provides the use of a hierarchical description of abstract actions (denoted methods) in sub-actions to obtain actions (i.e., corresponding to actions in PDDL). A method has a precondition and a set of sub-actions. For example, the method "travel" can be decomposed into two sub-actions "travel by road" or "travel by plane". From the user's goal, The HTN planner tries to apply methods and actions until the goal is expressed into a sequence of actions.

In order to produce a UI, the UI composition can be done after DSC. The idea is to take advantages of the plan dynamically computed by calling the UIs of these services in a second step. For example, [5] proposes to compose the UIs of the selected services in a same frame. In this way, a composed UI is computed from the services plan.

In contrast, CRUSe [16] introduces the notion of UI services and focuses on the composition of UI components by proposing a system architecture. However, CRUSe does not focus on the selection of UI services (i.e. the computation of the plan). It supposes the plan already computed.

Human Computer Interaction

At a higher level of abstraction, a UI is modelled as a *Task Model* [14, 2]. The *Task Model* (TM) is a recursive description of the *user's task* into parallel or sequential sub-tasks until obtaining *elementary tasks* (i.e., tasks that would be further decomposed into physical actions only). For example, in order to "get medical assistance", the user must "call the office" and "find route information". A user's task can be seen as a service provided by a *UI service*. In consequence, in order to dynamically compose new UI services, the computed plans must be trees of user's tasks instead of sequences only.

An adaptive UI is a UI able to adapt or to be adapted to the current context of use. Many works have focused on the adaptation of the task model at runtime [2, 12]. Thus all these works start with a complete task model. To our knowledge, no work proposes to compute the plan in terms of UI services.

Huddle [13] uses a PDDL planner in order to produce a sequence of actions that represent a valid configuration of the UI components to be composed. The goal is to automatically generate a UI for multiple appliances. However, the planner does not handle abstract actions such as HTN planner.

[15] presents how to dynamically produce a UI from Web Services. In particular, the authors show how to create abstract descriptions of user interfaces from a task model and to bind them to existing Web services in order to generate the UI implementation. In the same way, [9] does not use a planner but starts from a task model to produce a plan that describes how existing services can be composed to generate the application. Thus [15, 9] do not focus on the algorithm to compute a plan.

PROBLEM AND SOLUTION FORMALIZATION

Problem Formalization

The principle is to build a UI whose function is to bring the user from his/her current situation to a situation suitable to fulfil his/her needs. More formally, the current situation is the initial s_0 state of an exploration space. This state is represented as a set of logical propositions: $s_0 = \{has(Victor, Smartphone), internet(Smartphone), at(Victor, Philadelphia), Guidance\_Prompting(), \dots\}$

In the same way, the user's needs, i.e. his/her goal, are represented as a set of g propositions. The states containing g are called "s_g targeted states" :
$s_g = \{found(Victor, medical\_assistance), \dots\}$.

The exploration space is a graph of the changes of states whose nodes are states and the arcs are actions that the user can carry out using the UI (Figure 1).

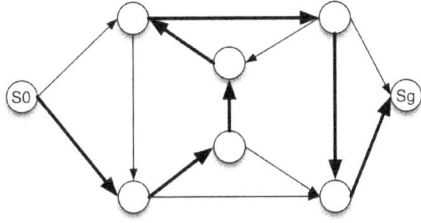

Figure 1. State change graphs.

An action a is defined by the triplet $(precond(a), add(a), del(a))$ where $precond(a)$ is a set of logical propositions which represent conditions to trigger the action: an action is applicable if and only if the state under consideration contains $precond(a)$. We denote $precond^+(a)$ and $precond^-(a)$ the positive and negative predicates. $add(a)$ and $del(a)$ are respectively the effects added to the current state. If an action a is applicable, the following state can be calculated by:
$$\gamma(s_i, a) = (s_i - del(a)) \cup add(a) = s_{i+1}$$

Therefore the problem lies in building a UI that reaches the targeted state from the initial state. That is to say π is a list that is the length of k of these actions and s is the current state; the next state is defined by:

$$\gamma(s, \pi) = \begin{cases} s, & \text{if } k = 0 \\ \gamma(\gamma(s, a_1), [a2, \ldots, a_k]), & \text{if } k > 0 \text{ and} \\ & a_1 \text{ is applicable to } s \end{cases}$$

In practice, the user expresses his/her needs. These are translated into a set of logical g propositions. The system perceives the context of use and represents it in the form of a set of s_0 logical propositions. The planning algorithm knows the actions that the user can carry out via the UI. The actions are expressed in intention in the form of *operators* and *methods*.

An operator o is in the form of $(precond(o), add(o), del(o))$. It is defined by its preconditions, what has been added and what has been taken away, which are sets of logical predicates of the first order. For example, a "$Call\_the\_office(?u, ?p)$" operator, the preconditions could contain the predicates "$has(?u, ?p)$ and $internet(?p)$" ; the user $?u$ and the platform $?p$ are variables linked to domains, i.e. to sets of constants. Thus, the "$Call\_the\_office(?u, ?p)$" operator represents the actions "$Call\_the\_office(Victor, Smartphone)$", "$Call\_the\_office(Victor, Wall)$", etc.

A method m is in the form of $(type(m), precond(m), subAct(m))$ where $precond(m)$ defines its preconditions and $subAct(m)$ breaks down the method in operators or methods to be accomplished to carry out m. The type of break-down expressed in $type(m)$ is either a sequence or a parallelism. As a sequence, the $subAct(m)$ methods or operators are ordered completely. As a parallelism, the $subAct(m)$ elements can be carried out in any order. For example, the method "$Get\_medical\_assistance$" corresponds to the sequence of "$Call\_the\_office$" then "$Find\_route\_information$".

(a)   **(b)**

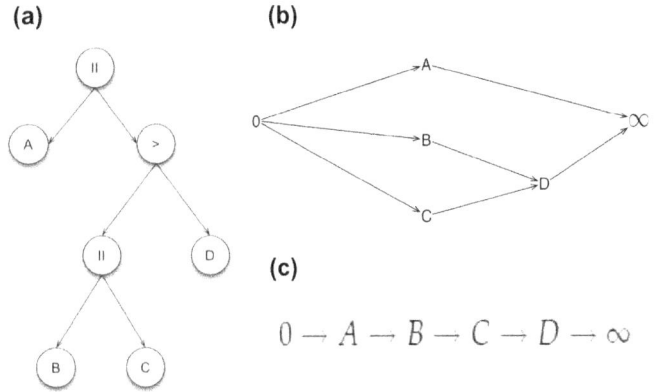

(c)

Figure 2. (a) Task tree obtained by the planner; (b) ρ projection of the task tree ; (c) linearisation.

Problem Solving Formalization

From the initial state s_0, from the goal g and from a set of methods and operators, the planning algorithm calculates a task model which allows the user to accomplish his/her goal. This task model is a tree. Each node corresponds to an existing UI component. For example, the task of "$Call\_the\_office$" corresponds to one UI. Once calculated, the task tree makes it possible to know the UIs that the root UI will contain. For example, here it will contain the UIs which correspond to the sub-tasks "$Call\_the\_office$" and "$Find\_route\_information$".

The task tree contains two types of nodes: internal and leaf. The internal nodes are completely instantiated methods (all variables are linked to constants) of type sequence ("¿") or parallelism ("II"). The leafs are actions, i.e. completely instantiated operators (Figure 2a). We call projection ρ of the task tree the set of partially ordered actions which come from it (Figure 2b). The ordering relationship "$C > D$" expresses that the C action precedes the D action. 0 and ∞ are formal actions which represent the beginning and the end of interactions. The linearisation of ρ is a set composed of the same actions completely ordered by the relationship of precedence. An example of this is given in Figure 2c. $L(\rho)$ is the set of linearisations of ρ. The composition issue is from there simply formalized: $P = (s0, g, A)$ a planning problem where s_0 is the initial state, g the goal and A the set of possible actions (in practice expressed in the form of methods and operators). Solving the problem means finding a ρ set (in practice a task model) such as: $\forall \pi \in L(\rho), g \subseteq \gamma(s_o, \pi)$

Intuitively, for finding a solution, it's necessary to compute all the linearisations (all sequences of actions) that can be carried out by the user to achieve his/her goal. In the case where no plan is found, the problem has no solution and no UI can be composed.

PLACID ALGORITHM

Based on the formalization of the problem, we propose the PLACID algorithm to solve the problem of the dynamic composition of UI services. Some notations are introduced in order to describe the PLACID algorithm.

Notations

A task can be a method or an action. The root of the task model (plan) to be computed is denoted by the *goal task* t_u. In practice, the projection ρ is a set of actions representing a task model. $\rho(t_u)$ denotes the projection where t_u is the goal task.

Once $\rho(t_u)$ computed, we can compute the effects and the preconditions of t_u. More formally, in order to compute the preconditions and the effects of a task t_u, two cases are considered if t_u is an action or a method:

- Case 1 (t_u is an action a): if $\rho(t_u) = \{a\}$ is a solution, then $precond(t_u) = precond(a)$, $add(t_u) = add(a)$ and $del(t_u) = del(a)$.

- Case 2 (t_u is a method m): let $t_1, \ldots, t_n$ the sub-tasks of t_u in $\rho(t_u)$. If $\rho(t_u)$ is a solution, then $precond(t_u) = precond(t_1) \cup \cdots \cup precond(t_n)$, $add(t_u) = add(t_1) \cup \cdots \cup add(t_n)$ and $del(t_u) = del(t_1) \cup \cdots \cup del(t_n)$ Intuitively, the preconditions (resp. effects) of t_u are the union of the preconditions (resp. effects) of its sub-tasks.

In order to check that two tasks can be composed in parallel, we adapt the notion of conflict already used in PDDL planning. If two tasks do not have conflict, they are independent. More formally: two tasks t_1 and t_2 are independent if and only if:

- $del(t_1) \cap (precond^+(t_2) \cup add(t_2)) = \varnothing$ and

- $add(t_1) \cap (precond^-(t_2) \cup dell(t_2)) = \varnothing$ and

- $del(t_2) \cap (precond^+(t_1) \cup add(t_1)) = \varnothing$ and

- $add(t_2) \cap (precond^-(t_1) \cup dell(t_1)) = \varnothing$.

Intuitively, two tasks are independent if an effect of one task is not in conflict with the effect or precondition of the other one.

Algorithm

Let $P = (s_0, t_u, O, M)$ be a composition problem where s_0 is the initial state, t_u is the goal task to achieve (a task is a method or an action, for example "get medical assistance"), O and M are the prexisting actions and methods. In order to compute the set of linearisations (the solution), the algorithm computes one linearisation and checks if there are no conflict between tasks partially ordered. More formally, $\rho(t_u)$ is a solution to P if and only if:

- Case 1 (t_u is an action a): a is applicable to s_0. Then $\rho(t_u) = \{a\}$.

- Case 2 (t_u is a completely instantiated method m): let $\{t_1, \ldots, t_n\} \in subAct(m)$; there are two cases if the method type is a sequence or a parallelism:

    - Case 2a (m type is a sequence) : m is applicable to s_0 and $\forall t_i \in subAct(m)$, $\rho(t_i)$ is solution to $P_i = (\gamma(s_0, t_{i-1}), t_i, O, M)$ with $\gamma(s_0, t_{i-1}) = s_0$ if $i = 1$. Intuitively, if t_u is a sequence, a solution is a classical linearisation.

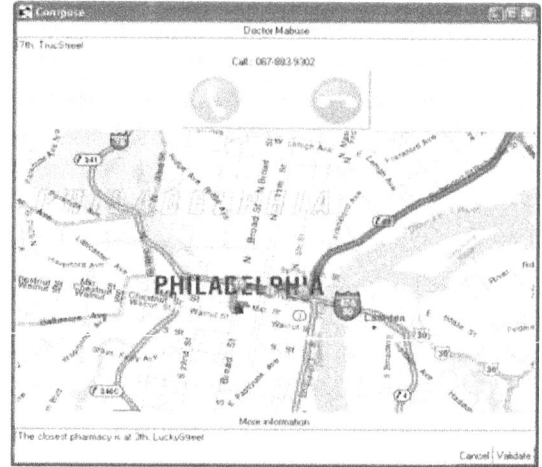

Figure 3. User Interface composed to contact the doctor.

    - Case 2b (m type is a parallelism): m is applicable to s_0 and $\forall t_i \in subAct(m)$, $\rho(t_i)$ is solution to $P_i = (s_0, t_i, O, M)$ and $\forall t_i, t_j \in subAct(m), i \neq j, t_i$ and t_j are independent. Intuitively, the algorithm checks that all subtasks in parallel are applicable to s_0 and there is no conflict between them. The conflicts are checked in order to allow the user to select the order between parallel UI services.

IMPLEMENTATION ON A CASE STUDY

PLACID is illustrated on a case study: Victor needs medical assistance while being on holiday out of his country. First, the case study is presented. Then, the implementation of the operators and methods is described. Finaly, the PLACID specificities are discussed.

Case study

Victor lives in New York. Suddenly he does not feel well in Philadelphia. He needs medical assistance. Fortunately, he has a system that can be of help to him. He specifies his goal "I want medical assistance" on the digital wall. In turn, PLACID dynamically computes a plan in terms of UI services. Each UI service describes the service it provides; in turn, the plan expresses the composed UI. For example, the composed UI allows Victor to choose a doctor. Once, the doctor is chosen, the system composes a UI that allows Victor to call the chosen regular doctor "Dr Mabuse" (figure 3; the number is pre-set see the top of the window), get guidance to reach the office (figure 3; see the map) and the nearest chemist (figure 3; see the address at the bottom of the window).

Implementation

In order to implement this case study, the developer needs to provide/reuse operators, methods and UI components. The following operators and methods are implemented in our case study:

Operator *Choose_the_city*: Parameters are a user (?u), a platform (?p) and a location (?l). The UI service requires that the user has a platform for its execution: has ?u ?p. Once the user has selected the location, a predicate is added to the state: $isChosen\ ?u\ ?l$.

Operator $Call$: Parameters are a user ($?u$), a platform ($?p$) and the person to call ($?pp$). The UI service requires that the user has a phone: $isPhone\ ?p$. The fact that the person pp has been called is added to the state: $isCalled\ ?u\ ?pp$.

Operator $Find\_route\_info$: Parameters are a user ($?u$) and a platform ($?p$). The UI service requires that the user has a platform with an Internet access: $isInternet\ ?p$.

Operator $Find\_nearest\_chemist$: Parameters are a user ($?u$), a platform ($?p$) and the chemist to display ($?o$). The UI service requires that the user has a platform ($has\ ?u\ ?p$) and that the chemist can be displayed on this platform: $isDisplayable\ ?o\ ?p$. The state is enriched accordingly: $isDisplayed\ ?p\ ?o$.

Method $Get\_medical\_assistance$: parameters are a user ($?u$) and a platform ($?p$). The UI service requires that the user has a platform for its execution: $has\ ?u\ ?p$. The sub-tasks are $Choose\_the\_city$ and $Contact\_the\_doctor$ in sequence.

Method $Contact\_the\_doctor$: parameters are a user ($?u$) and a platform ($?p$). The sub-tasks are $Call\_the\_office$, $Find\_route\_info$ and $Find\_nearest\_chemist$ in parallel. The component requires that the user has a platform for its execution: has ?u ?p. The UI service also requires that the platform has a large screen: isLargeScreen(?p).

From these methods, operators and user's goal, the algorithm computes a solution/plan in figure 4. Indeed, in order to check if the method "$Get\_medical\_assistance$" is a solution, the algorithm checks if a linearisation of "$Choose\_the\_doctor$" and "$Contact\_the\_doctor$" exists. "$Choose\_the\_doctor$" is applicable on s_0 and produces s_1. In order to check if the method "$Contact\_the\_doctor$" is applicable on s_1 and produces s_5, the algorithm checks if the actions "$Call\_the\_office$", "$Find\_route\_info$" and "$Find\_nearest\_chemist$" can be applied on s_1 and if the actions are independent. If there is no conflict, s_5 can be computed from one linearisation of these actions.

Discussion

Once computed, the plan can be mapped on UI components such as classical DSC approaches. Indeed, each UI service is provided by a UI component. A method expresses a way to compose the sub-UIs. For example, figure 5 displays a running UI that can be composed from the plan of UI services according to the COMPOSE prototype [6].

In contrast with classical functional planners that do not provide the method in output, PLACID computes a tree containing the methods. Indeed, the methods express the layouts, i.e. the way to compose UI components providing subservices. For example, the method $Contact\_the\_doctor$ expresses a frame that will vertically contain the UI components of the operators $Call\_the\_office$, $Find\_route\_info$ and $Find\_nearest\_chemist$.

In contrast with classical functional planners, PLACID composes UI services in parallel. Indeed, if two UI services are

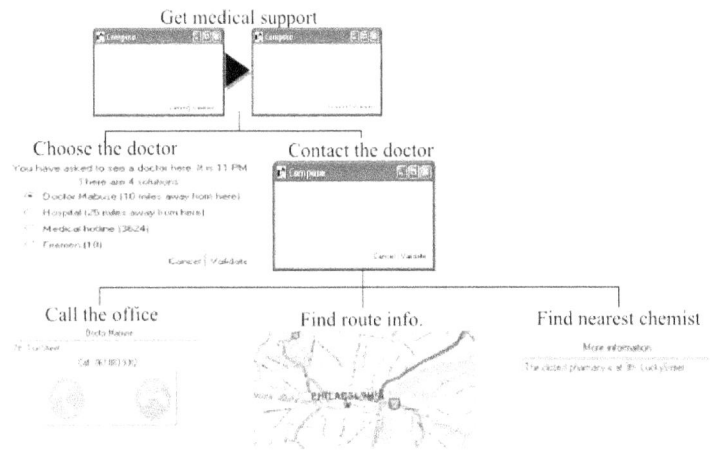

Figure 5. UI services provided by possible UI components.

not in conflict, the two corresponding UI components can be composed in the temporality (in the same frame or tab for example). For example, the system will not compose two UIs that need to use the speakers at the same time.

In order to produce a system that is able to dynamically compose a UI, the developer must implement the UI components, the corresponding UI services and a mapping between them. The UI components can be reused to provide many UI services. For example, the UI component that composes UI components vertically in the same frame will be often reused.

Up to now PLACID has been applied to simple case studies only. Its performances need to be further studied for a composition at runtime. By default, PLACID could be used at design time as a task models composer for helping the developers to model the user's tasks. This would be an interesting side effect as practitionners are not so familiar with task modeling.

CONCLUSION AND PERSPECTIVES

This paper has presented a solution for dynamically composing UI services. The two main contributions of this paper are, on one hand, a formalization of the problem and its solving by planning, and, on the other hand, the PLACID algorithm for computing plans from UI services. PLACID covers parallel and sequential composition of UI services (tasks) as two UIs can be composed in the same temporality/frame as well as in sequence. In order to compose two UI services in the same temporality, PLACID checks whether the user can use the UI services at the same time or not without any conflict. In the future, we plan to evaluate the algorithm performances.

REFERENCES

1. Bucchiarone, A., and Gnesi, S. A survey on services composition languages and models. In *in Proceedings of International Workshop on Web Services Modeling and Testing (WS-MaTe2006)* (2006), 51–63.

2. Calvary, G., Coutaz, J., Thevenin, D., Limbourg, Q., Bouillon, L., and Vanderdonckt, J. A unifying reference

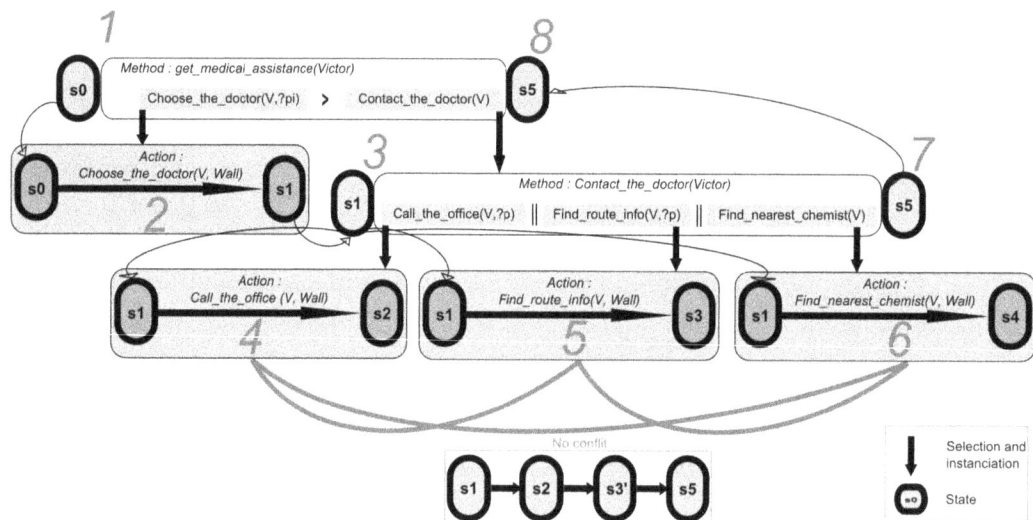

Figure 4. Execution of PLACID on the case study.

framework for multi-target user interfaces. *Interacting with Computers 15*, 3 (2003), 289–308.

3. Coutaz, J. Software architecture modeling for user interfaces. *Encyclopedia of software engineering* (1993).

4. Erol, K., Hendler, J., and Nau, D. S. Htn planning: Complexity and expressivity. In *AAAI*, vol. 94 (1994), 1123–1128.

5. Feldmann, M., Martens, F., Berndt, G., Spillner, J., and Schill, A. Rapid development of service-based interactive application using service ANNOTATIONS. 319–322.

6. Gabillon, Y., Petit, M., Calvary, G., and Fiorino, H. Automated planning for user interface composition. In *Proceedings of the 2nd International Workshop on Semantic Models for Adaptive Interactive Systems: SEMAIS'11 at IUI 2011 conference*, Springer HCI (2011).

7. Ghallab, M., Nau, D., and Traverso, P. *Automated planning: theory & practice*. Morgan Kaufmann, 2004.

8. Klusch, M., Gerber, A., and Schmidt, M. Semantic web service composition planning with owls-xplan. In *Proceedings of the AAAI Fall Symposium on Semantic Web and Agents, Arlington VA, USA, AAAI Press* (2005).

9. Kritikos, K., Plexousakis, D., and Paternò, F. Task model-driven realization of interactive application functionality through services. *ACM Transactions on Interactive Intelligent Systems (TiiS) 3*, 4 (2014), 25.

10. McIlraith, S., and Son, T. Adapting golog for composition of semantic web services. In *Principles of Knowledge representation and reasoning-Iinternational Conference*, Citeseer (2002), 482–496.

11. Medjahed, B. *Semantic web enabled composition of web services*. PhD thesis, Faculty of the Virginia Polytechnic Institute and State University, 2004.

12. Motti, V. G., and Vanderdonckt, J. A computational framework for context-aware adaptation of user interfaces. In *Research Challenges in Information Science (RCIS), 2013 IEEE Seventh International Conference on*, IEEE (2013), 1–12.

13. Nichols, J., Rothrock, B., Chau, D. H., and Myers, B. A. Huddle: automatically generating interfaces for systems of multiple connected appliances. In *Proceedings of the 19th annual ACM symposium on User interface software and technology*, ACM (2006), 279–288.

14. Paternò, F., Mancini, C., and Meniconi, S. Concurtasktrees: A diagrammatic notation for specifying task models. In *Human-Computer Interaction INTERACT97*, Springer (1997), 362–369.

15. Paternò, F., Santoro, C., and Spano, L. D. Engineering the authoring of usable service front ends. *Journal of Systems and Software 84*, 10 (2011), 1806–1822.

16. Pietschmann, S., Voigt, M., Rümpel, A., and Meißner, K. Cruise: Composition of rich user interface services. In *Web Engineering*. Springer, 2009, 473–476.

17. Rao, J., Küngas, P., and Matskin, M. Application of linear logic to web service composition. In *IWCS*, L.-J. Zhang, Ed., CSREA Press (2003), 3.

18. Rao, J., and Su, X. A survey of automated web service composition methods. *Semantic Web Services and Web Process Composition* (2005), 43–54.

19. Sirin, E., Parsia, B., Wu, D., Hendler, J., and Nau, D. Htn planning for web service composition using shop2. *Web Semantics: Science, Services and Agents on the World Wide Web 1*, 4 (2004), 377–396.

20. Thevenin, D., and Coutaz, J. Plasticity of user interfaces: Framework and research agenda. In *Proceedings of INTERACT*, vol. 99 (1999), 110–117.

Phone Proxies: Effortless Content Sharing between Smartphones and Interactive Surfaces

Alexander Bazo
Media Informatics Group
University of Regensburg
alexander.bazo@ur.de

Florian Echtler
Media Informatics Group
University of Regensburg
florian.echtler@ur.de

ABSTRACT

We present *Phone Proxies*, a technique for effortless content sharing between mobile devices and interactive surfaces. In such a scenario, users often have to perform a lengthy setup process before the actual exchange of content can take place. Phone Proxies uses a combination of custom NFC (near-field communication) tags and optical markers on the interactive surface to reduce the user interaction required for this setup process to an absolute minimum. We discuss two use cases: "pickup", in which the user wants to transfer content from the surface onto their device, and "share", in which the user transfers device content to the surface for shared viewing. We introduce three possible implementations of Phone Proxies for each of these use cases and discuss their respective advantages.

Author Keywords

casual interaction; smartphone; mobile device; interactive surface; NFC

ACM Classification Keywords

H.5.m Information interfaces and presentation (e.g., HCI): Miscellaneous.

INTRODUCTION & RELATED WORK

As large-scale interactive tables are increasingly appearing in public settings, the number of people having the opportunity to interact with such devices also grows. Due to today's pervasive availability of smartphones, most of these people can also be expected to own a personal mobile device. As these mobile devices are rapidly becoming the default storage location for personal media such as pictures, music or contact data, users will desire an easy way to share this content on the interactive surface. However, all current solutions to this task require a

EICS 2014, June 17–20, 2014, Rome, Italy.
Copyright is held by the owner/author(s). Publication rights licensed to ACM.
ACM 978-1-4503-2725-1/14/06...$15.00.
http://dx.doi.org/10.1145/2607023.2610276

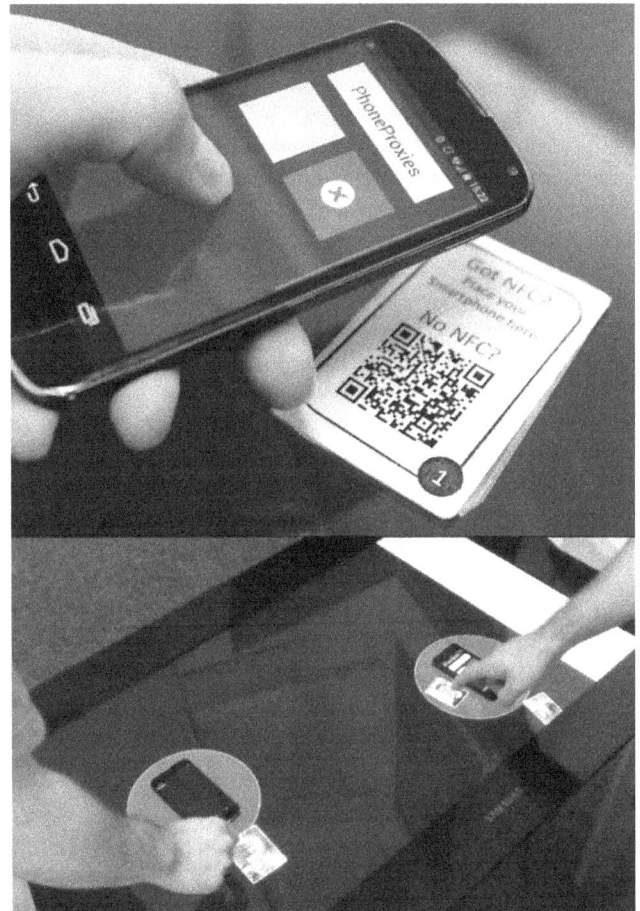

Figure 1. Connecting a mobile device to an interactive tabletop through a *Phone Proxy* (top). Transferring media between multiple phone proxies (bottom). Numbers on cards are used to visually identify the different tags.

complex setup process involving various combinations of stick-on marker tags, custom app installations and wireless connection procedures. Due to these lengthy setup requirements, scenarios involving casual interaction from first-time users are rare.

Our approach to this problem is called *Phone Proxies*, shown in Figure 1, which leverages the NFC reader integrated in more and more mobile devices in conjunction with the optical marker tracking available on many interactive surfaces. Devices access custom URLs embedded into the NFC tags, thereby allowing association between devices placed on the tags and the tags' position on the tabletop. For complex scenarios - where a custom app is still required - the NFC tag can also automate a major part of the app installation process and consequently minimize the user's initial effort.

We motivate this approach through two usage scenarios. In the first scenario, called "pickup", the user wants to transfer media shown on the tabletop surface to their own mobile device. In the second scenario, called "share", the user wants to transfer selected media from their own device to the tabletop and show it on the surface (with the additional option of later using this media in the "pickup" scenario of another user).

Numerous researchers have investigated the topic of establishing a connection between mobile devices and interactive tabletops. Most related work relies on a combination of optical detection of device presence on the surface with a secondary data channel for disambiguation. For example, Wilson et al. use infrared or visible light flashes [12] generated by the device's screen or IrDA port. Echtler et al. use Bluetooth signal strength information [5] in conjunction with knowledge about the receiver's antenna sensitivity, while Schmidt et al. present PhoneTouch which relies on acceleration data generated by touching the surface with the device [8]. More recently, Boring et al. [2] have focussed on connecting phones and public displays by means of QR (quick response) codes detected by the device's camera. However, all of these approaches require the prior installation of a custom application on the phone in order to access the various hardware sensors or output ports. While one variant of Phone Proxies still also requires a custom app, care is taken to reduce the user interaction required for installation to an absolute minimum.

Employing NFC tags for simplifying the connection process between mobile devices and larger displays in general has also been a topic of research. Several researchers have used a large grid of individually encoded NFC tags mounted behind a larger screen for coarse position sensing. Seewoonauth et al. have investigated this approach with a laptop display [9], while Broll et al. applied this concept to a large projection screen [3]. A broader overview of these techniques involving multiple tags and/or readers can be found in [4].

There is surprisingly little work, however, which attempts to directly merge interactive surfaces with NFC interaction. MobiSurf by Seifert et al. [11] uses a technique similar to PhoneTouch for coupling mobile devices with an interactive surface and uses NFC for direct data exchange *between* the mobile devices (similar to Android Beam[1]), but does not integrate the tags with the surface. EPawn, a French company, presents a flatscreen which claims to integrate NFC-like sensing functionality directly into the display[2] but provides little detailed information. A similar product, the "Dynamic NFC Screen" from think&go[3] also integrates individual NFC tags at fixed screen locations, but does not offer a way to dynamically move the mobile device during interaction.

IMPLEMENTATION VARIANTS

We present three implementations variants for Phone Proxies, each with their own specific drawbacks and advantages. We will discuss each of these implementations in the context of our "pickup" and "share" use cases.

All variants have been implemented on the Nexus 4 Android smartphone and the iPhone 5 (where applicable), a Samsung SUR40 (PixelSense) interactive tabletop system and credit-card-sized "Mifare Ultralight C" NFC tags (see figure 2). The software running on the SUR40 is written using the MT4J framework in combination with the Surface2TUIO adapter. The NFC tags carry a optical marker for the PixelSense tracker on their bottom side. When such a marker is detected by the SUR40 sensor, a halo is shown around the tag's position which acts as a "drop zone" in the pickup scenario and in which the shared images appear in the share scenario (see also figure 1). Data in the NFC tags is formatted according to the NDEF standard [7].

Bluetooth Tags

This implementation is based on NFC tags which contain NDEF "Bluetooth Out-Of-Band Pairing" data, storing the Bluetooth hardware address of the host device. When such a tag is read by the mobile device, a connection is opened to the stored hardware address and the Bluetooth pairing process is initiated. For security reasons, this process requires the user to enter a 4-digit PIN code which is printed on top of the proxy tag and which has been pre-defined on the host side. Although the NDEF standard also allows the tag to directly store the required encryption data and perform the pairing process without further user interaction, this feature is currently unsupported on Android.

Depending on the usage scenario, it may be desirable to differentiate between multiple tags which can be in use simultaneously. Since the only identifying information the standard allows to be stored in the NFC tag is the Bluetooth hardware address, this requires the use of one separate Bluetooth adapter per tag on the host side. However, as an USB Bluetooth adapter is currently priced at about 5 US$, this is possible with moderate additional cost even for a larger number of tags.

Once the Bluetooth connection has been established, the host can now initiate a transfer of arbitrary media data

---

[1]https://developer.android.com/guide/topics/
connectivity/nfc/nfc.html

[2]http://www.epawn.fr/products-2/
[3]http://www.thinkandgo-nfc.com/?page_id=472

Figure 2. A *Phone Proxy* tag (bottom view). The optical PixelSense tag is glued to the tag's center, while the NFC antenna and the NFC chip itself (top left) are visible through the transparent plastic of the tag.

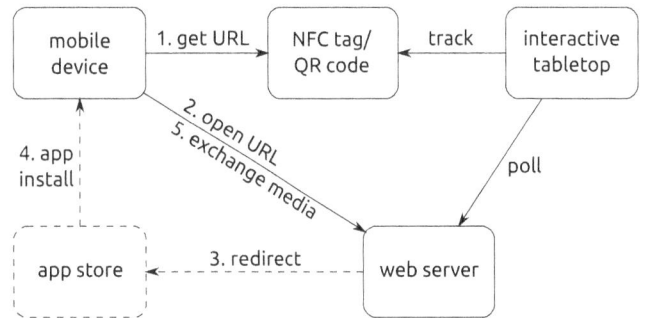

Figure 3. Data flow in an application using Phone Proxies. Steps 3 and 4 are only relevant for the app-based implementation variant.

to the device by means of the *OBEX Push* protocol [1], thereby fully supporting the "pickup" scenario on nearly every Bluetooth-enabled device. Although the Bluetooth/OBEX standards also specify the more complex *OBEX FTP* protocol which would allow the host to automatically browse and retrieve stored media on the mobile device in the "share" scenario, very few devices actually implement this protocol due to security concerns. Should a suitable implementation be available (either natively on the device or by means of a third-party app such as BlueFTP[4]), this second scenario can also be supported.

Custom App

The second implementation of our concept is the most complex, but also most flexible one. Advanced use cases will require additional functionality on the mobile device which can only be achieved through a custom app. However, installing such an app usually is a cumbersome process for the user which involves opening the app store, searching for the correct app and performing the actual installation.

[4]https://play.google.com/store/apps/details?id=it.medieval.blueftp

We accelerate this process by using pre-defined URLs integrated with the server infrastructure shown in figure 3. The URL pointing to this web server is encoded as a standard NDEF message on the NFC tag. When the URL from the NFC tag is scanned for the first time, it will automatically open in the mobile browser. The web server detects this special case through lack of additional POST data and redirects the mobile device to a URL starting with https://play.google.com/..., thereby directly launching the Android app store page for the custom app. The user then has to perform three actions in total: tap "Install", tap "Confirm" (for app permissions) and re-scan the NFC tag. As the final action (scan the tag again) is not self-evident and many users will just start the app directly after installation, this case triggers a message asking the user to re-scan the tag.

For devices without NFC support, it is possible to use a QR code on top of the tag and access the URL using a barcode app. To also support iOS devices, the web page at the initial URL could detect the browser type and redirect either to the correct iTunes store page or to a custom URL scheme which will then launch the app.

When the tag is scanned for the next time, the custom app will now start instead of the browser. This functionality is achieved by means of an URL filter registering the app as default handler for all URLs starting with the address of our local web server. At this point, our sample app implementation will then automatically push the three most recent images from the mobile device to the server without requiring any further user interaction for the "share" scenario. Obviously, this is a security issue and is only meant to demonstrate the capabilities of a custom app approach. In a possible real-world usage, the user may (pre-) select a certain folder or album, from which images - when placing the mobile device on to the NFC tag - are automatically pushed to the server. In addition, the app will monitor the server-side directory for images that have not been uploaded by the app itself and, if such images are detected, download and display them on the mobile device to support the "pickup" sce-

Table 1. Feature matrix for different implementation variants of Phone Proxies.

Implementation variant	supported scenarios	support for multiple tags?	OS support	Requirements (mobile device)	Interaction for first-time setup	Interaction for normal usage
Bluetooth Tags	Pickup[1]	yes[2]	Android	NFC, Bluetooth	PIN entry	-
HTML5 Sharing	Pickup, Share	yes	Android, iOS[3]	Internet access	-	image selection
Custom App	Pickup, Share	yes	Android, iOS[3]	Internet access	confirm install	-

[1] "Share" scenario only supported using third-party software
[2] extra Bluetooth dongle per tag required
[3] iOS support uses QR codes instead of NFC tags

nario. The data flow for this implementation variant is illustrated in Figure 3 involving steps 1 to 5.

To avoid having to upload multiple images over the potentially slow and costly mobile data connection of the device, our app provides optional support for the automatic connection to a local wireless network. The URL encoded in the tag can contain additional credentials (network name and passphrase) for a WPA2-secured WLAN. If these credentials are provided, the app will automatically enable the device's WLAN adapter, connect to the network and restart the synchronization process with the server.

HTML5 Sharing

The third - and most promising - implementation of Phone Proxies makes use of built-in functionalities of modern mobile devices and also relies on access to a web server like the previous variant. The stored URL points to a web page containing an HTML5 file upload form, accessed by one large touch-friendly image button. When this button is tapped, a file selection dialog opens, allowing the user to choose which files to share. Afterwards, the upload process will start immediately. The URL in every tag also contains an unique ID as additional parameter which is used to distinguish the different devices and to select the correct upload directory on the server side. When new images appear in the directory associated with a tag, they are displayed next to the tag on the interactive surface. For the "pickup" scenario, media dragged onto the tag's halo on the surface are placed into the tag's directory on the server and pulled onto the webpage by a custom JavaScript program. The user can then save individual images to the device using the browser's built-in dialog.

This implementations also supports older devices without an NFC reader or iOS-based devices by using additional QR codes printed on top of the proxy tag. Both variants, NFC and QR, encode the same URL. Scanning the code with a suitable app before placing the device on the tag will also direct the browser to the HTML5 page, thereby enabling a similarly seamless interaction scenario as with NFC-equipped devices. The data flow for this implementation variant is illustrated in Figure 3 involving steps 1,2 and 5.

To be used in this scenario, the user's device is only required to support web access and either NFC or QR capability. The possible field of application is limited, not by the the device's technical specifications, but its browser's support for different actions. We have chosen the example of image sharing, as it is supported by both Android's and iOS's stock browser. For security reasons most platforms do not support browser access to other providers such as contacts or calendar. However, this data may be accessible by integrating cloud services - e.g.: *Google Calendar* - into the web client.

Summary & Discussion

In table 1, we summarize the different features of our implementation variants for Phone Proxies.

The Bluetooth-based implementation is somewhat limited in terms of use cases, supported operating systems and flexibility. However, as Bluetooth adapters are nearly ubiquitous in today's computers, this variant is perhaps the easiest to set up. When a simple PIN such as "0000" is chosen and printed on top of the proxy tag, the one-time setup effort for each individual user is also quite small. For scenarios involving only one-way transfer of data to the mobile device, this variant is consequently a valid option.

The HTML5-based variant has the considerable advantage of not requiring any initial setup by the user. As soon as the tag is scanned, the corresponding web page will open on the mobile device and enable the user to exchange media with the tabletop system. Although some interaction is required to choose the media on the mobile side or save shared media to the device, this variant perhaps offers the best balance between complexity and features. However, it requires a high-bandwidth internet connection to be available on the mobile device.

For more complex scenarios, the implementation variant centered around a custom app is likely the best choice. Although a small amount of user interaction is required for the first-time installation of the app, all further interaction can be automated. In particular, it is also possible to automatically switch connectivity to a local wireless network, thereby increasing transfer speed and reducing bandwidth consumption on the mobile data link.

EXPERT REVIEW

In order to evaluate our concept and its prototypical implementations, we performed a short expert review with colleagues and students from our local university department. We chose to focus on the two advanced implementation variants (HTML5 & app) due to their higher flexibility and broader OS support. We collected opinions & feedback through semi-structured interviews from 4 participants using their own, unmodified devices (1 x Galaxy S3 and 3 x iPhone 5). Participants exchanged and discussed pictures with the interviewer who was using a Nexus 4 device.

All participants (P1-P4) expressed highly positive opinions of our concept, but also suggested enhancements which we aim to address in future work. For example, one participant expressed concerns over privacy ("Are these pictures being posted on Facebook right away?", P1) and a desire to explicitly delete pictures from the surface again. Two other participants requested a better visualization of pictures' origins, either through matching color-coded frames and haloes (P2) or through animations during transfer (P3). Interestingly, only one of the participants (P4) was bothered by the manual interaction required for sharing media in the HTML5-based variant. This suggests that the other reviewers were fine with this kind of interaction as it provides explicit control over which pictures are shared, as opposed to the automatic sharing afforded by the app-based variant. Finally, P4 also suggested to visualize information about albums or folders on the mobile device as segments of the halo.

In summary, we observe that nearly all feedback from our reviewers focused on the interactive surface and not on the mobile devices. At the very least, this suggests that our goal of unobtrusive sharing was achieved on the mobile side.

CONCLUSION & FUTURE WORK

We have presented Phone Proxies, a technique for effortless connection between mobile devices and interactive tabletop systems. By using the NFC reader increasingly available in mobile devices, various scenarios such as retrieving and sharing media on the tabletop can be supported. For more complex use cases, the automated installation of a custom app is also possible. Source code for tabletop and mobile app is available at https://github.com/alexanderbazo/portals.

As future work, we will also implement and test our third, app-based implementation variant with iOS. While some minor modifications to the URLs are required (redirect either to iTunes or to a custom URL scheme such as "phoneproxy://"), the general concept is still applicable. Some additional directions for future investigation are outlined below.

We intend to evaluate the quality and acceptance of our prototypical implementation by user tests. As our project emphasizes an easy-to-use and seamless approach to share content between personal mobile devices we suggest to study its capabilities in a natural environment. The utilized tabletop computer is easy to move and can be placed in a public and well-frequented place. We are planning to let random passers-by use both, the native app and the HTML5-based variant, to share images from their smartphones. For this purpose, we will modify the application to prevent accidental sharing of personal data. We hope to gain a deeper insight into how usable the proposed technique is and how well it is accepted by actual users.

In order to preserve users' privacy when they are no longer present at the table, it would be desirable to delete all shared data from the server when the mobile device is removed from the proxy tag. Removal of a device can be detected using the optical tracking system: as the device is noticeably larger than the tag, the secondary object outline detected in addition to the tag itself will rapidly shrink in area when the phone is picked up, thereby triggering a disconnection event for the tag in question. The same also applies if the tag is picked up together with the phone. Techniques such as Shield&Share [10] might also be employed here to provide users with better control over privacy-related issues.

Alternatively, it is also be possible to apply a sticky silicone coating to the top side of each proxy tag which will temporarily affix the tag to the phone on contact. While it should still be easily possible to peel off the tag from the phone's back, the tag will have to be picked up with the phone first. This action would remove the marker from the surface, too, thereby also triggering media deletion. If a coating with sufficiently strong adhesion is applied to both sides of the tag, it might even be possible to attach the entire phone-tag-combination to a vertical interactive surface, similar to the concept of *Vertibles* introduced by Hennecke et al. [6].

REFERENCES

1. Bluetooth SIG. Bluetooth Core Specification 4.0. https://www.bluetooth.org/docman/handlers/downloaddoc.ashx?doc_id=229737, 2012. Accessed 2013/07/31.

2. Boring, S., and Baur, D. Making public displays interactive everywhere. *IEEE Computer Graphics and Applications 33*, 2 (2013), 28–36.

3. Broll, G., Reithmeier, W., Holleis, P., and Wagner, M. Design and evaluation of techniques for mobile interaction with dynamic NFC-displays. In *Proceedings of the fifth international conference on Tangible, embedded, and embodied interaction*, TEI '11, ACM (New York, NY, USA, 2011), 205–212.

4. Broll, G., Vodicka, E., and Boring, S. Exploring multi-user interactions with dynamic NFC-displays. *Pervasive and Mobile Computing 9*, 2 (Apr. 2013), 242–257.

5. Echtler, F., Nestler, S., Dippon, A., and Klinker, G. Supporting casual interactions between board games on public tabletop displays and mobile devices. *Personal and Ubiquitous Computing 13*, 8 (2009), 609–617.

6. Hennecke, F., Wimmer, R., Vodicka, E., and Butz, A. Vertibles: using vacuum self-adhesion to create a tangible user interface for arbitrary interactive surfaces. In *Proceedings of the Sixth International Conference on Tangible, Embedded and Embodied Interaction*, TEI '12, ACM (New York, NY, USA, 2012), 303–306.

7. NFC Forum. NFC Data Exchange Format. http://www.nfc-forum.org/specs/spec_list/, 2006. Accessed 2013/07/31.

8. Schmidt, D., Chehimi, F., Rukzio, E., and Gellersen, H. PhoneTouch: a technique for direct phone interaction on surfaces. In *Proceedings of the 23nd annual ACM symposium on User interface software and technology*, UIST '10, ACM (New York, NY, USA, 2010), 13–16.

9. Seewoonauth, K., Rukzio, E., Hardy, R., and Holleis, P. Touch & connect and touch & select: interacting with a computer by touching it with a mobile phone. In *Proceedings of the 11th International Conference on Human-Computer Interaction with Mobile Devices and Services*, MobileHCI '09, ACM (New York, NY, USA, 2009), 36:1–36:9.

10. Seifert, J., Dobbelstein, D., Schmidt, D., Holleis, P., and Rukzio, E. From the private into the public: Privacy-respecting mobile interaction techniques for sharing data on surfaces. *Personal Ubiquitous Comput. 18*, 4 (Apr. 2014), 1013–1026.

11. Seifert, J., Simeone, A., Schmidt, D., Holleis, P., Reinartz, C., Wagner, M., Gellersen, H., and Rukzio, E. MobiSurf: improving co-located collaboration through integrating mobile devices and interactive surfaces. In *Proceedings of the 2012 ACM international conference on Interactive tabletops and surfaces*, ITS '12, ACM (New York, NY, USA, 2012), 51–60.

12. Wilson, A. D., and Sarin, R. BlueTable: connecting wireless mobile devices on interactive surfaces using vision-based handshaking. In *Proceedings of Graphics Interface 2007*, GI '07, ACM (New York, NY, USA, 2007), 119–125.

Formal Verification of UI Using the Power of a Recent Tool Suite

Raquel Oliveira [1,2,3]   **Sophie Dupuy-Chessa** [1,2]   **Gaëlle Calvary** [1,2]

[1] Univ. Grenoble Alpes, LIG, F-38000 Grenoble, France
[2] CNRS, LIG, F-38000 Grenoble, France
[3] Inria
Emails: FirstName.LastName@imag.fr

ABSTRACT

This paper presents an approach to verify the quality of user interfaces in the context of a critical system for nuclear power plants. The technique uses formal methods to perform verification. The user interfaces are described by means of a formal language called LNT and ergonomic properties are formally defined using temporal logics written in MCL language. Our approach moves towards the powerfulness of formal verification of user interfaces, thanks to recent tools to support the process.

Author Keywords

User interface; critical systems; formal verification; temporal logic; ergonomic properties; process language

ACM Classification Keywords

H.5.2. Information Interfaces and Presentation (e.g. HCI): User Interfaces; I.6.4. Simulation and Modelling: Model Validation and Analysis

INTRODUCTION

User interfaces (UI) play an important role in the Human Computer Interaction (HCI) [6], specially in safety-critical systems, where failures may have disastrous consequences. This calls for high quality of user interfaces, which can be ensured by several ways. For example, [13] proposes four ways of evaluation: *formally* by some analysis techniques, *automatically* by a computerized procedure, *empirically* by experiments with users and *heuristically* by looking at the UI and passing judgement according to an expert opinion.

Although each approach has advantages and drawbacks, formal verification is suitable for safety-critical systems [11]. It allows exhaustive reasoning on the system models, unveiling subtle bugs that could be undetectable by testing or by simulation. In [11], an experiment was performed to compare the effectiveness of formal verification and testing at discovering errors, showing how testing failed to find errors that were

found by formal verification. Besides, user testing can be expensive [15] considering that users in safety-critical systems are highly specialized and their time has a high cost.

Formal verification approaches can be seen as a complement of classical testing techniques to ensure UI quality. It allows an exhaustive analysis of the system, handling complex cases that are difficult for a human to reason about. For this purpose, it requires a model of the system to be verified. The formal model is an abstraction of the system's behavior. It is crucial for the model to be a meaningful approximation of the system in order to have a useful evaluation [15]. By using formal verification one can avoid the need for a runnable version of the UI, thus enabling design errors to be detected earlier in the development cycle.

In this paper we propose a formal approach to ensure quality of user interfaces in safety-critical systems. We revisit some techniques proposed in the '90s ([14, 8]), with changes in several directions. Besides, we use the newest versions of tools specialized in formal verification, namely the toolbox CADP (*Construction and Analysis of Distributed Processes*) [7], the formal language LNT (*Lotos NT*) [16], and MCL (*Model Checking Language*) [10], a language to express temporal logic formulas. We illustrate how features added in recent versions of these tools facilitate the formal verification of UIs. Our ideas are being applied in an industrial case study in the nuclear power plant domain.

The reminder of this paper starts by giving an overview over several ways to ensure quality of UIs using formal methods. Then it will present our approach step by step. A case study on which the approach has been applied will then be described to illustrate model checking in action. Finally the conclusion will summarize our current results and propose some perspectives.

RELATED WORK

Several approaches [12, 5, 11, 17, 9, 14, 8] propose to ensure quality of user interfaces using formal verification. Originally formulated for the modelling of user interfaces, and nowadays covering the modelling of full interactive systems (not only the user interfaces), the ICO (*Interactive Cooperative Objects*) formalism [12] enables one to prototype and to verify applications before they are fully implemented. ICO uses concepts from object-oriented approach to describe the static aspects of systems, and it uses high-level Petri nets to describe their dynamic aspects. The specification is validated using proof tools, by the analysis of Petri net properties. The use of Petri net properties has limitations [12]. In particular, the analysis is usually performed on the underlying Petri net (a simplified version of the original Petri net), and the verification of properties in underlying Petri nets does not imply that these properties also hold in the original Petri net.

Other approaches that use formal methods to verify safety-critical systems (in the avionic domain) are described in [5, 11, 17]. In [5] the authors explore the UIs-related causes of several air plane accidents. In the context of a NASA project, [11] proposes a framework to translate some graphical models (e.g. Simulink and Stateflow) into textual specifications that can be given as inputs to model checkers (e.g. NuSMV, BAT, Kind). These approaches do not verify properties over models, but rather offer a support for formal techniques. In [17], however, the authors propose the computer-aided verification of properties (written in CTL - *Computational Tree Logic*) over a safety-critical system model developed in the MAL (*Modal Action Logic*) Interactors language. Similarly, the approach described in [9] uses models that were originally developed using MAL, and proposes a method to verify some requirements in the context of medical devices regulators.

Closer to our approach than the aforementioned ones, in [14] (later enriched by [8]) the authors use model checking to verify properties of user interfaces. With this goal, the UIs are first represented by a CTT (*Concur task trees*), later used to generate a formal specification in the LOTOS formal language using the CTTE tool.

Once the formal model describing the UI behavior is created, properties that need to be verified on the UI are specified using the ACTL temporal logic. Properties like *continuous feedback, reachability, reversibility, etc.* are verified over the formal specification. Then the authors use CADP toolbox to verify the satisfiability of these properties on the UI model.

We revisit this technique using a more powerful support, which enlarges the possibilities of UI verification. The main differences between our approach and this one will be deeply detailed in the next sections.

OUR APPROACH
Our approach is illustrated in Figure 1. It consists in verifying properties over a formal model of the user interface. In the following sections, we detail it step by step.

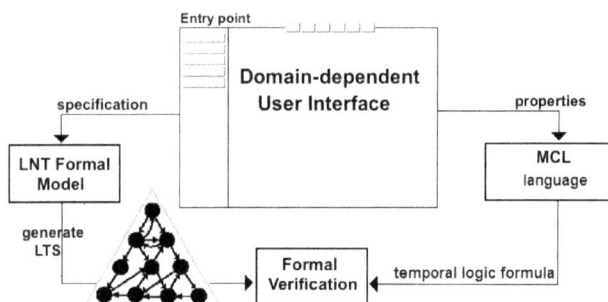

Figure 1: Formal verification of UI properties

Entry point
The starting point before any verification is to understand the UI in depth, i.e. the purpose and behavior of each UI element. This can be done using either the real system, or a prototype, or informal descriptions as entry point. We focus on the UI and thus consider only the UI and the parts of the functional core that have an impact on the UI behavior.

LNT Formal Model
Once the user interface behavior is well known, a model of it can be created. We use LNT to write the specification. Nowadays this model is manually written, in contrast to the work proposed in [14], that generates a LOTOS specification directly from a task model. In our case, a task model per se does not contain sufficient information to permit automatic generation of the formal model. It turns out that our formal model covers the user interface behavior and some aspects of the system's core. It is so written manually, to be as realist as possible.

The LNT model of the UIs is the first input of the formal verification in our approach. We apply model checking as technique, and for this purpose, a LTS (*labelled transition system*) of the formal model is needed. We use CADP [7] to generate the LTS from the LNT specification.

MCL Temporal Logic
With the UI formal model in hands, one can verify a set of properties on it. The right branch of Figure 1 illustrates this second input of our approach. A lot of works have been done [2, 1, 18, 13] to guide the identification of user interface properties. In our approach, the usability properties from the framework [1] was chosen. In contrast to [14], our approach suggest the usage of these ergonomic guidelines in order to identify UI properties, rather than defining them on demand.

In order to verify if the user interface satisfies the identified properties, the verification technique requires these properties to be written in a formal way too. We use MCL (*Model Checking Language*) to re-write them in a formal way.

Formal Verification
There are several techniques that can be used for verification, including (but not limited to) model checking, equivalence checking, visual checking [7]. Our approach applies model checking: we use CADP toolbox to reason over the LTS model of the UI and to verify properties satisfiability.

To end the process, as usual in model checking [14], once a property is not satisfied (meaning that it is false over the user interface in study), the tool provides a counter-example. A counter example is a set of ordered steps that should be followed, by interacting with the user interface, that leads to a UI state where the property is false. This diagnosis is one of the main benefits of using formal methods to verify UIs, furnishing a precise way to identify UI problems.

Advantages of our approach
The key enhancements brought by our approach is the usage of a more powerful support. In order to describe the UI behavior, we use the LNT formal language [16], which improves

LOTOS, and can be translated to LOTOS automatically. LO-TOS is a formal description technique originally devised to support standardization of OSI (Open Systems Interconnection), but that has been used now more widely to model concurrent systems. In [14] the authors point out how difficult it is to model a system using LOTOS, when quite simple UI behaviors can easily generate complex LOTOS expressions.

Our approach alleviates this difficulty, by proposing the usage of LNT, which is a more intuitive language. In terms of expressiveness, LOTOS and LNT are equivalent, but they differ in terms of format and appearance. LOTOS consists of two orthogonal sub-languages: the data part, based on algebraic abstract data types (using equational programming style) and the control part, based on process algebra. In LNT, both parts (data and control) share a common syntax, using the imperative programming style (easier to learn and to read). In [16] the authors deeply argue about the benefits of LNT over LO-TOS, notably the user friendliness and the richer data type definition, to mention only two advantages.

A user-friendly language decreases the learning curve of designers in the formal analysis domain, and it decreases the required labor time of writing a formal specification of the UI, enabling one to bypass the complexity of formal methods and more quickly take advantages of them.

The richer data type definitions of LNT permits more realistic UI models, thus widening the capabilities of verification, covering verifications on the data type of the UI fields, for instance.

Another point of improvement in our approach is the use of MCL to formalize the properties. MCL is more expressive than the ACTL logic used in [14]. As a matter of fact, MCL is an enhancement of the modal μ-calculus, a fixed point-based logic that subsumes all other temporal logics, aiming at improving the expressiveness and conciseness of formulas [10]. This allows us to identify, for example, the existence of complex unfair (infinite) cycles in the model's graph (i.e. the LTS generated from the formal model in Figure 1). An unfair cycle is an infinite sequence made by the concatenating sub-sequences satisfying the formula [10], e.g. a sequence of actions over the user interface that once started loops forever. For instance, in MCL it can be expressed that:

*The UI will potentially respond (meaning provide a feedback) after **at most** three user interactions (requests) occurring in any order.*

This is stated as follows in MCL:

$\nu Y(c : nat := 0).$

$\langle not(req_1 \vee req_2 \vee req_3)^* . resp\rangle true$

or

$((c < 3) \text{ and } [req_1 \vee req_2 \vee req_3] Y(c + 1))$

and read as follows:

"Starting from the initial state, there exists a path leading to a UI response before the user has interacted three times with the UI."

The interest of this property is that, for instance, when user's requests require a large processing time on the system (e.g. in a website), it is guaranteed that at most after three interactions the UI is able to give some feedback to the user. Under the chosen framework for our approach [1], this is an example of *robustness* property, more precisely, a *response time* property.

The support to data-handling mechanisms on temporal logic formula is another advantage of MCL language (i.e. the declaration and initialization of the variable *"c"* in the formula above). This is possible to be expressed on classical modal μ-calculus, but it requires bigger (thus more difficult to read) formulas, and it is not possible to express in ACTL [10].

The set of tools is important to support formal analysis. Rather than developing our own tool to perform formal verification, we work in collaboration with the authors of CADP toolbox. Their know-how in formal methods and the maturity of their tools increased the confidence in our approach. In particular, CADP has continuously evolved in the past years. The last published work covering a similar technique [15] uses an earlier version of the CADP toolbox that dates from 2001, while we used the latest version of CADP (2014-c). In [7] the authors list the capabilities of the toolbox added in the last ten years.

By taking advantage of the new capabilities added to CADP, it is now possible for example to perform *compositional verification* on individual processes of the model, enabling to handle much larger state spaces. As explained in the Subsection *LNT Formal Model*, CADP creates a LTS from the formal model, and the reasoning is performed over this LTS. The more complex the system under evaluation is, the larger its LTS will be. *Compositional verification* is a way to avoid state space explosion, by creating an equivalent LTS for each process of the model [7], replacing a state space by an equivalent but smaller one. In practice, bigger models can be handled, so that we can consider more realistic UI models.

CASE STUDY

Our approach has been applied on a system's prototype of a nuclear power plant control room. The main UI of the prototype is illustrated in Figure 2a (in French).

The main goal of the system is to provide a general overview of the plant status, advertising the control room operator in case of some discrepancies on the reactor [3].

On top of the user interface there are six tabs, namely RP, ANGV, ANRRA, API, APR and RCD. These tabs indicate the current status of the plant, which ranges from completely stopped to working on full capacity. For the purpose of this case study, we do not take into account neither who changes these states, nor how they are changed.

Depending on the plant status, different reactor's parameters are displayed in the middle of the UI. Each parameter is represented by the widget illustrated in Figure 2b. The top of the widget displays the name of the parameter (for instance, *Pth_Moy*, standing for *average thermal power*). The middle displays the current value of this parameter (90.00) and a line that shows the last values. This value varies between a min-

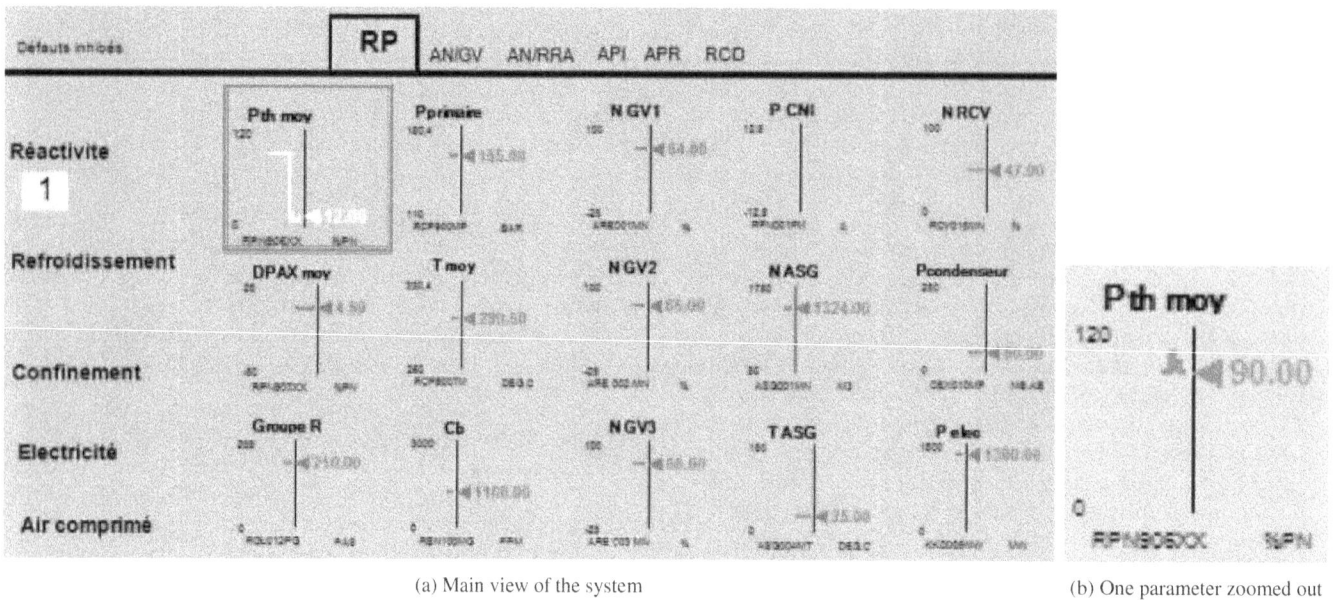

(a) Main view of the system   (b) One parameter zoomed out

Figure 2: UI prototype of a nuclear power plant overview

imum and a maximum range (0 – 120). Finally, the bottom of the widget displays the name of the sensor that monitors the parameter (*RPN906XX*) and also its measurement unit (*%PN*).

The system monitors the evolution of these reactor's parameters. If discrepancies occur in these values (for instance, if one achieves a value which is higher than the maximum expected value), then the parameter is highlighted in different ways, e.g. a colored frame around it (Figure 2a). Besides, the system generates an alarm signal in the reactor's function that is affected by this discrepancy, e.g. the box under the function *reactivity* (réactivite) in Figure 2a.

This system prototype has several other functionalities. However, we will not detail them here.

Formal model

Since LNT proposes a modular-based programming style [16] (inherited from LOTOS), the UI is described as several modules (Figure 3). Modularity is key for scalability. Which provides a means for structuring, abstraction, and reusability [16].

The modules are related to Presentation, Abstraction and Control, as defined in the PAC architecture style [4] (Figure 4). The *presentation* is in charge of the perceivable inputs and outputs for the user. The *abstraction* encompasses the functional core. The *control* ensures consistency between abstraction and presentation [4].

LNT modules

The modules are identified as follows (Figure 3): *Plan state* describes the area in the UI where the plant state can be chosen, i.e. the 6 available states, and the current one. The module *menu* models the left part of the UI, where the operator has

access to detailed views of the reactor according to the concerned function (e.g. reactivity, core cooling, confinement, etc.). This menu provides a hierarchical access to the UIs. By accessing a given function, for instance the menu option "reactivity", the user has access to other UIs that synthesize informations about this function [3], e.g. "boron concentration", "rods position", "boration/dilution" and "reactor control". The middle of the user interface is modelled by *reactor* and *generate signals* modules. The former has functions to evolve the reactor's parameter values in time, while the later generates discrepancies in these values, in order to simulate disturbances on the reactor. All those modules communicate with a central module called *selection*, that mediates the interactions on the UI and the calculations in the system's core.

PAC components

The separation of concerns is one of PAC's characteristic. Each one of the three components provides a way to address a different problem in the system under study. In our case, each LNT module of the UI is classified in the following way (Figure 4): *Plan state* and *menu* are in the *presentation* component, since they model the operator's input and the corresponding system's output in the UI. The *reactor* and *generate signals* are in the *abstraction* component, describing part of the functional core of the reactor. *Selection* is in the *control* component, providing the communication between *presentation* and *abstraction* components.

Beyond the PAC style, a special module called *user model* is included in the architecture, in order to describe part of the user's behavior. In this case study, the operator perceives the UI displayed by the system (arrow *interface* that exits the module *selection* in Figure 4) and reacts to it by interacting with the menu options (arrow *relevant menu options* that exits the module *user model* in Figure 4). This simulates a common monitoring activity of the operator [3]: the reaction to dis-

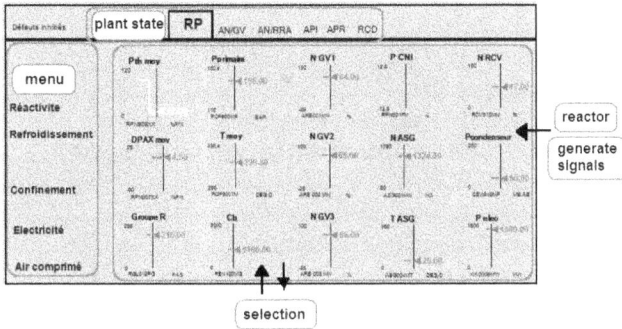

Figure 3: UI organized by modules

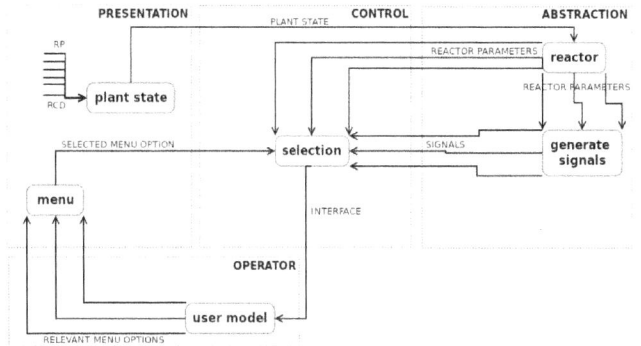

Figure 4: Formal model architecture

crepancies in the reactor. Consisting in accessing the views that have more details about the reactor failure.

The communication between the modules is done as follows: the *plant state* is set, and its value is passed to the module *reactor*. For its part, the reactor will evolve different parameters according to the plant state and to the scenarios that we have implemented. The parameters values are then passed to two modules: *generate signals* and *selection*. The former simulates failures in the parameters and the later identifies which UI should be displayed in order to monitor these failures. The *user model* module represents a human user, who perceives changes in the UI (e.g. the display of a failure), and interacts with the *menu* module to access the UI that provides detailed information about the failure. *Menu*, in its turn, passes to the *selection* module the option chosen by the operator, that in its part displays the corresponding UI.

All these modules are part of the whole LNT specification of the user interface, which contains 15 modules in total, and 3,339 lines of code.

Ergonomic properties

The properties that need to be verified have to be written in a formal way too. In our case, considering the framework [1], all the identified properties are classified as *robustness* properties, with the subcategory *observability>reachability*, which refers to the possibility of navigating through the observable system states of the system [1].

Five properties were identified as key for the project. We wrote them in MCL language. For example, the property:

"from any view, one can always go directly to the main view (i.e. without passing through any other view)"

is expressed in MCL in the following way:

$[true^*]$

$\langle (not(view))^* . 'GLOBAL\_SYNTHESIS' \rangle true$

and may be read as:

From every reachable state

$\langle$ *there exists a sequence of steps...*

...not passing through any view...

...and leading to the GLOBAL_SYNTHESIS view $\rangle$

This property ensures that, in all user interfaces, there is always the possibility to come back to the main view (called *global synthesis*, Figure 2a) with one single user interaction, i.e. without the need to access intermediate views before.

The other four properties are:

- a view is only accessible along the hierarchy of views [1]

- one can always come back to the parent view

- the SIGNAL DETAILS view is always directly accessible

- from any state one can always reach any view

Verification

We use CADP toolbox to perform formal verification. More precisely, we use OCIS (*Open/Caesar Interactive Simulator*, for step-by-step simulation with backtracking. We simulate scenarios over the formal model, and we test it interactively while an execution tree is created in the OCIS tool. This simulation allows one to explore all the possible executions of the model.

Another tool available in CADP is the EVALUATOR 4.0 model checker (for handling MCL formulas [7]). We used it to evaluate the formula over the LTS of the formal model. In the end, we had a diagnosis of the evaluation: an example of steps that lead to a state where the property is true, or a counter-example otherwise (meaning a sequence of steps that leads to a state where the property is false).

The five properties defined before are evaluated to **true** over the model in question. In the case a property is evaluated as false, one can reconsider the essential questions in formal verification: is it a pertinent property? Is the property properly written in MCL language? Is the formal model a meaningful representation of the real system? Is the formal model properly written in LNT? If the answers for these questions are *yes*, then the formal verification rigorously indicates a problem in the system under verification, with a precise way to reproduce it.

---

[1] See in Subsection *LNT modules* the concept of hierarchy of views

CONCLUSION

The approach described in this paper aims at verifying the quality of user interfaces for a safety-critical system using model checking. Specifically, we verify the satisfiability of some ergonomic properties over formal models of the UIs. The UI models have been conceived in terms of PAC architecture, while the LNT formal language describes it. The MCL language is used to write the usability properties formally. The model checker used belongs to the CADP toolbox. Our approach is supported by recent versions of those tools, moving towards the powerfulness of formal verification of user interfaces.

The technique is being applied and validated in an industrial case study in the nuclear power plants domain. This corroborates the advantages of applying the strong capabilities of formal methods to ensure the quality of user interfaces in a real case study. It can be generalized for other safety-critical domains, though.

The following for the approach is to enrich the formal model, to cover visual aspects of the user interface. This would allow one to verify "static" properties, i.e. not necessarily requiring user interactions, for instance, color or position of widgets.

There are also other features of CADP that we aim to explore, for instance, the `BISIMULATOR` tool, which performs equivalence checking over models. This would allow us for instance to verify if different versions of the same user interface are equivalent or not. Such an approach would be applicable for adaptive user interfaces.

ACKNOWLEDGEMENTS

This work is funded by the French Connexion Cluster (Programme d'Investissements d'avenir / Fonds national pour la société numérique / Usages, services et contenus innovants).

REFERENCES

1. Abowd, G. D., Coutaz, J., and Nigay, L. Structuring the space of interactive system properties. In *Proceedings of the IFIP TC2/WG2.7 Working Conference on Engineering for Human-Computer Interaction*, North-Holland Publishing Co. (Amsterdam, The Netherlands, The Netherlands, 1992), 113–129.

2. Bastien, J. C., and Scapin, D. L. Ergonomic criteria for the evaluation of human-computer interfaces. Tech. Rep. RT-0156, INRIA, June 1993.

3. Chériaux, F., Galara, D., and Viel, M. Interfaces for nuclear power plant overview. In *8th International Topical Meeting on Nuclear Plant Instrumentation, Control, and Human-Machine Interface Technologies 2012 (NPIC & HMIT 2012): Enabling the Future of Nuclear Energy*, NPIC & HMIT 2012, Curran Associates, Inc. (2012), 1002–1012.

4. Coutaz, J. Pac, an object oriented model for dialog design. In *Proceedings Interact*, vol. 87 (1987), 431–436.

5. Degani, A., Heymann, M., Meyer, G., and Shafto, M. Some formal aspects of human-automation interaction. *NASA Technical Memorandum 209600* (2000).

6. Galitz, W. O. *The essential guide to user interface design: an introduction to GUI design principles and techniques*. John Wiley & Sons, 2007.

7. Garavel, H., Lang, F., Mateescu, R., and Serwe, W. CADP 2011: A Toolbox for the Construction and Analysis of Distributed Processes. *International Journal on Software Tools for Technology Transfer 15*, 2 (2013), 89–107.

8. Markopoulos, P., Johnson, P., and Rowson, J. Formal architectural abstractions for interactive software. *Int. J. Hum.-Comput. Stud. 49*, 5 (Nov. 1998), 675–715.

9. Masci, P., Ayoub, A., Curzon, P., Harrison, M. D., Lee, I., and Thimbleby, H. Verification of interactive software for medical devices: Pca infusion pumps and fda regulation as an example. In *Proceedings of the 5th ACM SIGCHI Symposium on Engineering Interactive Computing Systems*, EICS '13, ACM (New York, NY, USA, 2013), 81–90.

10. Mateescu, R., and Thivolle, D. A Model Checking Language for Concurrent Value-Passing Systems. In *FM 2008*, J. Cuellar and T. Maibaum, Eds., vol. 5014 of *Lecture Notes in Computer Science*, Springer Verlag (Turku, Finlande, 2008), 148–164.

11. Miller, S. P., Whalen, M. W., and Cofer, D. D. Software model checking takes off. *Commun. ACM 53*, 2 (Feb. 2010), 58–64.

12. Navarre, D., Palanque, P. A., Ladry, J.-F., and Barboni, E. Icos: A model-based user interface description technique dedicated to interactive systems addressing usability, reliability and scalability. *ACM Trans. Comput.-Hum. Interact. 16*, 4 (2009).

13. Nielsen, J., and Molich, R. Heuristic evaluation of user interfaces. In *Proceedings of the SIGCHI conference on Human factors in computing systems*, ACM (1990), 249–256.

14. Paternó, F. Formal reasoning about dialogue properties with automatic support. *Interacting with Computers 9*, 2 (1997), 173–196.

15. Paternò, F., and Santoro, C. Support for reasoning about interactive systems through human-computer interaction designers' representations. *Comput. J. 46*, 4 (2003), 340–357.

16. Sighireanu, M., Chaudet, C., Garavel, H., Herbert, M., Mateescu, R., and Vivien, B. Lotos nt user manual. *INRIA, june* (2004).

17. Sousa, M., Campos, J., Alves, M., and Harrison, M. Formal verification of safety-critical user interfaces: a space system case study. In *Formal Verification and Modeling in Human Machine Systems: Papers from the AAAI Spring Symposium*, AAAI Press, AAAI Press (Stanford, 26 March 2014), 62–67.

18. Vanderdonckt, J. *Guide ergonomique des interfaces homme-machine*. No. 13 in Collection "Travaux de l'Institut d'Informatique". Presses Universitaires, Namur, 1994.

Mindless or Mindful Technology?

Yvonne Rogers

UCLIC, University College London, London, UK

Abstract

We are increasingly living in our digital bubbles. Even when physically together – as families and friends in our living rooms, outdoors and public places – we have our eyes glued to our own phones, tablets and laptops. The new generation of 'all about me' health and fitness gadgets, that is becoming more mainstream, is making it worse. Do we really need smart shoes that tell us when we are being lazy and glasses that tell us what we can and cannot eat? Is this what we want from technology – ever more forms of digital narcissism, virtual nagging and data addiction? In contrast, I argue for a radical rethink of our relationship with future digital technologies. One that inspires us, through shared devices, tools and data, to be more creative, playful and thoughtful of each other and our surrounding environments.

Categories and Subject Descriptors

H.5.2 User Interfaces

Keywords

Mindful technology; vision; creative technology, HCI

Short Bio

Yvonne Rogers is a Professor of Interaction Design, the director of UCLIC and a deputy head of the Computer Science department at UCL. Her research interests are in the areas of ubiquitous computing, interaction design and human-computer interaction. A central theme is how to design interactive technologies that can enhance life by augmenting and extending everyday, learning and work activities. This involves informing, building and evaluating novel user experiences through creating and assembling a diversity of pervasive technologies.

EICS'14, June 17–20, 2014, Rome, Italy.
ACM 978-1-4503-2725-1/14/06.
http://dx.doi.org/10.1145/2607023.2611428

Yvonne is also the PI at UCL for the Intel Collaborative Research Institute on Sustainable Connected Cities (ICRI Cities) which was launched in October 2012 as a joint collaboration with Imperial College.

She was awarded a prestigious EPSRC dream fellowship rethinking the relationship between ageing, computing and creativity. She is a visiting professor at the Open University and Indiana University. She has spent sabbaticals at Stanford, Apple, Queensland University, University of Cape Town, University of Melbourne, QUT and UC San Diego.

Central to her work is a critical stance towards how visions, theories and frameworks shape the fields of HCI, cognitive science and Ubicomp. She has been instrumental in promulgating new theories (e.g., external cognition), alternative methodologies (e.g., in the wild studies) and far-reaching research agendas (e.g., "Being Human: HCI in 2020" manifesto). She has also published a monograph (2012) called "HCI Theory: Classical, Modern and Contemporary."

From 2006-2011, Yvonne was professor of HCI in the Computing Department at the OU, where she set up the Pervasive Interaction Lab. From 2003-2006, she was a professor in Informatics at Indiana University. Prior to this, she spent 11 years at the former School of Cognitive and Computing Sciences at Sussex University.

Yvonne was one of the principal investigators on the UK Equator Project (2000-2007) where she pioneered ubiquitous learning. She has published widely, beginning with her PhD work on graphical interfaces to her recent work on public visualisations and behavioural change. She is one of the authors of the definitive textbook on Interaction Design and HCI now in its 3rd edition that has sold over 150,000 copies worldwide and has been translated into 6 languages. She is a Fellow of the British Computer Society and the ACM's CHI Academy: "an honorary group of individuals who have made substantial contributions to the field of human-computer interaction. These are the principal leaders of the field, whose efforts have shaped the disciplines and/or industry, and led the research and/or innovation in human-computer interaction."

Triangulating Empirical and Analytic Techniques for Improving Number Entry User Interfaces

Abigail Cauchi, Patrick Oladimeji, Gerrit Niezen, Harold Thimbleby
College of Science
Swansea University, Swansea, SA2 8PP, UK
csabi, p.oladimeji, g.niezen@swansea.ac.uk; harold@thimbleby.net

ABSTRACT

Empirical methods and analytic methods have been used independently to analyse and improve number entry system designs. This paper identifies key differences in exploring number entry errors combining laboratory studies and analytic methods and discusses the implications of triangulating methods to more thoroughly analyse safety critical design.

Additionally, a previously presented analytic method used to analyse number entry interfaces is generalised to analyse more types of number entry systems.

This paper takes "number entry" to mean interactively entering a numeric *value*, as opposed to entering a numeric *identifier* such as a phone number or ISBN. Many applications of number entry are safety critical, and this paper is particularly motivated by user interfaces in healthcare, for instance for specifying drug dosage.

Author Keywords

Number Entry; Medical Devices; Differential Formal Analysis; Empirical Trials.

ACM Classification Keywords

H.5.2. Information Interfaces and Presentation (e.g., HCI): Miscellaneous

INTRODUCTION

Best practice for designing effective and safe interactive systems uses methodologies that were developed primarily in office and consumer domains: iterative design, user evaluation (using both laboratory and field experiments), and so forth. International standards, such as ISO 9241, summarise current best practice. However, safety critical and dependable applications should be designed not just to be usable, but to be safe; design should reduce risk to be "As Low As Reasonably Practical," or ALARP, which is a legal requirement under the UK Health & Safety At Work Act (1974) and under comparable legislation in other countries. The relevant ISO Standards here are primarily concerned with assurance processes;

in contrast, in the present paper we are concerned with new methods.

Design for *dependable* interactive applications, we argue in this paper, require complementary methodologies in addition to what conventional usability approaches offer. For example, a standard laboratory experiment may find that users prefer one system to another, or that they make fewer errors or are faster. This is certainly useful information, but (except for very simple systems) a lab study cannot cover all features (let alone all states and transitions) of a system. Also, if the design has bugs — actual software bugs or poor boundary cases in the user interface — then human participant-based evaluation may not help enough. For complex systems, and for critical applications, reliance on user testing alone may not be good enough to assure a system has as few design defects as possible. In addition, much usability practice emphasises individual performance and preferences (UX), and in most dependable applications users are professionals, and their UX as such is less important than safe completion of tasks, including coverage of unlikely cases that cannot reasonably be tested in a reasonable laboratory experiment.

A common approach to evaluation is via empirical studies. With any method, its validity is an important issue. In a typical usability experiment researchers try to achieve validity by managing participant variability. For example, if the only participant was a university student, the results would not be representative of a typical consumer population; in general the smaller (and less representative) the population of participants the less reliable it is to estimate the significance of any results. In addition, running long or large trials is prohibitively expensive.

Software errors and UI features can have a significant impact on safety, which here is the ability of the user to successfully enter the number intended. We are concerned with improving user interface (UI) design to reduce number entry errors. Number entry is a very common task in healthcare, and incorrect drug doses and incorrect drug dose calculations are a significant contributory factor to unnecessary fatalities. There are many papers on the prevalence of prescribing errors [12], but very few on user interaction errors, since interaction errors are harder to measure as they generally do not leave a paper record that can be easily analysed. Vincente [11] estimates the probability of fatal number-entry errors on PCA pumps (patient controlled pumps) as between 1 in 33,000 to 1 in 338,800 (the large uncertainty is due to estimating reporting rates as many errors are not reported); or in absolute terms approximately 65–667 per year in the US or (scaling by population) 155–1,587 per year in Europe. By way of comparison, the probability of death from general anæsthesia is approximately 1 in 200,000–300,000.

This paper is concerned with number entry errors that can be quantified relative to the intended *value*: for example, an error that is 1% out is less significant than an error that is out by 10%. Relative error does not, however, apply equally well to all number types, tasks or all UIs: for instance, numbers may be used as *identifiers*, such as user identifiers, and here different design and analysis techniques than the ones explored in this paper should be used — as even a "low" numerical value error of 1%, unless detected, will result in an entirely different identifier. Many techniques, like check sum digits, that can help reduce identifier errors generally do not help reduce value errors, since they change the values.

Key contributions
Our key finding is that there is a significant variation in the safety of common number entry user interface design choices, at least under the assumptions used in this paper, which are based on real clinical data from infusion pumps. The results show that safety should be assessed by a triangulated combination of empirical and analytic methods, and it thus follows that better user interfaces can be chosen on the basis of the assessments. This result may be used by manufacturers (who wish to design safer systems), to procurers (who wish to buy safer systems), and to patients (who wish to have safer treatment). In the long run, one could imagine that assessments of safety would be displayed prominently on devices [9], thus increasing awareness and hence would encourage more appropriate choices of designs for the uses to which they may be put.

Of course, safety is a complex design trade-off, and higher or lower safety as we measure it has to be balanced against other criteria, including details of the user's task (e.g., entering a new drug dose rate is a different task than adjusting an existing drug rate). Nevertheless making at least some safety assessments available, even if not the whole story, is an important step forward.

The present work uses the combination of an analytic technique based on *Stochastic Key Slip Simulation* (SKSS) that is described in [1,8] and a lab study used in [5]. This analytic technique allows us to analyse number entry interfaces to a detailed level of abstraction and the setup of a lab study allows us to log all the keystrokes we need and know when a number is entered erroneously.

The implementation of the SKSS method has been further extended to work on different types of number entry interfaces, which gives insight into the types of systems that can be modelled using the method.

PREVIOUS WORK AND DEFINITIONS
KLM and GOMS, and their variants, [6] are well-established analytic methods that are useful for obtaining a measure of time to perform a specified goal. These techniques generally assume no use errors and evaluate unit tasks and typically measure time (CogTool is a tool that partly automates this process).

In reality, a user may make errors while entering a number and this requires analysis. The focus of the present paper is error rate rather than time: for many dependable applications, making a UI safer, and finding out how to make them safer, is more important than making them faster.

In safety critical systems, the safest design is not necessarily the fastest or most appealing to users. In safety critical domains, having a design that reduces errors is desirable. However, there are always design trade-offs and an appropriate balance between speed and safety is required. Often making a device safer will make it slower (car brakes are a good example).

Oladimeji *et al.* [4] performed a lab study that compared two different styles of number entry interfaces using the criteria of speed and numerical accuracy. The study indicated that error rates in lab experiments are low, and undetected error rates (i.e., errors users make that they do not notice) are even lower. Since the differences in interface designs are subtle implementation differences in interfaces, it is not practical to find the best design using lab studies because of the time it takes to perform experiments to get statistically useful results given the very low error rates.

In a follow up study, Oladimeji et al. [5] evaluated the performance of five different styles of number entry user interfaces with respect to both speed and accuracy of entry. Their study was carried out on interfaces that ran on a high fidelity physical prototype. Figure 1 shows three of the five interfaces evaluated in this study.

Cauchi *et al.* [1,2] studied the five-key number entry system (shown in figure 1c) by developing an analytic method to study different implementations of the same physical style of number entry. This gave insights into how a single UI can be implemented in several different ways, some of which are more likely to cause serious harm than others. Cauchi *et al.* compared 28 different five-key UI implementations . The method simulates users by injecting all combinations of keystroke slips (omission, repetition, transposition and substitution) with a uniform probability p per keystroke. The analysis makes a number of predictions and raises a number of questions that require validation through empirical data.

So far, the analytic evaluation of number entry interfaces has been carried out on five-key interfaces in [1,2] and on number pad interfaces in [8]. In the present work we are extending the analytic method from [1] to evaluate and compare the number entry systems studied by Oladimeji *et al.* in [5].

As described by Bolton *et al.* [19], current formal methods techniques that are used in interaction design are most frequently model checking and theorem proving. Bolton *et al.* [19] describe some of the shortfalls of using these methods for interaction design. In both cases, it is difficult to verify the formal descriptions of either the model that is being verified or the verification properties. Model checking and theorem proving guarantee that a property is true or false within a given system, however neither of these techniques can be used to make claims about the properties being verified. The analytic technique presented by Cauchi *et al.* [1] can be used to choose what properties to verify about a system from an interaction design perspective.

In contrast to Bolton *et al.* [18], which represents using model checking to analyse user errors, our approach combines conventional empirical data with statistical simulation methods. Our approach can be seen as a development or complement to routine experimental usability studies, and indeed one that generates data that can be understood in conventional statistical ways, whereas most formal approaches require a sophisticated understanding of formal methods as well as a substantial formal model of the systems under investigation. Like formal methods, our approach stands in contrast to usability studies, and therefore offers new insights for designers and evaluators, however our approach is sufficiently close to conventional empirical work that we use the term *triangulate*, since the "same" results are generated for direct comparison. This is not generally the case with formal methods.

An example of theorem proving used in safety critical interaction design can be seen in [15], where Masci *et al.* mathematically defined predictability, and explored how such a property can be verified on real systems through automated reasoning tools. The predictability property tests whether an expert user can tell what state the device is in from the perceptible output of the system, and hence accurately predict the consequences of an action from that state — normal human users can do no better. The analysis was performed on the formalisation of two real devices, and showed that devices, when closely examined, have many boundary cases where interactive functionality seems awkward. Here we explore the impact of errors, and assess in a systematic way if variations in the design of the numeric entry system can reduce harm when errors are made.

In Masci *et al.* [15], the importance of predictability in a safety critical interactive system is described based on literature. Although the predictability property is formally defined in [15] and verification claims made in that work are based on the given definition, the predictability property is not formally or empirically verified to be essential as a requirement. Using the method presented in Cauchi *et al.* [1], this sort of property can be verified as essential or not in terms of safety.

Lee *et al.* [16] and Cauchi *et al.* [2] have analysed medical device logs. Lee *et al.* [16] present valuable insight into how infusion pumps are used in hospitals, how we can gain insight into hospital infrastructure, how much it costs for nurses to attend to alarms over a period of a year and other interesting findings that can significantly improve healthcare systems.

Cauchi *et al.* [2] however, describe how commercial medical device logs fail to give useful insight into interaction design issues for designing infusion pumps. For the type of analysis carried out in [1], the logs analysed from infusion pumps from three different leading manufacturers do not give us enough information to study real world human error. One of the ma-

jor drawbacks is that two manufacturers only store the last 200 keystrokes and the third manufacturer does not provide any keystroke logs at all, making it impossible to determine how the clinician interacted with the device. The other drawback from analysing logs is that unless we can compare the numbers entered into the medical device to the relevant prescription, we cannot determine whether the logged number is correctly input or erroneous.

The study carried out by Wiseman *et al.* [14] and the work by Cauchi *et al.* [2] show that the numbers that are used in the medical domain are not uniformly distributed. Both Cauchi [2] and Wiseman [14] analysed two different sets of infusion pump logs collected from hospitals and found that some digits are more likely to occur in entered numbers than others. Digits like 1, and 5 are more likely to occur than 4 and 7, for example. Since this work aims at improving devices used in healthcare, it is important to run trials using numbers with distributions found in healthcare. In this study, the number pairs were of the type $(0, b)$, where b is a number uniformly selected from a pool of numbers representative of medical device logs and the same number set used in the lab study.

In safety critical medical device design, it is critical to triangulate number entry error from both theoretical and empirical perspectives. In doing this, insight into better use of the different methods and their role in the manufacturing process is presented in order to reduce unnecessary harm and death from bad interaction design.

Why triangulate?

Good practice in user interface design is *iterative design*, where a system is designed, evaluated and then redesigned or otherwise improved, and the process repeated. (Iterative design is covered in ISO standard 9241.) Thus iterative design acknowledges that we do not know how best to design — indeed, if we did, we would not need to evaluate designs and iterate them. Iteration also allows users to change their minds or express new insights into their requirements as they experience working prototypes. Equally, then, we ought to acknowledge we do not really know how to best evaluate a design either; why don't we also do "iterative evaluation," using and improving different techniques for evaluation — a sort-of meta iterative design? One way to do this would be to use contrasting techniques, and then explore their different results in detail. Discrepancies require exploration, and either indicate inappropriate or inapplicable aspects of the evaluation methodologies or indicate interesting aspects of the user interface design for further exploration. The point is: in a safety critical application, one really wants to discover blind spots in the design process. Radically different evaluation methods are likely to complement each other in their ability to contribute to improving dependability.

In dependable design we want to find designs that reduce the probability of design defects affecting users or the success of the tasks they perform. In particular, we want to reduce error and the consequences of error, and to ensure the probabilities of design defects inducing problems is as low as possible. Unlike conventional HCI, we are not primarily interested in understanding the user and their likes and dislikes, we want to find risky behaviours that may happen and make them less likely to happen (or happen and have unwanted consequences), for instance by designing constraints or safeguards into the system.

We therefore want to devise engineering features that reduce bad outcomes when a user interface is used. Unfortunately as we improve the safety of a design, the probability that users do unsafe actions reduces, and the time it takes to do statistically valid experiments with users therefore increases. We cannot rely on any user evaluation that finds zero defects, as we do not know whether this means there are no defects or that the experiment failed to find any. Logically, testing never shows the absence of problems.

One solution is to stress users so that their error rate is increased. This is problematic for two reasons: is their increased error rate representative of what users would really do without the experimental stress, and once we have stressed them to some rate and reduced measurable user interface problems to zero, what do we do as we try to further improve the design? We can never stress users more and more indefinitely! Rather than rely entirely on increasingly long and expensive experiments with human users, there is a point at which it becomes worthwhile and insightful to emphasise alternative evaluation methods that do not rely exclusively on human users. In this paper, we use statistical techniques. The human experiments give us an idea how users behave, and then we simulate human behaviour — along with human errors — using fast computer programs. It is then trivial to perform experiments that in a few minutes simulate impractically long conventional experiments. There is an interesting balance between the psychological validity and the scale and ease with which such experiments can be done.

Another way of looking at this triangulation process is to imagine a conventional usability experiment, say, with N users, maybe 10, as participants. Typically, one user turns out to be an outlier, and they are examined closely and then discarded as unrepresentative. In our approach, one of the users is a "robot" and of course is in that sense unrepresentative, but we know exactly why and how they are unrepresentative, so we can think through in detail whether for each feature we are interested in how and to what extent the robot performance is an indicator of required design improvements. As we explain below, there is a very useful feature of robots: we can precisely control the probability that they perform certain actions. We may then find that the best design changes are the same regardless (within broad limits) of some performance probabilities. In other words, sometimes we may parameterise the robot to be realistic (we got an initial value of some probability from real human performance) but it will sometimes turn out that exact parameters do not matter.

"Out by r error" definition

In healthcare, giving a patient a drug dose ten times too much (or ten times too little) is almost always a critical error regardless of the drug involved, and is called an *out by ten error*. More generally, if the number e a user enters is *at least $r > 1$* times higher or lower than the intended number we call this

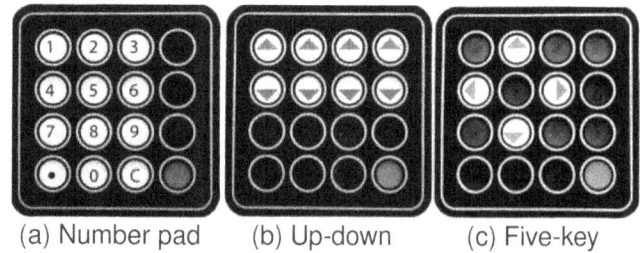

(a) Number pad   (b) Up-down   (c) Five-key

Figure 1. The different keyboard configurations of UIs used in this study. All keypad layouts were constructed using the same physical former. This figure does not show the the device itself nor its conventional numeric display.

Figure 2. The physical prototype used in the lab study.

an "out by r" error. For example, the user entering (at least) 100 when 10 was expected or (at most) 10 when 100 was expected has made an out by 10 error. Of course, entering 100 or more in error when intending 10 will also have made an out by 11 or out by 20 error, all of which are worse than "just" an out by 10 error. In general any out by r error is also out by $\leq r$ by definition.

Note that the measure of "out by r error" forces us to distinguish user error from the magnitude of its consequences. Some user errors have no significant consequences, either for the task or for the design.

TYPES OF NUMBER ENTRY USER INTERFACES

This paper focuses on three different number entry styles, as shown in figure 1 and discussed below.

Number pad UI

The number pad UI allows number entry using a 12-key numeric keypad in telephone-style layout (see figure 1a). It has a decimal point and a cancel key. The decimal point key appends at most one decimal point to the number on the display. The cancel key deletes the rightmost character on the display. Inevitably, if the user keys more than one decimal point, the cancel key's behaviour is defective, as it will delete more keystrokes than the user expects — this behaviour is typical of many number entry UIs with a cancel key.

Up-down UI

The up-down UI has eight buttons arranged in two rows and four columns. The top row buttons increase individual digits in the number, and the bottom row buttons reduce the the corresponding digits. In this UI, the rightmost column matches the hundredth place value and it is used to increase or decrease the value by 0.01. This UI uses the arithmetic configuration, described by Cauchi *et al.* [1], which means the effect of decreasing a digit from 0 or increasing a digit from 9 is carried over to adjacent digits: for example, if the display is 20.56, decreasing the 0 would change the display to 19.56, thus changing two digits in this case.

Five-key UI

The five-key UI has four buttons arranged in a navigation style (up, down, left, right) and a button to enter the number. The left and right buttons move a cursor on the screen which selects a place value in the number, and the up and down buttons increase or decrease the selected digit. Like the up-down interface, this UI works in the arithmetic configuration.

Chevron keys, knobs and other styles of UI

Chevron-key interfaces (typically with upward facing chevron buttons and downward facing chevron buttons in a row) are also commonly used in medical devices. In contrast to the three styles we have evaluated, chevrons use a continuous interaction style: values change while the button is held down, and often a button can be held down longer to change the value faster. This type of UI is better suited to dynamic closed-loop feedback analysis [10] and is not evaluated in the present paper.

Other types of UI

This list is not exhaustive, but since our study is based on the data from prior empirical experiments and data collection from actual infusion pump use in a hospital, it is beyond the scope of the paper to analyse other styles of UIs, such as those that rely on selecting from a menu of numeric values from lists, though it should be noted that some medical devices give the user a menu of standard values in this way.

EXPERIMENTS

In the present paper we extend the SKSS implementation from Cauchi *et al.* [1] to analyse more user interfaces that have been previously analysed empirically by Oladimeji *et al.* [5]. This section briefly describes the lab study from the previous work so that we can highlight the differences between running empirical and analytic experiments. We then describe how we extended the SKSS implementation to evaluate three of the user interfaces evaluated in the lab study.

Calibration using real data

We obtained log files from 60 syringe pumps in clinical use from a university hospital. The log files were anonymous and contained no personal information. We randomly sampled 30

numbers used as rate and volume settings from the logs to inform our analysis. All the numbers had a decimal part and ranged in value 0.26–83.3. A third of the selected numbers used had a precision of 2 decimal places. The same 30 numbers were used for both the lab study and the analytic trials.

Lab study

In the lab study by Oladimeji *et al.* [5], 33 participants (22 female) took part in the experiment. Participants were trained on each UI before commencing trials on the interface. Ten numbers were used in a practice session and 20 were used in the experiment. All participants experienced all the user interface styles and the same numbers were entered by participants on all the interfaces. The order in which the UIs and the numbers were encountered were randomised for all participants.

Analytic study

For the analytic study, the implementation of the Stochastic Key Slip Simulation method [1] was extended to accept a state machine described in JavaScript Object Notation (JSON).

We used the model discovery method, developed by Gimblett *et al.* [3], on the number entry user interfaces used in the lab study to generate a JSON state machine of each number entry interface. The SKSS implementation used these JSON state machine models to ensure that the number entry interface models used in both the lab and analytic study were identical. The representation of state machines followed standard practice [7], where each vertex represented every possible display of the number entry system and the arcs represented the transitions that happened after each button press.

In both the lab and analytic study, the number entry interfaces displayed numbers from 0 to 100 with a precision of two decimal places. Representing number entry systems state machines in the way we described leads to quite large state machines. Even though each number entry interface had the same range and the same precision, the state machines were of different sizes: the number pad state machine has 11,204 states, the up-down machine has 10,001 states, and the five-key machine has 50,005 states.

The five-key state machine is exactly five times the size of the up-down state machine. Both the five-key and up-down interfaces work in two steps, by selecting what digit to edit then editing that particular digit using the up and down buttons. The difference between the two is that in the up-down interface, the user selects the digit to edit by directly selecting the correct button to press, while in the five-key interface, the user selects the digit using the left and right buttons that will highlight the selected digits in turn. The five-key interface gives the user a visual cue of which digit is selected, while the up-down interface relies on the user looking at the buttons. In fact, the state machine of a five-key interface will always be n times bigger than the state machine of an up-down interface where n is the number of digits displayed.

The state machine for the number pad is a different size than the up-down and the five-key: the number-pad interface is

Error	Out by 2	Out by 10	Out by 100
All errors	83.7	16.3	0
Deletion	0	0	0
Repetition	100	0	0
Substitution	82	18	0
Transposition	0	0	0

Table 1. Percentage error rates for the up-down interface.

Error	Out by 2	Out by 10	Out by 100
All errors	58.2	35.8	6
Deletion	56.1	33.9	10
Repetition	49.8	50.2	0
Substitution	86.8	9.1	4.1
Transposition	48.4	51.6	0

Table 2. Percentage error rates for the number pad interface.

Error	Out by 2	Out by 10	Out by 100
All errors	69.7	29.2	1.1
Deletion	48.1	49.9	2.1
Repetition	100	0	0
Substitution	69.5	29.6	1
Transposition	99	1	0

Table 3. Percentage error rates for the five-key interface.

a form of sequential number entry where the decimal point has to be input explicitly by the user, leaving the possibility of states with missing or "naked" decimal points. Neither are possible in up-down and five-key designs, since both interfaces show a constant display width with digits after the decimal point.

The SKSS method works by randomly generating N pairs (a, b), where N is the number of tasks. A *solver* uses a *strategy* to generate an ideal key sequence to take the UI from showing a to showing b. In our experiments, the ideal key sequences used to set the values on each interface are the shortest possible to input that value in each individual interface.

Then, for each key in that key sequence, with a probability p per keystroke a key slip is injected which is: (1) repetition, where a key is repeated; (2) substitution, where another key is entered erroneously; (3) transposition, where the sequence of two keys is transposed; or (4) deletion, where pressing a key is omitted. After inserting random key slips with probability p, the resulting key sequence is used to simulate keying in that sequence on a design which starts from a display showing the number a. The resultant value, which may not be b if any of the injected errors has affected it, is then compared to the original intended value b to find out whether the error is out by r.

For this study, we ran SKSS with 10^5 such number pairs for each UI and 5 times for each interface design — note that this sort of scale of analysis is impractical for laboratory experiments.

In the first trial, all types of keying error (repetition, deletion, substitution and transposition) were set as equally likely to happen; and in the rest of the trials the key slip probabilities were manipulated individually to see how the types of error contributed to the results.

The basic keystroke error probability for SKSS was set to 0.01, though in [1,2] it is shown that the real-world empirical value of keystroke error probability does not matter, since a range of keystroke error probabilities were tried and the rankings for different designs did not change with the different probabilities.

RESULTS

Figure 3 shows a paired bar chart of the percentage of errors that occurred for each of the number entry interface styles, comparing the lab study results from [5] and the analytic study from the present work.

In the lab study, the errors on the up-down interface were mostly out by 2 errors. It had fewer out by 10 errors, and

no out by 100 errors. These proportions were the same in the analytic study but the percentage of errors in the analytic study were smaller for this type of interface. The up-down interface is the only interface that does not cause out by 100 errors in the analytic study. The reason for this becomes clear when we look at results from the other trials running each error category separately in the next subsection.

The number pad did not have any out by 2 errors in the lab study, but had a few out by 10 and out by 100 errors. In the lab study, the number pad turned out to be the user interface that caused high magnitude errors, the type that would be dangerous in the medical domain. In the analytic study, the number pad had errors at all magnitudes, and from this study it is also the interface with the highest out by 100 errors.

In the lab study, there were no errors at all for the five-key interface. In the analytic method, key-slip errors are injected with equal probability across all interface styles. With the same error injection probability rates across designs, five-key interfaces had more errors than observed in the lab study. This is expected since errors were deliberately injected in the five-key trial.

The percentage error rates of the two types of studies are different. In the lab trials, there were no errors on the five-key interface. Of course, if the lab trial was run for a longer period of time, there would have been errors; thus the lab study shows that the error rates for the five-key interfaces are low, possibly very low. Analytic methods can run trials that would take an unreasonably long time to do using lab trials, however, further work needs to be done to better inform the analytic methods with empirical results to simulate human behaviour more closely — or to determine if the absence of errors in the empirical experiment was a statistical artefact.

In the analytic results, each interface had mostly out by 2 errors, followed by out by 10 errors. Out by 100 errors were the lowest of the interfaces considered. Although the five-key interface had more out by 2 and out by 10 errors than the number pad, the number pad had more out by 100 errors. In the lab study, the up-down interface had mostly out by 2 errors, followed by out by 10 errors and then out by 100 errors

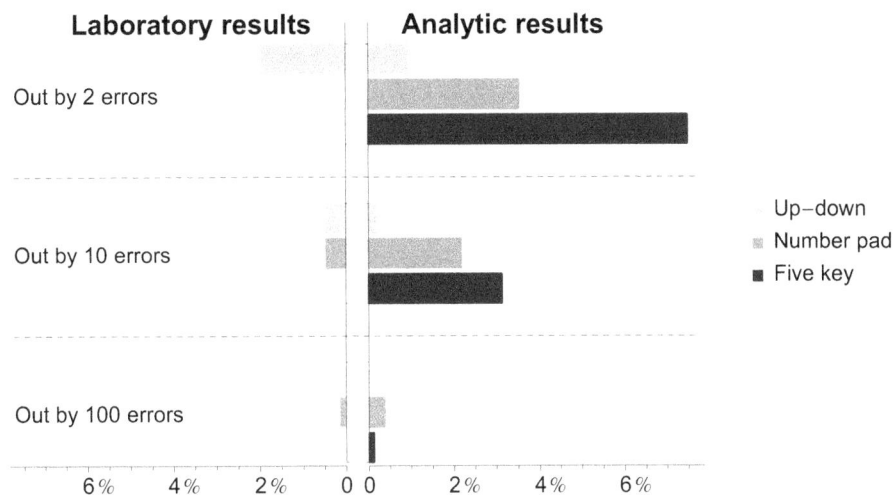

Figure 3. Comparing laboratory and analytic results, showing out by 2, out by 10 and out by 100 errors for each style of interface. The analytic results here are for the trial with each error occurring with equal probability.

but the number pad had fewest out by 2 errors (none), highest out by 10 errors and low out by 100 errors.

The lab results indicate that the number pad is more likely to generate higher magnitude errors, and the out by 100 errors observed in the analytic study confirm that number pads should be avoided in safety critical number entry systems.

Error analysis

We now focus on the analytic study to examine how each error type contributed to the results. This sort of analysis is difficult to do from a lab based study because error rates are too low, and without triangulation there is no "tension" to inform the analysis.

Tables 1, 2 and 3 show percentage of errors that occurred for five-key, number pad, and up-down interfaces when running individual trials with 10^5 numbers. The tables show how each error type (deletion, repetition, substitution and transposition) affect the combined result of all error types.

Figures 4, 5 and 6 show the ratios of out by 2, out by 10, and out by 100 errors respectively between all interfaces for the five different trials.

The up-down interface does not have any out by 2, out by 10 or out by 100 errors caused by deletion and transposition errors. Since the correct key sequence to enter any number in a trial is a sequence of ▲ buttons for each digit, deletion errors would be very small (less than out by 2). Transposition errors have a small probability of causing any error at all. If the hundreds digit is being incremented five times and one of those five keystrokes is transposed, this does not result in an error. A transposition error will only occur in the location in the key sequence where the two subsequent keys are different. In the case of the up-down interface this would be when one digit is set and the next digit is about to be set. Repetition errors in the up-down interface only cause errors of small magnitudes, and no out by 10 or out by 100 errors were de-

tected. In general, this interface is the least likely to cause high magnitude errors.

The number-pad interface has the highest proportion of out by 100 errors across all types of error. From the bar graph in figure 6 it is clear that the number pad consistently has a higher proportion of out by 100 error. However, from the analytic trial we can see that repetition errors do not cause any out by 100 errors in the number pad.

In five-key interfaces, repetition errors are very unlikely to cause high magnitude numeric errors. The analytic results for repetition errors detected no out by 10 or out by 100 errors. Transposition errors in this case are also much less likely to cause errors of high magnitude with 99% of transposition errors being out by 2 errors, 1% being out by 10, and there are no out by 100 errors. The cause for the errors in five-key interfaces being of lower magnitude in transposition and repetition errors is similar to what happens in up-down interfaces.

This error analysis therefore gives us insights into why the analytic study gave us the results it did. Up-down interfaces resulted in lower error rates because there are two types of errors (deletion and transposition) that do not generate any errors at all, even in a trial simulating 10^5 number entry tasks. The up-down interface "designs out" these two classes of error. Up-down interfaces also show that three types of errors do not produce any out by 10 or out by 100 errors, that is, high magnitude errors. This is a desirable property in a safety critical domain where high magnitude number entry errors can be fatal.

Discussion

Safety critical number entry is prevalent in the medical domain and elsewhere. Infusion pumps that are commonly used in hospitals worldwide use a variety of the number entry systems studied in this paper. The results from the previous lab study, that this current paper makes comparisons to [5], suggest that number pads should not be used in hospitals. The results presented in this present paper make an

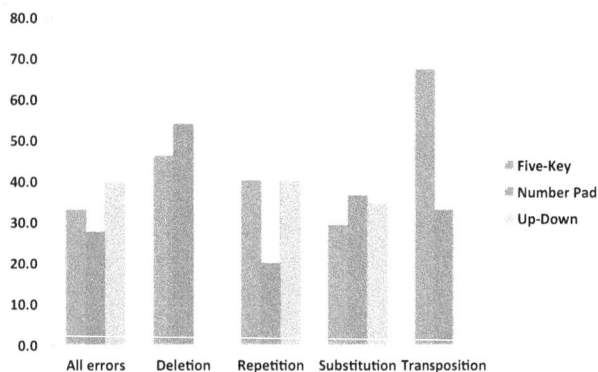

Figure 4. Out by 2 error rates for each design in the five separate trials. All errors refers to the trial that was run with the four error types occurring with equal probability while the rest of the trials were run with only one error type being injected.

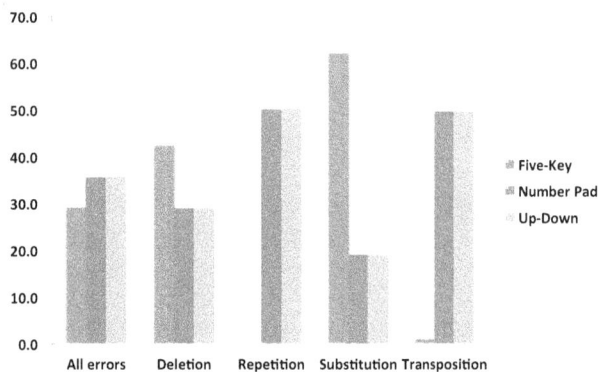

Figure 6. Out by 100 error rates for each design in the five separate trials. All errors refers to the trial that was run with the four error types occurring with equal probability while the rest of the trials were run with only one error type being injected.

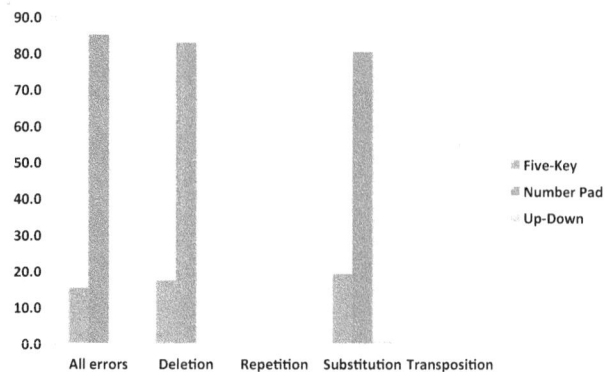

Figure 5. Out by 10 error rates for each design in the five separate trials. All errors refers to the trial that was run with the four error types occurring with equal probability while the rest of the trials were run with only one error type being injected.

analytic argument to further substantiate the claims made using the lab study.

Figure 6 shows that in the analytic trial, the biggest percentage of out by 100 errors are from the number pad user interface, which is true for all trials performed. Errors of this magnitude would be disastrous for many drugs, thus this style of interface should be avoided in medical device design.

Figure 4 is another graph drawn from the results in the analytic trial. Five-key interfaces are sensitive to substitution errors. This sensitivity can be reduced if the buttons on the device are designed to be far apart from each other, such as requiring two hands to input the number. The current implementation of SKSS does not take into consideration how far the buttons are on a device.

If the probability of the user making one error in an empirical experiment lasting t hours (including preparation, participant briefing, etc) is p, then the expected number of hours that experiments need to be performed to record at least one error is roughly t/p (t and p may not be constant, etc). For a typical $t = 1, p = 0.01$, the estimated time exceeds a working week, and practically one starts to have to run experiments over months or even years to get enough data to say statistically useful things. Seen like this, empirical experiments have

limitations just when they become important for dependability assessment; in contrast, analytic methods can simulate a user by computer program and can therefore be performed very fast, generating quantities of data for analysis. Interestingly, in experiments looking for design defects that may affect safety, the *actual* (situated human) probabilities of error are not as interesting as designing to *reduce* them. We have found that our analysis methods suggest insightful design recommendations despite the uncertainties of real user performance data. Illustrating this argument, below, we will show how our analytic technique identified some design problems with a five-key user interface that had not been detected by empirical experiments.

In safety critical domains such as hospitals, human error eventually happens. It is our aim to reduce the harm caused by human error, when it does occur. Even a well-designed lab study may not be able to sample all the errors that will occur during use for each interface. For example, during the lab study the five-key interface and number pad did not show any out by 2 errors; an implausible result. In general, it is not feasible to run a lab study for a long enough time, analytic studies can be used in complement to explore the bigger picture, instead of assuming that the interface design is error free.

Differences in results

The version of SKSS used simulates key slips in a user's task with equal probability and simulates the task many more times than is feasible in a typical user study. Consequently, and generally, the number of reported errors will be a lot more than in a lab study.

Analytic studies are important in the design process for engineering out error. By design, key slip errors due to repetition and transposition of keys are less severe on the up-down interface. Consequently from the SKSS analyses, most of the errors on the up-down interfaces were out by 2 errors. Empirical results complement this method. The low number of out by 10 errors on the up-down interface highlights a current limitation in the key slip injection mechanism used in the analytic study which is currently not as sophisticated as some of the errors that were manifest in the lab study. For example, on the up-down interface, some users made out by ten errors because they shifted the place values of the digits to be entered. One user entered 1.11 instead of 11.1 [5]. This means that SKSS is currently only reporting a certain class of fundamental key slip errors but misses out cognitive errors that users make when using devices. This reiterates the point in this methodology about iterative evaluation; modelling cognitive-type errors in SKSS based on user behaviour from lab studies would enhance the method to cover more types of error.

In modelling both up-down and five-key number entry systems we see that conceptually, the only difference between them is that five-key uses a visual cue on the display while the up-down interface does not. From an eye tracking lab study reported in [4] interfaces where users looked at the display while entering numbers led to fewer undetected errors. Currently, SKSS does not account for the differences in undetected error rates that are as a result of differences in interface design. The cursor based design of the five-key interface requires a level of user attention on the screen. This implies that users are probably more likely to notice errors on this interface than on the numeric keypad interface. An improvement on the SKSS method would vary the probability of error based on user interfaces to account for the possible differences in error detection rates, which can only be found out empirically.

CONCLUSIONS AND FUTURE WORK
Number entry user interface design can be improved by triangulating empirical *and* analytic methods for evaluation. In this paper, three types of number entry systems were used: the number pad, up-down, and five-key interfaces. A SKSS implementation was calibrated with a large hospital data set and applied to these three different styles of number entry user interface. The results were then compared to previous empirical lab-based results presented in [5].

We found that the coverage of an analytical method, such as SKSS as used here, can be far more exhaustive than the small sample of errors that can be studied in a user experiment. Conversely, we have also seen that the types of real user errors occurring in the lab are more complex than those currently modelled using analytical methods.

Empirical methods help in making sure that users understand the different designs while analytical methods help in designing the fine details of the systems that are essential in critical design such as those of medical devices. Such insights will help improve future versions of the analytic methods, especially with respect to typical use error types.

Real design — particularly safety critical UI design — calls for rigorous and insightful design methods. We have shown that empirical studies may be inadequate for revealing errors in a statistically significant way under normal cost-effectiveness resource limitations, and in contrast, SKSS, a simulation-based approach, can overcome these limitations, though at the expense of simulating user behaviour. Nevertheless, the types of result SKSS produces are directly comparable with conventional experimental results, and therefore the combined approach supports triangulation productively.

HCI contributions lie on a spectrum from practice to research. For research, this paper shows both analytic and empirical methods need developing, together, to more reliably understand safety critical design issues. For practical system development — where we wish to improve a particular design rather than uncover underlying design principles — the main insight is that designing number entry systems by using both types of analysis methods is essential, and while neither method is perfect, the combination of methods raises critical questions that will need to be addressed in further development.

Acknowledgments
Funded by CHI+MED: Multidisciplinary Computer-Human Interaction research for the design and safe use of interactive medical devices project, www.chi-med.ac.uk; UK EPSRC Grant Number [EP/G059063/1].

REFERENCES
1. A. Cauchi, H. Thimbleby, A. Gimblett, P. Curzon and P. Masci. Safer "5-key" number entry user interfaces using differential formal analysis. In *British Computer Society HCI Conference*, 29–38, 2012.

2. A. Cauchi, M. Harrison, H. Thimbleby and P. Oladimeji. Using medical device logs for improving medical device design. *Proceedings International Conference on Health Informatics*, 56–65, IEEE, 2013.

3. A. Gimblett, H. Thimbleby User Interface Model Discovery: Towards a Generic Approach. *Proceedings of the 2nd ACM SIGCHI Symposium on Engineering Interactive Computing Systems*. EICS'10, 145–154, Berlin, Germany, 2010, ACM.

4. P. Oladimeji, H. Thimbleby, and A. Cox. Number entry interfaces and their effects on error detection. *Proceedings of the 13th IFIP TC 13 international conference on Human-computer interaction*, INTERACT'11, 178–185, Lisbon, Portugal, 2013. Springer-Verlag.

5. P. Oladimeji, H. Thimbleby, and A. Cox. A performance review of number entry interfaces. *Proceedings of the 14th IFIP TC 13 international conference on Human-computer interaction*, INTERACT'13, 365–382, Cape Town, South Africa, 2013. Springer-Verlag.

6. S. K. Card, T. P. Moran and A. Newell. *The Psychology of Human-Computer Interaction*. L. Erlbaum Associates Inc., Hillsdale, NJ, USA, 1983.

7. H. Thimleby, *Press On*, MIT Press, 2007.

8. H. Thimbleby and P. Cairns. Reducing number entry errors: Solving a widespread, serious problem. *Journal Royal Society Interface*, **7**(51):1429–1439, 2010.

9. H. Thimbleby. Improving Safety in Medical Devices and Systems. *International Conference on Health Informatics*, 1–13, IEEE, 2013

10. G. Niezen. A continuous interaction approach to interactive medical device design. *MediCHI Workshop at ACM CHI'13*, Paris, France, 2013.

11. K. J. Vicente, K. Kada-Bekhaled, G. Hillel, A. Cassano, and B. A. Orser. Programming errors contribute to death from patient-controlled analgesia: case report and estimate of probability. *Canadian Journal of Anesthesia*, **50**(4):328–332, 2003.

12. B. Dean, M. Schachter, C. Vincent, and N. Barber. Prescribing errors in hospital inpatients: their incidence and clinical significance. *Quality and Safety in Health Care*, **11**(4):340–344, 2002.

13. E. M. Clarke Jr., O. Grumberg, and D. A. Peled. *Model Checking*. The MIT Press, Boston, NJ, USA, 1999.

14. S. Wiseman, A. Cox and D. Brumby. Designing device with the task in mind: Which numbers are really used in hospitals? *Human factors*, **55**(1):61–74, 2013.

15. P. Masci and R. Rukšėnas and P. Oladimeji and A. Cauchi and A. Gimblett and Y. Li and P. Curzon and H. Thimbleby. The benefits of formalising design guidelines: A case study on the predictability of drug infusion pumps, *Innovations in Systems and Software Engineering*, 1–21, Springer-Verlag London, 2013.

16. H. Thimbleby, P. Lee and F. Thompson. Analysis of Infusion Pump Error Logs and Their Significance for Healthcare *British Journal of Nursing*, **21**(8):12–22, 2012.

17. M. Bolton and E. Bass. Formally Verifying Human — Automation Interaction As Part of a System Model: Limitations and Tradeoffs, *Innovations in Systems and Software Engineering*, **6**(3):219–231, 2010.

18. M. Bolton and E. Bass. Generating Erroneous Human Behavior from Strategic Knowledge in Task Models and Evaluating its Impact on System Safety with Model Checking, *IEEE Transactions on Systems, Man, and Cybernetics: Systems*, **43**(6):1314–1327, 2013.

19. M. Bolton, E.J. Bass. Using formal verification to evaluate human-automation interaction, a review, *IEEE Transactions on Systems, Man, and Cybernetics: Systems*, **43**(3):488–503, 2013.

Extracting Behavioral Information from Electronic Storyboards

Jason Forsyth
Department of Electrical and
Computer Engineering
Virginia Tech
Blacksburg, VA
jforsyth@vt.edu

Tom Martin
Department of Electrical and
Computer Engineering
Virginia Tech
Blacksburg, VA
tlmartin@vt.edu

ABSTRACT

In this paper we outline methods for extracting behavioral descriptions of interactive prototypes from electronic storyboards. This information is used to help interdisciplinary design teams evaluate potential ideas early in the design process. Using electronic storyboards provides a common descriptive medium where team members from different disciplinary backgrounds can collectively express the intended behavior of their prototype. The behavioral information is extracted by a combination of visual tags applied to elements of the storyboard, analysis of storyboard layout, and natural language processing of text written in the frames. We describe this process, provide a proof of concept example, and discuss design choices in developing this tool.

Author Keywords

Prototyping; Interdisciplinary Design; Programming
Tools

ACM Classification Keywords

D.2.2 Design Tools and Techniques

INTRODUCTION

In this paper we present a novel information extraction process to create behavioral models of interactive systems from electronic storyboards. Our approach allows storyboards to serve as a common design tool for interdisciplinary teams and enable those teams to reason about system behavior or aid in implementation. We focus on the early stages of the design cycle where ideas are often in flux. As such, the artifacts generated by this process are not final products, but rough examples that are useful for generating discussion amongst the design team. This type of prototyping is important during the early stages of design when many ideas regarding form, function, and behavior are being evaluated [28].

In an interdisciplinary setting, the insight and experience of all team members is required, especially when creating and evaluating prototypes. The close proximity of technology and human experience, inherent in pervasive computing systems, necessitates that these systems be designed by the domain experts in the fields in which the systems will be deployed. It is not the engineers, who until now are the typical creators of pervasive systems, but the fashion designers, industrial designers, and architects that are trained to work in these domains. However, designing pervasive systems requires knowledge of computing technologies and programming languages that may be inaccessible to team members without a computing background. Without appropriate design tools and methods, the insights of non-computing team members may be lost.

To address these problems, many tools have been created that attempt to lower the barrier to learning programming languages [4, 21, 26], or are customized tools that target domain specific applications [16, 18, 24, 29]. However, these tools present their own difficulties. First, even a simplified programming language can be a barrier for team members who are not programmers. For these members, their understanding of the prototype's behavior is solely dependent upon how well they understand the programming language. Second, domain specific tools can be suitable for specific projects, but they may be cumbersome for a general design process where the target application can change between projects. Thus, a team may have a suitable tool for describing wearable applications, but then be forced to use a different tool for location-based systems.

We propose the use of electronic storyboards to enable interdisciplinary teams to collaborate in the designing and prototyping of pervasive computing systems. Electronic storyboards are a software design tool that allow an interdisciplinary team to electronically draw and depict how a user, or group of users, interacts with some pervasive computing system. Storyboards are advantageous because they can represent high-level behavior such as context, location, action, and temporal phenomena [12] [9, p.296] in multiple application domains and are a format in which team members can collectively reason about system behavior [14]. We intend for these storyboards to be employed during the early design stages when quick, low-fidelity prototypes are desirable.

Our work seeks to extend storyboards from a descriptive medium, where ideas are illustrated, to one that is generative and can be used to prototype design ideas. We achieve this by extracting behavioral information from storyboards to form a model of computation that describes the depicted prototype. This model can be used by the design team to reason about the prototype's behavior or it can be synthesized into source code using traditional model-driven engineering techniques [3, 8]. The ability to automatically create behavioral models from the storyboard reduces the time between design iterations and allows the team to produce more prototypes over time, resulting in better design outcomes [22]. Furthermore, the process of creating the behavioral model is interactive and may reveal missing or ambiguous information in the storyboard thereby facilitating discussion of intended behaviors.

In this paper, we address the key difficulty of extracting a suitable model of computation from electronic storyboards. We present an information extraction method where the team as a whole can collaborate on designing prototypes by "tagging" visual elements of the storyboard that represent specific computing domain concepts such as Event, Action, Time, and Context. Based upon the user tags, the layout of the storyboard, and the natural language processing of textual annotations, a timed automaton model of the prototype can be formed.

The remainder of this paper presents our process for creating the timed automaton and discusses design tradeoffs for this approach. The following sections present related work on prototyping tools and motivates the need for interdisciplinary design of pervasive computing systems. Next, we present an overview of the design challenges in extracting behavioral information from the electronic storyboards as well as a description of our approach. Finally, we provide a proof-of-concept example that describes how a timed automaton can be formed. While only a singular example, it showcases many common problems faced when extracting information and is representative of a wider class of problems.

BACKGROUND AND RELATED WORK
This section outlines the need for interdisciplinary design of pervasive computing systems, describes the drawbacks of existing prototyping tools, and discusses related work in storyboarding.

Need for Interdisciplinary Design
The goal of pervasive computing is to make interactions with computing technology subconscious, or cognitively and physically invisible. Weiser said that our computers should be "an invisible foundation that is quickly forgotten but always with us, and effortlessly used throughout our lives" [32]. Achieving these "invisible" interactions requires detailed knowledge about the needs and desires of the end user. To understand these needs, creators

of pervasive systems must "uncover the very practices through which people live and to make these invisible practices visible and available to the developers of ubicomp environments" [1]. Understanding these invisible interactions requires an interdisciplinary approach that includes not just technology researchers and engineers, but also designers, particularly but not limited to industrial design, architecture, and apparel. It is these practitioners who are trained to understand human behavior and the subconscious motivations and interactions of the end user [31,32]. Working in an interdisciplinary setting aligns with the foundations and goals of pervasive computing by combining a revolution in technology with a focus on human experience that makes human-computer interaction calming and supportive.

Existing Tools and Related Work
Creating meaningful pervasive computing interactions is a balance of constraints between the user experience, physical form of the system, and the underlying computational platform. In an interdisciplinary setting, the introduction of computing technology, such as microcontrollers, sensors, and actuators, may exclude team members from fully engaging in the design process as they are unfamiliar with particular technologies, or have a limited understanding of programming concepts. While it is not expected that every team member should be an expert programmer, or like-wise an expert designer, each member should have sufficient knowledge and tools to work across disciplines.

Several tools have been created that address these problems and fall into two large categories: either general programming languages that are aimed at novices, such as Scratch For Arduino [26] and ModKit [6], or custom tools targeted at a particular application domain, such as dTools [16], aCAPpella [11], CAMP [29], or Activity Designer [18].

In an interdisciplinary setting either of these approaches may still create difficulties. Requiring non-programmers to learn a programming language creates an additional barrier for those members to engage in prototyping. Depending on the level of abstraction in the programming language, team members may be caught up in the details of the underlying implementation, rather than reasoning about why a behavior did not work. As we will describe in later sections, our electronic storyboards address these issues by providing a high level of abstraction that describe systems in terms of State, Event, Action, and Context.

A similar difficulty is encountered by domain-specific tools as they are tailored to work well in a particular domain but may not be usable in all situations. Considering that pervasive computing applications span a wide range from wearable computers to ambient spaces, it is undesirable for design teams to switch tools when working on different projects. Electronic storyboards address this issue by utilizing the storyboard format that has been used to express applications in domains such as augmented reality [27], conditional events for location-based applications [33], mixed-media applications [7], or creating GUI applications [17, 23, 25]. Additional work, such as the MuiCSers framework and Timisto have focused on using storyboards as a general design tool by extracting task sequences, abstract user interfaces, and time sequences from storyboards [15, 30].

While electronic storyboards address several issues, they are not a replacement for all domain-specific tools or programming languages. For certain applications it may not be suitable to use a storyboard to describe the application. Furthermore, because our approach describes applications at a high-level of abstraction, certain domain-specific concepts may be difficult to implement or express. However, our electronic storyboard could still be useful as the behavioral models generated from our tool could serve as an input to existing tools.

MOTIVATION AND CHALLENGES USING ELECTRONIC STORYBOARDS

In the previous section, we discussed the need for interdisciplinary design of pervasive computing systems and the difficulties in existing design tools. To address these problems we advocate the use of electronic storyboards for interdisciplinary teams. Here we outline the requirements needed to extract behavioral information from electronic storyboards and how to map that information to a suitable model of computation. We intend these storyboards to be used across application domains, and to be employed during the early design stages when quick, low-fidelity prototypes are desirable.

In the remainder of this section we provide establishing definitions and discuss the design tradeoffs when using electronic storyboards. Specifically, we address the (1) tension between the ambiguous nature of storyboards, and the specificity of software systems, (2) how prototype complexity is represented in the storyboard, and (3) the need for storyboards to represent key semantics such as time, action, and context, and how that information maps to a model of computation.

Definitions and Assumptions

Electronic storyboards are a software design tool that allow an interdisciplinary team to electronically draw and depict how a user, or group of users, interacts with some pervasive computing system. A storyboard typically contains a set of frames, with each frame containing textual and visual annotations. Visual annotations encompass all the drawn elements of the storyboard, while textual annotations are the words and phrases placed in and around the frame.

A simplifying assumption made in this paper is that the storyboard is drawn electronically using some computer application. By using an electronic medium, the drawings and markings on the storyboard can be recognized as independent objects, such as words and images, and

Keyword	Description	Example
Person	name of a person	Jimmy, Mom, Dad
Context	name of a context	Meeting, Outside
Location	physical location	At Home
Temporal	time interval	Later, Meanwhile
Event	triggering event	Push a button
Action	prototype's response	Display a Message
State	prototype state name	Idle, Waiting, Alert

Table 1: Supported tags for storyboard objects

not as a collection of individual strokes. This assumption removes the need for sketch recognition in the storyboard, and makes the challenge one of sensemaking and deriving high-level meaning.

Software Specificity vs Storyboard Ambiguity

When using storyboards to describe pervasive computing systems, one of the most significant tradeoffs is between the current practice of storyboarding, and the need to accurately capture the semantics of the pervasive computing system. Storyboards are often ambiguous and leave details to the reader. In practice this can be useful as ambiguity serves as a focal point for discussion between team members and moves the design process forward [9, p.117]. However, when describing pervasive computing systems, this ambiguity is a barrier to correct implementation of the intended system behavior. Prototypes of these systems often require assembling hardware and software components, where ambiguity in the implementation may create incorrect or undefined behaviors.

Our approach strikes a balance between the needs of the design team, and the requirements of correct implementation through a combination of keyword "tags" applied to visual elements of the storyboard, and natural language processing of text throughout the storyboard. When creating a storyboard, the design team can "tag" visual elements within the storyboard to indicate that image contains important information. Our example tags are shown in Table 1 and allow the design team to indicate semantic information about a prototype's behavior using State, Event, and Action tags, or indicate important contextual information using Person, Location, Temporal, and Context tags. This tagged information is supported by natural language processing (NLP) [10] of text within the storyboard. Any words, text, or labels contained within the storyboard are parsed using NLP to identify additional information regarding events, locations, or time. These NLP results supplement the information from the tags and allow the design team to incompletely describe a prototype, either intentionally or not, and thus enable the storyboard to retain some ambiguity. Given the inaccuracy of the natural language tools, their results are considered less authoritative than elements tagged by the design team. We resolve this issue by querying the user before any NLP information is accepted when creating the behavioral model.

Complexity of Behavior within a Storyboard

When using an electronic storyboard, the design team depicts the intended behavior of their prototype using frames, images, and text. Depending on the complexity of the intended behaviors, the storyboard can be rather large. Simple storyboards describe simple prototypes, but as the number of behaviors increases for the prototype, so does the complexity of the storyboard. While storyboards do not necessarily enable concise descriptions of a prototype, they do enable the description to be understood across disciplinary boundaries.

The complexity of the prototype is most readily apparent in the layout of the storyboard. Typical storyboards have a linear flow, meaning that are read left to right. When used to describe interactive behavior, the layout lends itself to expressing behaviors in a linear and causal order. An example of this linear layout in shown in Figure 1a. However, when developing interactive systems, there are often conditional or iterative behaviors that need to be expressed. For example, a device should make a choice between two inputs, or should continue a behavior until some condition is met.

Keeping the linear structure of a storyboard would make expressing these situations more difficult. To address this problem we have added arrows to connect frames with conditional events as shown in Figure 1b. In this way, the linear structure can be extended to exhibit branching behavior. These arrows can also be used to express looping behavior where the storyboard returns back on itself as in Figure 1c. By augmenting the traditional structure of storyboarding we can allow design teams to express additional "computational" behaviors without sacrificing existing practice.

Mapping Storyboard and Model Semantics

Earlier in this section we discussed how information in storyboards can be expressed through keyword tags, natural language processing, and the layout of the storyboard. To enable these information sources to aid in generating a behavioral model, their information must be mapped to a suitable model of computation. A "good" model of computation must have several properties: (1) support easy transformation of storyboard information to model information, (2) capture key prototype behaviors such as action, response, time, and context, and (3) support code generation to enable rapid creation of the prototype. For our approach, we selected timed automata to represent the prototype's behavior within the storyboard. A timed automaton describes a system as a series of states, with each state having trigger conditions and responsive actions between states. These models can be considered an extension of finite state machines as they allow transitions based upon time.

Timed automata are flexible and can be used to describe moderately complex systems [5]. Additionally, several of the keywords in Table 1 map directly to timed automaton concepts as shown in Figure 2. The keywords State, Event, and Action directly map to timed automaton states and transitions, whereas contextual information can be represented as a superstate that enables the timed automaton. Furthermore, timed automata can capture temporal phenomenon contained in storyboards. While frames are typically rendered in a linear order, their content can be highly variable with regard to temporal information. Timed automata are advantageous because transitions between states occur based upon an independent clock that is external of user input. In situations when there are temporal relationships between automata, for example some behavior must occur before another, we have adopted an interval algebra [2] that is used to specify how those automata should be ordered and executed. Finally, timed automata can be used to automatically generate code [3, 8] that can facilitate implementing the prototype once the model has been formed.

INFORMATION EXTRACTION METHOD

In this section, we discuss our approach for extracting behavioral information from an electronic storyboard. We describe how storyboard information, expressed through a series of keyword tags and natural language processing of textual information can be transformed into a timed automaton. Figure 2 provides a graphical description of how storyboard information can be mapped to the timed automaton. As we will discuss later in this section, images that have been tagged in the storyboard can directly map to timed automaton elements, while textual information must be parsed before use.

The process described in this section has been implemented using the Eclipse Graphical Editor Framework [13] which allows users to electronically draw and annotate a storyboard. A screenshot of the GUI as seen by the user is shown in Figure 3. The remainder of this section describes the specifics of how the storyboards are implemented in GEF, and how the storyboard model is transformed into a timed automaton.

Electronic Storyboards in Eclipse GEF

An implementation of electronic storyboards has been created in GEF that allows users to draw a storyboard using frames, images, and text. Images placed on the storyboard canvas can then be "tagged" using the set of keywords in Table 1 where each tag reflects a specific type of information. In addition to images, users can also place labels that contain arbitrary text, and frames to contain both the images and text and provide a structure to the storyboard. The design team can then "compile" the storyboard from within Eclipse and interact with the tool using the console.

Visual annotations and labels can be placed on the storyboard canvas by dragging and dropping elements from the palette shown on the right-hand side of Figure 3. These elements can be easily resized and moved in and out of frames. Specific information about each annotation, such as a Person's name or a particular Location

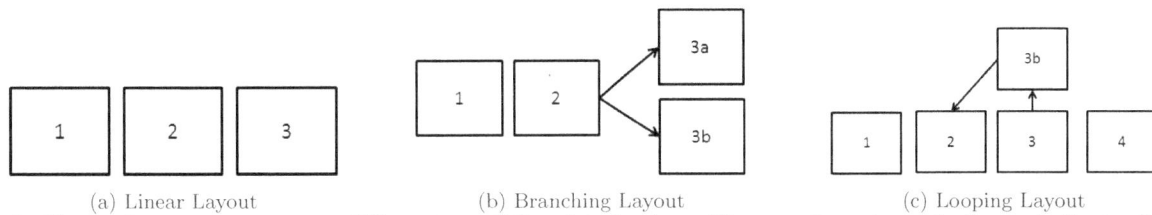

(a) Linear Layout   (b) Branching Layout   (c) Looping Layout

Figure 1: Frame layouts to express different conditional behavior. The numbers in each frame indicate the order in which they would be "read" by the storyboarding tool. (a) shows linear storyboard frames that are read left to right. (b) allows for conditional behavior to branch away from the linear layout. (c) uses arrows to loop back on the storyboard.

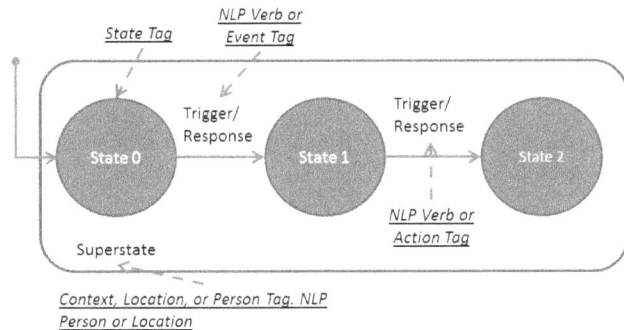

Figure 2: Mapping from storyboard objects onto a timed automaton

can be modified in the Properties View below the canvas. In Figure 3, the Properties View shows the model information for a State tagged image, and allows the user to give the state a name, resize the image, and identify what device it belongs to. The attributes for each image change depending upon the keyword tag applied. For example, an image tagged as a Person could be given the attribute "John", or a tagged State as "Idle" or "Running". The attributes given to Context and Location objects have more significance as they help partition the storyboard into different sets of behavior. In addition to existing storyboard objects (frames, text, and images), we have added arrows that connect frames across the storyboard. These are used to indicate conditional behaviors in the storyboard that may not be directly indicated from the layout.

Transforming Storyboards into Timed Automata

In the previous sections, we discussed how electronic storyboards are implemented in Eclipse. This section presents a method for converting electronic storyboard information into timed automata. The first subsection describes how storyboard information corresponds to timed automaton objects. The timed automaton can then be synthesized in two phases: first, the layout of the storyboard is partitioned into regions of similar time and context then each region is compiled into an automaton.

Mapping Storyboard Objects to Timed Automata

Within electronic storyboards, there are two main types of information: visual images that have been tagged by

the design team and the results of natural language processing from any text or words placed on the storyboard. Figure 2 shows how these two sets of information can be mapped to a timed automaton. Using the keywords in Table 1 tagged visual annotations within the storyboard can be directly mapped to timed automaton elements, e.g. State, Action, Event, and Context. For example, an Event tag corresponds with a state transition trigger, while an Action tag maps to a responsive action by the automaton.

Textual annotation are parsed using Semantic Role Labeling (SRL) and Named Entity Recognition (NER) using the Senna Natural Language Processing (NLP) tool [10]. SRL identifies the structure and content of a sentence, such as verbs, direct object, indirect object, temporal modifiers, or locations. NER identifies words that are a person, location, or time indicator. These natural language results aid in capturing behavioral information that is not explicitly tagged by the design team. For example, if an Action or Event is not tagged, its existence could be inferred by a verb clause found by SRL.

Because of the ambiguity in natural language processing results, this information is considered less authoritative and does not automatically map to timed automaton concepts. When parsing the storyboard, if certain tagged information is missing, the NLP results are consulted for the missing information. However, as we will see in the following section, the user is queried before any NLP information is used to create the timed automaton.

Partition Based Upon Time and Context

The first step in creating the timed automaton is to partition the storyboard into regions of similar context and time. At present, partitioning is done by "reading" the storyboard frame by frame. For a group of frames, the first context or time interval encountered is set as the initial value. If new contexts or time intervals are encountered, the previously read frames are partitioned into their own set and a new set is created with the newly encountered time or context.

Context and time information can be found from Context, Temporal, or Location tags, or from location results from natural language processing. Currently, the tool can identify that some information is related to context or time, but it cannot distinguish between different contextual information. For example, two contexts "at home" and "at work" that are tagged by the design team are easily recognized, but the tool itself has no means to distinguish these contexts and requires the design team to differentiate between the two. A semantic understanding of these contexts could be accomplished through tools that enable novice users to define contexts of interest [11], or existing architectures to recognize and disseminate context [19]. However, an implementation of these approaches is beyond the scope of this work. Regarding temporal information, our approach does determine relationships between time intervals by using interval algebra [2] to provide a formal definition of temporal ordering.

Building Local Behavior

After the storyboard has been partitioned into sets of similar time and context, each set is analyzed to build a timed automaton. The storyboard is read according to its layout and each frame is analyzed for information relating to the behavior of the prototype. The tool looks for State, Event, and Action tagged images which correspond to states of the automaton, the triggering events between states, and the actions taken by the system. Parsing continues until one of two stop conditions is reached: two states have been found, or an event and action have been found. Each condition reflects that a state transition has occurred indicating the depicted prototype executed some behavior. With two states, it is known that a transition has occurred, but the triggers and responses may be unknown. With an event and action the transition is described, but its originating and next states are unknown. In the absence of tagged objects, the textual annotations within the storyboard are queried based upon SRL and NER parsing results. If NLP information is not available, or the user does not select any NLP results, the user will be asked to manually specify the missing information. Additionally, if multiple tagged events and actions or available, the user will be asked to specify which events and actions cause the transition.

FEASIBILITY OF EXTRACTING INFORMATION FROM A STORYBOARD

This section showcases an example of how to use electronic storyboards to synthesize a timed automaton. We have developed a Java-based proof-of-concept tool in Eclipse GEF that implements the information extraction process described in the previous section. The tool reads an electronic storyboard and interacts with the user to resolve ambiguous or missing information in the storyboard. The example storyboard, as shown in Figure 3, is taken from an interdisciplinary product design course [20] and has been re-created by the authors with keywords to describe the prototype's behavior and provide a proof-of-concept for our approach. No other changes have been made to the original storyboard.

While this section only examines a single example storyboard, it has been intentionally chosen as it highlights many common difficulties encountered when synthesizing electronic storyboards. Based upon our experiences working with college-level product design teams and recent work with middle school students, most storyboards will be incompletely tagged and fall under the same class of storyboard as our example here. It is important in this example that the tags applied to the storyboard do not fully specify the prototype. As we will see, there are missing "event" tags in the first three frames, and no tags for "event" or "action" in the later frames. This forces our tool to rely on natural language processing and to query the user for missing information. As this paper is a study of the feasibility of using electronic storyboards, and this example is representative of many common storyboards, our methodology must show that it can address these types of storyboards to be a viable design tool.

The example storyboard in Figure 3 shows a child interacting with a smart watch. The storyboard illustrates how a father and son can communicate to keep up to date on the son's blood glucose levels. The parts of the storyboard shown illustrate the response of the watch when it receives a message and how the son can push a button to display and read the message.

In Figure 3, tagged elements of the storyboard are indicated by arrows pointing to different visual annotations. In the first frame there are three tagged elements. The image of the child is tagged as a Person and given the name Jimmy. The picture of the watch is tagged as a State of a device and assigned the name Idle. Finally, the first image with the sun is tagged as a Context and assigned the name Outside. Once these elements are tagged, their information persists across the storyboard. Thus in the second frame, the watch is known to be in an Idle state without having to re-tag the visual annotation. In addition to tagged storyboard elements, the results of the NLP parsing are shown in Table 2. For the SRL and NER results, V indicates a verb, A0 a direct object of the verb, A1 an indirect object of the verb, TMP a temporal modifier, and LOC a location.

As described in the previous section, the storyboard is automatically converted into a timed automaton in two phases. First, the storyboard is partitioned into sets of frames that occur under the same context and during the same time interval. After the frames have been partitioned, each set of frames is parsed to isolate behavior about the prototype. Each frame is searched for states of the prototype, events that it responds to, or actions that the prototype performs. For our example storyboard, the timed automaton in Figure 4 is generated by the process. We illustrate how that automaton is created in the remainder of this section.

Partitioning Based Upon Time and Context

Beginning with the first frame, the storyboarding tool searches for context and time information. Initially the

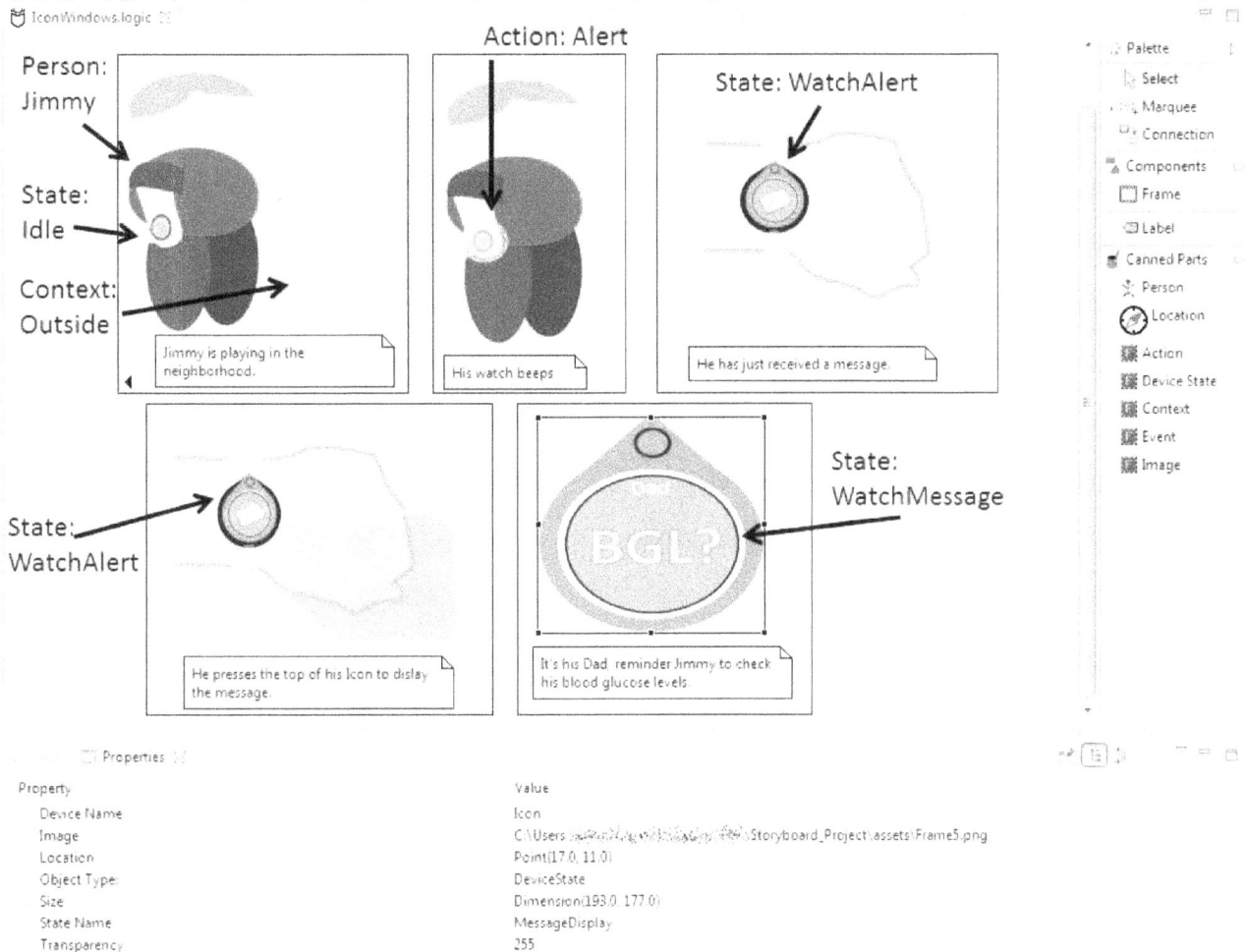

Figure 3: Screenshot of electronic storyboarding tool in Eclipse showing an example storyboard, palette, and properties view. Arrows indicate the type of tagged object and its value.

tool does not have any understanding of time or context, but adopts the first meaning that it finds. From that point forward, new time intervals or contexts are compared with the current to see if they are similar. Using the information in Table 2, the tool searches for frames that provide information regarding time or context. Time information is found from any tagged Time keywords, or any NLP result with the TMP tag. Similarly, context information is found from any Context, Location, or Person tags or any NLP result with the LOC tag (indicating location).

The Context "Outside" is created as the initial context, as it is found from tags in Frame 1. However, within the same frame, a location "in the neighborhood" is found from the NER results. Presently, our method cannot determine the difference between contexts based solely upon name, so the user is queried via the console to determine if they are different. For this storyboard containing the contexts "outside" and "in the neighborhood" the user would respond that they are equivalent contexts so the tool continues through the storyboard. As no new

contexts are encountered through the remainder of the storyboard, all the behaviors within the storyboard are assumed to occur under the context "outside". This is represented by the superstate in Figure 4 that contains the whole automaton.

Building Local Behavior

After partitioning the storyboard, the tool scans each frame for State, Event, or Action information until one of two stop conditions is reached: two states have been found, or an event and action have been found. Each condition indicates that a change in behavior has occurred. With two states, it is known a transition has occurred but the triggers and responses may be unknown. With an event and action the transition is described, but its originating and next states are unknown.

Returning to the example storyboard in Figure 3, the tool reads Frames 1 to 3 and encounters two states and an action. Frame 1 shows the smart watch in the Idle state. Frame 2 shows the Action alert, and Frame 3 provides a new state called WatchAlert. Currently, two states are known (Idle and WatchAlert) along with the

Frame	Tags	Semantic Role Labeling	Named Entity
1	Person:Jimmy, Context:Outside, State:Idle	A0: Jimmy V: playing LOC:in the neighborhood	Jimmy:Per
2	Action:Alert	—	—
3	State:WatchAlert	A0: He V: received A1: a message	—
4	State:WatchAlert	A0: He V: presses A1: the top of his Icon	—
5	State:WatchMessage	A0: Jimmy V: check A1: his blood glucose levels	Jimmy:Per

Table 2: Information extraction from an example storyboard (V=verb, A0=direct object, A1=indirect object, LOC=location, TMP=temporal, PER=person)

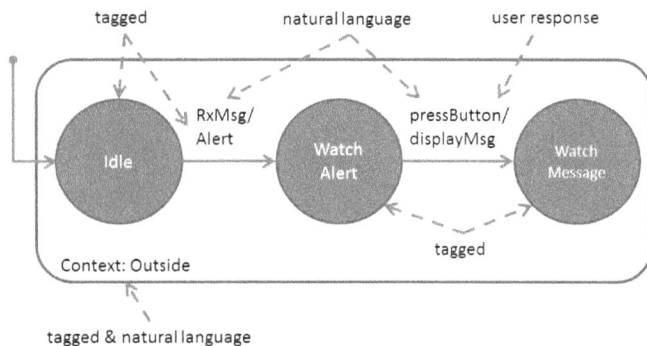

Figure 4: Timed automaton derived from example storyboard. Information sources are indicated with dashed arrows.

Action "Alert", which is the watch's response to the state change, but the trigger of the state change is unknown. With no tagged information to guide it, the tool asks the user for the triggering event. Since the action "Alert" is known the tools asks "Does the following statement cause the action Alert?" This question is posed for each SRL result in Table 2 and the user is asked to respond 'yes' or 'no'. For the example storyboard, the user is asked whether "playing in the neighborhood" or "received a message" caused the Action Alert. The user would respond that "receive a message" is the correct trigger. Using this process, the tool has found that the watch moves from State Idle to State WatchAlert when "received a message" occurs and should respond with an Action called Alert. This information is represented in the timed automaton in Figure 4 as a transition between the two states Idle and WatchAlert. After creating this behavior, the tool continues parsing the storyboard.

Beginning in Frame 4 the tool encounters State WatchAlert and then State WatchMessage in Frame 5. In contrast to the earlier frames, there are no tagged events or actions to indicate what causes the transition between these states. The tool attempts to resolve this issue by asking "Does the following event cause the system to transition from WatchAlert to WatchMessage?" using the SRL results in Table 2. Thus, the user would be asked whether "presses the top of his Icon" or "check his blood glucose levels" is the triggering event of the transition. Here the user responds that "presses the top of his Icon" causes the state transition. However, the

transition cannot be completed as a responsive action is still missing. The behavior implied by the storyboard is that the message should be displayed after the button is pressed. In this situation the tool would continue to ask the user if the remaining SRL result, "check his blood glucose levels", is the responsive action. As this is not the expected behavior the user would decline these result. Having exhausted all information resources, the tool will ask the user to manually specify the action. The user could then manually type a response such as "display the message" on the console. This final behavior can now be added to the timed automaton in Figure 4 as a transition between WatchAlert and WatchMessage, caused by pressing the button, and the user supplied response.

After reading Frame 5 the parsing of the storyboard is finished. The automaton in Figure 4 represents the behavioral model produced by this process. Additionally, source code can be generated from the automaton. Program 1 shows a portion of generated code that shows the transition logic for the automaton using the Arduino programming language [4]. The code initially checks to if "outside" is the current context and then executes the logic defined by the automaton.

DISCUSSION

In the previous section we showed the feasibility of extracting behavioral models from an electronic storyboard. While the process of deriving the model can seem involved, from the perspective of the user, creating the timed automaton takes less than a minute. The time required to create the automaton is dependent upon the information content of the storyboard. If all the necessary States, Events, and Actions are already tagged, then producing the automaton is automatic. However, if information is missing, the user will be queried until the information is found, which may be cumbersome if there are many NLP results.

While the example storyboard could be complied into an automaton, not all storyboards can be. In particular, the tool has difficulty identifying State information that is not tagged. Events and Actions can be easily found from verbs in natural language processing, but State information does not have a natural analogue. Without tagged States, the tool cannot separate events and actions into individual transitions. The primacy of state

```
State currentState=INITIALSTATE;
State nextState;
void loop(){
  if(isOutside()==true){
    currentState=Idle;

    switch(currentState){
    case Idle:
      if(receivedAMessage()==true){
        alert();
        nextState=WatchAlert;
      }
      break;
    case WatchAlert:
      if(pressesTheTopOfHisIcon()==true){
        displayTheMessage();
        nextState=WatchMessage;
      }
      break;
    case WatchMessage:
      break;
    }
  }
  currentState=nextState;
}
```

Program 1: Arduino code created from the timed automaton in Figure 4

information requires that when using the tool teams take care to tag States and may need specific instruction to do so.

Finally, one drawback of our electronic storyboarding approach is that generated models and code are general and do not represent a specific domain. While this allows design teams to describe applications across domains, our approach does not facilitate automatic implementation of a fully functioning prototype. For the code shown in Program 1, the design team would need to implement the functionality to check for a message, beep, or display the message. Given that the time required to synthesize the storyboard and generate the code is short, our approach can reduce the time between prototypes by automatically implementing the logical structure of the prototype.

CONCLUSIONS AND FUTURE WORK

In this paper, we have presented a process for automatically extracting behavioral information from electronic storyboards of pervasive computing systems. We have validated this approach by implementing a proof-of-concept tool that parses an electronic storyboard, generates a timed automaton of the storyboard, and automatically synthesizes code for the prototype. We have pursued the use of electronic storyboards because we believe automatic synthesis of storyboards will reduce the time between prototypes and increase the number of prototypes that can be created by an interdisciplinary team, thereby improving their ability to explore the design space.

For future work, we plan to evaluate our storyboarding tool with novice and expert users to assess how the tool impacts their design processes. We also plan to improve the tool's capabilities by providing shared views of the design from various perspectives. It would also be useful to have changes in the timed automaton cause the storyboard to change, so that a team can see how changes in the model affect the storyboard or vice versa. Finally, we would like to integrate physical CAD tools (e.g., 3D renderings) with the storyboard tool so that a change in the form factor of the design would propagate to the storyboard.

ACKNOWLEDGMENTS

The authors would like to thank the reviewers for their helpful comments on this work. This material is based upon work supported by National Science Foundation under Grant No. EEC-0935103 and the Virginia Tech Institute for Creativity Arts and Technology.

REFERENCES

1. Abowd, G., Mynatt, E., and Rodden, T. The human experience [of ubiquitous computing]. *IEEE Pervasive Computing 1*, 1 (Jan 2002), 48–57.

2. Allen, J. F. Maintaining knowledge about temporal intervals. *Commun. ACM 26*, 11 (Nov. 1983), 832–843.

3. Amnell, T., Fersman, E., Mokrushin, L., Pettersson, P., and Yi, W. Times: A tool for schedulability analysis and code generation of real-time systems. In *Formal Modeling and Analysis of Timed Systems*, K. Larsen and P. Niebert, Eds., vol. 2791 of *Lecture Notes in Computer Science*. Springer Berlin Heidelberg, 2004, 60–72.

4. Arduino. www.arduino.cc.

5. Arney, D., Pajic, M., Goldman, J. M., Lee, I., Mangharam, R., and Sokolsky, O. Toward patient safety in closed-loop medical device systems. In *Proceedings of the 1st ACM/IEEE International Conference on Cyber-Physical Systems* (New York, NY, USA, 2010), 139–148.

6. Baafi, E., and Millner, A. A toolkit for tinkering with tangibles and connecting communities. In *Proceedings of the fifth international conference on Tangible, embedded, and embodied interaction*, ACM (New York, NY, USA, 2011), 349–352.

7. Bailey, B. P., Konstan, J. A., and Carlis, J. V. DEMAIS: designing multimedia applications with interactive storyboards. In *Proceedings of the ninth ACM international conference on Multimedia*, ACM (New York, NY, USA, 2001), 241–250.

8. Behrmann, G., Cougnard, A., David, A., Fleury, E., Larsen, K., and Lime, D. Uppaal-tiga: Time for playing games! In *Computer Aided Verification*, vol. 4590 of *Lecture Notes in Computer Science*. Springer Berlin Heidelberg, 2007, 121–125.

9. Buxton, B. *Sketching User Experiences: Getting the Design Right and the Right Design.* Morgan Kaufmann, 2007.

10. Collobert, R., Weston, J., Bottou, L., Karlen, M., Kavukcuoglu, K., and Kuksa, P. Natural language processing (almost) from scratch. *Journal of Machine Learning Research 12* (Nov. 2011), 2493–2537.

11. Dey, A. K., Hamid, R., Beckmann, C., Li, I., and Hsu, D. a cappella: programming by demonstration of context-aware applications. In *Proceedings of the SIGCHI conference on Human factors in computing systems*, ACM (New York, NY, USA, 2004), 33–40.

12. Dow, S., Saponas, T. S., Li, Y., and Landay, J. A. External representations in ubiquitous computing design and the implications for design tools. In *Proceedings of the 6th conference on Designing Interactive Systems* (June 2006), 241–250.

13. Eclipse Graphical Editor Framework. http://www.eclipse.org/gef/.

14. Haensen, M. *User-Centered Process Framework and Techniques to Support the Realization of Interactive Systems by Multi-Disciplinary Teams.* PhD thesis, Universiteit Hasselt, 2011.

15. Haesen, M., Coninx, K., Bergh, J., and Luyten, K. Muicser: A process framework for multi-disciplinary user-centred software engineering processes. In *2nd Conference on Human-Centered Software Engineering and 7th International Workshop on Task Models and Diagrams*, Springer-Verlag (Berlin, Heidelberg, 2008), 150–165.

16. Hartmann, B., Klemmer, S. R., Bernstein, M., Abdulla, L., Burr, B., Robinson-Mosher, A., and Gee, J. Reflective physical prototyping through integrated design, test, and analysis. In *Proceedings of the 19th annual ACM symposium on User interface software and technology*, ACM (New York, NY, USA, 2006), 299–308.

17. Li, Y., Cao, X., Everitt, K., Dixon, M., and Landay, J. A. Framewire: a tool for automatically extracting interaction logic from paper prototyping tests. In *Proceedings of the 28th international conference on Human factors in computing systems*, CHI '10, ACM (New York, NY, USA, 2010), 503–512.

18. Li, Y., and Landay, J. A. Activity-based prototyping of ubicomp applications for long-lived, everyday human activities. In *Proceedings of the SIGCHI conference on Human factors in computing systems* (April 2008), 1303–1312.

19. Lim, B. Y., and Dey, A. K. Toolkit to support intelligibility in context-aware applications. In *Proceedings of the 12th ACM international conference on Ubiquitous computing*, ACM (New York, NY, USA, 2010), 13–22.

20. Martin, T., Kim, K., Forsyth, J., McNair, L., Coupey, E., and Dorsa, E. Discipline-based instruction to promote interdisciplinary design of wearable and pervasive computing products. *Personal and Ubiquitous Computing* (December 2011), 1–14.

21. Modkit. http://www.modk.it/.

22. Moggridge, B. *Designing Interactions.* MIT Press, 2007.

23. Nam, T.-J. Sketch-based rapid prototyping platform for hardware-software integrated interactive products. In *CHI '05 extended abstracts on Human factors in computing systems*, ACM (New York, NY, USA, 2005), 1689–1692.

24. Obrenovic, Željko and Martens, Jean-Bernard. Sketching interactive systems with sketchify. *ACM Trans. Comput.-Hum. Interact. 18* (May 2011), 4:1–4:38.

25. Schmieder, P., Plimmer, B., and Vanderdonckt, J. Generating systems from multiple sketched models. *Journal of Visual Languages & Computing 21*, 2 (2010), 98 – 108.

26. Scratch for Arduino. http://seaside.citilab.eu/scratch/arduino.

27. Shin, M., soo Kim, B., and Park, J. Ar storyboard: An augmented reality based interactive storyboard authoring tool. *IEEE / ACM International Symposium on Mixed and Augmented Reality 0* (2005), 198–199.

28. Tohidi, M., Buxton, W., Baecker, R., and Sellen, A. Getting the right design and the design right. In *Proceedings of the SIGCHI conference on Human Factors in computing systems*, ACM (New York, NY, USA, 2006), 1243–1252.

29. Truong, K., Huang, E., and Abowd, G. Camp: A magnetic poetry interface for end-user programming of capture applications for the home. In *Proceedings of Ubicomp 2004* (2004), 143–160.

30. Vogt, J., Haesen, M., Luyten, K., Coninx, K., and Meier, A. Timisto: A technique to extract usage sequences from storyboards. In *Proceedings of the 5th ACM SIGCHI Symposium on Engineering Interactive Computing Systems*, EICS '13, ACM (New York, NY, USA, 2013), 113–118.

31. Weiser, M. Some computer science issues in ubiquitous computing. *Communications of the ACM 36* (July 1993), 75–84.

32. Weiser, M. The world is not a desktop. *Interactions 1*, 1 (Jan. 1994), 7–8.

33. Welbourne, E., Balazinska, M., Borriello, G., and Fogarty, J. Specification and verification of complex location events with panoramic. In *Pervasive Computing*, vol. 6030 of *Lecture Notes in Computer Science*. Springer Berlin / Heidelberg, 2010, 57–75.

Supporting Design, Prototyping, and Evaluation of Public Display Systems

Morin Ostkamp
Software Engineering Lab
Münster University of Applied Sciences
morin.ostkamp@fh-muenster.de

Christian Kray
Institute for Geoinformatics
University of Münster
c.kray@uni-muenster.de

ABSTRACT

Public displays have become ubiquitous in urban areas. They can efficiently deliver information to many people and increasingly also provide means for interaction. Designing, developing, and testing such systems can be challenging, particularly if a system consists of many displays in multiple locations. Deployment is costly and contextual factors such as placement within and interaction with the environment can have a major impact on the success of such systems. In this paper we propose a new prototyping and evaluation method for public display systems (PDS) that integrates augmented panoramic imagery and a light-weight, graph-based model to simulate PDS. Our approach facilitates low-effort, rapid design of interactive PDS and their evaluation. We describe a prototypical implementation and present an initial assessment based on a comparison with existing methods, our own experiences, and an example case study.

Author Keywords

Public Display Systems; rapid prototyping; immersive environments; toolkit

ACM Classification Keywords

H.5.m. Information Interfaces and Presentation: Miscellaneous

INTRODUCTION

Public display systems (PDS) are a common sight in many places nowadays. Often, they allow for interaction via touch overlays, WiFi and Bluetooth interfaces, or body tracking cameras, for example. These means of interaction add complexity to the software that runs the public display and to the user interfaces. As with any software, PDS need sound design and testing to guarantee a certain level of reliability and to ensure a good user experience. There are best practices and approaches (e.g., unit testing and participatory design) to develop and test conventional software. Yet, many of these practices only partially address a key aspect of PDS, i.e., their situatedness and their inherent interaction with the context they are deployed in.

Alt et al. [1] compared various evaluation methods for PDS and analyzed them with respect to how well they are suited to answer specific research questions (e.g., audience behavior or user acceptance). One aspect they highlighted is the importance of ecological validity for PDS, which usually comes at the expense of external or internal validity. In this paper, we propose a novel approach to increase the degree of 'situatedness' in lab-based PDS studies. It supports the design and evaluation of PDS at early development stages by combining panoramic images or video footage with a light-weight, graph-based model to simulate public displays in an immersive video environment (IVE). We also present the *Immersive Public Display Evaluation and Design (IPED) Toolkit* as an initial implementation of our approach. We demonstrate the benefits of the toolkit in terms of rapidly designing and evaluating PDS with relatively little effort.

In the remainder of this paper, we first position our research within related work and discuss some key challenges in designing and evaluating interactive public displays. After introducing our approach and its initial implementation (the IPED Toolkit) we report on experiences gathered from using immersive environments for evaluation, summarize findings from a field trial, and apply the IPED Toolkit to an example case study. We conclude by discussing limitations and implications of the approach. We also summarize our contributions and outline promising directions for future work.

RELATED WORK

This section focuses on related work that covers designing, prototyping, and evaluating PDS. After discussing these areas in more detail, we will briefly summarize the main advantages and drawbacks of the reviewed approaches (cf. Table 1).

Design

A fundamental property of signage in general is its legibility. Xie et al. [23] investigated (static) emergency signage and its legibility. They proposed and validated a geometrical model that captures relevant aspects of sign visibility. Such an approach could be applied during the design phase of a PDS to assess and predict whether the shown content can be perceived. The same is true for agent-based models (cf., e.g., Penn and Turner [13]), which can simulate pedestrian movement in general, but can incorporate visibility assessment as well. As such models often only rely on geometrical computations, combining them with our approach would facilitate the investigation of contextual factors as well. Stahl and Haupter [19] used a 3D model of intended deployment sites in which they inject screen contents of existing PDS. This is similar to the approach proposed here. However, their system lacks visual fidelity, does not incorporate sensor readings, and does not easily support different scenes at the same location (e.g., daytime vs. nighttime). A (scaled-down) replica of a planned deployment site can also be used in the design phase. Hamhoum and Kray [7] applied this approach to a PDS that supports navigation at densely crowded sites. They were able to gather insights into properties of the full-scale system (e.g., the relative density of displays) based on the physical simulation. While the approach proposed in this paper could be used to design and evaluate the system presented in [7], simulating the users' locomotion is still difficult.

Prototyping

The Proximity Toolkit [9] is based on a theory of proxemic interaction. It allows for rapid prototyping of applications that make use of the ideas and concepts of proxemics, e.g., the user's location and orientation in front of public displays. While this approach was successfully used to prototype different PDS, it only focuses on one type of interaction and does not consider contextual factors, display contents, or the deployment location of the PDS. This last aspect is picked up on by Nakanishi [11] who proposed to use miniature models of real locations to facilitate frequent prototyping and testing. Not all relevant aspects can be covered in a miniature model, which is why they suggested to analyze a corresponding virtual model as well. This virtual model can then be used to assess the ideal positioning of interactive devices, while the miniature model can be used to eliminate discrepancies between the virtual and the real space (such as "optical attenuation"). Their approach is subject to some limitations, as the virtual model and the small scale physical model may lack some realism. Moreover, in contrast to the approach presented in this paper, their system requires designers to work with two models rather than just one.

Harrison and Massink [8] proposed stochastic models as a means of prototyping and evaluating ubiquitous systems prior to deployment. The idea is to reduce risks during the development, as some design flaws can be identified early. However, constructing usable models of this type may require considerable effort and might not capture all relevant contextual factors. In contrast, the approach we propose facilitates a rapid development of simulations and integrates different contextual factors. The APEX framework [16] is a related approach for model-based rapid prototyping of ubiquitous environments. It enables users to experience an envisioned system in a 3D simulation and is based on three components: the virtual environment, the behavior, and the communication/execution. These components bear some resemblance to the architecture described in this paper. However, the model of the framework is based on a (potentially complex) Coloured Petri Net (CPN) in contrast to the lightweight, graph-based model presented in this paper.

Evaluation

Alt et al. [1] presented a survey on how to evaluate PDS based on an extensive literature review. They identified a set of typical research questions that often occur when evaluating PDS and classified how such research questions could be

evaluated. They also discussed external, internal, and ecological validity and provided a small number of guidelines for studying PDS with users. Though they did not consider IVEs or formal models, they covered a broad range of evaluation methods and highlighted the relative benefits and drawbacks of different methods. One of the most popular evaluation methods they identified was to record all interactions (e.g., via log files or video recordings). This approach has been used in many different settings (cf., e.g., [4, 6, 20, 22]), in particular in combination with extended deployments such as reported for the Wray photodisplay [21], the Hermes system [5], SPAM [2], and MobiDiC [10]. A key advantage of an approach based on recordings is a high degree of ecological validity, since the interactive PDS is analyzed in its target environment. Drawbacks include privacy concerns, inherent limitations in terms of what can be recorded, as well as the effort and time required for long-term deployments. Our approach can make use of such recordings to simulate physical environments in the lab and also supports recording interactions in the lab. Singh et al. [17] combined immersive video and surround audio to create "a realistic simulation of a ubiquitous environment". The IPED Toolkit presented in this paper is based on the design by Singh et al. However, while Singh et al. focused on prototyping and evaluating context-aware apps on mobile devices, the IPED Toolkit supports the design, prototyping, and evaluation of PDS.

All of the presented methods for design, prototyping, and evaluation of PDS have their strengths and weaknesses. Table 1 summarizes the characteristics of each method and contrasts them with the approach described in this paper.

CHALLENGES

While scrutinizing the related work, we identified a number of challenges *(C1-C8)* that may occur during the design and evaluation processes of interactive PDS. Though the following list might not be exhaustive, we believe it covers key issues in the context of PDS.

(C1) Public displays always posses a certain *situatedness* (cf., e.g., [5, 10, 21]) that can only be simulated partially in a different location (e.g., a lab). *(C2) Form factors* of public displays may vary significantly, e.g., ranging from desktop-sized monitors to wall-sized facades. *(C3) Fixed environmental factors*, such as surrounding buildings or vegetation, may have an impact, e.g., by limiting the viewing angle or interaction area (cf., e.g., [11, 18]). *(C4) Dynamic environmental factors*, for example, passersby, weather, or the time of day may have an influence (cf., e.g., [8, 9, 10, 11]). The approach introduced in this paper can be used to assess challenges *(C1-C3)* via simulating corresponding scenarios in immersive video environments. Challenge *(C4)* can be assessed at least partially, as dynamic environmental factors could be represented by corresponding footage (cf. "event shots" [17]).

(C5) The interaction and communication between public displays and *mobile devices* (cf., e.g., [10, 12, 15]) is particularly challenging due to two reasons: (1) The communication stack that is required to facilitate the actual interaction (e.g., via WiFi or Bluetooth) adds some extra complexity to

Table 1. Overview of evaluation and design methods for public display systems.

System	Pros	Cons
Marquardt (Proximity Toolkit) [9]	rapid prototyping possible	limited interaction; lack of context
Hamhoum & Kray [7]	supports locomotion	effort required to construct physical small-scale model
Harrison & Massink (PEPA, Fluid Flow) [8]	prototyping and a priori evaluation based on stochastic model	effort required to create model; may require expert knowledge; lack of context
Nakanishi [11]	rapid prototyping of interactive public display systems	requires analysis of miniature and virtual model rather than just one; interaction limited
Taylor (Wray) [21], Faisal (Hermes) [5], Cheverst (SPAM) [2], Müller (MobiDiC) [10]	results with high external and internal validity	inherent limitations of logging; effort and time required for long-term deployments
Stahl & Haupter [19]	rapid evaluation of display and content visibility	limited coverage of other design and evaluation aspects
Silva et al. (APEX) [16]	precise (3D) model of evaluated system	based on (complex) Coloured Petri Net (CPN)
Singh et al. [17]	rapid and low effort prototyping of context-aware mobile apps; no physical deployment needed	applicable to mobile apps only; not accessible to non-experts; locomotion limited; predefined locations; limited applicability to research questions defined by Alt et al. [1]
IPED Toolkit	rapid and low effort prototyping of interactive PDS; accessible for non-experts; no physical deployment needed	locomotion limited; predefined locations; limited applicability to research questions defined by Alt et al. [1]

the software system and the user interface; (2) The great diversity of mobile devices (e.g., various operating systems and screen sizes) can make the testing process a daunting task. The toolkit presented in this paper helps to assess challenge *(C5)*, as developers of such interaction means can rapidly prototype and evaluate their mobile apps precisely and in a repeatable manner. This way, the user's performance can be analyzed more reliably than in situations (e.g., field studies) with fluctuating parameters (e.g., varying network connectivity, weather conditions, or passersby). For example, the user's task completion time could be influenced by bad WiFi reception, which is likely a negligible factor in an HCI study.

(C6) Multi-display networks introduce unique design challenges (cf., e.g., [4, 6, 20, 22]). In contrast to single displays, multi-display networks offer an extended set of possibilities: If the system ensures continuity and synchronicity between all attached displays, users may benefit from a continuous experience throughout a building, for example. Testing these large scale deployments may be time consuming and expensive, as deploying and updating the numerous installations can take a significant amount of time. Moreover, the acquisition as well as the maintenance and management costs for display networks can also be a major roadblock. Our approach allows to assess challenge *(C6)* by simulating multi-display deployments cost efficiently. Additionally, the early development process can be accelerated, as changes to the system's behavior, for example, can be reflected on all simulated displays with little effort. Our approach may also help to assess the user's performance regarding, e.g., error rates, as external factors or disturbances, such as (involuntary) interactions with passersby, can be controlled more precisely. Aspects

that require locomotion of the user are however difficult to replicate with our approach.

(C7) Public displays are usually exposed to certain audiences in specific environments. To increase the *acceptance* of a public display within a social group, it may be beneficial to let these people participate in the early design process, for example, in order to determine well-suited installation sites (cf., e.g., [5, 15, 21, 22]). A realistic preview of the public display and its environment could be used to create a common base for further discussion and design steps. While our approach can support addressing *(C7)*, it is not suited to provide deeper insights in terms of general user acceptance, e.g., users noticing or actually using displays while performing certain tasks.

(C8) Depending on the context, a public display may be subject to specific *legal constraints*, such as privacy and security laws or content regulations. As long as those constraints can be mirrored in a virtual simulation as proposed in this paper, our approach can be used to assess challenge *(C8)*, e.g., by relocating installation sites, varying form factors, or simulating different contents.

APPROACH

Our approach to design, prototype, and evaluate public display systems aims at replicating real-world scenes in the lab with a high degree of audiovisual fidelity to provide designers and participants with an immersive experience similar to being in situ. The approach consists of the following core elements. A state-transition graph connects real-world scenes (represented by the nodes of the graph) to one another via edges that indicate a direct transition from one state to another. Each node is linked to photo or video footage of a specific real-world place in a specific state. Additionally, further information such as the location of public displays in the virtual scene or sensor data recorded in the real-world are stored in each node. We decided to use this graph-based approach because of its light-weight and extensible characteristics. Moreover, traversing the nodes in the graph mirrors the physical transition between locations and situations in the real world. The content and behavior of the simulated public displays can be controlled with different approaches (e.g., manually, via Wizard-of-Oz, or by a (semi-)functional prototype). Figure 1 visualizes the process of preparing footage in order to use it for a simulation of a specific use case. In the following, we will describe the core elements of our approach in more detail and then review how the approach can be applied and integrated at different stages of the development process (i.e., design, prototyping, and evaluation).

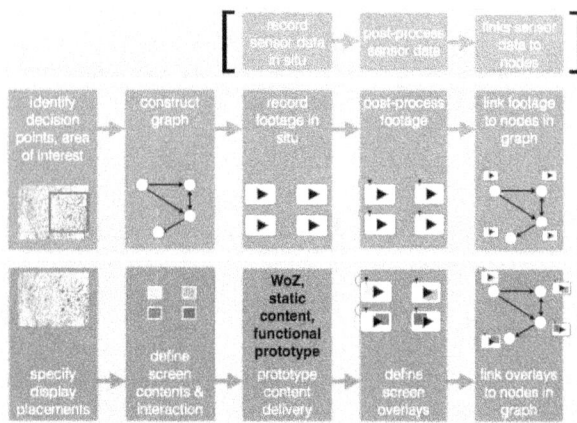

Figure 1. Process of preparing the simulation environment and the integration of a PDS prototype: The top two rows illustrate the construction of simulated environments; The bottom row outlines how to integrate a PDS into such environments (see text for more information).

Core Elements

Our approach is based on a state-transition graph that encapsulates the different states in which the simulated world can be in (e.g., daytime vs. nighttime). Locations are usually situated in a specific area of interest, i.e., the area where a PDS is meant to be deployed. It seems reasonable to focus on these locations only, as the inclusion of all possible locations would result in a very large (and cumbersome) graph. Instead, we focus on decision points and places that have a specific relevance in the investigated application scenario *(C3)*. Consider, for example, a PDS that facilitates the use of a public transport network in a city. It appears reasonable to include locations that are served by public transport in the graph, for example. A single physical location can be represented by more than one node as explained below, e.g., to capture different states or contexts of this location.

The edges in the graph represent transitions from one node to another. As each node corresponds to a location or state, an edge basically determines whether it is possible to move from one location or state to another (since one location can be represented by multiple nodes to encode different states *(C4)*). In the public transportation scenario, an edge might

connect two nodes that represent two adjacent bus stops on a particular bus route. Equally, an edge might connect nodes representing different states of the same location, e.g., one node represents the location while a bus arrives and another node represents the same location with no buses at all.

The graph describes physical and logical connections, events, and other links between different scenes. Designers can use this structure to describe specific use cases or scenarios for their PDS. Users can experience the virtual world by "moving" through the graph. Users can only be in one location or state at a time, i.e., they can only be at one node of the graph. The graph thus represents the envisioned installation site of a PDS by connecting users, displays, locations, and states.

The basic graph structure also provides a framework to organize and attach audiovisual (and other additional) data to locations. Moreover, it allows for the integration of public displays in the simulated world. Audiovisual material such as video footage, photographs, or audio recordings can be captured at the locations of interest and can then be used to simulate locations and their states during design, prototyping, and testing. In the context of the public transportation scenario, for example, several short video clips could be recorded at a bus stop for each of the relevant states, e.g., one showing a bus arriving, one showing the stop without a bus in sight, and one showing the bus departing from the stop. Further data can also be recorded on site, such as GPS and orientation information, or environmental factors, such as temperature or signal strength of cell towers. This data can also be linked to a specific node in the graph and can then be used during the development process. In the context of the bus stop scenario, the GPS and orientation data could be used to design and evaluate the behavior of an augmented reality (AR) app that visualizes actual bus routes and departure points on the screen of the user's smart phone, taking into account which information is being shown on a public display at the bus stop.

Public displays are specified within the frame of reference, which is defined by the visual data linked to a location. For example, regions in the footage can be labeled as public displays. During design, prototyping, and evaluation, they can be replaced by the envisioned content. Our approach does not specify how the content is generated, but only how it is integrated in the simulated world. Content can be generated in a variety of ways, e.g., Wizard-of-Oz style (WoZ), static imagery, a functional system that serves content adapted to various locations, etc. The public displays can be placed via the frame of reference within the visual data in different ways as well. A simple option is to use the pixel-coordinates of a video frame or photograph. Alternatively, a set of depth layers can be defined on top of a video scene or photograph. Public displays could then be placed in each layer. Finally, a 3D model can be associated with the visual material. This 3D model describes all visible surfaces (e.g., walls or tables) geometrically; public displays can then be attached to these surfaces. For example, if the video footage shows the view from a bus stop looking at buildings across the street, a simple 3D model could include the facades of those buildings. Public displays could then be attached to one of the virtual facades at a particular location *(C1, C2)*. The frame of reference is also important to facilitate the interaction with simulated public displays: Within a specific scene, the relative location of a person in front of a (virtual) public display can also be specified within the given frame of reference. It is thus possible to realize distance- or orientation-based interaction with the virtual public display. For example, the content of a time-table display at a bus stop may change depending on how close a person stands to the display.

The proposed approach also facilitates the integration and interaction with mobile devices *(C5)* by connecting the devices to a PDS via the state-transition graph. Developers can thus develop, test, and amend their software more rapidly as these steps can be carried out in the lab rather than at a (remote) deployment site. Multi-display setups *(C6)* can be simulated cost-efficiently, since the array of required devices is purely virtual. Furthermore, it is possible to change many characteristics, e.g., the form factor *(C1)* or the position and rotation quickly and easily. This way, the (physical) effort as well as costs for development and user studies can be reduced. Since the approach can simulate the appearance of the public display system realistically, even technically less savvy people (who are not involved in the actual development) can experience and use the system at early development stages prior to its actual installation. Designers can pinpoint possible design issues early on, e.g., by varying certain characteristics such as the display form factor *(C2)* or by modifying certain environmental factors *(C4, C5)*. This may positively influence the user acceptance once the system is deployed. Similarly, designers might be able to assess legal constraints *(C8)*, e.g., legibility or distraction caused by displays.

Creating Simulated Environments

Unlike fully synthetic simulations (e.g., 3D renderings based on textured geometric models), the proposed approach requires considerably less effort to generate realistic simulations while providing means to easily modify and test key characteristics of a PDS. The following paragraphs describe the process of creating such simulated worlds in more detail.

The creation of simulated worlds consists of five steps (see the blue boxes in the middle row in Figure 1). If the simulated world should include sensor data (e.g., GPS or compass information), three additional steps have to be performed (see the green boxes in the top row in Figure 1). The first step is to *identify decision points* that have a specific relevance in the analyzed application scenario. Looking at the public transportation scenario, for example, the relevant decision points could be the stops of a particular bus line. The next step is to *construct the graph* with its nodes and edges. A node represents a particular decision point in a specific state. An edge represents a possible transition between two decision points or a transition between two states of one particular decision point. The third step is to *record* the actual decision point in situ. Depending on the hardware being used and the goals being pursued, the recording can be done with one or more (video) cameras, audio capturing devices, or other sensors. Once the recording is complete, the footage has to be *post-processed*. This may include steps such as adjusting the res-

olution, performing panoramic stitching, format conversions, or creating seamless video loops. The final step is to *link* the recorded footage to the corresponding nodes in the graph.

In case the recorded footage is complemented by sensor data, the *recording* step has to be extended with appropriate devices, e.g., a GPS tracker or a compass. This additional sensor data may also require *post-processing*, for example, to align the measured samples to certain time codes in the video footage. Finally, the sensor data needs to be *linked* to the corresponding nodes in the graph as well.

Integrating Public Display Systems

In order to integrate PDS in the simulated world, designers have to carry out five steps that correspond to the five steps explained above. The first step is to specify the *placement* of a PDS at designated decision points. This is important since the placement may have some influence on the actual video recording, e.g., in terms of distance or perspective. The next step *defines the screen content* and ways of *interaction* with the PDS. In terms of the local transportation scenario, this could be to define whether the simulated public displays show the bus schedule of a specific route or rather instructions on how to interact with this schedule. The third step in the process is to *create the screen content*. This can be done in different ways, for example by using fully functional systems, prototypes of varying fidelity, or simple (static) mockups. The fourth step is to *define the display overlays*. This includes, for example, to specify the exact position and spatial dimensions within the frame of reference. Finally, the fifth step *links the overlays* to the nodes in the graph so that the simulated PDS is shown whenever the user "arrives" at the corresponding node. In practice, most of the steps may take little time. Post-processing the footage, for example, could only require to crop it so that it can be looped infinitely.

Application

Our approach can be applied to different phases of the development. In the following, we review how it can be used during the design, prototyping, and evaluation of PDS.

Design

The design of an interactive PDS is a complex task that is influenced by many aspects such as, e.g., the location, orientation, form factor, background, or content of the public display. Our approach facilitates the manipulation of multiple parameters with ease and at low cost. In terms of the local transportation example, it would be possible to adjust the height of a public display effortlessly until it suits the needs of physically impaired people. Also, the visual appearance of a public display could be easily altered in order to determine the size, color, or shape that attracts people the most. Similarly, sensitive content (e.g., personalized information) can be analyzed and immediately revised in a realistic simulation of a public environment. This can also support the legal assessment prior to public exposure. Thus, the proposed approach can help to address challenges *(C1-C4)*, *(C6)*, and *(C8)*.

Prototyping

Closely linked to the design process is the prototyping of a PDS. Our approach supports this phase with realistic simulations of the behavior of interactive PDS. Looking at the bus stop example, our approach could help to prototype a multi-display network that is spread throughout the city to deliver up-to-date arrival and departure times. The graph of the simulated world could be used to let users take a virtual walk (or bus ride) through the city in order to test the interaction between the users and the interactive PDS (e.g., via touch screens or different mobile devices). Thus, the proposed approach helps to address challenges *(C5)* and *(C6)*.

Evaluation

The simulation at the heart of our approach allows for manipulating various parameters such as the location of the public display, its orientation, content, or interaction mode. The approach can thus complement conventional controlled lab tests or field studies. Previous research shows that people who are exposed to an IVE can actually feel immersed under certain conditions (cf., e.g., Snowdon and Kray [18]). This facilitates the evaluation of non-functional characteristics of an interactive PDS. Regarding the public transportation scenario, our approach could thus be used to evaluate how users perceive a multi-display network depending on its presence at certain (sensitive) points of interest within the city.

THE IPED TOOLKIT

The *Immersive Public Display Evaluation and Design (IPED) Toolkit* is an initial prototypical implementation of our approach. This section describes the toolkit, its core elements, its design and evaluation processes, and the current implementation in more depth. Figure 2 provides an overview over the architecture of the toolkit.

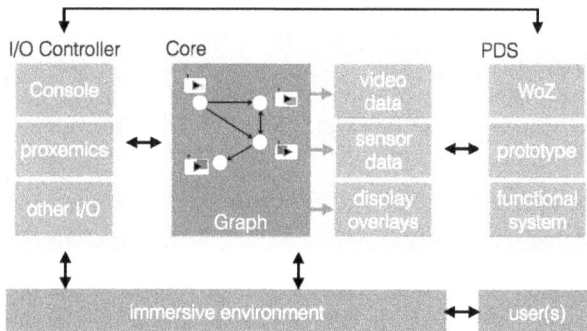

Figure 2. Architecture of IPED Toolkit: I/O Controller encapsulates different means of interaction; Core contains graph and data defining simulated world; different PDS control behavior of simulated system.

Architecture

The IPED Toolkit consists of several components as depicted in Figure 2. The Core component maintains the state transition graph that defines the simulated world and manages all information that is attached to the graph. In particular, it contains the (video) footage that represents the real-world locations and their states as well as the positions of virtual public displays. Optionally, it can store additional sensor data that has been recorded at particular locations. Finally, it maintains the user's position in the simulated world.

The PDS component controls the content of the virtual public displays that are embedded in the simulated world and it reacts to any interaction. Content can be generated in different ways, for example, via a Wizard-of-Oz (WoZ) approach, i.e., that a human "wizard" selects appropriate content in response to what a user does in order to simulate a functional system. Alternatively, prototypes of different degrees of sophistication can (semi-)automatically generate the screen contents. Equally, it is possible to use a fully functional version of a PDS to generate screen contents and react to the user's input. Content can be represented as a web page or video, for example. This way, it can be displayed via standard web browsers within the overlays that represent virtual public displays.

The I/O Controller component encapsulates different means of interaction between the simulated world and the PDS. It incorporates a Console application that can be used to configure the simulated worlds and to control the user's movements within those worlds. Additionally, the I/O Controller includes a simple mapping API that different interaction mechanisms may use to control various aspects of the simulated worlds (e.g., moving between locations and states or triggering specific actions). The latter capability allows for interaction with a PDS via proxemics, for example: The user's location in the lab can be translated to the corresponding location in the simulated world and thus trigger a reaction of the PDS in turn.

Users experience the system via an immersive environment (see Figure 3). They can interact with the system in a variety of ways. What they see is determined by their position within the graph (managed by the Core component) and by the content of simulated displays (generated by the PDS). The overall architecture thus decouples the simulated world, the display placement and content, as well as the way in which people interact with a PDS. This structure provides a high degree of flexibility with respect to designing a PDS and modifying aspects of it. It also facilitates the re-usability of components and the reuse of simulated environments.

Figure 3. Panoramic video footage presented in an early version of the immersive video environment (IVE).

Immersive Video Environment

The IPED Toolkit uses on an immersive video environment (IVE) that simulates PDS and their environments (see Figure 3). The IVE presented in this paper is inspired by the system presented by Singh et al. [17]. Panoramic video footage recorded at real-world locations is played back in order to immerse users into these settings. Three back-projection screens (200 cm x 150 cm) are arranged in a semi-circular manner, spanning a viewing angle of about 114°. The resolution of each screen is 1280 x 1024 pixels, resulting in an overall resolution of 3840 x 1024 pixels. The corresponding footage is recorded using three standard DLSR cameras (Canon EOS 550D) mounted on a custom-made tripod. The angles between the cameras are adjusted to match the angles of the three IVE screens. To minimize visible seams between the three videos, the footage is post-processed using standard video editing software. Finally, the video footage is scaled down to the native resolution of the IVE. A high quality surround audio recorder (Zoom H2n) is used to capture ambient sounds in decent quality. Both, audio and video material, is then played back on a single desktop PC, equipped with a graphics card that can drive multiple displays.

Implementation

The current implementation is based on several open-source components. The VLC player[1] handles audio and video playback. One instance of the player is launched for each of the three screens. The simultaneous playback of all instances is orchestrated by a custom application that remotely controls the media players. The virtual public display systems are realized as overlays on top of the video footage; each overlay consists of a polygon that defines its boundaries and a web page that represents its content. The web page is rendered in a standard browser and can be generated by the PDS in a variety of ways. The overlay component is written in Java and uses the additional data (e.g., location and perspective information) in the edges of the graph to create the overlays that correspond to a specific location or state.

Currently, there are three ways to control the simulation, i.e., to move around in the simulated world: (i) Wizard-Of-Oz, (ii) a mobile UI, and (iii) an experimental gesture-based control mechanism. Methods (i) and (ii) both use a simple web interface to the custom control software that is based on JQuery mobile[2]. The interface can be accessed either from a standard desktop PC or from a mobile device. The difference between both methods is that the web interface is either controlled by one or more experimenters or by the participants themselves. The experimental gesture based interaction (iii) can be used in two modes: (a) The authoring mode allows designers of public displays to incorporate their envisioned systems into immersive video environments. It is based on a set of gestures that enables users to position and scale displays on top of the video footage and to select content that should be shown on the displays. Once the design of the public display system has been created, participants use the (b) experience mode to explore the designed system. In the latter mode, they can perform gestures to interact with the location and the display (e.g., to move around). The software can switch between the authoring and experience mode fluidly in order to allow for a rapid prototyping of PDS.

In its current version, the IPED Toolkit can simulate the following aspects of potential relevance when developing a PDS: In terms of the actual display, the toolkit can incorporate the location and orientation at a specific site (C1), the

size, shape, and form factor (C2), as well as the content (C5-C8). Contextual factors that can be simulated to some degree include visual environmental properties (C3), ambient noise, time of the day, and (in a very limited way) passersby and bystanders (as recorded in the used footage). Some events, such as an arriving bus or an opening door, can also be simulated (C4). However, quite a few contextual factors cannot be simulated easily, for example, temperature, precipitation, or the negotiation of a crowded place. The IPED Toolkit facilitates the interaction with public displays via mobile devices (C5), gestures, and also via proxemic interaction – though the range of locomotion is limited considerably. In addition, it supports the rapid development of multi-display networks (C6) within the limitations outlined above.

EXPERIENCES & ANALYSIS

Though the toolkit does not yet fully implement the proposed approach, we have been using preliminary versions of it in a number of different contexts. In addition, systems based on immersive environments have been successfully used in the past to evaluate various systems. This supports the idea of applying such an approach in the development process of PDS. Finally, applying our approach to an example scenario can also provide evidence for its usefulness in the context of developing PDS. The following sections thus review these aspects in more detail.

Experiences With Immersive Environments

Video- or photo-based environments have been used in the past to evaluate situated technology, in particular mobile systems. Snowdon and Kray [18], for example, used such an environment to assess a mobile system that provides hikers with information about natural environments. Even without sound or moving images – the simulation used panoramic photographs only – they reported on a high degree of immersion amongst the participants, evidenced by the way in which they referred to objects depicted on the screens. In particular, the language people used to describe the scene and to identify and locate objects shown on screen strongly resembled what they would use if they actually were at the location in the real world. For example, in some scenes participants would refer to objects as if standing at the top of a hill looking down into a valley rather than just describing what they see on a screen. It therefore stands to reason that certain contextual factors (such as the structure of the environment where a public display is installed) can be replicated well inside an immersive video environment. Thus, it can also be used during the development and evaluation of PDS when applying the approach proposed in this paper.

Early versions of the toolkit were demonstrated to different user groups on a number of occasions (e.g., a regional trade fair focused on Smart Cities). In this case, an earlier version of the toolkit was used, which included the gesture-based control mechanism described above. The mechanism enabled users to place various objects (including public displays) inside an urban scene that was depicted by captured video footage. While the interaction mechanism caused some issues (e.g., sensors not recognizing people and their gestures correctly), the general principle of augmenting video footage

---

[1] http://www.videolan.org/vlc, accessed 30 Mar 2014
[2] http://jquerymobile.com, accessed 30 Mar 2014

with objects to discuss, design, and experience (e.g., public displays) was easy to grasp for the participants. This is in line with observations from a series of demonstrations at our lab (with different audiences) and provides initial evidence that the approach proposed here is also accessible to non-experts.

Example Scenario

In order to illustrate how the proposed approach can be applied to different stages of the development process of a PDS, we can consider the following example scenario. Let us assume a network of public displays is to be installed at a large hospital in order to replace static signage. One key function could be to provide individuals (e.g., patients, visitors, or employees) with personalized directions. Using our approach, the first step would be to identify the sites in which the system should be installed (e.g., where current static signage is mounted). Next, we would acquire the required video footage. One option would be to reuse existing footage that was previously recorded, for example via a public repository. However, since the hospital is a very specific scenario, it is unlikely that suitable footage exists. Thus, the required footage would have to be recorded in situ. Usually, a few minutes per site are sufficient to create seamless loops. After recording videos at the identified locations, the footage has to be processed, e.g., in order to play it in a seamless loop. In most cases, it is only necessary to crop videos so that the beginning and the end of the clip are visually similar or identical. Then the graph that links the different sites (and recordings) has to be constructed. The nodes of the graph correspond to the decision points identified earlier. They are linked to the corresponding video footage. The edges between two nodes represent the physical or logical connections between the decision points (i.e., adjacent locations are most likely connected by an edge). In its current implementation, the graph is constructed and stored in a XML-based configuration file. Creating a node or an edge thus corresponds to entering a line of text. Once completed, the graph contains the required information for simulating the deployment site. It can now be easily reused in other contexts, too (e.g., to develop a PDS managing waiting times in the same hospital or to develop an application in a more generic hospital scenario).

Once these steps are completed, the IPED Toolkit can be used to test and discuss the placement and shape or size of public displays at different locations *(C1, C2)* by overlaying corresponding designs over the recorded footage. Using the toolkit greatly simplifies designing and prototyping at this stage, as designers do not need to be at the actual deployment sites. They can rather place (virtual) displays freely and rapidly without physical efforts. The placement and configuration of each public display is stored within the corresponding node. This data can be reused in different contexts as well, since the content of the displays is controlled and generated independently. As the development of the system progresses, designers and users can use our approach to test, inspect, and discuss the system at various stages. For example, at early stages, a static mock-up of the proposed dynamic signage system could be used to assess whether the interface design fits the targeted installation site *(C8)*. Once a functional dynamic prototype exists, it can be connected to the display overlays

within the simulation to replace the static mock-ups for further analysis. If there are multiple recordings for one location (e.g., representing busy vs. quiet office hours), these recordings can also contribute to the evaluation of the system prior to its actual deployment *(C4)*. In the hospital scenario, it would be possible to test whether the content of the public displays is unambiguous and thus suitable to guide visitors through the building. This could be done by assessing the user's performance in terms of task completion times (how long it takes them to determine which way they need to go at each display) or error rates (how often they take the wrong direction at a display).

Finally, the proposed approach also supports the integration of different means of interaction. In the hospital scenario, designers might want to test an interface based on proxemics (cf. Marquardt et al. [9]): If a person steps closer to a display, its content could change to provide more detailed directions for that person. Sensing the relative position of a person to a screen in the lab can be achieved easily, e.g., by using a depth camera. These sensors could then be connected to the prototype of the PDS, which in turn adapts the screen content that is shown in the simulation accordingly. Once connected, a sensor is available at all simulated locations without the need to physically deploy it multiple times – which would be necessary for field trials. Compared to designing, testing, and evaluating PDS in the real world, the proposed approach can thus reduce effort at several stages. It simplifies the integration of sensors and allows for covering large areas without the need for extensive hardware deployments. At the same time, the toolkit can simulate and control context realistically. It also facilitates the reuse of simulated installation sites and simulated displays. While the approach can thus complement existing methods well, it is also subject to some limitations. For example, locomotion is only possible within very narrow limits, as is the simulation of physical aspects (e.g., temperature, texture of surfaces, or precipitation). Furthermore, appropriation and user acceptance can only be assessed in a limited way. The interaction with passersby and other users is subject to constraints as well.

DISCUSSION

Alt et al. [1] identified a number of research questions that are relevant in public display research. Our approach can help – at least to some degree – to address questions relating to *user performance* (e.g., task completion times or error rates), *user experience* (e.g., analyzing different interaction techniques), *user acceptance* (e.g., using a virtual prototype to support focus group discussions with a more "realistic" feel of the system), *privacy* (e.g., estimating threats such as shoulder surfing while entering data), and *social impact* (e.g., how to foster social interaction between strangers using the system for a specific task). Our approach is less well suited to answer questions relating to *audience behavior* (requires "real" audiences in "real" settings) and *display effectiveness* (often assessed by observing people's behavior in "real" settings).

Based on experiences we gathered so far, specific drawbacks and advantages of our approach can be identified. One key limitation is the lack of support for locomotion. This is an inherent problem of virtual environments and has been a research subject for a long time (cf., e.g., [3, 14]). While omnidirectional treadmills are a (still very expensive) way to address this, using photos or videos to construct simulations further limits user movement, as only the recorded views can be experienced without distorting images. Consequently, our approach is better suited to investigate scenarios where locomotion is not essential. In terms of privacy analysis, the proposed approach can be used to carry out controlled studies (e.g., simulating shoulder surfing in a specific situation). It is, however, not well suited to assess audience behavior, display effectiveness, or social impact as those aspects heavily depend on various characteristics of the actual installation site. The current IPED Toolkit implementation does not support 3D augmentation of video footage. It only allows for placing "flat" 2D representations of displays within the simulation. These 2D representations can be panned, scaled, rotated, and skewed to create the illusion of perspective and depth. Consequently, if displays have to be shown at an angle, their content needs to be adapted manually. A further limitation is the lack of sophisticated transitions between locations. Instead of "teleporting" users between recorded locations, smooth transitions (e.g., similar to Street View[3]) might help users to create a mental map of the simulated area.

In our opinion, however, these drawbacks and limitations of our approach are outweighed by its benefits. Compared to a design, prototyping, and evaluation process based on field studies, our approach would facilitate reproducibility while providing a high degree of visual realism. It thus offers a way to reduce the trade-off between internal and ecological validity. In the context of the local transportation scenario, for example, it would be interesting to analyze people's performance while using different versions of the system (e.g., different UI implementations) in a stressful situation (e.g., shortly before a bus arrives). While it would be difficult to repeatedly expose participants to this situation in a real environment, our approach can easily facilitate this while immersing people in a realistic audiovisual simulation of the intended deployment site. At the same time, the effort required to carry out such a study is greatly reduced compared to a conventional field study: There is no need to transport people or equipment to study sites, for example. While some aspects, such as appropriation or the impact of unforeseen factors, can only be fully assessed in field studies, our approach can thus complement such studies in the ways described above, particularly at the early stages of the development when a functional version of PDS is not available yet. Compared to lab-based studies, our approach increases the visual realism while providing means to record a variety of factors at the same level of detail.

Based on these considerations and our experiences with using our approach, we can infer that it rather complements than replaces existing approaches to designing and evaluating PDS. As previous work has pointed out (cf., e.g., Alt et al. [1]), field studies are necessary to fully assess audience behavior, appropriation, or social impact, for example. Lab-based stud-

ies are very well suited to rigorously test hypotheses while exerting full control over a large number of variables. Our approach offers a middle-ground that combines aspects of both field and lab studies and may offer some key benefits particularly during the early development of PDS. Initial experiences also suggest that this way of prototyping public display systems is accessible to designers and laypeople. In addition, the approach would lend itself well for a combination with model-driven approaches such as the ones introduced by Harrison and Massink [8] or Silva et al. [16]. Assessing the qualities and possibilities of such a combination, however, requires further studies.

Whether prototyping and "deploying" PDS in the virtual world is actually faster than a "quick and dirty" deployment at actual installation sites does not only depend on the target locations, but also on the authoring tools available to designers. The current version of the IPED Toolkit only provides very rudimentary support (e.g., text-based definition of the graph), so that the assessment of the efficiency of the proposed approach is currently limited. Nevertheless, once deployment areas have been recorded and the corresponding graph has been created, it can be easily re-used to design and develop further PDS. For example, testing an alternative system (to the PDS for which the simulated environment was originally created) would simply require connecting the new PDS to the existing simulation.

CONCLUSION & FUTURE WORK

In this paper we reviewed approaches to design, prototype, and evaluate public display systems (PDS). We also proposed a novel approach to engineer such systems based on realistic audiovisual simulations and a state-transition graph. Our key contributions include a systematic analysis of approaches to engineer PDS, a novel approach that integrates many of the benefits of previous approaches, an architecture for a toolkit implementing the approach, and an initial assessment of the approach based on an example scenario and our own experiences from using it. Key benefits of our approach include high re-usability of simulated environments, reduced effort to "construct" deployment sites and scenarios, as well as support for a broad range of prototypes (e.g., of varying fidelity) and design and evaluation methods. Our work can thus contribute towards simplifying and accelerating the development of (interactive) PDS.

In addition to expanding the existing version of the toolkit, there are a number of further directions for future research. One of them relates to simulating movement within the IVE (e.g., via a treadmill and footage of movement) and with extending the field of view of the IVE (i.e., by using a head-mounted display). Closely linked to this aspect is the investigation of different ways to visualize movement (e.g., via different cinematographic transitions or via footage of actual movement). A further interesting line of work concerns the way in which different people can interact with the system, e.g., groups of designers discussing alternatives or end-users providing input during the early stages of a participatory design. Finally, and possibly most importantly, there is a need to systematically compare different design and evaluation meth-

---

[3]`http://maps.google.com`, accessed 30 Mar 2014

ods for PDS via controlled user studies. In particular, it would be very valuable to clearly establish similarities and differences between field studies and studies carried out in the IVE (e.g., with respect to quantifying the impact of different contextual factors).

REFERENCES

1. Alt, F., Schneegaß, S., Schmidt, A., Müller, J., and Memarovic, N. How to evaluate public displays. In *Proc. PerDis '12*, ACM (2012), 17:1–17:6.

2. Cheverst, K., Clarke, K., Fitton, D., Rouncefield, M., Crabtree, A., and Hemmings, T. SPAM on the menu: The practical use of remote messaging in community care. In *Proc. CUU '03*, ACM (2003), 23–29.

3. Chim, J., Lau, R. W. H., Leong, H. V., and Si, A. CyberWalk: a web-based distributed virtual walkthrough environment. *IEEE Transactions On Multimedia 5*, 4 (Dec. 2003), 503–515.

4. Davies, N., Langheinrich, M., Jose, R., and Schmidt, A. Open display networks: A communications medium for the 21st century. *Computer 45*, 5 (May 2012), 58–64.

5. Faisal, T., and Cheverst, K. Exploring user preferences for indoor navigation support through a combination of mobile and fixed displays. In *Proc. MobileHCI '11*, ACM (2011).

6. Friday, A., Davies, N., and Efstratiou, C. Reflections on long-term experiments with public displays. *Computer 45*, 5 (May 2012), 34–41.

7. Hamhoum, F., and Kray, C. Supporting pilgrims in navigating densely crowded religious sites. *Personal and Ubiquitous Computing 16*, 8 (2012), 1013–1023.

8. Harrison, M. D., and Massink, M. Modelling interactive experience, function and performance in ubiquitous systems. *Electronic Notes in Theoretical Computer Science 261* (2010), 23–42.

9. Marquardt, N., Diaz-Marino, R., Boring, S., and Greenberg, S. The proximity toolkit: prototyping proxemic interactions in ubiquitous computing ecologies. In *Proc. UIST '11*, ACM (2011), 315–326.

10. Müller, J., Jentsch, M., Kray, C., and Krüger, A. Exploring factors that influence the combined use of mobile devices and public displays for pedestrian navigation. In *Proc. NordiCHI '08*, ACM (2008), 308–317.

11. Nakanishi, Y. Virtual prototyping using miniature model and visualization for interactive public displays. In *Proc. DIS '12*, ACM (2012), 458–467.

12. Ostkamp, M., Bauer, G., and Kray, C. Visual highlighting on public displays. In *Proc. PerDis '12*, ACM (2012), 2:1–2:6.

13. Penn, A., and Turner, A. Space syntax based agent simulation. In *in M. Schreckenberg and S. Sharma (Eds.), Pedestrian and Evacuation Dynamics, 99-114* (2001).

14. Schellenbach, M., Krüger, A., Lövdén, M., and Lindenberger, U. A laboratory evaluation framework for pedestrian navigation devices. In *Proc. Mobility '07*, ACM (2007), 495–502.

15. Seichter, H., Grubert, J., and Langlotz, T. Designing mobile augmented reality. In *Proc. MobileHCI '13*, ACM (2013), 616–621.

16. Silva, J. L., Campos, J., and Harrison, M. Formal analysis of ubiquitous computing environments through the apex framework. In *Proc. EICS '12*, ACM (2012), 131–140.

17. Singh, P., Ha, H. N., Olivier, P., Kray, C., Kuang, Z., Guo, A. W., Blythe, P., and James, P. Rapid prototyping and evaluation of intelligent environments using immersive video. In *MODIE Workshop at MobileHCI '06* (2006), 36–41.

18. Snowdon, C., and Kray, C. Exploring the use of landmarks for mobile navigation support in natural environments. In *Proc. MobileHCI '09*, ACM (2009), 13:1–13:10.

19. Stahl, C., and Haupert, J. Simulating and evaluating public situated displays in virtual environment models. In *MODIE Workshop at MobileHCI '06* (2006), 32–35.

20. Storz, O., Friday, A., Davies, N., Finney, J., Sas, C., and Sheridan, J. Public ubiquitous computing systems: Lessons from the e-campus display deployments. *Pervasive Computing, IEEE 5*, 3 (Sept. 2006), 40–47.

21. Taylor, N., and Cheverst, K. Creating a rural community display with local engagement. In *Proc. DIS'11*, ACM (2010), 218–227.

22. Ten Koppel, M., Bailly, G., Müller, J., and Walter, R. Chained displays: configurations of public displays can be used to influence actor-, audience-, and passer-by behavior. In *Proc. CHI '12*, ACM (2012), 317–326.

23. Xie, H., Filippidis, L., Gwynne, S., Galea, E. R., Blackshields, D., and Lawrence, P. J. Signage Legibility Distances as a Function of Observation Angle. *Journal of Fire Protection Engineering 17*, 1 (2007), 41–64.

SecSpace: Prototyping Usable Privacy and Security for Mixed Reality Collaborative Environments

Derek Reilly[1], Mohamad Salimian[1], Bonnie MacKay[1], Niels Mathiasen[2],W. Keith Edwards[3], Juliano Franz[1]

[1]Faculty of Computer Science,
Dalhousie University
Halifax, Canada B3H 3P8

[2] Trifork
Margrethepladsen 4, 8000,
Aarhus, Denmark

[3]GVU Center, Georgia Institute
of Technology
Atlanta GA 30308 USA

{reilly, rizi, bmackay, franz}@cs.dal.ca nm@nielsmathiasen.dk keith@cc.gatech.edu

ABSTRACT

Privacy mechanisms are important in mixed-presence (collocated and remote) collaborative systems. These systems try to achieve a sense of co-presence in order to promote fluid collaboration, yet it can be unclear how actions made in one location are manifested in the other. This ambiguity makes it difficult to share sensitive information with confidence, impacting the fluidity of the shared experience. In this paper, we focus on mixed reality approaches (blending physical and virtual spaces) for mixed presence collaboration. We present SecSpace, our software toolkit for usable privacy and security research in mixed reality collaborative environments. SecSpace permits privacy-related actions in either physical or virtual space to generate effects simultaneously in both spaces. These effects will be the same in terms of their impact on privacy but they may be functionally tailored to suit the requirements of each space. We detail the architecture of SecSpace and present three prototypes that illustrate the flexibility and capabilities of our approach.

Author Keywords

Usable privacy and security, mixed reality, mixed presence, software toolkit, smart room, framework

ACM Classification Keywords

H.1.2; K.6.5

INTRODUCTION

Mixed presence collaboration, or collaboration between collocated and remote individuals, is becoming commonplace. In healthcare, telepresence has long been a topic of research [1], and is now supported by a variety of specialized systems. Virtual classrooms link groups of students and educators across distances, sometimes using immersive video or virtual worlds [2]. In the office, meetings often include remote participants connected via videoconference and/or shared desktop software.

During co-located collaboration, many physical privacy-related actions occur. These include managing the visibility (and sharing) of documents with others in a room, and using one's position and orientation relative to others to glance at personal information in private. During extended collaborations, smaller groups may also wish to achieve visible and/or audible privacy, or signal that they wish privacy based on their position relative to those in the larger group [3]. We are also cognizant of the current and likely future locations and actions of our collaborators and of others. For example, we maintain an awareness of who else is in a meeting room to manage sharing of sensitive information, and rely on social norms inherent in the collaborative activity and/or the environment: for example strangers in a cafe may eavesdrop on our conversation, but they are less likely to walk up to our table and peer intently at the work we are doing. Beyond individual meetings, physical information security policies are often in place in institutions (such as hospitals) that share large amounts of sensitive paper materials, and architecture also considers ways to support the need for privacy and security.

In mixed presence collaboration we have to manage privacy and security across two "channels"—the physical or co-located, and the virtual or remote—simultaneously. The privacy mechanisms used in each channel often differ. For example, once content is shared on the network we become concerned with encryption and access permissions. We are also challenged to maintain situational awareness across both channels. While we may know who is in the room with us, we can often be unaware of who is in the room with our remote collaborator(s). Technologies providing security policy specification and enforcement are often too brittle to apply during synchronous collaboration due to the negotiated and situated nature of privacy in these situations.

Recently, the technology for co-presence has advanced to the point where physical (and possibly virtual) collaborative spaces can be combined into a spatially fused environment (a shared or *blended* space as defined by O'Hara et al. [4]). Mixed reality environments blend physical and virtual spaces, such that they together form a hybrid space [5][6][7]. Mixed reality has been used quite extensively in locative games [35] , and increasingly as a mechanism to encourage a sense of co-presence during mixed presence collaboration [8][9][10]. Mixed reality holds several potential benefits as an approach for mixed presence collaboration, including: not requiring expensive and identical technical setups at each linked physical location, not requiring a video presence while still providing a visual representation of collaborators, providing a shared repository for work that can be spatially meaningful, giving a sense of a shared "place" for collaboration that can exist beyond a single meeting, and supporting both asynchronous and synchronous collaboration.

Further, mixed reality offers interesting potential solutions to the multiple channel problems when managing privacy. Specifically, since the virtual/online channel is manifested as a space—and more specifically, the virtual is connected spatially to the physical place where co-located work happens—we might be able to transfer the physical privacy/security mechanisms so that they exist in physical and virtual simultaneously. Consistency in how privacy and security are achieved may make it easier for remote collaborators to understand what is happening in the physical space, and for local collaborators to understand what is happening in the virtual space. It may also reduce the overhead for privacy and security: those collaborating locally act within a single channel (the physical) and remote collaborators act solely in the virtual, knowing that their actions will affect both spaces. Mixed reality collaborative environments pose specific challenges to collaboration, however: actions and representations in a virtual space can be misinterpreted due to a literal interpretation of the spatial metaphor. Even though the physical and virtual may look the same and/or are linked together spatially, the expressive capacities of physical and virtual spaces are very different. Therefore, it is not a straightforward matter of replicating physical privacy mechanisms in the virtual. For example, in the physical world one can selectively show a portion of a document by folding it or holding one's hand over a sensitive portion of the document, while doing the same in a virtual world would likely require a number of user interactions to secure a portion of a document's content before displaying what one wishes to share.

According to Bødker [11] and McCarthy and Wright [12] , we should emphasize experience during user-centered design of ICT tools. Often privacy and security mechanisms do not clearly reflect this user-centric approach: instead they focus on establishing secure procedures that users should follow, specifying proper security policies, and providing end-user assistance with these procedures or specifications [13][14]. Our broader research goal is to explore potential designs to support privacy in heterogeneous, document-centric, mixed presence collaboration. In particular, we want to determine how people 'naturally' manage security and privacy while performing some of these tasks both in the digital and real world. Therefore we want to use an exploratory approach to look for physical patterns of security-related behavior and to generate and evaluate design ideas pertaining to user-centric privacy and security for mixed reality collaboration.

In order to do this, we have developed a framework that allows the rapid development of privacy and security mechanisms that are manifested in both physical and virtual. The primary contribution of our work is the SecSpace framework, permitting rapid prototyping and evaluation of usable privacy and security mechanisms for collaborative mixed reality.

We also introduce several physical privacy and security mechanisms that might be useful in collaborative mixed reality. We illustrate these mechanisms through a set of three SecSpace prototypes. They serve to show the capabilities of the framework, and are not presented here as validated security mechanisms.

The first prototype considers mixed presence collaboration around a whiteboard. This carries a number of implicit security-related issues. For example, we can see who is using a whiteboard and decide whether or not to share information (orally or on the whiteboard). This changes when the whiteboard's content is mapped onto to a whiteboard in a virtual world.

The remaining prototypes consider mixed presence collaboration around a table. While collaborating around a table participants manage what documents to share and when. When the document content on the table is mapped to a table in a virtual world these practices break down. For instance placing a document in the middle of a table normally implies that collaborators are allowed to view the document, while taking the paper back normally implies that the view permission is now expired. There is no guarantee that the same is achieved in the virtual space.

There are several key challenges to achieving a shared experience in these types of scenarios, in particular:

- how to manifest the physical cues employed by collocated collaborators in the views used by remote collaborators,

- how to enable remote collaborators to easily and naturally generate cues that are visible to and understood by the collocated group, and

- how to ensure that collaborators are aware of how their actions are manifested in the other space.

SecSpace allows researchers to explore ways to address each of these challenges.

BACKGROUND

Co-located Collaboration

A number of privacy and security approaches have been considered for co-located collaboration at a range of physical and temporal scales.

UbiTable [15] provides different levels of security and privacy when sharing documents. UbiTable defines three sharing semantics: private, personal, and public. Private documents will not be accessible or visible to others, personal documents (semi-private) are located on the side of the table close to the owner and can be shared if the owner chooses, and public data are accessible and visible equally to all users.

Semi-Public Display [16] promotes awareness and collaboration in small co-located group environments. Building on practices such as email status reports, shared calendars, and instant messenger status, the display is divided into a space for reminders, a collaboration space, a graphical representation of group activity over time, and an abstract visualization of planned attendance at shared events. The system protects the privacy of group members by using abstract visualizations and icons, such that casual viewers will not easily decipher its contents.

Virtual walls [17] provides a metaphor for user-defined privacy policies in sensor-rich pervasive environments. Users are given control over their digital footprints by defining how "visible" they will be in different regions of the physical space.

Shared Spaces

Shared space techniques seen in research prototypes like VideoArms [18], ShareTable [19], WaaZam! [20] and Carpeno [21] attempt to create the illusion of a single fused space, where interaction is identical in all connected locations; however, this is not possible when one or more parties do not have the required technical infrastructure. Furthermore, when a group of people are co-located and are working (or playing) with just one or two remote collaborators, it may be desirable to allow the collocated group continue to use the spaces and tools in their environment (like real playing cards, for example), while not requiring remote collaborators to do the same. This heterogeneous experience is not supported in many shared space tools, and while some permit alternative setups (VideoArms.[22], [12] for example), they often require significant resources such as calibrated cameras and large screens at each node.

Tools for remote collaboration on the desktop emphasize user-driven privacy and security through explicit sharing settings (e.g. Screen Sharing Item [23] for the Community Bar system). Shared spaces introduce new privacy and security concerns, and the absence of desktop-style interaction requires that we reimagine how to support privacy and security. For example, the ShareTable [16] system consists of video chat and a shared tabletop space. Targeted for communications between a separated parent and their children, it provides facilities for drawing, learning support, and physical document sharing. ShareTable raises some issues about the privacy of those around the users, and of the users themselves, with respect to what they are saying and doing.. To overcome these issues the authors suggested placing the system in the child's room and arranging the best time to make calls, but this kind of measure may not be feasible in all circumstances. While some guidelines exist for managing

privacy in always-on media spaces [38], more research is required to identify privacy and security mechanisms for shared spaces and mixed presence collaboration.

Mixed Reality

Benford et al. [24] categorize shared spaces based on three attributes: *transportation, artificiality*, and *spatiality*. Transportation means the possibility of moving a group of objects and participants from their local space into a new remote space to meet and collaborate with others. Artificiality considers the degree to which the environment is synthetic or relies on the physical world. For example, video conferencing is seen as the physical extreme while Collaborative Virtual Environments (CVEs) are seen as the synthetic extreme. Spatiality is the degree of support for physical spatial properties such as containment, topology, distance, orientation, and movement [24]. Mixed Reality can be seen as a form of shared space that combines the local and remote, the physical and synthetic—merging real and virtual worlds to create an environment for physical and virtual objects to interact in real time. While privacy is identified as a concern in mixed reality collaboration, to our knowledge SecSpace is the only reported framework targeting research in this area.

Privacy Approaches in Mixed Reality Environments

To help promote the exploration of how people naturally manage privacy in mixed reality collaborative spaces, we derived five strategies, inspired by our own ethnographic research into privacy issues in office work and healthcare and the co-design of collaborative mixed reality concepts for these domains [32][37]. This is not meant to be a complete list, and we are not recommending that all approaches be present in a single usable privacy solution. Rather, they form a core set of requirements for SecSpace. In the interest of space we list the strategies here: 1. use privacy mechanisms that are appropriate to the physical and virtual worlds, 2. visually represent the current policies in both worlds, 3. build on social norms when negotiating privacy mechanisms between the worlds, 4. enforce privacy mechanisms based on context, and 5. provide simple authentication and permission controls.

SYSTEM IMPLEMENTATION

Creating smart interactive spaces for collaboration has been a research topic in Ubiquitous Computing for some time; iRoom [26], NIST smart room [27],i-LAND [28] are examples of earlier projects in this area. However, these systems are useful for collaboration between people who are located in a single smart space. Connecting a virtual world to a smart room has been proposed as a way to bring mixed presence collaboration to these spaces. Virtual worlds can provide accurate, real time information about the location and orientation of participants and their actions in the virtual world, as a form of virtual sensing [5]. Recent advances in localized indoor tracking of both objects and humans make it possible for physical interactive smart rooms and virtual worlds to behave similarly, and in many respects give the feeling of being in one location to all participants.

SecSpace is an extension of the TwinSpace software framework for collaborative mixed reality applications [25]. TwinSpace provides a flexible mapping approach between objects and services in linked virtual and physical environments, allowing for example the movement of physical objects to cause linked virtual objects to move, or dynamically remapping how the virtual environment is manifested in a connected physical space based on the activity taking place. The architecture of TwinSpace is detailed in [25]. It is built using a document-centric collaborative virtual world called OpenWonderland [26], a blackboard model distributed messaging backbone (EventHeap [29]), and a context engine built using Semantic Web technologies (Apache Jena). In this section, we consider four core features of TwinSpace, and detail how each feature is exploited in SecSpace.

Distributed Communication

TwinSpace provides a distributed physical-virtual communication mechanism. This allows virtual entities to take part in distributed sensing and control, and includes a model of virtual Observers and Effectors that serve as counterparts to sensors and actuators in the physical world.

SecSpace defines Observers that detect events relevant to privacy and security and communicate these via the distributed communications channel. For example, the ProximityObserver detects when avatars come within a specified range of a location or entity. A set of Effectors is used to apply privacy and security policies in the virtual world in response to commands coming from the distributed communications channel. For example, the PermissionEffector can set global, group or individual permissions for a shared document. The set of Observers and Effectors currently available are listed in Table 1.

Table 1: SecSpace virtual Observers, Effectors and Proxies. Modified TwinSpace components are marked by *.

Category	Name	Description
Observers	Login	User logs on or off
	Proximity	User approaches object
	UICapture*	User interacts with object
	ObjectCreated*	Object is created
	NewlySecured	Objects is secured
	Permission	Object permission change
Effectors	AddSecurity	Secures target object
	AddUICapture*	Log all object interaction
	Permission	Change object permission
	Movement*	Move object in world
	Creation*	Create new object
	Destruction*	Destroy object
Proxies	Display*	Virtual display
	CardGame	Manages game events

Observers and Effectors combine to form privacy and

security mechanisms in the virtual world. For example, the PermissionEffector can set which users can read a document; and the UICaptureObserver can then be used to determine whether a document will reveal its contents when clicked, or if a warning message appears instead. Similarly, a ProximityObserver and MovementEffector can be used to keep objects or avatars away from a given location.

Security-related messages coming from virtual Observers, physical sensors, and applications get placed on the distributed messaging backbone, as do security-related commands and policies coming from either the physical or virtual spaces, to be interpreted by corresponding virtual Effectors, physical actuators and applications. This model provides a great deal of flexibility in defining how entities communicate, share data, enforce and apply rules. For example, a dedicated server can manage all privacy and security by receiving all messages, determining relevant actions and communicating them via the backbone. A completely decentralized model is also possible, by letting each entity determine what messages it will listen for and how it will translate these into privacy and security-preserving actions. Mixed models are also possible, and developers can define and evolve specific approaches over time, facilitating prototyping and policy experimentation.

Importantly, SecSpace does *not* provide secure distributed communication. While it is possible to integrate SecSpace with middleware security technologies (e.g. the Event Heap iSecurity model [30]), this is not the goal of our work. SecSpace is a framework for exploring usable privacy and security approaches within the context of mixed reality collaboration.

Shared Ontology

TwinSpace [25] defines a common ontology for addressing, manipulating and linking physical and virtual objects, allowing a single set of rules to be defined that can be applied in both physical and virtual spaces. The ontology has evolved from a subset of the SOUPA ontology for pervasive computing applications [36], including classes for Location, Person, Document, among others. A set of proxy objects permit common concepts (such as Display, CardGame) to be used across physical and virtual environments when these concepts are not directly present in one environment, or where they are present in very different ways. Proxy objects typically wrap a set of Observers and Effectors that together provide the expected behavior for the object.

The ontology is also used for reasoning across objects and events in both spaces, for example to infer activity. An inferencing component called the Context Engine pulls relevant tuples from the backbone, adding them to the context state. Rules are evaluated which can generate commands to specific entities or classes of entity.

SecSpace uses this feature to define privacy rules once for both physical and virtual spaces, to link shared resources that have physical and virtual manifestations (paper and digital documents, for example), and to respond to contextual events (such as the approach of an unidentified person) that can occur in physical, virtual, or both spaces simultaneously. For example, both physical display and virtual Displays (proxy objects) share the same ontological class. We could define a rule such that when an unidentified Person enters either space, all Displays display a notification. Alternately, we could define a rule that displayed a notification only on those Displays with the MainDisplay attribute. We can then link a specific physical display to a specific virtual display by assigning this attribute to each of them. If we use the Context Engine component, rules are interpreted and applied dynamically. Because of this, it is possible to replace or update rules at runtime, which is useful for both *ad hoc* testing and controlled experiments. To continue with our example, one experimental condition may apply the global Display notification policy, while another condition applies the MainDisplay notification policy.

Interface Mechanisms

TwinSpace provides a set of lightweight interface mechanisms that link physical and virtual. These include virtual world clients that can be used as addressable portals in a physical environment, and mechanisms for dynamically linking input devices to these clients. The virtual world clients can listen for relevant messages on the distributed communication backbone, and can be connected to using a dedicated communications channel (typically OSC) where a high degree of control and responsiveness is required.

SecSpace can control how interface mechanisms function, as a way of enforcing privacy policies in the connected physical space. For example, a smartphone app reads touchscreen events and converts them into control commands for a virtual portal's camera. SecSpace can control which portal(s) are controlled by which phone(s), and can define allowable camera paths or ranges. In this way, we can experiment with policies that apply to collocated groups as a whole, and to define access permissions to individuals in collocated groups.

Decoupled Components

TwinSpace offers a great deal of flexibility when deciding how to prototype mixed reality interaction. For example, most early prototypes do not use the Context Engine, connecting physical and virtual entities more directly via the messaging backbone to save one level of indirection. While the ontology helps maintain consistency in messages across distributed code, a developer can decide not to use it when testing out an idea. When the interaction between physical and virtual is minimal, all communication can take place through a single virtual world client, rather than use the backbone to communicate with the virtual world server. OpenWonderland's module-based extension feature allows us to package a subset of TwinSpace's functionality to suit a specific application.

When using SecSpace, developers can choose to use the elements of the framework that best suit their purpose. If the research involves context inference (for example, determining when a group splits into subgroups) or adaptive privacy policies (either when evaluating candidate policies in a comparative study or as a feature of a prototype's design), the Context Engine is useful. The messaging backbone is useful if a prototype needs to respond to simple, discrete events (such as someone entering a room), or when non-VW visualizations and applications form part of a prototype (for example, maintaining a 2D abstract visualization of activity progress). If a prototype emphasizes providing a visual indication of what is happening remotely (for example when choosing to share the view of a specific remote collaborator), the addressable portals are most useful.

PROTOTYPE EXAMPLES

To demonstrate the capabilities of SecSpace we describe four prototypes. The prototypes were built for two specific mixed reality environments. One was designed in collaboration with Steelcase, Inc. [32], and is an example of a "project room" [33], a dedicated space for synchronous and asynchronous collaboration around a single project. The room features several distinct 'collaboration regions', including an area for brainstorming equipped with an interactive whiteboard (used in the "Cone of Engagement" prototype), and an area for active table work (used in the "Card Game" prototype). The second environment mimics a more public mixed reality setting, linking a virtual public space (a café), manifested on large displays surrounding an interactive tabletop in our lab. The Card Game prototype was ported to the café setting, and two additional tabletop prototypes were developed inspired by this configuration (a guessing game and a facility for sharing portions of paper documents). The Cone of Engagement, Card Game and Guessing Game prototypes are presented in turn below. We discuss the privacy mechanisms inherent in each prototype, and consider how SecSpace supports them.

Privacy around a physical/virtual whiteboard

We embedded a virtual whiteboard in a physical space by linking it with a physical interactive whiteboard, such that collocated and remote collaborators can edit and discuss whiteboard contents in real time. Projecting a straight-on view of the virtual whiteboard onto the physical whiteboard "links" the physical and virtual whiteboards. Because of this, in-room collaborators have a limited perspective on the virtual environment when using the whiteboard.

While it is clear who is working at the whiteboard in the physical team room, we considered several ways to advertise when a remote collaborator joins the group at the virtual whiteboard. Our ultimate design was to directly translate the physical act of approaching the whiteboard into the virtual environment, and augment this with visual aids and event triggers: the remote collaborator moves their avatar into a visible "cone of engagement", which fans out to the virtual whiteboard from a point in front of it. The cone of engagement is contained within the field of view of the 'camera' that presents the virtual whiteboard on the physical interactive whiteboard (see Figure 1). This provides a simple engagement cue: when an avatar enters or leaves the region they become visible on the periphery of the physical whiteboard. In the virtual environment, we can build further on the act of approaching the whiteboard to introduce access control. A collaborator in the physical environment must move close enough to a whiteboard in order to view all of its contents. Similarly, the cone of engagement can be used to control access to the content on the whiteboard for remote collaborators. Specifically, their avatar must enter the cone of engagement before being able to view and/or edit the whiteboard's content. This threshold mechanism can also be used to check access permissions and grant access only to those who have sufficient privileges, whether or not their avatar has entered the cone.

By inferring a relationship between an avatar's proximity to the virtual whiteboard and the visibility of the content of the whiteboard, we create a space in which the privacy of the discussion around the whiteboard can be negotiated. In this way, users do not have to understand and manage security policies or learn a secure procedure. They can derive and negotiate their own rules in an ad hoc manner. For instance, a group can decide to only discuss topic A while persons X and Y are not present, or decide not to speak of an especially controversial topic if persons who were not present during the entire meeting engage partway.

To disable the whiteboard for remote participants while their avatars are not near the whiteboard is indeed constraining the way activities can take place in the virtual world, and one may argue that it is not smart to introduce such constraints for dynamic group work. However, work at a physical whiteboard already has implicit constraints. A person standing several meters away may not be able to see and hear all details, and people even further away will likely not be able to participate at all. Thus collaboration

Figure 1. The Cone Of Engagement

around a physical whiteboard is also constrained, and importantly these constraints are used to negotiate and manage security and privacy.

Using SecSpace, a ProximityObserver detects when an avatar enters or leaves the cone, and then a PermissionEffector updates access to the whiteboard for that individual accordingly. In our prototype, two objects are used for the whiteboard: an image that those outside the cone can see (displaying a "whiteboard in use" message), and the real whiteboard for those inside the cone. Note that all of this takes place within the virtual world: if desired, we could move control over authentication and response out to the Context Engine. This would be particularly useful if we wanted to combine whiteboard proximity triggers in both the physical and virtual spaces, for example to evaluate rules of engagement based on who else was collaborating and on the content being shared.

Privacy around a physical/virtual table

We are exploring three privacy scenarios involving sharing documents to people located around the physical table and with remote people who are connected using a virtual environment. We are focused on how to ensure privacy and security when using both physical and digital documents during mixed presence collaboration. The collocated participants around the physical table mainly use paper documents while the remote players share their documents digitally. Within this general setup we are exploring three types of privacy and interactions between people: 1) individual privacy and sharing with the world; 2) sharing with one individual/subset within a group; and 3) sharing partial information with others in a group. We discuss the first two of these in this section due to space constraints.

Individual Privacy and Sharing with the World

This involves keeping some information private while sharing other information globally. For example, a card game embodies this kind of privacy. While playing cards, a player hides cards from others until they decide what to share. We built a card game prototype, where people seated at the table could play the game using physical cards, while a remote participant uses a virtual world client.

An advantage of SecSpace is that we can quickly implement different versions of a concept as it is explored. In the first version of the card game, the virtual world tabletop was top-projected onto the physical game table. In this approach, we attached fiducials (visual markers that can be tracked by cameras) to the picture side of a deck of cards. An overhead camera recognized cards thrown on the table facing upwards. When this happened, the corresponding card was displayed on the top of the virtual table so that the remote participant could see the card. Permissions were set so that only the remote player saw the digital copy, to avoid projecting on top of the physical card. A second camera was placed in a box with a transparent top, making a virtual scanner. When the physical cards were dealt, the remote participant's cards were placed on

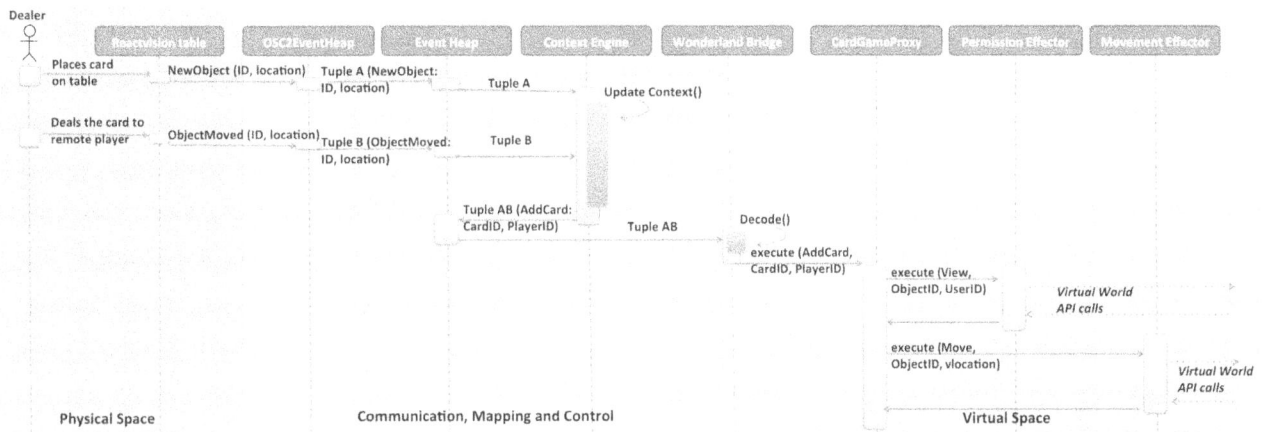

Figure 2. Sequence diagram for card game implementation. The Dealer deals a physical in the table region designated for a remote player, generating a virtual world command. In the virtual world, the card becomes accessible to the remote player, and is placed in a dedicated region showing their hand. Here, a physical privacy action corresponds to a different virtual one.

the box facing downwards, recognized by the camera in the box, and displayed to the remote participant in a dedicated region. Cards dealt to the remote participant were visible only to them until they were played. When the remote participant clicked one of the cards it was "thrown on the table" and set to be visible to all, making it visible on the physical tabletop as well.

This first version was limited in that it was cumbersome to pass cards back and forth between digital and physical, and for the remote player to swap unwanted cards for new ones, limiting the kinds of games that could be played. We began developing a new version on a touchscreen tabletop. We designed an Arduino LED app for the scanner box so that played or selected digital cards would trigger a flashing LED below the corresponding physical card. SecSpace facilitated this approach by requiring that the scanner listen for CardPlayed events already coming from the CardGame proxy object – these events were generated by remote players clicking on the card or by local players touching the digital card on the touch table. Similarly, if a remote player selects the digital version of another player's card, the area around the physical card glows on the tabletop. After initial testing we found that the scanner surface was too small and wanted a way to place all cards directly on the table. We then simply attached fiducials to both sides of the deck of cards. While cards might be recognized by the fiducial marker, we were only interested in this implementation for a short controlled study—a final implementation could use a tracking camera beneath the tabletop surface. Instead of a dedicated device, the remote player was assigned a dedicated region of the table; the dealer placed the remote player's cards face down in that region. The same system of indicators (glowing regions around cards of interest) was used to allow players to communicate and play together with physical and digital cards (see Figure 3). Figure 2 shows a sequence diagram of the event sequence that takes place when the dealer deals a physical card to the remote player in this current implementation.

Just like in card games in the physical world, the game rules were player-enforced (i.e., the system did not enforce any rules). Players manage their own security and privacy and negotiate it with the other players. A player can show one of his cards to a local player by showing it physically or to a remote player by placing it face down in the remote player's region of the table temporarily. For instance if a player is amused by how fortunate she is to end up with an ace, she can show the ace to selected players in order to share her amusement and still not ruin the game.

Share with certain individuals within a group.

When people are in a group there may be times when they only want to share information with one person or a subset within a group. In particular, how would someone share information with both a real person and a virtual person and at the same time while hiding it from others and the world?

To explore this scenario, we created a guessing game prototype. Two players share categories (each has a set of category cards they can share) and decide on an item (e.g., a movie title) for another player to try to guess by asking questions up to a maximum number.

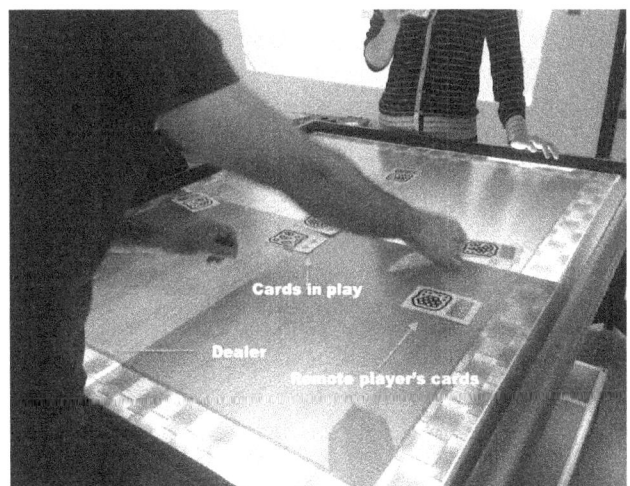

Figure 3. The final Card Game implementation.

SecSpace facilitates this by placing ProximityObservers around virtual table regions. Remote players move a category card into one of the regions to make it legible on the physical table. We place physical dividers around these table regions to prevent eavesdropping (Figure 4). Local players share their category cards with remote players by placing the category card face down in the remote player's dedicated table region (a fiducial is placed on the back of the category card as with the card game)

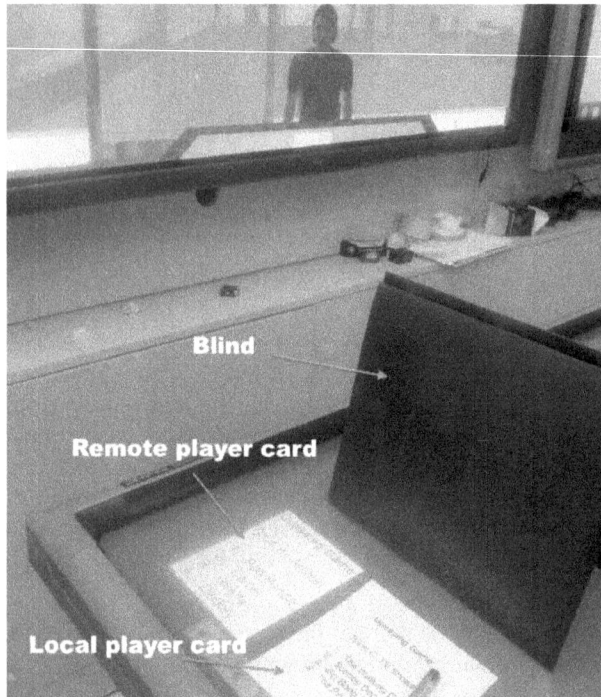

Figure 4. The Guessing Game

DISCUSSION

The use of SecSpace has allowed us to rapidly develop a range of prototypes exploring privacy in mixed presence collaboration. This has helped to build hypotheses that can be explored in future controlled studies and other evaluations. First, we are interested in how physical privacy behaviours (around paper documents, for example) can be sensed and translated into counterpart virtual privacy actions.

Second, we believe that design for management of privacy (rather than enforcing policies) may make security and privacy dependent artifacts more usable. Using SecSpace, we were able to design and prototype mechanisms that made it possible for users to negotiate and thereby manage their own privacy in a tangible (in the card game example) or embedded (in the whiteboard example) way. The two implementations do not guarantee security or privacy, however—they place that responsibility in the hands of the users, who can determine the actual need for security or privacy.

While we believe SecSpace provides a number of benefits in its current form, there are a number of technical limitations still to address. We outline these here.

Limitations

Learning curve

There are a lot of technologies (OpenWonderland, Event Heap, Jena, OSC) that prototype builders need to become familiar with in order to use SecSpace to its fullest extent. It is often difficult to know "where" the best place is to write logic, interface code, or privacy policies. Through the development of a number of TwinSpace and SecSpace prototypes (involving approximately 70 individuals with widely varying expertise) we have found that developers typically start with a very simple model at first and then (if necessary) move to more comprehensive use of SecSpace. Typically, a developer will capture a physical interaction, and generate an OSC message that a specific virtual world client will receive and respond to, or generate an EventHeap message that a specific Effector will handle in the virtual world (see Figure 5); alternately the developer will write simple code that responds to an EventHeap message coming from the virtual world via an Observer. We plan to define abstraction layers (for example, hiding the communication mechanism through a factory pattern) to simplify engagement with more of SecSpace earlier.

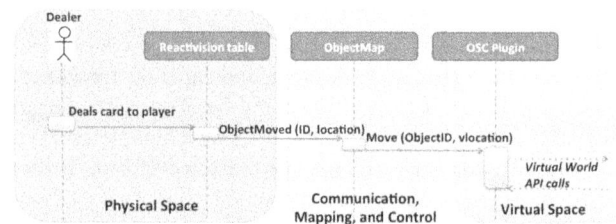

Figure 5. Sequence diagram showing dealer dealing a card in initial card game implementation. Here, moving physical cards maps directly to virtual card movements.

Difficulty transitioning between reduced and full feature set

When prototypes are developed using simple models, it is often difficult to encourage engagement with the larger feature set of SecSpace, and this may reduce the ability of the system to flexibly evaluate alternative privacy mechanisms. For example, the card game began using the model shown in Figure 5. While straightforward, it requires a fair bit of custom glue code between the physical and virtual pieces, and custom code on the virtual world client to enable interaction with cards. The first card game version used Observers and Effectors, but did not use the Context Engine, instead placing the mapping, privacy and game logic in the glue code. Moving this code to the Context Engine and a Card Game proxy object was tedious and challenging. It is useful that SecSpace decouples components to give flexibility, but well-defined, clear best practices and supports need to be available.

Distributed model: sometimes robust, often opaque

Developing a prototype using all of SecSpace requires configuring a number of distributed components. The decoupled message passing of the Event Heap and redirection capability of OSC permits robustness when some components aren't present, but this will depend on the way the prototype is designed. Complex prototypes with deeply interlocking components benefit less from these features, and can be difficult to set up correctly and to debug. Finally, while SecSpace (and TwinSpace) were designed to permit different rendering and virtual world engines, they were built using OpenWonderland. This means that certain features (specifically the mechanics and capabilities of particular Effectors and Observors) will be reliant on the availability of features (such as document editing and related permissions) on the base platform. We plan to port SecSpace to a Unity-based platform in future, and will be able to better assess the generality of our model.

CONCLUSION
We have presented SecSpace, a software framework for prototyping usable privacy and security mechanisms for mixed reality collaborative environments. Its key features are distributed communication, shared physical-virtual ontology and reasoning, a set of interface mechanisms for real-virtual interaction, and a high degree of feature decoupling permitting a range of development strategies. We demonstrated the value of SecSpace through the description of three prototypes, one focused on a shared whiteboard and the others a shared tabletop. Developing and modifying prototypes using SecSpace has contributed to our understanding of usable privacy in mixed presence collaboration, inspiring targeted research. We also identified a number of current limitations that we hope to address in future work: a high learning curve, difficulty transitioning between simple and more complete system models, and difficulties understanding system status when developing highly interconnected prototypes.

ACKNOWLEDGEMENTS
This work is funded in part by Boeing and GRAND. Earlier work was supported by NSF grant IIS-0705569, and a research collaboration grant from Steelcase Inc.

REFERENCES
[1] P. Garner, M. Collins, S. M. Webster, and D. A. D. Rose, "The application of telepresence in medicine," *BT Technol. J.*,154, 181–187, 1997.

[2] A. Petrakou, "Interacting through avatars: Virtual worlds as a context for online education," *Comput. Educ.*, vol. 54, no. 4, pp. 1020–1027, May 2010.

[3] J. Lang, "Privacy, Territoriality and Personal Space – Proxemic Thoery," in *Creating Architectural Theory: The role of the behavioral sciences in design*, New York, 1987, pp. 145–156.

[4] K. O'hara, J. Kjeldskov, and J. Paay, "Blended interaction spaces for distributed team collaboration," *ACM Trans. Comput. Interact.*, 181, pp. 1–28, Apr. 2011.

[5] J. Lifton, M. Laibowitz, D. Harry, N.-W. Gong, M. Mittal, and J. A. Paradiso, "Metaphor and Manifestation Cross-Reality with Ubiquitous Sensor/Actuator Networks," *IEEE Pervasive Comput.*, 83, pp. 24–33, Jul. 2009.

[6] Z. Pan, A. D. Cheok, H. Yang, J. Zhu, and J. Shi, "Virtual reality and mixed reality for virtual learning environments," *Comput. Graph.* 0, pp. 20–28, Feb. 2006.

[7] C. Sandor, A. Olwal, B. Bell, and S. Feiner, "Immersive mixed-reality configuration of hybrid user interfaces," in *Fourth IEEE and ACM International Symposium on Mixed and Augmented Reality (ISMAR'05)*, 2005, pp. 110–113.

[8] I. Wagner, W. Broll, G. Jacucci, K. Kuutii, R. McCall, A. Morrison, D. Schmalstieg, and J.-J. Terrin, "On the Role of Presence in Mixed Reality," *Presence Teleoperators Virtual Environ.*, 184, pp. 249–276, Aug. 2009.

[9] O. Oyekoya, A. Steed, R. Stone, W. Steptoe, L. Alkurdi, S. Klare, A. Peer, T. Weyrich, B. Cohen, and F. Tecchia, "Supporting interoperability and presence awareness in collaborative mixed reality environments," in *19th ACM Symposium on Virtual Reality Software and Technology - VRST '13*, 2013, p. 165.

[10] P. Van Schaik, T. Turnbull, A. Van Wersch, and S. Drummond, "Presence Within a Mixed Reality Environment," *CyberPsychology Behav.*, 75, pp. 540–552, Oct. 2004.

[11] S. Bødker, "When second wave HCI meets third wave challenges," in *4th Nordic conference on Human-computer interaction changing roles - NordiCHI '06*, 2006, pp. 1–8.

[12] J. McCarthy and P. Wright, "Technology as Experience," Sep. 2004.

[13] E. Chin, A. P. Felt, V. Sekar, and D. Wagner, "Measuring user confidence in smartphone security and privacy," in *Eighth Symposium on Usable Privacy and Security - SOUPS '12*, 2012, pp. 1–16.

[14] J. Goecks, W. K. Edwards, and E. D. Mynatt, "Challenges in supporting end-user privacy and security management with social navigation," in *5th Symposium on Usable Privacy and Security - SOUPS '09*, 2009, p. 1.

[15] K. R. Chia Shen, Katherine Everitt, "UbiTable: Impromptu Face-to-Face Collaboration on Horizontal Interactive Surfaces," in *UbiComp 2003*, 2003, pp. 281 – 288.

[16] E. M. Huang and E. D. Mynatt, "Semi-public displays for small, co-located groups," in *conference on*

Human factors in computing systems - CHI '03, 2003, pp. 49 – 56.

[17] A. Kapadia, T. Henderson, J. J. Fielding, and D. Kotz, "Virtual walls: protecting digital privacy in pervasive environments," pp. 162–179, May 2007.

[18] S. G. Anthony Tang, Carman Neustaedter, *VideoArms: embodiments in mixed presence groupware*. Springer London, 2007, pp. 85–102.

[19] S. Yarosh, A. Tang, S. Mokashi, and G. D. Abowd, "'almost touching'," in *2013 conference on Computer supported cooperative work - CSCW '13*, 2013, pp. 181 – 192.

[20] K. Hunter, S., Maes, P., Tang, A., and Inkpen, "WaaZam! Supporting Creative Play at a Distance in Customized Video Environments.," in *SIGCHI Conference on Human-factors in Computing Systems 2014*, 2014.

[21] H. Regenbrecht, M. Haller, J. Hauber, and M. Billinghurst, "Carpeno: interfacing remote collaborative virtual environments with table-top interaction," *Virtual Real.*,102 pp. 95–107, 2006.

[22] A. Tang, C. Neustaedter, and S. Greenberg, "VideoArms: Embodiments for Mixed Presence Groupware," *People Comput. XX — Engag.*, pp. 85 – 102, 2007.

[23] K. Tee, S. Greenberg, and C. Gutwin, "Providing artifact awareness to a distributed group through screen sharing," in *2006 conference on Computer supported cooperative work - CSCW '06*, 2006, pp. 99 – 108.

[24] Steve Benford, Chris Greenhalgh, Gail Reynard, Chris Brown, and Boriana Koleva. 1998. Understanding and constructing shared spaces with mixed-reality boundaries. *ACM Trans. Comput.-Hum. Interact.* 5, 3 (September 1998), 185-223.

[25] D. F. Reilly, H. Rouzati, A. Wu, J. Y. Hwang, J. Brudvik, and W. K. Edwards, "TwinSpace: an infrastructure for cross-reality team spaces," in *23nd annual ACM symposium on User interface software and technology - UIST '10*, 2010, pp. 119 – 128.

[26] B. Johanson, A. Fox, and T. Winograd, "The Interactive Workspaces project: experiences with ubiquitous computing rooms," *IEEE Pervasive Comput.*, vol. 1, no. 2, pp. 67–74, Apr. 2002.

[27] N. A. Streitz, J. Geißler, T. Holmer, S. Konomi, C. Müller-Tomfelde, W. Reischl, P. Rexroth, P. Seitz, and R. Steinmetz, "i-LAND: an interactive landscape for creativity and innovation," in *SIGCHI conference*

on Human factors in computing systems - CHI '99, 1999, pp. 120–127.

[28] V. Stanford, J. Garofolo, O. Galibert, M. Michel, and C. Laprun, "The NIST Smart Space and Meeting Room projects: signals, acquisition annotation, and metrics," in *2003 IEEE International Conference on Acoustics, Speech, and Signal Processing, 2003. Proceedings. (ICASSP '03).*, vol. 4, pp. IV–736–9.

[29] B. Johanson and A. Fox, "The Event Heap: A Coordination Infrastructure for Interactive Workspaces," In *Mobile Systems and Applications, 2002.* p. 83, Jun. 2002.

[30] O. F. Yee Jiun Song, Wendy Tobagus, Der Yao Leong, Brad Johanson, "isecurity: A security framework for interactive workspaces," 2003.

[31] "The OpenWonderland Project." [Online]. Available: http://www.openwonderland.org.

[32] D. Reilly, S. Voida, M. McKeon, C. Le Dantec, J. Bunde-Pedersen, W. K. Edwards, E. D. Mynatt, and A. Mazalek, "Space Matters: Physical-Digital and Physical-Virtual Co-Design in the Project." *IEEE Pervasive Comput 9(3)*, 2010, pp. 54–63.

[33] G. Olson and J. Olson, "Distance Matters," *Human-Computer Interact.*, 152, pp. 139–178, 2000.

[34] W. K. Edwards, E. S. Poole, and J. Stoll, "Security automation considered harmful?," in *2007 Workshop on New Security Paradigms - NSPW '07*, 2008, pp. 18 – 21.

[35] Benford, S., Magerkurth, C., & Ljungstrand, P. (2005). Bridging the physical and digital in pervasive gaming. *Communications of the ACM*, 48(3), 54-57.

[36] Chen, H., Finin, T., & Joshi, A. (2005). The SOUPA ontology for pervasive computing. In *Ontologies for agents: Theory and experiences* (pp. 233-258). Birkhäuser Basel.

[37] Reilly, D, Salimian, M., and Brooks, S. (2013) Document-Centric Mixed Reality and Informal Communication in a Brazilian Neurological Institution. Beyond Formality: Informal Communication in Health Practices Workshop, CSCW 2013, San Antonio, TX, USA

[38] Neustaedter, C., & Greenberg, S. (2003, January). The design of a context-aware home media space for balancing privacy and awareness. In *UbiComp 2003: Ubiquitous Computing* (pp.297-314). Springer Berlin Heidelberg.

Towards a Measurement Framework for Tools' Ceiling and Threshold

Rui Alves   Claudio Teixeira   Mónica Nascimento   Amanda Marinho   Nuno Jardim Nunes

Madeira-ITI, University of Madeira

Polo Científico e Tecnológico da Madeira, floor -2, Funchal, Portugal

rui.alves
@m-iti.org

claudioteixeira7
@gmail.com

monica.nascimento
@m-iti.org

amanda.zacarias
@gmail.com

njn@uma.pt

ABSTRACT

Software development tools are not catching up with the requirements of increasingly complex interactive software products and services. Successful tools are claimed to either be low-threshold/low-ceiling or high-threshold/high-ceiling, however no research to date addressed how to define and measure these concepts. This is increasingly important as these tools undergo an evaluation and adoption process by end-users.

Here we hypothesized that the evaluation and adoption of tools is associated with the threshold (learnability). To assess this we conducted a learnability and usability study using three commercial Platform-as-a-Service tools. In this study we used an augmented think-aloud protocol with question asking where ten subjects were asked to create a simple web application.

Our data shows that most learnability issues fall into two categories: *understanding* or *locating*. No evidence was found that usability defects correlate with the tools learnability score. Though we found an inverse correlation between the amount of issues and the learnability score.

Author Keywords

CASE tools; threshold; ceiling; learnability; PaaS.

ACM Classification Keywords

H.5.m. Information interfaces and presentation (e.g., HCI): Miscellaneous.

INTRODUCTION

Software development tools are key in increasing the productivity and manageability of complex interactive software products and services. Applications and services today are built using a myriad of tools, from text editors to integrated development environments (IDE) including all sorts of modeling, editing, debugging and testing tools. Despite the high level of sophistication, interactive software development tools are not very different from 25 years ago and many feel that opportunities for better tools are being lost to stagnation.

In a classical paper about the past, present and future of user interface software tools Myers et al postulated about the themes that seem to be important in determining which tools were successful [11]. A highly relevant theme was how the threshold and ceiling of tools concepts were important in evaluating tools. The threshold is how difficult it is to learn how to use the tool, and the ceiling is how much can be done using the tool. In the late 90s the authors suggested that the most successful tools seem to be either low-threshold and low-ceiling, or high threshold and high ceiling [11]. However, we are still struggling with some of the basic challenges of 25 years ago. We still need tools that support developers in acquiring and sharing HCI and software engineering best practices. They ought to help refine and evolve basic methods to make them fit into particular project contexts [13].

In this paper we describe our efforts to increase our understanding of the usability of interactive software development tools. Despite the amount of research in learnability and usability we found little evidence about defining and evaluating techniques to measure the threshold and ceiling of tools. For this purpose we decided to focus specifically on platform-as-a-service (PaaS) tools because they fall into an important and emerging market segment of low-threshold tools. PaaS are becoming highly popular in cloud computing. Since their business model relies on their adoption to make money (as opposed to sold units in shrink wrapped tools), adoption as a function of learnability is crucial to PaaS vendors.

The next section discusses the state of the art in terms of tools adoption and in particular ceiling and threshold. The following section discusses the hybrid research protocol we devised to conduct our research case study, which is the focus of the subsequent section. We then present the results in detail and provide a discussion before the conclusion.

STATE OF THE ART

Computer-aided software engineering (CASE) refers to tools that provide automated assistance to software development [1]. The goal of CASE tools is to reduce the time and cost of software development and enhance the quality of the systems developed [1]. Nevertheless, both software engineers and designers often complain that their tools are unsupportive and unusable [11]. Despite the evidence that technology reasonably improves product quality and consistency, the relationship between practitioners and their tools has always been troublesome. While many studies have analyzed and tried to better support general software development practices [4,13], qualitatively studies about user interface related practices in software development are relatively rare. Seffah and Kline showed a gap between how tools represent and manipulate programs and the software developers' actual experiences [13]. Their work quantitatively measured developers' experiences using heuristic and psychometric evaluation. However, they did not specifically addressed threshold and ceiling related issues, which is the focus of this research.

In the last two decades several authors addressed multiple CASE tool adoption issues [2,4,5,8,11]. This prior research suggest that: (i) few organizations use CASE tools; (ii) many organizations abandon the use of the tools; and (iii) countless developers, working for organizations that own CASE tools, do not actually use them [8]. Moreover, back in late 90's, Jarzabek and Huang argued that CASE tools should be more user-oriented and support creative problem-solving aspects of software development, as well as rigorous modeling, in order to better blend into the software development practice [5]. Furthermore, CASE tools were expected to be based on sound models of software process and user behavior [5]. Yet, figures on these tools adoption seem to contradict the goals driving their development. Nevertheless, a new breed of tools emerged, in particular PaaS, which claim to bridge previous gaps and promise easier and faster development, even for non-technical users. Intrigued by these apparently conflicting forces, we found room to contribute with research that could advance the state of the art in CASE tool adoption. Here we investigate the facts providing evidence on the association between PaaS tools adoption and the ceiling and threshold classification levels of these tools. In the following subsection we further detail these two central concepts.

Ceiling and Threshold

In the previously mentioned study about UI design tools, Myers et al stress the dichotomy between the sophistication of what can be created (the usefulness of a tool) against the ease of use (the learnability). This is directly related to the threshold and ceiling of tools. The threshold deals with the difficulty to learn how to use a tool, whereas the ceiling is how much can be accomplished with it [11]. The optimal approach is building tools that provide both low-threshold and high ceiling, however this is at the same time a grand challenge for modern software engineering [12].

RESEARCH QUESTION

In this work we hypothesized that threshold is associated with tool's learnability, thus its adoption. If our hypothesis is confirmed, we could reposition learnability as a cornerstone success factor for low-threshold and high-ceiling tool, such as PaaS. As a matter of fact we claim that the success of a PaaS tool is directly related to effective tool adoption (in the sense of actual usage), not commercial success nor number of issued licenses.

This initial effort focuses on learnability. A longitudinal study would be required in order to assess adoption. Due to time constraints, this longitudinal study was not performed, thus it is not covered by the work described in this paper.

TEST PREPARATION AND SAMPLE

In our study, we have exposed ten subjects to three distinct PaaS tools, namely Knack, Mendix Business Modeler 4.7.0 and OutSystems Studio 8.0. These tools were chosen among several alternatives surveyed by our team. Since we are aiming at studying initial learnability the subjects were first time users (they never saw any of these three tools before). The test duration was around two hours and a half per subject, during which they were challenged to create a simple web application, which was meant for a small store (inventory of products and prices).

Subjects had to create this web application three times, one per tool. To accomplish it, we handed-out a set of high-level tasks, as exemplified in Table 1, to guide them in what to do, but not how to do it. As such, they were free to complete the tasks the way they deem more appropriate.

Task	Description
T1	Create a database and populate it with the existing spreadsheet.
T2	Create pages for products with and without price. Add buttons to set price and add new product.
T3	Create the page to add new products.
T4	Create the page to set the price.
T5	Protect the set price page with a login.

Table 1: Scenario tasks description.

Such a long test (almost three hours) is demanding, namely on subjects' engagement and motivation. Upon surveying the literature, we have decided to augment the think-aloud protocol with the question-asking protocol [7]. The rational for this decision was to keep subjects highly motivated and truly engaged. The fact they could preview the result of their work as they progressed was a plus to achieve it. All these factors combined proved effective thus reducing the risk of subjects dropping the test.

A coach and an observer supported this process. All test sessions were video and audio recorded, upon subjects' consent. Screen casts were also recorded in order to aid the process of identifying both learnability issues and usability defects.

Sample

Our sample of ten subjects, six males, was divided in two groups of five elements each comprising both genders. The first group includes people who run small businesses. The other group was composed of IT users (software engineering master students). Their age ranged from 22 to 38 years old, with an average age of 28. Regarding the professional experience, 50% had worked for less than one year, 30% had four to nine years of experience, while the remaining 20% had worked for more than 10 years. In terms of academic background, 10% are not graduated and the same percentage holds a masters degree, while 80% had a bachelor degree.

We inquired subjects about their experience regarding the creation of simple web sites. As such, 50% had experience in web applications. Among these subjects, IDEs, such as Netbeans (60%), Dreamweaver (40%) and 20% use content management systems (CMS) were the tools used to develop such applications. The most popular language to create these applications is PHP, known by 80% of the users.

METHODOLOGY

We used a repeated measures design, since individual scores in one condition, can be paired with scores in the other conditions (using one or another tool). The study procedure included four major activities:

1. Record subjects' activity while being tested.

2. Collect pre-test and pos-test surveys per subject.

3. Elicit learnability and usability issues from recordings.

4. Process and analyze data.

We performed three pilot tests in order to iteratively improve the participant's and coach instructions as well as measure the test duration. The tests were done in a meeting room where subjects used a 15" laptop with built-in video, screen and audio recording software. These devices are not intrusive, thus subjects did not felt observed. Subjects gave informed consent for recording the test.

Subjects were asked to perform the same tasks sequentially on the three tools. In order to neutralize the aggregated experience bias we shuffled the order of execution among our sample. This means that, for instance, our first subject was presented with PaaS1, PaaS3 and PaaS2, whereas the second participant used PaaS2, PaaS1 and PaaS3 and so on. All subjects used the same operating system and computer. Both the operating system and tools were setup in English.

Scenario and Procedure

Upon arriving to the test room, subjects were briefed, to act as shop owners through a scenario. The shop owner wants to replace his spreadsheet to manage products, with a simple web application. This application uses a database and two major pages (one to display products without price and another page for products with price). Finally, subjects should set security settings in the set price page, since only the owner can set prices.

The coach sat side-by-side with the participant, to see user actions and provide help, if needed. An HCI researcher sat in a location where he did not interfered and was *invisible* to the participant, as observer. The observer controlled timings and breaks and was taking notes regarding usability defects and learnability issues.

In the beginning of the test the protocol rules (Table 2 and Table 3) were explained verbally to the subject. Then, printed copies of the high-level scenario instructions were handed-out to him. From this point on, the coach talked with the subject in order to follow his progress in the scenario tasks and they reported what they were thinking during the execution of the tasks. Whenever users got blocked or tried to accomplish an action without success and needed help, the coach encouraged them to ask questions in order to avoid any stress, which could lead to a decrease in motivation to finalize the task. The coach was authorized to answer questions with minimum instructions only to allow subjects to proceed.

a) Moderately verbalize the rational behind your main actions, intentions and thoughts.
b) Focus on completing your tasks as if you were creating this for your own business project.
c) Do not attempt to use built-in application support or online help, instead ask the coach.
d) Ask for help whenever you feel that you cannot progress, but only after trying to do it.
e) Ask only specific questions related to the tasks.
f) Off-topic conversations are not allowed.

Table 2: Protocol instructions for the participant.

a) Whenever the participant is completely stuck, ask him if he wants help to accomplish the task.
b) Whenever participant laps into silence, remind him to talk about the main actions he does.
c) Do not make participant nervous or stressed.
d) Avoid forcing the participant to talk all the time.
e) Do not help if participant do not ask for help.
f) If a task is incomplete or incorrect but is required to accomplish the next tasks, complete it quickly.
g) Do not tutor or explain with details.
h) Keep participant motivated.
i) Answer with minimum procedure actions.
j) Keep focus on the task completion flow and avoid distracting the user.
k) Do not encourage off-topic conversations.

Table 3: Protocol instructions for the coach.

This approach provided equal control conditions and well-defined tasks, thus reducing bias. For each tool, each participant went through a tutorial (around fifteen minutes per tool) followed by approximately 30 minutes to create the application proposed in the scenario. These timings were obtained as result of the three pilot tests we conducted before deploying the actual study. Still, users were not forced to complete the test scenario within 30 minutes, as we have not set any time limit. We did five minutes breaks between distinct PaaS, so that subjects could relax.

RESULTS

Four datasets are analyzed in this study, namely (1) learnability scores, (2) learnability issues, (3) performance and (4) usability defects. Two groups are presented: (G1) which refers to IT subjects, (G2) business. Additionally, due to privacy issues, the data is anonymous, both regarding subjects and tools involved, to which we refer to as PaaS1, PaaS2 and PaaS3 from here on.

Learnability Score

Among several learnability metrics [3], we have selected two metrics: (M1) the percentage of users who complete a task without any help and (M2) percentage of users who complete a task optimally. In M1 users cannot ask any kind of task-flow related questions, whereas in M2 users must complete the task straightforward, without help [10].

After gathering M1 and M2 percentages the scores were averaged from all users in both groups, where each metric had a weight of 0.5. This formula enabled us to plot the combined percentages from M1 and M2 to a 0-100% scale. For instance, if a group of *n* users complete all tasks without help but not optimally the system will have a learnability score of 50%. Conversely if the group completes all tasks optimally, the tool will have a score of 100% and if half of users complete optimally and the other half without help, system will end up with a 75% score. We classified the tools learnability score in four levels: (i) extremely difficult to use [0 to 24%], (ii) difficult to use [25 to 49%], (iii) easy to use [50 to 74%] and (iv) extremely easy to use [75 to 100%].

Table 4 summarizes the computed data for all three PaaS. Remarkable is the fact that in PaaS1 results do not vary across groups or when aggregating all subjects. The opposite happens with PaaS2, where G1 results position this tool as easy to learn, whereas for G2 it is an extremely difficult tool to learn. PaaS3 presents a blend of results, yet following PaaS2 results, yet with less extreme values.

Group	PaaS1	PaaS2	PaaS3
G1	Easy 66%	Easy 62%	Easy 62%
G2	Easy 68%	Ext. Difficult 20%	Difficult 42%
All	Easy 67%	Difficult 41%	Easy 52%

Table 4: Learnability Scores with Classification

Based on these results, empirical evidence seems to indicate that for first time users, PaaS1 and Paa3 are easy to learn whereas PaaS2 is difficult to learn.

Learnability Issues

Along with learnability scores we have identified also learnability issues. We have reused Grossman's et al classification schema, where issues are classified according to five categories: (i) understanding, (ii) locating, (iii) awareness, (iv) transition and (iv) task-flow [3]. *Understanding* is when a user is aware of some functionality but could not understand how to use it.

Locating is when a user is aware of some feature that was available in the tool but could not locate it in the interface.

Awareness is when a user is not aware of some feature, which is available to use in order to complete some action. *Transition* covers issues when the user is aware of some feature but chooses other features to complete the task (often more time consuming and difficult). Finally, a *task-flow* issue is when a user is knowledgeable of the task high level but do not know how to start it or the sequence of actions to achieve it [3]. In Table 5 we summarize all identified learnability categories weight, per tool and group.

Category	PaaS1		PaaS2		PaaS3	
	G1	G2	G1	G2	G1	G2
Understanding	22%	**52%**	17%	11%	**33%**	**52%**
Locating	**33%**	22%	**45%**	**38%**	17%	9%
Awareness	22%	0%	14%	6%	17%	16%
Transition	17%	9%	3%	9%	0%	0%
Task Flow	6%	17%	21%	**36%**	**33%**	23%
Total	18	23	29	47	24	44

Table 5: Learnability issues.

Aggregating all values per category, we found that transition issues are the less frequent. By computing a ratio between the all categories and *transition*, we found what types of learnability issues hinder users the most (see Table 6). Likewise we also computed a weighted average, where G1 accounts for 25%, G2 another 25% and all together 50%. Because we have five subjects in each group and ten in total, thus the average is evenly weighted.

Category	G1	G2	All	Average
Understanding	3.6	6.7	5.0	1.7
Locating	4.7	4.0	4.4	1.5
Awareness	2.6	1.3	2.0	0.7
Transition	1.0	1.0	1.0	0.3
Task Flow	3.0	4.4	3.6	1.2

Table 6: Learnability issues frequency.

Given these results, the most frequent learnability issues are related to understandability, closely followed by *locating*, *task-flow* is the third, followed by *awareness* and *transition* issues. On G2 *understanding* issues are 6.7 times more frequent than *transition* issues, whereas in G1 *locating* issues are 4.7 times more frequent than *transition* related problems.

Performance

Within the scope of our test, performance stands for the elapsed time to complete a given task. The first fact is that IT users (G1) performed faster in all cases. In rough numbers, the difference between these two groups, ranged from 25% up to 50%. We realized that G1 performs better than G2 subjects in 66.6% of all tasks of the complete test.

Usability Defects

Table 7 summarizes the total and average usability defects per user, for all evaluated tools.

Group	PaaS1		PaaS2		PaaS3	
	$\sum$	$\bar{x}$	$\sum$	$\bar{x}$	$\sum$	$\bar{x}$
G1	27	5	30	6	40	8
G2	35	7	50	10	70	14
Total	62	6	80	8	110	10

Table 7: Usability Defects Encountered per User

Figures show that PaaS3 has more usability defects, followed by PaaS2 and PaaS1. We have clustered the usability defects according to their relation to the interface.

Category	PaaS1		PaaS2		PaaS3	
	G1	G2	G1	G2	G1	G2
Icons	7%	0%	13%	26%	15%	**21%**
Bars/Windows	4%	9%	13%	12%	20%	16%
Canvas	0%	0%	0%	0%	10%	14%
Menus/Commands	22%	26%	**33%**	**30%**	15%	14%
Interaction	**41%**	**37%**	7%	12%	15%	17%
Text/Feedback	26%	29%	**33%**	20%	**25%**	17%
Total	27	35	30	50	40	70

Table 8: Usability Defects

Most usability defects in PaaS2 are related to commands, while in PaaS3 the most common fall into the icons and text categories. In PaaS1 *interaction* aspects standout (Table 8).

Usability defects that fall into the *icons/graphics* category are related to a graphical design issue (similar icons). Under the *bars/windows* category we clustered defects that are directly related to using bars or high level commands which belong to the tools' window (positioning of properties box). Defects classified as being *canvas* refer to the design area of the interface (egg. cannot drag items to put them above the table). When the defect was related to buttons or input fields then it was categorized as *menus/commands*, whereas defects classified as *interaction* are related to the interaction paradigm (. double clicking of an object creates something without questioning the user). Finally, the *text/feedback* category refers to issues on the textual terminology and text feedback from the interface. In addition we also measured each tool ceiling.

Ceiling

Ceiling is inherently a function of features: "how much can be done using the system" [11]. In order to be able to classify and compare the three tools under analysis, we propose a simple method to determine the ceiling. We extract the contextual features (e.g. centralized app governance, Service oriented architecture refactoring tools) from the three tools and identify an extra tool, which is supposed to be one of the most complete in the PaaS context. From this extra tool we

extracted the contextual features. After merging the previously extracted four sets of features we then created a checklist in order to match each tool's features with the ones in the merged list (highest number of features).

We have applied this technique in our study which provided the following results: from a total of 31 features, PaaS1 matches with 29, PaaS2 matches with seven features and PaaS3 matches with 31. Therefore PaaS1 gets a ceiling score of 0.94, PaaS2 a score of 0.23 and 1.0 for PaaS3. A four level scale approach was used to classify the tools, namely: (i) extremely low ceiling [0 to 24%], (ii) low ceiling [25 to 49%], (iii) high ceiling [50 to 74%] and (iv) extremely high ceiling [75 to 100%]. In this scale PaaS2 is extremely low ceiling, while PaaS1 and PaaS3 are both extremely high-ceiling. Upon analyzing all this data we concluded that our results could be threatened by our sample size. As such we further investigated our sample size adequacy.

Threshold and Ceiling Classification

Table 14 summarizes our test results, namely threshold and ceiling classification. Threshold is obtained by inverting the learnability scores, i.e., 100% learnability score means *low threshold*, as threshold a measure for how difficult is to learn a tool. Ceiling is determined directly, i.e., 100% matching of features is *high ceiling*. We have classified the tools according to the groups under evaluation in terms of ceiling and threshold. It's important to remark that this classification is only valid for this experiment context, i.e. for the first time usage of the tools (initial learnability).

Group	PaaS1	PaaS2	PaaS3
G1	Low-Ceiling Low-Threshold	High-Ceiling Low-Threshold	High-Ceiling Low-Threshold
G2	Low-Ceiling Low-Threshold	High-Ceiling High-Threshold	High-Ceiling High-Threshold
All	Low-Ceiling Low-Threshold	High-Ceiling High-Threshold	High-Ceiling Low-Threshold

Table 9: Ceiling and threshold classification matrix

Having these classifications, one cannot argue that PaaS2 is a high-ceiling and high-threshold as it is a generic classification, since as stated before this classification only applies to initial learnability. Additionally we would like to remark also that, according to literature [12], an optimal software tool should have a high-ceiling and low-threshold which we can observe in the following table several times in G1 but not for G2. The target audience of the tools under study is both G1 and G2, so any conclusions made from this table should be handled with this under consideration.

DISCUSSION

We found that the most frequent learnability issues are related with *understanding* issues. Thus, PaaS providers should pay special attention to this aspect, in order to increase their tools learnability, thus increasing their adoption chances. Moreover, *locating* issues are also common, which provides evidence that poor interaction design is being devoted to build these PaaS tools. Furthermore, by relating learnability scores to learnability issues, we observed that, in general, the greater amount of issues, the lower the learnability scores.

Regarding the ceiling/threshold discussion, our results are in line with Myers et al, who claim high-threshold tools also have a high-ceiling [11]. This reinforces the problem both academia and industry are still struggling with, and failing, to build tools that provide both low-threshold and high ceiling [12]. Having low-threshold and high ceiling, basically means that users can do development quite easily. This goal is proving to be a demanding challenge. Thus, further research is required to properly address this issue.

As thoroughly discussed by Jeng, there is no consensus on what are the attributes that characterize usability but the most relevant attribute is learnability (53% of these authors support it) [6]. Yet, according to our data, when it comes to usability defects, no patterns were identified. This points towards a preliminary conclusion that, despite the intrinsic relationship between learnability and usability, in our experiment we have not found evidence that correlates usability defects with tools learnability score, learnability issues or performance. Further research will be needed to investigate the reasons behind these findings.

In what concerns users' performance, we found that the IT group (G1) performed faster in all cases. The difference between G1 and G2 users ranged from 25% in PaaS3 to 34% in PaaS1 and 48% in PaaS2. The post-test survey suggests that users from G1 have experience with look-alike tools, such as IDE tools. Another possibility is that G1 may be more familiar with the terminology and domain, yet we do not managed to gather evidence on this hypothesis.

In our study we had no access to users' performance standards (real users performance). Jeng claims that learnability is inferred from the amount of time required to achieve user performance standards [6]. In order to have standard performance figures we would need to perform an extended test with more tools and users. Nevertheless, our goal for this phase was to measure initial learnability, not a longitudinal study.

One possible weakness of the presented work is the sample small size. These figures were constrained by the available time but are is in line with the fact that the first four to five subjects in an usability study discover around 80% of all usability defects [14], including the severest usability defects. Our sample size is adequate for covering 70% of learnability issues, according to Lewis [9].

CONCLUSION

Our ongoing work aims to improve the state of the art in assessing tools' ceiling and threshold. We found that most learnability issues fall into two categories: *understanding* or *locating*. Additionally, we found an inverse correlation between the amount of issues and the learnability score.

We plan to expand the sample size and do a longitudinal study to validate identified trends and gather statistical evidence on existing correlations. We believe this work is valid to other tools thus increasing our understanding on how to design the tools of the future.

REFERENCES

1. Banker, R. and Kauffman, R. Reuse and productivity in integrated computer aided software engineering. *Information Systems Working Papers Series, Vol,* (1992).
2. Campos, P. and Nunes, N.J. Practitioner tools and workstyles for user-interface design. *Software, IEEE 24,* 1 (2007), 73–80.
3. Grossman, T., Fitzmaurice, G., and Attar, R. A survey of software learnability: metrics, methodologies and guidelines. *Proceedings of the SIGCHI Conference on Human Factors in Computing Systems*, (2009), 649–658.
4. Iivari, J. Why are CASE tools not used? *Communications of the ACM 39,* 10 (1996), 94–103.
5. Jarzabek, S. and Huang, R. The case for user-centered CASE tools. *Commun. ACM 41,* 8 (1998), 93–99.
6. Jeng, J. Usability assessment of academic digital libraries: effectiveness, efficiency, satisfaction, and learnability. *Libri 55,* 2-3 (2005), 96–121.
7. Kato, T. What "question-asking protocols" can say about the user interface. *International Journal of Man-Machine Studies 25,* 6 (1986), 659–673.
8. Lending, D. and Chervany, N.L. The use of CASE tools. *Proceedings of the 1998 ACM SIGCPR conference on Computer personnel research*, (1998), 49–58.
9. Lewis, J.R. Evaluation of procedures for adjusting problem-discovery rates estimated from small samples. *International Journal of Human-Computer Interaction 13,* 4 (2001), 445–479.
10. Linja-aho, M. Evaluating and Improving the Learnability of a Building Modeling System. *Helsinki University of Technology*, (2005).
11. Myers, B., Hudson, S.E., and Pausch, R. Past, present, and future of user interface software tools. *ACM Trans. Comput.-Hum. Interact. 7,* 1 (2000), 3–28.
12. Myers, B.A. and Rosson, M.B. Survey on user interface programming. *Proceedings of the SIGCHI Conference on Human Factors in Computing Systems*, ACM (1992), 195–202.
13. Seffah, A. and Metzker, E. The obstacles and myths of usability and software engineering. *Communications of the ACM 47,* 12 (2004), 71–76.
14. Virzi, R.A. Refining the test phase of usability evaluation: how many subjects is enough? *Human Factors: The Journal of the Human Factors and Ergonomics Society 34,* 4 (1992), 457–468.

Presenting EveWorks, a Framework for Daily Life Event Detection

Bruno Cardoso
CITI, Departamento de Informática
Faculdade de Ciências e Tecnologia
Universidade Nova de Lisboa
2829-516 Caparica, Portugal
b.m.pinto.cardoso@gmail.com

Teresa Romão
CITI, Departamento de Informática
Faculdade de Ciências e Tecnologia
Universidade Nova de Lisboa
2829-516 Caparica, Portugal
tir@fct.unl.pt

ABSTRACT
In this paper we present EveWorks, a new framework for the development of context-aware mobile applications, focused on the detection of events on people's daily lives. In our framework, events of interest are expressed through statements written in a simple domain-specific language that, being interpreted, allows for changing an application's reactive behavior at runtime. Instead of being focused on programming through technology of framework-specific components, our approach allows developers to express events in terms of more natural constructs – intervals of time where some data invariants are true, articulated through the operators of James Allen's Interval Algebra.

Author Keywords
Context awareness framework; daily life event reaction; time interval algebra; mobile application development.

ACM Classification Keywords
D.3.3. Language Constructs and Features: Frameworks

INTRODUCTION
Intertwined as they are in our daily lives, smartphones are an ideal platform for the deployment of meaningful and valuable interactions. Besides their availability, which has been increasing in the last decade [10, 14], research has found that they accompany their owners for most of the time – Dey et al.'s study revealed smartphones to be on the same room as their owners for about 90% of the time [6]. Needless to say, this translates to a valuable potential for delivering the right interaction at the right time, and this becomes especially true for context-aware applications. However, what this "right time" may be, depends on a high number of factors, such as the intention behind the application and the nature of the interaction itself. For instance, whereas an application designed to deliver

advertisement would perhaps find a good opportunity by the time its user enters the mall, a weight logging system would possibly fare better if it prompted its user to log his/her weight when s/he leaves his/her bedroom, first time in the morning.

The programming of such interactions, however, may be a demanding task. Beyond the matters of context acquisition and processing, there is also the challenge of developing a flexible enough architecture to support the detection of different events for different application-specific interactions. An important observation can be found in Carlson and Lisper's work [4], who state that the separation between the mechanisms for event detection and the rest of the application logic constitutes a systematic approach and facilitates design and analysis of reactive systems. Acknowledging this, the research community has proposed a number of frameworks, conveying very elaborate architectural solutions (see Related Work). However, as most of those frameworks interface with the rest of the system's code through Application Programming Interfaces (API), the code implementing the interaction between the application and the framework will have to be written in the application's own source code. This approach, of course, may limit the frameworks' potential for cross-platform portability. Moreover, because this code is compiled along with the rest of the application's sources, the latter's reactive behavior will have to be defined at compile time and will be static once the application has been deployed.

While we do believe that these solutions are valid and adequate for applications requiring only static reactive behavior, they do not provide immediate answers for systems with more dynamic requirements. Finally, note that these approaches require the event detection logic to be implemented through framework or technology-specific constructs. This, of course, may pose as a difficulty for programmers unfamiliar with a particular framework's mechanics. We argue that, when programming an application's reactive behavior, developers should not be concerned about framework or environment-specific constructs; rather, their minds should be set on higher level, more natural descriptions of the events they wish to detect.

In this paper we present a new framework, EveWorks (an acronym of Event Framework), targeted to the detection of daily life events, that offers a powerful set of functionalities to context-aware application developers. Like most of the examples found in the literature, EveWorks also encapsulates the complex mechanics of contextual data acquisition and event matching. However, our framework interfaces with the embedding application's logic through statements, written in its own runtime-interpreted scripting language. This enables an application to change the set of events it's listening for, after it has been deployed to a user's smartphone – thereby granting context-aware applications an adaptability potential.

RELATED WORK

Most of the frameworks found in the literature are not designed to run on platforms with relatively limited resources, like smartphones. A good example of one such framework is Dey and Abowd's Context Toolkit [5], a framework designed for rapid development of context-aware applications. The Context Toolkit is composed of five different functional abstractions, each having specific purposes: context widgets retrieve context information, thereby insulating applications from context acquisition concerns; interpreters produce additional levels of abstraction for context information – for instance, location may be expressed at low level of abstraction, through geographical coordinates, or at higher levels, through street names; aggregators combine related contextual information into a common repository; services execute actions on behalf of applications or, more specifically, they control or change state information on the environment; and, finally, discoverers, which are responsible for maintaining a registry of what capabilities exist in the framework, which is useful for distributed context-aware systems. The Context Toolkit is mainly focused on the problem of providing functional abstractions to ease the task of context gathering, rather than the expression and detection of events, as is the rationale of EveWorks.

Of course that, given the privileged relationship that smartphones enjoy with their owners [6], a number of context-awareness frameworks targeting these platforms can also be found in the literature. For instance, Wissen et al. developed the ContextDroid, an interesting expression-based, context-aware framework, targeted for the Android platform [14]. Context, as understood by the framework, is composed of context entities which are collections of context information – for example, the user's location expressed in terms of latitude, longitude and altitude; context readings, composed of a value representing the state of the entity, a timestamp and a time of expiration, with the context reading being valid from the timestamp to the time of expiration; context conditions provide some abstraction over the context readings, since they realize Boolean evaluations over a set of parameters; evaluators, which are simple interfaces for the evaluation of context conditions; and, finally, context expressions for combining context. Contrary to what happens with EveWorks, ContextDroid's expression-based approach is tightly coupled to the Java

language, with expressions being built through the instantiation of classes provided by the framework and the invocation of methods on the instantiated objects. Granted, because they are written directly in the application's source code, event expressions will be compiled and, therefore, to alter the set of events an application is listening for will require manipulating the source code.

Kramer et al. presented a layered, rule-driven, generic context acquisition engine [10]. Similarly to ContextDroid, the engine was also implemented targeting the Android platform. It is an interesting approach, as the engine was designed to be used as a standalone instance capable of context capturing, composition and broadcast to any listening context-aware applications running on the same device. The engine's infrastructure is based on the idea of self-contained context components and, because it is organized in a tree hierarchy, it allows for the building of hierarchically structured context data, in which low level, simpler context components are loosely coupled to form higher level, composite context representations. It has three conceptual elements: the context component, the composite component and the context engine manager. The context component is a self-contained implementation which deals with the tasks of acquiring raw context data from context sources, mapping raw context data into a finite set of predefined values and broadcasting the processed information, in case the new value differs from the last. Composite components are combinations of loosely coupled context components, whose main role is the handling of aggregated, high-level context information. They can be constructed, assembled and defined at runtime and the combination of context components is based on sets of rules that define the composite component's behavior, as the values of their respective lower-level context components' change. Finally, the last component is the context engine manager, which deals with the distribution of context information to any listening applications. Although addressing the authors' objective of having a single, centralized context acquisition engine for various applications, it is important to note that the rule-based context composition may raise an application's complexity.

As a last example, we mention Ferreira's AWARE framework [7]. AWARE is an instrumentation middleware, aiming to streamline the effort of developing mobile logging tools. The framework is architecturally distributed, featuring two main components: AWARE client and AWARE server. The AWARE client is used as a context data gatherer and the collected data may be stored locally on the device's storage, or it can be sent to the server and remotely stored and processed. The client can be extended with new context sensors which, in essence, are subclasses of the Android platform's Service class. The sensors collect and abstract data and may reuse context data from other context sensors, thereby creating new, higher-level contexts. In turn, the AWARE server is targeted to researchers and developers and is a distributed infrastructure designed to share and reuse context data with other applications and devices. As previously cited, AWARE is mainly focused on the development of logging tools whereas EveWorks is focused on the detection of events on people's daily lives. Moreover, like the previously presented frameworks, AWARE also targets the Android platform and some of its core concepts are tightly connected to some of the Android platform's components.

EVEWORKS

Design Decisions

Since we aim our framework to provide support for the implementation of reactive behavior on mobile, user-oriented systems, we will draw a running example, inspired by the recent trend on mobile health managing systems [11], that will help us illustrate our design decisions: imagine an application (rather simplistic) intended to reduce excessive daily coffee consumption through the timely display of warning messages. As people´s lives are a constant flow of events, an effective detection system must be able to distinguish interesting events from the multitude of non-interesting ones. To this end, there is an objective necessity to provide developers with (1) means for expressing sets of conditions that an event must satisfy. Following this logic, we propose a trigger for our message: the intervention should occur when the user approaches a coffee machine (we are assuming, of course, that we have all of the necessary technological resources to perform such an assessment).

In practice, however, this interruption mechanism may result rather poorly. Indeed, our system would trigger on regular coffee drinking habits, when only excessive consumptions should be regarded. Noting that an event may assume different meanings when temporally articulated with other events (2), we can devise a more sophisticated formulation. For instance, if we assume the number of times that a user is near a coffee machine, within a given time span, to be a good indicator of excessive coffee consumption, we could have the application trigger its programmed action upon detecting that the user is near the machine for the third time within, say, 1 hour (this strategy, of course, merely serves to illustrate our point – that events may gain significance when related to other events).

There is still, however, another subtlety to be noted; indeed, the detection of the amount of times that a user is near a coffee machine within an hour timespan may still be too simple a strategy. Truly, it may so be that the path to the user's workplace forces him to pass near the coffee machine and, on a particular day, s/he just happened to have passed three times near it. In order to account for such eventualities, we should also (3) allow for events to have temporal depth – a duration quality. With this in mind, we may decide that a better indicator for coffee consumption would be to detect if the user spends more than, say, one minute near our hypothetical coffee machine. Therefore, on a final restatement of the triggering conditions we say that the message should be presented whenever the user stands more than four times near the coffee machine, spending more than one minute each time, within one hour.

On the preceding discussion, we have pointed out some important considerations about the nature of the events we are interested in, namely (1) the event detection mechanism must allow the expression of conditions; (2) there must be a mechanism to allow the expression of temporal articulations within an event and (3) events may have temporal depth. From here, we argue that events can be more accurately expressed if their conditions are associated to time intervals where a number of conditions are satisfied – that is, periods of time where some data invariants hold – rather than to points in time. Moreover, even though the final trigger for our example was expressed through a simple before-after chaining of time intervals, many more relations are possible between interval pairs. Acknowledging this situation, James Allen proposed an approach that has become very influential – the Interval Algebra [1]. The Interval Algebra is an interval-based calculus for reasoning about temporal descriptions of events, where thirteen different relations between pairs of time intervals are defined: *is before, meets, overlaps, starts, during, finishes,* plus their respective converses *is after, is met by, is overlapped by, is started by, contains, is finished by* and, finally, the thirteenth relation *equals* (which is its own converse). All of these basic relations are *distinct*, because no pair of fully defined intervals can be related by more than one; *exhaustive*, because any pair of definite intervals can be described by one of the relations; and they are *qualitative* – rather than quantitative – because no numeric time spans are considered [2]. It should be stressed here that, whereas Allen's focus was knowledge representation, our interest lies in building a mechanism for event detection. Thereby, in addition to implementing all of the Interval Algebra's basic operators, EveWorks also supports numeric time quantities.

From the Interval Algebra's influence also derives one of the most important design decisions we have made – and one of the most distinctive characteristics of our framework: in the scope of EveWorks, all data is represented as a time interval. We believe this rule simplifies formal thinking about the events that may interest a particular application, as the developers are only required to define the data invariants that are true on each time interval and the temporal relations that hold between those intervals.

EveWorks was designed to be integrated into an application's environment, running in parallel (it is a periodically called process), while interfacing with the embedding application through statements written in its own Domain Specific Language (DSL). According to Martin Fowler's definition [8], DSLs are computer programming languages of limited expressiveness focused on particular domains. A good example of a mature and widely used DSL can be found on the domain of database management systems: the Structured Query Language (SQL), a declarative language with the sole purpose of data management. Likewise, the DSL implemented on EveWorks is used to express events of interest through the specification of data invariants over intervals of time and the relations that hold between those intervals. EveWorks DSL was designed with simplicity and legibility in mind and, since it is not based on any platform's programming environment, it has the advantage of having a platform independent syntax – much like SQL statements, which may be constructed independently of the language environment or the operating system whereupon the database management system happens to be deployed. Since our DSL is an interpreted script (EveWorks features an integrated parser and interpreter), it allows for runtime modification of the events it is listening to. This feature allows for a set of event statements to be maintained out of the application's code – for instance, on a server - and then be accessed and interpreted whenever is fit.

Framework Architecture

EveWorks uses "probes" for gathering values for context attributes. Probes are functional abstractions that encapsulate the logic of accessing context data sources that can be anything, from the system's location services (GPS, for instance) to a website containing weather information or even other probes - namely, our indoor location probe produces its results out of readings produced by the Wi-Fi probe. New probes can be added to EveWorks and then used on event statements, provided they implement the required interfaces. Probes also implement the processing logic that creates context attribute values out of the gathered data, including the management of any eventually necessary data storage resources (e.g., for a weather probe, a temperature of less than 10°C could be labeled and outputted as the attribute value 'cold weather'). Another construct worth mentioning here are the "trace tables", which are circular buffers, kept in a database, containing sequential readings for each probe.

The core mechanics of EveWorks are implemented as a routine that runs periodically, having three basic steps: *read*, *match* and *clean*. On the first step, *read*, the set of currently active events are evaluated in order to extract which probes must be read and, afterwards, those probes are queried for data. This, of course, saves the running device's battery, since it keeps the framework from activating unrequested sensors; at the end of this phase, the gathered context data is stored in the trace tables. On the *match* step, the trace tables are queried in order to conclude if a given event has occurred (see section Event Detection). Finally, during the *clean* step, EveWorks automatically eliminates outdated readings from the trace tables (by default, the trace tables will store timestamped readings from the last 24 hours – although this is configurable).

DSL Syntax

In order to create a simple and expressive syntax, we designed the expression of events as structured statements; therefore, all EveWorks statements follow the same structure. Moreover, we have introduced some visual cues into the language, inspired by conventions found on the field of Mathematics. As it is, every interval is delimited by square brackets (e.g. [A] means "the time interval identified by A"). All statements are structured compositions of the following clauses:

LET Clause (time interval declarations): The LET clauses state the interval building conditions (i.e., the interval's data invariants). They follow the general structure LET [<id>] BE [<predicate-expression>], where <id> is an interval identifier written in non-punctuated text and <predicate-expression> stands for a Boolean expression of predicates, complying with the following syntax <attribute> <boolean-op> <value>, where <attribute> is a context attribute, <boolean-op> is a regular SQL Boolean operator and <value> is a value to evaluate the attribute against. E.g., "LET [A] BE [location='home' OR location='workplace']", means that the interval identified by A corresponds to any time interval where the location attribute is either "home" or "workplace".

WHERE Clause (temporal relations): This clause declares the temporal relations between the intervals declared on the statement's LET clauses. The WHERE clause has the following syntax: WHERE <expression>, where <expression> is a Boolean expression of temporal relations and attributes. These relations, in turn, have the syntax: [<id1>] <relation> [<id2>], where <id1> and <id2> are interval identifiers and <relation> is one of the Interval Algebra's thirteen operators. For instance, the clause "WHERE [A] IS BEFORE [B] OR [A] MEETS [B]", means that either the ending time of interval A precedes the starting time of B, or that the ending time of A is the same as the starting time of B.

ON Clause (anchor to present time): This clause sets the conditions that must be satisfied at present time in order to trigger the event. Its syntax is: ON <id-expression>, where <id-expression> is a Boolean expression of interval identifiers. For instance, "ON [A] OR [B]" means that the event will trigger if either the data invariants of intervals A or B hold at current time (that is, either A or B or both are true at present time).

WITHIN Clause (timespan): This clause sets a timespan for the retrieval of readings from the trace tables, which will have to have been timestamped within the indicated timespan. All intervals will be constructed from the retrieved set of readings. The clause's syntax is as follows: WITHIN <timespan>, where <timespan> is any time span. Exemplifying, "WITHIN 10min" means that all event intervals will be constructed out of the set of individual readings that have been recorded within the last 10 minutes.

CALL Clause. This clause informs EveWorks about the actions to perform, when an event is triggered. Its syntax is CALL <target>, <arg-list>, where <target> is the application's construct that will receive the event matched notification, and <arg-list> stands for the list of arguments that will be forwarded to it. This clause's syntax may vary, in accordance with the platform where the application embedding EveWorks is running.

Examples

We now present a couple of snippets that illustrate the syntax of EveWorks' statements. In order to keep it free from platform-specific details, we will omit the CALL clauses.

Example 1. This example detects when the user enters a specific location (in this case, a place where the location probe produces the value 'lab').

```
(1)  LET [out] BE [location != 'lab']
(2)  LET [in]  BE [location = 'lab']
(3)  WHERE [out] MEETS [in]
(4)  ON [in]
```

Here, (1) means that *'out'* is *"any time interval where the 'location' probe's reading was different from 'lab'"*, (2) states that *'in'*, is *"any time interval where the 'location' probe's reading was 'lab'"*, (3) indicates that *"the ending time of interval 'out' meets the starting time of interval 'in'"* and (4) means *"trigger when interval 'in' is true at present time"*.

Example 2. For this example, we will fetch the context of the coffee addictive behavior example that we have stated earlier. The statement would be like:

```
(1)  LET [I1] BE [location = 'coffee']
(2)  LET [I2] BE [location = 'coffee']
(3)  LET [I3] BE [location = 'coffee']
(4)  WHERE [I1] IS BEFORE [I2]
     AND [I2] IS BEFORE [I3]
     AND DURATION OF [I1] > 1min
     AND DURATION OF [I2] > 1min
     AND DURATION OF [I3] > 1min
(5)  ON [I3]
(6)  WITHIN 60min
```

Again, the clauses (1) to (3) mean *'I1'* to *'I3'* are *"any interval of time where the probe 'location' has returned 'coffee'"*, (4) indicates the temporal relations that hold between the intervals (a simple before-after chaining) and each interval's durations, (5) means that the event will trigger after the user has arrived at 'coffee' for the third time, standing there over one minute, and (6) means that *"all intervals must be composed of readings recorded within the last 60 minutes"*.

Event Detection

We have modeled our event detection process as a constraint programming problem [12], where time intervals are represented by pairs of variables (one for each interval's start and end time), and the temporal relations between intervals are modeled as constraints between their variables. The domains of these interval variables (the set of all possible values that each variable may take) are built out of the timestamps of the trace table readings that satisfy the interval's conditions – in fact, the start and end time of sequences of consecutive readings satisfying the interval's data invariants. For example, suppose we are interested in detecting an event described by the occurrence of two time intervals, A and B, with A taking place before B. EveWorks will model this problem by associating four variables (one to each of the two interval's start and end time – $A.start$, $A.end$, $B.start$ and $B.end$). Then, EveWorks will process the trace tables and extract sequences of consecutive readings that satisfy A and B's data invariants. Finally, the constraint $A.end < B.start$ will be imposed, and a search for a solution will be initiated by an embedded constraint programming solver (since our prototype was built on Android, we have used JaCoP, a Java constraint programming solver [13]). Continuing our example, suppose that A's conditions are satisfied by readings {0, 1, 2, 3} and that B's conditions hold in readings {6, 7, 8}. Then, $A.start$ variable's domain will be the single-valued set {0}. Similarly, $A.end=\{3\}$, $B.start=\{6\}$ and $B.end=\{8\}$. Since the imposed restriction only requires $A.end$ to be less than $B.start$, the final solution will be immediate: $A.start=0$, $A.end=3$, $B.start=6$ and $B.end=8$. Since these values satisfy the restriction, the event succeeds and its action will be triggered.

EVALUATION

Aware of the novelty of our approach and in an effort to ascertain if our concepts are easy to understand, a study was conducted in which participants were asked to answer a set of questions regarding our DSL's usability [3]. In a nutshell, the questionnaire was answered on a website and its usability evaluation part consisted of 3 multiple choice items (1-3) where participants were asked to find, among the available options, the DSL statement that would detect a described event; one item (4) that asked the participants to explain a provided statement using their own words; and another item (5) that asked participants to write a DSL statement (the site featured a parser for our DSL's syntax, that detected and stored the number of errors). Our study had 84 participants (73 male) with ages ranging from 20 to 59, averaging 25.6, and the number of years of programming experience ranged from none to 25, averaging 6.9. The most notable results were that participants did not manifest any particular difficulty, in spite that almost none declared to have had any experience with similar technologies. Items 1 to 3 (associate a statement to a verbal description) respectively registered 90.5%, 100% and 90.5% of correct answers, item 4 (read and interpret a statement) had 97.6% of correct answers and, finally, on item 5 (write a statement), 71 participants wrote the statement at first try, with no syntactic errors, while the remaining 13 users averaged 1.7 errors.

We have also performed evaluations on the framework's performance: a test application was developed, embedding EveWorks, which was programmed to listen to 20 different events, with varying levels of complexity, simultaneously. The smartphone running the test application – a Sony Ericsson Xperia Arc S (LT18i) – was carried by the users across our faculty campus while they rehearsed the behaviors that would satisfy the events' triggering conditions. The test results were encouraging, with most of the alarms being raised when expected. Indeed, of the 20 programmed events, 18 triggered consistently at the right moment; the remaining two events occasionally did trigger when not supposed to (false positives). Rather than a problem in the concept of EveWorks, this behavior turned out to be a well-documented difficulty of distinguishing between adjacent indoor locations solely through Wi-Fi readings (an issue that will require further study).

CONCLUSION AND FUTURE WORK

This paper is intended to provide a first glance upon EveWorks, a new framework that aims to simplify the task of developing context-aware mobile applications. Our framework provides, as far as our tests have shown, a systematic and comprehensive approach to event detection. The Interval Algebra's operators proved to be easily understood, and so were time intervals as building blocks for more complex events. The success registered on the field testing was also proof that EveWorks performs as expected. Even though we take our usability study's results to be very encouraging, we acknowledge that there are still many aspects to work out. As EveWorks is an ongoing project and its DSL is still in its earlier versions, we naturally expect it to evolve, both syntactically and semantically, as need arises. We are currently developing the syntax and the mechanics to express absence of events – for instance, to allow the detection of an event like "the user has left his/her workplace and arrived home without stopping by the gym".

On a last note, we acknowledge that we have used highly subjective context labels in our examples throughout the paper (for instance, the use of a location value of 'lab', which will likely correspond to different places for different users). Since we intend EveWorks to support the detection of events on people's daily lives, our framework must have a mechanism that allows it to communicate its requirements, either directly to the users of its embedding application or, as we do not know the nature of the latter beforehand, to the application itself. A hypothesis under consideration is the creation of a functional component to act as an interface between EveWorks and the application. In this setting, our framework would register its requirements on this component and, afterwards, the application could request them and eventually trigger the necessary interactions with the user.

ACKNOWLEDGMENTS

This work has been funded by FCT/MEC through grant SFRH/BD/73177/2010 and CITI (Pest-OE/EEI/UI0527/2011).

REFERENCES

1. Allen, J. 1983. Maintaining knowledge about temporal intervals. *Communications of the ACM* 26, 11, 832-843

2. Alspaugh, T. 2005. Software support for calculations in Allen's Interval Algebra. *ISR Technical Report UCI-ISR-05-02*. Institute for Software Research, University of California, Irvine.

3. Cardoso, B. and Romão, T. 2014. The Timeline as a Programming Interface. In *CHI '14 Extended Abstracts on Human Factors in Computing Systems* (CHI EA '14). ACM, New York, NY, USA.

4. Carlson, J., Lisper, B. 2004. An Event Detection Algebra for Reactive Systems. *Proc. of the 4th ACM international conference on embedded software* (EMSOFT 04). ACM, New York, USA, 147-154.

5. Dey, A., Abowd, G. 1999. The Context Toolkit – Aiding the Development of Context-Aware Applications. *Proc. of Human Factors in Computing Systems*, 434-441.

6. Dey, A., Wac, K., Ferreira, D., Tassini, K., Hong, J., Ramos, J. 2011. Getting closer: an empirical investigation of the proximity of user to their smart phones. *Proceedings of the 13th international conference on Ubiquitous computing (UbiComp '11)*. ACM, New York, USA, 163-172.

7. Ferreira, D. 2013. AWARE: A Mobile Context Instrumentation Middleware to Collaboratively Understand Human Behavior. *Ph.D. Dissertation*. University of Oulu, Finland.

8. Fowler, M. Domain Specific Languages. 2010. Addison-Wesley Professional.

9. Frosini, L., Manca, Marco. and Paternò, F. 2013. A framework for the development of distributed interactive applications. *Proc. of the 5th ACM SIGCHI symposium on Engineering interactive computing systems* (EICS '13). ACM, New York, USA, 249-254.

10. Kramer, D., Kocurova, A., Oussena, T. Clark, T., Komisarczuk, P. 2011. An extensible, self-contained, layered approach to context acquisition. *Proceedings of the Third International Workshop on Middleware for Pervasive Mobile and Embedded Computing, M-MPAC '11*, ACM, New York, USA.

11. Klasnja, P and Pratt, W. January 2014. Managing health with mobile technology. *Interactions* 21, 1, 66-69.

12. Rossi, F., Beek, P., and Walsh, T. 2006. *Handbook of Constraint Programming (Foundations of Artificial Intelligence)*. Elsevier Science Inc., New York, USA.

13. Szymanek, R., Kuchcinski, K. JaCoP - Java Constraint Programming Solver. http://jacop.osolpro.com

14. Wissen, B., Palmer, N., Kemp, R., Kielmann, T. and Bal, H. 2010. ContextDroid: an expression-based context framework for Android. *Proc. of PhoneSense 2010*

Engineering Interactive Systems with SCXML

Dirk Schnelle-Walka
TU Darmstadt
Hochschulstraße 10
64289 Darmstadt, Germany
dirk@tk.informatik.tu-
darmstadt.de

Stefan Radomski
TU Darmstadt
Hochschulstraße 10
64289 Darmstadt, Germany
radomski@tk.informatik.tu-
darmstadt.de

Torbjörn Lager
University of Gothenburg
Box 200, SE-405
30 Gothenburg, Sweden
torbjorn.lager@ling.gu.se

Jim Barnett
Genesys
21 King Street
Auburndale
MA, 02466, USA
jim.barnett@genesyslab.com

Deborah Dahl
Conversational Technologies
1820 Gravers Road
Plymouth Meeting
PA 19462, USA
dahl@conversational-
technologies.com

Max Mühlhäuser
TU Darmstadt
Hochschulstraße 10
64289 Darmstadt, Germany
max@informatik.tu-
darmstadt.de

ABSTRACT
The W3C is about to finalize the SCXML standard to express
Harel state-machines as XML documents. In unison with the
W3C MMI architecture specification and related work from
the W3C MMI working group, this recommendation might be
a promising candidate to become the "HTML of multi-modal
applications".

Author Keywords
SCXML; Dialog management; Multimodality, Standards.

ACM Classification Keywords
H.5.m. Information Interfaces and Presentation (e.g. HCI):
Miscellaneous; D,2,2 Design Tools and Techniques: State di-
agrams

INTERACTIVE SYSTEMS WITH SCXML
The W3C MMI Working Group suggests the use of
SCXML [1] to express the dialog control of multimodal applications. The overall approach has already been shown to
be suitable i.e. to decouple the control flow and presentation
layer in multimodal dialog systems [6]. It has been used in
several applications to express dialog states [3] or to easily
incorporate information [5] from external systems.

As SCXML approaches formal W3C recommendation status and more applications employing SCXML start to appear, we would like to gather experiences, short-comings especially related to established and current dialog modeling

techniques and in general areas where clarification, further
standardization or extension is needed or opens new perspectives, like [4].

WORKSHOP CONTENT
The workshop will provide a forum to discuss submissions
detailing the use of SCXML, in particular, multi-modal dialog systems adhering to the concepts outlined by the various
W3C standards in general and related approaches of declarative dialog modeling to engineer interactive systems.

We are interested in tooling such as own implementations or
tools to ease the development with SCXML as well as usages
in interactive systems. We regard interaction within a web
browser, on the desktop, mobile or beyond the desktop. This
includes applications in robotics and adjacent spaces of interactive systems. In order to disseminate already established
knowledge and first experiences, we are interested also in integration of SCXML into existing technologies, especially related W3C standards, e.g. the W3C standard for Multimodal
Architecture and Interfaces [2].

PARTICIPANTS AND WORKSHOP PUBLICITY
The workshop will have interdisciplinary appeal. We expect
about 20-30 participants from the areas of EICS, UIST, IUI,
HCI, UbiComp and related areas. The program committee
comprises researchers that are active in these research areas and who moreover plan to encourage researchers, also
from their institutes, to submit to this workshop. Moreover,
the chairs also include leading experts from the respective
SCXML working groups who will promote this workshop in
their companies. Thereby, we ensure active participation in
preparation and execution of the workshop. We will especially encourage young scientists and Ph.D. students to submit papers to explore their research topics with distinguished
experts from research and research related industry. The call
for papers and participation will be distributed through well-
established mailing lists and websites in various research

EICS 2014, June 17–20, 2014, Rome, Italy.
ACM 978-1-4503-2725-1/14/06.
http://dx.doi.org/10.1145/2607023.2610287

communities, including EICS, IUI, CHI, UIST and UbiComp as well as via suitable W3C mailing lists. We also plan to promote the workshop through our website and OSNs and setup a web site to publicize the event.

FORMAT

We plan for a full-day workshop with submissions in the following three categories: (i) position papers and posters (2 pages) focusing on novel concepts or works in progress, (ii) demo submissions (2 pages) and (iii) full papers (4-6 pages) covering a finished piece of research.

Our goal is to attract a wide range of submissions related to the declarative modeling of interactive multi-modal dialog systems to leverage the discussion and thus to advance the research of modeling interactive multi-modal dialog systems. To stimulate discussion between the workshop participants we plan a poster and demo session to spark further in-depth discussions on selected topics that will be collected during the workshop

We also plan to summarize the outcome and publish it on the workshops website and our publication server at the TU Darmstadt to ensure that the submissions can be cited. This publication strategy will attract higher quality submissions, and increase the exposure of the workshop before and after the event.

The following agenda details how the workshop will run:

9:30am - 10:45am	Introduction, Paper Session I
10:45am - 11:00am	*Coffee Break*
11:00am - 12:00pm	Paper Session II
12:00pm - 1:00pm	*Lunch Break*
12:30pm - 1:15pm	Demo Session
1:15pm - 1:30pm	Selection of topics to discuss
1:30pm - 2:15pm	Discussion on selected topics
2:15pm - 2:30pm	*Coffee Break*
2:30pm - 3:30pm	In-depth discussion (continued)
Evening	*Workshop Dinner*

ORGANIZERS AND PROGRAM COMMITTEE

The organizers are early adaptors of SCXML as well as leading experts from the SCXML working group.

Dirk Schnelle-Walka leads the "Talk&Touch" group at the Telecooperation Lab at TU Darmstadt. His main research interest is on multimodal interaction in smart spaces.
Stefan Radomski is a PhD candidate at the Telecooperation Lab at TU Darmstadt. His main research interest is about multimodal dialog management in pervasive environments.
Torbjörn Lager is professor of general and computational linguistics at FLoV, University of Gothenburg. His main research interests include computational logic, web technology and state machine technology for building web-based multimodal systems.
Jim Barnett is a software architect at Genesys, a contact center software company. He is the editor of the SCXML specification.
Deborah Dahl is the Principal at Conversational Technologies and the Chair of the W3C Multimodal Interaction Working Group. Her primary technical interest is practical appli-

cations of speech, natural language and multimodal technologies.
Max Mühlhäuser is full professor and heads the Telecooperation Lab at TU Darmstadt. He has over 300 publications on UbiComp, HCI, IUI, e-learning and multimedia.

The list of program committee members is as follows:

- **Rahul Akolkar** (IBM Research, USA)
- **Kazuyuki Ashimura** (W3C, Japan)
- **Stephan Borgert** (TU Darmstadt, Germany)
- **Jenny Brusk** (University of Skövde, Sweden)
- **Sebastian Feuerstack** (Offis, Germany)
- **David Junger** (University of Gothenburg, Sweden)
- **Stephan Radeck-Arneth** (TU Darmstadt, Germany)
- **David Suendermann-Oeft** (DHBW Stuttgart, Germany)
- **Raj Tumuluri** (Openstream, USA)

PC members will help the organizers to publicize the event in more scientific communities and allow for a competent peer-review process.

ACKNOWLEDGEMENTS
Our efforts around SCXML have been partially supported by the FP7 EU Large-scale Integrating Project SMART VORTEX[1] co-financed by the European Union.

REFERENCES
1. Barnett, J., Akolkar, R., Auburn, R., Bodell, M., Burnett, D. C., Carter, J., McGlashan, S., Lager, T., Helbing, M., Hosn, R., Raman, T., Reifenrath, K., and Rosenthal, N. State chart XML (SCXML): State machine notation for control abstraction. W3C working draft, W3C, Feb. 2012. http://www.w3.org/TR/2012/WD-scxml-20120216/.

2. Bodell, M., Dahl, D., Kliche, I., Larson, J., Porter, B., Raggett, D., Raman, T., Rodriguez, B. H., Selvari, M., Tumuluri, R., Wahbe, A., Wiechno, P., and Yudkowsky, M. Multimodal Architecture and Interfaces. W3C recommendation, W3C, Oct. 2012. http://www.w3.org/TR/mmi-arch/.

3. Brusk, J., Lager, T., Hjalmarsson, A., and Wik, P. DEAL: dialogue management in SCXML for believable game characters. In *Proceedings of the 2007 conference on Future Play*, ACM (2007), 137–144.

4. Radomski, S., Schnelle-Walka, D., and Radeck-Arneth, S. A Prolog Datamodel for State Chart XML. In *SIGdial Workshop on Discourse and Dialogue* (Aug. 2013).

5. Sigüenza Izquierdo, Á., Blanco Murillo, J. L., Bernat Vercher, J., and Hernández Gómez, L. A. Using scxml to integrate semantic sensor information into context-aware user interfaces. In *International Workshop on Semantic Sensor Web, In conjunction with IC3K 2010*, Telecomunicacion (2011).

6. Wilcock, G. SCXML and voice interfaces. In *3rd Baltic Conference on Human Language Technologies, Kaunas, Lithuania* (2007).

---

[1] http://smartvortex.eu

Engineering Gestures for Multimodal User Interfaces

Florian Echtler
Chair for Media Informatics
University of Regensburg
florian.echtler@ur.de

Dietrich Kammer
Chair of Media Design
TU Dresden
dietrich.kammer@tu-dresden.de

Davy Vanacken
Expertise Centre for Digital Media
Hasselt University - tUL - iMinds
davy.vanacken@uhasselt.be

Lode Hoste, Beat Signer
Web & Information Systems
Engineering Lab, Vrije
Universiteit Brussel
{lhoste,bsigner}@vub.ac.be

ABSTRACT

Despite increased presence of gestural and multimodal user interfaces in research as well as daily life, development of such systems still mostly relies on programming concepts which have emerged from classic WIMP user interfaces. This workshop proposes to explore the gap between attempts to formalize and structure development for multimodal interfaces in the research community on the one hand and the lack of adoption of these formal languages and frameworks by practitioners and other researchers on the other hand.

Author Keywords

gestures; formal languages; APIs; multimodal user interfaces.

ACM Classification Keywords

D.2.2. Software Engineering: Design Tools and Techniques: User Interfaces; H.5.m. Information Interfaces and Presentation (e.g. HCI): Miscellaneous

WORKSHOP TOPIC

During the last five years, interest in multimodal user interfaces (MMUIs) has increased significantly in research as well as in a commercial context. Popular examples are smartphones which usually provide a multitouch screen, speech input and motion sensors, or the Microsoft Kinect, which enables full-body interaction with a game console. However, the design of development tools and application programming interfaces (APIs) has not kept pace with this new trend. Most widely used APIs such as the Android SDK or the Microsoft Surface SDK still follow the decades-old paradigm of triggering event-based callbacks and support a few hard-wired gestures at best. While numerous research projects have attempted to address these issues, they have so far failed to gain widespread adoption, with the possible exception of the low-level TUIO protocol [4]. Reasons for this low rate of adoption may include complex programming paradigms, lack of support for diverse input devices, inflexible GUI libraries or limited availability for popular operating systems.

EICS'14, June 17–20, 2014, Rome, Italy.
ACM 978-1-4503-2725-1/14/06.
http://dx.doi.org/10.1145/2607023.2610288

We wish to stimulate a discussion on these issues by inviting position papers between 2 and 6 pages in length on any of the following topics:

- Definition of and relationship between gestural and multimodal user interfaces

- Novel programming paradigms for MMUIs, e.g. reactive programming or visual programming

- Architectural concepts for multimodal UI APIs

- Studies on performance of different programming paragdigms

- Analysis of limitations of existing multimodal API concepts

- Improved event structures for MMUIs

- Formal languages and concepts for describing multimodal interaction

- Arguments for/against formalization of multimodal user interfaces

- Reports on real-world deployment scenarios using existing APIs

- Standardization efforts regarding multimodal UIs by ISO, W3C, ...

WORKSHOP AIMS & GOALS

We hope to foster a lively discussion on the issues of multimodal interface development with the ultimate goal of developing a set of design guidelines that multimodal UI APIs should follow. We aim to include framework developers who *provide* such APIs as well as application developers who *use* these APIs to avoid an "ivory tower" discussion which might lead to the most elegant, formally rigid or most universal API design without taking the real-world requirements of application developers into account. The combined knowledge and experience of the workshop participants should lead to a modular and extensible concept for programming gestures for multimodal user interfaces.

WORKSHOP FORMAT

This workshop follows in the footsteps of the "Engineering Patterns for Multitouch Interaction" workshops at EICS 2010 and 2011. We envision a half-day workshop with approximately 8 - 12 participants. The first part (about 2 h) will consist of short presentations in Pecha Kucha style and questions on the submitted papers, while the second part (also about 2 h, after a coffee break) will consist of 3 - 4 small discussion groups who each focus on a different sub-topic (selected from submitted position papers). After a second coffee break, a final wrap-up session (about 1 h) will reconcile the outcome of the discussion groups into a set of design recommendations for multimodal APIs. Total duration including breaks is estimated to be about 6 h.

Possible contributors to the workshop are researchers and practitioners in the area of multimodal framework development. A number of researchers have published individual approaches before, who will be explicitly invited to participate in the workshop. Among these approaches are Proton [7] by Kin et al., GDL [6] by Khandkar and Maurer, Midas [9] by Scholliers et al., GISpL [2] by Echtler and Butz, GeForMT [5] by Kammer et al., [10] MARIA by Spano et al., ICO [8] by Navarre et al., NiMMiT [1] by De Boeck et al. and GestureAgents [3] by Julià et al.

ORGANIZER CV
Florian Echtler is an assistant professor at the Chair for Media Informatics at University of Regensburg. His research interests focus on formal languages for gesture descriptions and design of multimodal development frameworks. Additional topics include computer vision for HCI applications, sensor technology and rapid prototyping.

Dietrich Kammer is a postdoctoral researcher at Technische Universität Dresden, affiliated with the Chair of Media Design. His research is focused on the formalization of gestural input, especially with regards to multitouch technology. Further areas of research are semiotics in HCI, computer graphics, and information visualization.

Davy Vanacken is a postdoctoral researcher at Hasselt University, affiliated with the HCI group of the Expertise Centre for Digital Media (EDM). His research is primarily focused on multi-touch and mid-air gestural interfaces for public and shared interaction spaces.

Lode Hoste is a PhD student at the Vrije Universiteit Brussels within the Web & Information Systems Engineering laboratory (WISE) and the Software Languages Lab (SOFT). His research focuses on software engineering abstractions for multimodal interaction, ranging from programming language design to modular and reusable framework architectures.

Beat Signer is Professor of Computer Science at the Vrije Universiteit Brussel (VUB) in Belgium, where he is co-director of the Web & Information Systems Engineering laboratory (WISE). His research interests include pen-based gesture recognition, multi-touch and multimodal gesture frameworks as well as cross-media information architectures.

WORKSHOP OUTCOME
The primary outcome is a set of design recommendations for multimodal user interface APIs. These recommendations as well as selected notes on their development process will be published on the workshop website along with the submitted position papers. An extended version of the design recommendations will also be submitted to an appropriate computer science journal or scientific conference for further dissemination of the results.

ACKNOWLEDGEMENTS
On behalf of Dietrich Kammer, this work was supported by the European Union and the Free State Saxony through the European Regional Development Fund (ERDF).

The work of Lode Hoste is funded by an IWT doctoral scholarship.

REFERENCES
1. J. De Boeck, D. Vanacken, C. Raymaekers, and K. Coninx. High-level modeling of multimodal interaction techniques using NiMMiT. *JVRB - Journal of Virtual Reality and Broadcasting*, 4(2007)(2), Aug. 2007.

2. F. Echtler and A. Butz. GISpL: gestures made easy. In Proc. TEI '12, page 233–240, New York, NY, USA, 2012. ACM.

3. C. F. Julià, N. Earnshaw, and S. Jordà. GestureAgents: an agent-based framework for concurrent multi-task multi-user interaction. In Proc. TEI '13, page 207–214, New York, NY, USA, 2013. ACM.

4. M. Kaltenbrunner, T. Bovermann, R. Bencina, and E. Costanza. TUIO: a protocol for table-top tangible user interfaces. In Proc. GW '05, 2005.

5. D. Kammer, J. Wojdziak, M. Keck, R. Groh, and S. Taranko. Towards a formalization of multi-touch gestures. In Proc. ITS '10, page 49–58, New York, NY, USA, 2010. ACM.

6. S. H. Khandkar, S. M. Sohan, J. Sillito, and F. Maurer. Tool support for testing complex multi-touch gestures. In Proc. ITS '10, page 59–68, New York, NY, USA, 2010. ACM.

7. K. Kin, B. Hartmann, T. DeRose, and M. Agrawala. Proton++: a customizable declarative multitouch framework. In Proc. UIST '12, page 477–486, New York, NY, USA, 2012. ACM.

8. D. Navarre, P. Palanque, J.-F. Ladry, and E. Barboni. ICOs: a model-based user interface description technique dedicated to interactive systems addressing usability, reliability and scalability. *ACM Trans. Comput.-Hum. Interact.*, 16(4):18:1–18:56, Nov. 2009.

9. C. Scholliers, L. Hoste, B. Signer, and W. De Meuter. Midas: a declarative multi-touch interaction framework. In Proc. TEI '11, page 49–56, New York, NY, USA, 2011. ACM.

10. L. D. Spano, A. Cisternino, and F. Paternò. A compositional model for gesture definition. In Proc. HCSE'12, page 34–52, Berlin, Heidelberg, 2012. Springer-Verlag.

HCI Engineering: Charting the Way towards Methods and Tools for Advanced Interactive Systems

Jürgen Ziegler
University of Duisburg-Essen
Duisburg, Germany
juergen.ziegler@uni-due.de

José Creissac Campos
Universidade do Minho
Braga, Portugal
jose.campos@di.uminho.pt

Laurence Nigay
Univ. Grenoble Alpes, LIG
CNRS, LIG, F-38000 Grenoble
laurence.nigay@imag.fr

ABSTRACT

This workshop intends to establish the basis of a roadmap addressing engineering challenges and emerging themes in HCI. Novel forms of interaction and new application domains involve aspects that are currently not sufficiently covered by existing methods and tools. The workshop will serve as a venue to bring together researchers and practitioners interested the Engineering of Human-Computer Interaction and in contributing to the definition of a roadmap for the field. The intention is to continue work on the roadmap in follow-up workshops as well as in the IFIP Working Group on User Interface Engineering.

WORKSHOP TOPICS AND SCOPE

Engineering interactive systems is a multidisciplinary endeavor positioned at the intersection of HCI, software engineering, usability engineering, interaction design, visual design and other disciplines..

The field of Human-Computer Interaction Engineering (HCI-E) is concerned with providing methods and tools for the systematic and effective design, development and evaluation of interactive systems in a wide range of application areas. The aim of such methods and tools is twofold: (1) Improve the process of designing, developing and evaluating interactive systems (2) Improve the quality of the user interface of interactive systems, including usability properties and software properties (also called external and internal properties respectively in [1]).

Traditionally, HCI-E methods and tools have mainly addressed standard graphical, mobile, multimodal and multi-device interactive systems, as well as special themes such as safety-critical systems in the medical domain and automotive user interfaces. In recent years, the range of interactive techniques available and their applications has broadened considerably and can be expected to grow even further in the future. While new interaction techniques offer the prospect of improving the usability and user experience of interactive systems, they also pose new challenges for methods and tools that can support their design development and evaluation in a systematic engineering-oriented manner. This is aggravated by the fact that they are increasingly being applied in novel and less understood application domains (e.g., wearable medical devices and in-vehicle applications).

Examples of innovative interaction techniques with little methodological support so far include:

- tangible and mixed-reality interfaces;
- 3D interaction;
- perceptual interfaces based on computer vision, speech recognition, or the measurement of biosignals;
- visualization techniques and their application to big data, e.g. social media applications.

The techniques mentioned above as well as many other novel forms of interaction involve aspects that are currently not sufficiently covered by existing HCI-E methods/tools such as design spaces, task models, model-based generation of user interfaces, toolkit, evaluation methods. This may require new methods/tools or adaptations/extensions of existing methods/tools.

In addition to emerging interaction techniques, there are remaining HCI-E issues for more established interaction techniques (e.g., mobile interaction, multimodality, collaborative interaction). For instance prototyping techniques and approaches for designing mobile applications was the topic of a workshop at the last MobilHCI conference [3]. While prototyping tools exist for GUI, they require adaptations and extensions to cover the range of issues involved in mobile HCI and Ubiquitous Computing (e.g., multi-touch gestures, usage of sensors for interaction).

GOALS OF THE WORKSHOP

The workshop aims at identifying, examining and structuring the engineering challenges related to novel forms of interaction or to emerging themes in HCI due to new application domains. An intended outcome of the workshop is an organized overview of engineering challenges and of areas that currently lack systematic method or tool support. These results shall serve as a basis for drafting a roadmap for engineering advanced interactive systems, consolidating, structuring and prioritizing open research questions.

While it is not realistic to cover all methodological and tool-related research questions in depth in a one-day workshop, the intention is to continue work on the roadmap cither in follow-up workshops as well as in the context of the IFIP Working Group on User Interface Engineering [2] where external participants are welcome.

FORMAT AND ORGANIZATION

Soliciting and Selecting Contributions
We will solicit contributions from the HCI-E related communities and we would be very interested to welcome both researchers and practitioners for a fruitful discussion. To do so we will dispatch the call to the usual channels including announcements in mailing lists, conferences and personal contacts (in particular for practitioners).

Prospective participants should submit a 2-page position paper describing their interests in and views on future engineering methods/tools, as well as related previous work (including their own) where appropriate. At least, each position paper should describe a major engineering-related challenge to be further elaborated at the workshop. We will select participants on the basis of the abstract's quality, their response to the list of issues and the diversity of their backgrounds, aiming thus at an interdisciplinary group. A further criterion will be the stated intention to continue work on elaborating and updating the roadmap after the workshop.

Pre-workshop activities
We will compile and publish a list of the challenges submitted by the accepted participants on the workshop website prior to the event. The selected presenters will be asked to provide an extended 5-page position paper two weeks before the workshop. These position papers will be circulated in advance to all participants to obtain an understanding of the mutual views and to provide a starting point for the discussion.

Structure and schedule of the workshop
The workshop will last one day and will comprise brief position statements by the participants followed by a plenary discussion and an initial structuring of the topics. Breakout groups will further refine the different research areas. Based on the reports from the breakout groups, the research field will be further structured with the aim of producing an initial version of a research roadmap for HCI Engineering.

Plan for dissemination
We will make the workshop results available on the workshop website and plan to publish extended paper versions electronically after the workshop. We also plan to produce a publication, e.g. a journal paper, summarizing and consolidating the contributions in the form of an Engineering HCI roadmap. Furthermore, the results will serve as inputs to future work and discussions in the IFIP Working Group on User Interface Engineering [2].

ORGANIZERS BACKGROUND AND EXPERIENCES
José C. Campos is an assistant professor at the Department of Informatics of Universidade do Minho, and a member of HASLab / INESC TEC. His main area of research is the verification and validation of interactive computing system. Among other roles, he was general co-chair for EICS 2012 and tutorials co-chair for INTERACT 2011. He was awarded an International Excellence Award by the BCS HCI Group, for his paper on Systematic Analysis of Control Panel Interfaces Using Formal Tools at DSVIS 2008.

Laurence Nigay is a full Professor in Computer Science at Université of Grenoble 1. She is the director of the Engineering Human-Computer Interaction (EHCI) research group of the Grenoble Informatics Laboratory. From 1998-2004, she was vice-chair of the IFIP working group WG 2.7/13.4 User Interface Engineering. Her research interests include new interaction techniques, Multimodal and Augmented Reality (AR) user interfaces. She has received several scientific awards (including the CNRS Bronze medal in 2002 and the UJF gold medal in 2005) for excellence in her research.

Jürgen Ziegler is a full Professor in Interactive Systems and Interaction Design at the University of Duisburg-Essen. His main areas of research are context-adaptive interaction, recommender systems, information visualization and user interfaces for semantic data. He has served in various functions for all major HCI conferences and has co-organized workshops at CHI, IUI, INTERACT and other venues. Currently, he is also chair of IFIP Working Group 2.7/13.4 User Interface Engineering.

REFERENCES
1. Gram, C. and Cockton G. Editors. 1996. Design Principles for Interactive Software. Chapman & Hall.

2. IFIP WG 2.7/13.4 Working Group on User Interface Engineering. http://ui-engineering.org/index.html

3. Workshop on Prototyping to Support the Interaction Designing in Mobile Application Development (PID-MAD 2013) http://hciv.de/pidmad/

Author Index